THE ENGLISH ATLANTIC
1675–1740

THE
ENGLISH ATLANTIC
1675–1740

An Exploration of
Communication and Community

IAN K. STEELE

New York   Oxford
OXFORD UNIVERSITY PRESS
1986

Oxford University Press

Oxford   New York   Toronto
Petaling Jaya   Calcutta   Madras   Karachi
Kuala Lumpur   Singapore   Hong Kong   Tokyo
Nairobi   Dar es Salaam   Cape Town
Melbourne   Auckland

and associated companies in
Beirut   Berlin   Ibadan   Nicosia

Published by Oxford University Press, Inc.,
200 Madison Avenue, New York, New York 10016

Oxford is a registered trademark of Oxford University Press

Library of Congress Cataloging-in-Publication Data
Steele, Ian Kenneth.
The English Atlantic, 1675–1740.
Includes index.
1. Communication and traffic—North America—History.
2. Communication and traffic—West Indies, British—History.
3. Great Britain—Colonies—America—Commerce. I. Title.
HE202.S74   1986   380.3′09171′241   85-25828
ISBN 0-19-503968-8

2 4 6 8 10 9 7 5 3 1

Printed in the United States of America
on acid-free paper

To

Colin and Ken

Who have always competed
successfully with this book
in more ways than they can know

PREFACE

This study began as a simply inquiry into the nature of communications in the first British Empire, just an elementary question or two to be solved before proceeding to something more general and supposedly more significant. Years later, this tentative exploration of some aspects of English Atlantic communications is offered to illustrate a promising perspective from which to understand the English Atlantic world and central features of early American history.

Although history is ostensibly about people, it has tended to become overwhelmingly about "lands." Countries are given histories that can portray areas of soil as living social, economic, and political beings, whereas oceans are viewed primarily as vast and empty moats between those histories. Although I cannot support the antidote offered by Lucien Febvre when he sought "reconstructions of the histories of the Oceans considered as real entities, historical personalities, primary factors in the collective efforts of men,"[1] there is a need for some reappraisal. The land-oriented bias derives from some realities and from most surviving sources, but it has also been exaggerated by nineteenth-century revolutions in land transport and political ideas. Maritime empires have come to be regarded as unnatural creations whereas continental empires are seen as fulfilling natural destinies and, if they succeed, are not called empires at all. The assumption that land united and water divided is dubious for early modern times, and the seaborne empires are much more understandable if the assumption is challenged.

Did the Atlantic Ocean make the United States of America a foregone conclusion? Thomas Paine, a recent migrant to America on the eve of the American Revolution, thought so.

> Even the distance at which the Almighty hath placed England and America is a strong and natural proof that the authority of one over the other, was never the design of Heaven.[2]

Nineteenth-century historians often sought the colonial origins of the United States, and of liberty, in the lives of provincial Englishmen. This preoccupation with the ways in which colonials were different from other Englishmen, rather than the ways in which they were similar, was understandable. The width of the Atlantic was no longer a conscious explanation for American independence, but rather the ocean became a vast social moat by supposition. Twentieth-century interpretations of colonial America are numerous, and most of them are suggestive. Those scholars who assert the creative pragmatism of the isolated colonial situation confine the English influence to the cultural luggage of the Stuart migrants. A major opposing view is that the ideas brought by the initial migrants became themselves the treasured bases of American uniqueness. Both of these contending interpretations, which together constitute a central dichotomy in the analysis of early American history, assume that the ocean effectively insulated the colonies from England.

The nineteenth century has imposed upon the eighteenth in another historiographical tradition. The development of the English sugar islands was so blatant a display of economic preoccupations that Marxist scholars have found it a prime example of their thesis. Yet a class analysis of a seaborne economy has been diverted, or aborted, by the assumption that classes, like "peoples," seem to end at the water's edge. Marxist notions of imperialism can overwhelm Marxist notions of class. Colonies are seen as exploited by mother countries or peripheries by centers. Countries are considered to be in conflict rather than classes, ranks, or people. Colonizers are too quickly seen to be the colonized. Scholars who describe an oceanic political economy and who claim that social and ideological perceptions are derivative of economic fundamentals still manage to see the ocean as a complete social barrier.

Early American social history has been exploded by a generation of local studies as eighteenth-century English political history was exploded by the Namierites. "Colonial America" has melted easily, as that anachronism should, before the careful demography and thick description of life in villages, towns, and counties. New calibrations of many aspects of local life have armed historians with enticing information that was not available to their subjects. Because new information for its own sake is little valued, these group portraits have been framed in social theories that seek to explain differences over space and time. Comparisons between England and America have become central in this work as are the study of shared origins. Yet the shared experiences within the empire, as distinct from the shared inheritances, have received very little attention from social historians.

"Anglo-American" and British imperial historians have unraveled innumerable transatlantic networks of business, politics, religion, and family during the colonial era. Like the oceanic political economy, these ties were born and sustained by letters and travel. Yet the connecting ocean, like the insulating one, has been asserted without study of the pace and pattern of English Atlantic communications; without appreciation of the changes in communication over time; and without realizing that the pace, pattern, and change in the spread of news had implications for political, economic, and social relations. The three parts of this inquiry initiate discussion of these forgotten essentials.

The first British Empire has been a peculiar institution in the eyes of many historians, a political economy that was not a society. Yet the Anglo-American relationship lasted for seven generations and did not tear cleanly through Thomas Paine's liberating ocean. As many New World colonies stayed within the empire as left, and in the revolutionary colonies there were many of all ranks who could not accept the separation when it finally came. This study concerns the lifetime of people who died within the first British Empire, without knowing what their grandsons would do later. Despite the valuable insights that can come from studying longer periods, there is a very real sense in which everyone is dead in the *longue durée*. A study that ends in 1740 avoids the teleological preoccupations that the American Revolution has imposed on much of the study of American colonial history, yet communications continued to develop after 1740, with erratic but substantial growth in shipping, newspapers, and postal services and the coming of a regular packet-boat service to New York after 1755. Those of us who (with the aid of instant electronic communication) have witnessed the evaporation of empires built in the age of sail can appreciate that increasing familiarity can breed discontent.

Although this work challenges existing preconceptions about English Atlantic communications, it can only illustrate some of the myriad aspects and implications of this perspective. As a result, this study is an exploration and an invitation to further research. Yet I hope that this book will be of help to those trying to analyze the emergence of American social and political identity or understand the longevity of the first British Empire and the lives of those who lived within it.

Footnote citations attempt—rather inadequately—to indicate the help received in developing this study. The archival research has depended on the generous support of Canada Council Leave Fellowships and a Killam Senior Fellowship. I am grateful to the *Journal of British Studies* for permission to reprint Chapter 6. The University of Western Ontario has supported this project with research grants and library accessions, and the university is primarily the people who have asked, listened, and helped. Special debts must be acknowledged to Gerry Mulcahy and George Robinson of Weldon Library; Barry Arnett, who introduced an innocent to computers; and Jeanette Berry and Lori Morris, who have expertly retyped the text, and Patricia Chalk for help with the maps. The curiosity and enthusiasm of many students have helped to sustain me, but Adrian Fraser and Terence Wister have assisted in special ways. Parts of the manuscript have been given particularly valuable criticism by Professors Jack Bumsted, Samuel Clark, Fred Dreyer, Roger Emerson, David Flaherty, Richard Johnson, Ken Lockridge, Alison Olson, Jacob Price, Peter Russell, Craig Simpson, and the late David Alexander. I am very grateful for all this thoughtful advice, especially that which I have declined to follow.

Without the help of my family, this book would have been finished years ago, which is only one of the many ways they have improved what follows. All rights to surviving errors and weaknesses are, in accordance with cruel convention, reserved exclusively by the author.

London, Canada   I.K.S.
September 1985

CONTENTS

ILLUSTRATIONS

THE ENGLISH ATLANTIC
1675–1740

1 · Introduction

As the old 40-ton barque *Palm Tree* rode at anchor in her busy home port of Plymouth, England, in October 1699, she seemed a most unlikely bearer of her exotic name. Built at nearby Fowey a quarter of a century earlier, she was rather broad for her 35-foot length, square-sterned, and unarmed. Although her mizzenmast carried a lateen sail that could use crosswinds effectively,[1] the other two masts that rose from her cramped deck were square-rigged as if to announce that she was not intended for challenging navigation. Biscuit, cider, and a pack of serges made up the suitably prosaic cargo, and the master, William Lewis, had only a five-man crew when they weighed anchor on October 14. Yet the *Palm Tree* was sailing on its third English Atlantic circuit in as many autumns.[2]

Plymouth was a superb English port from which to commence such a voyage. From Plymouth Sound there was plenty of sea room to the south, making the westerlies an ally rather than the persistent enemy they were further into the Channel. The *Palm Tree* sailed across the westerlies on her way south, then worked the lighter and more variable winds off the Portuguese coast while welcoming the aid of the Canaries current to reach Madeira. Sighting that island would confirm Lewis's navigational competence, correct his reckonings, and prompt all on board to think of refreshment and news ashore. From Madeira the course would be shaped to the southwest though the trade winds would not fill the square-rigged sails in that season until the *Palm Tree* moved into the tropics. Improved speed would make this the quicker half of the crossing, as though the old ship were answering to her name in these latitudes. Master Lewis began more regular observations now, seeking a reading of 13°N latitude. When this was reached, the course was changed to the west, and the *Palm Tree* held to that course until Barbados appeared.[3] The *Palm Tree* arrived at Bridgetown, Barbados, without incident on December 11 after an eight-and-one-half-week crossing that was average for merchantmen on that route.[4]

The *Palm Tree*'s arrival at Bridgetown probably caused little more stir than had her departure from Plymouth. Admittedly, a little barque could carry a great deal of news, and the *Palm Tree* was the first vessel into Barbados directly from the English West Country ports in more than three months.[5] But even if she were carrying personal or business news for Barbadians with West Country links, her London news had already arrived by several ships directly from the metropolis. The *Palm Tree*'s voyage had been successfully timed to bring her cargo of provisions to a market not yet flooded with the Irish provisions that would come with the English sugar fleet in the next month or so. Lewis's cargo was sold quickly, and, less than two weeks later, the *Palm Tree* left the island. The local naval officer has left the only record of the barque's visit, bonding Lewis and noting the *Palm Tree* was bound to Virginia with a cargo of rum, sugar, and molasses.

The *Palm Tree* likely followed the easier January course leading westward from Barbados, out through the Mona Passage into the Antilles current and the Gulf Stream, then working around Cape Hatteras and into Chesapeake Bay. The *Palm Tree* arrived in Virginia after being noted tersely in the logbook of the captain of the royal guard-vessel HMS *Essex Prize* and carefully entered into customs on the James River.[6] The 34-day passage from Barbados was very close to the average on that route; again, this atypical little vessel on its own odd assignment was charting the average pace of English Atlantic shipping.

Her size, though not her shape, would make the *Palm Tree* appear as a colonial coasting vessel amid the big tobacco ships that were loading on the James River. It was nearly four months before the barque was again noted by the quill of the customs officer, this time on her way out of the James River loaded with tobacco. With 56 other tobacco vessels, the *Palm Tree* was convoyed back to England by HMS *Essex Prize*.[7] With the westerlies pushing her and the North Atlantic Drift assisting, this tubby, aging, and heavily laden little barque was carried northeasterly and then east across the North Atlantic to enter customs at Plymouth within 65 days. On this arc of her sailing circle, the *Palm Tree* bettered the average time by some 18 days.[8] In all, her men had been away from the ship's home port for 9 months, though they had spent only 5 of those actually at sea or waiting for usable winds after clearing customs.

The *Palm Tree*'s 10,000-mile circuit of the North Atlantic did not make history.[9] As a sea story, it was as mundane as the ship itself. The various customs officers who clocked the *Palm Tree* in and out of three English Atlantic ports may well have kept track of this duly bonded little trader, thinking that someone in London would pore over all the records of all the ships traveling to all the ports of the English Atlantic empire, but no one did. This apparently successful voyage provoked no lawsuits against the master from either disappointed owners or unpaid crewmen, and hence left no traces in Admiralty or mayoralty court records. The five crewmen who sailed the ocean to sell biscuit, rum, and tobacco have left no account of their workaday voyage. If William Lewis kept a ship's log, it has disappeared like almost all other merchantmen's logs for this period, perhaps as fuel for some fire. Were the men of the *Palm Tree* daring fools or stoic heroes aboard a lucky little ship that managed to escape all the well-known perils of the Atlantic? Or was theirs the usual and obvious story of thousands of seamen, a story that was not thought worth recording then and has now come to be regarded as the odd, the unlikely, and the obscure?

Common sense and surviving historical records seem to support three widely held suppositions about early modern Atlantic communications—that they were slow, infrequent, and dangerous. However, it is worthwhile to survey the support for each of these assumptions and to notice some awkward questions that they leave unanswered.

Nothing appears to be more obvious than the slowness of Atlantic communications. The *Palm Tree*'s nine-month sailing circle seems proof enough in itself and can be supported from thousands of sources. One major source for English Atlantic history, the government papers summarized in the *Calendar of State Papers, Colonial Series*,[10] includes more than three thousand letters exchanged between colonial governors and the Lords of Trade in London during the 63 years following 1675. They include many references to lost letters, shortages of shipping, convoy restrictions, and unexplained silences from the metropolis. There are no accounts of splendid communications save from the manager of the West Indies mail packet service in its best years.[11] Although governors were quick to complain when the service began to falter,[12] there had been no extravagant praise at the launching of this ambitious mail sloop service. The perspective of governors will be studied later, but it illustrates the support given to the perception of communications as slow.

Yet the speed of communication was bound up with legitimate expectations, and one assumption that is central to modern assessments of early modern communications is a Newtonian view of time as an abstracted constant. Although time perception is very complicated, it is a learned social value developed from observable motion.[13] The English language remains littered with anachronistic metaphors for speed that involve mice, hares, deer, winks, and winds. These were not just quaint sayings in the Atlantic empire of the first Georges. At that time, the pace of human communication could not challenge the old metaphors for speed.

Did the pace at which mails, news, and gossip traveled have to be "accepted" or "tolerated with resignation?"[14] Had travel been quicker earlier? Feats of speed, daring, endurance, and recklessness performed on a lathered horse or on a crank sloop were the subjects of wagers, crowds, and comments. In 1745, for example, Cooper Thornhill of Stilton, Huntingdonshire, wagered that he could ride a 213-mile course to London and back in 15 hours. After he accomplished the trip in less than 12½ hours, a contemporary recorded the following in amazement:

> This is deservedly reckon'd the greatest performance of its kind ever known. Several thousand Pounds were laid on this affair; and the roads for many miles lined with people to see him pass and repass.[15]

This breakneck race, which must have exhausted a number of horses as well as innkeeper Thornhill, was run at an average speed of 17.3 mph. It may be asking a great deal, but unless we can share their surprise, we cannot appreciate the communications of the period that preceded that ride.

Thornhill's achievement grows when it is placed in context. A royal courier on a frantic ride from London to Plymouth averaged 7.7 mph.[16] Average speeds of 6 miles per hour were possible for postriders or light coaches on the comparatively good roads of the London area, but most of the carrier wagons averaged less than 3. In Cornwall, in most of England north of the Wash, and in the sister kingdoms, the reach of London was slower, wagons and coaches were of less use, and pack trains were still common on many routes.[17] Infrequent travel, rather than longer traveling time, meant that remoter areas of Scotland and Ireland were as far from London news as were Barbados and Massachusetts. Many British migrants to the New World had only moved from one of London's provinces to another.

Ships could not match Thornhill's speed, but some of them could average the speed of a postrider and maintain such averages for weeks on end.[18] When Edmund Dummer proposed a 100-day schedule in 1702 for his West Indies packets to Barbados, the Leeward Islands, and Jamaica, his pace for the North Atlantic circle was considered impossible. He was understandably proud when his sloops accomplished that speed with some regularity in all seasons and regarded the service as "commanding time."[19] Even conventional merchantmen brought the West Indies closer to England than the Levant was at that time,[20] and the width of the English Atlantic in 1700 approximated the same number of days as had the Mediterranean during the reign of Philip II.[21]

The ocean that William Lewis sailed has changed much less since 1675 than have the perceptions of it. The main patterns of the winds, currents, and marine biology have altered relatively little in the centuries since the discovery of the New World.[22] Norse colonization of Greenland had spanned remarkably warm centuries (1200–1400) for the North Atlantic, but collapsed from a cooling trend more than a century before the noticeable beginnings of what some have called "the Little Ice Age (1550–1850)" in Western Europe.[23] In this cooler phase the wind patterns of the North Atlantic were apparently a little less regular, the belt of westerlies and polar easterlies reached slightly farther south in winter, and the proportion of north and east winds in winter over southern England was higher than has been usual since 1850. The strength of the Gulf Stream also seems to have lessened in this cooler period, which may help explain the intermittent loss of knowledge of it between the early sixteenth and mid-eighteenth century. Although the Gulf Stream was certainly there, more of its waters stayed in the central Atlantic circle at some times, strengthening the Carnaries current and giving less to the North Atlantic Drift.[24] Rather dramatic contrasts did occur between the cold English winters of the 1690's and the warm ones of the 1730's, indicating shorter-term variations in wind patterns and water temperatures. Lesser changes due to shoreline erosion, continental tilt, or river silting have hardly redrawn the edges of the ocean, nor have the more dramatic earthquakes like those that drowned parts of Port Royal, Jamaica, in 1692 or Lisbon in 1755. The main characteristics of the North Atlantic remain as they appeared to the early modern navigator.

The great sailing circle of the *Palm Tree* corresponded well with the cosmic clockwise gyro of winds and currents circling the usually calm waters of the Sargasso Sea. This mammoth circle of air and water meshes with the two anticlockwise gyros that flank it to form the three linked circles of the Atlantic in the age of sail, circles that crocheted together the political economies of four continents. (See Figure 1.)

Favorable winds were more crucial, if less reliable, than ocean currents in the age of sail. A broad, seasonally migrating belt of equatorial calm and low pressure separates the North Atlantic from the South Atlantic just north of the equator like some cosmic objection to the slave trade. Although this is the narrowest part of the ocean, these equatorial calms helped make "middle passages" some of the longest and saddest westward crossings, and not only because they were passages into slavery. The Bermuda-Azores high pressure area is the core of the North Atlantic wind system, for the descending air establishes a clockwise circulation of surface winds that includes both the trades and the westerlies. These northeast trade winds constitute an unending attempt to equalize the equatorial low and are a standing invitation for Europe to visit the Caribbean. Although this situation forced English mariners past the coastlines of their rivals, the English made the trades their major route to the New World. The prevailing westerlies, blowing most of the time in the 50°N belt, urged the English either to stay home or go home. Although there were seasonal variations and many interruptions caused by pressure cells tracking eastward across the Atlantic, the westerlies and the northeast trades were part of the navigational climate. A vessel from an English port that could make its way south to Madeira or the Canary Islands could cross the Atlantic to the Caribbean on the trades in any season. If a vessel could work its way up the North American coast to 40°N, it would find the westerlies with which to sail back to England. The essential link between these two wind belts was a region of variable winds blowing above helpful and constant ocean currents.

The dominant ring of North Atlantic currents revolves, more reliably than the wind circle, around the warm, usually calm, and weed-cluttered, Sargasso Sea. (See Figure 1.) It is flanked on the west by one of the world's greatest currents, the Gulf Stream, which can add 130 miles a day to the speed of a ship.[25] This gargantuan water jet swings toward the east as it leaves the continental shelf near Cape Hatteras and begins to slow and meander off the south coast of Nova Scotia until it becomes indistinguishable in the warm North Atlantic Drift beyond the Grand Banks off Newfoundland. The North Atlantic Drift is a one-mile-an-hour tangent off the central Atlantic circle, part of the route home from the New World for both ships and debris. The Canaries Current is the weakest arc of the North Atlantic circle, yet even here the waters that stay within the great circle move fast enough to add 40 miles a

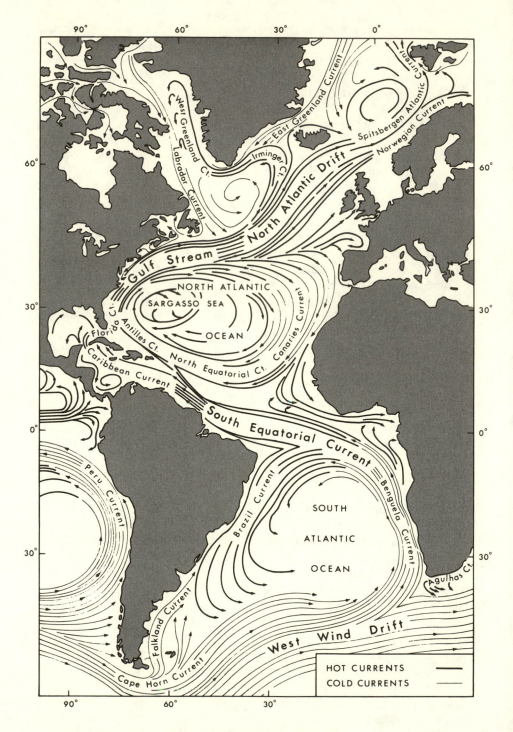

Figure 1. Major Atlantic Currents.

day to the pace of a southbound sailing ship groping for the trade winds. The North Equatorial Current was less needed but helped westward-bound vessels. Those waters that stay outside the fence of the Antilles chain of islands flow northwesterly as the Antilles current until joining the Gulf Stream north of the Bahamas. Although the central Atlantic water circle is not self-sustaining, it did encourage one-way traffic around the North Atlantic and offered aid to Stuart mariners like William Lewis, especially in making headway along established routes in the latitudes between the westerlies and the northeast trades.

For an experienced mariner like William Lewis, there was a natural pace to the voyage of the *Palm Tree*, not unlike the agrarian cycles. Speed of individual ships was constantly being compared, particularly within convoys, and passages were compared with previous voyages. Yet the *Palm Tree*'s nine-month circuit of the English Atlantic would fit very well within the legitimate expectations of the crew, their families, and the ship's owners. It seems fair to ask whether English Atlantic communications were always slow.

Infrequency of shipping is another assumption that seems self-evident and, like the notion of slow communications, well supported by much of the surviving evidence. By the nearly unanimous consent of both contemporaries and historians, the English Atlantic has been regarded as a seasonal phenomenon. Whenever fleets fell victim to privateers, diseases, or storms, the assessment of the disaster usually included the poor choice of sailing season for the convoy or expedition. Convoy arrangements usually required choice of the single "best" month for sailing in a trade. Although the decision might follow long and acrimonious debate about the relative merits of various sailing dates, the results were statements of the single best month for sailing.

Seasons for the ships and seasons for the various New World staples appear to have demanded the seasonality of English Atlantic communications. The English Atlantic trades seemed regulated by nature's effect on ships and their crews. The Hudson Strait allowed vessels through its ice flows during only three to four months of summer and autumn, then arbitrarily, but decisively, closed the icy channel again whether or not ships were still within the bay. Pack ice and winter's westerly gales helped define the fishing and whaling seasons of the northwest Atlantic, and winter ice could close harbors north of the Chesapeake for weeks, if not months. Where winter was not villainous, the summer was. In the Chesapeake, teredo worms destroyed ships while fevers destroyed crewmen. The hurricanes of August and September should have frightened shipping from the sugar and tobacco ports by midsummer, enabling them to reach English harbors long before the onset of the North Atlantic winter gales.[26] Winter, summer, and the winds themselves seem to have commanded seamen to respect the seasons of the Atlantic.

Colonial cargoes for the ships also had seasonal rhythms that reinforced the logic of seasonal Atlantic travel. Cod appeared off Newfoundland coasts in May, as did West Country fleets in search of the greatest possible catch with the least unnecessary expense.[27] The New Hampshire mast fleets moved their strategic cargoes only when the rivers disgorged the winter's wooden harvest. Shipmasters anxious to load the first Chesapeake tobaccos left England in September, and sugar merchants knew that the West Indian crop was ready for shipping beginning in January. Did the mariners actually do what they and subsequent historians have regarded as safe and commercially prudent, making the Atlantic a seasonal communications network?

Although the last years of the seventeenth century gave England a series of very severe winters, nature seldom closed English ports. An incomplete record indicates that cargoes for the New World were dispatched from English ports around the calendar, with more activity in November and December. (See Table 1.1.) Yet even in the quietest months of April and June, some vessels were clearing English ports for transatlantic destinations. These sources suggest more seasonality to the return of ships and news to English ports from across the Atlantic. Ships seldom arrived in the spring and were most likely to dock between midsummer and late autumn. The few arrivals in late winter were generally tobacco and sugar ships from the winterless colonies.[28] This preliminary evidence suggests that Atlantic shipping might not conform to ideal seasonal schedules, and the various routes might bear closer examination.

How often could transatlantic correspondents hope to write each other? Experienced correspondents adjusted to the rhythms of particular routes, and there are some indications of more general expectations. Promoters of colonies occasionally gave clues of what proud settlers thought was a very good level of communications and presumably what they thought their readers would also find acceptable. William Bullock's *Virginia Impartially Examined* (London, 1649) misled his readers by claiming that New England's links with England were also Virginia's and that "men shall seldome misse passage for New England from London once in two Moneths."[29] Richard Ligon, describing the much less isolated Barbados colony at about the same time, argued that "ships will be every month, some or other, coming for England."[30] A monthly opportunity to correspond seems to have become an objective in the later Stuart empire. Boston's first attempt at a newspaper, written by an experienced London journalist used to weeklies there, was to be a monthly unless "any Occurrences happen oftener."[31] A monthly correspondence was the objective of the packet boat services to the West Indies initiated in 1702 and again in 1744 and also of the North American packets after 1755. In the early months of 1734, colonial worries about the outbreak of war could be allayed by a report from Barbados claiming that it must be peace because they have not had a packet from England for more than 30 days.[32] A migrant about to leave London for New York 30 years later could reassure his brother in Scotland

> As to the Distance from Great Britain, that is not so great as to prevent our frequently hearing from one another as there is a Packet Boat once a month to and from New York.[33]

Whatever the performance of ships or correspondents, it would appear that one opportunity each month was thought adequate in the case of major colonies.

The *Palm Tree* voyage of 1699–1700 suggests something else about the frequency of sailings. She was neither built nor sailed to be a sugar ship. She was quite small for an Atlantic sailor but a reminder that small vessels continued to operate in that trade. The *Palm Tree* left Plymouth to arrive at Barbados before the sugar fleet in order to bring her English exports to a better market at a winterless port. The loading time at Barbados suggests success in this marketing plan though other ships were doing likewise. The frequency of ships, like their speed, was an effort to meet expectations of that time, not of ours. From that perspective, neither success nor failure was a foregone conclusion.

Was it the dangers of Atlantic travel that dominated all other considerations and firmly established the ocean's role as a great barrier between worlds? From the days of their first expeditions, the English had paid a grim tribute in lives to the unknown Atlantic.[34] The annals that were gathered and popularized by Richard Hakluyt and Samuel Purchas may well have been intended to inspire the daring and energetic, but the stories of Thomas Cavendish, Richard Grenville, Humphrey Gilbert, John Hawkins, and Francis Drake all ended in death at sea. Although mariners always risked their lives, the "Western Ocean" meant a host of new dangers. Unknown shorelines, with their uncharted currents, shoals, and reefs, were more dangerous than an unknown ocean. Despite all that the English had learned from the Spanish and the Portuguese about Atlantic travel, many mariners were lost in the discovery of the best routes and the safest harbors of English America.

As chroniclers of Atlantic passages, the Tudor explorers were succeeded by Stuart landsmen. Although thousands of seventeenth-century Englishmen made their living aboard trading and fishing vessels on the Atlantic, they and their contemporaries regarded their work as unremarkable and unexceptional. Literate officers still occasionally published their impressions of new lands, but the published sea journals of the time, both real and fictitious, described voyages beyond the "Western Ocean."[35] It was the landsmen who explored and settled the New World who came to write most accounts of Stuart North Atlantic travel. These men often found the Atlantic crossing itself one of their most frightening ordeals, and deliverance on dry land was regarded as a mercy of God.

Surviving a sea voyage came to be regarded as a special providence by many devout travelers, be they Puritan, Quaker, or Anglican. William Bradford's brief description of the *Mayflower*'s unexceptional passage of just under two months is a moralized tale of suffering and deliverance. John Winthrop's journal of a comparable passage on the *Arabella* shows more confidence. Winthrop thanked God on occasion but regarded crossing the Atlantic as within the competence of man.[36] Perhaps belief in the "errand into the wilderness" presumed a passable ocean. But Winthrop's jottings of what he found curious or interesting were converted into religious allegory later. The theme of spiritual deliverance found in Bradford, Thomas Shepherd, Roger Clap, or John Hull would be imposed on Winthrop in Cotton Mather's *Magnalia Christi Americana.* Here the *Arabella* becomes an ark of Noah, and the crossing of the Atlantic becomes a divine dispensation greater than the parting of the Red Sea for the ancient Israelites. The whole enterprise, indeed the whole American continent, becomes part of God's plan for a New Jerusalem. England becomes Babylon, and Winthrop is Nehemiah leading his people out of slavery and into the promised land.[37] Yet part of the colonial history of Boston is the story of vain efforts to insulate a growing seaport town from influences that were never far enough away. A broad and frightening ocean was useful to the New England Puritan perspective in 1700 and would have related uses long afterward.

Most Quaker travelers who published memoirs were "ministering friends" who traveled the Atlantic as they had traveled the British Isles and continental Europe to share their vision of Christ and encourage their coreligionists. Their memoirs were spiritual autobiographies designed to be exemplars.[38] No other type of travel account can be quite as devoid of description or wonder at the worlds encountered. For George Fox, whose journal set the pattern for most Quakers on similar missions, the ocean was the scene of divine deliverance from storms, pirates, and other enemies.[39] With their religious hope, the chroniclers are usually the only ones aboard who remained calm. Like evil men, the ocean tried to hinder the progress of truth but failed.

Anglican divines were less drawn to spiritual autobiography, but some could sound like their Puritan or Quaker counterparts. In 1736, John Wesley recorded his party's reaction to the storms of a passage to Georgia.

> We returned God thanks for our deliverance, of which a few appeared duly sensible. But the rest [like true cowards] (among whom were most of the sailors) denied we had been in any danger. I could not have believed that so little good would have been done by the terror they were in before.[40]

The purposeful contrast between godly passengers and cursing seamen was common enough.[41] It remains hard to imagine the able seaman, who was up in the sheets in all weather, being as terrified as this embarrassed landlubber. The religious representation of the ocean was hostile, was printed, and was widely accepted.

Despite supporting evidence and its social utility, the notion of the deadly ocean creates some difficulties. Members of the colonial elite—the fortunate few of a time when few were that fortunate—made their wills, prayed, and bade tearful farewells before setting out on ocean voyages. They went to lobby for colonial appointments or causes; to supervise the buying and selling of cargoes; or to gain status-giving education, friends, or experience.[42] Were these people daredevils driven by vanity and greed? Was Edward Randolph, son of a Kent physician and eventually a pugnacious surveyor general of customs in America, desperately possessed to cross the Atlantic 17 times?[43] John Smith, a Harvard graduate and prominent Boston dry-goods merchant, risked a regular annual trip to London on business.[44] And what folly led Captain Bryant of New York to complete 55 voyages from his home port to London, for a total of 110 Atlantic crossings?[45] For those of us cursed with the desire for solid statistics, these examples may not convince. Yet there may have been many John Smiths and Captain Bryants even if mercy demanded that there were not many Edward Randolphs.

If the people at the captain's table are puzzling, the same is certainly true of the men in the fo'c'sle. There is plenty of evidence that theirs was a hard life, and the journal keepers among them often reflected on their unwise choice of work as they scrambled from a wreck, were taken prisoner once more, or pulled on the oars of an Algerian galley.[46] Yet some 10,000 English-speaking seamen worked ships in Atlantic waters at the turn of the eighteenth century.[47] Some may have joined to escape even more desperate circumstances ashore, and some, like Robinson Crusoe, may have been lured by a free passage to the unknown.[48] English merchant seamen were able to price their risks; they gained major wage concessions from wartime risks. A merchant seaman's peacetime wages of 24 shillings (s.) per month jumped to 45s. on the outbreak of war in 1689 and reached 55s. when naval convoy protection was particularly ineffective. Mariners also successfully refused to sail without an agreed scale of "smart money" for possible wounds.[49] War apparently made the sea a great deal more dangerous than ocean travel itself. Colonial wage scales for seamen are yet to be compiled, but the pool of desperate men could not be large enough to man the ships of a port like Boston.[50] Some of those who might have lived on a frontier farm or on Walden Pond actually chose to go to sea instead.

Although some people suffered and died in the Atlantic, were the risks still of the same magnitude by later Stuart times? Improving English knowledge of the oceans was symbolized by two events of 1675. The first was the establishment of the Royal Observatory at Greenwich, at once the fruit of the gentlemanly science of the Restoration and an unfulfilled promise to navigators. The second event was the publication of John Seller's *Atlas Maritimus*, the first English sea atlas and one printed by the man who had launched that eminently practical and popular *The English Pilot*.

The founding of the Royal Observatory was an indication of the theoretical and practical ambitions of the Royal Society. The failure of the gentlemanly scientists to discover a practical measure of longitude should not mask their contribution to the understanding of the English Atlantic. In the 1660's the society was very anxious to receive mariners' observations, and directions expressly for shipmasters were published in 1667.[51] If the Royal Society gradually drew away from some of the practical maritime problems, Edmond Halley was an outstanding exception who made great efforts to understand the ocean.[52] In 1686 he built on the earlier work of Vossius to attempt an explanation of the trade winds. This paper included the first general chart of the wind systems of the world.[53] Thanks in part to Halley's work, and that of

William Dampier, maps and globes dated after 1700 often showed the wind systems of the oceans in their general patterns. Explanations for these observed movements of winds and waters were less urgent, and little was accomplished until the efforts of George Hadley and Colin Maclaurin.[54] Halley's careful plotting of the compass variations of the North Atlantic proved of little value in the search for measurable longitude but nevertheless helped navigators.[55] The most significant navigational improvement, Hadley's octant, became available commercially by 1734,[56] and the first Atlantic trials of Harrison's chronometer began in 1736. The chronometer would greatly assist the explorers of the Pacific but brought belated precision for the mariners of the North Atlantic. Scientists and ingenious mechanics had made some progress in the decades before the chronometer, but the necessary practical knowledge was already widely available to those who wished to learn on the decks of men-of-war and merchantmen.

From the mid-1670's English chartmakers were not only increasing their productivity, but their subjects were becoming much more global as well. John Seller was a leading initiator of the trade in English printed charts; his *Atlas Maritimus* of 1675 has been called the first English sea atlas, and it was a digest of the first two volumes of his more ambitious *The English Pilot*. Seller went no further with this five-volume work himself but had launched this very enduring "Sea Waggoner for the whole World." It was the fourth volume, by John Thornton and William Fisher, that became the standard marine atlas of the English Atlantic from its first appearance in 1689 through its 37 legitimate and three pirated editions during the next 105 years. A growing market and improved charts by leading cartographers, including Herman Moll and Cyprian Southack, caused more frequent editions after 1706 than had been the case earlier. Labeled for pilots, rather than for learned navigators, this book included profiles to help identify islands sighted, channels and soundings of significant ports, and descriptions of routes and approaches. Here was an aid to any practical master mariner sailing the English Atlantic.[57]

Improving English knowledge of the oceans brought a better understanding and reduced risks on the most familiar ocean. For the English, the "Atlantic" was only the North Atlantic through most of the eighteenth century. Most English maps of the period labeled their nearest ocean the "Atlantic," the "Western," the "Great Western Ocean," or the "North Sea."[58] All or part of the South Atlantic was usually labeled the "Ethiopean Sea," the sea into which slavers ventured. William Dampier, English buccaneer and observer whose maritime career began in 1674, correctly argued that the width of the North Atlantic had been exaggerated and also attempted to expand the range of the term "Atlantic Ocean."

> . . . I use that name not only for the North-Sea, as 'tis called, but for
> this whole Ocean, on both sides of the Equator between Europe and
> Africk on the one hand, and America on the other. If I be questioned

for taking this Liberty, I should think it enough to say, that I wanted a general name for this whole Ocean, and I could not find one more proper.[59]

His bold effort did not convert English mapmakers. Even the maps in Dampier's volume, maps made by the famous Herman Moll, still labeled the "Ethiopian Sea." There were other reasons why the North Atlantic was considered the only Atlantic. Dampier's own instructions on the difficult maritime crossing of the equator illustrated how the winds resisted his enlarged Atlantic.[60] In European diplomacy the equator had become "the Line" beyond which their fragile international civility did not venture. The equator also seemed to be the limit of the ambitions of the later Stuart monarchs.[61] Daniel Defoe wisely placed Robinson Crusoe on an imaginary island at the edge of the relatively familiar ocean; imagination gained its freedom some miles south of Barbados though just north of the equator.[62] It is also significant that "the Line" did not extend eastward into the Gulf of Guinea. The "Ethiopean Sea" was in the beyond for many reasons, however valuable those returning slavers would be after they recrossed the equator. Imagination, diplomacy, bureaucratic ambition, and moral frontiers all reinforced the English Atlantic as defined by the mapmakers, the currents, and the winds.

While scholars and mapmakers worked, hundreds of shipmasters equipped with the instruments of their Tudor predecessors sailed the routes of the North Atlantic using experience rather than science. More numerous lighthouses improved maritime safety; by 1740 there were 40 lights aiding shipping around the British Isles, and the first English colonial lighthouses were operating at Boston (1716) and Tybee Island, Georgia (1740?).[63] Edmond Halley was one who urged more navigational sophistication, as when he complained to Samuel Pepys about the primitive methods

> used by masters of ships to find their ports and you will know how tenaciously or rather obstinately they resolve to make use of no other than the Common Plain Chart as if the earth were a flat, when at the same time they all know and allow that they sail on a Globe, and they content themselves that those that knew no more have yet brought their ships home safe. Whence they conclude that any further Art, as they calle it, is superfluous.[64]

Halley's complaint was understandable, yet parallel sailing sufficed on the main routes of the North Atlantic; it would certainly have been enough for William Lewis as master of the *Palm Tree* in 1699.

Although the dangers of Atlantic travel were no longer those of explorers, the landsman's understandable fear of the sea remained. George Alsop ridiculed "my poor Mechanick Countreymen" who bragged of their fearlessness as soldiers but found the idea of a sea voyage an instant laxative.[65] The

Reverend Charles Wolley, Anglican chaplain to the New York garrison in 1679–1680—and no seaman—recognized that prospective migrants might be worried about the voyage.

> . . . but oh the passage, the passage thither, *hic labor, hoc opus est*: there is the timorous objection: the Ship may flounder by springing a leak, be wreckt by a Storm or taken by a Pickeroon: which are plausible pleas to flesh and blood, but if we would examine the bills of mortality and compare the several accidents and diseases by the Land, we should find them almost a hundred for one to what happens by Sea, . . .[66]

Wolley's statistics are doubtful, but our reading of surviving ships' logs could be improved. Sea logs and diaries provided evidence for captains and owners, as well as courts, on the management of ships at sea. Lawsuits were often launched by merchants whose goods arrived damaged, implying that arrival itself was not taken as a miracle. The logs also determined pay owing to deceased seamen and, incidentally, served as a parish register because of that. In this function, the ship logs read like the registers of all-male parishes—all deaths and no births.

Wolley's timorous travelers were real, but some could be converted. John Dunton describes his very healthy fear of the ocean as he set off from London for Boston, Massachusetts, in 1685; but as he left Boston on the return trip, his doggerel included the following:

> Look how on the shore they hoop and they hollow.
> Not for joy I am gone, but for grief they can't follow.[67]

It is also interesting that, by the early eighteenth century, colonial doctors were recommending sea voyages for the recovery of one's health, and ships' surgeons were being eliminated as unnecessary for most transatlantic merchantmen though they were still used on Hudson Bay, Mediterranean, African, and Indian voyages.[68] Chaplain Wolley concluded his account of the dangers of the sea with one of Lord Bacon's apothegms. In this, a mariner mentions that his great-grandfather, his grandfather, and his father all died at sea. The landsman's reaction was, "If I were you, I would never go to sea." When challenged as to where *his* ancestors had died, the landsman proudly announced that they had all died in their beds. The mariner's obvious retort was, "If I were you, I would never go to bed."[69]

In the exploration of English Atlantic communications, there are special advantages in focusing on the period after the *Palm Tree* was built in 1675. By this time, what Pierre Chaunu has called "the first Atlantic" was being succeeded by a second, more diverse, primarily Northern European Atlantic— and one eventually dominated by the English.[70] By this time the tentative and often tragic beginnings of isolated English colonies were in the past. Although the populations and economies of Jamaica and the Carolinas indicated that they were still just beginning by 1675 and though Pennsylvania, Georgia, and Nova Scotia were still to be founded, the outlines of the political economy of the English Atlantic empire were already developed. The staple trades in sugar and tobacco had proved their worth in developing internal imperial markets, government revenues, and reexport profits. The drive to exclude foreigners from this carrying trade had begun with legislation and war in the early 1650's. By 1675 the trade wars with the Dutch were over, the Navigation Acts had been established and strengthened, and the administrative machinery was being created to improve enforcement. The establishment of the Lords of Trade in 1675 as a permanent office of colonial administration was just one more sign of increased royal interest in colonial affairs in the last decade of Charles II's reign. Bacon's rebellion in Virginia the following year was stark testimony that the subletting of authority to governors could be dangerous. Both Charles II and his brother, James, usually encouraged those who sought tighter control of the English Atlantic political economy in the name of the king. This somewhat spasmodic drive to centralize would succeed in creating the vice-admiralty court system, creating colonial agencies in London to facilitate business, and had considerable initial success in bringing proprietary and charter colonies under closer London scrutiny. This last objective would outlive these kings but would remain under active consideration long after England's governments denounced the centralizing efforts of Charles and James as tyranny.

By 1675 the English had declared and defended an Atlantic maritime empire. In this process, many Dutch merchantmen were taken prize, providing much-needed tonnage for an English merchant fleet that was initially unable to service the declared shipping monopoly.[71] The rather vulnerable and cumbersome Dutch flyboats were not important in the English Atlantic trades, but these additions freed more English-built ships to join the colonial-built fleets in the subsequent growth of colonial trades. The ships of the English Atlantic trades did not change much in size in the lifetime after 1675, so that any increase in staple production and colonial population brought increased traffic in direct proportion, adding to the opportunities to receive news, to write, or to travel. Innovations in the ships themselves were limited although the development of headsails and of the helm wheel did improve the control of ships from early in the eighteenth century. Innovations in ship design were minimal between 1675 and 1740 and had little effect on the speed, frequency, or safety of Atlantic crossings.

From a number of perspectives, then, it seems valuable to examine the nature of English Atlantic communications between 1675 and 1740. Initially, it is advisable to study the various routes of the English Atlantic as separate entities with different traffic patterns, levels, seasons, and passage times. As the seventeenth century drew to a close, these routes were still largely independent of each other, like bent spokes of some giant rimless wheel. Part I of this study will explore the separate evolution of these routes. Part II focuses on the conscious, even strenuous efforts made to improve communications through postal services, newspapers, and mail packet boats. These efforts reveal expectations, possibilities, and implications. Each part concludes with a case study of the spread of news in the English Atlantic empire. These inquiries are followed, in Part III, by an attempt to indicate some of the political, economic, and social aspects and implications of the findings of this investigation.

PART I

News by Merchantman

Cet Océan, qui semble mis au milieu des terres pour en faire une éternelle séparation, est au contraire le rendez-vous de tous les peuples, qui ne pourraient aller par terre d'un bout du monde à l'autre qu'avec des fatigues, des longueurs et des dangers incroyables. C'est par ce chemin sans traces, au travers des abîmes, que l'ancien monde donne la main au nouveau, et que le nouveau prête à l'ancien tant de commodités et de richesses.

—François de Salignac de La Mothe-Fénelon (1713)

2 · Sugar Routes

The central Atlantic ring of currents and winds had remained the main route for transatlantic travel from the days of Columbus. Nature's invitation to the Iberians was so obvious that later Spanish convoys made little improvement on the passage times of Columbus's expeditions.[1] The same Canaries Current that drew Spanish galleons into the trade winds would also bring them back after an elliptical clockwise circuit that was almost the shortest distance to and from the New World. (See Figure 2.) This route had not been a sugar route of consequence for the Iberians. Indeed, when the Dutch, French, and English launched the Caribbean sugar industry in the seventeenth century, one of the incentives was that this sugar would be much closer to European markets than was the major Brazilian sugar industry.[2] Caribbean sugar routes became the main Atlantic routes of the English and of their competitors.

Although nature invited the Spanish to the Caribbean and objected little to French participation, the English were not invited by the wind and waves of the Channel. Although the *Palm Tree*'s great sailing circle was natural enough, it was traveled in peacetime and originated from Plymouth. English access to the central routes was objected to most persistently by the westerlies and most forcefully by French privateers in wartime. Both these objections were most effective in the Channel, but London controlled the English sugar trade despite the geography of Atlantic navigation. London's predominance derived from the power to raise capital, distribute goods, and influence government.

The Channel has been called "the highway to the ocean" but, with the currents running to the east and the westerlies reinforcing these 74 percent of the time with speeds averaging 14 knots in summer and 25 knots in winter,[3] it might be better named the highway from the ocean. The westerlies launched Thames shipping, then becalmed it in the Downs. A wind from the eastern half of the compass, the once-famous "Protestant wind" more likely in winter, carried London's shipping into the Channel as surely as it brought French privateers out to harass them in wartime. Once in the Channel, the

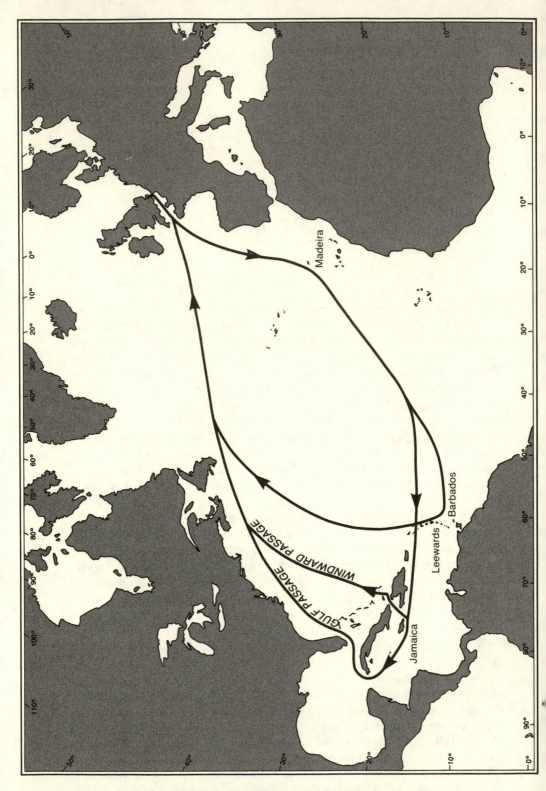

Figure 2. Main English Sugar Routes.

square-rigged sugar ships were likely to be stalled, if not threatened, by the westerlies. Many an outward-bound passenger lamented the irritating, lengthy, and expensive sojourns at Channel ports. The well-to-do tended to join their ship at Portsmouth and thereby avoid much of the delay. Letters, orders, and news were often sent on to Plymouth or Falmouth by post rider; even bad roads could be better than the narrow, choppy Channel waters, known to old tars as the "sea of sore heads and sore hearts."

As the Channel widened at Lyme Bay and Plymouth Sound to give sea room to the south, the westerlies became usable not only for nimble sloops and brigs with their fore-and-aft rigging but also for ships and barques like the *Palm Tree*. As the mail packets for the West Indies would demonstrate, vessels could operate out of Falmouth and Plymouth in all seasons with minimal delay for favorable winds. By contrast, Bristol ships had to fight the westerlies in negotiating the Bristol Channel although it was shorter and safer than the gauntlet run by London ships. Inland distribution and Irish trade advantages helped Bristol to remain the premier outport, even though both Plymouth and Liverpool ships could maneuver out of their home port much more effectively in the face of the westerlies. The advantages of the ports of the Southwest, the West Country, and the major Irish ports would give them a greater place in the seasonal distribution of news than in the distribution of sugar. In peacetime, these ports were one or two weeks closer to the West Indies than was London. During war, when London shipping paid for its nearness to government by convoy and embargo restrictions that were most effectively enforced in the Thames,[4] the western outports benefited even more.

A sugar convoy illustrates the outward voyage. Four men-of-war and a dozen merchantmen weighed anchor in Plymouth Sound and bore away for Barbados on 16 June 1694.[5] The only thing at all out of the ordinary was the sailing date in June. A detailed study of the last five years of the century indicates that, of 251 vessels clearing English customs for the sugar islands, more than one third sailed in the favored months of November through January. The season April to June was the least favored, with 37 clearances in 5 years, but these were proof enough that ships laden with goods, passengers, and news could and did leave England for the West Indies in any month of the year.[6]

Any English sugar fleet clearing Plymouth was off on a voyage measured better in days than miles, and half the sailing time would be spent covering one third of the distance: the third that led to Madeira and the entrance to the central Atlantic circle. Although paced by its slowest merchantman, the 1694 convoy accomplished something very close to an average passage. The 26 days from Plymouth to Madeira at an average speed of 2 knots was not slow, though individual merchantmen had occasionally tripled that speed.[7] If summer sailing across the westerlies made for slower initial progress for the big square-riggers, the northerly summer winds off the Portuguese coast, known as the Portuguese trades, would more than compensate.

Madeira was a Portuguese island, but the subjects of the king of England dominated its anchorages. Not only were most of the ships trading at the island English, but visits from outward-bound English colonial governors were not uncommon.[8] The sight of Madeira would quickly bring logbooks back into unison after the cumulative differences that the log-and-line reckonings had created. Refreshment, news, and the opportunity to send home word of their progress were reasons enough to stop at Madeira. Crews of the larger ships would also have loaded pipes of the island's famous wine, which improved during the sea voyage and was popular in West Indies markets.[9]

After a week at Madeira, the Barbados convoy of 1694 set out on a southwesterly course, urged on by the trade winds that blow from outside of the tropics in the summer. Averaging twice the speed achieved between Plymouth and Madeira, the fleet bettered 100 nautical miles a day. Although some individual merchantmen were faster than this,[10] this convoy's total time of 60 days compares well with passages of merchantmen clearing Channel ports for Barbados in all seasons once peace returned. (See Table 2.1.)

The diagonal crossing between Madeira and the eastern Caribbean was one of the few major seventeenth-century routes of the English Atlantic that deviated very far from "parallel sailing" along lines of latitude. It took the constancy of the trade winds to lure shipmasters away from the land and sea breezes in coastal waters and from the navigational reassurance of the occasional headland to confirm celestial navigation.[11] The more direct diagonal route to the West Indies required a precise latitude reading as a vessel made and held the latitude of 13°N in order to make the final approach to Barbados. The Davis quadrant, which was popular among English-speaking shipmasters, had to be used within one minute of noon in such a low latitude, in order to get a reliable reading from the fast-moving tropical sun. James Logan, in advocating a Pennsylvanian improvement on the Davis quadrant in 1734, commented:

> And yet, perhaps, no Parts of the World require more Exactness in taking the Latitude than is necessary in Voyages to the West-Indies: For it is owing to the Difficulty of it, that Vessels have so frequently miss'd the Island of Barbados, and when got to the Leeward of it have been obliged to run down a thousand Miles further to Jamaica, from whence they can scarce work up again in the Space of many Weeks, . . .[12]

If missing the island was a rather obvious and expensive embarrassment, it is surprising that the supposedly frequent misses are not better recorded. In 1701, however, one such incident was reported. A shipmaster approaching Antigua missed the island but was apparently so convinced and convincing about the accuracy of his navigation that all those abroad, as well as the people of Philadelphia where he docked, believed for a time that the island of Antigua had been completely destroyed by an earthquake.[13]

Although the main route to the West Indies was southwesterly from Madeira, there were ships other than slavers that continued southward from

Madeira to the Cape Verde Islands, particularly to load free salt at the Isle of May. Dampier's estimate that 100 English ships a year stopped at the Cape Verdes may be generous, but at least one comparatively well-informed English visitor was convinced that the Isle of May was an English island.[14] Slavers left the central Atlantic circle beyond the Cape Verde Islands, and those few slavers who chose to beat their way back there before a "middle passage" to the West Indies were taking the longer route despite the maps.[15] Most slavers approached Barbados from the southeast, having returned to the North Atlantic on the South Equatorial Current. Seldom were slavers able to bring English or English-American news to the West Indies.

When the 1694 Barbados convoy carrying the new governor, Sir Francis Russell, dropped anchor in Carlisle Bay in August, they found a fleet of 26 other ships preparing for a convoyed voyage back to England.[16] Why all this activity at Barbados at the onset of the hurricane season? What cargo could the arriving fleet expect when the perishable muscovado sugars are ready only in January and the clayed sugars by June? And what of the ships that was outward-bound in mid-August?

The worst hurricane in a generation smashed into Barbados six weeks later at the end of September. The dazed survivors must have feared that God had gone over to the French. Twenty-six ships were lost, and the frenzied waters completely destroyed the stone breakwater at Bridgetown. Gales lashed the island for four days, and the hurricane raced off to the north in pursuit of the ships that had left the island in August. That convoy was caught some 400 leagues to the north, where it had been becalmed. Twelve Barbados merchantmen and the mammoth 800-ton East Indiaman *Medina*, which was coming home *via* Barbados for protection against French privateers, all went down with all hands. The other 13 shattered and scattered ships were left to fend off privateers as best they could.[17]

Had war forced these fleets to defy the natural law of the sugar seasons? When the opportunity arose to blame the Admiralty rather than the Almighty for their substantial losses, the London merchants made it sound as though such hurricanes came to Barbados as surely and regularly as did September. Most surviving materials and historians' opinions based on them have claimed that Barbados shipping had a clearly defined season.[18] Midsummer brought epidemic mortality among visitors to the West Indies; August to October was the hurricane season and, therefore, no time to be in Barbados waters; and in winter, gales on the North Atlantic were to be avoided. Indeed, the first months of the year would seem to be the only safe time for a ship to be in or near Barbados or the other English islands.

How well were shipmasters able to schedule sailings to avoid these predictable hazards? Even in the years 1695–1700 when memories of this Barbados convoy disaster were still vivid, most ships clearing English ports for the sugar islands did not time their departure to meet the new sugars in the spring. Of 482 ships arriving at Barbados, 67 arrived during the hurricane season. There were more arrivals in the first half of the year than in the last, but English ships were arriving at Barbados in every month of the year in peacetime.[19] The relatively even distribution of entries from Britain, compared with the uneven pattern of departures from Britain for the islands, was the result of stopovers by some vessels in Ireland or the islands of the eastern Atlantic. With upward of 100 ships a year sailing from Britain to Barbados at the end of the seventeenth century,[20] the island was well placed to receive cargoes, news, and gossip regularly. Like the *Palm Tree*, a number of ships were timing their voyages to maximize profit on their cargoes to Barbados.

Yet seafaring men had not forgotten the hurricane. British-based shipping may have arrived at Barbados at all times of the year bringing news, bills of lading, and orders from the metropolis, as well as merchandise, but there was some respect for the hurricane season in the timing of their departures from the island. In the convoy-free years of 1699 and 1700, more than half (86 of 167) of the clearances from Barbados destined for Britain were in the spring. Vessels that arrived at the island late in the year nearly always waited there over the northern winter and returned with the new sugars in the spring. Still, it is important to notice that nearly half of the vessels did not adhere to this pattern, and there were vessels leaving Barbados for Britain every month of the year except January. In peacetime, Barbadians had monthly opportunities to write, ship, or travel to England.

The shortest version of the sugar routes across the English Atlantic was that taken by the ships that returned directly to England from Barbados or the Leewards. The northeastward route was a great nonstop arc that began with the fully laden merchantmen heading northwest across the trade winds. The course shifted toward the north, but winds lightened, and calms were usual as the ships worked northward in search of the westerlies, the highway home. Convoyed passages of six to seven weeks were not uncommon, but eight to nine weeks proved the average. In times of emergency, a hired, sloop-rigged packet boat was expected to cut two weeks off the time, but this expensive expedient was seldom used.[21] Except for ships in distress, Bermuda was too far to the west on the route back to England, and the Azores were out of sight to ships passing to the north. The English route from the eastern Caribbean was only marginally shorter than the route outward: The difference can be accounted for by the outward-bound stop at Madeira rather than the Channel difficulties, which were offset by the speeds achieved while sailing with the trade winds. Unlike communications with the rest of the Atlantic empire, the English routes to and from the eastern Caribbean were about the same length, eight to nine weeks.

At the end of the seventeenth century, the winds and currents of the central Atlantic circle brought more ships to Barbados from the New World than from the Old, and most of the former came in from New England. (See Tables 2.2 and 2.3.) New England shipmasters arriving at Barbados from their home ports had completed a voyage that was nearly as far as, and more difficult to navigate than, the English sugar route to Barbados. From the New England ports the ships ran before the westerlies, working as far south as these winds would permit. Near mid-ocean, which had to be determined without any longitudinal measurement, the masters drew the vessel away from the westerlies toward the south. The light and variable winds of the "horse latitudes" were better used by fore and aft sails in making headway south and east in search of the edge of the trade winds and the main English route to Barbados. As a ship sailed southward, none of the available instruments helped determine when the ship was far enough to the east to be safely windward of Barbados. Even the compass varied from 10° west of true north at Boston to 5° east of true north at Barbados, according to Edmond Halley's isogonic chart of 1700. Nor were there Atlantic islands to help on this trip. The Azores were an unnecessarily long arc for a direct passage to Barbados and were even less frequent as a triangular approach to Barbados than the little-used New England-Madeira-Barbados route.[22] Sighting of Bermuda or any other Caribbean island would end all hope of a reasonable voyage to Barbados and do nothing for the master's reputation with his crew. The 3800-mile voyage from Massachusetts ports to Barbados, double the direct distance, was no coasting voyage. In peacetime, the average passage time from New England to Barbados was just over six weeks, at an average speed of better than 3.5 knots.[23]

Bridgetown and Boston were usually first to be favored with news from Stuart England, and the volume and seasons of their shipping connections with each other further enhanced their advantage as sources of news. Of some 70 New England-owned vessels entering Barbados annually at the end of the seventeenth century, 56 had come directly from their home province. Thirty-five years later, although Barbados had lost its place of primacy as an English sugar island, there were 75 ships arriving at Barbados from New England ports in addition to the 10 from New York and 22 from Philadelphia.[24] (See Table 2.3.) As English North American ports grew, so would their links with each other and with Bridgetown. As a result, comparatively good connections became even better.

As if in deliberate defiance of the hurricanes, the New Englanders actually favored July as well as January for entering Barbados. Again it is important to notice that some ships came in from New England in each calendar month in peacetime. January was the favored month for New England vessels, avoiding the idle time of the northern winter with a single annual Caribbean voyage that could sell fresh provisions to sugar ships. Many July entries were by vessels continuously employed in the West Indies trade and accomplishing two six-month round-trips each year. These New Englandmen were arriving when most of the English ships were not, thereby maximizing the island market for their provisions. Their European news would be rather stale although their information on northern colonial markets would be eagerly sought.[25]

New England shipmasters could trade news at Barbados and would sometimes learn more than they taught. Most Barbados clearances for North America were in July, August, and September: to bring rum for the continental harvest; apparently to test the Lord's mercy in the midst of the hurricane season; but not to bring any "fresh advices" from Britain via the West Indies. Between November and February, few cleared Barbados directly for New

England, for the option of loading salt at Salt Tortuga Island off the Venezuela coast was popular in that season.[26] But those who did brave the direct winter passage back to New England brought English news, mail, and newspapers with them in addition to West Indian information. When important European news occurred in early winter, as was the case in the winter of 1688–1689, the Northern colonies would learn of it first by way of the West Indies, and in the seventeenth century the English West Indies would likely learn of it first by way of Barbados.

Barbados was the premier colony on the sugar routes of the later Stuart empire, producing over half of the sugar imported into England and needing imported provisions for its 65,000 people. Whether it was news concerning market prices of sugar, merchant or naval shipping that had entered the Caribbean, threatening French squadrons, or changes in the political winds in England, Barbadians were well placed to be among the first to know the westbound news. English or English colonial shipmasters anxious to maximize the safety and yield on their ventures could learn much at this island drawing 300 ships a year in all seasons from England's Atlantic empire.

As English Atlantic news passed to the Leeward Islands and on to Jamaica, so, too, would the primacy in the sugar trade of the English Atlantic. Without any noticeable decline in sugar exports before the 1730's, Barbados had been surpassed by the rapid growth of sugar exports from the Leeward Islands and Jamaica. This development would shift attention to Antigua as the center for news in the English Caribbean, but Barbados kept its remarkable level of communications with Britain until the 1730's and its trading connections with North America continued strong. (See Table 2.2.) As the main route into the English Caribbean shifted north from Barbados, that island saw less of what was passing to leeward. The launching of the *Barbados Gazette* in 1731[27] coincided less with a growing demand for news than with the first signs of a diminishing supply.

Spreading news from Barbados to the Leeward Islands had been simple enough as the English government recognized when sending urgent expresses for all West Indian governments by packet to Barbados. The hundred leagues northwesterly from Bridgetown to English Harbour, Antigua, was a few-days' sail with the trades as a usable crosswind. In the peaceful years 1699 and 1700, an average of one vessel a week made the trip. This predominately local traffic between Barbados and the Leewards was not impeded by seasons, but it could be entirely disrupted in wartime by the French privateers based along the route at Martinique, Guadeloupe, and Désirade. The return trip to Barbados was more difficult, but it was possible for the small fore-and-aft rigged sloops and ketches of the islands and the mainland colonies. For example, in 1700, a year with light sugar crops that made ships work harder for freight, there were 57 entries to Barbados from the Leewards, including at least one vessel each month.[28]

The English Leeward Islands emerged from their varied and vulnerable beginnings to become even more important than Barbados to the English sugar trade. Although the four main Leeward Islands are as much as 40 miles apart, they were a single freight market, had a single governor, and normally exchanged news easily. In the 1670's the variety of crops grown there and local supplies of provisions made the islanders less dependent on imports than were the Barbadians but also limited their access to news. The approximately 19,000 people living on the islands late in the 1670's were being visited by about 100 ships a year from all quarters. Half of this traffic was to Nevis, the island that was then leading the Leewards in the shift toward more sugar, which meant more slaves and more ships.[29] As late as 1690, when the English government was calculating the wartime shipping allowed to go to the English West Indies, the Leeward Islands were allocated only one seventh of the total, 23 ships amounting to 1710 tons.[30]

The tripling of the sugar exports from the Leeward Islands in the first third of the eighteenth century (see Table 2.4) did not mean an end to local provisions crops, but the growing specialization and interdependence increased shipping dramatically. In the year following Ladyday 1719, for instance, the island of Antigua alone had 130 entrances and 159 clearances of ships in the oceanic trades with England and North America. These ship movements were distributed throughout the calendar except for February. Ships were in from North America in all months, and entries from and clearances for Britain occurred in all months except December and February.[31] In the next two decades, St. Kitts would come to produce more sugar than Antigua, but the old capital would keep its place of primacy.[32]

Antigua came to replace Barbados as the usual source of the "freshest advices" in the English Caribbean in the years after 1714. Expansion of the Leeward Island sugar production was part of the reason; the growth of Jamaica was another. The general routes of ships from old and New England bound for the Caribbean were little changed, but the 17°N latitude became the approach for more of the vessels, and the voyages were 100 leagues and a few days shorter as a result. Antigua, with its position to windward of the English Leewards and its fine harbor, became a major port of call for Jamaica-bound ships from Britain. Antigua's rising status was clearly demonstrated by the development of the first British naval station in the eastern Caribbean at English Harbour from the late 1720's.[33] The changing naval strategy, which included the emergence of overseas naval bases at Jamaica, Antigua, and later Halifax, was at once an admission that occasional expeditionary forces were no longer adequate and an assertion that imperial priorities could be maintained by instructions and by Atlantic communications. These bases also indicated that naval, merchant, and pirate ships were in the Caribbean year-round.

Jamaica was separated from the other English sugar islands by more than the 300 leagues of the Caribbean. Born as a bellicose challenge to New Spain in 1655, the English colony served this purpose first for buccaneers and then for the Royal Navy. The trade winds that brought news from Barbados or Antigua in less than a fortnight were the same winds that could bring Jamaica an invasion overnight from the French or Spanish communities on Hispaniola. Jamaica was the isolated and vulnerable frontier of the English

Empire in the Caribbean. Because her shipping had to run the gauntlet of all the Caribbean freebooters in peace and of all the same enemies battle-dressed as privateers in war, Jamaica needed to be more self-sufficient than the other English islands. With eight times the area of all the other English sugar islands combined, though much of her land unsuitable for growing sugar, Jamaica could become the premier sugar producer of England's empire in the eighteenth century without ever being as dependent on imported provisions as was Barbados.

When Edward Barlow signed on as a mate of the 280-ton *Cadiz Merchant* in 1681, he began his fourth voyage from London to Jamaica in as many years. The three earlier voyages had followed the main sugar route south to the tropics, but this time northwesterly winds and fear of Algerian pirates prompted a course to the north and west of the Azores. Nonetheless, the *Cadiz Merchant* was thereafter worked more to the south than was usual until the thirteenth parallel and Barbados were reached, allowing Barlow his third visit to Barbados in four Jamaica voyages. This passage of 43 days to Barbados and just under 8 weeks from Plymouth to Jamaica was a good merchantman's passage, for the average was between 9 and 11 weeks. Mail packets, by comparison, averaged exactly 8 weeks to Jamaica in 41 passages from ports in southwest England, and these trips included brief stops at Barbados and each of the four Leeward Islands.[34]

The *Cadiz Merchant* ended its seven-week stay at Jamaica and set off on the longest English Atlantic passage of them all after a parting feast for the captain, who had contracted an English Atlantic marriage and was leaving as his bride in Jamaica a gentlewoman he had met on the outward voyage. Barlow would log 6256 miles on each of his two passages from Jamaica to the Downs in the *Cadiz Merchant*. This fourth voyage gave Barlow his first experience of the Windward Passage between Cuba and Hispaniola, "it being the nearest way to England, but troublesome to come a great way against the wind and sometimes the current likewise . . ."[35] After five days of trying, the *Cadiz Merchant* and her two consorts altered course, passed Port Royal harbor again, and sailed northwest around Cuba and through the Straits of Florida, as Barlow had done in each of the last three years. A hard "norther" in the straits, together with the fast current and heavy seas, made this his worst passage through the gulf. Once the worry of the Bahama shoals had passed, the *Cadiz Merchant* would see no land until the Scilly Isles. HMS *Richmond* parted company with the merchantman in latitude 32°N. This naval frigate bound for Barbados, like slavers bound from Jamaica to Africa, traveled a great northward arc that took it near the latitude of Bermuda. The *Cadiz Merchant* continued in a northeasterly route until well north of Bermuda, when the course shifted more to the east.[36] On the first of Barlow's Jamaica voyages, he marveled, as an experienced mariner might, at the strong current that hurried them through the Straits of Florida, pushed them northward much farther than their log-and-line let them calculate, and gave them a "strong easterly current beyond our expectations" and a 62-day passage to the Downs, "which was a very quick and good passage from thence."[37] Discovering the Gulf Stream was not that easy; on his next three voyages Barlow lost the ocean river soon after leaving the straits themselves. Although there were some subsequent signs of improved information about the Gulf Stream, no major progress was evident before the middle of the eighteenth century.[38] Even without the Gulf Stream, Barlow's 75-day passage in 1682 compares well with his own previous voyages and with average times of 14 weeks recorded a generation later. Dummer's mail packets would use the Windward Passage and achieve a surprising average of only six weeks in the crossing to the southwest Channel ports.[39]

Throughout most of the period, when news was freighted in merchantmen, if not in wartime convoys of merchantmen, English news took between 9 and 11 weeks to reach Jamaica, and the return trip was 12 to 14 weeks. Comparative isolation may account for the emergence of the first English West Indian newspaper in Jamaica,[40] but the fact that London was farther away from Jamaica's news than Jamaica was from London's helps account for the squadron on station there by 1701 and the packet service during the subsequent war.

The passage times, however, mattered only if shipping opportunities existed. In Barlow's time, Jamaica was already the second-ranking English sugar island although also exporting logwood, hides, cotton, indigo, pimento, and ginger.[41] In the two years after Michaelmas 1685, there were 307 vessels importing goods into Jamaica, and 101 of them came directly from England or Ireland. At least 1, and as many as 10, vessels entered Jamaica from Britain in each of these 24 months. At least 2 ships a month arrived from Britain in the hurricane season though more arrived after October, and spring was the busiest season. (See Table 2.5.) As was the case at Barbados, the fully laden ships seldom cleared Jamaica customs during the hurricane season, yet at least 1 ship cleared Port Royal for Britain in 20 of 24 months. The seasons of shipping, like the passage times, made it a little easier for English administrators, merchants, or relatives to contact Jamaicans than it was for the islanders to reply. Nevertheless, with ships in from Britain every month and others bound out for England almost every month, Jamaicans were regularly in touch with England in the 1680's.

English Jamaica's first generation of development had been satisfactory, but, in the bellicose 30 years after Barlow's visits, the Jamaica trade refused to grow. In the 1680's the island exported to England about 5000 tons of sugar a year in 50 ships. In the interlude of peace that ended the century and in the first years after the Peace of Utrecht, approximately the same number of English merchantmen arrived at Jamaica.[42] In the decades of peace that followed 1714, Jamaica sugar exports would triple. (See Table 2.4.) In the wars beyond 1739, Jamaican trade would continue to grow, and ships would also be larger, but the sugar trade in general and the Jamaica trade in particular had suffered a great deal in the first two Anglo-French wars. The stationing of several men-of-war at Jamaica after 1701 helped with both local security and communications with England, as would the packet boats that ran during the subsequent decade of war.

Jamaica was bound, somewhat loosely, to the other English colonies in America by the demands of trade and security. Barbados and the Leeward Islands were Jamaica's listening posts, forwarding news that could arrive within a week or two on the numerous ships coming in through the Caribbean from England, Africa, or occasionally from North America; there was little traffic directly from Jamaica back to the other English sugar islands. The one-way traffic was usual in the Caribbean although there were exceptions that were tributes to the sailing abilities of the sloops and sailors of the area. As the voyage of HMS *Richmond* in 1681 illustrated, the route from Jamaica to Barbados was by way of Bermuda. The Jamaica Council put the matter succinctly during the distress of the Port Royal earthquake, stating that "it often takes as long for a ship to beat to windward to Barbados as to sail to England."[43]

Jamaica's trade with English North America developed a healthy reciprocity. Colonial ships brought timber, naval stores, horses, and some provisions to trade for molasses, rum, and sugars. Both the growth of this trade and the southward shift of leadership among the North American ports that dominated it are evident from Table 2.6. Although this intercolonial trade was small in comparison to Jamaica's sugar trade with England, the colonial trade grew comparably. New England ships were the most numerous in this trade, but New York, Philadelphia, Norfolk, and Charles Town (today Charleston) accounted, in turn, for more than their share of the increase in traffic. This southward shift reflected the advantages of shorter routes once development provided the cargoes needed for the Jamaica trade. The voyage to Jamaica through the Windward Passage was six weeks from Boston, just over four weeks from New York or Philadelphia, and noticeably less from Norfolk or Charles Town.[44] The return trip from Jamaica would be shorter than the outward voyage for ships from Charles Town, but longer in the other cases.

The seasons of Jamaica's trade with North America were, given its volumes and the limited postal connections south of Philadelphia through most of this period, especially important in considering the news-bearing potential of the trade. In the 36 months ending September 1688, there was at least one vessel into Jamaica from New England or New York every month.[45] Though the distribution was fairly even throughout the year, slightly more arrivals were recorded in midwinter and in midsummer than in other months. These seasonal variations were less pronounced than in the Barbados trade, where rum was a more significant preharvest export to North America. Peacetime traffic between Jamaica and the English North American ports represented a regular opportunity to send news, an opportunity that became more frequent with the increase in the volume of trade after 1714, and correspondence had also improved with the intercolonial postal service that had linked Boston to New York and Philadelphia after 1693 and eventually connected Charles Town with Piscataqua by 1738.

Charles Town's entry into the West Indies provisions trade continued a history that had bound South Carolina to the sugar islands and to the sugar routes of the English Atlantic. English settlement of the Carolinas had just begun in the last third of the seventeenth century, and the familiar problems of finding a merchantable staple and laborers would not be solved for a generation. Isolated by land from the other English mainland colonies and ill-served by sea until the rise of Charles Town, the Carolinas developed very little local shipping and did not attract much from elsewhere in the empire by the end of the seventeenth century. Only four vessels a year cleared England for the Carolinas at the end of the century, though these colonies had a population of some 16,000 by then.[46] With so little shipping, no clear seasonal pattern was yet evident, although a ship could be expected to leave England for Carolina in one of the last four months of any calendar year.

South Carolina's best communications were with Barbados in the generation after the founding flotilla stopped at that island on the way to the colony. The Carolina proprietors maintained an agent in Barbados, migrants from Barbados formed a substantial element in the settlement, and shipping timber and provisions to Barbados was an early Carolina trade. Yet only eight ships a year cleared Barbados for Carolina at the end of the century, including three London ships that had followed the main sugar route to Barbados on the way to Carolina to load deerskins. The traffic from Carolina back to Barbados was even lighter, and these sloops venturing to Barbados were doing so with less knowledge of market conditions than was usually available to Charles Town's competitors in this trade.[47] In 1700 those Carolinians living south of Cape Hatteras would get most of their English, European, and West Indian news by way of Barbados, and they could expect to be among the last English subjects living in the New World to hear such news.

The emergence of rice as the dominant staple of South Carolina and the rise of the naval store industry in North Carolina after the English government bounties of 1705 would both bring marked improvements in intercolonial and transatlantic shipping and communications in the area. New England traders had been important to North Carolina settlement and trade from the 1660's, and there had been an occasional ship to South Carolina from New England before 1700.[48] By the early eighteenth century, New England was as valuable as Barbados in transmitting news. Charles Town became the most active port for its size in North America in the generation after the Peace of Utrecht. Although Charles Town's population nearly doubled during that time, it still numbered only 6800 people in 1742. (See Table 4.1.) Nevertheless, the port was handling as many ships as the much larger ports of New York and Philadelphia. (Compare Tables 2.7, 4.7, and 4.12.) Charles Town's connections with the British West Indies also remained strong throughout this period, accounting for at least a quarter of the ship entries and clearances and representing the busiest trade until the mid-1730's. By then there were more ships arriving at Charles Town from North American ports, though direct return traffic to northern destinations was usually much lighter. (See Table 2.7) Charles Town's growing export trades, especially the transatlantic rice trade, prompted multilateral trading by vessels returning from Europe to other parts of English America before reentering at Charles Town.

More ships left Charles Town for Britain after 1715 than from any other North American port except Boston, and by the later 1730's Charles Town had surpassed even Boston. Although the legalization of direct rice shipments to southern Europe increased that traffic after 1730, most of the ships left Charles Town for England either to satisfy the English market or to clear English customs before going to northern European ports. This shipping headed for London itself or for the Channel ports of Poole, Cowes, or Dover. Bristol was a significant importer, but there was very little direct traffic from Charles Town to other English outports or to Ireland. London merchants were central to the reexport trade, making returns to shippers and merchants of other participating colonies. A Boston shipowner took Carolina rice as freight to Cowes and Amsterdam, expecting to be paid by a London merchant exporting to Boston. The ships touching at Channel ports forwarded mail packets to London, and the whole trade organization made communications between Charles Town and London particularly good.[49]

Although the rice trade concentrated much of Charles Town's transatlantic traffic into months that were winter elsewhere, the port's links with Britain in peacetime went well beyond the seasons of the rice trade. A calendar of Charles Town's shipping with Britain, limited by the nature of the surviving records, suggests that one monthly arrival from Britain could usually be expected except for one summer month when the toredo worm riddled wooden hulls in the salt water harbors of the southern colonies.[50] The much more numerous clearances for Britain offered similar writing, shipping, or traveling opportunities. (See Table 2.8.)

Passages from Charles Town to Britain were marginally longer than those from the more northerly ports but a short 5 weeks compared to the 9 to 11 weeks that were common on direct return voyages. Charles Town could not be a serious rival to Boston in the receiving of European news except during winter months. Then European and West Indian news, together with local information on the rice crop and the levels of shipping and freight rates, traveled aboard the intercolonial coasters, reinforced finally by postal links to the north in 1738.

By 1740 the Carolinas had ceased to be the southern frontier of English North America in several ways. Nearly 100,000 people lived in the Carolinas, including 60,000 slaves, whose presence and efforts were testimony to the extent of export-oriented plantation agriculture.[51] This community was visited by shipping that averaged more than one ship each week from the northern colonies and the British West Indies, with approximately one vessel each month in from Britain and southern Europe. A strong export trade to Britain maintained regular communications. These had more than local significance during the northern winter, which coincided with the peak of the Charles Town rice-exporting season. The number of ships in this trade, as well as the passage times compared to those of return voyages, meant that Charles Town was much better positioned to communicate with London than was London to communicate with Charles Town. Arrival in Charles Town of those twin communication improvements, a newspaper (1732) and postal connections with the other colonies (1738), reflected and reinforced the change of the Carolinas from an annex to the sugar routes into a vigorous and well-connected part of the English Atlantic political economy.

War could impose seasons on the English Atlantic sugar routes much more effectively than could the economy of sugar or the climatology of hurricanes. The British Empire was at war with the French for nearly one third of the 65 years between 1675 and 1739. Although war intensified the need for efficient communication of intelligence, shipping embargoes and convoys were part of government efforts to protect shipping and prevent the spread of damaging news. This was bound to disrupt the flow of information from England to the sugar colonies, and it would be even more of an imposition on colonists trying to write to London. In wartime, as in peacetime, the British government could send a light navy frigate, hire a sloop, or grant a pass to an adequately armed merchantman to sail without convoy in return for carrying dispatches. This could be expensive, and certainly subject to capture, but it was always possible. Governments of the sugar islands seldom undertook such an expense. The returning convoys and guardships were the only naval vessels there, and they had assigned duties. Throughout the War of the League of Augsburg, the English government made no further provision for imperial communications. The results help explain the launching of an unprecedented transatlantic packet service during the next war.

The worst shipping disasters for the sugar trade in the war years occurred not in the Indies, not in the 1694 hurricane, but in the English Channel. In the generation after the battle of La Hogue, commerce raiding was a major feature of French maritime strategy.[52] In the year commencing in the autumn of 1694, English West Indies traders counted 66 ships lost to French privateers at a value of nearly £600,000. In the spring of 1697, French Channel privateers were powerful enough to scatter the main West Indies-bound convoy, bringing additional suffering to the provisions-short islands.[53] French privateers in the English and St. George's channels were in a position to afflict all the sugar trade, for the route around Scotland that was an alternative for North America was no help for an outward-bound sugar fleet. English naval protection was gradually increased in "the Soundings," but the privateers were not effectively checked. For trade and for communications, the seasons of war were hard on London, the center of England's connections with her overseas political and economic hinterlands.

Barbados, the island with the most to lose from any disruption of communications, tasted the worst of wartime isolation and fear in the last two years of the War of the League of Augsburg. The year 1696 was a very bad one with few vessels in from England; even the Admiralty advice boat sent to warn the island of De Ponti's expedition was taken by French privateers off the English coast.[54] The year 1697 was even worse. (See Tables 2.9 and 2.10.) The flow of ships from all English ports had been severely disrupted, and London merchants and administrators could not learn of every outport sailing in time to have letters aboard. From Table 2.9 it is clear that Ireland had a special place in communications between Britain and Barbados in this year. Nine of these 17 ships were English-owned but had stopped in Ireland to load provisions. Their provisions were fresher than their English news.[55] The other 8 ships to Barbados from Ireland that year were Irish (4), Barbadian (3), and a Marylander. These ships could bring important news for members of the Irish community in Barbados, and could bring Irish and English newspapers but would not be carrying letters from London.

Barbados itself was comparatively safe for ships coming in from the east, being south of the main routes of England's rivals bound for the Greater Antilles and to windward of both friend and foe. It was leaving Barbados that was difficult. The route from Barbados for almost all ships was initially northwesterly across the trades and across the path of the French privateers based at Martinique and Désirade.[56] These privateers were the crowning argument of those anxious to divide the sugar convoy from England rather than have all of it go out by way of Barbados. Small craft that worked out of Barbados in peacetime were entirely immobilized by war. (See Table 2.10.) Respect for the corsairs added to the effectiveness of the island's shipping embargoes and to its isolation. In April of 1697 the Barbados Council wrongly claimed that no vessels had left the island for Europe in the preceding seven months in accordance with a royal order that merchantmen were to sail only if adequately protected.[57] Table 2.9 shows some disruption, but it also shows that four English vessels began unloading goods from Barbados in the first three months of 1697. The four ships were each reentering their home ports of London, Newcastle, Lyme, and Plymouth. Given England's postal service, these ships could distribute news beyond their own hinterlands, so the silence from Barbados was broken. Although the island was at war until the end of the year, the English entries from Barbados indicate numerous individual sailings to England, and probably there were others to Ireland. War could cut the shipping to Barbados to a mere one third of the flourishing traffic of a year like 1700 (see Table 2.10), but ships were still sailing without convoy. Contacting a friend, a merchant, or a political ally in England by any means other than the convoy was difficult for Barbadians, but it was not impossible.

The problems of writing England from the islands in wartime can be further illustrated by the attempt to report the death of Governor Russell of Barbados, who died 7 August 1696. A convoy had been preparing for a month and was nearly ready to sail (in August again), but the Barbados Council intended to send an express ahead of the fleet. Merchants objected that the fleet would be endangered if the express were captured. The council agreed, "thinking that fourteen days' earlier notice was not worth the hazarding of the fleet."[58] The fleet sailed on 10 September, but its fastest ships were outsailed by the *Spy Galley*, a small merchantman that left Barbados one day after them and reached Bristol one day before the convoy made Plymouth. *Lloyd's News* told the business community of the governor's death three days later, and it was the next day before the Lords of Trade and Plantations first heard of Russell's death.[59] The governor had been dead nearly 12 weeks by then; war held the news in Barbados for 5 weeks; the *Spy Galley* had brought the news from there to England in only 6 weeks. At its worst, war could leave

Barbadians without news from England for 2 to 3 months, and the news that came often amounted to little more than what was known in the pubs and on the wharfs of Plymouth, Bristol, or Cork. Barbadians had comparable difficulty finding opportunities to write to correspondents in England.

War's impact on the sugar islands' association with English North America was naturally of the same kind as its influence on maritime traffic elsewhere, but there were differences. The number of ships on these routes diminished during wartime. Colonial shipping embargoes and the need for convoys broke the usual flow of shipping and could, given lower wartime volumes, bring silences of a couple of months between the most active colonies. North American ships bound for the islands were safer as they left their own ports than were English West Indiamen, although they faced the same problems once in the Caribbean. The closely linked colonies of Massachusetts and Barbados serve to illustrate the problems at the end of the War of the League of Augsburg. In the last two years of the war, ships entered Barbados from Massachusetts about half as often as during the subsequent peace.[60] On hearing of major French squadrons bound for the New World in each of the summers of 1696 and 1697, Massachusetts had imposed embargoes on all outward-bound shipping.[61] The results were periods of two calendar months each year without any entries into Barbados from Massachusetts and with the elimination of the usual summer surge in entries. Significantly, the winter traffic from England was not as disrupted. Although traffic levels were lower than during peace, the monthly exchange of news continued, preserving the special place of Barbados in providing New England with European news in winter. If the arc of colonies between Pennsylvania and New Hampshire, linked as they were by post rider from 1693, are regarded as a single communications area, their wartime links with Barbados seldom weakened to the point of a full calendar month without a ship sailing from one area to the other. As Table 2.10 indicates, Barbadian wartime links with English West Indian colonies were much more disrupted than were those with North America.[62]

Leeward Islands shipping suffered less than Barbados shipping in the first war with France. A veteran Nevis planter could write this to his sister in England in 1704:

> I am not averse to coming home, but since Warr time is money time
> here; I think it sinfull to goe Counter to God's Providence.[63]

He was wrong about what Providence had in store for Nevis, but the tripling of sugar prices during the previous war had been the grounds for his optimism.[64] The privateers of Martinique who stilled the fleet of Barbados in these war years also crippled communications between the Leewards. A Nevis planter complained in 1702 that privateers

> are so thick amongst these Islands, that we can't sail from Island to
> Island but with more hazard than between England and this place;
> hardly a vessel in three escapes.[65]

When the West Indies packet service was instituted later that year, its scheduled stops at every one of the Leewards were mute testimony to the truth of the complaint. Surviving shipping records for Nevis in 1705 suggest that the island's links with Britain were tenuous. There was a two-month period late in the year without any entries from Britain, and there were no sailings for Britain during the two months before and one month after the September sailing of the convoy. News to and from North America was scattered throughout the year, and only about one third the level of traffic to Barbados. Clearances to North America occurred each month except for a three-month lull from September to November.[66] Compared to Barbados, the Leewards were more isolated from friends and more vulnerable to enemies.

Jamaicans, downwind of almost all the trouble that could come to the Caribbean in war, would have even more difficulty in communicating with Britain or fellow colonies. When Port Royal was shattered by an earthquake on 7 June 1692, for instance, the crippled colony could not even cry for help. Fearful that the French might invade from St. Domingue at the opportunity the quake afforded, the Jamaica Council intensified the existing embargo on ships bound for Europe to include all local traffic as well.[67] Two years later, when that feared invasion did come, Jamaica was months away from any help.[68] As this punishing war drew toward its close, the governor lamented the lack of English and North American shipping. He blamed fear of disease and of impressment, but he might well have added fear of the privateers who were infesting both the Windward Passage and the Florida Straits. The isolation became a siege by January of 1697, when Governor Beeston claimed that the island had received no direct news from England in nine months.[69]

The War of the Spanish Succession would be different for the sugar islands and particularly for Jamaica. A naval squadron, based at Jamaica from before the war, provided defense and aggressive trade protection for ships trading with New Spain. The squadron also would be cause and means for better communication between Jamaica and England. Merchantmen would be subject to convoys and shipping embargoes, as before, and the flow of news was disrupted again. Links with North America were less disrupted than was trade with England.[70] The growing importance of Jamaica after the turn of the century was initially due less to the increased productivity of the island than to the expansion of the English trade to Spanish America through Jamaica. Both the value of this trade and the strategic importance of this English outpost in the Western Caribbean meant that the English government needed better information of developments there than the recent wartime experience suggested was possible without extraordinary measures.

War was an ambiguous visitation on the seaborne English Atlantic empire. War with colonial neighbors and fear of European fleets made the English Caribbean more dependent on England, and the war itself made efforts to communicate more difficult. In strategic terms, the most important news was a warning that England could send to the islands. Although this message was subject to capture, the English watch on French naval preparations could result in timely colonial defense as well as English reinforcement. Colonial news for England was more likely to be sad news about something that could no longer be helped. Colonial isolation was worse in the War of the League of Augsburg, when few extraordinary measures were taken to bolster the frequency of sailings to and from the Caribbean at a time when convoys were necessary. Although communications were never as infrequent as the convoy system intended, they were certainly less frequent than the winter-free Caribbean expected in peacetime. The development of a packet boat system in the War of the Spanish Succession, as will be seen, reduced the disruptions that were the cause of constant complaint during the earlier war. The English Atlantic needed better communications than it had had from 1689 to 1697. The packet boats were to preserve, or restore, a level of communication that had come to be regarded as necessary.

The sugar routes were the year-round highway between England and English America. War severely disrupted communications in the 1690's, particularly for Jamaica, but the lifetime after 1675 saw great improvement in transatlantic links. If a monthly arrival was an acceptable level of contact, the sugar ships provided good communications between England and both Barbados and Jamaica from 1675. The volume of shipping was still too light to the Leeward Islands, but, by the end of the generation of war with France, the Leewards were also receiving and sending a minimum of one ship a month to England.

The sugar routes were generally slightly better for sending news to the New World than they were for sending it back except at Charles Town, South Carolina. The passage times each way were comparable for the Eastern Caribbean, and the trip "home" from Jamaica was longer than the trip out. When shipping levels were low, either in the early stages of the development of an island or when war cut the number of ships traveling, ships bound to the sugar islands were more evenly distributed throughout the calendar year than were the vessels leaving for England. The Royal Navy, the English government's financial resources, and the wartime slack in the English shipping industry all meant that the English government was better able to send urgent wartime news by "express" to the sugar islands than these islands were able to reciprocate.

The growing volume of the sugar trades ensured regular peacetime traffic between England and her Caribbean islands, and the related trades in molasses and barrel staves ensured that the links between developed sugar islands and New England would be as good as transatlantic connections. Boston and Bridgetown had a level and frequency of ship exchanges that defied hurricanes and historians. As the Leeward Islands sugar industry developed, the same was true there. In winter, the Caribbean became New England's first source of European news. The rise of Jamaica would coincide with, if not contribute to, the southward shift in the growth of North American ports trading with the islands. Carolina's access to news improved dramatically with her West Indian trade as well as the emergence of her own staple trade. The impact of the development of the sugar trade on the communications of other North American colonies would be uneven though generally favorable.

The sugar routes were the standard against which administrators, merchants, shipmasters, and travelers could judge transatlantic communications, and this standard was rising between 1675 and 1740. High-volume, all-season traffic on the sugar routes reached what contemporaries called "constant communication" in peacetime.

3 · Tobacco Routes

Tobacco fleets that cleared the Chesapeake for England were among the most awesome displays of the economic and fiscal fruit of English expansion. This great staple trade fulfilled the hopes of those who saw economic specialization and interdependence as the road to greater prosperity. Yet the traffic between England and the Chesapeake was much better designed for circulating tobacco than information. An examination of the volumes, routes, seasons, and passage times of these routes reveals some paradoxes and some striking changes in the movement of news through the tobacco colonies.

For most of a lifetime after Bacon's rebellion, the significant changes in the tobacco trade were not changes in its scale. Scattered evidence from the decade before 1686 suggests that about 100 ships a year were needed to carry the tobacco imported into London. With an additional 60 to 70 ships importing Chesapeake tobacco to English outports, the tobacco trade employed more shipping than the sugar trade before the wars with France began.[1] (See Tables 3.1 and 2.2.)

There was spasmodic expansion of the trade down to 1700, but wartime dislocations of the European markets exaggerated cyclical weaknesses in the trade to produce stagnation for a generation. Growth resumed after the Peace of Utrecht; British tobacco imports first exceeded 40 million pounds a year in 1721 and first reached 50 million pounds six years later.[2] The changes in the volume of the trade over 75 years were considerable, and increased traffic would improve the circulation of information somewhat, but the number of tobacco ships had been high compared to other colonial trades for decades. Paradoxically, the seasons, routes, passage times, and intercolonial traffic all worked to minimize the ability of those in the Chesapeake to gain information or send it to Britain or to other colonies.

If the volume of tobacco shipped suggested that four of five ships a week might enter the Capes of Chesapeake Bay, the seasons of the trade definitely did not. Seasonal rhythms were very strong in tobacco planting, marketing, and shipping. Transplanting the young plants was to be finished by the end of May; harvesting, by mid-September; and curing could last into late winter and early spring. Although fully cured tobacco kept much better than the partially refined muscovado sugars that dominated West Indian exports, there were good reasons to sell the tobacco crop while it was fresh and heavy.[3] Because Chesapeake Bay seldom froze in winter and the gathering of cargoes took a matter of months, ships arrived in the autumn after the 1630's.[4] It was advisable to be within the capes before the beginning of November. Thereafter the winter westerlies not only brought gale damage but also could prevent entry into the Chesapeake for weeks on end. After a winter spent assembling a cargo, the ships left in the spring, hurried by fear of the summer, when the teredo worm attacked the ships while fevers attacked the crews. Surviving material suggests that this very seasonal pattern held, through the shifting fortunes of the tobacco trade, down to the 1690's.[5]

The Chesapeake shipping season would undergo revolutionary changes in the eighteenth century despite all the factors that made the earlier seasons inevitable. These changes came from the generation of war with France that followed 1689. The coming of war brought a doubling of the wages of merchant seamen and even greater increases in the costs of insurance. These increased costs hit at the same time that the closure of some European markets left wholesalers with a glut of tobacco and prices fell. With freight rates forced up and prices forced down,[6] the trade was dislocated even before very substantial losses to French privateers occurred. As J. M. Price has persuasively argued, these losses were long-term investments in giving the French smoker a taste of superior tobacco, and they ultimately created a major market there; the initial results, however, were more misery and higher costs. Under all these pressures, it is not surprising that one of the costs that was being scrutinized was the cost of the long loading season in the Chesapeake. Whether they were arguing for a different convoy pattern or the establishment of towns as ports, critics noted that "it is an usual thing with Ships to lye three or four Months in the Country, which might be dispatch'd in a Fort-night's Time, . . . and this inhances the Freight to almost double the Price of what it needed to be, if the Ship had a quick Dispatch."[7]

The demands of war on the Royal Navy would also tend to shorten the seasons of Chesapeake shipping. The Admiralty regularly objected to the length of the layover in the bay because it cost sailors' wages and victuals, as well as preventing other uses for the much-needed men-of-war. To minimize the commitment of ships, the navy used the guard-vessel assigned to Virginia as part of the convoy arrangements and drew homeward-bound men-of-war from Jamaica or New York into the tobacco convoy. Yet the need for outward-bound convoys and for strong escorts for the homeward-bound fleets meant that much of the protection for the tobacco fleet had to be sent from England specifically for that purpose.

Convoy planning inevitably drew merchants and bureaucrats into discussion of the ideal month for the sailing of the tobacco fleet. Full-scale debate on the timing of the tobacco convoy occurred three times in the course of these wars. Naturally, some of the argument had to do with immediate problems like the shortage of seamen or the lateness of the return of a current fleet, but the differences went well beyond such contingencies. The proposal that ultimately won the endorsement of the government called for a single annual convoy to go out in late summer and return the following spring. This represented a victory of London merchants over the outports, for the latter preferred to sail in January.[8] Without the same dependence on a seasonal easterly wind in the Channel, with a shorter voyage and usually a smaller ship, the outports merchants could trim months off wage and victualing bills. The policy accepted by the government also represented a victory for merchants who traded on their own account rather than for those acting simply as factors.[9] The longer time in the Chesapeake, which allowed for months of market analysis and tactics, would be less relevant for the country factor system that developed after 1714. Early autumn sailing also favored the Virginia producers over those from Maryland. The Maryland crop tended to be a few weeks later into the cask, and a later convoy would improve the competitive position of the Marylanders. The Maryland Council also showed much more reluctance to impose shipping embargoes on outward-bound tobacco ships than did their counterpart in Virginia.[10] At times the range of opinion expressed to the Board of Trade was baffling. In theory at least, the government made its preferences clear by 1707, and those with the most influence were preferred.

Far beneath the speculations on the ideal convoy arrangements for the tobacco trade was the real world of fitting, provisioning, and deploying men-of-war and politicking for delays in sailing. Even after settling the policy, the Board of Trade confessed to the acting governor of Virginia that "the merchants here have such different interests, and opinions, that we may justly fear it will not be so punctually observed as it ought."[11] Surviving logbooks for men-of-war convoying 21 of the fleets to the Chesapeake in these war years suggest the pattern that emerged. (See Table 3.2.) In this generation of war, the convoys cleared England for the Chesapeake most often in the spring, presumably satisfying few of the interest groups who wanted sailing in August–September or in January. Although the season for clearing the capes for England came closer to uniformity, it is evident that half of the convoys left the Chesapeake just after a summer of teredo worms and fevers. Wartime contingencies had forced experiments in different seasonal patterns for the tobacco trade.

The Peace of Ryswick allowed the tobacco trade to operate without convoys, at least until rumors of war in 1700 prompted tobacco ships, including the *Palm Tree*, to accompany a man-of-war on the voyage home.[12] English port books for this period survive from the outports although not from London. Port book notations on 139 outward-bound merchantmen demonstrate clearly that the months from August to January saw almost all the clearances for the Chesapeake, with October by far the most popular month for leaving an English outport for the tobacco colonies.[13] Naval officers' records for Virginia confirm this picture of a return to the earlier pattern of autumn sailings from England and spring sailings from the Chesapeake during this peace. In the last two years of the century, fully 83 percent of some 143 ships clearing Virginia for England did so in the four months beginning with March.[14] Compared to the sugar trades, the tobacco trade was sharply focused into seasons. This staple trade, unlike that of the sugar islands, was not a market for English or Irish provisions and, therefore, lacked off-season transatlantic traffic in peacetime. War would shift the seasons and prove that the navigation was possible but would not increase the number of months in which the Chesapeake colonies would receive direct news from England.

A dramatic shift occurred in the seasons of the tobacco trade in the early eighteenth century, a shift in both the times of ship arrivals in the Chesapeake from Britain and in their departure. As Table 3.3 illustrates, the autumnal westward crossings of the end of the seventeenth century became much less popular, replaced by spring arrivals in Virginia. The change in departure timing, toward late summer clearances, is also significant.[15] Explaining this change is more intriguing and more speculative than discovering it. The wartime experience of convoyed merchantmen often conformed to the timetable that became popular later in peacetime. The attraction of lower wage and victualing bills, so crucial in wartime, would still operate in peacetime. The incentives were considerable.

The teredo worm had been one major obstacle to summer loading of tobacco. There were a number of methods of combating the worm that were generally known. Robert Beverley offered four suggestions as early as 1705. A good coat of "Pitch, Lime and Tallow, or whatever else it is" was effective against the honeycoming insects provided the coat was entire. Anchoring large vessels in the fastest tidal areas prevented damage, too, though small craft were better pulled ashore for the six-week period of concern. Beverley also suggested singeing the hull at the end of the worm season. Finally, he suggested that ships sail up the rivers far enough to escape salt water during this period, thereby escaping the worm attacks. Although his was not an exhaustive list, Beverley's concern indicates the significance of the problem during the enforced summer shipping of the wartime convoys.[16] Expansion of tobacco acreage further up the rivers eventually made Beverley's fourth suggestion an economic trip rather than a retreat from the worms. This expansion upriver also brought increased danger of winter ice above the salt water as the losses and damage to ships in the cold winter of 1736–1737 demonstrated.[17] Nonetheless, the teredo worm had lost its veto on summer shipping in the bay.

The new tobacco-loading season, shorter than the old, was also made possible by marketing changes in the trade. Much of the local negotiating of freight was eliminated by the increased use of resident merchants, storekeepers, and factors who bought up tobacco in advance of the ships' arrival.[18] This facilitated quicker loading and often meant the ships were hired in England and Scotland with designated tobacco cargoes to be picked up. Here was a productivity change in the shipping industry. The striking change in the seasons of the tobacco ships was not isolated from other observable changes of consequence in the shipping to the Chesapeake from Britain. Changes in the routes to the bay have been noticed but can profitably be connected with other changes in the trade, including the changing season and the shift of the British termini for the trade to the northwest.

British ships bound on a Virginia voyage had such a wide variety of routes available that a fairly direct passage could be undertaken that would allow a sighting, or watering stop, at Barbados, one of the Leeward Islands, Madeira, the Azores, or even Newfoundland. (See Figure 3.) These options meant that masters could take advantage of a favorable wind (if it promised to be sustained—though the winds did not always keep their promises) and shape a course accordingly. The choices available for this comparatively long Atlantic route also allowed the shift of seasons mentioned earlier.

From the first days of English expansion, the English followed the Spaniards on the great tropical routes to the New World. The founding voyages of Sir Richard Grenville, Christopher Newport, and Leonard Calvert all showed that the Chesapeake was linked to the West Indies as motive, rest stop, and supply depot on the most familiar routes outward to farthest America.[19] The *Palm Tree* of Plymouth made a profitable use of this route to Virginia in 1699. The 250-ton *John* of London was in the tobacco trade regularly at that time, and Richard Reswick had been her master on at least two recent voyages there before setting out again in November 1700. The outward voyage was on the main sugar route. The leisurely passage out, of 87 days, included a stop at Madeira. Although only a few vessels would load wine there in quantity, the uneven contest between Madeira and Fayal wines for the table of prosperous Virginians was, in part, a contest between routes to Virginia. The *John*'s three-week stopover in Barbados was an opportunity for fresh provisions and some trading; outward-bound tobacco ships usually had plenty of stowage space. Almost the whole of February 1701 was spent at Barbados before the *John* went on to Virginia in a quick 19-day passage. The *John* had been four months on the outward voyage, but about a third of that time was spent in port at Madeira and Carlisle Bay.[20] Here was the southern route to tobacco at its longest but not its hardest. This was not a convoy route to Virginia, but it is instructive that men-of-war in two separate winter convoys bound for the Chesapeake by more northerly routes in 1697–1698 and in 1703–1704 were forced to abandon the effort in the teeth of the winter westerlies and make for Barbados and a more southerly route.[21] Newly appointed governor of Maryland, John Seymour, would share one of these sad passages with his family and the crew of HMS *Dreadnought*, a passage totaling nearly six months.[22] For the *John* or for the *Palm Tree* a year earlier, this route to Virginia was a sound and potentially profitable route with some trading along the way. For a few ships like these and for a few bedraggled survivors of North Atlantic winter gales, Barbados was on a transatlantic route to the Chesapeake.

Although a voyage via Barbados or one of the Leeward Islands was a viable route to the Chesapeake, the most popular southern routes westward to that bay had no West Indian landfall. All these routes followed the sugar route as far as Madeira outward-bound and involved a passage westward in

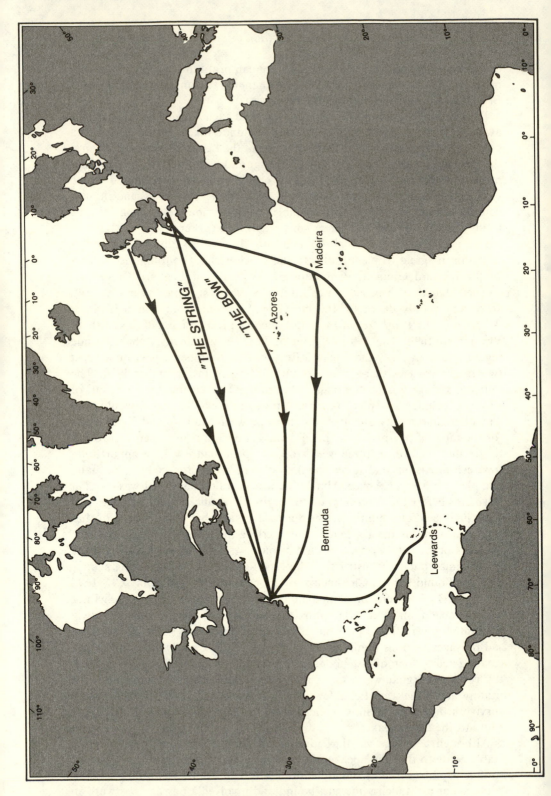

Figure 3. British Routes to the Chesapeake.

an arc that could be very flat or might involve sailing just within the tropics to catch a bit of the trades in a winter passage. In 1609 the Virginia Company pioneered a crossing westward from the Canaries.[23] As on all these subtropical passages, Bermuda could provide refreshment, navigational aid, and danger. Later versions of this route did not take the ships as far south as the Canaries on the east side of the Atlantic and had no Bermuda or Bahamas landfall on the west. Parallel sailing was gradually modified on this route, but observed latitude remained the crucial part of the navigation. Without much surviving details of routes, it is difficult to relate passage times to the routes taken. However, it is interesting that of 19 recorded crossings westward to the Chesapeake accomplished by men-of-war between 1676 and 1715, the shortest passage was on this route. HMS *Shoreham* made a seven-week passage from the Lizard to the Capes of the Chesapeake, sighting Madeira and keeping north of 27.32° in a very flat arc.[24] Naturally, this was a summer passage accomplished in June and July of 1715, when the trades blew in that latitude.

The claim that these southern routes were superseded was made prematurely by William Bullock in his deceptively titled *Virginia Impartially Examined* (London, 1649). Voyages by way of Madeira remained common during the later Stuart period. During the last years of Queen Anne's reign, three of the major convoys went by the southern route, as did HMS *Shoreham* in 1715 and HMS *Hector* in 1738.[25] The last years of Queen Anne's War had seen major attacks on convoys by French privateers, yet three of five convoys bound to the Chesapeake in those years are known to have gone by way of Madeira.[26] The survival of the subtropical southern route to the Chesapeake seems certain well into the eighteenth century. As late as 1787, Governor Thomas Pownall printed a map offering two routes to the Chesapeake. One, which he labeled "Upper course from Britain to Carolina and Virginia," ran from Plymouth to Madeira, then west to Bermuda and the Chesapeake. The other, called the "Usual course from Britain to the West Indies, Carolina and Virginia for the sake of the Trade Winds," went to Antigua from Madeira on the outward passage. Pownall's route map[27] missed both the Scottish route and the western routes to the Chesapeake, but it does suggest that the southern routes remained part of the English traffic to the Chesapeake. Madeira was a much better source of current European news than were the Azores, and the subtropical route could occasionally bring fresh advices to the tobacco colonies.

A westerly route from England to the Chesapeake had much to recommend it. In the long years of war with France, a westward-bound convoy reduced the risks that were inherent in voyaging southerly past the Biscay ports of the enemy. A northerly approach to the Chesapeake Bay also avoided the pirates and privateers operating out of the Caribbean, as well as the treacherous navigation around Cape Hatteras.

William Bullock, enthusiastic about Virginia and anxious to advocate the quickest routes, urged migrants in 1649 to consider going out with the Newfoundland fishermen on a cheap, quick, and early passage. He then went on to discuss a route available in March.

> Your Passage will be pleasant, both for fair weather, and shortnesse,
> since now you go not out of your way to the Azores as in the Winter
> voyage: But you go straight way, for these two ways differ just as the
> Bow and string, and your voyage is sometimes under a Moneth,
> seldome above: in this time of the year the winds hang Easterly from
> our Coast, which follows you all the way . . .[28]

These, then, are three seasonal western routes that competed for traffic to
Virginia.

Bullock's mention of the Newfoundland trade might have been intended to
urge the impecunious to spend a summer fishing or unship themselves in
St. John's and seek out a stray Virginia-bound vessel, but it is more likely
that he was advising a route, as is true in the rest of his statement. The oft-
reprinted fourth book of *The English Pilot* (1689) offers nothing on the
transatlantic routes to the Chesapeake except considerable caution as the
coast is approached. But there is an interesting indirect reference in its
detailed description of Newfoundland. Trepassey Bay, on the south coast of
the Avalon Peninsula, was described as a good harbor and the most southerly
on the island at 46° N latitude "and most convenient to receive our Shipping
from *Virginia* and the Bermuda Islands, because they usually pass in sight of
the Land of Trepassie, and in return likewise make the said Land."[29] There is
not much surviving evidence to support this claim. Virginia merchants did
petition the English government for a convoy outward to Newfoundland in
August 1694, but none of the surviving logbooks for convoying men-of-war
operating in the tobacco trade sailed on that route in the generation after the
appearance of *The English Pilot*. Individual merchantmen did go on to
Virginia when their westward voyage to Newfoundland did not bring them to
the market they had anticipated,[30] but a route to Virginia via Newfoundland
did not develop.

There is every reason to believe that the other two routes mentioned by
Bullock, the "bow" and the "string," did become important in the century
after he wrote. Bullock considered the bow, an outward-bound passage via
the Azores, as a winter voyage. Logbooks of six convoys to the Chesapeake
between 1676 and 1715 indicate that they stopped at, or sighted, the Azores.
One of these was an early winter passage, one was a late winter passage, and
the others were late spring voyages. These passages via the Azores showed no
marked advantage over the other routes, averaging 11 weeks.[31] The route via
the Azores could be a spring route evidently and cannot be eliminated as one
of the routes that would be used extensively when the season of ship arrivals
in the Chesapeake shifted dramatically to the spring.

Bullock's direct spring route, which he called the string, was also used by
some of the tobacco convoys. Six convoys that attempted a southwesterly
course from the Channel averaged 10-week crossings. Their season of sailing
varied, as did their route, but none of them approached Bullock's month
passage. William Byrd's "short and pleasant passage" of 28 days early in 1688
was probably on this route, but John Fontaine's crossing from Bristol to

Virginia was certainly on this route, was begun in March (1715), and ended 13 weeks later after short rations of water and biscuit. By this time, however, Hugh Jones could describe this route as though it were the only one and "may be esteemed as easy a voyage as any."[32]

Despite all that Jones or Bullock had to say in favor of the WSW route from the English or St. George's channels, this route would lose out to a better one in the years that followed the Peace of Utrecht. Twenty years earlier a customs official at Liverpool had reported to the Admiralty that a tobacco ship of his port had been taken by privateers near Tory Island off the Donegal coast of northwest Ireland. He went on to mention that all the tobacco ships bound for Liverpool, Lancaster, and Whitehaven return on this route.[33] All three of these ports traded tobacco with Ireland as well as their own hinterlands, and Whitehaven traded tobacco with Scotland before the Union allowed Glasgow to begin its rise to dominance in the trade.[34] The northern Ireland route proved to be shorter by two to three weeks than sailings from the same ports southward through the Irish sea.[35] The difference was not primarily due to distance, for the mileage of the northern route was no shorter.[36] This route did allow conventional ships to use the westerlies a little more effectively than on a course shaped even closer to the wind. The prime advantage was that a late winter voyage could often meet with north-easterly winds or at least with interrupted westerlies and more variable winds. This quicker route cut costs and gave merchants of the northwest information on the state of the crop and colonial market demand weeks before the same information was available in London or Bristol. The rise of Glasgow in the tobacco trade was built on advantages in financing and trade organization, but the shift of the tobacco trade to the northwest in general was due to the superior route to the Chesapeake, a route that also encouraged a shorter loading time in the colonies.

Were there any changes in ship rigging or design that might help explain the northerly shift in routes to the Chesapeake? There were three developments that improved the ability of relatively large ships to sail a course close to the wind. The development of the jib and headsails was a clear and significant development that superseded the spritsails of the seventeenth century. The headsails on ship-rigged vessels meant that even the less handy vessels could sail within six points of the wind.[37] This change would be especially important on the westerly routes and would help to explain the growing popularity of the direct route to the Chesapeake. A ship that could hold close to the wind could tack less with less loss of time.

Another major change that emerged in the English Atlantic in the early eighteenth century was the development of the schooner. Although the type of rigging was in use in various combinations earlier, the term "schooner" first appears in colonial usage in 1718. These gaff-rigged vessels would begin as rather small craft, and the improvement did not affect the tobacco trade until the later development of the Baltimore clipper-schooner.[38]

Ironically, it is harder to document the appearance of a major new invention in ship-handling, the helm wheel. The wheel dramatically increased rudder control on larger vessels and certainly was introduced by the opening of the eighteenth century. The earliest surviving model dates from 1703, there are printed references as early as 1743, and the wheel's place in the ship is well described and taken for granted before William Falconer's *An Universal Dictionary of the Marine* appeared in 1769.[39]

All these developments would improve the ability of ships to sail in the teeth of the westerlies. They would be most significant on the crossings from England to Newfoundland, New England, New York, and Pennsylvania although they would improve the time on the northern tobacco routes via the Azores or the direct WSW route. The changes were not as important in the emergence of Britain's northwest ports and the northern Ireland route to and from the tobacco colonies. This route hoped for a later winter weakening in the westerlies, as did "the bow" and "the string." The new pattern seldom matched the boasts of ships from the Clyde arriving to supply Chesapeake factors every six months. In the generation before 1740, the advantages of the northwest were not fully exploited, and the north of Ireland route was less traveled than the WSW one, the Azores route, or the southern ones via Madeira. Technology helped a little, but there were not revolutions in passage time. The new routes saved a little westward passage time and a great deal of loading time. The power of war to raise costs and lower tobacco prices, as well as inspire legitimate fears, would seem to have encouraged a significant enduring cost efficiency in the tobacco trade.

The Chesapeake colonies were, with Jamaica, the Carolinas, and Hudson Bay, in farthest English America in terms of passages westward. William Byrd was understandably enthused about his 4-week passage to Virginia in 1688, for it would seldom be equaled. A 5-week crossing from London was not unheard of, but was very rare,[40] and a 7- to 8-week passage was less than usual. The fastest of the convoys discussed earlier made a 7-week passage, but the average was 11½ weeks, and the longest was 25 weeks. Because an individual merchantman could hope for an 8- to 10-week crossing westward to the Chesapeake and because the seasons of arrival there tended to be more sharply defined than in most parts of America, the Chesapeake colonies were slower to receive most European news than were the rest of English America save only Hudson Bay. William Byrd could lament in 1690 that "Wee are here att the end of the World, and Europe may bee turned topsy turvy ere wee can hear a Word of itt,"[41] and his son could later echo this by claiming he lived "quite out of the latitude of news, nor can pick up one dash of scandal to season a letter withall . . ."[42]

The speed with which a Virginian scandal would be current in London was, however, another matter. As was the case with all of English North America, but not the West Indies, the voyage eastward to England was markedly shorter than a westward passage. Without needing a wide range of routes, ship design changes, or shifting British destinations, the direct route from the Chesapeake to England was a relatively simple and speedy passage urged by the westerlies. The best-recorded passage for a later-Stuart merchant ship bound from the Chesapeake was the 20-day passage of the *Content* of

London to Cowes in 1682.[43] If this is only a week quicker than the best westward passage, the differences are clearer if the eastward passages of the convoys are investigated. The average of 18 convoy passages by naval escorts sailing between 1676 and 1715 was 46 days from the capes of Virginia to the Lizard. The average for the convoys was 6½ weeks compared to a westward passage between the same points averaging 11½ weeks. Whereas these westward passages ranged from 49 to 178 days, the range of the return voyages was only from 31 to 64 days.[44] If this contrast allowed many Virginians to feel relatively close to England while limiting their fear of metropolitan interventions or if it made planters feel close to their markets and far from their English creditors, there is no convincing way of measuring these feelings. Perhaps this situation helps explain Virginian and Maryland resistance to improved intercolonial posts[45] and also the fact that defense of the vital tobacco fleets and revenues never provoked a packet-boat service comparable to those for the West Indies, New York, or Charles Town.

The tobacco ships usually contributed less to the general transatlantic communication network than their numbers might suggest. In the seventeenth century, when the fleets wintered in the Chesapeake, the late autumn arrival of European news was difficult to convey northward or southward because of lack of postal services. The tobacco fleet, like the New Hampshire mast fleet, did represent a well-armed wartime opportunity to write to England early in the spring, but spring was the time for much of North American shipping to sail in peacetime. As the connections by land with neighboring colonies improved in the eighteenth century, the arrival and departure seasons of the tobacco fleet came to coincide with the other northern transatlantic shipping seasons. By the 1730's it would be Charles Town that often provided the Chesapeake, as well as its northern neighbors, with winter news.

Limits of intercolonial land communication were not offset by intercolonial shipping. Although Virginia was the most populous English colony throughout the Stuart and early Georgian period, she did not attract much intercolonial traffic. Until the development of wheat surpluses for export to New England in the 1730's, the limited intercolonial tobacco trade and the Chesapeake market for West Indian products succeeded in drawing some 30 vessels a year to Virginia from other colonies.[46] Virginia's own fleet was small, numbering about 15 craft in the late 1690's, with only one vessel over 100 tons besides that unique mammoth, the *Indian King*, which was monarch of the transatlantic tobacco trade at 650 tons.[47] Coastwise shipping could not provide Virginia with regular news from other colonies because there was so little traffic, and one third of it was within the Chesapeake.

Massachusetts and Barbados, the English colonies with the most traffic, naturally accounted for the origin and destination of most intercolonial traffic to Virginia from colonies outside the bay. Ships in from Barbados were evenly, if sparsely, distributed around the calendar in 1699 and 1700 except for a silence in January and February, and a similar pattern was evident in the heavier traffic on that route later. (See Table 2.3.) Virginia vessels clearing for the eastern Caribbean preferred summer departures with an emphasis on August. The harvesttime market for rum seems to have prompted the taking of these risks as was true of other North American traffic to the British West Indies.[48] By the 1730's, when the British ships were favoring arrival in Virginia in May and departure in September, vessels entering from other colonies had shifted to that time as well. From the ship movement material in the *Virginia Gazette*, it would seem that intercolonial traffic was coming in the spring for tobacco and in the summer for provisions and grain. It is essential to realize that there were few vessels and that they showed the same seasonal restrictions as evident in the transatlantic fleet. The colony was isolated by land and by Virginia's limited seaborne trade with her neighbors, aggravated by the seasonal clustering of that traffic. The shifting of the active shipping season showed that economics, and not geography, determined the seasons of shipping at Virginia. These seasons meant that for much of the year, Virginians would not have as ready access to political or economic information as would the elites of New England, the Middle Colonies, or the Caribbean. Here there was a season for news, which coincided with the season for much else. There may have been cultural reasons for the delay in the launching of a newspaper in Virginia until 1737, but it represented growing access to news that marked the end of a period that had been different.

Maryland's communications were not exactly the same as those of Virginia. Although no rival to Virginia in tobacco production, Maryland's near 15,000 people in 1675 were in the tobacco business. The colony fed itself, exported provisions in limited quantity, but met the world through the sale of tobacco. Population would grow to 116,000 by 1740[49] though tobacco production grew less rapidly than the grain trade. By the end of the seventeenth century, 75 to 100 ships a year came to take away nearly 10 million pounds of tobacco.[50]

The Maryland tobacco trade focused the arrival of ships and news from Britain as was the case with Virginia. Records for the last five years of the seventeenth century suggest that Maryland tobacco shippers were already showing a preference for early spring arrival although ships still came in during the autumn. Fully one quarter of clearances for England were in June in this period although Maryland also had its upriver "freshes" that allowed a safe retreat from the teredo worm. The later months of summer were the worst for receiving direct English news in Maryland, and the latter half of the year provided few opportunities to send letters to England. (See Table 3.4.) Maryland's direct seaborne contact with England had a similar pattern to that of Virginia, with similar seasonal difficulties.

Intercolonial seaborne traffic was small out of Maryland, but it would bring news from North America and the West Indies in all seasons. Late summer and early autumn brought more vessels in from North American colonies than other seasons and must have provided the cargoes of news to be chewed by the fire for the next few months.[51] Much of this traffic was in the hands of northern shippers, who were resented locally for bringing in trade goods just before the arrival of the tobacco ships, buying up the local tobacco, and then reselling this to English traders for European goods. The New Englanders who might have provided goods and news at other times of the year were speeding the loading of the tobacco ships at the planters' expense. There was a local fleet, of some 161 craft counted in 1697,[52] which did not range widely but could gather news, passengers, and cargoes from across the Chesapeake or up the Delaware River.

It was Maryland's access to news by land that made the most difference to the communications of this tobacco colony. Until 1695, land travel northward from the head of the bay to young Philadelphia was very irregular but possible, and in that year a regular post began to ride between the Potomac and Philadelphia. Although Reverend Hugh Jones praised the roads of sandy-soiled Maryland in 1699 as allowing 100 miles a day travel in summer, traffic was light, and traveling could be dangerous.[53] The link with Philadelphia was a link with the northern posts all the way to Piscataqua, an advantage over Virginia that was not reduced until the through post to Williamsburg was established in 1717. The advantage was not in the organizing of ferries,[54] but in the fact that Maryland had fewer major rivers than Virginia. The rise of Philadelphia would draw much of Maryland into its communications hinterland both by water and land—until the rise of Baltimore—but even for most of the period under discussion here, Maryland had better connections with the northern colonies than had the tobacco colony across the bay.

Maryland's links with the other continental colonies outside the Chesapeake were not as strong as her connections with the British Caribbean islands at the end of the seventeenth century. Although the island trade in timber and provisions was not major, entries into Maryland from the Leeward Islands equaled those from Massachusetts in the last six years of the century, and the shipping in from the islands was more evenly distributed around the calendar. Most of the Caribbean traffic, totaling 77 entries in those six years, came in from Barbados, the Leeward Islands, and Tobago. Maryland apparently had very little direct trade with Jamaica. (See Tables 2.3 and 2.5.) During seasons other than those that drew the tobacco ships from England, Maryland could receive European news by ricochet. This would be more likely to be by way of the eastern Caribbean than by way of Massachusetts.

The tobacco colonies had a special relationship with the island of Bermuda, the island on the southerly tobacco route where settlement had begun as an accidental offshot of the Virginia colony, launched a tobacco industry, and then proved unable to develop an alternative staple export once its tobacco proved uncompetitive. Without a staple trade to draw transatlantic shipping, Bermuda had very little direct merchant traffic with England in peacetime and even less during war.[55] By the 1730's, when Bermuda's population approached 8000,[56] the colony was averaging only one sailing for Britain every second spring. (See Table 3.5) In these circumstances, an island that theoretically might send a ship to England in less than two weeks was actually quite isolated from England. Yet there were six times as many ships (still fewer than three ships a year) arrived from Britain en route to other colonial destinations. These arrivals seem unhampered by season, but the traffic was very light. Except when naval packets were sent expressly to Bermuda on their way to the tobacco colonies, as was the case with important news in 1689 and 1712, Bermuda's transatlantic communications justified Governor Robinson's complaint that "for news we lye soe remote & Soe small a rock yt we hardly hear anything."[57]

The special frustrations Bermuda's governors felt about communications with England, frustrations that could border on paranoia in the case of Governor Bennett,[58] came from the fact that Bermuda was not an isolated island at all. In two important respects, the island deserved its reputation for "the best intelligence of any place in America."[59] In the first place, Bermuda was on the main shipping route of most of the English Atlantic's homeward-bound staple trade. The island's governors never tired of reminding the British government that the American trades could be entirely disrupted by any enemy in possession of Bermuda, and the Barbados Council declared the same in 1696.

> Not only the trading ships between Europe and those parts, but all the small craft that ply between the North American Colonies and these Islands . . . always pass within thirty or forty leagues of Bermuda, and ten times out of twelve actually within sight thereof, sometimes even stopping there.[60]

English American news or informal communication of doings in Europe were available off the Bermuda coast in most seasons. Bermuda also had good commercial information because the island's people had become seafarers. The famous cedar sloops built in Bermuda were marketed throughout the English Americas, but enough of them remained under Bermudian ownership to afford a flourishing intercolonial traffic through their home port. Approximately 70 vessels of Bermudian ownership traded with English colonial ports at the end of the seventeenth century, and between 300 and 400 small, two-masted craft were estimated as being used for fishing and local traffic. Bermuda's own fleet may not have increased much in the next 30 years,[61] but the records of intercolonial traffic through Bermuda then suggest an active exchange with a wide variety of colonial ports. Bermuda's place in intercolonial commerce was not large, but more than a hundred vessels a year visited Bermuda on their way to or from other colonies. (See Table 3.5.) It should also be noted that these figures are for vessels that entered or cleared customs. Vessels did not need to do so to exchange news. In the colonial traffic through Bermuda in the 1730's, there was a special emphasis on trade with the Leeward Islands, the Bahamas, and Virginia.[62] Bermuda had benefited from the improvements in communications that the early eighteenth century brought to the distribution of information among the British North American colonies, as well as from the development of the Leeward Islands.

Bermuda could be a source of Caribbean news of value to her neighbors. In September 1694, for instance, the governor of Bermuda sent a sloop to Barbados with news of the French devastation of Jamaica, news that was so appreciated that the Barbados Council and Assembly took the unusual course of paying for the sloop's voyage.[63] In March 1709 word arrived at Bermuda from Curaçao indicating that a Spanish and French raid on South Carolina was planned. Bermuda's governor sent an express to warn the intended victims. In October 1730 it was learned in New York by way of Bermuda that a 50-gun Spanish man-of-war having nearly a million pieces of eight on board had been cast away near Point Pedro, Jamaica. Of course, a sloop with 100 men aboard had left Bermuda to investigate before the news was relayed to North America.[64]

Bermuda may have been closer to England than the tobacco colonies were, but the lack of traffic meant that Bermuda would seldom hear important news directly from England. Bermuda was like the tobacco colonies in having a longer wait for news from England than the time it took to get news to England. It was the considerable and varied traffic between colonies that made Bermuda's merchants and shipmasters among the best informed on New World markets and politics. It is hard to tell whether the evasion of the Navigation Acts there was on a scale to attract many unrecorded ships, but that reputation certainly existed.[65] In any event, Bermuda displayed the possibilities for seaborne news gathering on what might have been a comparatively isolated island. The contrasts with the tobacco colonies, which had so little intercolonial traffic in the seventeenth century and such strong shipping connections directly with England, illustrate the variety available on a single route to America.

Although the tobacco colonies began with communications seasons and routes that were similar to those of the sugar routes, the differences between the communications patterns in the two staple trades are striking. Because there was no provisions trade to the Chesapeake luring English or colonial ships to venture in the off-season of the staple trade, the Chesapeake colonies had a season for news that coincided with the season for loading tobacco. When the tobacco ships wintered over in the Chesapeake, the limited maritime and landward connections between the tobacco colonies and their northern neighbors had meant that the differences in shipping season were of little help in forwarding Atlantic communications.

The dramatic change in the season of the tobacco trade to spring arrivals and summer sailings meant that Chesapeake traffic was on a schedule that added little to the news conveyance of the ports further north that had to suffer winter and enjoy the traffic of the summer. The rising port of Charles Town would gradually assume the role of the main winter news source for the whole region. War may have contributed to the change of seasons in the tobacco trade, but the convoy restrictions made less difference in the availability of news in the Chesapeake area than was true of the English sugar islands. The changes in the tobacco routes reduced the news gathering that was possible on the westward passages, and the emergence of new British termini for the tobacco trade tended to slow Chesapeake communication of political or economic news directly to the south of England. The impressive expansion of communications through the Chesapeake did not come from the more numerous merchantmen in the tobacco trade. It was the new landward postal services of the 1730's, which had been actively resisted in the Chesapeake for so long, which all but eliminated the seasons of communication between residents of the Chesapeake and their correspondents elsewhere in the English Atlantic.

4 · Western Routes

The *Sarah Galley* was bound for her Boston home port when she sailed from London on 18 March 1730. After a relatively short wait of 3 days in the Downs, she sailed into the Channel with some 40 vessels that had been waiting for favorable winds in order to proceed westward. A week out of London, the *Sarah Galley* put into Torbay to ride out contrary winds for 2 days. Yet as she passed the Lizard only 11 days out of "the pool of London," the experienced master John Erving could be pleased with the progress to date. As he seems to have done on all his crossings on this route, Erving changed his logbook from a cryptic journal of passing promontories to a full sea log that would do justice to a man-of-war.[1] Under the daily heading of "Transactions at Sea," Erving listed the ship's speed as checked every two hours, with notes on winds, weather, course, currents, and major rigging changes. Each day's entry also included ships seen or "spoke with," a review of the weather, total running miles, and corrected nautical miles logged to westward, as well as the observed or estimated latitude of the ship.

Erving, who completed two round trips to London from Boston in the *Sarah Galley* in 11 months, was taking his ship on a very good merchant sea crossing of 45 days and a total London-Boston time of exactly 8 weeks. The ship-rigged *Sarah Galley* was, nonetheless, probably being passed by all eight of the vessels she met with, most of which were bound westward for Newfoundland. Certainly fore-and-aft rigged vessels should have outsailed the *Sarah Galley*,[2] and the average passage time from London to Boston for 132 news-bearing merchantmen was only 52.5 days. (See Table 4.4.) A good passage need not be uneventful, and the *Sarah Galley*'s passage included calms that let the ship gain only 14 miles a day, a storm that broke the mizzen yard and left her riding with bare poles, and "I Rackon we have gon Nothing this 2 days to ye Wstard," as well as fresh gales from the ESE that let the ship make her top speed of 8 knots and better 150 miles a day.[3] But the passage, like the two other westward crossings of the *Sarah Galley* that were well recorded, was generally a struggle at 2 to 4 knots, holding as close to West-by-South as the head winds and seas allowed. This could occasionally mean eight course changes in a day, but that was unusual. On this trip Erving logged 2700 nautical miles before ending his log on meeting a Salem fishing schooner 45 to 50 leagues east of his destination.

Like westward crossings to New York or Philadelphia, the 2850-mile ocean crossing from the Channel to Boston was arduous to the point of being regarded as uphill by seamen who just as correctly saw the trip from Boston to London as downhill. Ships could log an average of 500 additional miles on the westward trip compared to the eastward, and the ship-rigged *Sarah Galley* completed westward trips between the Channel and Boston averaging nearly twice as long as her eastward voyages.[4] The power of the westerlies could certainly overwhelm shipping in a variety of ways. In August 1728 the 55-ton ship *Katherine* left Londonderry for New England. Seven months later, when she ran aground on the Galway coast, only 14 of her initial 123 passengers and sailors were still alive.[5] The same year another emigrant ship from Londonderry bound for Philadelphia was 23 weeks at sea, desperately short of provisions, and eventually made Jamaica instead of her original destination. The ship's company might well be included in the note that "the Ship was a mere Wreck, and could not be made capable of putting to Sea again." A "Cloud of New-England Men" arrived unintentionally in the Leeward Islands in December 1732, and a Dutch vessel bound from England to Newport, R.I., that same winter had her sails so tattered that she had to make for Charles Town, South Carolina, instead.[6] Improvements in rigging, the use of headsails, and the development of the schooner, as well as the coming of the helm wheel, would all be applied to the westerly routes before 1740,[7] but the westward trip remained one against nature for most of the year.

Boston competed with New York and Philadelphia for maritime dominance in English America. All three ports grew in the six decades before 1740, contending for economic hinterlands producing exportable commodities for West Indian and European markets and also for the local markets for English, European, and local manufactures. As is well known, the three cities grew at very different rates, challenging a general rule that urban growth respects the rank order of city size in the development within a single economic system. Boston remained the largest city in English America down to 1740 although Philadelphia grew phenomenally, matching lagging New York by 1740 and challenging Boston as the largest city in English America by 1760.[8] (See Table 4.1.) Growth in population of these competing seaports was linked to their maritime trade fortunes, although not exclusively so.

The economic strength of a leading port should have been self-reinforcing as long as ship traffic was the main source of information about opportunities for seaborne commerce. The growth of Philadelphia at the expense of New York is particularly interesting in this context, especially because it is now clear that the later rise of New York in the nineteenth century was greatly assisted by its place in the circulation of overseas information, especially business information.[9] The rise of Philadelphia, the slow growth of New York, and the continued leadership of Boston are due to numerous factors, but some aspects of these processes can be illuminated by exploring the patterns of trade and information on the "western routes."

The three contending ports of English North America were all susceptible to winter ice, which interrupted information movements, but the differences between the ports were noteworthy. None of these harbors were automatically closed by winter ice. River ice in a broad zone from Portland, Maine, to the Chesapeake occurs in "short, discontinuous and variable periods" through the season.[10] A frozen harbor was a matter of weather and immediately became news for the local papers and those of the rival ports. A rare hard winter could affect all three ports, as was the case in the winter of 1732–1733. Before the end of November, ship movement had ceased at Philadelphia, and wood prices there soared because of the surprisingly early winter that was destined to last until early March, when the port reopened after a dramatic breakup of 15-inch-thick ice with attendant flooding.[11] By Christmas of that winter the rivers of Maryland were frozen, and the Chesapeake Bay at Annapolis "near stopt up with Ice."[12] At New York, the sound was so full of ice that sloops were damaged while attempting to sail, and other vessels waited for the ice to clear. At Boston people were walking on the harbor ice as January 1733 began, and horse-drawn sleighs crossed from Boston to Charlestown. By 18 January, moderate weather had reopened the harbor, and work was under way to cut away the ice at the docks.[13] This uncommonly cold winter gave different weather and different problems to each of the three ports. New York shipping was encumbered for a few days, Boston shipping stopped for three weeks, and Philadelphia closed for more than three months. Yet this had been a very hard winter with uncommon difficulties that could not affect general expectations of merchants or shipmasters.

As a hard winter suggests, Philadelphia had much more trouble with winter ice than the other major ports though it was the most southerly of them. A Philadelphia merchant urged his sea captain and partner in a 1699 West Indies venture to be back before the December frosts or else make for Virginia, Maryland, or even Bermuda, where he was empowered to unship the crew and sell the cargo.[14] In the 20 years after 1719, there were only three winters during which Philadelphia was still open to ship traffic by the first of January. New York and Boston had newsworthy stoppages to ship traffic in only 5 of those 20 years, including 1719–1720 and 1732–1733, when all three ports had difficulties.[15] Philadelphia's location 100 miles up the Delaware River meant more river ice there than at the saltwater ports.[16] Vessels leaving Philadelphia could take advantage of a thaw, but vessels generally did not attempt to make Philadelphia during January. Although less emphatic, the same wintertime trend of more clearances than entries was also true of New York and Boston. As will be seen, there were disadvantages of some consequence in Philadelphia's comparative position but nothing that seriously slowed the rise of that city during this period. The crucial elements in the intercity competition are more evident from a closer examination of the trade and communication of each.

Boston was the premier port of Massachusetts and of British North America down to 1740, whether the dominance is measured in population, shipowning,[17] or ocean traffic. (See Table 4.2.) Boston owed a great deal of its dominance to its continuing control of the import trade in British goods. Boston had the largest immediate market for English goods of the three rivals and the strongest earnings of credit in England through the colony's trade with the West Indies and the fish trade to southern Europe.[18] These advantages for Boston's British trade were reinforced by the fact that news-bearing passages from England to Boston averaged 10 days less than similar crossings to New York and were quicker than similar Atlantic crossings to Philadelphia by 4 additional days.[19] Boston entries from British ports (Table 4.2) were few compared to the staple trades traffic to Bridgetown, Barbados, or the capes of the Chesapeake, but they were numerous in comparison with New York or Philadelphia. At the opening of the eighteenth century, much of New York business with Europe was still conducted through Boston.[20] In the years 1717–1719, Boston completely dominated the sailings from London for the northern American colonies.[21] A decade later, Boston was still entering more than four times as many ships from London as either New York or Philadelphia.[22] The level of communications between Boston and Britain in 1730 would not be surpassed until the 1760's, and at no time between 1697 and 1739 did the combined imports of Philadelphia and New York from Great Britain equal the value of British goods imported into Boston.[23] By that time only 1 vessel in 10 entering Boston's harbor was bound in from a British port, but Boston was still the leading entrepôt of goods and news throughout the northern colonies.

The Atlantic traffic between England and New England was not dominated by the seasons of any commodity, but winter was an important factor. The incomplete evidence offered in Table 4.3 suggests that the fear of one of Boston's harder winters imposed on traffic into Boston much more than the reality of most winters imposed on traffic bound from Boston to Britain. Yet the westward traffic seems to have shifted from a midsummer focus to spring and fall entries into Boston. For a conventional vessel like Erving's *Sarah Galley*, it was possible to make two round-trips a year on the North Atlantic route. This shift of season would not only suggest increased efficiency in some ship utilization and improvement in market conditions and rate of capital returns, but it also seems to have been a move toward seasonal passages that tended to be somewhat faster. The passages analyzed in Table 4.4, for news-bearing ships as identified in the *Boston News-letter* reveal the seasonal advantages of the emerging sailing seasons noted earlier, as well as confirming that winter passages westward were not common.

When English political exigencies demanded a winter passage to Boston, such a voyage was possible. The capture of Captain William Kidd, who was accused of piracy during a privateering expedition financed by leading Whig officeholders, was a political sensation in London in the winter of 1699–1700. News of the capture at Boston reached England at the beginning of September, and the idea of sending a frigate out to bring Kidd and his associates back to England for trial was broached immediately, including the notion that sending a frigate from Plymouth or from Ireland would cut westward voyage time in half.[24] When Governor Bellomont heard the HMS *Rochester* had been dispatched, he replied that the winter storms on the New England coast "are more violent than in any part of the world." The frigate was disabled by bad weather even earlier in the intended voyage and was forced back to Plymouth. With the House of Commons investigating the matter in December, HMS *Advice* was sent to Boston for the prisoners. She arrived after a very good six-week winter passage and had the prisoners back in London for examination by the Admiralty Board on 14 April.[25] This was a very unusual winter initiative, revealing that the passage could be made if the very real risks were judged to be worthwhile.

Boston sustained its position in the importation of British goods through earnings from seaborne trade to the West Indies and southern Europe and from communications advantages over her rivals for the English trade. Boston was closer to England than was either New York or Philadelphia, giving some information advantages and savings on freight. Boston operated as a port more of the year than Philadelphia although New York's winter advantages in this respect would matter subsequently. What is also clear is that Boston was closer to England than England was to Boston. Although this disparity between eastward and westward passages is true of all North American traffic with Britain, it was especially true for Boston. Boston could contact London by ships leaving any month, and the trip would be nearly half that of vessels attempting to bring metropolitan replies, objections, or shipments to Boston during only nine months of the year.

Boston's trade with the West Indies had been a major source of commercial capital for Boston's import merchants from the earlier days of the Massachusetts Bay Colony. Island demand for timber, fish, beef, pork, and cereal products helped establish and expand New England commerce, shipping, and industry. As Table 4.2 suggests, more than half of the entries into Boston in 1687–1688 were from the West Indies. In the subsequent half century this traffic would increase, but it did not keep its share of trade to the rapidly expanding English sugar islands. Boston's traffic from the West Indies fell from more than half the port's entries in 1687–1688 to a third of the entries by 1718–1719 to a quarter one decade later, and one fifth by 1737–1738. Here was a preliminary indicator of the stagnation of Boston, the stalled growth that became more dramatically evident in the 1740's. (See Tables 2.2 and 4.2.)

Boston's general place in the West Indies trade was bound to change. As timber stands disappeared in the immediate area, the focus of the timber, staves, and shingles would shift northward to subsidiary ports in Massachusetts, New Hampshire, and Maine. Congestion in Boston would strengthen the place of Salem and Marblehead in the shoreline-consuming fishing industry, and the growth of whaling would also center outside Boston as the industry grew.[26] These developments did not necessarily mean that Boston capital and Boston ships were not as active as ever or that they were not necessarily expanding at a comparable rate with Massachusetts growth. What it does suggest is that Boston's ship traffic, with its attendant refitting services and the distilleries that depended on imported molasses, were not growing as fast, and the economics of communication with the West Indies was no longer as favorable for Boston as it had been.

Further evidence of the changing place of Boston in the West Indies trade can be seen by a closer look at the changing patterns of Boston trade with that area. The most dramatic growth was in the number of ships entering Boston from foreign West Indian ports after 1714. As Table 4.5 documents, the loading of salt at the unsupervised Spanish island of Salt Tortuga was the major venture outside of the English island colonies for Boston shipping to the West Indies late in the seventeenth century.[27] The growth of Boston trade in from Surinam after the Peace of Utrecht was considerable, reaching 24 ships a year in 1729–1730. Surinam became an occasional source of European news for the *Boston News-letter*, and on one occasion during war it was even the route by which some English court news was first learned in Boston.[28] The dramatic drop in the entries from the foreign West Indies after the Molasses Act of 1733 is ambiguous evidence. Certainly, the earlier drift of Boston's traffic to the foreign West Indies confirms the claims of the planters of the British Islands that their molasses was not drawing the continental traders. Because evasion of the molasses duties involved declaration of false quantities and delivery of cargoes to ports with the poorest customs supervision (especially Newport, R.I.), the number of ship entries from foreign West Indies into Boston may not have been falsified, and Boston clearances to the foreign West Indies did not decline. For Boston, the Molasses Act apparently meant fewer sailings in from the foreign West Indies.[29]

The growth and decline of Boston's shipping traffic to the English Caribbean in the half century after 1690 is as striking as the change of focus from the eastern to the western end of the Caribbean. This decline does not relate to the British sugar islands growth rate at all. The drop in Boston traffic with Barbados predates any decline in the level of activity on that island. Even before the Molasses Act, Boston's share of the traffic in from Barbados to northern colonial ports had dropped dramatically and was being closely challenged by both Philadelphia and Virginia shipping.[30] Boston failed to gain anything in the dramatic growth of Leeward Island shipping early in the eighteenth century, and she gained little from the growth of Jamaica. (See Tables 2.3 and 2.5.)

Boston had initially enjoyed primacy in the trade to the Caribbean that was overwhelming in comparison with the newly conquered port of New York and the nascent Quaker town of Philadelphia. The only effective competition was with Irish provisions, and in this the Bostonians had seasonal advantages and good supply from the then-dependent bread colonies. The growing control over their own West Indian export traffic by New York and Philadelphia merchants was not simply a matter of commercial maturity. The transfer of provisions to Boston, in order to enjoy the economies of bilateral trading from there to the West Indies, was a cost that would go up with the growing need for imported grain for Massachusetts itself from early in the eighteenth century.

A New York shipper had another advantage in the contest with a Boston merchant for a specific Caribbean market. The route from New York to Barbados was approximately one week shorter than the trip of his Boston rival, and the New York vessel would probably be home four or five days earlier than a Boston ship clearing Barbados for home on the same day.[31] Not only would this constitute a 15 percent average saving on wages and victuals, but the advantage in market information would make the New York merchant much better able to respond to market changes, including the very literal "windfall profits" to those who traded to the hurricane belt. Boston was to suffer from a communications problem in this major trade, and the levels of her traffic from the eastern English Caribbean would be low enough by the 1730's to cost her the previous advantage of first receiving winter English news by way of the islands.

As if the competition were not tough enough for the traffic of the eastern Caribbean, Boston would also suffer from the shift to the western Caribbean, particularly Jamaica, by the 1730's. (See Table 4.5.) The passage from New York to Jamaica was a full 10 days shorter than the Boston passage to the new center of the English Caribbean, and the return voyage was four days shorter on an average.[32] This amounted to a 15 percent advantage again for the New Yorker over the Boston merchant and a more valuable gain in economic information. In this case, Philadelphia could very legitimately be expected to be even better situated. The West Indies trade was the arm of Boston commerce that most clearly foretold the stagnation of trade and development that was to come.

The most dramatic transformation of shipping to Boston in the half century after the "Glorious Revolution" was the sevenfold increase in ships entering Boston from North American ports. (See Table 4.6.) Here, in general terms, was a revolution in traffic that entirely eclipsed the stabilizing of the port's traffic with Britain and the decline of its West Indies shipping. The traffic growth is out of all proportion to the growth in Boston's population or to that of the colony, and it is not at all connected to the traffic or value of imports from Britain.[33] This growth is not generally due to complex shipping patterns through Boston, for the clearances from Boston for North American ports are generally comparable with entries, supporting other evidence of essentially bilateral trades.[34] The changes occurring in Boston's links with other North American colonies are more clearly evident from a regional treatment of the subject.

Of the continental plantation colonies, South Carolina was the farthest from Boston throughout the provincial period. Connected to the West Indies in origin and later developing a rice industry with a completely transatlantic direction, South Carolina would attract comparatively little shipping directly from Boston.[35] Without land communications with the north and with light ship traffic with Boston mainly in winter, Charles Town and Boston had few commercial links and little purpose for improving communications.

Although Boston's economic and maritime hinterlands did not reach to South Carolina, the trade of North Carolina was a significant part of Boston's commerce in the eighteenth century. As Table 4.6 indicates, the traffic was born before 1719, by which time it constituted nearly one third of the shipping to Boston from North America. The explosion had been in the naval stores industry of North Carolina. Without a harbor fit for oceangoing vessels, the pitch, tar, and turpentine producers of North Carolina came to depend on the New England coasters for export. The English government bounty on colonial naval stores after 1705 made these attractive exports with which Boston merchants earned London credits, and the shipbuilding industry of Massachusetts absorbed considerable quantities as well. Acquiring naval stores by selling New England and European goods to the growing population of North Carolina made this a particularly attractive trade for Boston.[36] Initially, this trade provided winter employment for Boston vessels in northern coastal trades and a destination a little less hazardous than the West Indies for a winter voyage in war. This tendency remained as traffic volumes increased after the Peace of Utrecht, but there were ships entering and clearing Boston in the North Carolina trade in each of 10 months of the year by 1718–1719, and every month of the year by 1737–1738.[37] The expansion in Boston's traffic with North Carolina between those years should not obscure the fact that this trade fell from accounting for nearly one third of Boston's traffic from North America to less than one fifth. Boston's place in providing news would also change from the days when Yankee shipmasters brought the gossip of Boston taverns and the *Boston News-letter* to a relatively isolated group of settlements. With the opening of postal service from Williamsburg to Edenton, N.C., in 1738, the earlier pattern of communications might be said to have ended. *The American Weekly Mercury* and the *Pennsylvania Gazette* were but the first intruders, with the newspapers of Williamsburg and Charles Town following. Charles Town's hinterland had previously included portions of North Carolina; the rise of Norfolk, Virginia, as the entrepôt for North Carolina was the more direct challenge.[38] Despite the continuing importance of North Carolina in Boston's trade, the strange empire in the south was fading by the 1730's.

Boston never enjoyed the position in the Chesapeake Bay that had been hers in the trade of North Carolina. The intercolonial commerce of the tobacco colonies had, for the period before 1740, been very ancillary to their trade to Britain. Boston's trade with the Chesapeake was less an entrepôt trade in European goods than the export of New England fish, rum, and timber products. As the most populous English colony, Virginia was an outlet for these goods in the 1680's, but Boston's traffic in from Virginia in the next half century suggests that the connection did not grow. The growing food deficit of Boston and surrounding towns would be offset by grain imports. Virginia was not prominent in this traffic, but Boston's connections with Maryland were stronger and grew in proportion to Boston's traffic with her North American neighbors. In this more diffused and diversified tobacco economy, the New Englanders found a place as middlemen in the tobacco gathering. Maryland also became a major source of grain for Massachusetts.[39] By the 1730's, Boston's traffic with the Chesapeake amounted to entries and clearances almost every month.[40] The place of the Chesapeake colonies as a source of winter news from Europe had dwindled from the 1680's, but the exchange of local news by land and sea definitely improved. The plantation staple colonies maintained the direct connection with Britain intended by government decree and royal officers and supported by economics. Boston's empire was not strong here.

Boston's traffic to her middle colonies rivals could not be expected to be major. As an established supply center, Boston had a place in the building of Philadelphia, but a place that would not be maintained in the subsequent growth of either city. New York's position would be somewhat different. Ships to Boston from New York grew in numbers even as Boston's political and economic superiority waned. The sloops that exchanged New York flour and grains for New England fish at Boston wharves were seldom exchanging news that had not already reached either city. The weekly post rider was usually quicker with the letters and the newspapers. In winter, when that service fell to a biweekly one, the coastal traffic between New York and Boston was also slowed to the odd vessel.

Boston's shipping links with other parts of English North America grew very unevenly in the period after 1675; the phenomenal growth occurred in the traffic with her more immediate neighbors and what can easily be regarded as Boston's new empire to the northeast. Even if the figures before 1719 in Table 4.6 suggest some underreporting of entries from Rhode Island and Connecticut, this traffic grew mightily. Boston served as entrepôt of European goods in these trades, with Connecticut serving as provisioner and Rhode Island as subsidiary commercial and manufacturing center. Newport also became a receiving port for Boston's foreign West Indian ventures after the Molasses Act. Boston was growing with New England. Connecticut and Rhode Island ports were oriented toward the same West Indian trades as Boston itself, and the waterborne commerce between these New England ports would not be a major source of usable commercial news.

Boston's expanding shipping to the northeast showed solid growth in the years between the one Boston-inspired conquest of Port Royal and the other of Louisbourg. The growth of this traffic in fish was not well represented by figures of the entries into Boston from that area, for the markets were elsewhere, and the preparation of the cargoes was done during the fishing season on or near the fishing grounds. The entries into Boston from those areas do, however, indicate the opportunities for news to reach Boston from the international fisheries and indirectly from Europe. An English newspaper aboard a fishing vessel bound for St. John's could be Boston's first source of important court news, as in 1702.[41] Here, too, was access to news from La Rochelle, Lisbon, or Cadiz that could affect the fish market of southern Europe. Lisbon also provided Boston with English news frequently, for many English and colonial merchantmen entered at Lisbon, and there was an English mail packet service there.[42] Winter certainly stilled the fishery traffic from Boston although an occasional vessel came back to Massachusetts from this area in winter's lulls.[43] The emphasis was on the last half of the year, meaning that news from England via the sack ships to Newfoundland in May or June could reach Boston relatively quickly.

The growth of Boston ship traffic in the period after 1675 was substantial, but the early eighteenth century was marked by significant changes in the directions of growth. Claims that the first British Empire was being outgrown by colonial commerce are only partly true in the case of Boston. This port was not expanding its trade with England, was slowing down in the West Indies trade, and had lost some of the entrepôt function for English North America that had been important before the rise of Boston's rivals. Boston's strength by 1740 was in her own region, from Connecticut to Louisbourg, and traffic here had increased remarkably. This new pattern for Boston's shipping was itself a symptom of decline, for these comparatively short voyages used less tonnage, earned less freight, and paid less in wages than the longer oceanic trades. A contraction of trade with southern Europe in the years of war that followed 1739 would mark the decline of Boston; the earlier retreat to a regional, specialized economy in the face of the rising entrepôt functions of New York and Philadelphia would make that contraction more distressing. Yet in the years of the Peace of Utrecht, Boston's communications with her trading world remained at least as good as they had ever been before and were weaker than her rivals' news gathering only in the West Indies trade.

New York's commercial growth in the three generations after the English conquest was decidedly modest. Perhaps the geography and economics of the port under the Dutch had already built a center that was large for the human neighborhood it served.[44] The population of the city doubled between 1660 and 1700 and would double again to reach 10,000 by 1742, but this was not rapid growth by the standards of English American colonies nor of the colony of New York itself. After the first English conquest—and perhaps even after the second—there were commercial changes that were bound to retard the prosperity of the city's established traders and to advance the fortunes of those who could easily establish trade on credit in England. Yet these problems, though explaining some of the context for Leisler's Rebellion, are not enough to explain the pathetic shriveling of the city's tax base from £95,867 in 1677 to a mere £38,671 by 1708.[45] Customs collectors at the port blamed the war for the drastic fall in shipping in the 1690's, adding that the growth of Philadelphia had cost New York her "mart" in Pennsylvania and the Jerseys and that short crops in the West Indies during the Peace of Ryswick aggravated matters. The sketchy evidence on New York shipping for most of the 1680's and 1690's does suggest that the active New York fleet was falling and that the local influence of Boston was growing.[46]

Compared to the evidence for the late seventeenth century, the surviving shipping records for New York's first four decades of the eighteenth century are full. (See Table 4.7.) The shipping activity of 1701 can be taken to represent the very lean times of the later 1690's, for the limited evidence suggests that the Peace of Ryswick did not help New York shipping as much as had been hoped.[47] Continuing complaints in Queen Anne's reign suggest that the level of recovery accomplished by 1718 was all achieved after the Peace of Utrecht. Thereafter the level of traffic into New York grew very little, and comparisons with Boston were even less encouraging. (See

Table 4.2.) Even more striking was the failure of the port of New York to attract shipping in proportion to the growth of the colony or the city in the generation after 1720.[48]

Direct shipping between Britain and New York was very limited as governors through the period repeated and Table 4.7 makes plain. Even the direct imports from Britain in 1718 and 1728 actually represent vessels that had stopped at a Channel port to legitimize their trade between the Netherlands and New York.[49] It is also true that most of the evident growth in traffic to Britain and Ireland between 1728 and 1738 was growth in traffic to Dublin and Belfast.[50] Direct political, economic, or social correspondence between New York and London was infrequent compared to the Boston connection with the metropolis.

New York's seasonal advantages over Boston, which would later give New York a dominance in the early-spring flaxseed trade to Ireland and the terminus of the transatlantic packet service,[51] was not at all evident through this period. (See Table 4.8.) New York did gain extra weeks of shipping mobility by a location that put both winds and tides to work clearing the saline harbor of whatever ice did develop. James Birket, an Antiguan traveling in North America, noticed this and added, "The vessels by this means in the winter are Soon into the Harbour, And Soon out when the wind Serves, when in other ports they are frequently frose up."[52] It was possible for New Yorkers to walk across the ice to New Jersey one week in January and have no ice whatever in the Hudson the next week.[53] This was not an advantage used in the trade with Britain in this period. When upbraided for not writing more often to the Lords of Trade and Plantation, Governor Cornbury replied:

> I intreat your Lordships to consider that but few ships goe directly from this port to England, So that I must depend upon Boston and Philadelphia Posts for conveying my letters to such ships as may be going to England; and some times both those Conveyances faile.[54]

Cornbury was not an assiduous correspondent and would suffer from wartime disruptions of traffic as well, but his complaint was fair as far as it went. It is not surprising that the British government found it necessary to organize a packet service to New York when a major military initiative was under way in 1710.[55]

Infrequent traffic with London reflected another New York disadvantage. Although the nineteenth-century differences in fast packet sailings to Boston or New York from Liverpool were minimal,[56] the differences in London passage times to the two colonial ports early in the eighteenth century were significant. (Compare Tables 4.4 and 4.9.) Although a four-week passage was the shortest to either destination from London, passages to New York averaged eight days longer, were longer on average for ships arriving in any month of the year, and were much longer for the occasional winter crossing.

Although the evidence is inadequate to sustain anything but a tentative explanation, it seems likely that the route to New York often included a stop at Madeira and an approach to New York from the southeast.[57]

Certainly Lord Cornbury would never have been chided about his infrequent correspondence if he had not been preceded in office by a man who went to great lengths to write London often. The Earl of Bellomont thought a winter crossing to New York too dangerous, but he had alternatives. He advised the secretary of the Board of Trade on sending winter mail to him at New York.

> When 'tis either towards winter or in the latter end of winter, by way of Virginia or Barbados or both, which was the course taken in Sr Edmund Andros's time here, and, excepting in the dead of winter, there come sloops hither from Barbados every month in the year, and two or three months earlier in the beginning of the year than any ships come from England to Boston or this place.[58]

Were New Yorkers pursuing a West Indian trade that took full advantage of their winter shipping season?

Trade with the Caribbean was, in good times and bad, the major trade of colonial New York. Cadwallader Colden said as much in 1723,[59] but it appears to have been true for the whole period under study here. Local sources of grain, flour, bread, and most meat made the trade convenient, and advantages over Boston mentioned earlier gave New York merchants opportunities that were exploited. In the first four decades of the eighteenth century the percentage of ship entries into New York directly from Caribbean ports ranged between about one third and one half of the total traffic inward.[60] The trade was even more important than these figures suggest because ship deployment, freight earnings, and crews' wages and victualing for this trade would be high compared to coastal traffic. Despite the place of the Caribbean trade in the New York economy, the traffic did not grow as might be expected during the Peace of Utrecht. After dramatic growth and recovery by 1718, the number of New York entries from the Caribbean stabilized at about 100 vessels a year. (See Table 4.10.)

The decline of Barbados in New York's trade was quicker after 1725 than in the trade of Boston (see Tables 4.5 and 4.9), although Barbados had earlier been significant in New York's communications world.[61] New York was not gaining its share of the expanding prosperity of the Leeward Islands or of Jamaica, though in the latter traffic New York traders had a substantial place. (See Table 2.5.) In terms of access to European or eastern Caribbean news, there was a relative decline in the New York position in the 1720's and 1730's. In 1697 an English wine merchant in Madeira heard of the loss of a ship near Barbados by letter via New York; Bostonians would first hear of the murder of Governor Parke of the Leeward Islands in March 1711 by way of New York, and these exceptions at the opening of the century would remain exceptions in the next three decades.[62]

The shift in the focus of New York Caribbean trade toward Jamaica expanded the seasons of entries from the British Caribbean islands. (See Table 4.11.) Lord Bellomont had rightly claimed that sloops were into New York from Barbados in all months save "the dead of winter" at the end of the seventeenth century. That lull could then be four months long, and the traffic peaks were in spring and in August, like those in the Boston trade to the English Caribbean. The same pattern held for the larger traffic of 1718, but by then only two months passed without any ships in from the British Caribbean. By the end of another decade, which saw less Barbados traffic, at least two ships a month entered New York from the British Caribbean. New York's access to Jamaica market information and the diplomatic encounters between New Spain and Jamaica-based English men-of-war and merchant-men of the English Atlantic would be better in the 1730's—and more necessary. Although the British government sought to keep its naval commanders at Jamaica well informed—and hence some information became available to local authorities and merchants—Jamaica was seldom able to relate fresh English advices to New York before these had arrived by other routes. New York would not usually have European news for Jamaica either, given the length of the voyage between them.[63]

It is the foreign, especially the Dutch, West Indies that has been assumed to be the area of growth for the New York provisions trading. This was a significant part of the import trade in 1718 but grew little in the next decade, and the questionable figures for 1738 show either the deception of those evading the Molasses Act or the caution of those trading in the range of the increasingly bellicose Spanish *guarda-costas*. (See Table 4.7.) If foreign West Indian goods came in disguised as British, there was no great number of ships claiming to come in that year from the British islands either. Although the New York trade with Holland survived the transfer of power by a very long time, the trade with the Dutch and other foreign West Indian islands was not so much a survival as a new growth—and not a particularly vigorous growth.

As with Boston, the most substantial growth in New York shipping entries in the first four decades of the eighteenth century was in the trade from other English North American ports. (See Table 4.7.) Neither the scale nor the rate of growth of this traffic into New York compared with the explosion of regional traffic into Boston in the first decades of the eighteenth century, but the New York development was also a sign of regional interdependence. At the opening of the century, two thirds of New York's entries from North America were from Massachusetts. The 16 ships in from Boston in 1701 were a reasonable average even 40 years later. New York shipping to Boston had increased to carry the grain there, but the direct return traffic had not grown.[64] With post riders linking New York and Boston throughout the period, the ship letter would be for discussing cargo and for less urgent communications; the occasional ship coming into New York from Boston in winter did not necessarily bring much news. New York would, as the century progressed, gain some trade from the new developments in the Carolinas and Georgia, but to 1740, at least, these were marginal sources of news or trade.

As with Boston, New York traffic from Rhode Island was the most significant development between 1700 and 1740. From one entry a year in 1701, New York customs men came to record 31 entries in 1738. Rhode Island's growing place in the coastwise trade of the contending centers of Boston and New York is intriguing. If the bases of the rise of Newport were lax customs administration, a fertile archipelago of grazing lands, and a good harbor, the town's rise in the West Indies trade was preceded by Newport's growing importance to the neighboring giants. This growth precedes the Molasses Act by enough years to reduce the importance of that stimulus.[65] Yet West Indian produce was certainly part of this traffic from Rhode Island to New York, and both the commodities and the news would have been processed to the advantage of the Newport merchants before being sent on to New York.

In the lifetime after 1674, New York's staple had shifted from fur to bread, flour, and meat, and its communications focus shifted to the Caribbean. Despite the best all-season harbor, New York did not capture her share of the West Indian market. New York had her own maritime hinterland in East Jersey, Long Island, and parts of Connecticut, but this whole area was within Boston's hinterland as well. By postrider and by ship entries in all months of the year, New York and Boston were firmly linked together economically before and after the Dominion of New England was tried as political cement. Development of Newport, Rhode Island, on this line of communication was at the expense of New York in the West Indies trade. Before the establishment of Philadelphia, merchants in the new English colony of New York dealt in Delaware tobacco, served as conveyors of European goods to West Jersey, and could expect a growing place in the Chesapeake trade. The burgeoning new port of Philadelphia would foreclose these prospects. By 1700, West Jersey was clearly in the sphere of the new city as was even the Iroquois trade of the upper Susquehanna.[66] Philadelphia was also carving out a place for herself, at the expense of Boston and New York, in the Caribbean trade. The postriders into New York from Pennsylvania would bring latest news on West Indian markets, to be traded there for Boston and Newport news of the Old World and New. New York's position was damaged less by the rise of Newport than by the development of Philadelphia between New York and its Caribbean trade.

Pennsylvania and its capital would rise mightily in the sixty years after 1680, weaving a new and powerful web of Atlantic maritime commitments. From little more than a notion in the fertile mind of its founder in 1680, the colony grew to over 85,000 people by 1740, with a capital city of 9500 clearing some 200 ships a year to Britain, southern Europe, the West Indies, and neighboring North American colonies. The lack of surviving customs records for Philadelphia creates a problem in tracing the meteoric rise of what would become the premier city of colonial America. The general outline of that process, for Philadelphia and its immediate hinterland at least, has been summarized as establishment down to 1700, stagnation from there to 1730, and expansion from 1730 to 1760.[67] With this general pattern in mind,

Table 4.12 can be used to gain a closer view of the components of Philadelphia's trade.

Establishment and growth of Philadelphia as a seaport owed much to the Caribbean trades as was true of New York and Boston. The trade was an excellent match of needs and resources for the new town on the Delaware. Between 1696 and 1700 an average of 16 vessels a year entered Barbados from Pennsylvania. A tendency to arrive at the island in January or in July and August suggests a hurricane-defying rhythm similar to that of the New Englanders there.[68] Although the surviving evidence is only suggestive, Philadelphia's trade to the West Indies seems to have developed somewhat differently from that of Boston and New York by the 1730's. Philadelphia's shipping entries from the Caribbean did not match those of her rivals before 1740, but much more of her traffic was with the English West Indies.[69] Philadelphia was not a major distillery town, so the lure of foreign West Indian molasses would not be as strong as was the market for good Barbados rum. Before the end of the 1730's, Philadelphia received more ships from Barbados and the Leeward Islands than did either of her rivals. Although better evidence than we have would be necessary to sustain this argument, its implications could be important. Not only would Philadelphia's shipping suffer less disruption because of the Molasses Act of 1733, but there would also be less fear from *guarda costas* in the subsequent years. The West Indies trade would earn more London credits for Philadelphia merchants, and the eastern Caribbean would provide Philadelphia with news from Europe and the eastern Caribbean in most months of the year. From the early eighteenth century, Philadelphia sent at least a monthly cargo to Barbados except in January, and the connections with the Leewards and Jamaica were comparable. In 1738, Alexander Spotswood could urge Virginians to use the newly improved posts to Philadelphia, "from whence Vessels are almost always going to one or other of the Islands."[70] By this time spring and early summer were particularly busy for those involved in the West Indies trades out of Philadelphia, but some traffic was active in all save the icebound weeks, which varied from winter to winter. Because Irish provisions would arrive in the West Indies as the year opened, Philadelphia's trouble with river ice was of limited consequence for her place in that trade. Links with Maryland, New York, and Newcastle (lower on the Delaware) would bring information in when ships were frozen out of the port. Philadelphia's competition with New York for the trade of the Caribbean did not involve much advantage in passage times or routes[71] although both of these ports had clear advantages over Boston. An average difference of 10 days on a round-trip could well be the difference between two and three trips a year. The West Indian trade of Philadelphia was central to the development of the mercantile community there, would still account for a third of the ship movements in the later 1730's, and would become the leading trade to the Caribbean from North America in the subsequent generation.[72]

Philadelphia's coastal commerce with neighboring British colonies grew between 1720 and 1739 (see Table 4.12.) and would grow even more thereafter. Delaware Bay was Philadelphia's maritime core, and Maryland was drawn into the orbit of the Pennsylvania capital as was West Jersey.[73] In the 1690's Pennsylvania had a significant role in provisioning the homeward-bound Maryland tobacco fleets,[74] a role that would fade with Maryland's increased production of grain. There was some growth in trade with the Carolinas in the 1730's, but it was Massachusetts that led Philadelphia's coastal trade with a dozen or more vessels arriving each year, most of them for grain. (See Table 4.6.) There was some growth in traffic with the Carolinas in the 1730's, but the scale was not large. In general, Philadelphia's coastwise trade must be considered as light in comparison to New York's and very light in comparison with that of Boston. (See Tables 4.2 and 4.7.) Philadelphia's hinterland was landward. Her maritime connections with a wide range of neighboring colonies were slight in terms of shipping employed and too thin to represent a communications channel nearly as useful as the postriders who linked Maryland and New York with Philadelphia. The occasional movement of grain cargoes between Philadelphia and New York on news of price advantages was an indication of an improving market system;[75] Philadelphia's best postal communications were with continental cities she competed with rather than with her markets. Nonetheless, Philadelphia merchants were able to gather market information on shipments to the West Indies, as well as news on conditions in the islands at least as quickly and reliably as their competitors to the north.

Another branch of Philadelphia's maritime trade grew remarkably in the first 40 years of the eighteenth century although the scale was still small in 1740 compared to its place by 1770 as second only to West Indian commerce. This was the trade in wheat and flour with southern Europe. (See Table 4.12.) Lisbon, with such strong ties to the English in the wine and fish trades that it could be considered an English Atlantic port, was the preferred destination for Pennsylvania wheat cargoes because it was an information center, a major market itself, and comparatively safe from pirates and privateers. Voyages left Philadelphia any month the port was open although a preference for June and December was evident.[76] The westerlies encouraged a passage to Lisbon that was a direct and comparatively prompt crossing. The Iberian and Mediterranean grain market was very complex, with major suppliers in Sicily, North Africa, and England all able to respond more rapidly to opportunities than could a Philadelphia merchant. Price and supply information was important as this trade developed as was southern European diplomatic news. The risks were taken, in part, because grain was often cheaper from North America despite the freight costs and because payment was usually in good bills on London as the English wine trade was always in serious imbalance.

As the general pattern of Philadelphia shipping makes clear, the freight returns were a much more complicated matter than the financial balancing of the southern European trade. Salt and wines from the "Wine Islands" (which were not considered European by the Navigation Acts and, therefore, could export directly to the American colonies whereas Iberian sherries and ports had to go through England) constituted the only significant direct returns, and these tended to be oversupplied at Philadelphia because of the comparatively large returning fleets from the 1730's. Table 4.12 suggests that much of the excess shipping returned to Philadelphia by way of England. The wheat trade to southern Europe, in which Philadelphia took an early lead over New York,[77] like the Carolina rice trade to that same area, represented a significant expansion of trading horizons beyond the British Empire. Yet the place of English merchants in both of these trades is a reminder of the limits of that initiative and the vulnerability of these trades to market conditions that could not be adequately forecast. There were merits to English factoring, which could work effectively in trades with a higher margin of profit.

Philadelphia's direct trade with Britain was modest throughout the period from the town's founding until 1740—and remarkably slight on closer investigation. Philadelphia had very little in the way of cargo that could be profitably shipped to English or Scottish ports. In the last five years of the seventeenth century, for instance, all the English outports received only one recorded cargo from Pennsylvania, a load of logwood and tobacco imported into Newcastle upon Tyne.[78] In the next few years, according to surviving evidence, reexported Maryland or Lower Counties tobacco or furs and skins were the only bulk cargoes that could be offered as return freight for ships bringing migrants and manufactured goods from Britain.[79] Thereafter the ship traffic (see Table 4.12) was always unequal, and this did not even represent the extent to which the trade itself between Britain and Pennsylvania was overbalanced in favor of the metropolis. Ships bound for Lisbon, Cadiz, Madeira, or Gibraltar would earn some of the returns, and Philadelphia's Irish trade would contribute as well. Legalizing of direct trade to Ireland in nonenumerated goods after 1730 caused this traffic to grow rapidly in the next decade. From nothing before 1730, this trade grew to account for an average of 11 ships a year from Philadelphia in the early 1730's and 20 ships a year bound eastward to Ireland in each of the next five years.[80] This trade with Ireland accounted for all the growth in ships bound from Philadelphia to Britain and Ireland between 1730 and 1739. The direct traffic to England had not grown at all.

In November 1739 the London-bound lieutenant governor of Pennsylvania, Patrick Gordon, and his party went aboard the *Constantine*, Edward Wright commander. The *Constantine* was moored at Chester, downriver from Philadelphia, as a precaution against early ice. Gordon's choice of ship was an endorsement of regular and reliable experience, for Wright and the *Constantine* had been making an annual crossing for at least 11 years since she was advertised in July 1729 as offering "Extraordinary Accomodations for Passengers, and is to return Early next Spring, directly from London to this City."[81] Although hardly a passenger "liner," the 130-ton *Constantine* was the first vessel advertising for passengers for a regular transatlantic voyage from North America. Perhaps it was the lightness of merchant traffic from Philadelphia to London that prompted the *Constantine* and its imitators[82] to begin this kind of service out of Philadelphia. The infrequency of direct voyages for England, together with a longer winter than that of her competitors, did mean that Philadelphia was less able to contact London than was either New York or Boston. As the Iberian and Irish trades developed in the 1730's, this commercial weakness remained although the level of English sailings *to* Philadelphia increased the flow of information about those markets.

Ship traffic from England to Pennsylvania was well below that to Boston throughout the period and lighter than the shipping to New York until after 1715, but the volume grew to average 27 ships a year in the early 1730's and to 40 ships a year later in that decade. (See Table 4.12.) By this time a vessel a month could be expected in from Britain except for the first three months of the year.[83] These voyages averaged a few days longer than those to New York on similar routes, but the fastest recorded passage for a news-bearing ship from London to Philadelphia before 1740 was a full 12 days longer than those bound to Boston or New York.[84] (Compare Table 4.13 with Table 4.4 and Table 4.9.) If it was important to hear some European news before competitors in New York or Boston, Philadelphians could not usually expect to succeed. Yet the regular correspondence between William Penn and James Logan early in the eighteenth century indicated possibilities although it demanded awareness of all possible conveyances.[85] A similar level of contact could be maintained with less effort by the 1730's.

Philadelphia's growth down to 1740 revealed some differences from the pattern of competitors. She did not achieve parity in the West Indies, coastwise, or in British trades by any count of ship traffic or trade statistics. The English Caribbean held its place as the main overseas trade out of Philadelphia, and Barbados and the Leewards could be sources of European news for Philadelphia throughout the period. The development of wheat export trades to southern Europe and to Ireland in the 1730's brought more multilateral trading across the Atlantic than had been general before except for the New England fish trade. Philadelphia was not as close to Britain as was Boston, yet it was developing a strong Atlantic communications network. When Andrew Bradford launched his *American Magazine* in 1741 from Philadelphia, he certainly was not deciding which city to choose by its correspondence. Yet his claims for his city were not false.

> As the City of Philadelphia lies in the Center of the British Plantations, and is the Middle Stage of the Post, from Boston in New-England Northward, down to Charles-Town in Carolina Southward, and as that City, besides its frequent Intercourse with Europe, drives a continual Commerce with the West-India-Islands, & has also a considerable Commerce with the rest of the Colonies on the Continent; We, Therefore, fixed upon it as the properest Place, and more commodiously situated that [*sic*] any other, for carrying on the various Correspondences, which the Nature of the Work renders necessary.[86]

The three rival ports of English America were engaged in a contest for hinterlands of agricultural produce for a variety of West Indian markets and eventually those of southern Europe as well. In this competition the lean soils of Massachusetts were destined eventually to lose to New York and especially to Pennsylvania. Boston held its entrepôt function throughout the period 1675 to 1740, importing and distributing English products to a populous regional market reachable by coastal shipping. Fishing was not only the major method for making multilateral returns to English creditors, but it also symbolized a commercial method. Although some market information would help determine whether a fishing venture would be undertaken at all and market information at Lisbon, Cadiz, or Barbados would help determine the ultimate place of sale, the taking and marketing of fish were processes over which very little careful control of supply was possible, and, once taken, the perishable cargo demanded a quick market regardless of conditions. Although the fishing industry gave a multilateral aspect to Boston commerce from the beginning, it should be emphasized that this was also the city that maintained the strongest commercial ties with England of all the towns of temperate America. Nor need it be considered ironic that political relations seemed more often strained where commercial relations were closest. Boston also kept her lead in ships clearing for the Caribbean although both of her rivals were better positioned to receive and use market information as soon as the number of their ships in the trade became at all adequate. As English shipping to the West Indies became less seasonal, markets for colonial provisions could not be presumed to work in certain seasons without fail. As North American rivals increased their shipping to the islands in all seasons, the markets were being tightened in ways that worked to the prejudice of ports further away from news of those markets. Venturing fish or other cargoes on ships bearing appropriate names like *Faith*, *Hope*, or *Hopewell* would become less rewarding than had been the case earlier. Yet Boston was the leading port of British America before 1740, and that leadership was based on superior links with London as well as entrepôt functions dependent on those links.

Despite the best harbor, an easily accessible agricultural hinterland, and clear British government preference in matters of defense spending, sponsored settlement, and even mail packet services, New York did not grow at the rate of her rivals. Boston had a better position in the trade with Britain, and New York lacked a European trade to earn English credits before the 1730's although New York's position in the Caribbean trade remained stronger than that of Philadelphia. Nevertheless, the increasing oceanic trade of Newport and Philadelphia were cause, symptom, and consequence of New York's relatively limited growth before 1740.

The growth of Philadelphia over New York was not reflected in total ship entries and was not built on any advantages in passage times to the West Indies. Indeed, Philadelphia developed in spite of more winter disruption of traffic and persistent disadvantages in trade with Britain. In the contest for growth, Philadelphia drew more immigrants than New York, and the marginally richer and more accessible hinterland not only helped draw people but also gave some marginal advantage in very competitive markets.

Communications advantages were supportive, but hardly decisive, in the emergence of Philadelphia before 1740. Yet Philadelphia improved its business information faster than it increased its shipping. The emergence of regular postal facilities after 1693 and newspapers after 1720 began two processes. On the one hand, correspondence from rival ports improved the understanding of supply for as competitive a market as that to the West Indies. Whether it was a receipt of ship preparations from a friend or agent or simply the shipping news on vessels leaving the rival ports, this was more information than was available earlier. This separation of information from ship arrivals was not complete, and receiving ports still had opportunities to respond first, but a beginning was being made. Communications improvements were also making the knowledge of the state of specific markets more accessible as competition increased. Although information was still imperfect and sometimes worse than no information at all would have been, a transformation had begun where it was needed. This was not in the staple trades of the south or the north but in the trades of the three rival ports of the western routes. The growth of all three ports and the connections between them would also multiply their opportunities for political, economic, and personal correspondence with Britain although the direct trade remained dominated by Boston.

The merchant shipping out of the ports of Boston, New York, and Philadelphia indicated how the western routes were unlike other colonial trades. None of these ports had a direct trade with Britain in a staple commodity that would establish a major fleet of merchantmen in a direct transatlantic trade. The merchant-shipowners of these North American ports had nothing resembling an export monopoly, so they could not be complacent about gathering market information as carefully and quickly as their competitors in their own port and the rival centers. Although their shipping operated bilaterally wherever possible, trading was much more multilateral for merchants in these ports than for those in colonial staple trades. The West Indies provisions trade; the fish trade to southern Europe; and the later transatlantic trades in wheat, rice, and flaxseed were all connected to earning credits for the imports from England that were a source of significant profit and a major aspect of intercolonial traffic out of these colonial entrepôts. Although venturing unsolicited cargoes was still undertaken, the growing competition for trade was increasingly a competiton for fresh and accurate information.

Together these ports would not have entered 250 vessels in 1675, yet they entered nearly 1000 vessels a year by the end of the 1730's. (See Tables 4.2, 4.7, and 4.12.) The most dramatic growth had been in sailing between North American ports, a development that improved the sending and receiving of news from Britain or the Caribbean as well. By 1738 there were more than 350 sailings a year south to the Caribbean, helping shipowners, masters, and crew to avoid winter ice and idleness, providing European news during the lull in direct traffic between old England and new, and building intercolonial connections and dependencies that strengthened the rim of the English Atlantic. The burgeoning intercolonial shipping laced together the different routes of the English Atlantic, improving the flow of news, particularly to those parts with seasonal interruptions in oceanic traffic.

Direct traffic between the three leading North American ports and English ports was comparatively light before 1740, growing to about 100 sailings a year late in the 1730's. The eastward passages averaged about one half of the 8- to 10-week westward passages on these routes, and sailings eastward could commence from Boston in any month although westward passages in winter were uncommon. Boston's position as the leading North American port had numerous causes, most of which are well known. Her advantage in communication with England was an asset that deserves more emphasis. Her competitors would benefit more from the strenuous and expensive improvements in the colonial postal service, would exploit their marginal advantages in the Weste Indies trades, and would force Boston merchants to improve their information. Yet until 1740 Boston's primacy in colonial shipping and in access to seaborne news was mutually reinforcing. In particular, Boston's advantages in communication with and through England helped maintain the town's maritime leadership among the colonial ports on the western routes of the English Atlantic.

5 · Northern Routes and the English Atlantic

The northern staple trades of the English Atlantic had communications patterns that were very different from those of the developing ports of the western routes or the warmer trades for sugar, rice, or tobacco. Both Newfoundland and Hudson Bay were primary trades and not colonies, and it was here that winter imposed its most compelling tyrannies over ships and people. Yet Newfoundland and Hudson Bay were profoundly different from each other. The English Atlantic was at its narrowest between Newfoundland and England and its widest between London and the Hudson's Bay Company factories at the bottom of James Bay. The fishery was a vast and unruly concourse of international competitors, and most of the English among them were from the outports that sent ships into a multilateral trade marked by volatile markets, perishable products, and very severe limits on available information about current markets. By contrast, the Hudson Bay trade was miniscule and under close monopoly control held firmly in London despite the limitations imposed by distance and winter. These contrasts should, on closer examination, reveal features of communications in the higher latitudes as well as illuminate some aspects of English Atlantic communication along all its routes.

Insistence that Newfoundland was not a colony was English government policy in support of West Country interests anxious to operate freely on the beaches and shores of Newfoundland. Actual English settlement was slight, numbering fewer than 2700 people in the summer of 1698 and nearly half of these would not stay over winter. By 1738 four of five summer residents were people who lived there permanently, and the population had nearly doubled, but both the growth rate and the population were small. The poor growth of Newfoundland population in the two centuries before 1700 and the slow growth down to 1740 are a telling commentary on the country itself and the perceptions of the Atlantic. For all the threats of maritime travel, nearly half of those who came to fish at Newfoundland from England and Ireland found the risks of two Atlantic crossings a year worth taking in order to winter in the home country.[1] This was, indeed, a nursery of seamen.

If northern European fishermen had been lured into the Atlantic in search of rich virgin fisheries, the progress of their harvesting would lead them around the northern rim of the Atlantic to the New World. In the Atlantic basin, warm lands are generally washed by relatively lifeless seas, and, as if by way of compensation, the harder lands are fringed with waters teeming with life. A broad irregular arc of plankton-rich, cooler waters that are stirred by contact with the warmer North Atlantic Drift reaches from the North and Norwegian Seas, through the Faeroe Islands and Iceland's rich coastal fisheries, to the Greenland coast and on to the fishing banks and coasts of Newfoundland, Nova Scotia, and the Gulf of Maine.[2] Fishermen venturing progressively further along this arc—as overfishing, warfare, or minor climatic variations lessened the catches closer to home—were actually tracing the northerly route to Newfoundland and the Hudson Bay as well.

Routes to Newfoundland were necessarily designed to lessen the sailor's confrontation with the westerlies, and the northern route was one early solution. This may have been the favored route in the sixteenth century and seems a logical extension from the old fifteenth-century English presence in the Icelandic fisheries. A northerly course from Ireland allowed ships to catch the polar easterlies, which blew strongest in the first months of the year in the latitude of about 60°, and both the East Greenland and Irminger currents assisted.[3] (See Figure 4.) Either on sighting Cape Farewell or encountering the Labrador current, the fishermen could then follow that cold current south to Newfoundland. From the first days of discovery, it seems evident that a direct westerly course was often taken, with either Dursey Head, Ireland, or the Lizard as points of departure. In the right circumstances, this could be a very quick passage indeed as seems to have been the case with John Cabot's *Matthew* in 1497. When Humphrey Gilbert sailed a similar course for St. John's in 1583, he was forced into long traverses in the face of the westerlies.[4] Here was a course to test the weatherliness of a ship, for those that could not sail close to the wind were often on a long voyage.

The route that came to dominate the English approach to the fishery by later Stuart times involved a WSW course shaped from the Lizard or Lundy Island in Bristol Channel. The ship would try to hold to that course, shared by traffic to Boston, New York, or Philadelphia, until her estimated position was from 50 to 60 leagues west of the Azores and the latitude approximately 43°. Newfoundland-bound shipping changed course then, sailing NW until the latitude was read or estimated at 46° 30', at which point the course became westerly until the 100-fathom line assured the master that he had arrived on the Grand Banks. Wind shifts would divert the fishing or "sack" ship from this arc as recommended in *The English Pilot, the Fourth Book* (1689), but this was the route favored by those who could not afford the pleasanter and slower passage by way of the Azores.[5]

These comparatively direct routes to Newfoundland did not preclude some

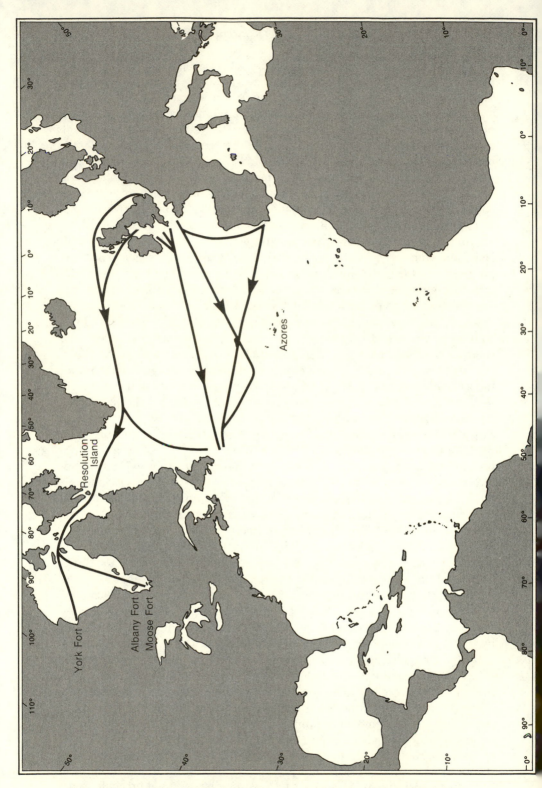

Figure 4. Main English Routes to Newfoundland and Hudson Bay.

multilateral approaches to Newfoundland by English ships. The Staffords of Topsham sent out three ships to the Newfoundland fishery in 1698. The 90-ton *Elizabeth and Mary*, Phillip Stafford master, cleared from Barnstable near the end of January 1698. This rather early start for the English fishery was caused by a need to buy foreign salt. For the *Elizabeth and Mary*, the family's 250-ton *Daniel and Henry*, and 24 other English vessels in the trade in that year of peace, salt from the French islands of St. Martin and Île d'Oléron was close at hand at the beginning of the voyage. Other ships in the English fishery that year had ranged further for salt, relying on the Portuguese (19 English ships arrived at Newfoundland that year by way of Portugal) and Cape Verde Island salt (7 ships) as had become essential during the recent war with France. These sources, together with the West Indian salt from Salt Tortuga, provided the English fishery at Newfoundland with its comparatively expensive salt.[6] These ships would bring in old news from England, but the Portuguese stop may have provided some tentative information on some aspects of fish markets there.

While two Topsham vessels commanded by Staffords headed to Newfoundland with salt, Ben Stafford took the *Peace* of Topsham, 70 tons and 21 men, to the fishery via Cork, where he loaded provisions, if not fishermen. Fully one vessel in six of the English Newfoundland fishing fleet came in that year via Ireland,[7] favored as a place to take on provisions and extra hands for the fishery. Stopping in Ireland afforded fresh Irish news for countrymen in the fishery but, like the voyages by way of salt sources, made the news and gossip from Western English ports of origin of little social utility on the Grand Banks.

Although the ships came from a variety of ports by a variety of routes and fished a vast area off Newfoundland's coast, the English fishery there was a major source of news from all parts of the North Atlantic. The English fishery at Newfoundland was, if commentators, participants, and historians are correct, in decline in the Restoration era and did not recover until the 1730's.[8] Although the French fishermen, privateers, and occasional squadrons were a real threat, they were less important in most submissions than the growing competition from English colonies. The Newfoundland settlers were regarded as interlopers in the English preserve as were the New England and Irish fishermen and traders. The decline of the English fishery was, to some degree, a matter of semantics. Englishmen resident elsewhere in the English Atlantic were sharing in the fishery.

The number of vessels involved in that part of the Newfoundland fishing industry that operated out of England was quite variable from year to year between 1675 and 1740. (See Table 5.1.) English fishing vessels may have competed with boats of the local inhabitants, but much of the latters' catch would be shipped to market in the sack ships that came out expressly to buy fish taken by others. Although statistical evidence is fragmentary and suspect, there seem to be adequate grounds for concluding that English shipping to Newfoundland did not match its reported level of some 175 ships in 1675 until the short period of peace that marked the end of the century. Wars with

France were particularly hard on the English fishery, attracting perhaps fewer than 40 ships from England in the worst years of the War of the Spanish Succession. In the first years after the Peace of Utrecht, which seemed so decisive a victory for British interests in this fishery, the recovery was not back to the volumes of 1699 or 1700. By the late 1730's the English catch was up to new highs, and it would be safe to assume that at least 300 vessels a year were involved then.

Ocean passages of the Newfoundland fleets were short in comparison with other crossings of the English Atlantic empire. The outward passage time of Phillip Stafford's *Elizabeth and Mary* is not recorded, but the average direct passage from England to Newfoundland was approximately five weeks. Sir George Peckham made a revealing comment on the Tudor mariner as well as on Newfoundland when he said, in 1583, "the passage is short, for we may goe thither in Thirtie or fortie dayes at the most, having but an indifferent winde, & returne continually in twenty or foure & twentie dayes at the most."[9] Whether or not subsequent travelers regarded the crossing to Newfoundland of more than a month as "short," they could hope for a passage of as little as three weeks. For the westward passage of gossip, newspapers, or copies of bills of exchange or correspondence, the shortness of the passage to Newfoundland made it the first area to hear European news in certain seasons and the first to suffer its consequences. On occasion, Newfoundland could supply English America with fresh news although the short fishing season, the scattered nature of the fishery, and the relatively low levels of New England bilateral merchandizing voyages meant that the entrepôt of news could not fulfill its potential. When a packet service to Newfoundland was under brief consideration in 1705, it was regarded as an isolated and independent service. If the westerlies held the outward-bound English ships to averages of less than 4 knots, those same winds hurried the fishermen home with news from the fishery. When Stafford's *Elizabeth and Mary* put into Barnstable on 28 October 1698, she had probably completed an average passage of about three weeks.[10]

While the routes, volumes, and passage times of the traffic between England and Newfoundland all suggested a strong connection, the seasons of that traffic did not. In 1716 an English chaplain at Newfoundland claimed:

> This pt of America, being only an Island & having no Communication wth any other pt of The Known World, save in Ye Summer time, . . .[11]

The season for sailing to Newfoundland usually began later than the *Elizabeth and Mary*'s date of 26 January 1698. This was not due to the problems of navigation, which were real but regularly overcome by French fishermen who braved the winter westerlies and Newfoundland ice in their January and February crossings. The well-known differences between the French "wet" fishery packed aboard ship in heavy salt and the English "dry" fishery involving use of drying stages ashore were not simply matters of taste and salt supply. The French were Grand Banks fishermen, because of their technique, and the cod are on the Grand Banks all year round. To catch for the Lenten market in France, the Normandy and Breton fishermen left home in January. The English in the seventeenth century were primarily involved in the on-shore fishery for cod on the Newfoundland coast itself. This is not a year-round fishery at all—and not just because the onshore ice is there until April. The cod does not come into the bays of Newfoundland to feed until May. Therefore, the seventeenth-century English fishermen were most efficient if they arranged to arrive in the bays of Newfoundland slightly before the cod in order to prepare the drying "stages" ashore. In the half century after the Peace of Utrecht the English fishery would shift its emphasis to Grand Banks fishing, and simultaneously the resident islanders increased their share of the catch.[12] The technique did not change with the English expansion into formerly French fishing areas, nor did the seasons of English shipping shift to catch a "wet" fishery market (this was an almost exclusively French rather than Iberian and Mediterranean market in any case); the Newfoundland residents did some earlier fishing each year. Winter English news would not come to Newfoundland earlier in the eighteenth century though the English fishing season was a little longer.

Although the Staffords and a number of others in the fishery arrived at Newfoundland by way of salt-supplying islands or Ireland, most came out from "the West of England" directly and did so beginning in March and April of each year. Convoys were a standard feature of this trade, even in peace-time, to enforce a minimum of civility on the English fishery and protect English interests in this international fish bazaar. Yet even in dangerous times the fishing and sack fleets left England piecemeal. (See Table 5.2.) The advertisement issued at the Royal Exchange, that the convoy for Newfound-land would sail from the Downs by the first fair wind after 1 April,[13] was an official launch to the season, but no one sailing with the convoy had the opportunity to become the season's "admiral" in a bay at Newfoundland—a worthwhile prize of local control for the first ship there each year. At the end of a bitterly cold March passage that ended amid ice masses, ship surgeon James Yonge and his fellows found they were not near being first. Those in ahead of them provoked the comment "mad Newfoundland men are so greedy of a good place they ventured in strangely."[14] The earliest ships could, on occasion, be a chance source of winter news for New England and its neighbors. Although London correspondents would find it difficult to know when specific ships sailed from the dozens of West Country ports for the fishery, letters or orders sent to major ports in the first half of the year would be aboard a boat bound for Newfoundland that season.

Communications from Newfoundland to England were very constrained by the season of sailing, as well as the southern European destination of many vessels. Autumn was the only time that news went home to England from Newfoundland. (See Table 5.2.) For merchants or sea captains, the fishery received spring news and early summer news, and there were several opportunities to reply in late summer before sailing home. For the few in-

habitants of Newfoundland, whose numbers would grow as the eighteenth
century wore on, the whole year offered no more communication with
Europe than that available to the summer people.

In the fall and winter of 1696–1697, for instance, the English inhabitants
were attacked and captured by powerful French squadrons of privateers and
men-of-war. The attacks began at Bay Bulls on 5 September, and neighboring harbors were attacked before Ferryland was taken on the twenty-first.[15]
The first exaggerated accounts stirred London by Tuesday, 20 October. By
Thursday the capital heard calmer versions via Bideford and Bristol. By
Saturday London learned that 170 refugees had arrived at Falmouth that
Monday. Petition and inquiry were the only immediate signs of response as
winter set in. Then, on 10 January the battered *Betty* of Bideford was towed
into Dartmouth harbor. Aboard were 250 men, women, and children who
were the majority of those in St. John's when it had surrendered to French
forces on 30 November. The news was spread in London by the fourteenth[16]
and the plans for revenge were under way almost immediately. Winter news
from Newfoundland was almost invariably bad, and there would be no
government response for months even if fishing vessels were already preparing to sail for the new season.[17] Communication between Newfoundland and
England was seasonal as a rule. Tragedy could cause winter crossings like that
of the *Betty*, but the eastbound traffic from Newfoundland to England was
very light in the first half of the year.

English fishing fleets were usually large enough that the opportunities to
write westward in the first half of the year and eastward in the second half
were frequent even if many ships did not return directly to England. Of 242
English fishing ships surveyed by Commodore Norris in 1698, only 60 expressed an intention of returning directly to England, whereas 150 were
bound for Spanish (93), Portuguese (42), or Italian (15) ports.[18] Especially
while the Falmouth-Lisbon packet boats ran, summer links between Newfoundland and England—or occasionally between New England and Old—
could be shorter by way of Lisbon and Falmouth.

Attraction of English fishing fleets to Newfoundland early in the spring of
the year meant that English and European news could readily come to other
English American colonies by way of Newfoundland. At the accession of
Queen Anne in 1702, a newspaper received in Boston by way of Newfoundland brought Massachusetts and its neighbors the unwelcome news of William
III's death and Anne's accession.[19] In May 1712 the *Orange Tree* came in
to Boston from Newfoundland with London news enough to preoccupy two
issues of the *Boston News-letter*.[20] Colonial shipping was, in general, not
attracted to Newfoundland in any numbers, so that the fishery functioned as
a news source in spring only for New England. Barbados had some direct
trade with Newfoundland (see Table 2.3), but there appears to have been little
traffic between the other West Indian islands or the continental colonies
outside of New England. Even New England vessels figure much more
prominently in the laments of the English traders involved in the fishery than
they did in surviving evidence of ships at Newfoundland in this period. In

1698, a year of very active English involvement in the fishery, there were 10 vessels into Newfoundland from New England, 7 from Barbados, and 7 more from all other English colonies.[21] Fifteen years later there were again a total of only 24 colonial vessels trading to Newfoundland, and of these 8 were from Boston, 8 from Barbados, and 8 from all other colonies.[22] Boston's traffic to Newfoundland may have tripled between 1718 and 1729 (see Table 4.6), but most of the traffic was bound to the fishery in the spring and back in the fall, limiting the opportunity to deliver spring news to Boston from the Grand Banks.

Newfoundland was located so as to be favored in the transatlantic spread of news and often drew a fleet of ships that certainly would be the envy of any other colonial community of but 2000 to 4000 residents. Yet the seasons of that shipping were so confined and the fishery was so scattered that the number of vessels in the trade exaggerates the communication facilities available. When war with France prompted active consideration in 1705 of a packet boat service to give mail regularly to Newfoundland, even the optimistic projector Edmund Dummer was not inclined to try it, "the place being sufficiently frequented in the summer, and that navigation being almost impracticable in the winter."[23] Traffic was one way in the spring and the other in the fall; here was the caricature of English Atlantic communications. Although less rigid than the rules nature imposed on Hudson Bay navigation, the seasons of shipping at Newfoundland were narrower than those allowed to traffic elsewhere in the English Atlantic.

English trade and communications with the Hudson Bay was unlike any other English Atlantic trade. If the explorers had not established the reputation of the area as treacherous for navigation, the early years of the Hudson's Bay Company were their own grim testimony.[24] In the spring of 1682, a year that would result in two more wrecks in the company service, the managing committee insisted on quick unloading and return of vessels sent to the bay. They wanted to "recover the good Opinion, and take of[f] the direfull apprehensions" that made it difficult and expensive to hire ships, masters, and seamen for the trade.[25] The absolutism of nature's seasons was nowhere more complete than in Hudson Bay. Very low shipping volume, short seasons, and a commercial monopoly excluding all intercolonial shipping meant that servants of the company on the bay were among the most isolated of Englishmen anywhere in the Atlantic. The annual ship bringing its annual letter was all that could be hoped for, and even those modest hopes could be killed in the ice floes of the strait or the bay. In that same unhappy year, 1682, the Hudson's Bay Company governor, John Nixon, showed admirable restraint when he wrote, "I am greatly desierous to heare how my letters and my service is accepted with yow, it is hard for a man that is in my place to be three years before he can have ane ansuer of his letters, . . ."[26] Hard indeed. Isolation would seldom be that bad again as experience brought system to routes, seasons of shipping, and trading operations. Yet the most ill-informed stereotypes about the infrequency of English Atlantic communications are nearest to the truth in the case of Hudson Bay.

It would take more than 50 years before the route to Hudson Bay became firmly fixed. Shipping of the London-based company set out from the Thames. The Channel, or "west-about," route was usually suggested as optional in the company's sailing orders before 1732.[27] A timely east wind could be utilized as far as it blew, and this route meant an ocean course that was northwesterly to Cape Farewell and less in the teeth of the prevailing westerlies than the "north-about" route required. Yet the Channel route was much more vulnerable to French privateers and English press gangs, in addition to the navigational problems mentioned earlier. The Hudson's Bay Company shipmasters were seldom required to use this route although such orders were issued annually between 1715 and 1719 when Jacobites and their Spanish allies were regarded as threats.[28] Aside from this brief period, the Channel was seldom safer than the Scottish route and was little used on the outward voyage.

The "north-about" route had been used on the initial 1668 voyage of the *Nonsuch* and was subsequently favored as avoiding the westerlies in narrow seas and avoiding privateers. Early in the War of the League of Augsburg (1690–1691), late in the following war (1708, 1710–1712), and again during the Anglo-Spanish war (1727–1728), Hudson's Bay Company shipmasters were ordered to go "north-around" outward. This route was the more usual when masters were given the freedom to choose, and some recruiting of Orkneymen, inured to isolation, became traditional. Company orders after 1732 specified the use of what Captain William Coats could consider by 1751 as the only route to Hudson Bay.[29]

Whichever route was taken around the home island, the westward crossing was the northernmost trading route to the New World. Initially the company provided no specifics, but in 1698 they ordered their masters to keep north of the 60° parallel, where favorable currents and winds could be expected. Fortunately, the order did not produce any of the predictable wrecks on Cape Farewell, Greenland, though the order lasted until 1701.[30] The commanders of the 7 ships sent out in the next 11 years were urged to keep north and make Resolution Island before entering Hudson Strait. Without any related losses, the company's sailing orders changed completely on this issue in and after 1714. Masters were henceforth ordered to keep to the *south* of 57° 30′ (raised in 1722 to 59°).[31] This order was to avoid ice off Cape Farewell. Once to the west of that cape, the ships were to be sailed for Resolution Island. By pulling northward to make that island, the dangers of the Labrador Current and coast were avoided, and the approach to the Hudson Strait would be less encumbered with ice. The ocean crossing, from the Downs to Resolution Island, averaged just over 6 weeks and ranged from 1 to 2 months.[32] Although this meant that more than half of the total westward passage time was spent gaining Resolution Island, in terms of risk, the worst was still to come.

The *Hudson's Bay*, the fourth ship to bear that name, was captained by the experienced William Coats when she arrived at Resolution Island on 18 June 1736. Although she had started the voyage early, it took the very good passage of 38 days to bring the ship to Resolution Island at this unprecedented early date. Within six days, the *Mary* and the *Seahorse*, which completed the Hudson's Bay Company fleet that had sailed together from the Downs to the Orkneys, came into the rendezvous, and the captains undoubtedly consulted during the next week about the annual decision that should have given the island its name.[33]

The *Hudson's Bay* led the way into Hudson Strait, but she went only six leagues before becoming entangled in ice. Although the winds were calm, ice blocks crushed in the sides of the hull, and she sank in 20 minutes. It was 3 July, early but not the earliest recorded date for a successful passage of the strait. Fifteen years later, Captain Coats still advised entering Hudson Strait on 6 July, "a few days sooner or later, as the season will admit."[34] He had not forgotten 1736 or his six attempts to enter the strait in the first half of July 1739. He was trying to maximize the shipping season that the strait dictated to the bay. Pilots of modern steel-hulled ships still face the same problem. The 1955 edition of the *Labrador and Hudson Bay Pilot* notes:

> The central portion of the Strait does not freeze over; however, for about eight months of the year it is rendered practically impassable by great ice floes, carried back and forth by the tidal currents.[35]

The monopoly of the months July to October was stricter than the monopoly of the Hudson's Bay Company.

Captain Coats would prepare a volume of advice intended to help his sons gain and keep employment as Hudson Bay shipmasters. He made it clear that if there were any danger whatsoever of being entangled in ice in the first 15 leagues of Hudson Strait, it was best to return to Resolution Island. Once within the strait, there were some strategies for survival. An impressive array of ice hooks, cables, axes, and chisels was advocated. The tides must be prepared for, and the lookout must be sharp. The real enemy was large ice blocks, big enough to smash the hull yet small enough to be free moving in the tides that were particularly fast in the narrower parts of the strait. Coats regarded small ice in quantity as the best defense against the blocks and recommended getting well into small ice when the tide was about to turn.[36]

The sinking of the *Hudson's Bay* cost no lives, for the consort ships picked up the crew. The company's sailing orders had urged the ships bound for the west main and the bottom of the bay posts to sail together through the strait, and the practice was understandably common. Except for the years 1699–1712, when company fortunes were low, fur prices were poor, and most of their forts had been captured by the French, at least two ships went out to the bay each year.

Maneuvering through Hudson Strait's less than 400 nautical miles could be very tedious indeed. The average westward passage through the strait before 1740 was 17.6 days, at an average speed of less than one knot. The range, however, was from 4 days for the *Mary*, Captain William Coats master, in 1740, to 39 days for the *Seahorse*, Captain Christopher Middleton master, when she accompanied the doomed *Hudson's Bay* in 1736. Trading with

Eskimos became an authorized feature of the slow procession westward each July, a month when the westerlies are mercifully less persistent in the strait,[37] which forces ships to face those winds with limited room for "transversing." For all its dangers, the Hudson Strait claimed only the one ship in half a century before 1740. Yet the strait demanded respect; regulated entry into the bay; set the pace of spring preparations in England; and hurried the unloading, loading, and letter writing at the posts in the bay.

English shipping into Hudson Bay concentrated on two areas, the western shore posts of York Fort (now York Factory) and Churchill and the bottom of the bay factories at Albany, Rupert House, and Moose River. Ships entering the bay together parted company off Mansfield (now Mansel) Island to make their way to each area. The westward crossing of the bay in July was usually quicker than the passage down to James Bay. York Fort, on the Hayes River but well located for Nelson River traffic as well, was the center of English interest in the western shore before and after the French possession of the post from 1697 to 1713. Crossing the bay to York Fort was not usually difficult, and little more than the tedium of contrary winds tended to be reported. Two years, 1714 and 1715, were different. In August 1714 the *Union*, a 240-ton ship, failed in the first efforts to make York Fort and was unable to get through the bay ice to either Churchill River or the Severn River. On the second try that month, the *Union* reached York Fort after being held in the ice for several days. The following year the new *Hudson's Bay III* actually failed to reach the western shore at all and returned to England without delivering supplies or mail.[38] Aside from these two incidents, the shipping bound for Churchill (1717), York Fort, or both in turn reported no difficulty with the remains of the winter ice. Although there were threats to the ships in the immediate vicinity of the far-from-excellent anchorages, the last stages of the 75-day average passage from the Downs to York Fort or Churchill was not particularly difficult.

The company occasionally specified that vessels were to leave for home by the middle of September, an order issued more regularly by conditions. Captain Coats advised shipmasters to be out of the bay by then, for gales became severe and frequent, and hard frosts prevented working of the ships "when blocks are locks, and ropes are bolts, and sails can neither be taken in nor left out, is surely the last extremity . . ."[39] These urgings from nature came first to the western coast factories, and ships trading there very seldom wintered in the bay.[40] Off in mid-September at the latest, the ship or ships from the western coast would usually be home in about six weeks.[41]

In terms of seasons of shipping, the James Bay posts gained little by being further south. Wind-driven "rafted ice," sometimes as high as 30 feet, barricaded the shoreline to leeward. Although the winter ice was usually gone by the beginning of July, the rafted ice was there for another month.[42] The voyage out to Albany Fort or Moose Fort averaged a week longer than the passage to the western shore posts[43] although the passages back to England were comparable. The bottom of the bay was much more vulnerable to French overland raids than the western posts, and occasionally ships were ordered to winter there to provide men and guns for defense or to trade on the Eastmain. Gilpin's Island, and Charlton Island were favored for wintering vessels in comparative safety. Thus, there were need and opportunity for ships to winter in James Bay. When wintering of a ship was by local initiative rather than the Hudson's Bay Committee, the lateness of the season and fear for the safety of the ship and cargo were presentable arguments. Yet it is interesting that between 1689 and 1715 nine ships wintered in the bay whereas none did so between 1716 and 1740. In both periods, sloops that were stationed for communications between posts wintered over, but the contrast in the wintering of the ships is instructive. In 1713, the *Hudson's Bay (II)* arrived at Albany Fort with news of the peace with France that was just a month old at sailing time. The ship wintered at the bottom of the bay. Captain Knight of York Fort wrote the Albany Fort governor that the wintering "was three thousand Pounds out of ye Compies Way one with another, by hireing a Ship to come hither, and so many Mens Victuals & Wages as they must pay."[44] The *Port Nelson*, Captain James Belcher, would winter over 1715-1716, but the Hudson's Bay Committee wrote the governor of Albany Fort to ensure that the ship was speedily unloaded and dispatched, "it being of the utmost Importance to us to have our ships Return to Us the Same Year."[45] In the next 25 years of peace with France, no ships wintered in the bay except the sloops intended for local use. The navigation to the bottom of the bay clearly did not require wintering over, nor was it a considerable risk in so well-organized a trade.

Despite the light shipping volumes entering the bay each year, the company's control over their forts was remarkably direct. Letters of an official kind and letters of instruction to newly appointed or promoted fort governors were not general delegations of powers and authority. These letters dealt with immediate problems of management and accounting and named personnel and specific abuses. In the busy fortnight when the vessel or vessels were being unloaded and reloaded, the governor was expected to read and implement the committee's orders. The fur ship moored in the river was an express waiting to carry accounts, justifications, and retiring company servants back to London with the cargoes. The governor could not expect to be able to consult London as problems arose, but the peculiarities of Hudson Bay shipping and fur trading meant that the company could and did expect prompt action on their own orders and inquiries.

From the bottom of the bay, as from York Fort and Churchill, the ships set out for Mansfield Island's leeward passage by early September. The Hudson Strait was usually open until the middle of October, when ice floating down from Foxe Channel clogged the western end of the strait.[46] Again the strait dictated the timing and forced the company ships out on what was a comparatively quick passage to England with the westerlies in pursuit. In time of war, or rumor of war, the ships carried orders to return by way of the Orkneys, either to gain information of the state of things or to put into a Scottish harbor and await convoy. Those orders were given in only nine years between 1690 and 1740, however.[47] The company ships usually came up the Channel to the Thames, then up the Thames to Ratcliffe Dock. Between 1719 and 1740, some 35 recorded passages homeward averaged six weeks, or half the time for the outward voyage to the bottom of the bay. Seamen who worked this trade could not expect more than five months' pay per year out and home.[48]

After severe difficulties in communications in its first years, this small trade came to be very efficiently organized and reliable. During the War of the League of Augsburg and its successor, the company sent no ship at all during six scattered years[49] and held on to only one and then the other of its two areas of trade. But between 1713 and 1740 there was an average of three ships a year sent out. In those 28 years only four vessels were wrecked,[50] none involving loss of life. The Hudson Bay posts were isolated, yet they had regular and predictable opportunity to write and receive letters once a year. Despite the isolation that drove good men to drink, there are no complaints of bad communications by the fort officers of that generation. Their expectations were being fulfilled, and nothing more could reasonably be expected.

The routes of the English Atlantic carried news at a variety of speeds and frequencies within England's Atlantic empire, and the differences between major clusters of routes were greater than the considerable changes within a single lifetime on any one of these routes. Having discriminated between the various routes and the expectations they could legitimately provoke, this study appropriately offers some comparisons by way of summary. Each of the four elements of the preceding chapters (routes, passages, seasons, and volumes) deserves attention in turn.

The main routes changed comparatively little between 1675 and 1740. The sugar routes were unaltered although the number of vessels visiting the various English sugar islands did change, and the number using the sugar routes as a first leg of voyage from England to North America fell after 1714. From that time Charles Town also emerged as a major factor in English transatlantic shipping, adding a new route to England and back as well as increasing multilateral intercolonial traffic on the westward crossing to Charles Town. The tobacco trade experienced the only dramatic shift in routes as the routes between Britain's northwest and the Chesapeake developed as the eighteenth century opened. These routes and those attempting a direct WSW passage from the Lizard were part of a growing trend to sail into the westerlies to North America from Britain rather than taking the route of the *Palm Tree* or routes tropical enough to catch the edge of the trade winds. This tendency, encouraged by war and comparatively minor improvements in ship-handling, may also have benefited from a change in weather patterns. This change would affect the Chesapeake trade the most but was also influencing routes to Charles Town and Philadelphia and would make the more southerly transatlantic routes to New York less popular. The routes to Boston and Newfoundland, most of which had always been close-hauled to the westerlies, changed little as did the Arctic approach, which had once been a significant part of the Newfoundland fishery but had become the preserve of a few whalers and the Hudson's Bay Company. These modest changes in the westward Atlantic crossings were considerable when compared to the persistence of the routes that the westerlies provided to carry ships eastward to England. Emerging southern European markets for rice and grain from America, as well as the emergence of a considerable traffic to Ireland from Philadelphia and New York, all represented increased variety in destinations and more multilateral trading on the return voyage. As was true of the transatlantic fish trade of England and New England, the need for European market information, as well as arrangement of return of proceeds and laden ships, all gave English merchants and their agents a role to play in what were colonial initiatives diversifying trade from an English center.

The English Atlantic can only be measured fairly by its passage times, and these produced different oceans. A ship leaving the English Channel for an Atlantic crossing was generally entering a wider ocean than a vessel leaving a colonial port for England. This was particularly true for all crossings north of the Chesapeake. From Philadelphia north to Hudson Bay the westerlies made the Atlantic only half as wide with the wind as against it. Here the English Atlantic was at its narrowest from Newfoundland (averaging approximately 5 weeks westward and 3 weeks eastward) and at its widest to and from Albany Fort in Hudson Bay (12 weeks westward and 6 weeks eastward). The disparity between the ocean from England and from America was also evident in the traffic of the southern mainland colonies though the differences between westward and eastward passages were less pronounced. The new tobacco routes saved between 1 and 2 weeks of ocean travel, but the more significant savings there came from shorter loading times in the Chesapeake. The Caribbean colonies had a different schedule. Barbados and the Leeward Islands were about 8 weeks from England, and England was also 8 weeks from them. Although these islands were no further from England than Boston was, in terms of the time it took to get to the colony, a Barbadian was twice as far away from England as a Bostonian contemplating a voyage to London. Jamaica was a special case. The average voyage to Jamaica from England was about 10 weeks, not very different from an English passage to Charles Town or Philadelphia and generally a little shorter than a voyage to Virginia or to York Fort on the western coast of Hudson Bay. The Jamaican intent on traveling to England, however, had to prepare for a crossing that averaged 14 weeks. Nowhere else in the English Atlantic was further away by sea, and nowhere else did it take longer to go to England than to return. With a range of *average crossings* from 3 to 14 weeks, the English Atlantic routes were through very different oceans.

Seasons of the English Atlantic varied more with route than with the changing volumes of traffic on any one route. Nature's attempt to impose seasons was completely effective in the cases of Hudson Bay and Newfoundland trades. Winter icing of ports between Boston and Philadelphia was variable but a real deterrent to arriving ships that could not have usable information on these conditions. Winter traffic out of these ports was also reduced although connections with the Caribbean and the Carolinas were strong in winter and crossings from Boston to Britain were common early in winter. This bias in favor of eastward crossings in winter reinforced the bias of speedier eastward passages. If winter insisted on sharp and narrow shipping seasons in Hudson Bay, imposed on the Newfoundland fishery, and slowed traffic on what have here been termed the "western routes," it was human necessities that gave boundaries to the seasons of the tobacco trade. Here the season was radically altered, in seeming defiance of the tobacco-processing season and the teredo worm, yet a shipping season remained clearly defined. At ports from Charles Town to Barbados there were seasonal rhythms to the level of traffic, but shipping was never stilled by climate. Here a year-round exchange of information connected England to her empire, and here intercolonial shipping brokered news to the northern colonies. War or the threat of war was a season that disrupted traffic tremendously. Although it made colonies especially anxious for European news, it funneled much of the traffic into convoys. The change would be much more pronounced in the winterless ports although war's impact on life and communications was powerful throughout the empire. In peace, the English Atlantic was not a seasonal phenomenon south of Newfoundland. The major ports of continental North America built a strong trade with the winterless colonies and also benefited from efforts made to build communications that were independent of ship movement at any individual port.

It is clear that the number of English transatlantic and intercolonial voyages accomplished in any one year rose dramatically in the lifetime before 1740. Transatlantic traffic to the West Indies more than doubled although fewer vessels were visiting Barbados by the 1730's. Charles Town emerged from nothing to a substantial port, sending 80 ships a year to England. The new English colonial ports of Philadelphia and New York had comparatively little direct traffic with Britain although their Irish trade grew notably in the 1730's. Boston's dominance of the continental American traffic with England held through the period, during which the number of voyages doubled and the seasons expanded. Recovery, rather than growth, in the English fishery at Newfoundland was pronounced by the end of the 1730's although the deliberate lack of government and relative isolation of the fishery from the rest of English America limited the transfer of news even in the fishing season. The transatlantic tobacco fleets grew by 50 percent over the period though the shift to a summer shipping season limited the news-bearing potential of this mighty traffic. England's traffic with her Atlantic empire had numbered fewer than 500 ships a year in the 1680's. Although this was a considerable number, it must be remembered that nearly half of these ships were in the very seasonal tobacco trade. By the end of the 1730's, Defoe's boast that 1000 ships a year were involved in these trades now seems a modest estimate, with one third in the sugar trade, one third in the tobacco trade, with the fishery, Charles Town, and Boston attracting most of the others in that order.

Intercolonial shipping grew even faster, apparently tripling in this same period, from some 500 to perhaps 1500 voyages a year. Intercolonial traffic into Boston accounted for nearly one third of all of this traffic, with Barbados second with an annual peacetime average of some 200 vessels in from English colonies. New York and Philadelphia grew in intercolonial trades, with links to the West Indies growing faster in the latter's case than trade with continental North America. Despite Boston's visible retreat to her own vicinity, the expanding intercolonial trade bound the continental ports even more closely to the Caribbean islands and to each other, multiplying the opportunities to make the flow of news throughout the English Atlantic empire less seasonal for colonists living between Maine and the Chesapeake. Even the growing multilateral trading with southern Europe, which broke the bounds of imperial trade in ways that had portent, actually increased the connections between colonies as more ships returned from Europe by way of other colonies in the traffic to a port like Charles Town.

Increasing transatlantic and intercolonial shipping shrank the English Atlantic between 1675 and 1740. More ships promoted a widening of the seasons of communications in most trades as ship managers sought the least congested port facilities and merchants sought the best markets. Expanding intercolonial shipping helped free correspondents on both sides of the Atlantic from the limits imposed by light traffic or seasonal ice at some colonial ports. Certainly, the contemporaneous development of postal services by land and sea, together with the emergence of newspapers, were, as will be seen, central to the freeing of news from the routes and seasons of any single trade. Yet the transformation of the English Atlantic empire—from a rimless wheel of dissimilar trades into a linked community challenging the seasons nature prescribed for crops and ships—owed a great deal to the increasing merchant shipping on and between almost all the major routes of the English Atlantic.

6 · Communicating Revolution, 1688–1689

The *America* of Boston, bound from its home port to London in December 1688, began taking soundings that were political as well as nautical as she approached England. Two weeks before an English port was reached, first news was heard from a ship in from Barbados sharing what they had heard earlier from an English vessel out of Galloway. The passengers of the *America* heard that William of Orange had landed at Torbay early in November, that the prince had taken England, and that King James was dead. The truth, the guess, and the false rumor all came aboard with equal credibility.[1] They were only four days from port before they first learned that the king was not dead although the source was a five-week-old report from the Canary Islands. The occupants of the *America* could still be buffeted by strange and disturbing tales when they were only one day from Dover. The master of a pink that was two weeks out of Liverpool gave the date of the prince's landing as three weeks later than the event, gave William's force as an astounding 50,000 men in 600 ships, and told the apprehensive colonials that the drowned bodies of Englishmen were being found tied back-to-back and that French men-of-war were cruising with commissions from King James II. All this worrisome "news" proved erroneous but accompanied an account that would prove correct, that the king was not dead but had fled to France.[2] Even colonials anchored in the English Channel were sharing in the unavoidable confusion that accompanied the four-and-one-half-month English monarchical crisis.[3]

Spread of news during the revolution of 1688 presents a particularly instructive case study in later Stuart Atlantic communications. The importance of the news made it comparatively well recorded although the suspension of some record keeping, the deliberate suppression of news, and the subsequent distortion of both the news and the timetable of its receipt all tend to complicate efforts to understand exactly what became known to whom and when. In Maryland and the Dominion of New England, where revolu-

94

tions occurred, the motives and risks taken by the rebels can only be evaluated after determining how much they knew of the progress of the long monarchical crisis. Charges that failure to proclaim the new monarchs helped provoke the risings can be tested by comparison with colonies in which there were tensions but not actual revolutions. The spread of news in that winter of war, rumors of war, and administrative disruptions describe communications at their weakest. Dispersal of the "Glorious Revolution" to the English new world can serve particularly well to illustrate the problems and possibilities of communications in that empire before the establishment of colonial posts and newspapers.

Surprisingly little attention has been paid to exactly what the colonial rebels knew of English events when they overthrew the governments of Edmund Andros, Francis Nicholson, and William Joseph. Were the revolts daring objections to the empire of James II, undertaken despite genuine risk of reprisal? Were the colonials responding to William of Orange's manifesto without knowing that he had succeeded? Or were the uprisings rather safe and self-serving confirmations of William's known victory, used by alternative elites to maximize their advantage over those who could be expected to suffer for their visible allegiance to an ousted king?

Defenders of the revolutions were not always explicit about how much was known, but the risings in Massachusetts, New York, and Maryland all involved rebel charges that the chief executives knew that William had succeeded but were keeping the news from the people.[4] Although the revolutionaries maintained that William's coup was widely known before they rose in his name, they also wanted to claim to have joined William in his risks. Defenders of the fallen administrators unwittingly reinforced this notion by asserting that no reliable news had been received, that the rebels were attacking royal authority as such, and that the pretended enthusiasm for William and Mary was a subsequent convenience.[5] Modern studies tend in the same direction by emphasizing the compelling local economic, social, and political tensions that were vented in the risings.[6] "Delays" in receipt of public news are regarded as catalysts of suspicion or triggers for revolt[7] but have not been carefully examined. "Delay" is a judgment based on expectations. Some measure of the legitimate expectations for transatlantic winter communications in 1688–1689, as well as the actualities, can be taken from what is known of the dispersal of England's revolutionary news to all her colonies.

A whole collection of news items was involved in the spread of this revolution. Unless he received regular shipments of undistorted news in chronological order, any colonial governor of a royal or proprietary colony would have had a tense and frustrating time in 1689. Royal governors announced England's uncertainties when they published James II's proclamation of 28 September 1688, warning of the intended Dutch invasion.[8] News that William had landed at Torbay on 5 November or that the king had arrived at Salisbury, marshaling his forces on the nineteenth, would be of intense interest to colonials. However, it would also remind them of the disastrous failure, three years earlier, of the duke of Monmouth's challenge to James.

News of James's retreat from Salisbury on 23 November or of his foiled attempt to flee the country on 11 December would upset governors and encourage their enemies but would prompt no action by either group.

Even the most casual reading of the *London Gazette* of 13 December 1688, a copy of which might be sent by a well-wisher too cautious to send anything over his own name, would convince its recipient that something dramatic had happened. Although the printer was still James II's licensee, Edward Jones, the paper included the text of the 11 December Guildhall declaration of the Lords, announcing that James had withdrawn himself from the kingdom and that they were supporting Prince William and Protestantism. The same issue also included the telling news that Judge George Jeffreys had been taken and put in the Tower. James's welcome on being returned to London was reported in the *London Gazette* of 17 December, but the trend of events against him became increasingly obvious thereafter. The news out of London between 13 December and the end of the month, when William had accepted control of the administration, was extremely favorable to those who were upset with the colonial remains of James II's reign.[9]

None of the December news was sufficient to allow any governor to make a formal pronouncement. A governor could not write anyone in England without fearing that the treasonous stories he had heard were false, in which case the governor would destroy himself; or, if these stories were true, his correspondent might be in the wrong camp, disgracing the governor by association. Only one governor is known to have responded to the news of the Torbay landing with a letter to his king offering to come home to help resist the invader. This letter only speeded that royal governor's resignation.[10] William Penn's new governor of Pennsylvania, John Blackwell, wrote the proprietor more cautiously: "I have not thought fitt, under covert to your self, to comitt anything to writing . . . which falling into other hands may be improved to your owne or your friends prejudice." Blackwell sent a more complete account to his own wife, who was to be careful about how the letter was passed on to Penn.[11] Most governors apparently followed the dictates of prudence even further, neither writing nor proclaiming anything until matters in England seemed settled. Royal governors did not announce the new regime at least until they had received William of Orange's formal letter of 12 January 1689, which declared that he was in control of the administration and that he confirmed officeholders who were not Roman Catholics. This letter could also be challenged as inadequate as it was in Jamaica and Bermuda. In these cases, the decisive communication was the Privy Council order to proclaim William and Mary, dated at Whitehall on 19 February 1688/9.[12]

News from England to its empire in the winter of 1688–1689 was not hastened by any government-sponsored advice boats after November.[13] The news can best be followed along the gigantic North Atlantic clockwise circuit of winds and currents in that season, aboard the outward-bound sugar ships. After spreading through the taverns of Madeira and the Canaries, the stories could be expected to go to the West Indies and then on to continental North America.

Excellent communications, good fortune, and personal flexibility combined to allow the unpopular lieutenant governor of Barbados, Edwin Stede, to weather the winter of England's revolution with apparent ease. Despite Stede's lavish public celebration of the birth of the Prince of Wales and his full reporting of the same to London, this local agent of the disliked Royal African Company was not challenged during the monarchical crisis that ousted both his prince and his king.[14] English communications with Barbados suffered neither from winter nor from embargo; in the three months after Christmas 1688 7 ships arrived directly from England, and 20 more with Irish provisions that were probably fresher than their English news.[15] Stede was also fortunate in his association with William Blathwayt, a seasoned royal administrator who survived the crisis. Stede was able to recount, with understandable gratitude, that he had received King James's proclamation of 28 September and letter of 15 October, a subsequent packet of gazettes by way of Ireland with news to mid-November, and a letter from Blathwayt's clerk enclosing more gazettes that described William's unopposed approach to London in mid-December. This last packet seems to have been brought by the 200-ton *Blake* of and from London, which arrived in Barbados on 9 February. It was not until 15 days later that Stede debarred papists from office and arrested two of their leaders.[16] The *Castle Frigate*, another London merchantman, arriving from its home port on 4 March, brought a full account from Blathwayt's secretary describing William's seizure of power and also included the prince's own letter announcing his control of the administration.[17] Internal tranquillity was not disturbed at Barbados in the two months between the announcement of this news and the proclamation of William and Mary on 9 May. On this island, the first signs of England's crisis were seen by mid-November, the confusion was over by early March, and the new monarchy was proclaimed six months after the first signs of trouble. Barbados served as a source of news for English America[18] and can serve as a standard against which to compare the spread of the revolution elsewhere.

Although the duration and timing of revolutionary tension in the Leeward Islands were very similar to that in Barbados, there were telling differences. Governor Nathaniel Johnson was a loyal supporter of James II. When he heard of the Torbay landing, he wrote the king what would become an embarrassing letter, offering to come home and help. He later reported that it was "some weeks" after this December letter to James before he learned of the "present alterations of the Government."[19] News of William's "happy proceedings in England with his entrance there" was, according to a visitor,[20] current in the Leewards by February. This would appear to be the news of mid-December, which was comparable to what was known in nearby Barbados at the same time. It is likely that this news included the *London Gazette* of 13 December with its Guildhall declaration of the peers in favor of William. Both the governor and the visitor suggest as much. Governor Johnson's loyalty to James was deep enough to prompt him to send a copy of his letter to France by way of the French governor of Martinique.[21] This effort, made before 10 April, confirms that James's flight to France was known in the Leeward Islands before that date. Johnson's Jacobitism would become a serious problem after war commenced between England and France, but he was still at his post when he belatedly received Prince William's clarifying letter of 12 January and the following month's Privy Council orders to proclaim the new rulers. William and Mary became known as king and queen in the Leeward Islands on 10 May. War with France would bring the resignation of the governor and a revolt by Irish Catholics in St. Christopher (St. Kitts) later that summer, but there had been no tumult during the six months when those islands—and Barbados—shared the uncertainties of the English political crisis.

Jamaica also had six months of uncertainty, but an embattled acting governor reacted differently and survived what was undoubtedly the worst political factionalism in the English Caribbean. The duke of Albemarle's disastrous year as governor had ended with his death in October 1688. He had encouraged a party of buccaneers and small planters at the expense of the planter elite. Prominent planters left for London, where they had gained a royal order repudiating the man and measures of Albemarle's administration. King James's orders of 30 November and 1 December, which were repeated exactly by the Prince of Orange when he took over the admininstration, amounted to Jamaica's version of the glorious revolution.[22] King James's letters arrived in Jamaica in February 1689 to challenge the power arrangements of Albemarle's deputy, Sir Francis Watson. The underattended council joined Watson in delaying implementation of the orders, no doubt because the orders were unwelcome and because news of the Torbay landing made hesitation possible. When those favored by the royal orders objected to the action, Watson promptly proclaimed martial law.[23] Watson hung on tenaciously, apparently ignoring the prince's orders as he had the king's. It was only after notification of the accession of William and Mary had been received and proclaimed at the end of May, that Watson finally ended martial law. This device, which Watson attempted to justify either by citing James's warning concerning the Dutch or by emphasizing fears of the French and Spanish,[24] allowed a superseded and comparatively uninfluential Watson to fend off both local faction and London orders as long as uncertainty remained. It is noteworthy that no other colonial governor, including the soldierly Edmund Andros and his deputy, Francis Nicholson, used this recognized military defense against political turmoil.

All the sugar colonies had six months to wait between the news of a feared Dutch landing and the proclamation of William and Mary. Although there were no revolts in the English West Indies, one of James's governors had died before the trouble began, another was forced to resign without waiting for London approval, and a third spent most of the period exercising martial law.

The sugar colonies had a frontier of their own in this period, a place where English news could be expected to come later than it did to the busier centers of the sugar routes. Carolina's governor in 1689, James Colleton, was another prominent Barbadian who had recently migrated to Carolina. Sir Nathaniel

Johnson, ex-governor of the Leeward Islands and future governor of Carolina, sailed for that colony before the end of July 1689, bringing some English news of the crisis with him. Lieutenant Governor Stede of Barbados reported to England that a vessel that left Carolina in July 1689 had passed on the information that

> all is quiet there, but the people have not yet knowledge of the accession of their Majesties. So little converse have they with their neighbours—for New England, New York and Virginia proclaimed their Majesties some months since.[25]

The Lords Proprietors of Carolina had ordered the proclamation of the new monarchs promptly enough, but it was more than a year and a half before they learned that their colony had joined the reign of William and Mary. Carolina was effectively insulated from tensions concerning the revolution. Although the colony was one in which political turmoil was endemic, there was no trouble that could be directly attributed to this proprietary colony's very long wait for official word of the new reign.[26]

Communication of the news and reaction to it were remarkably different in each of the tobacco colonies. The Chesapeake was at the end of one of the longest passages in the Atlantic empire, and the gathering of ships into convoyed fleets further reduced the opportunities to communicate, yet Virginia's experience in this political crisis indicates some of the advantages of comparative isolation. At the Virginia Council meeting of 27 February 1688/9, the leadership was still proclaiming the birth of King James's son. Yet "the unsteadiness of ye times" was noted: the councillors considered the five-month-old royal letter about defensive preparations against the Dutch.[27] The royal letter apparently came together with a good deal more information, as well as rumor. The letter had been in London, awaiting transport, for a month when the Privy Council ordered that a boat be pressed to take dispatches to Virginia.[28] As the vessel could not have left before that order of 15 November, it was certain to be carrying news of the Torbay landing and seems to have brought news of the king's military preparations at Salisbury to confront William's forces.[29] There were disturbances in Stafford County, Virginia, where people armed themselves against a conspiracy they feared would destroy the Protestant inhabitants. Although this fear seems to have been spontaneous and indigenous, a new element entered the rhetoric by the beginning of April. Claims that there "was neither King, Law nor Government," suggests that the English news of mid-December had arrived in some form.[30]

Danger to Virginia's stability did not evaporate entirely with the arrival of a spring fleet on 26 April with orders to proclaim William and Mary. By the end of that day not only was the proclamation ordered for the next day, but the arrest of the leading Stafford County insurgents was also ordered. Proclamation of the new monarchs was not enough to end all the trouble, but it was a necessary stabilizing influence.[31]

If Virginia came close to serious disorder, it was not because of a prolonged period of uncertainty. This colony was the first to proclaim William and Mary, doing so two weeks before the government of the favored colony of Barbados and after the shortest period of confusion of any colony in the empire save Hudson Bay. As Virginians heard of James's warning, a vessel was already leaving England with orders to proclaim William and Mary. Its arrival two months later meant that the colony's uncertainties had lasted only half as long as had England's.

Virginia's abbreviated version of the English revolution contrasted with, and contributed to, the agonizing politics of its neighboring tobacco colony. As a proprietary colony, Maryland was not sent King James's warning about the Dutch. Yet on 7 January, seven weeks earlier than any news was presented to the Virginia Council, the Maryland Council discussed "the present juncture of Affaires in England and the Invasion thereof threatned by the Dutch or some others . . ." This news almost certainly came to Maryland from Barbados, where James's warning was public knowledge in November.[32] The news further worried an already nervous council, which acted too quickly and too cleverly. Their proclamation of 19 January spoke of an impending war between England and unspecified enemies as reason for a recall of all public weapons for repair. The council admitted to the proprietor privately that they were misleading the people into submitting arms that would only be reissued "into such hands as shall faithfully serve the King your Lordsp and the Country."[33] Within two weeks of this proclamation some people in Maryland had learned the news that had come with James's last packet boat to Virginia, reporting that William had arrived in England and that James had gone to Salisbury. The proclamation in Maryland not only began the season of uneasiness very early, but it caused legitimate suspicions of the council as well.

These suspicions became part of a wave of those fears that spread in March throughout the Protestant communities along the Potomac in both tobacco colonies. There is no surviving evidence that any additional English news arrived in the next seven weeks. It was not until 28 March that Councillor Henry Darnell revealed the arrival of some additional information in his letter to the deputy governor, William Joseph, and the rest of the Maryland Council. In the midst of efforts to calm the agitated, Darnell wrote:

> I thanke your honr for the good newes imparted to me and I doe heartily rejoyce at the safety of his Maty whose happy restoration without bloodshed I most earnestly wish . . .[34]

This would appear to be news that James II had arrived in France, which happened on Christmas Day 1688. Although this report may have arrived divorced of any other knowledge of English events of the fortnight before Christmas, Darnell and his correspondents could view the king's arrival in France as good news only if they had already heard some report that was very unwelcome from their Catholic and proprietary perspective.

If a coterie of Maryland councillors had heard of the tumultuous English events of December before the end of March, this news would be common knowledge within a month. A few days after Darnell's letter, a Virginia report indicated that the ouster of James was known in Stafford County, which bordered on the most agitated area in Maryland. Yet the claim that the Maryland "Association in arms for the defense of the Protestant Religion, and the Asserting the Right of King William and Queen Mary to the Province of maryland and all the English dominions" was founded in April is debatable.[35] Until Virginia's proclamation of William and Mary on 26 April was known in Maryland, the form of the new English monarchy could not be clear.

Given the close-knit leadership of the Maryland Association, and the litany of grievances that scholars have assembled to explain their revolution,[36] it is tempting to ask why nothing happened for two and one-half months after the "trigger" of the Virginia proclamation had been pulled. Did the movement have well-motivated leaders long before it had followers who felt that the delays in proclaiming the new monarchy had been long enough to suggest foul practice?

Perceived delay in proclaiming William and Mary appears to have helped raise and sustain the opposition to William Joseph's proprietary regime in Maryland. The uncertainties had lasted for six months before the rebellion occurred. Although this was no longer than the experience of the West Indies, it was three times as long as the period of confusion in neighboring Virginia. The Glorious Revolution may well have been no more than an opportunity for the disgruntled Protestant elite to lead the Maryland revolt and gain the fruits of office that they sought. To their followers, who were essential to the success of the July rising, the leaders of the revolt used the failure to proclaim the new monarchy as lure, hope, and justification.

Bordering Maryland to the north was Pennsylvania, another proprietary colony surviving in James II's reorganized empire. Here, as in proprietary Maryland, there was no official letter warning of a Dutch invasion. Yet here an embattled and poorly led proprietary party[37] weathered one of the longest periods of imperial disquiet experienced anywhere in the Atlantic empire and defended the interests of an English proprietor who was more closely bound to the ousted monarchy than were the Calverts.

Pennsylvania remained factiously but firmly in the reign of James II until astounding news arrived with the *Mary* from London on 23 February 1688/9. The *Mary* had left London about 12 December carrying both news of the Orangist success near Reading and an inquisitive passenger named Zachariah Whitepaine. Like others aboard the ship, he had heard of James's attempt to flee the country on 11 December and of the Guildhall declaration. Whitepaine also heard something of James's recapture while the *Mary* was anchored off Deal. He went ashore and hurried to Canterbury. There he missed the party returning the captured king but was able to confirm what he knew and to learn of the latest developments. The *Mary* left the Downs on 23 December, with Whitepaine back on board and no doubt sharing the knowledge that the business of government was being conducted by a committee of peers who had ordered the royal army disbanded. What Whitepaine tried to add to his information as the *Mary* sailed down the Channel in the last days of December and the first days of January was less reliable, indeed no better than the information being gathered by the *America* coming up the Channel to Dover at about the same time.

Within hours of Whitepaine's arrival in Philadelphia, his news spread without restriction although probably not without embellishment. The next day, Whitepaine appeared before the Pennsylvania Council to tell his story and sign a copy of it.[38] Clear and accurate as we know Whitepaine's story to have been, it could only have the status of an exciting first report in need of confirmation. Governor John Blackwell forwarded Whitepaine's news to Lieutenant Governor Francis Nicholson at New York, but Blackwell insisted that the diverse reports arriving during the next month still meant "we should wayt theire being rendered more certaine."[39] Yet his wait had just begun. In mid-August Blackwell reported that people in the Lower Counties were expressing dissatisfaction that William had not been proclaimed. Blackwell had replied that without orders he did not know how to proclaim William "and that he feared he might either Exceed or fall short of the titles ought to be given him which would be treason in either case."[40] When news of war with France arrived at the beginning of October, the question of the accession became entangled with the special difficulties war brought for the Quakers and their governor.[41] A month later a councillor still argued that he would do nothing "until he knows who is king." The governor's answer, that he believed that William and Mary were monarchs, brought the retort "We are not to believe but to be certain in such matters."[42] The governor was denied any assistance in preparing for war, and it was not until 2 November that Blackwell ordered Pennsylvanians to obey William and Mary and to conduct legal business in their names. The colony that had been first to hear that William of Orange was winning the contest with his father-in-law was the last to know officially after an interval of more than eight months.

There had been no serious threat of revolt in Pennsylvania although the political atmosphere included a number of ingredients shared with both her neighboring colonies, where revolt did occur. An alien, authoritarian, and politically unsophisticated governor had, with some encouragement from the proprietor, upset the dominance of a well-led Quaker merchant elite. The proprietor was intimately linked to the ousted English monarchy, and lack of news prompted rumors that Penn had lost his life or his charter or that he was delaying news that was unfavorable to himself. Yet the angry opponents of Governor Blackwell did not seriously threaten revolt. Quakerism discounted direct violence, but that had not eliminated political bloody-mindedness. The particular advantages that James II and William Penn had offered Quakers made the Glorious Revolution a less usable tool for the local elite in consolidating itself in power. It is also evident that the wily Quaker councillors were more than a match for their blunt new Puritan governor. Pennsylvania's elite neither wanted nor needed to revolt, and the life of the governed was not disrupted by the political hiatus. The very long, unused opportunity of 1689 eloquently argues for an essential confidence among the elite of that very young colony and suggests that it was still insulated by both political structures and attitudes from the full impact of a political convulsion at the empire's center.

The colonial political tumult of 1689 centered on the Dominion of New England, that vast and uneasy new government stretching from the uncertain boundaries of Acadia to the Delaware River. The perambulatory satrap, Governor Sir Edmund Andros, was not always well located to receive news, but he was the only one who could decide when or if sufficient reliable news had been received to warrant a public declaration in favor of the new rulers in England.

As 1689 began, the *Richard* arrived in Boston from London with James II's proclamation warning of a Dutch invasion and also with letters, including one anticipating the English revolution "out of wch: new Engld may I hope find deliverence."[43] For the next month there would be little news arriving in New England by sea or traveling overland from New York. The first significant news reached New York from Virginia on 5 February. Lieutenant Governor Nicholson apparently damned the messenger and ordered him to keep silent. Within a week the outlines of the story were confirmed from Maryland, prompting Nicholson to take formal depositions[44] and forward the news to Andros in Maine and Fitz-John Winthrop in New London. To Winthrop, Nicholson reported on 16 February:

> Wee have a flying reporte from Virginia that the Prince of Orange was landed in Tarr Bay and had dined at Exeter; his Majesty had set up his standard upon Salisbury Plaine. But this news I want to have confirmed.[45]

That same day the city of Boston heard of the Torbay landing from the first ships returning from a winter voyage to the West Indies.[46] Within a week the news was confirmed by another vessel in from Barbados and St. Christopher. The deputy secretary of the Dominion of New England reported confidently:

> All is well here, save that some ill spiritts appear in scattering & publishing seditious & rebellious libells, for wch some are in custody.[47]

News of the Torbay landing itself did not rouse many Bostonians, and news of Bostonians' reaction did not cause Andros to interrupt his military campaign against the Indians.[48] The story told by Zachariah Whitepaine in Philadelphia on 24 February and relayed through Nicholson on 1 March was more serious.[49] If Andros received this news before he left Pemaquid on 16 March, as seems likely, the information would hasten him to Boston without allowing him to do anything decisive on arrival.

There are several puzzles concerning communications to Boston between

23 February and 4 April 1689. Apparently, this busiest port in English North America—and one that often had shipping arriving from the West Indies in February—heard nothing for seven weeks. It is well known that the crucial letter of 12 January from Prince William and the next month's order to proclaim the monarchs were never sent to Andros because of the lobbying of Increase Mather and William Phips in London. Yet is it coincidence that Increase Mather's correspondence with his son Cotton and Cotton's diary for this period seem to be have been deliberately destroyed?[50] Increase Mather had, by the end of February, much London news that would have delighted his friends in Boston. Although there was no shipping embargo and such a passage was commonplace, there appears to have been no news directly from England before the April uprising.[51]

There is evidence, however, that the flow of information had not stopped entirely. On 25 March John Nelson, who would be a prominent leader in the revolt, wrote from Boston that William was victorious and that James had escaped to France.[52] By then, the Boston printer Richard Pierce had reprinted one of Increase Mather's tracts from London, appending to it *An Address of the Nonconformist Ministers* to Prince William, which was dated 2 January 1689.[53] These shards of evidence suggest that some prominent Bostonians who opposed Andros knew of William's complete victory at least three weeks before they took charge of a popular rising in the town. This knowledge probably came by way of the West Indies, but its conveyance in comparative secrecy remains a puzzle.

The long public silence in Boston was broken on 4 April, when a ship came in from Nevis. A young passenger, John Winslow, later recounted being in Nevis in February, when a ship arrived from England. It brought "the Prince of Orange's Declarations, and brought news also of his happy proceedings in England with his entrance there." Being bound for New England and recognizing how welcome the news would be there, he "gave four shilling six pence for the said Declarations, on purpose to let the people in New-England understand what a speedy deliverance they might expect from Arbitrary Power." Winslow was taken before Governor Andros; Andros was unable to stop the spread of Winslow's news but had the young man imprisoned for "bringing Traiterous and Treasonable Libels and Papers of News."[54]

After Boston's revolution, John Winslow's account would be featured in the subsequent struggle to justify that revolution and to regain the charter. The incident was, naturally, presented as evidence that Andros was stifling news of William's landing in England. It was also claimed that, on this notice of the prince's intended expedition, "New-England manifested an earlier zeal for Him and It, than any of all the American Plantations," moved by these words of William's declaration "All Magistrates who have been unjustly turned out, shall forthwith Resume their former Employments, as well as all the Burroughs of England shall return to their antient Prescriptions and Charters."[55] This direct justification for returning to government by charter would be combined with a claim of devotion to William's cause while it was still in doubt. William's declaration of October 1688 was actually being presented as more important than what Winslow called "news also of his happy proceedings in England with his entrance there" and what Andros called "Papers of News."

What real news did Winslow bring back from Nevis in February? The Governor of the Leeward Islands had long since known of what he called "the present alteration of the government,"[56] which was English news of late December. A visitor to Boston writing four days after Winslow arrived commented that there had been recent confirmation from Barbados and Virginia of what had been known in Boston already, and he added that "the prince of orange is now Commander in chiefe in England."[57] One comprehensive defense of the Boston revolution included a reference to people's fear, "when they had notice of the Late King James's being in France," that Andros would serve his king and betray his colony to the French.[58] This was news from the end of December, by which time William's success was complete. It is not certain just how much of the news of late December came from the West Indies by early April, but the news of 11–13 December apparently arrived with Winslow or the other ships into Boston about that time from the other colonies.

The printing press played a role in Boston's revolution that it could not play elsewhere: The prince's declaration was printed in Boston within days of Winslow's arrival.[59] This encouraged some, but apparently not many, of the discontented in and around Boston. Yet there was another two-page printed sheet that deserves special attention in this context. Samuel Green, a respected Boston printer, reprinted the *Declaration of the Nobility, Gentry and Commonality at the Rendezvous at Nottingham, November 22, 1688*. This declaration, which was the only attempt made during the English revolution to justify the use of force,[60] included a numbered list of grievances against the government of King James. These complaints were used to justify this English county's elite in giving allegiance to the Prince of Orange. On the back of this reprint, Green copied the Guildhall declaration of the "Lords spiritual and temporal" in favor of William. Green also added a copy of the order given by these lords to the *London Gazette*'s printer, Edward Jones, dated 12 December, requiring him to print their declaration, which he had done on the thirteenth.[61] It is not known exactly when Samuel Green reprinted and sold this sheet, but there is reason to suspect that it was before the revolution of 18 April. On that day Green printed the *Declaration of the Gentlemen, Merchants, and Inhabitants of Boston and the Country Adjacent. April 18, 1689*. The numbered grievances show imitation of the Nottingham declaration in format as well as in title. Boston's declaration gives a more direct clue:

> . . . we ought surely to follow the Patterns which the Nobility, Gentry and Commonality in several parts of those Kingdoms have set before us, though they therein chiefly proposed to prevent what we already endure.

This specific reference, in a document intended for Bostonians, would make sense only if Samuel Green had already sold copies of the Nottingham declaration and the Guildhall declaration. This, together with the similarity in title and format of the two declarations, suggests a date of publication in Boston of the Guildhall declaration during the week or two preceding 18 April. The Boston revolutionaries' declaration that "we have understood, (though the Governour has taken all imaginable care to keep us all ignorant thereof) that the Almighty God hath pleased to prosper the noble undertaking of the Prince of Orange" can, therefore, be given more precise meaning than the apologists of that revolution wished to convey.[62]

The Boston declaration of 18 April was printed by Samuel Green for one Benjamin Harris, a bookseller whose place in the history of English Whiggery makes him an especially interesting transatlantic figure in this rising. Harris had been prominent as an antigovernment publisher and bookseller in London during the Popish Plot and the Exclusion Crisis. With the lapse of the Licensing Act in 1679, Harris had launched the Whig *Domestic Intelligence: or News both from City and Country, Published to Prevent false Reports*, an opposition newspaper that would survive for nearly two years. Harris became something of a Whig celebrity in 1680, when he was tried and pilloried for publishing a pamphlet in support of the duke of Monmouth.[63] With the accession of James II, Harris had migrated to Boston, an unlikely refuge, where the press was directly controlled by the loyal and authoritarian Edmund Andros. Harris printed nothing himself in Boston before 1689 and had published only one almanac, which Green printed for him. Yet Harris claimed later in 1689 that he had suffered under the Andros regime simply for wishing William of Orange well. Whatever Harris's part in the distribution of news before 18 April, he was prominent in the printed aspects of the rising thereafter. Not only was Boston's *Declaration* itself printed for him, but it was probably soon thereafter that Green printed copies of the 1629 Masachusetts Bay charter on Harris's order.[64] Within the next few weeks, Harris made his own public declaration for William. *The Plain Case Stated: Of Old—but especially of New England, in an Address to His Highness the Prince of Orange* was a broadside of verse extolling the liberator and proclaiming that Boston had but followed his example. The sheet is subscribed "Boston, Printed for and Sold by Benjamin Harris at the London Coffee-house."[65] Green likely printed this for Harris as he had all Harris's other imprints of that year, including *The New England Primer*. Harris's Whig credentials in London would make him a worthy ally for those seeking to consolidate there the changes in Boston of 18 April. It seems unlikely that Increase Mather would be without copies of this verse for distribution to Whigs of the appropriate sort in London. The embryonic press of Boston had played a part in the popular rising, though less impressive than the place the printing press played in the subsequent justifications.

Boston's revolutionaries had not joined William before they knew he was in power. William had previously invited those dispossessed of positions or charters by "popery and slavery" to take them back, and so they did. This happened only three months after Andros's proclamation had marked New England's importation of England's unsettled politics. Although Andros was correct in arguing that reliable news had not been received, what had arrived was more than enough to promise success and justification for a seizure of power by the discontented. The opportunity that was seized was to confirm, to extend, and to import England's new political arrangement. Yet Bostonians knew less than the revolutionaries in Maryland knew before they rebelled, and ordinary Bostonians reacted much more quickly after encouraging news had been received. This would suggest either that the monarchical crisis mattered more to Boston's rising or that the resistance to the Andros regime was much further developed than opposition elsewhere so that the opportunity could be more quickly acted upon—or both. The smooth orchestration of the revolt supports the notion that the better-informed local elite quickly seized control of the popular rising.

The whole Dominion of New England was destroyed by Boston's revolution of 18 April 1689. Expediency, preference, reference to the prince's declaration, and imitation of Massachusetts all led the governments that had recently been subjected to the Dominion to revive their old charters until more was heard from England.[66]

One government could not do this. New York had belonged to King James as a proprietary colony before his accession and then as a royal colony that had been merged with the Dominion of New England. Lieutenant Governor Francis Nicholson had gathered information, forwarded it to Andros, and prevented circulation of news locally. Nonetheless, news of the Torbay landing was current late in February, and by mid-March it was widely known in New York that "there is a total Revolution att home."[67]

On 26 April, the very day that Virginia led the colonies in proclaiming the new monarchs, New York City heard that there had been a revolution in Massachusetts a week earlier. This news brought no convulsions to the city though freeholders in Suffolk County, Long Island, seized local control and similar changes occurred in Queens and Westchester during the next three weeks. As this threat of local disintegration developed, Nicholson's working authority became based on his council, New York City officials, and militia officers, including Jacob Leisler. A small dispute occurred at the end of May that led to a revolt by part of the militia and their seizure of the fort.[68] This first decisive step in the revolution was not related to the arrival of any additional news from England or Boston.

Within four days of the militia capture of the fort, a sloop arrived from Barbados bringing several printed papers, including the *London Gazette* of 14–18 February, which contained the proclamation and speeches attending the accession of William and Mary.[69] Although this was the kind of information that had been lacking, neither the militia colonel Leisler nor Lieutenant Governor Nicholson were willing to bolster their positions by proclaiming the new monarchs immediately on receipt of this very good evidence.

Leisler did join in the preparation of an address to the monarchs that was designed to justify the seizure of power. The rebels claimed to be responding to Prince William's declaration of 10 October 1688, which had been known for at least a month before the rising. They also claimed that the unanimous declaration of the English Parliament had prompted the seizure of the fort although that news is known to have arrived only four days after the takeover had occurred.[70] The fort had been seized when the rebels knew as much as the Boston leaders had known when they rebelled. Yet in New York, this English news had been current for at least a month, as had the news of Boston's revolution. The timing of Leisler's coup showed no immediate links to the receipt of imperial news, however much this was claimed. Emergence of an opposition came after the opportunity presented itself, unlike the pattern of events in other centers of revolution.

Although hardly a colony at all, the isolated outposts of the Hudson's Bay Company were rude and remote stations that the political shock waves of the English coup did not reach. If politically volatile Carolina gained peace from being remote, these trading posts were even more immune to revolution. The annual ships, vestiges of the earlier days of colonization elsewhere, set out for Hudson Strait and Bay in June 1689 carrying this news:

> Surprizeing changes have happened in this Kingdome vizt. the Prince of Orange comeing hither with an Army many of the Nobility and Soldiery Sideing with him King James leaveing the Kingdome and the Prince & Princesse's of Orange being Advanced to the Throne, for particulers referr you to the Printed papers herewith sent.[71]

This cryptic note, together with a new commission and oath of allegiance for all men around the forts, was all there was to the revolution by the time it reached Hudson Bay. The two outward-bound vessels bearing this news were attacked by French privateers, who took one ship and forced the other to limp back to England without crossing the Atlantic. This encounter, signifying that the new war would affect the forts of Hudson Bay much sooner than would the new monarchy that launched that war, simply postponed the importation of the new reign for another whole year—without any anguish or apology.[72]

Comparative study of the spread of news from England to the American colonies does not support the notion that some extraordinary delays in the receipt of news provoked those risings that did occur in 1689. Maryland's revolution was the only one that owed much to perceived delays in announcing what was certain. Marylanders who rebelled after six months of anxiety had found the "delays" intolerable only because Virginia had proclaimed the new monarchy months earlier. Yet coincidence had made Virginia's receipt of news "early," even earlier than that at the busy winterless anchorages of Barbados. "Delays" occurred only where comparisons could have been made, and Pennsylvania's eight-month wait suggests that perceived delay was not in itself a significant incentive to revolt. In genuine isolation, like that of the politically frozen little Hudson Bay posts, news that was a year old could still be fresh.

The Boston and New York coups occurred with the definite knowledge that William had succeeded in gaining control of the English administration though neither the rebels nor the governors thought they had enough exact information to be able to proclaim the new monarchs. It is also evident that apologists for the Boston and New York coups exaggerated the difficulty of Atlantic communications in order to claim the virtue of joining William of Orange in his risks. Englishmen who did not join William until the end of December hoped to do so inconspicuously. Colonials who did what amounted to the same thing claimed that they were passionate partisans of the new regime. Although the future would see Leisler executed, the new Massachusetts charter limited, and both Andros and Nicholson exonerated, the colonial rebels initially succeeded in pressing their version of the story on the English Court.

The colonial rebellions of 1689 were not daring objections to the rule of King James II or his appointees. It is also evident that these colonial risings were not even timed to take advantage of an imperial power failure in order to redress local grievances. Although the reconstruction of the spread of England's revolutionary news to her empire remains exasperatingly incomplete, what is known is revealing. Weeks before their uprising, a number of Bostonians knew that James II had fled to France and that William of Orange had become England's commander in chief. New York's delayed reaction to the disintegration of the Dominion of New England was begun with as much—or more—information about William's victory. The Maryland rebellion did not occur until long after it was common knowledge in the colony that William and Mary had been proclaimed monarchs. Despite the colonial rebels' later claims that they had joined in the risks of England's revolution, the colonial revolutionaries faced only the evaporating power of local representatives of the ousted English regime. The North American rebellions were dramatic local variations on a theme that played throughout the colonies, the importation from England of William of Orange's success.

Variety of experience in the English colonies attending the Glorious Revolution in England is suggestive. The West Indian colonies all went through a six-month period of uncertainty without actual revolution although the leaders of Barbados proved to be much better informed than those of the more troubled governments to leeward. The English sugar islands played a special role in the spread of this winter news to the continental colonies. The range of experience in the North American colonies emphasizes their relative isolation from each other that winter. Turbulent Carolina was almost entirely in a world of its own for a year. Express riders might carry private messages all the way from Virginia to Maine, but public information available in the Chesapeake had little impact further south or north, and Whitepaine's account did not spread southward from Philadelphia. The effectiveness of Francis Nicholson's control of information in New York owed much to the limited land and water traffic between New York and Philadelphia that winter. The Dominion of New England died with comparative speed, indicating that the administrative unity was paralleled by news channels along which a ripple of revolution restored charters where possible. Boston was the only center in which a local press contributed to the spread of news, merely hinting at the possibilities that might come in the next generation with the spread of printers, newspapers, and intercolonial posts. News to the Hudson Bay posts represented the persistence of a level of isolation that had already become a faint memory elsewhere. The Glorious Revolution would have bypassed most of the North American colonies, as it did Hudson Bay, if winter had stilled English Atlantic shipping as effectively as many historians have presumed.

In the half century after 1689, increasing ship traffic would markedly improve the spread of news in the English Atlantic, as would the development of posts and papers. Yet merchantmen had carried the news of England's revolution in the winter of 1688–1689 along routes that were still comparatively isolated from each other with much more efficiency than was subsequently admitted.

PART II

Commanding Time

It seems the Gen.^{ll} Humour of Men to Judge of such intricate undertakings off hand, and to despise what they do not easily Comprehend, but if a Just reflection be made upon the Advantages and Disadvantages wch depend upon the article [Time], in all Humane affaires this Service well perform'd will be as acceptable in peace as now in Warr for 'tis but commanding time & every mans Inclination and Interest is commanded with it.

—Edmund Dummer urging the British Treasury to continue support for his West Indies packet service, 24 February 1703/4.

7 · The Posts

Developments within the English Atlantic community between 1675 and 1740 transformed the flow of information even more dramatically than did the substantial increases in merchant shipping. The posts, the papers, and the mail packet boats were all services designed specifically to transmit news. In their origins and structures and in their methods and fates, these initiatives illustrate the various needs and purposes they were intended to serve, some of the changes that came quickly, and some of the problems of innovation in a variety of settings. Increased shipping brought more sailors, travelers, and migrants who carried information orally, though not without considerable filtering, to the illiterate. The ship letter brought more information more accurately transmitted to the literate, and available for careful and repeated review. Emergence of communication services enhanced the obvious advantages of literacy, transformed the pace and risks of business, and made transatlantic politics into a more responsible and exacting activity.

A shipmaster's mailbag, hanging on a nail in a tavern in London, Bristol, Plymouth, Bridgetown, Boston, or New York, represented the postal facilities of the English Atlantic in 1675. The bag was an invitation to write correspondents near a specific destination or destinations, for few correspondents wrote letters unless there was a means of sending them. News of a sailing would come first to those owning, sailing, or freighting a vessel, but the word would spread through the maritime community of a provincial port. In the event of prolonged loading times caused by repairs to a vessel, embargoes, or other delays, correspondents in the immediate hinterland could hear of a sailing and write letters to catch the opportunity. Although "advice boats" could be dispatched with vital government news and naval convoys, guard-vessels, or squadrons provided additional opportunities to write, most letters were entrusted to merchant shipmasters who sailed for purposes other than the speedy and safe delivery of mail.

"Ship letters" were still the usual method of Atlantic communication by 1740, but several important changes had occurred in the preceding 65 years. First, the traffic levels had increased substantially on almost every route, as has been discussed earlier. This not only increased opportunities to write, but it also allowed those writing to frequented destinations to write when they wished, confident that a ship was usually loading for that destination. For instance, Virginians were advised in 1738 to send letters for the West Indies by way of Philadelphia "from whence Vessels are almost always going to one or other of the Islands."[1] The flow of political, business, or personal correspondence quickened even if most travel times remained the same.

Another major change that affected the sending and delivery of letters in the English Atlantic was the development of the postal services in England and their creation in the North American colonies. Both of these changes have rightly been seen as part of the political and economic unification of England and colonial America respectively. Yet these developments were also part of the integration of the English Atlantic.[2] Once the major centers of England and of America were linked by regular postal services, a ship bound to major English or American ports could carry mail for the others.

The emerging English postal service suffered from the conflict between several royal purposes in addition to the vagaries of royal fortune itself in the seventeenth century. Royal initiatives in postal matters were often military in orientation, as was the case with the first regular post to Scotland in 1481; in the relatively frequent Irish mails; and in the transatlantic packet boat services launched amid war in 1702, 1710, 1744, and 1755. As much as the court wished for speedy information and a facility for sending messages to troublesome provinces, the Tudor court was also anxious to deny such information to those internal enemies who were capable of treason. These considerations militated against a public post service like those established by wealthier and more secure powers. In times of trouble, the king's postmasters could be forbidden the private traffic in letters entirely, or private letters could be opened. Postmasters were also to be direct sources of news for the king, so that the whole service could be seen as a system of court spies.[3] Free distribution of printed gazettes and favored newspapers and the denial of franking rights to opposition newssheets was a significant part of the information control of the Restoration secretaries of state.[4] In season and out, the crown wanted that direct power of the posts that the origin and evolution of the service made natural enough.

Although the crown's monopoly of the posts would stand, the arguments for a restricted inland post were not sufficient to counter the fiscal and political attractions of a better service to those who could afford it. The establishment of regular horse posts on the main roads of England, in imitation of the continental posts, was attempted under Charles I, effected under Cromwell, and confirmed by the Post Office Act of 1660.[5] A service that had been farmed in 1653 for £10,000 brought £21,000 from 1660.[6] Assignment of the rental revenues to the king and the duke of York[7] added yet another dimension to royal concern for the post. By farming the posts to prominent courtiers, the restored Stuarts gave real benefits to their friends without loss of the intelligence-gathering aspects of the posts. As a source of royal patronage, the post office would become part of the hereditary revenues after James's accession in 1685, and it would remain a significant aspect of royal revenue until 1760. In these comparatively stable times, the service would gradually improve although much of the revenue was being diverted from the service that produced it. The revenues themselves, as indicated in Table 7.1, more than doubled between 1687 and 1744.

Although the growing proceeds may have satisfied the managers of the postal revenues and some historians, they are deceptive. The Post Office Act of 1711 introduced very substantial increases in postal rates, and these increases resulted in less mail even if they produced more revenue. In terms of the volumes of mail carried, the level reached in 1703–1704 was probably not equaled again before 1747.[8] The growth of the mail service under the later Stuarts appears to have halted for the whole of England's longest peace of the eighteenth century.

For English Atlantic communications, the patterns of English posts were more important than the growth and stagnation of the English postal revenues. London, at the center of the wheel of post roads, gathered the news of its hinterland and reached to England's coasts for overseas news. The needs of government, the wholesale traders, and the merchant bankers were being met by these lines of communications, and the capital was the unchallenged exchange center of news. As the capital of financial resources, banking, and insurance and as the center of political lobbying as well, London was vital to provincial and colonial producers and customers. English outports could compete in the colonial staple trades only if they could provide their colonial correspondents with insurance, reliable accounts of business with London, payments in London, and goods to compete with those of London. All these services could be provided only if and when reasonable communications between the outport and the capital existed.

The capital's internal exchange of news was many-faceted, but the development of William Dockwra's penny post in 1680 indicated a desire for a level of news exchange that was remarkably high. There were hourly mail collections at more than 400 houses, with four to eight deliveries in the city and "To Inns of Court, and places of business in Town, especially in Term or Parliament-time, 10 or 12 times a day."[9] It was probably a combination of political and economic motives that prompted a successful legal challenge to the service as an infringement of the monopoly of the General Post Office. After an interruption of only a few days in November 1682, the penny post reopened as a separate part of the post office.[10] The capital city was well equipped to circulate its own news, including that brought in from the counties and the world along the main post roads.

Of the six main post roads out of London, the two that led to the east were of least consequence to English Atlantic communication. The rather short, 71-mile route to Harwich had not been a post road under Elizabeth[11] but was used more during the Restoration and became the major route of European military, diplomatic, and commercial news after 1689. The packet boats that ran once a week between the spacious and well-defended port of Harwich and Hellevoetsluis in Holland were important in the intrigues that brought William III to England and in the wars with France that came with him. Early in the eighteenth century "it was easier for a London merchant to trade with Holland than with the remoter parts of his own country."[12] Some of the most important news for the English Atlantic had come down this road to London, but seldom would it go out to the empire by that route.

London's other post road to the east, the Dover Road, was the same length as the road to Harwich, but was older, better, and busier.[13] As the main route of European news to the capital and the main route to the continent for messengers, ambassadors, and travelers, the Dover Road maintained its primacy among English post roads through the seventeenth and eighteenth centuries. From the Restoration there was a daily post six days a week for Dover[14] and improved service to shipping in the Thames estuary and the Downs. Gravesend and Chatham anchorages had been reached by the Dover-bound posts earlier, but the new services to Sheerness[15] and especially to Deal were important to English Atlantic communications. The Downs was a major anchorage for shipping bound down the Channel and for London-bound shipping awaiting winds or pilots to help them up the Thames estuary. For ships' passengers and their well-wishers, for official and private correspondents, the post road to Deal was a way to postpone partings, add final words of good wishes or orders, and narrow the Atlantic slightly.

The Great West Road, out of London by way of Staines and Salisbury for Exeter, Plymouth, and Falmouth, had special importance in English Atlantic communications. This was the road down which royal messengers would race with second thoughts and urgent news to be delivered aboard outward-bound ships days—and occasionally weeks—after they had left the Thames or the Downs. The attempt to change Drake's instructions as he sailed out on his Cadiz raid in April 1587 and the attempt to stop the sailing of Admiral Hugh Pigot in May 1781 are noted examples of this common use of the Great West Road.[16] Whitehall's messages to fleets and convoys bound for Atlantic or Mediterranean destinations could often reach the western Channel ports more quickly and safely by post than by water, especially if the Channel were infested with enemy privateers or swept by hard-blowing westerlies. The Great West Road brought in the Iberian, Mediterranean, and colonial news as well.[17] Tudor and early Stuart courts did not always maintain posts along this 269-mile road to Falmouth, for the cost of its 18 stations was high; it was the merchants of London trading with the Levant who found it worthwhile to launch a semiweekly foot post to Plymouth early in the seventeenth century. Defense of the royal postal monopoly helped prompt the establishment of the crown system of horse posts on all the main roads of the kingdom in the 1630's.[18] By the Restoration a horse post left Plymouth for London three times a week, and these mails were to reach the capital in little more than two full days.[19]

By the end of the seventeenth century the Corunna and Lisbon packet boats returning to Falmouth and Plymouth fed "fresh advices" onto the

Great West Road for London, but local merchants were in a position to gain from the information, too. War in the Channel may have been part of the encouragement for some London merchants to maintain Plymouth agents, and it was certainly part of the reason why precious cargoes of transshipped European luxuries were sent from London to Plymouth by carrier wagon in order to be put aboard the West Indies packet boats for Jamaica and the Spanish Main.[20] The Corunna and especially the Lisbon packets could also bring in North American news brought to the Iberian ports by Newfoundland or New England fish carriers.[21] The packets also allowed English owners of vessels in the Newfoundland trade to mail advice for their captains at their intended Iberian ports of call.[22] In the Restoration period and especially in wartime, Plymouth had an important role to play in London's links with the Atlantic trades. Yet Plymouth's hinterland did not allow her to exploit mercantile information to anything like the same degree as her rival Bristol.[23]

Bristol's primacy among the English outports was built on the effective improvement of natural advantages. Ready access to the resources and markets of southern Wales, northern Devon, and southern Ireland was matched by river access to the valleys of the Severn and the Bristol Avon. Compared to the commerce within this trading basin, the English Atlantic trades did not build Bristol. Yet the city was of special importance to the Atlantic empire; it was the Atlantic outport nearest to London. In the Restoration period, Bristol was 30 hours from London and was served, like other main routes, with three posts a week.[24] The post road from London was more than an advantageous link with metropolitan services, for it continued west through the main centers of southern Wales to Milford Haven and then by boat to Waterford in Ireland. This route served London's political and military needs for Irish information, but its commercial mail would serve Bristol before it served London.

The Bristol Channel was not safe from privateers during the wars, but at least vessels from the New World that came around the north of Ireland to English outports ran fewer risks than those using the English Channel. This served to reinforce the position of Bristol in the Atlantic trades, a position won long before in the fisheries, in the traffic in Irish provisions and servants to the colonies, in the market for specifically West Country products to West Countrymen who emigrated to the New World, and in processing colonial staples for Englishmen in Bristol's expanding commercial hinterland.

Bristol's place was illustrated and reinforced by the development of two major crossposts in the 1690's. Until 1696 communications between Bristol and Exeter were private and expensive or by way of the posts through London, paying twice the normal postage and providing rather slow service between cities that were less than 70 miles apart. The beginning of a direct horse post by stages between the cities in 1696 meant two mails a week each way,[25] giving Bristol access to some news arriving in Cornwall more than a day before the same would reach London. In 1700 this profitable cross post was extended further to the north through Worcester and Shrewsbury to Chester.[26] This extension gave Bristol merchants access to Irish news from

Dublin by way of the Holyhead packet service, improved Bristol's links with important towns to the north, and gave this premier Atlantic port ready access to news that might arrive at the comparatively small ports of Chester, Liverpool, or Lancaster. This major cross post, which linked the three important western post roads, represented a major breach in London's dominance of news and allowed the Atlantic outports to coordinate markets and supplies over a wider area and to satisfy Irish and colonial market needs and payments with less delay and less coastwise ship movement after wind, weather, or enemy privateer had prompted a change of destination.

The London road through Chester for Holyhead and the sailing packet to Dublin had long been a major strategic route.[27] Chester's silting waterways would seldom be stirred by the ships of the Atlantic empire, but the eighteenth century would witness the phenomenal rise of Liverpool as an Atlantic trading port.[28] Liverpool did not have links with London comparable to those of Bristol, but the nearness of the London–Chester road put the new port at little more than 180 miles from London and able to communicate with other outports through the Chester-Bristol-Exeter cross post after 1700. Liverpool became Chester's port and enjoyed the same advantages in its growing Irish trade as Bristol did on the more southerly post road to Ireland. Although Liverpool was not isolated from the main postal network through this period, it was not a place to dock with London-connected cargoes. Liverpool's Atlantic trade was as Manchester's port and a midland entrepôt.

If Liverpool showed less evidence of being a London-linked outport, the same is even more true of Glasgow. The Scottish tobacco port had three foot posts a week setting out on a two-day trip to Edinburgh before 1717, when these became horse posts on a 10- to 12-hour ride.[29] Once arrived in Edinburgh, a London-bound letter was still 400 miles and some 85- to 135-hours travel from its destination.[30] It is not surprising that later Stuart London merchants complained to their colonial correspondents about returns made to Scottish ports.[31] The Great North Road was the longest of the six main roads, but its mail was seldom related to the Atlantic trades before the rise of Glasgow in the middle of the eighteenth century. Although merchantmen sailing out of the northeastern English and Scottish ports for transatlantic cargoes to satisfy their home markets might bring back mail or freight for London merchants, this was not common. Although the Great North Road linked the ports of Carlisle, Berwick, Newcastle upon Tyne, York, and Hull directly and indirectly, the road was not a significant route of regular colonial news. A north-about convoy or stray vessel might put into Newcastle upon Tyne and write London for naval assistance and merchant patience, and a Hudson Bay-bound vessel could put ashore reassuring packets on the way north or make a plea for a convoy for the rare return on this route, but these were not regular occurrences.

The English postal services of the Restoration period gave regular and frequent opportunities for the exchange of letters between the main English ports trading to the New World. This meant that payments, bills of exchange, and even small valuable commodities could be exchanged regularly. This service, though not cheap and becoming more expensive after the Post Office Act of 1711, also meant that a colonial correspondent anxious to contact a relative, a mercantile agent, or a political lobbyist in England could send a letter by most vessels bound for English ports with reasonable confidence of safe delivery. A duplicate or two would ensure delivery and be a lesson in the relative speeds by different routes. By 1700, England as a whole could be an effective target for a letter to any particular urban correspondent; this was hardly true of the mail headed from England to the English colonies.

The lines of communication between England and her colonies became increasingly clear and effective as time went on. The metaphor of a rimless wheel might describe the communications of the Restoration empire, when England's postal services brought together England's news of the Atlantic trades. Yet substantial intercolonial shipping already connected the English Americas, and news ricocheted by sea and land around the English Atlantic, whether shouted over a gunwale, exchanged in a tavern, or posted in a captain's mailbag. The emergence of colonial postal services would greatly expand the opportunities for intercolonial correspondence in the eighteenth century, advancing the spread of English, European, and colonial news.

Islands of people on the English Lesser Antilles were less isolated than those who lived on the North American sea of land. Shipmasters' mailbags were adequate to carry letters to the Caribbean islands and between them without the costs of postriders, post offices, bridges, ferries, or roads. Here in miniature was the cost efficiency of water transport. The English islands had little need for a post office, and the story of the development of the intercolonial posts is primarily the story of connecting the major centers of English North America. Before turning to that larger topic, however, attention should be given to the rather different character of the postal arrangements of the English Caribbean islands.

Small islands with relatively few correspondents, most of whom were involved in the sugar trade, were the ideal situations for the informal postal arrangements of the English Atlantic under Charles II. Shipmasters bringing consignments of goods, bills of lading, or servants with indentures were at no extra trouble to bring letters. Delivery was simple, and the sugar ships loaded slowly enough to give ample warning of the time for replies to be ready. Sporadic initiatives to organize a postal service[32] would not noticeably disrupt this system before the middle of the eighteenth century.

There were more initiatives to organize a postal service in Jamaica, the largest of the islands as well as the most insecure politically and socially. In 1671 the marshal was ordered to gather all letters from incoming ships and post a list of them. In 1683, again at local initiative, a letter office was opened to handle ship letters and local mail. James II's postmaster general, the earl of Rochester, appointed one James Wales to be deputy postmaster in Jamaica. Something of the adequacy and economy of the ship-letter system was revealed by the sequel. Port Royal merchants protested that their mail was being held "on Pretence of Postage," and the Jamaica Council all agreed that "there is no Post Office" in the island.[33] Rochester had his power to appoint a deputy in any colony confirmed by the Privy Council and the attorney general, as well as having postage rates for Jamaica specified, but July 1688 was not a good time for James's minister to be commencing a minor political campaign in Jamaica.[34]

It was not local need that brought about the establishment of postmasters in each of the English islands in 1705. Edmund Dummer's packet boats to the West Indies, to be discussed later, went over to a contract system at this time. The packets were on tight schedules in the islands, and it was necessary to have a postmaster who would gather mails for the packet and deliver mails after the boat left on its scheduled run to each of the English Caribbean islands. Dummer was to pay the postmasters himself, but they were appointed by the postmasters general and subject to their instructions.[35]

The recognized difference between the islands and the North American mainland, as seen by the postmasters general, was nowhere clearer than in the sequel to these appointments.[36] In March 1706 the English postmasters general were forced to replace their deputy at Barbados with a man nominated by the holder of patent powers granted to Thomas Neale 14 years earlier.[37] The postmasters general had monitored that patent throughout its life, yet they had never even considered it as involving the Caribbean until 1706. That would also be the year they bought out the remnants of the patent.

Ports of English North America received news from other colonies and from England by the same methods as did the English Caribbean islands. The flow of news depended on the merchant shipping levels, patterns and seasons already discussed. In a study of the development of an intercolonial horse post between the major towns of later Stuart America, several peculiarities should be noted. The maritime connections between these centers were competition for the posts, providing inexpensive or free service along lines of trade and requiring no capital or operating costs whatever. Ship letters also maintained their dominance in the long-distance business and personal correspondence in a way that was not true of most of England, Scotland, or Ireland after the emergence of the post office. In addition, the crown's military and political concerns were much more limited in the North American setting than in England itself. There was less likelihood that postal services would be launched or subsidized in the colonies to support the distribution of court newspapers or the gathering of political intelligence. The colonial postal services clearly predated the first colonial newspapers despite their connection. If they are seen in the context of legitimate expectations and the limited political and commercial need, the surprise is that comparatively expensive horse posts, connecting small settlements that were far apart, developed as soon as they did in English North America.

Massachusetts was the first colony to show interest in a postal service, but the 1639 appointment of Richard Fairbanks's tavern as the place to deposit and receive ship letters was primarily a political favor as was his more lucrative monopoly on the sale of liquor in Boston, which he had gained the previous year.[38] The postal concession was to allow Fairbanks to collect a penny for each letter; no monopoly was intended, simply security of delivery for those willing to pay for it. For inland communications with Massachusetts towns, with the overland migrants in New Haven, or with the colonies of dissidents or frontiersmen to north or south, early Boston had no regular connection at all. Indian runners, paid servants, or passing travelers carried the occasional letter; but communications were more often by water to the Maine frontier, to Rhode Island, or to the Connecticut River valley. When efforts were made to link Boston to New York by postriders in 1673, 1685, and 1693, the initiatives were from New York.[39] When the earl of Rochester made Edward Randolph his deputy postmaster general in North America, Randolph was just gathering a sinecure for himself.[40] There is no evidence that he, nor Richard Wilkins whom the Massachusetts General Court appointed postmaster to succeed him in 1689, did much to establish postal services.[41] Boston depended on the sea for most of her news, as for much else.

Launch of the first regular post between Boston and New York early in 1673 was at the initiative of Governor Francis Lovelace of New York. Lovelace had been unhappy with his communications with England, which he described as occurring, like the production of elephants, once in two years.[42] With the outbreak of what proved to be the last Anglo-Dutch war, Lovelace rightly feared that the Dutch would attempt to retake their former colony. As the first winter of that war began, Lovelace initiated a monthly postal delivery to Connecticut and Massachusetts.[43] Lovelace provided a salary for the lone postman, expecting him to charge for carrying private letters. The carrier, described by Lovelace as "active, stout and indefatigable," had a 250-mile route through New Haven, then north to Hartford and Springfield, and east through Worcester and Cambridge to Boston. The postman was to find and blaze the best route, and he was to make 500 miles a month. Whether he rode or walked, he must have averaged 25 miles a day.[44] If the service lived up to Lovelace's expectations, it lived only a few months and brought intelligence of the invasion that ended his governship abruptly in August 1673. Horses were being used along part of this route in Connecticut a year later although not as intercolonial posts.[45] If this post road had its uses, the post itself cannot have served many compelling and profitable purposes. Although Governors Dongan and Andros would promote revivals of intercolonial posts in the 1680's for the Dominion of New England, nothing very regular emerged.[46]

The intercolonial posts of English North America owed more to English opportunism than colonial necessity. Thomas Neale, MP, was a courtier, a placeman, and a "projector." He had been groom-porter to Charles II and had gained his prize as placeman in 1686, when he became master of the Mint. He kept his place under William III; sat as a Whig in Parliament from 1689 until his death a decade later; and was active in banking, lotteries, and building projects.[47] The royal patent that he received for the colonial posts, dated 17 February 1691/2, was more a projector's scheme than a placeman's reward.

Neale chose well when he nominated Andrew Hamilton to be his deputy in the New World. Hamilton had been an Edinburgh merchant until he migrated to East Jersey in 1685. Linked to the proprietors as a "fractioner," he soon was involved in the government of the colony as an investigator, then as governor. In the spring of 1692 he was elected governor of the East Jersey and West Jersey colonies by the proprietors. That summer he was appointed Neale's deputy, and in September he sailed back to America and his various tasks.[48] Although this last term as governor was long and difficult (1692–1701), he was active in organizing and promoting the postal services.

Neale's patent limited postal charges to those established in the English Post Office Act of 1660 "or such other rates or sumes of money as the Planters and others will freely agree to give for their letters or Pacquetts upon the first settlement of such Office or Offices . . ."[49] Hamilton applied to the colonial legislatures for support, and their response with post office acts was an indication of the perceived value of the service and a tribute to Hamilton's diplomatic skills. New York's response was quick and favorable, reflecting wartime fears once again. In November 1692, New York passed an act that confirmed the monopoly and exempted postmasters from excises on liquor and from watch and jury duties. The postal rates were 4½d. within 80 miles of the city and from Philadelphia, 9d. from Boston, Maryland, or overseas, and 12d. from Virginia, all in New York money. The 9d. rate for overseas letters seems most excessive when compared with the 2d. that would be allowed for similar mails in Massachusetts, New Hampshire, and Pennsylvania. Perhaps the New York legislators presumed that most overseas letters for New York would be put into the post offices at Philadelphia or Boston. New York's act was initially for three years, but regular renewals kept the intention in force until superseded by the parliamentary Post Office Act of 1711.[50] New York's response to the Neale patent was indicative of the city's needs and in keeping with the previous wartime initiatives of New York governors.

Postal service between New York, Massachusetts, and New Hampshire was launched 4 May 1693, while other colonies were still considering postal acts. Hamilton had traveled the route to Boston himself, and his negotiations with the governments of Massachusetts and New Hampshire resulted in post office acts within six weeks of the beginning of the service.[51]

The postrider eastbound from New York followed the earlier post route as far as New Haven, but instead of heading inland there for Hartford, he held close to the Connecticut coast and made for Saybrook, where the Boston rider exchanged mails with him. The Boston rider had come through Providence, Stonington, and New London on his route to Saybrook, a route that was superior to the northerly one in mail potential and had become possible once ferries operated over the Thames at New London and over the Connecticut River at Saybrook.[52] A two-year experiment that caused the Boston-to-Saybrook rider to alternate his routes each trip—first by Providence and New London, then by Springfield and Hartford—was ended in December 1716. In the winter, when service was always cut to once a fortnight, this experiment meant a drop from a weekly to a monthly service for John Winthrop in New London. He complained:

It is a great inconvenience to have it thus. Almost as good as none if it must be thus Stated. And Abundance of people that use to be good Customers to Campbels News papers, along this road, are now Resolved to have no more. And they send all their Letters by Travellers now Rather than by the post.[53]

The triumph of the coastal route through Connecticut was dictated by postal and newspaper revenues and represents the victory of the less isolated coastal towns over Hartford and Springfield. As with the entire service, the settlers with best access to seaborne news would also have best access to the mails of postriders.

The postal service from New York to Boston, weekly in nine months of the year as verified quietly by datelines in the *Boston News-letter*, was not necessarily the eastern terminus for a letter. A weekly service to Piscataqua was visible testimony to Boston's commercial hinterland. Carrying mailbags for the postmasters at Ipswich, Salem, Marblehead, and Newbury, the postrider tied together the major ports of Massachusetts,[54] and the Piscataqua lumber trade and mast fleet. Here, even more than on the road from New York to Boston, the post served economic integration. Boston's congestion and prices could be avoided by Boston merchants who could operate their capital in the shipbuilding, lumbering, and fishing trades out of the smaller ports.

The postal routes between New York and New Hampshire were first in establishment and in usefulness, but the actual levels of mail are not easy to establish. Detailed postal receipts for the first four years are ironically the only ones that survive. As indicated in Table 7.2, postage collected from New England recipients of mail grew quickly to £273.4.1 by the fourth year of the service. This figure does not include official correspondence or the cost of overseas letters, for which the postmaster paid the shipmaster 1d. each, which was likely no more than recouped in the postage collected because of the numbers of letters to addressees who had moved, died, or simply refused their mail.[55] Although the postal receipts could be regarded as an average of about a halfpenny per person for the whole year, participation in letter receiving was limited by literacy and even more by cost.[56] At 6d. for a letter from Rhode Island or New Hampshire to Boston, a letter would cost an able seaman nearly half-a-day's pay.[57] If all the New England postal revenue had been raised on such letters, the postmen of New England would have delivered nearly 11,000 paid letters[58] a year. This was only a letter a year for one New Englander in eight, but it was more than has often been appreciated.[59] Certainly, for the merchant gentlemen of Boston, who would send and receive much of this mail, the postal service was an asset of consequence.

Links between the trading communities of Boston and New York had one of their clearest demonstrations on 5 February 1704/5. The New York post for Boston set out for Saybrook with what must have been one of his heaviest mailbags ever. That day a royal proclamation fixing the price of silver coin in the colonies was issued in New York. Apparently anticipating the event,

Boston merchants had prompted New Yorkers to buy up the coin at the low, regulated price and send it by the postrider, who set out on schedule that night loaded with all the coin he could carry.[60] Boston, like New York, could use the opportunities that might arise anywhere along the 300-odd miles of what New Yorkers called the eastern post.[61]

New York's mail service south to Philadelphia did not commence until nearly four months after the first rider had left for Boston.[62] If the Philadelphia post were seen initially as an aspect of that royal power that brought Governor Fletcher of New York to be Governor of Pennsylvania that year, these reactions did not prevent the passage of a post office act in the spring of 1693 that was comparable to those of New York and Massachusetts.[63] Hamilton must have been disappointed with the early operations on this route. Not only did he feel "forced" to replace the postmaster in Philadelphia twice in the first 54 months of operations, but he must also have been very disappointed with the low postal revenues collected.[64] From 1697 the Pennsylvania governor allowed £20 a year toward the losses in providing a service to trade and commerce and raised rates, but the Philadelphia office was unprofitable during the life of the Neale patent.[65] Although it lost money, the weekly postal delivery down the 94-mile road[66] between New York and Philadelphia assisted the political and economic elite of the colony and its neighbors. In the midst of his vital transatlantic politics in 1700, William Penn assured his London agent "next to those comeing Directly to Our own River there is no conveyance safer than by Vessels to New York and Boston & from thence by post hither."[67]

New York was the center of the post in North America in the 1690's in a number of respects. Location between Boston and Philadelphia naturally allowed some brokerage of news. The war with Canada sharpened the colony's need to seek help from neighboring colonies. This need, together with the powers given Fletcher in Pennsylvania and Lord Bellomont in Massachusetts, made the posts serve New York political interests. The awareness of the value of the post was seen in the prompt and comparatively generous initial subsidy of £50 a year given the postal service by the New York government, amounting to at least twice the grant given by any other provincial government. If the initial location of the administrative center of the modest North American post office at New York owed much to the fact that the first deputy postmaster general was simultaneously governor of the two New Jersey colonies, the choice was entirely appropriate.

The postal revenues gathered by the New York postmaster, William Sharpas,[68] are the clearest evidence of the value of the post to some New Yorkers. In the first four years of the operation of the posts, the revenues collected in New York doubled to reach £112.17.0 in the year ending 1 May 1697.[69] This total is modest compared to the proceeds of the New England posts that year, but the differences are striking if populations are taken into account. New Yorkers averaged postal payments that were 3 times those of New Englanders and 10 times those of people paying for letters delivered out of the Philadelphia letter office.[70]

The history of the Neale patent in the Chesapeake colonies was shorter and sadder than that of efforts north of Philadelphia although the government of Virginia would also pass a post office act in the spring of 1693. It would appear that Thomas Neale appointed Peter Heyman to be his deputy post-master in Virginia and Maryland, and the appointment, at an annual salary of £100 sterling, was effective sometime in 1692. Governor Andros of Virginia proclaimed Heyman's appointment on 12 January 1692/3, and Heyman's petition about the posts two months later prompted Virginia's Post Office Act.[71] The Virginia government established postal rates and conditions on the basis of some knowledge of the Neale patent but without sight of it or Hamilton's commission as deputy. The result was a post office act that, if it was not actually intended to forestall the effective launch of a postal system (which was likely), was designed in a way that contributed to the failure of the initiative to link Virginia with the northern colonies by post. The Post Office Act approved by Governor Andros in April 1693 had been subjected to amendments made in the House of Burgesses and negotiated compromises.[72] The postal rates were low and concerned nothing but postal service within Virginia. The rivers, which made the informal waterborne postal arrangements more like a system in Virginia than in any other mainland colony, were barriers to a riding post that could be overcome only by establishing ferries at considerable expense. Without a monopoly of internal mail of the colony and without any subvention at all from their government,[73] the posts of Virginia were unlikely to run. Although Andrew Hamilton began his negotiations with the Virginia government within two months of the original legislation, nothing more was accomplished. In July 1695 the Virginia Council

> declared that the Postmaster had been wanting, not having settled the post-office in Virginia in pursuance of the Royal Patent nor the ferries which are vested in him. Order for the Secretary to write to Colonel Hamilton accordingly and to ask what his intentions are.[74]

This inquiry may well have prompted the end of Peter Heyman's appointment, and no successor was appointed. Virginia's legislators were not anxious enough to have a postal service within the colony and were even less impressed with the links to the north, where there were military problems. In its response to the Neale patent, the legislators of Virginia revealed a hostility to a postal service that would reappear more than once in the next generation and a view that was shared by the Maryland political elite as well.

Maryland's response to the Neale patent was unique but ultimately little more productive than that of the Virginian legislature. There is no evidence that Hamilton or Heyman approached the Maryland Council before September 1694, when the council read the royal letter of 1692 that had been part of Heyman's credentials in Virginia and they also read Andrew Hamilton's proposal to establish a post under the Neale patent. The House of Burgesses received these items in October but did little more than read them then—and again in May 1695—when they once again postponed consideration until the following session.[75] The question of a royal patent running in a proprietary colony (the government of which had been resumed by the crown) would have been complex enough to prevent a quick solution even if enthusiasm had existed for the Neale patent. Yet this time the delay was not a simple postponement.

Eight days after resolving to postpone consideration of Hamilton's proposal, the Maryland House of Burgesses decided to establish its own postal service between the Potomac and Philadelphia. A Captain John Perry was sought for the task, and within two days an agreement had been struck between Perry and the House of Burgesses. Within another two days, the governor and council proclaimed the establishment of the postal service, to run eight times a year.[76] The Maryland Assembly paid Perry £50 sterling a year to perform these eight round-trips and carry expresses to neighboring colonies as required by Governor Nicholson. Perry was to charge no postage at all on letters from Maryland to Philadelphia or for letters brought back to his "stages" along the route. The proclamation, to be made public by the sheriffs, was for a free postal service in Maryland. Until his death in 1698, Perry had his contract renewed regularly each year and he performed numerous missions for Governor Nicholson to Virginia and New York, including the delivery of gazettes and funds to Governor Benjamin Fletcher of New York.[77] Perry seems to have been highly regarded by the House of Burgesses and the governor, which cannot be said for Perry's successor, Joseph Mann, who did not last long before the service collapsed. For the three years that they had a postal service, the House of Burgesses of Maryland showed themselves willing to pay handsomely from the public purse for their own postman. While it lasted, the service could be seen as the fruit of the Neale patent in the Chesapeake Bay. Despite some effort and some expense by Neale, the Chesapeake did nothing for him, and his patent did little for the Chesapeake. Perhaps it was too early although there was still strong resistance to a postal service 20 years later, when it was no longer a private patent.

Thomas Neale's attempt to cultivate a profit by inventing the place of colonial postmaster general was unsuccessful, proving that even a very experienced placeman could fail in a project. Neale, like Edmund Dummer after him, would in the end appear to have been a public benefactor. In the accounts submitted to the English Treasury and the postmasters general, Neale calculated his losses at over £2360 in the four years to May 1697. When the postmasters general suggested that the governors might support the service more strenuously if it were not in private hands, Neale was quick to offer to sell to the crown, noting that revenues were rising.[78] By 1706, when the crown did buy out the Neale patent, Neale and Hamilton had both died. The North American postal service that Hamilton had created would survive for a generation without much change. As the colonial newspapers amply testified by the dating of intercity news, the mail service between Philadelphia and Piscataqua ran on Hamilton's route and schedule, with the occasional disruption.[79] Evidence of the scale of this early postal service is sketchy but suggestive. Table 7.3 offers very tentative estimates that suggest impressive growth in the first decade, even with correction for population growth. It is equally clear that the postal service could serve only the well-to-do at the prices, and an average of only 1 colonial in 10 received one letter a year in colonies served by the post. The less expensive private ship letters were bound to remain dominant in these circumstances as the repeated complaints of the postmasters made clear to everyone. Yet the colonial post tied together the merchant communities and the political leaders of the mainland colonies and multiplied the opportunities for correspondence between members of the English, West Indian, and North American elites.

Expansion of the English-American posts was expansion southward in the first decades of the eighteenth century against barriers that defeated several initiatives. The four great navigable rivers of Virginia, the James, the York, the Rappahannock, and the Potomac, were main avenues of trade and communication with Britain, being navigable from 60 to 110 miles into the country. It was via these rivers that anything could be delivered to a Virginia gentleman from a major English port "with less trouble and cost, then to one living five miles in the country in England."[80] These same rivers were formidable barriers to traffic between Virginia and her neighbors to the north. Ferry services across these rivers could not be profitable or reliable for two generations after 1675, and the ferrying of horses across these rivers was particularly dangerous. Even without political resistance, the costs of ferries and riders defeated the Neale patentees and their successors.[81]

Royal governors were one vocal group who were particularly unhappy with the isolation of the Chesapeake from the northern colonies. Francis Nicholson, who had suffered from the news embargo as lieutenant governor of New York in 1689 and had established Maryland's free post in 1695, was lieutenant governor of Virginia as the Peace of Ryswick faded in 1700. Nicholson traveled north that fall, as did William Penn, to discuss a variety of problems with Governor Bellomont in New York. Worries about intercolonial competition in the pricing of silver coin and about the pursuit of criminals and debtors across colonial borders were indicators of difficulties that were not new but that were aggravated by improving intercolonial communication and could be dealt with only by even more efficient communications.[82]

Nicholson would suffer acutely from his relative isolation once again when the war he expected finally came in 1702, and he would travel north to consult with the new governor of New York, Lord Cornbury, in the spring of 1703.[83] During this war, the isolation of Virginia from the north would also deprive the New York governor of what was seen as one of the safest opportunities to write to England. Cornbury, upset by the accusation that he should have written to the Board of Trade more often, explained that

the least I have known any express take to go from hence to Virginia has been three weeks, soe that very often before I can hear from Col. Nicholson what time the fleet will sail and send my packets, the fleet is sailed. I hope we shall find a way to remedy that shortly, for Col. Nicholson and Col. Seymour [Maryland] have wrote me word

that they will be here Sept., and I doe then intend to propose to them
the settling of a post to goe through to Virginia, by which I shall have
opportunity to write to your Lordshipps by every ship that sails from
this Continent.[84]

Expresses to Virginia were sent with a certain regularity while a packet boat
was operating between Bristol and New York in 1710–1711, but a regular
postal service was still more than a decade away.

It was September 1717 before Colonel John Hamilton, who had long since
succeeded his father as deputy postmaster general for North America both
under the patent and under the crown, met with the governors of Virginia and
Maryland in Philadelphia to discuss extending the post southwards.[85] The
post was to run from Williamsburg through Annapolis for Philadelphia and,
as the *Boston News-letter* advertisement noted, this meant that a letter from
Williamsburg could be in New York in 12 days and in Boston in a total of 19.
The Williamsburg-to-New York service was to be once a fortnight—and once
a month during the winter—but does not appear to have run regularly that
winter and was gone by spring.[86]

Although a Pennsylvanian like Jonathan Dickinson had applauded this
new service with the quiet pride that presumed the advantages this service
might bring his city,[87] John Custis of Williamsburg railed against the "damn'd
confounded, pretended Post Office here."[88] Opposition was widespread and
vocal among the gentlemen of Virginia and went much further than the
earlier unwillingness to support a public post. The strenuous objections were
to the rates of the new post office. The British Parliament had, in its
comprehensive Post Office Act of 1711,[89] established postal rates for Britain
and the colonies that were substantially higher than prevailing rates. It is not
clear what impact this change had on the colonial use of the existing posts. It
might safely be suggested that the loss of the previous power of each assembly
to establish the postal schedule would be nearly as unwelcome as the increased rates.[90] Virginia was, however, the only colony to attempt to destroy
its new post by act of assembly. Governor Alexander Spotswood may have
been one of the first governors to hear the argument that Parliament had no
right to tax Virginians without the consent of the colony's assembly. The
House of Burgesses and Virginia Council both accepted a rather ingenious
bill that made effective operation of the post office impossible. Spotswood
vetoed the bill,[91] but it was the Virginia Assembly that killed the postal service
once again. Two years later

> William Hill of Philadelphia Publisheth that he is willing to serve
> any Gentleman, as a swift and Trusty Messenger on Foot or Horse,
> to any of the Kings Colonies on the Continent upon reasonable
> terms, and is to be spoke with at the Post Office; . . .[92]

William Hill could safely assume that most of his courier services would be
southward from home.

Concern for the southward expansion of the North American posts may have had little bearing on the choice of a successor to John Hamilton in 1722, but the new incumbent deputy postmaster general was John Lloyd of Charles Town, South Carolina. Lloyd had served as secretary to James Craggs, Sr., joint postmaster general of Great Britain. Lloyd's rapid rise in the politics of the newly royal colony of South Carolina owed something to his ambitions as merchant and politician and something to his links with the Craggs family.[93] Lloyd was appointed one of the colony's agents in 1720[94] and was in London when Hamilton resigned. Lloyd arrived in Boston in September 1722, bearing his new title,[95] and may have inspected his postal system on the route back in Charles Town.[96]

Under John Lloyd there were no efforts made to link Charles Town with the northern colonies, but there were two revealing attempts to extend the posts south from Philadelphia as far as Annapolis. The first of these was announced to readers of the *American Weekly Mercury* in February 1722/3, and echoed two weeks later in the *Boston Gazette*. A fortnightly service was promised beginning that spring, and "All Merchants and others, who have any Letters or Parcels to send are desired to put them in the Bag for that Purpose at the Post Office in Philadelphia."[97] Whether the service commenced or not, it did not flourish. More success attended the attempt to revive this service in 1728, providing additional evidence of the value of linking the posts and the newspapers in colonial American business. The post that started in May 1728 had as its terminals "the House of Andrew Bradford in Philadelphia, and William Parks in Annapolis,"[98] the publishers of the *American Weekly Mercury* and the *Maryland Gazette*, respectively. The fortnightly service ran down the western shore of the Chesapeake to Annapolis and returned to Philadelphia by way of the Eastern Shore.[99] The service seems to have run until the following January at least and was probably suspended with William Parks's visit to England in 1729.[100] Parks would return to build his business and the postal services further to the south.

Alexander Spotswood, whose lifetime corresponds to the general boundaries of this inquiry and whose interest in improving postal services through Virginia was well established,[101] succeeded Lloyd as deputy postmaster general early in 1730. It was the summer of 1732 before Spotswood revealed his ambitions as well as some of his methods. In July a weekly post from Philadelphia to Williamsburg was launched, this one to go and return by the western shore, leaving mail for the eastern shore at Newcastle. Plans to extend the service to Edenton, North Carolina, and "in time for Charlestown itself" were also revealed. Spotswood claimed to have hired postmasters committed to their work, issued a tight schedule demanding that riders accomplish five miles an hour, and promised a printed schedule of rates posted for public view. He also invited advertisements and "hue-and-Cry's" that would also be posted at any or all stages.[102] Although the newspapermen Andrew Bradford in Philadelphia and his father in New York were evidently active in this project, the service seems to have failed before long.[103] It would be revived five years later, when Spotswood had two other printers to work with.

Spotswood appointed Benjamin Franklin as postmaster in Philadelphia in

November 1737 and immediately revived a monthly post from Philadelphia south as far as Spotswood's own residence at Newpost, Virginia, below the falls of the Rappahannock.[104] The following spring Spotswood announced a biweekly service on this route and the beginning of an extension further to the south. William Parks, who was now printer of the *Virginia Gazette*, was to launch a monthly service south from Williamsburg to Edenton, North Carolina. Parks undertook this postal service as a "farm" from Spotswood and promptly launched a monthly post all the way to Charles Town.[105] Franking privileges for a postmaster's newspaper could carry the post further than the ambitions of a deputy postmaster general who had to cover costs of new services out of his own rewards.[106]

Linking the horse posts from Piscataqua to Charles Town might appear the slow work of a whole lifetime, but it was a noteworthy and significant achievement. With low volumes of mail and incredibly long routes in comparison with their English model, the intercolonial posts succeeded in linking three of the major shipping routes of the English Atlantic. As in the case of the English cross posts through Bristol, access to news was altered noticeably. As the postriders added winterless routes (the Williamsburg-to-Charles Town route made no scheduled concessions to winter) to their network, the flow of transatlantic news would be even less seasonal.

As the routes extended, the center of gravity of the network necessarily shifted southward. The place of New York as inspiration and newsbroker was strong in the Neale period but was gone by 1740 although it would be deliberately resuscitated by the route of the transatlantic packet again after 1755. Although Lloyd and Spotswood were based further south, it was Pennsylvania that became the center of the network, especially Benjamin Franklin's city and business. The disruptions caused by Philadelphia's susceptibility to winter could now be minimized. The colonial posts gradually enlarged and unified the market for goods, allowing prompter response to price differentials and better ship management without a return to home port. For business and for government, the North American colonies were being drawn closer together in amity and in conflict.

English and colonial postal services developed rather different business structures. The development of the posts in England had been linked with hostelry for good and obvious reasons. The provision of post-horses and stabling of them was unlikely to be profitable in itself. Innkeepers not only benefited from the "baiting" and bedding of travelers who rode with the post but could also attract neighbors to get their own mail, share that of others, or learn the contents of the latest prints. All this sold ale. Although similar connections developed in the posts of the North American colonies, hostelry was not enough. From Duncan Campbell to Benjamin Franklin, there was a clear connection between the postmasters and the printers in major colonial centers. In Campbell's case, it was the postmaster who became the publisher of the *Boston News-letter*. In William Parks's case or William Bradford's or Benjamin Franklin's, a printer showed interest in the posts. In some areas at least, it would appear as though the colonial newspapers came to allow, to subsidize, and to need the expansion of a postal service.

Development of postal services greatly enlarged the number of opportunities and speeded the delivery of letters bound anywhere within the English Atlantic empire. The English postal services appear to have been initially designed to enhance London's advantages in access to news, but the Restoration post office greatly simplified colonial correspondence with any sizable community in England. The intercolonial postal services joined several of the routes of the English Atlantic together, defying the seasons, levels of ship traffic, and passage times wherever these had interfered with correspondence between ports.

The very considerable benefits of the improving posts were definitely exclusive. Those prominent in government in England and the colonies often had free use of the posts. The postal rates were expensive even before the major increases of the 1711 Post Office Act ensured that many of the literate would not be able to receive letters. Despite the occasional exception or complaint, the posts were also generally effective in keeping communication private. This represented very real economic, political, and social power for those with the literacy, the resources, and the time to maintain correspondence with kin, friends, partners, agents, patrons, and clients who were similarly blessed and living elsewhere within the progressively more integrated English Atlantic.

8 · The Papers

Isaac Pummatick and his companion, Peter, sought to escape from their lives on the Maine frontier and so began a bizarre journey in December 1705. Isaac was a short, slight Indian who had lived with English colonists in Hingham for a time and spoke very good English. When he deserted from garrison duty under Captain Joseph Brown, Isaac did not flee to the neighboring woods. Instead he set out southward through New Hampshire and was seen at Newbury, Massachusetts, wearing good English clothes, including a nearly new, black hat. He was accompanied by Peter, about 20 years old, of average height, also fluent in English, and adequately dressed in a mixed gray homespun coat, white homespun jacket and breeches, dark stockings, and French shoes. He, too, was wearing a black hat. Only Peter's "pretty brown Complexion" betrayed that he was the runaway slave of William Pepperrell of Kittery, Maine.

Whether by plan or by accident, Isaac and Peter gained passage on a southward-bound vessel out of Newbury or a neighboring Massachusetts port.[1] They probably took ship with one of the many traders bound for North Carolina and then headed southward on foot although it is possible that they were aboard the *Nonesuch* when it left Boston that winter directly for South Carolina. In any case, this pair from the margins of the English Atlantic empire must have felt confident that, when they reached the frontier colony of South Carolina, they had put a great deal of distance between themselves and their story.

Yet before that winter had left the forests of Maine, the escape of Isaac and Peter had ended in failure. It was not simply that they had come to a most peculiar place of refuge for a strange Negro and a native American; they probably intended to go further. They had been pursued southward by a December issue of North America's only newspaper, *The Boston News-letter*, which included ads for the runaways. Four months later the paper advertised itself when it trumpeted the capture of the pair in South Carolina, where the governor had secured them "for the Owner."[2] Peter and Isaac could be excused if they did not understand the concept of freedom of the press, but they had learned that the paper gave their master a very long arm.

Newspapers were by far the most powerful and extensive public communications innovation that developed within the English Atlantic empire between 1675 and 1740. Newspapers intended to make news available to a wide audience and to do so without the continuing distortions that affected word-of-mouth transmission. Papers went beyond their initial subscribers by being read in taverns and in the streets and also by being sent on to acquaintances further from the source of the news. For example, a copy of the *London Gazette* passed on from an English fisherman at Newfoundland to a Massachusetts shipmaster brought Boston more than the news that William III had died and that Anne was queen. As the court's paper printed the proclamation of the new monarch, Boston officials could proclaim the new monarch correctly and could do so long before the official packet would arrive.[3] Incidental transmission of all kinds of news increased with the growth of ship traffic and the postal services but especially as more of the ports of the English Atlantic imitated their metropolis by producing and distributing newspapers.

Those writing about the beginnings of newspapers have had good practical reasons to isolate London, English provincial, Scottish, Irish, and American papers from each other.[4] Yet comparisons between these various branches of the English-language newspaper industry are suggestive even if they cannot be comprehensive in this study. The following sketch of the origin and development of the newspapers is primarily concerned with the place of the papers in communications and in encouragement of cosmopolitan and local identities. The tendency of the literature to view London papers as integrating England while the rest of the English-language papers are developing local or regional identities only invites the suspicion that both aspects might be inherent in the subject although not equally interesting to its historians.

If a newssheet of weekly frequency is accepted as the definition of a newspaper,[5] Amsterdam had the first English-language newspaper in 1620. *The Corrant out of Italy, Germany, &c* and its early English imitators were alike in the European news they carried and in the wise precaution of not carrying any English news at all.[6] Such a precaution was not enough to ensure that an early Stuart newsbook could be published with safety, but it was a prerequisite. Royal hostility to newspapers in England was more ferocious but less enduring than its opposition to postal services, perhaps because printing was easier to control. James I gained a Dutch ban on the export of corantos to England, reminded his subjects of existing ordinances for licensing and controlling the press,[7] and imprisoned the publisher of the first English newspaper for doing so without royal license.

By the time Nathaniel Butter and his associates began printing English translations of the Dutch corantos in the fall of 1621, London and its immediate environs contained a quarter of a million people, the seat of government, the largest port in the country by a very great deal, as well as being designated the main center for printing. With these overwhelming advantages and political caution, Butter and his associates would issue news-books down to 1642. Joseph Frank has suggested that "it is likely that the average newspaper of the 1620's had a circulation of about 500, though when business was bad this might have slipped to 250."[8] Although circulation amounted to only a copy for every 500 to 1000 Londoners, the papers were profitable enough to be continued, defended against competition, and kept sufficiently innocuous to avoid political trouble.

London's market for printed news had not been effectively tested between 1620 and 1640 because of the ban on English news and the close governmental control of the licensed press. A better measure of the possibilities can be gathered from the experience of the 1640's. By early 1644 there were a dozen competing newspapers in the city, selling perhaps 6000 copies a week in total. As the decade wore on, most of these papers would disappear before better competitors and an increasingly effective parliamentary control. This early flowering of the London press would not survive the political climate of the 1650's, to say nothing of that beyond, but its scale is worthy of note. The newsbooks of the 1620's might have sold a copy for each 500 people living in London, but the newspapers of the 1640's were selling at a rate comparable to a copy for each 60 to 70 persons living in a larger London.[9]

It would be nearly half a century before London's appetite for newspapers would again be fed in relative freedom, but a number of developments in the meantime would affect the shape of the newspaper business that would emerge after 1695.[10] Three of these features call for particular mention: the reassertion of executive authority over the press, the impact of the official *London Gazette* on subsequent notions of the function and format of a newspaper, and the improved distribution system of the royal mail and its uses to newsmen.

As with other aspects of government initiative that are often reproachfully assigned to the later Stuarts, the development of a controlled official press was a legacy of the Commonwealth and Protectorate periods. The "official" papers of Marchmont Needham and Cromwell's increasingly efficient censorship under Secretary Thurloe could have provided Charles II with adequate precedent for executive control of the press.[11] Ironically, Charles preferred to continue the licensing of news by act of Parliament and gained all the power that he could have wished by the Licensing Act of 1662. Only 20 master printers were allowed in the kingdom, and all of these were to work in London save those allowed the two English universities, the city of York, and the King's Printer. The licensing of news, which amounted to prepublication censorship, was divided among the religious, judicial, and political authorities. For newspapers, this meant that the secretaries of state had control of what was printed.[12] The appointment of Roger L'Estrange as chief censor the following year tightened the real control, especially after an exemplary victim had been brutally executed.[13] The Licensing Act compromised royal authority because it needed renewing, and in 1679 a Parliament animated by the growing Exclusion Crisis failed to renew the law. Charles then resorted to a royal proclamation that controlled the press from May 1680 to the end of his reign and thereby effectively reasserted the prerogative power that would support colonial governors in this matter.[14] From 1685 to 1695 both James II and William III were able to supervise the press through the revived Licensing Act. This control assured the continuing dominance of London in the possession of the printers and presses that made papers possible. Controls also encouraged the related trade in manuscript newsletters, in which franker and fuller discussion of political events was possible. Yet perhaps the most significant legacy of this period was that it produced the *London Gazette*.

The *Oxford Gazette*, soon renamed and relocated as the *London Gazette*, was the last newspaper adventure of Henry Muddiman. Interest in his own successful private newsletter[15] may well have encouraged Muddiman to adopt the model of the Amsterdam and Paris gazettes and foster the safe preoccupation with foreign news that had been de rigueur under the early Stuarts. The safer focus on imported news, both in space and in the order of news in the paper, would also appeal to provincial and colonial newspapers. For the *London Gazette* and for its imitators, only government documents and announcements could take precedence over imported news. Muddiman used his own correspondents in the English outports to provide him with shipping news, including colonial items,[16] but such accounts disappear with the removal of Muddiman from the paper in 1666. Without the services of an experienced and concerned newspaperman, the *London Gazette* failed to fulfill its potential, but its monopoly made both market and influence secure. Although it did not deserve total denunciation,[17] the court's paper was formal and foreign for the most part, and even its ads came to be less revealing than those in its eventual competitors. Yet the style and the name would carry to the colonies even more evidently than to the counties.

For most of its first 30 years, the *London Gazette* was the only newspaper legally printed in the whole of the country. The literate—and some of their illiterate hearers—could be in possession of the same information at nearly the same time. The developing postal system allowed distribution that was quick and efficient, and the coincidence of postmasters being innkeepers meant that the paper was distributed in a manner that maximized its impact. The only real competition was from the very popular manuscript newsletters. These gave much more English news and gave better coverage of matters that would embarrass the crown, but the *London Gazette* was not marketing such news, was cheaper, and was often post-free.

Unfortunately, there are no circulation figures for the *London Gazette* in what might have been its halcyon days, so that its exact impact on its named city, the counties, and the colonies is difficult to estimate. Roger North, in writing of Cambridge University in the 1660's, suggests that (at least in retrospect): "The trade of news also was scarce set up; for they had only the public Gazette, till Kirk got a written news-letter circulated by one Mudiman."[18] But many could sympathize with the isolated colonial officeholder who wrote a London correspondent in 1688:

S[r] Yor Gazetts if you please to Comand your Serv[t] to Enclose what
you have already perused though old to you Wil bee new to mee, and
heartily welcom[19]

Broadsheets of news from the *London Gazette* were occasionally printed
by Irish and colonial printers who saw a market for a particular piece of news
or who were ordered to print the same by local authorities.[20] For those who
could read and afford any regular news, the *London Gazette* was much
cheaper than the newsletters and provided fairly reliable, if limited, news of
European events as well as English court function, appointments, and so
forth. The paper also affirmed the place of the metropolis as source for the
whole country's news. This notion was established by 1695, when the expiry
of the Licensing Act meant both that the London press would offer much
more in the way of newspapers and that provincial towns could have papers
of their own.

Although the lapsing of the Licensing Act in May 1695 was certainly not
the result of a political decision to "free" the press,[21] the event marked a
fundamental change in the trade in London itself and provincial English
towns.[22] Within days of the expiry of the law, five new newspapers appeared
in London, including one edited by Benjamin Harris, whose migration back
to London from New England was as well timed as his flight had been a
decade earlier.[23] By 1704 there were some 70 printing houses in and around
London, and the city had 9 newspapers (including the world's first daily)
issuing 27 editions a week.[24] Within another five years there were 55 editions
a week of some 19 London papers, almost all of them privately sponsored
and presenting some political bias.[25] Quite naturally, it was the politics of this
reading revolution that roused recorded concern and has attracted most
subsequent attention.[26] Between 1695 and 1712, London newspapers established new markets in the city and in the English countryside. These markets
would come to be shared with the country newspapers, but the main impact
of the London newspapers had been to raise an audience for news. The scale
of the transformation can be sensed in a very general way by comparing the
scattered statistics that survive for the London newspapers with the best
estimates of the city's population. Table 8.1 suggests a marked growth in the
total audience for London newspapers, but this audience certainly included
an expanding market for these papers outside of London.

London newspapers had been distributed outside the metropolis since the
days of the early Stuart newsbooks, and some Civil War newspapers had
organized distribution in the hinterland.[27] The *London Gazette* competed
with handwritten newsletters, and the flow of newspapers quickened
markedly after 1695. The most popular of the new London papers, the
Whiggish *Postman* and the Tory *Postboy*, had names and production on post
days to suggest their out-of-town audience.[28] By 1712 the *Night Post* and the
Evening Post were catering even more to the country market for the freshest
news available on post nights. Subsequently, the *St. James Evening Post*, the
London Evening Post and the *Whitehall Evening Post* were all anxious to

compete for the same markets. Late in the 1730's, Robert Walker went further in the London press struggle for a specifically country market. His *Warwick and Staffordshire Journal, Shropshire Journal, Derbyshire Journal, Lancashire Journal*, and *Northamptonshire Journal* were all printed in London.[29]

Political interventions in the newspaper trade suggest the importance of the export of London papers into the politically vital electoral hinterlands. By 1712 the government had developed several weapons to control the London press, cut its variety, and buy the writers of the papers to promote its own perspective. These measures provided very little control over the country newspapers, but the government apparently expected to drown out the opposition papers in the country from London. John Toland summarized some of the remaining problems for the government in 1717, when he complained that there were still too many papers; the stamp duties were being evaded by some London papers and almost all those of provincial towns; and the evening papers were a scandal, sometimes issuing more virulent editions for the country than they sold in town.[30] The success of the opposition press in London, as well as its influence in the countryside, was of continuing concern to the government.

The only way that London papers could be sent to country customers cheaply was by the posts, and herein lay real power for the government. The very popular antiministerial *Craftsman* claimed that post office personnel interfered with the delivery of their paper and even substituted papers more favorable to the government.[31] As the postal rates were themselves prohibitive, the exploitation of the franking privileges was another important feature of the war for the news. Franking was allowed to MPs, to government offices, and to the post office clerks of the roads. In the political crisis of 1733, opponents claimed that some 1400 copies of the government-controlled papers were being franked every week. This may well have risen further after a letter from the comptroller of the post office to all postmasters in the country, dated 9 October 1733, asked them for the names of any coffeehouses, so that these could be provided with free copies of government papers.[32] Figures are not available on the scale of this operation, but it was a considerable traffic in Walpole's last decade in power, during which he also dispensed some £50,077.18s. directly to writers and printers.[33] One scholarly estimate suggests that by 1764 some 35,000 papers a week were being franked from London, a figure that may nearly have matched the total production of the thriving provincial newspapers of that time.[34]

London papers were definitely serving to unite the community that was England as they competed to serve a national audience. The political biases and preoccupations meant that governments found it irresistible to tamper with the flow of London papers by curbing part of it and by flooding the country with papers loyal to themselves. There is considerable evidence that this technique promoted an antiministerial provincial press (unlike the early colonial papers), but the total effect may well have been to contribute to the stability that the era has become famous for. In any case, the London papers remained a major feature, source, and competition for the new English provincial press. Particularly in the 1730's, the London press may well have curbed the development of new provincial newspapers.

Growth of English newspapers outside London was a major development that followed the suspension of the Licensing Act in 1695. The act had applied only to England and Wales, so that Scotland, Ireland, and the colonies were not directly affected. As none of these communities had a functioning newspaper at the time and all would have them soon, there is merit in viewing the spread of the English language newspaper comparatively. It is noteworthy that certain towns already had printers—and hence the potential to produce a paper. In England the three towns were Oxford, Cambridge, and York. In Scotland there were presses in Edinburgh, Glasgow, Aberdeen, Campbeltown, and Maybole. Belfast, Cork, Kilkenny, Limerick, and Waterford all had printing presses in 1695, adding to those of the Irish capital. There were printers in both Cambridge and Boston in Massachusetts, in New York City, in Philadelphia, and in St. Mary's City, Maryland.[35]

The growth of a provincial press, officially or unofficially bound to the London metropolis, was a shared experience of the provincial English towns, the main centers of the other kingdoms, and the colonies. The official papers of Edinburgh, Dublin, Boston, New York, Philadelphia and St. Mary's City all gained and lost for having government support. As has been seen in the struggles to dominate the London papers, the government's ability to harass its enemies and help its friends was very considerable in the application of law, the awarding of posts or pensions, and the conduct of the postal service and enlistment of postmasters. In this respect, the English provincial press was less controlled than were the official papers of London or the administrative centers of the empire, and the English provincial press was more like the privately sponsored subsequent papers in the government centers.

Between 1695 and 1700, London-trained printers migrated out to the English towns of Bristol, Shrewsbury, Exeter, and Norwich.[36] Ten years later Norwich had three papers, Exeter had two, and Bristol had one. Five other towns (Yarmouth, Worcester, Stamford, Newcastle upon Tyne, and Nottingham) had papers by this time, and the only papers that failed were one in Shrewsbury and a second paper for Yarmouth.[37] The first towns have been called "progressive cities over a hundred miles from London,"[38] and distance from London was a continuing factor that might help explain why Oxford and Cambridge did not launch papers. Yet distance, size, and a printer were not enough to bring a newspaper to York before 1719.[39] To identify reasons for the launch of the provincial press, Norwich will be looked at more closely, not only because it was first but also because it was sustaining three papers in 1710 while another was thriving in nearby Yarmouth.

Norwich was the second city of England in 1700, with a population of some 30,000. The city's economy was dominated by the textile industry and by the cattle and grain trades, all of which were linked to the London market. The size of the mercantile and gentry group in the city could support a newspaper, but Norwich also had a sizable dissenter community, literacy among the weavers, and a county population of over 200,000.[40] Perhaps it was also significant that Norwich's need for regular and full news from London was not directly met by the post office, for Norwich was served by a privately contracted "bye post" from Colchester, a diversion from the main post road between London and Harwich.[41] It is noteworthy that John Houghton's trade-oriented *Collection for Improvement of Husbandry and Trade* (1692–1704) was sold by London hawkers and had only one out-of-town agent—in Norwich.[42] It would seem that Norwich needed more London news than was readily available, and the multiplication of London papers left rural audiences anxious for a sensible digest of the best of them at a lower cost than subscribing to very many of them.[43] All three of the first Norwich papers appeared on Saturday, the major market day, and all were reprinting from papers that left London on Thursday night.[44] Norwich needed a newspaper badly enough that Francis Burges could launch the first one in peacetime despite the overwhelming advantage that wartime news gave to the emergence of most newspapers. The other indicator of the primacy of Norwich was the fact that this major center could support three competing newspapers while the very idea of county town newspapers was still novel. Norwich was the first town to have a newspaper for a variety of reasons. Its economic and social connections with London, its size, and its inland location off the main post roads all contributed to its people's willingness to buy reprinted London news.

Bristol and Exeter reveal that the emergence of a newspaper need not display a preoccupation with the capital of the proportions inescapable in Norwich. Bristol was a metropolis with a West Country, Welsh, Irish, and colonial hinterland from which it derived goods and to which it supplied others, as well as transport, capital, and insurance.[45] Bristol's 20,000 people were bound to include a number who had caught what one wit called the "athenian itch"[46] for the latest news, but that group would be supplemented by many more whose prosperity was threatened by the war that commenced in the spring of 1702. William Bonny had established a printing shop in Bristol in 1695. He did printing for the local authority[47] and launched the *Bristol Post-Boy* in November 1702. The paper survived through a decade of war, coming to an end late in 1712. That last summer the paper was averaging 288 copies a week, which may explain why no competitor emerged although a successor was prompt enough.[48] As the second seaport and third city of England, Bristol took its rightful place among the earliest English towns to have its own newspaper. The seaborne commerce of the port created a community that was particularly interested in the foreign news of the war that came by way of the London papers down the fine post road to Bristol. The competition between the London papers and the *Bristol Post-Boy* can only be surmised, but those London papers were also to give Bonny the news he sold throughout the war. There seem to have been limits to the market for news in Bristol, at least in comparison with the other pioneer towns of the English provincial newspaper. Although the tendency to compete with existing papers was usually stronger than the compulsion to launch a town's first newspaper, Bristol had only one newspaper of its own for most of the years before 1740.[49]

The same could certainly not be said for the smaller southwestern port of Exeter, where eight different papers were launched between 1704 and 1736, and the town usually had two or three papers to choose from after 1709.[50] Like Norwich, Exeter was a center for the new draperies in the seventeenth century. Although Exeter had a hinterland that reached out from the valley of the Exe to Dartmoor and north to Barnstable or Bideford Bay, its draperies industry was export oriented.[51] Although smaller than Bristol in population and in shipping traffic,[52] Exeter's economy was even more dependent on continental European happenings than was that of Bristol. Here, too, the main post road from London would provide both fresh news and competition. Yet here that competition was not strong enough to limit the contest between rival local papers. The cross posts to Bristol may well have assisted in distribution of news from the western Channel ports northward.[53] The early attempt to start the fourth provincial newspaper in Shrewsbury in 1705 and the successful *Worcester Postman* (1709) suggest the attraction of locating on the route of the new Exeter-Bristol-Chester cross post.

The pioneer provincial papers of Norwich, Bristol, and Exeter suggest no single pattern to the location of newspapers although distance from London was a prerequisite for some time.[54] By 1710 eight English towns had newspapers, including the ports of Bristol, Exeter, Yarmouth, and Newcastle upon Tyne and the inland market county towns of Norwich, Worcester, Stamford, and Nottingham.[55] The commencement of provincial newspapers owed something remote to the end of the Licensing Act, something immediate to the commencement of the War of the Spanish Succession, and something more to the calculations of ambitious printers.

If the purpose of early English provincial papers were to be gathered by their contents, they were as preoccupied as the colonial papers would be with satisfying a thirst for foreign and London news.[56] These papers were not parochial; indeed, there seemed to be a ban on local stories in the early days. Provincial printers were subject to local courts and pressures that were lessened if the news was not local and especially if it was confined to what had been printed (and presumably permitted) in London. Although the "gagging" of the local papers was real, it is also true that local news could circulate fast enough that its appearance in the weekly newspaper would suggest embarrassing tardiness rather than the speed of posts, courants, or mercuries. The provincial press also avoided too strong a local flavor because the search for larger circulation and advertising revenue led far afield. It has been estimated that the average circulation of the provincial newspapers of the first two decades of the eighteenth century was between 100 and 200 copies. By 1725 highly successful papers like the *Gloucester Journal* and the *Reading Mercury* could claim weekly sales of between 350 and 400 copies. In 1739 the *Newcastle Journal* boasted near 2000 purchasers a week although the average circulation of English provincial newspapers at mid-century was only about 400.[57] In the growth of circulation, these papers soon went beyond the simplest methods of distributing by sale at the weekly market or by street hawkers. Generally, as has been mentioned, the provincial papers were not distributed by post.[58] What did develop was an elaborate network of news-people and agents who carried provincial newspapers to neighboring towns and rural subscribers with enough speed and regularity to become a delivery service for other goods and for letters. The leading provincial papers became an important part of reading in neighboring counties as well. This phase of the newspaper trade would end in most areas by mid-century. Although circulation would continue to grow, most papers were serving a narrower geographical area because of the emergence of more local competition.[59] It was only after this change had occurred that these papers could, in any serious sense, become truly local papers.

Although cosmopolitan in content, English provincial newspapers accorded space to colonial events only when British military adventures like Cartagena (1739) or Quebec (1759) happened to be colonial.[60] Shipping news of the provincial ports would include ships in from the colonies and occasionally their news. Bristol, the premier western outport early in the eighteenth century and one with particular interest in colonial trade, seems to have been an early exception. Surviving copies of *Sam. Farley's Bristol Post Man: or Weekly Intelligence* indicate that he and his readers were concerned about a treaty of peace with the South Carolina Indians, a merchantman that ran aground approaching Philadelphia but "got safe off again," and the death at Piscataqua of Ichabod Plaisted, who was particularly distinguished by having a paragraph of obituary in a paper that did not seem given to that art form. One of the six surviving copies of the paper carried three stories datelined from New York.[61] All three of these stories were reprinted, with the customary lack of acknowledgment, from three successive issues of the *Boston News-letter*.[62] Sam Farley and the Bristol papers of his family would lead in another development in the import of colonial news. In 1725 he had a correspondent in Philadelphia, and the following year he had another in New York.[63] The process would go one step further in 1747, when *F. Farley's Bristol Journal* could declare

> the Boston Correspondent (as also the Printer at Philadelphia) has engag'd to supply us with the most early Intelligence from their Parts of the World by all Opportunities.[64]

Provincial English newspapers were not a regular source of news for colonial papers, but there were connections as well as parallels. At times like the Jacobite risings of 1715 and 1745 there was particular interest in northern reports, and reprints from the provincial press were more frequent than usual. Most English provincial news would come via the London papers to the colonial papers. Yet one early example of the occasional importance of an English provincial newspaper was the *Boston Gazette* of 27 April 1721, which had received its stories datelined from London, Rochel, and Paris by a copy of the *Exeter Mercury*, which had arrived by way of Bristol.[65] The circulation of news in England was improving as was the freshness of the advices that left aboard vessels for the Atlantic colonies.

Another connection between the provincial and colonial press besides the occasional use of each other's news was the conscious comparisons between them. After one year in business as proprietor of the *Boston News-letter*, John Campbell compared his price and product with *Sam. Farley's Exeter Post-Man*, which had begun about the same time.[66] Most of the pioneering colonial newspapermen served an apprenticeship in London, as did those who launched the first provincial English newspapers. William Parks, who would found both the *Maryland Gazette* and the *Virginia Gazette*, was unusual in running the *Ludlow Postman or Weekly Journal* and the *Reading Mercury* before migrating to commence his career as a colonial printer.[67]

Patterns of development of Irish newspapers in the early eighteenth century bear outlining as part of the spread of English-language newspapers from London. Dublin may have been late to develop a newspaper by population, having over 60,000 people by the time *The News-letter* appeared in July 1685, but it was by far the first of the papers to be printed outside London.[68] Starting a paper in peacetime that focused on London suggests that, despite Dublin's substantial trade with the continent, there was a major market for London news because of the powerful links Dublin's trade, government, and Protestant community had to London. The suspicion that the beginnings of the Dublin press were more akin to the interests of Norwich readers than to those of Bristol is supported, too, by the fact that Dublin was also a market for reprinted English newspapers on a scale found nowhere else in the empire.[69] Dublin's pirating of English books may have aimed at English markets, but the reprinted newspapers were sold in Dublin itself. Indeed, to a degree unequaled elsewhere, Dublin papers were for Dubliners. Sale of papers by hawker and printing days planned for arrival of the postal packet from Holyhead rather than to fit local market or post days—both point to the city market for the papers. Through the 1690's a number of successors to *The News-letter* appeared, all of them castle organs operating without local competition, but faced the very real competition of the London papers that were imported directly.[70] The outbreak of the War of the Spanish Succession, which contributed to the expansion of English provincial newspapers, brought a new phase to the Dublin press. Numerous papers competed for the Dublin market, and publication days shifted to Tuesday and Saturday, the days the posts left Dublin for major towns of the island. Although surviving evidence does not suggest that there was a great market outside Dublin, Protestant Ireland was seeing the beginnings of a national press. Dublin's array of newspapers throughout the first half of the eighteenth century was remarkable both for the number of papers started and for good papers like *Pue's Occurrences*, which survived for more than a half century from its beginning in 1703.[71]

Ireland's major towns, like those of the American colonies, were all seaports. The war that activated the newspaper business in provincial England and in Dublin brought forward no attempts to establish newspapers in any Irish center outside Dublin. Eight newspapers started in Cork in the first half of the eighteenth century, and papers attempted in Limerick and Waterford, did not survive for very long.[72] Belfast, which arguably had a more literate audience, had no newspaper before 1737.[73] Although it is not entirely clear whether the Irish provincial newspapers suffered more from the comparative illiteracy in their communities or from the hostility of the majority to these papers, the experience of these papers serves as a reminder that early papers did not need to succeed just because they were a communications revolution. Even towns as sizable as these could be without an audience of the 100 to 200 needed to sustain a newspaper.

Scottish Protestantism had a concern for literacy and education that should have made the Scottish lowlands a special place in the spread of English-language newspapers. In the generation after 1642, Edinburgh had shown more interest in newspapers than had any other English-speaking city outside London. The Leith papers of 1642 indicated an early market for London news, and the Cromwellian press based there had a richer and longer life than did a parallel beginning in Cork.[74] Certainly, the 21 issues of *Mercurius Scoticus* warrant special attention as a Scottish-produced paper that ran through the last five months of 1651, but the interest in printed news is better revealed by the Leith reprintings of Marchmont Needham's London papers continuously between 1653 and 1660. Undoubtedly, papers were coming to Edinburgh from London in the posts to private citizens as well as to the printers. After the false starts and speedy ends to experiments around the time of the Restoration, Edinburgh's local newspaper of the 1660's was *The Kingdom's Intelligencer*, initially a reprint of Roger L'Estrange's *Kingdom's Intelligencer* of London but outlasting its source by at least a year.[75] Up to this point, Edinburgh and its port of Leith were clearly leaders in the local press even if the market for distant news made reprints satisfactory as a major source. It is also noteworthy that this paper was run by the keeper of the Edinburgh Post Office, Robert Mein.

It is not at all clear when and why *The Kingdom's Intelligencer* ceased publication, but it is even more puzzling that no newspaper was printed for a period of at least 14 and perhaps 24 years with the exception of the short-lived *Edinburgh Gazette* of 1680.[76] The grant of a 41-year monopoly to Andrew Anderson in 1671 was an encumbrance on the printing of a newspaper but less so than the Scottish Privy Council's censorship, which went beyond prepublication censorship to control of manuscript newsletters. These restraints on Edinburgh printing of newspapers may well have been bearable and profitable for Robert Mein because improved postal service from London ensured a supply of newspapers franked by the clerks of the roads. In any case, Edinburgh did not maintain the commanding lead she had once enjoyed in English newspaper production outside London. The launching of the *Edinburgh Gazette* in 1699 amounted to a new beginning, behind Dublin and just ahead of a number of provincial English and American colonial newspaper beginnings.

When the first copies of the *Edinburgh Gazette* were being sold on the streets of Edinburgh, the city was about the size of Dublin and much more populous than any English city outside London.[77] Publisher James Donaldson was proud to have business so well organized that within four or five hours of the arrival of the post from London, the *Edinburgh Gazette* would be issued from James Watson's printshop.[78] Donaldson's evident dependence on the London papers was perfectly natural as was his need for speed to compete with the London papers that came in the mail for sale in Edinburgh. Donaldson also revealed that the press run could have been substantial.[79] With the first issue of the *Edinburgh Courant* in February 1704/5, the city had two authorized newspapers. Although their competition was fierce and their careers were interrupted, Edinburgh was generally served by two competing newspapers from then on. Censorship encouraged the preoccupation with foreign news through much of the generation before the '45.

Although not enough is known about the circulation of Edinburgh papers, it seems safe to assume that Edinburgh printers were increasingly appealing to out-of-town audiences. The early competition between the Edinburgh papers was decided by control over the street hawkers, revealing the essentially city market of the papers. Despite the existence of printers in Aberdeen, Glasgow, Campbeltown, and Maybole[80] from the middle of the seventeenth century, Edinburgh would be the only Scottish city producing newspapers throughout most of the first half of the eighteenth century. Edinburgh's communications hinterland was fully demonstrated by the distribution arrangements of the Edinburgh reprinting of Daniel Defoe's *Review* in the summer of 1709.

> The counties of Northumberland and Westmoreland are also supplied with this paper from Scotland together with the towns of Belfast, Carrickfergus and the city of London-Derry in Ireland.[81]

Although such a wide range could not be presumed for Edinburgh's newspapers, the ease of communication to Glasgow probably hindered the growth of a newspaper in that very substantial city.[82]

Edinburgh and Dublin held a virtual monopoly on newspapers within their countries early in the eighteenth century. Both cities were large enough to sustain papers by street sales, but the papers produced were not concerned with local news or local perspectives. Prudence in these castle cities discouraged reporting of matters that irritated watchful governments.

The newspapers of England, Scotland, and Ireland at the opening of the eighteenth century represented more variety in structure and distribution than in content. The London newspapers fought for access to post office franking to augment the sales based on London street vending. Dublin and Edinburgh papers were more closely controlled and primarily reprinted items from the London press. English provincial papers developed distribution systems separate from the posts and thrived only when far enough from London to make postal rates for newspapers from the capital excessively expensive. Papers also seemed to locate where links with London were particularly important and where the news of the War of the Spanish Succession was likely to have an interested audience of mercantile and maritime customers. In all cases, the war news and London news were prominent. The newspapers of Queen Anne's kingdoms were not vehicles of local identity but paper windows on the world.

Newspapers have been given a special place in the history of English America. Did the American colonies have a special attachment to newspapers as the cultural form that suited a comparatively literate and egalitarian corner of the English empire? Colonial America had a place in the freeing of the press, and the press had a place in the freeing of America, yet the earliest newspapers of English America have not attracted much scholarly attention. By examining these early papers as the communications innovations they were and by studying their origins, content, and markets in comparison with English, Scottish, and Irish papers of the time, some new questions will be answered and some old answers will be questioned.

Massachusetts became the newspaper center of English America, but this was not evident in the seventeenth century. Although Stephen Daye began printing in Cambridge, Massachusetts, in the spring of 1639, the modest output of that earliest English American press reflected the religious concerns of the college and the book buyers.[83] The colony's intense interest in the English Civil War did not provoke local broadsides reprinting English news. As long as printing was confined to Cambridge, there was no possibility of printing news profitably. Even if printing had been allowed in a Boston of 3000 people in 1660,[84] with no postal services to give regular access to rural readers there could not have been anything more than the occasional broadside. If censorship by the Massachusetts General Court prevented the launching of anything resembling a newspaper before 1675, the unknown victim was likely being saved from economic misadventure.

Boston gained its first printing press in May 1674, when the Massachusetts General Court finally succumbed to the persistent petitions of Marmaduke Johnston. Although Johnston lived to enjoy his license for only a few months, neither he nor his successor, John Foster, gave any indication that they were interested in producing a newspaper for the town. Samuel Green began printing in Boston in 1681 under a license granted to Samuel Sewall.[85] Green's first newssheet was a broadside reproducing the *London Gazette* of 9 February 1684/5, the issue announcing the accession of James II, which so shocked the leaders of Boston.[86]

Boston printers Samuel Green and Richard Pierce played a significant part in bringing the Glorious Revolution to Boston early in 1689.[87] By the fall of that year the revived General Court was concerned about "disorderly printing" of material hostile to William and Mary. In addition to threats, the General Court had Samuel Green issue a broadside entitled "The Present State of New-English Affairs," which gave a very encouraging picture of the English reception of Boston's revolution.[88] This broadside included extracts from a letter of the colony's agent in London and other news reports, including an item from something called the "London Newsletter."[89] In the excitement of 1689, news would be printed and sold in Boston as occasion warranted, but such a crisis market was different from that for a regular newspaper.

In 1690, Boston was a town of some 7000 with no regular post linking it to other settlements in New England or New York. Benjamin Harris, the Whig refugee publisher from London who had been active in printing during Boston's version of the Glorious Revolution, ventured what proved to be a single issue of an intended newspaper. The extremely brief career of Harris's *Publick Occurrances, both Foreign and Domestick* was not ended by the automatic suppression of yet another itinerant radical who dared invade the tranquillity of Boston's restored leaders.[90] Harris had acclimatized well to the Boston market, publishing religious and political items that had made him a notable asset to the revolutionary government. Harris was publishing some of Cotton Mather's work in 1690, would continue to publish for him and for Increase Mather after *Publick Occurrances* was suppressed, and would serve as printer to the Boston authorities in 1692 and 1693.[91]

The appearance of Harris's *Publick Occurrances*, dated 25 September 1690, needs more explanation than does its demise. The timing exploited thirst for news of the Bostonians' attack on Quebec. Earlier that year Harris had published a manual of military discipline,[92] and he would have gained a sense of the market for local military exploits after publishing *A Journal of Proceedings of the Late Expedition to Port-Royal* that summer.[93] Harris, who had earlier published a paper twice weekly in London and would do so again, revealed his acclimatization to Boston by promising a monthly paper "or if any Glut of Occurrences happen, oftener."

This Boston paper was unlike any of its successors for half a century in both format and content. The overwhelming concern with local news, which was wisely avoided by all successful pioneers of English or colonial newspapers, suggests that Harris was more concerned with the current local market for military news than with publishing a regular newspaper. Even Harris's reputation as a "brisk asserter of English Liberties"[94] does not explain the foolishness of his paper's report on Mohawk reluctance to join the forces under General Winthrop, then attacking Canada. The report itself would comfort the enemies of the Massachusetts Bay colony in the midst of a campaign, but Harris's concluding barb at the Indians was even less prudent.

> And if Almighty God will have Canada to be subdu'd without the
> assistance of thos miserable Salvages, in whom we have too much
> confided, we shall be glad, that there will be no Sacrifice offered up
> to the Devil, upon this occasion; God alone will have all the Glory.[95]

This was most irresponsible, and Harris's immediate disclaimer about the quality of the reports received only admitted and aggravated the offense. Perhaps Harris's earlier printing of *Propositions made By the Sachems of the Three Maquas . . .* had represented a confidence that proved misplaced.[96] Cotton Mather would defend Harris's paper as "not a Word said of the Maqua's, but what wee ought to say To them, or else wee bring Guilt upon oursels.'''[97] But even a friendly government could not have a printer determining diplomacy and weakening morale this way. The government order formally prohibited the paper on the obvious ground that it was unlicensed although other unlicensed printing had occurred.[98]

Some, like Cotton Mather, may have hoped that the ban on Harris's newspaper would be temporary, but the project was a rash one on other grounds than the rashness of its publisher. The military news was bad and would only get worse. The town of Boston in 1690 was small among English-speaking communities that launched a sustained newspaper in the next half century. Without a regular postal service, the news from and through neighboring ports would not be available, nor would there be posts to distribute the paper to a wider market than those in Boston who were interested and could afford a newssheet. The marriage of postal service and early newspapers in America and the official government sanction and support of the pioneers were essential features that were missing in Harris's venture. Given Harris's continuing influence on the colony's government in the four years after his first paper was stopped, it seems fair to suggest that he had other reasons than government prohibition for not attempting a newspaper in Boston again. His propensity for publishing a newspaper would remain, for he was publishing *The London Post* soon after returning to London in 1695. If his Boston paper was a serious attempt to begin the industry in English America, it was only a prototype and a warning. Its inappropriate organization, its dangerous localism, and its provoking editorializing would all be avoided by successful early colonial newspapers.

The *Boston News-letter* has a very special place in the history of English Atlantic communications. As the first English colonial newspaper and the only one for nearly 14 years after its founding in April 1704, the paper reflected views about the nature and age of news, as well as serving as an obvious model for its eventual competitors.

John Campbell was a Scottish-born Boston bookseller who followed his relative Duncan Campbell in the town's book business and the position of postmaster.[99] Within a year of becoming postmaster in 1702, John Campbell was sending hand-written newsletters to governor Fitz-John Winthrop of Connecticut, and it is likely that Campbell had other customers as well.[100] A successful newsletter service probably led Campbell to approach Bartholomew Green about printing his *News-letter*.[101] Although the perfectly logical connection between newsletter writing and newspapers had been made in London and the postmaster of Edinburgh had been involved in an early newspaper there, Campbell's was a new development. London newsletter writers thrived on providing information that could not be printed, and English provincial postmasters distributed newspapers from the capital, thereby discouraging local newspapers. Campbell's venture was different. His audience wanted the news, and Campbell was in no position to send along a regular supply of London papers. Wartime shipping embargoes and convoys made London papers even harder to obtain, making comparatively reliable news even scarcer and more precious than usual. While writing his manuscript newsletter, Campbell cited the *London Gazette*, the Whiggish *Post-man*, *Votes of Parliament*, the *Edinburgh Gazette*, and London newsletters, copies of which had been acquired by shipmasters at Lisbon or the Azores.[102] Campbell also gathered news directly from shipmasters, as well as from travelers and correspondents using the postal routes that now tied his town to those of New Hampshire, Rhode Island, Connecticut, New York, and Pennsylvania. Even before his own newsletter was printed, and needed postal distribution, the marriage of post office and news service was necessary just to gather information post-free. As the early colonial printers were bound to the local government by printing contracts, so the link between newspapermen and the post office became customary.

The *Boston News-letter*'s ties with the Massachusetts government have distracted students from the considerable merits of this social document. Certainly, it was subject to prepublication censorship by the colony's secretary, and the publisher was vulnerable as a postal officeholder.[103] It was also a kind coincidence that the paper began just as Governor Dudley was pressuring the Massachusetts General Court for increased defense spending in the wake of the Deerfield massacre. Boston was more at war in 1704 than she had been at any time since Harris's paper lived its short life in 1690. Yet it must be remembered that Campbell did not have a large local population from which to gain subscribers. He could not have sold anything as official as the *London Gazette* had become. His venture was more akin to the official papers of Edinburgh and Dublin although his search for subscribers was in a town little more than a tenth the size of these cities. Amid the considerable official influences, Campbell knew he had to sell papers well beyond the governor's circle and beyond the town of Boston. The governor did not buy all the papers.

The monopoly of the *Boston News-letter* was preserved for nearly 16 years because it was a precarious venture, not because of government controls. Printers in New York and Philadelphia watched the Boston pioneer build his market but were not tempted to compete. Direct evidence supports the suspicion. If there were two printings of number 1 of the paper,[104] there was soon no need to print in those volumes. At the end of his first year of publication, Campbell moaned about the trouble he had been at; defended his price in comparison with *Sam Farley's Exeter Post-Man*, which had started at the same time; and noted that he had lost money and needed more subscribers or a higher price.[105] A year later, when he successfully petitioned the Massachusetts General Court for a consideration as postmaster, Campbell described his paper as a money-losing public service.[106] In May 1711, when he was back to the authorities again for an allowance as postmaster and newspaper publisher, Campbell claimed to be disappointed with his seven-year-old newspaper "the charge and trouble whereof is very considerable, and income very small, seeing he cannot vend two hundred and fifty copies of one impression."[107] In August 1719, after 15 years of publishing without competition and less than 6 months before that monopoly would be shattered, Campbell told his customers that he was not selling 300 copies per issue.[108]

When it is remembered that most English provincial newspapers were selling approximately the same number of copies as Campbell sold after 1711, that he was selling more copies than the publisher of the Bristol's sole paper in 1712, and that his town was smaller than most of those boasting newspapers in England in 1719, his ambitions seem unrealistic. If the range of addresses of those advertising in the paper can be taken as a gauge of the range of regular subscribers, Campbell was selling most of his papers in Boston and those towns of Massachusetts, New Hampshire, Rhode Island, and Connecticut that were along the major post road. Copies reached New York and Philadelphia regularly and would scatter much further afield but not in sufficient numbers to prompt advertising. Whatever is made of the censorship to which Campbell submitted, it must be recognized that he succeeded in selling his paper regularly to from 200 to 300 New Englanders who could afford his price and were interested enough to pay.

The news that Campbell printed is very revealing in its emphasis, the order in which it was received, its age, and how Campbell explained all this to customers he dearly wanted to keep. He had, of course, a very clear pattern of what a newspaper was supposed to be, derived from those he had received, including the *London Gazette*. Although Campbell usually followed the prevailing practice of taking items from other newspapers without acknowledging the source, he did reveal his sources when he advertised in no. 67 that he was selling

> the Monthly Mercury's, London Gazette, Flying Posts, Observators, Post Man and Post Boys, either in Setts by the year or single; so that any person in Town or Country, in this or the Neighbouring Provinces, may have them on Reasonable Terms . . .[109]

Such an array represents a major improvement over the resources he had when writing his manuscript newsletter in 1703 and supports his claim that he ordered English newspapers by several ships bound to any ports between New Hampshire and Pennsylvania during the war.[110]

From sources that usually overwhelmed the space he had to transmit it in, Campbell selected materials that can be said to represent what he, the colony's secretary, and his customers regarded as worthy news. The first and usually the largest section of the two-page print was news from London, provincial English cities, Edinburgh, or Dublin. When explaining his priorities early in 1717, Campbell stated what had always been the case, that it was the chief news of Great Britain "which most nearly concerns us."[111] Occasionally, items from the English Caribbean were included here, as well as the odd story originating in Africa or even India. The English Atlantic empire outside North America seemed to dominate this major category of news, and the London metropolis was the dateline for most of the stories, as well as the source for most of the stories datelined elsewhere. Court news, addresses to the monarch, or proceedings of the English Parliament often gave the paper the look of one of its major sources, the *London Gazette*, as did elaborate coverage of diplomatic negotiations. Campbell probably pleased himself and his audience by including more news of the activities of the Scottish kirk than would come from London papers. In its early years, the *News-letter* included complete membership lists of the English House of Commons, which might consume most of the space in two issues. Prominent English marriages, appointments, or deaths were also a continuing feature of the paper, affording the politically active New Englanders the opportunity to write a courtesy note or redirect a request. As was true of all newspapers, natural wonders, curious inventions, and particularly barbarous crimes were regular features. Most of the crimes reported in the *Boston News-letter* were English—and especially London—doings. Although it might be argued that these stories of victims and villains were told as though some of the readers might know these people and all the readers could feel a comfortable moral superiority to their capital, it was also common to have crimes reported without any mention of names, as if to teach morality and immorality in general. There is no doubt, however, that the reader of the *Boston News-letter* was being encouraged to see news that was presented without special category, decorative divider, or special spacing as news of the English empire outside North America.

Generally, the *Boston News-letter* included some European news presented in a separate section and sometimes labeled "Foreign Advices." The military, diplomatic, and dynastic happenings of continental Europe were often excessively brief, though more elaborate accounts were used to fill a winter's issue long after the English news had been extracted and reprinted from the same issues of the London papers. The Boston merchants who were making marketing decisions in the fish trade would naturally rely on returning ship commanders for information and would get prompt news in Campbell's paper of the outbreak or threat of war in southern Europe, but they must have visited him for more than their mail when news-bearing ships brought packets of English papers. Although the treatment of the news from beyond the English and French spheres might be whimsical, Campbell presumed geographical knowledge. European cities were datelined, but the countries they were in were presumed. Very occasionally, an item from the beyond was given an explanation, like a later story from Chile, described as "a great Colony of South America, to the South of Peru, Subject to the King of Spain."[112]

A third major element in the *Boston News-letter* of the days of its monopoly was what was occasionally labeled "domestic advices" or "home news." The first of these labels covered stories from English colonies in North America or the Caribbean, and the less common "home news" tended to be New England stories.[113] Neither of these labels was used regularly; rather the British colonial datelines followed a space or decorative divider. Before competition emerged, the paper carried a small but regular report brought by postrider from New York and Philadelphia, including news items that arrived at those ports from the Caribbean or Britain, as well as a few local happenings and wonders. This whole category was usually less than an eighth of the small paper, and Boston news dominated there. Campbell was following the best practice of the English provincial press in staying clear of most local political news and confining much of his local material to shipping news. As with English provincial papers, local news would travel within the town faster than a weekly paper could hope to pace, and Campbell was reaching for a readership that was largely outside Boston itself.

The format and content of America's first newspaper reveals a concern for London news that is so striking that scholars of American colonial history have tended to dismiss the paper from serious consideration. The focus on London owed something to the war with France and something to the official nature of the paper, but it also represented the news that mattered most in English Atlantic centers.

In one most fascinating way, the *Boston News-letter* was a unique adventure into news, and it can be made to reveal aspects of time perception that other newspapers never faced as directly, painfully, or publicly. Campbell was faced with too much news for his half sheet (that is, two page) weekly, with news that literally came in shiploads that were irregularly spaced and with news that resolutely refused to come in order.[114] The editor explained to his readers how he was presenting news, which is nearly as revealing as the discussions of the age of the news in this first newspaper primarily concerned with transatlantic news.

Campbell told his readers in December 1706 that he would interrupt the orderly presentation of news whenever ships arrived from England, Portugal, or the Caribbean if there was news from the West Indies packet boats. At those times, he would summarize "the most remarkable Occurrences" and then return to where he had left off. By keeping a file of the paper, the reader would have the sequence of European or West Indian news.[115] Eighteen months later he left his readers in the middle of an exciting account of the Jacobite expedition to Scotland, lamenting that he wished he could go over to a full sheet when important news arrived but could not do so without more subscribers.[116] It would be 10 years before Campbell could go over to a full sheet every second issue, but a year thereafter he proudly announced that the extra space had allowed him to improve the freshness of his news from beyond Great Britain. Rather than being 13 months behind, he was now only 5 months behind and anticipated catching up within another 6 months.

Even after the arrival of competition, Campbell remained very concerned that his readers be able to grasp the "train of occurrences." In April 1722 the paper devoted a major portion of four issues to an index of foreign news items appearing the previous year, offering them by country and by month so that the holder of the year's papers could read the news from any country in dateline order. Clearly not pressed for space at this time, Campbell went on to give a summary of the past year and then to provide an index of British colonial news.[117] Bartholomew Green, who late in 1722 became publisher of the newspaper he had long been printing, gradually went further than Campbell had. By the spring of 1724, the *Boston News-letter* kept British news as up-to-date as possible. When he printed European news, it was in strict dateline order.

The struggle to impose so much order on the chaos of incoming foreign news did not end until the beginning of 1727, when Green changed the name of the paper to *The Boston, New England Weekly News-letter*. In the first issue under the new title, Green admitted that the old attempts to keep a thread of occurrences "has not been very acceptable to the Publick, nor Satisfactory to its Encouragers." He promised that he would henceforth print the latest and most remarkable foreign and domestic news as received, provided it was well attested. He would soon fall into the popular habit of presenting older European news under the dateline of the London paper the story came from. The colonial reader had been thought too interested in British news ever to have accepted its presentation so schematically; after 1727 the readers would have no editorial help with piecing together their own "thread of Occurrences" in European news either.[118]

The freshness of news was a much more general concern than was the *Boston News-letter*'s preoccupation with the order of news, but the two were intertwined in ways that make Campbell's frankness most interesting. Late in the summer of 1719, Campbell had proudly commented on the quickening pace at which he was presenting European news, and by September he was pleased to be only three and a half months behind the London datelined foreign news.[119] England was now at war with Spain again, which heightened the interest in the news and, by the end of the year, brought the birth of the rival *Boston Gazette*. As in the English provinces, it was safer to launch a rival paper in a town that had one already than to venture in a new area, and, again as in the English provincial towns, the new rival sold itself as the opponent of stale news.[120] Campbell was sensitive to the charge. His removal as postmaster of Boston in September 1718 meant that Campbell had less colonial news to offer and devoted more space to bringing more European news more quickly. By June 1720 Campbell proclaimed:

> He is now but about two Months short of London, and Vessels passage are sometimes three, and allowing two more Months from Foreign parts of Europe to London, which is often three, makes now the Thread of the News but four Months behind, so that every one that has this Intelligence by the Year, will be furnished with what is Material for them to know, in all the Publick Prints of London.[121]

If he believed this himself, he did not long remain convinced that his customers were. In less than a month he was back to the subject again, inviting people to notice the datelines,

> which some Persons may perhaps call old, seeing it give Accounts of Actions of Europe done in December last, six months past, which Occurrences were three Months before they came in Print to London, and from thence hither in the March Mercury, by the last Ships, and two Months more being allowed for their usual passage hither, brings the six Months to one.[122]

There is something jarring in this line of argument, and it is tempting to dismiss Campbell as hopelessly unconvincing. Here is one place where the differences in time-perception between Campbell's period and ours is a factor. He was not inclined to leave out a story on the grounds that it was embarrassingly old but rather sought to convince those whose doubt he anticipated. The following winter he prefaced two news items with defensive remarks about their age. The explanation that most clearly shows differences in time-perceptions concerned a year-old story from Sweden.

> The following Intelligence for this part of the World, tho' now a Year old as to time, cannot well be reckoned very old, considering it was three Months old ere they had it in London, in the March Mercury, and allowing other three Months the usual passage of Ships from thence hither, will make it but about six Months old.[123]

News that had been in Boston for six months could, if it concerned some place as remote as Sweden, be used to fill a midwinter issue of the paper as would certainly have been the case earlier. But now there was competition, and the item needed an explanation. The explanations reveal that news did not go stale nearly as quickly then, for Campbell could store some remoter items for six months and still sell them.

English America's second newspaper was no direct threat to John Campbell and has remained unknown to many historians of colonial newspapers. Robert Baldwin, who had just established a press in Kingston, Jamaica, with the special encouragement of the new governor, printed and published *The Weekly Jamaica Courant*, beginning May 1718. Baldwin was government printer of votes, speeches, and addresses, but he also produced broadsides, pamphlets, and almanacs and sold a wide range of stationer's wares. Baldwin distributed his paper in neighboring parishes by runner and conducted some postal service as well. His readers were paying 30s. a year for reprinted London news, official Jamaican proclamations, and local maritime news and death notes, as well as advertisements. A variety of North American newspapers would acknowledge reprinting items from the *Courant* during the next 20 years, and the paper may well have run longer.[124]

The Weekly Jamaican Courant of the new town of Kingston suggests several things about early colonial newspapers in addition to proving that this slave majority town of some 5000 people had a press by 1718. Jamaica was the furthest English Atlantic colony, and impending war made it further from British news that year. Kingston's place in newspaper publishing, ahead of Philadelphia and New York, challenges the easy assumptions about the "precocious development of the American newspaper" being related to mass literacy, scattered settlement, or rivalry between capitals of colonial politics and commerce.[125] The *Courant* began as a by-product of government printing as would all early newspapers started in English America to the south of Philadelphia. A newsman like Samuel Keimer would have preferred Barbados as a location from which to gather and dispense news to the English

American empire. Although little is known about Jamaica's *Courant*, this very early paper is proof that a small community that is literate, well-to-do, and hungry for London news could sustain a newspaper if the government printer were its publisher. All this would not have been much comfort to John Campbell, displaced Boston postmaster who did not do his own printing. He would need his very different setting to survive against direct competition.

The competition that exploded on the *Boston News-letter* late in 1719 would signal the beginning of a major transition for Boston's founding newspaper. The loss of the postmaster's place was something Campbell now deeply resented. His sources of colonial news seemed to diminish promptly, and he did not regularly send papers out by post thereafter although he did print some copies on a full sheet, leaving half blank so that purchasers could write letters and mail the whole to correspondents outside Boston. What was lost in intercolonial news and markets—and it became increasingly apparent that this was considerable by 1725—did not make the *Boston News-letter* more parochial as might be suggested by the later evolution of English provincial papers. Instead the paper focused more on overseas news than ever. It is significant that his paper was able to survive in competition with the better-connected *Boston Gazette*, which also was predominantly based on London news. The market for such news had definitely expanded.[126]

A dramatic change in the British colonial newspaper occurred in 1719. In June the colonies learned that they were at war with Spain[127] and almost immediately Campbell had become defensive about the age of his news. The beginning of Andrew Bradford's Philadelphia-based *American Weekly Mercury* on 22 December 1719, as will be seen, represented an attack on Campbell's weakest and least important market, that beyond Connecticut to the west and south. The challenge that was the most threatening, datelined the day before Bradford's first issue, was the first number of the *Boston Gazette*, published for the man who had succeeded Campbell as postmaster, William Brooker.

The fierceness of the initial verbal battling suggests that the antagonists thought Boston did not have room for two newspapers. Without granting any special level of literacy for this capital of Congregational education, Boston should have been ready for a second newspaper. With a population of 12,000 in 1719 and an established newspaper for 15 years, Boston had a market comparable with that of several English provincial towns. Norwich, Bristol, and Exeter, those towns that had led the movement to provincial newspapers, all supported two papers by 1719, with three in both Norwich and Exeter. Although the larger cities of Bristol and Norwich might not inspire a Boston newspaperman as a fair basis for comparison, Campbell's own earlier comparison with Exeter would be with a town having three papers in 1719.[128] Even more interesting was the case of Nottingham. A town of less than 9000 and one that did not have a paper before 1710, Nottingham boasted both a *Weekly Courant* and a *New Mercury* in 1719. Boston would continue to maintain more newspapers than any other English colonial city. However much he had complained about his circulation, Campbell had launched his paper in the right place and had built the beginnings of what would become a thriving and competitive business.

The *Boston Gazette* paid Campbell the compliment of fashioning itself after his paper to a very large extent. Brooker's introduction made it clear that his possession of the postmaster's position, which allowed him to serve a market outside Boston and to gather information from other postmasters on the continent, was a major inducement to launch a paper some 15 months after Campbell had been replaced. The only specific promise of new material, the inclusion of regular prices current for various commodities, met some immediate opposition from merchants and was carried out rather irregularly.[129] The new paper was official, would be printed for five different postmasters in succession, and would demonstrate its own caution and the success of the format that Campbell had begun and was continuing. The younger paper initially had the advantage in the controversy over old news, for it had nothing to catch up on itself. As Table 8.2 indicates, the difference in the age of their overseas news was noticeable but not dramatic. Competition between the first two papers in Boston had not caused one to become antigovernmental, had not prompted one to reach for a more literary market in essays, and did not prompt any dramatic improvement in the speed with which Bostonians were provided with the news that had arrived in the London papers. The format remained much the same although over time the newer paper included more official speeches, proclamations, and addresses concerning other colonial governments and offered a little more colonial news than Campbell had ever done regularly—and much more of this than Campbell was doing by 1719.

There was some evidence that postal connections to neighboring colonies helped to build the intercolonial market for the *Boston Gazette* at least by 1725. Advertisements for runaway servants, always a major feature of newspaper advertising, suggest the spread of the hinterland of the *Gazette*. Masters as far away as Trenton, New Jersey, Philadelphia, Annapolis, and even Newport, Virginia, advertised in this Boston paper for their missing servants.[130] Newspapermen themselves advertized for runaway servants in newspapers in neighboring colonies, perhaps with special reason, and were prepared to presume that fellow printers would help in returning the wayward servant.[131] The prize for the advertisement in an early colonial paper from farthest afield would have gone to the *Boston Gazette*, which carried the following item in August 1738:

> This is to Inform (as well as to Recommend) All Persons bound from this and the Neighbouring Colonys, who may happen to Land at or near Dover in England, That they may be Accommodated with suitable Entertainment: Also with Coaches and Horses to go from then[ce to] any part of England, by Mr. Thomas Jennings, at the Ship Inn and Post House in Dover aforesaid.[132]

The *Boston Gazette* illustrated another change that was coming over the production of newspapers. As more newspapers developed in England and

America, the newspapers became the premier source for each other. In the early days of the *Boston News-letter*, ship captains were asked for news; travelers and private correspondence were used to gain knowledge of happenings. Increasingly, the arrival of a ship with "the latest prints" was the source of news.[133]

Boston's first two papers were competing for essentially the same market. The *Boston Gazette* was a postmaster's paper,[134] as its competitor had been, and both provided a news service with a minimum of comment to an audience that must have been growing. The *Gazette* had effectively replaced the *News-letter*, but the town's first paper survived largely on London news. Their similarity, even in stiff competition, suggests that the news that readers in Boston and neighboring towns wanted remained essentially the same.

A striking new departure was made with the commencement of James Franklin's *New England Courant* in August 1721. Franklin had printed the *Boston Gazette* briefly[135] and now showed a shrewd sense of timing in starting a paper devoted to witty denunciation of ministers and governors of Massachusetts. Earlier that year the differences between the governor and the General Court had stalemated a censorship case,[136] and this, together with the popular resistance to smallpox inoculation urged by some leaders of the Boston community, gave Franklin the opportunity to imitate the *Spectator* of London at the expense of the powers of Boston. His claim, that he was selling more copies than either of his competitors, cannot be confirmed. He was running a paper without many ads for revenue and with an audience that must have been largely in Boston itself. Yet it is interesting that Boston would be given three papers each Monday as 1721 drew to a close, an output that must have exceeded 700 copies in all. It is not surprising that the three would come to choose three different days of the week before long.[137] Franklin's *Courant* promptly became a target for efforts to constrain publishing and is remembered as the launching pad for younger brother, Benjamin, but it should also be seen as accomplishing two other intriguing things. On the one hand, it represented a secular and sophisticated importation of English journalism of a pointed, witty, and satirical bent. On the other hand, its preoccupations with Massachusetts made it a local and a political paper to a degree not seen before. This was the first English-language newspaper anywhere to print a legislative division list.[138] The *Courant* did not live beyond June 1726; it was crippled by Benjamin Franklin's flight to New York and killed by James Franklin's migration to Newport, Rhode Island.

If Boston's first literary newspaper was begun by one displaced printer of the *Boston Gazette*, the successor to the *New England Courant* would be launched by another. Samuel Kneeland lost the printing of the *Gazette* on the death of Thomas Lewis in 1727, and in March he began publishing the *New England Weekly Journal*. Without the animus or antiministerial bias of the *Courant*, the new paper offered essays on morals and human foibles with some wit. Kneeland would soon take in T. Green as a partner in a paper that would run until 1741, when these partners bought out the *Boston Gazette* and merged the literary and news paper.

A clearer and sharper migration from literary essay to news paper could be seen in the life of the next Boston paper, The *Weekly Rehearsal.* Launched in September 1731 by Jeremiah Grindley, future attorney general of Massachusetts, this was a paper concerned with original and entertaining essays in its first year. From there the paper moved quickly to become a source of news not much different from the *Boston Gazette* and the *Boston News-letter*, with which it competed.[139] The market for intelligence was strong enough that Thomas Fleet, soon printer and by April 1733 proprietor of the *Weekly Rehearsal*, was able to find a market for this and for the more popular *Boston Evening Post*, which he replaced it with in August 1735. Boston also provided a market for yet another paper of foreign and domestic news when the postmaster Ellis Huske started another newspaper in October 1734. This *Boston Weekly Post-Boy* would go on for 20 years providing the town of Boston with yet another intelligence sheet.

Boston's appetite for news had been growing at a remarkable rate. The town supported two newspapers from 1719, three from 1721, four from 1731, and five from 1735. Two former postmasters, Campbell and Boydell, had continued to publish their own newspapers after losing control of the paper that it now was presumed every postmaster of Boston would produce. Two former printers of the *Boston Gazette* also launched papers of their own with apparent success.[140] The circulation figures for these papers are not known, but the vigorous expansion of papers did not lead to the destruction of any of them. By 1735 Boston was a port of some 15,000 people that was now well beyond English provincial towns in supporting five newspapers.[141] Although there was considerable variety available and all were not published on the same day of the week, all were essentially sources of English, European, and colonial news, with essays playing a minor role of particular use when news was thin. With posts reaching further south and with intercolonial shipping going through Boston at a rate of more than 300 ships a year, Boston's papers would scatter news widely even if the papers were initially sold in Boston. The incidental spread of English, European, and colonial news would be increased without distortion. The papers in this period, with the notable exception of James Franklin's *Courant*, which was also the shortest-lived of these papers, did not focus on being papers of New England news. The general circulation of information of value to the whole English Atlantic community seemed a marketable objective for all of Boston's papers by this time.

If, as R. M. Wiles has argued, the provision of fresher news was a common justification for launching a competing newspaper, Boston was treated to a number of such opportunities, and the pioneering *Boston News-letter* had to face all the competition. There was another pressure for speeding the printing of news already received although its dimensions cannot be clearly defined. Back in 1690, when Benjamin Harris began his *Publick Occurrences*, he gave his address as the London Coffee House in Boston. It might be tolerable to assume that his paper and prints that he might acquire from England were intended to be available to the clientele of this coffeehouse. Stronger evidence of this practice, which was common to inns and taverns as well as in coffeehouses in England, Scotland, and the colonies, is provided by an innocent ad in the *Boston Gazette*. In June 1726, Thomas Selby of the Crown Coffee-House in Boston advertised that he

> hath been and still is at considerable Pains and Expence in procuring the London & Boston Newspapers for the Entertainment of the Publick . . .[142]

and went on to complain that copies were being taken away to the prejudice of other readers. Five years later, Mrs. Read opened a "Chocolate House," where customers "may Read the News, and have Chocolate, Coffee or Tea ready made any time of the Day."[143] If Thomas Selby and Mrs. Read were able to provide newspapers from London for such as visited their premises, the publishers of Boston's newspapers were in a race to provide news before it was everywhere in town.

Competition among papers, coffeehouse reading, and the increase in shipping into Boston, as well as the increased availability of news from other colonies with the birth of their newspapers and improved posts, all contributed to a speeding up of the appearance of news from the London papers in those of Boston. The age of London-datelined news in the *Boston News-letter* from the first year of the paper down to 1739, shows a very dramatic improvement. Figure 5 indicates that the average age of London news dropped from 162 days in the hard years of the War of the Spanish Succession to 128 days by 1717 and continued to fall until the average was 83 days by 1739. Neither ship speed nor the number of ships arriving in Boston from Britain had changed greatly by 1739. The increased number of newspapers in England and the colonies was circulating information more quickly. The *Boston News-letter* proprietors were not postmasters in the 20 years after 1719, so this paper would have nothing but the proprietor's determination to assist him in this improvement. For Boston, the newspaper revolution was significantly shrinking the English Atlantic.

It was, in some ways, a new beginning. In a colonial town of 10,000 that had sustained printers for decades, a printer began a newspaper focusing on international news in the midst of a war. Andrew Bradford of Philadelphia began his *American Weekly Mercury* in December 1719. Bradford had apprenticed with his father, William Bradford, a former Philadelphia printer who was the official printer for New York in 1719, who then assisted his son with the launch and distribution of the *American Weekly Mercury*, and who would publish the *New York Gazette* from 1726 to 1744.

Andrew Bradford's paper combined an introductory essay or a speech by a British or colonial official with a general emphasis on the latest news. Foreign news always included good coverage of London events, but these were given a little less prominence than in the Boston papers and usually appeared after continental European news. News from other British colonies was a regular

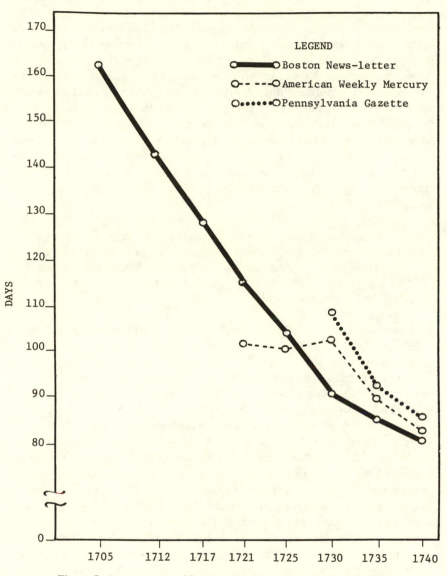

Figure 5. Average Age of London-Datelined News in Colonial Papers.

feature, with special emphasis on New York. Ship movements for Philadelphia and New York were given regularly, with sailings from other colonial ports noted often in winter. Bradford also attempted to provide prices current for commodities. Although the Philadelphia prices appeared frequently and those of New York, Boston, or Barbados were offered occasionally, this service was not regular enough to allow their systematic use either by merchants then or historians now. Bradford's paper gave considerable space to advertising, developing detailed woodcuts for that part of the paper as well as the well-known panel that was eventually atop the front page. Although the paper had room for Cato's letters and included an occasional original essay, the paper was very like the contemporary Boston offerings. News of England and the courts of Europe were the basic staple. One local scribbler, who successfully argued for space to describe a medicinal spring, began defensively:

> As I conceive our homeward News would be acceptable, and have a Place in your Mercury, as well as the Accounts of foreign Transactions, Leagues, Alliances, and the Course of the Politics of Nations, which perhaps will never affect us in these far distant, rough and woody Parts of the World . . .[144]

Although he was allowed to tell his story, this contributor's perspective was never shared by the editor. The distribution of news from abroad was, there as in Boston, what sold papers.

The masthead of the *American Weekly Mercury* was appropriately decorated with both Mercury and a postrider. Mercury reflected the ambitious title, which was probably a conscious imitation of the popular Whig *British Weekly Mercury* published in London by the Sun Fire Office. The postrider more accurately symbolized the paper. With his first issue, Bradford revealed his ambition to have customers from Hampton in Virginia to Newport in Rhode Island. Although he was not yet himself a postmaster, he was using postmasters as agents to take subscriptions and distribute papers.[145] It is also suggestive of the marketing anticipated that Bradford had no agents anywhere in Pennsylvania except himself. The paper was so closely bound to the postrider that the day of publication shifted from Thursday to Tuesday with the winter change in postal schedules, and publication was delayed as much as two days while waiting for the arrival of the New York post.[146] With a riverine location that was more susceptible to freezing, Philadelphia would have newsmen who were particularly anxious for winter news by way of New York and Boston. The inequality of these winter exchanges of newspapers would not last, for Philadelphia would have more winter news to exchange when the regular postal service was pushed south after 1730. Even if the tobacco fleets were not wintering over any longer, there were individual vessels from Britain and the West Indies into the Chesapeake when the Delaware was frozen.

The connection between New York and Philadelphia newspapers was made particularly strong by the family partnership between Andrew Bradford and his father. Jointly published books were advertised, as were services and property in New York. William Bradford became more formally linked to his son's paper as advertised salesman and joint owner between 1721 and 1725.[147] Despite his London training, William Bradford had not shown much interest in publishing a newspaper during his long career as a colonial printer to this point. He once reprinted a single copy of the *London Gazette*, but the timing of the first issue of the *New York Gazette*, of 8 November 1725, suggests that the 65-year-old Bradford had grown into the newspaper business by way of his son's venture.[148] The *New York Gazette* added nothing to the way colonial newspapers of an official type were conducted, but he found a market for news on the model of the earlier papers. Although he was not satisifed with his rate of return or the number of subscribers, his venture was expanding the number of colonials who could possess the same news at about the same time by the industrious reprinting of newspaper accounts by all the papers. The *New York Gazette* was a Monday paper timed to reprint news arriving by post, reminiscent of the *American Weekly Mercury* and the early Edinburgh papers.

William Bradford's period of local monopoly in New York lasted eight years, shorter than that of Boston or Philadelphia pioneer papers. In the case of New York, a new factor contributed substantively to the emergence of a second paper. Politics of opposition, so important to the multiplication of newspapers in London, first shows itself in full colonial battle dress in the emergence of the *New York Weekly Journal* late in 1733.[149] Governor William Cosby had not been in New York long before the alienation of many prominent leaders began. The "official" status of William Bradford's paper began to mean that the governor's position was printable, and his opponents' was not as accessible. The notion that pamphlet controversy was not enough to promulgate one's perspective is a comment on the growing strength of the newspaper. Deposed Chief Justice Lewis Morris and his friends contributed money; James Alexander, much of the writing talent; and John Peter Zenger, formerly an apprentice of William Bradford, served as printer. In these circumstances, the paper could begin without the usual market concerns and would soon benefit from the marvelous popularity of attacks on the governor. Unable to respond adequately in kind, Cosby would launch the abortive effort to silence Zenger that afforded that printer more immediate and eventual signficance than his modest talents might otherwise have warranted.[150]

William Parks, the most experienced originator of English provincial newspapers to bring his printing business to the colonies, was the first to launch newspapers south of Philadelphia. The beginning of his *Maryland Gazette*, probably in September 1727,[151] is a particularly interesting development in the emergence of the early newspapers of colonial America. Parks had been the pioneer editor of the first newspapers in two English towns, contributing the *Ludlow Post-Man* from October 1719 and the *Reading Mercury* from July of 1723. He and his wife, Elizabeth, migrated to Maryland by early 1726, at which time Parks was negotiating for government printing work. It was more than a year before opportunities developed for Parks. In September 1727 he launched his newspaper, timed to catch both the interest derived from yet another Anglo-Spanish war and the news of the death of George I.[152] Within a month of launching his paper, Parks was made printer to the government. It need not be thought that the colony's only printer was being leashed with the patronage of official printing. By the spring of 1728, Parks was also postmaster in Annapolis.[153] Yet it is important to notice that Parks proceeded from being a newly arrived printer to a newspaper publisher fairly quickly and that his positions as official printer to the government of Maryland (1728–1731) and postmaster of Annapolis (1728–1732) were subsequent to the launch of his paper.

Starting a newspaper in Annapolis, Maryland, in 1727 was a task that would require all the notable talents of William Parks. The town itself, with perhaps 3000 souls, was a much smaller immediate market than any attempted colonial newspaper to date. The lack of postal services in the colony and beyond it was also a considerable and unique problem. Within seven months of starting the paper, Parks was cooperating with Andrew Bradford in establishing a postal service between Philadelphia and Annapolis once a month.[154] Comparative isolation was more than offset, at least for modern critics of colonial newspapers who find the *Maryland Gazette* comparatively literate and literary, by Parks's introductory essays. As much as half of the four-page paper was devoted to essays on a wide variety of subjects, including the popular "Plain Dealer" essays. News coverage emphasized "foreign Affairs," with a London focus. The paper gave less space to commodity prices current and ship movements and more to local poetry and prose. Universal themes were stronger in this more isolated paper. Although the circulation of the paper cannot be estimated and the advertising quickly became as significant a part of the paper as of most of the day, there are signs that the venture was ahead of its market. Publication was suspended in 1731 and 1732. Even before that, Parks began printing in Williamsburg as well. He became public printer for the colony of Virginia in 1732 and would hold that post until his death in 1750. Although the *Maryland Gazette* did not end until 1735, Parks had left Annapolis in 1732. He would go on to establish the *Virginia Gazette* in 1736, his fourth newspaper pioneering venture and the one that would last the longest, for he was still publishing it in 1750.

The short life of the *Maryland Gazette* was not at all typical of colonial newspapers[155] but rather suggests that in Annapolis even a very good newspaperman could not yet start a paper that would survive his immediate attention. The very good paper he produced was his own, and its literary pieces were often by locals. His news was less comprehensive than that available elsewhere, but it was the best available in the Chesapeake Bay. Williamsburg would allow him more of a market even before the postal services he helped to initiate reached both north to Philadelphia and south as far as Charles Town. For sources of information and for markets, these new developments certainly helped confirm the recent wisdom of Parks's migration from Annapolis to Williamsburg. He had ventured into the Chesapeake ahead of an effective postal system, would help develop it, and reaped the rewards. How very different from the sequence established by earlier papers in the colonies, and how similar to the beginnings of the *South Carolina Gazette* further to the south.

Between the beginning of Parks's *Maryland Gazette* and the start of the *South Carolina Gazette*, the most significant development in colonial newspapers occurred in Philadelphia. By 1723 two migrants had arrived in Philadelphia who would affect printing and newspapers in the town that had to date been Andrew Bradford's preserve. The first of these was Samuel Keimer, a London-trained printer who was soon printing contentious pamphlets, selling books, but hardly presenting a challenge to Bradford's business at this stage.[156] Benjamin Franklin, who has dominated the records with his version of the story, worked for Keimer on Franklin's first arrival in Philadelphia and again after his return from London. According to Franklin, he himself had the idea of challenging Bradford's *American Weekly Mercury* with something weightier. By 1728, Franklin and his friend Hugh Meredith had begun the third printing house competing for the business of the Quaker capital of about 11,000. Whether Keimer stole Franklin's idea or not, the former sold the first issue of his *The Universal Instructor in all Arts and Sciences; And Pennsylvania Gazette*, dated 24 December 1728. Keimer sought to emphasize the lead articles, giving much space to extracts from the new Chamber's dictionary. The market was not there for this type of paper, or at least Keimer was unable to gain 100 subscribers after running the paper for nine months.

Franklin, whose plans to launch a newspaper of his own had been disrupted by Keimer's venture, first aided Bradford by ridiculing the new rival. Franklin and Meredith then bought out Keimer's newspaper business and began the paper known simply as the *Pennsylvania Gazette*. Keimer had apparently not prospered in Philadelphia,[157] and, with the sale of his newspaper, he migrated again, this time to Barbados. His *Barbados Gazette* provided Bridgetown and its visitors with what was the first paper in America to publish regularly twice a week. Keimer continued to publish until the end of 1738. He died soon after, but his last paper lived on. There is much to explain the success of this first paper in Barbados by a printer who could not succeed as the second newsman in Philadelphia, when his competition was both the postmaster and government printer. The beginning of a semiweekly paper at Bridgetown reflects the news-gathering strength of this first English Caribbean landfall. Keimer's success is easier to explain than the fact that this opportunity still awaited him.

Franklin certainly grasped the advantages over his remaining competitor in Philadelphia. Franklin soon managed to displace Bradford as postmaster of Philadelphia and, in 1730, as government printer. Whereas Franklin emphasized his own ability and industry, his rapid rise was also built on political shrewdness. Yet both Bradford and Franklin would prosper in Philadelphia.

Contracts for government printing had often been related to the emergence of a newspaper in the colonies. Colonial governors and assemblies showed an interest in having their proclamations and laws printed. This concern may have been related to the assumption of an adequate number of literates to inform the other colonists, and it may also have been related to the weakness of the legal practice that made an acquaintance with the laws as much a necessity as an avocation among those planters and merchants who could not rely on attorneys, stewards, or others to bring familiarity with law, especially colonial law, to the conduct of affairs. This government concern had brought William Bradford to New York, had encouraged Andrew Bradford and then Benjamin Franklin in Philadelphia, was central to William Parks's adventuring to Maryland and his migration to Virginia, and would be particularly important in the beginning of printing and newspapers in Charles Town, South Carolina. Leonard Levy's assertion that it was the colonial legislatures that most harried the printers is true, but it should also be remembered that legislators also encouraged printers.

The government of South Carolina considered seeking a printer as early as 1712, and a decade later an unsuccessful effort was made to attract a printer to Charles Town with an offer of a substantial loan to aid with establishing a press.[158] In 1731, when fast-growing Charles Town was still a town of less than 5000, the government renewed its search with better terms and much better results.[159] Eleazar Phillips, born and apprenticed in Boston, won the South Carolina government subsidy and published the *South Carolina Weekly Journal* (no copies of which have survived) for some six months before his death in July 1732. Thomas Whitmarsh was a London-trained compositor whom Franklin hired as a journeyman in 1730 and who went to Charles Town as Franklin's partner in a new business.[160] Although initially unsuccessful in winning the subsidy, Whitmarsh did launch the *South Carolina Gazette* in January 1731/2, and soon succeeded Phillips as government printer.

The *South Carolina Gazette* was modeled on Franklin's *Pennsylvania Gazette*, meaning that it afforded some space to essays, letters, and poems while maintaining a primary concern for news. The *South Carolina Gazette* announced a special concern for merchants and fulfilled this with fairly regular prices current and some export statistics, as well as ship movements. Like Parks's ventures in the colonies, the new Charles Town paper had more space for literary materials than was customary further north. It is plausible to attribute this to southern cultural preference although the absence of regular postal facilities certainly fostered the habit. Boston's first paper, by way of contrast, had been prone to fill in winter issues with older European news in the war years. After 1720 the appetite for such news did not compare with the popularity of the wittily written essays, letters, and poems that became a characteristic element of some colonial papers and some English provincial papers and had been inspired by several specialized London papers.

Whitmarsh was not long to enjoy the success of his joint venture with Franklin, for he died within days of printing the eighty-sixth weekly issue of his paper on 8 September 1733. Franklin soon despatched a new partner, who would collect a new subsidy and reestablish the *South Carolina Gazette* in the hands of a family that would edit the paper for the rest of the colonial years. Lewis Timothy was a Dutch printer, another journeyman recruited by Franklin, in this case to replace Whitmarsh when he had gone south to Charles Town. Timothy had been in charge of Franklin's very unsuccessful venture with a German language newspaper.[161] Although Lewis would live less than five years after reviving the Charles Town paper, his widow and then his son, whom Franklin had wisely included in the original agreement, continued the work.

Like William Parks's pioneering papers of the south, the *South Carolina Gazette* was begun with the arrival of printing to its city and in advance of postal connections with the shipping and news centers further north. Indeed, the paper began with no distribution system at all. Town subscribers were invited to "send a Negro" for copies on Saturdays after 3 P.M., and country subscribers were told that copies would be held for them at the printing office.[162] Seven years after the Charles Town paper was begun, the postal links through Edenton, North Carolina, to Virginia were established with notable participation by both William Parks and Peter Timothy. Again the pioneeer printer of the south valued access to regular news from the north more than he feared the competition of the newspapers carried by postriders.

Thirteen newspapers were being printed in English America in 1739. Presses in Bridgetown, Kingston, Charles Town, Williamsburg, Philadelphia, New York, and Boston were gathering, scattering, and exchanging news. Many more newspapers would be added in the next generation, and the papers would come to serve powerful local political purposes.[163] It is valuable to recognize the place of the challenges to authority that in retrospect make pioneers like Benjamin Harris, James Franklin, or John Peter Zenger memorable among the earlier journalists; but it is equally important to emphasize that they did not represent their peers, most of whom derived a living from supplying a growing colonial interest and need for the "freshest advices" of the outside world, especially news of the empire of which they were a part.

The pioneering newspapers of Boston, Philadelphia, and New York had all come some time after printing in those towns. The papers arrived at a time that does not at all suggest any special colonial hunger for newspapers. The towns were of a size comparable with some English provincial towns that pioneered newspapers, and competition had not come early to these colonial newsmen. By the mid-1730's, however, Boston was second only to London in the number of newspapers published in any city of the English Atlantic empire. Boston's strength in the newspaper industry rested not only on access to sizable local and regional markets but also on the city's advantages in access to news from England.

The overwhelming similarity between the various colonial newspapers of the period down to 1740 illustrates how they imitated each other as well as

English papers. In some respects, the *Boston News-letter*'s struggles with the train of occurrences and the age of its news revealed more uniqueness than most colonial papers. Emergence of the essay in the colonial papers was imitative of English practice, but afforded the likes of Benjamin Franklin and William Parks an opportunity to display colonial talent for universal themes and also revealed that local identity was definitely not being cultivated by the colonial papers of this period, even when they ran out of news.

Physical and political geography invited some considerable differences in the pattern of colonial and British newspapers. With the possible exception of some English sugar islands, where the supply of English papers may have limited the development of a local press, the colonial newsmen did not face much competition from London papers. Presence of copies of them in the coffeehouses may have urged prompt coverage of major items by the colonial paper, but there is no evidence of a distribution system in the colonies for London papers comparable to those functioning in England, Scotland, and Ireland.[164] London was the capital of colonial culture, as the papers constantly demonstrated, but the capital was not controlling the emergence of the colonial press to anything like the degree that the capitals of the centralized kingdoms of Scotland and Ireland did. Boston was the first and the greatest colonial newspaper town, but neither politics nor geography helped Boston papers control other colonial markets for news.

Government played a varied role in the emergence of newspapers in England and her dependencies. The potential of a court-controlled news organ was realized soon after James I was as unsuccessful in halting the import of news as he was the import of tobacco. The emergence of a controlled official press may well have reached its apex in the *London Gazette*, an organ that also suggests the sterility that such patronage and control can allow. After 1695, when English newspapers developed rapidly, a predictable politics of newspapers developed almost immediately. The English provincial press tended toward the opposition and was harder to control from London than was the case with the Scottish and Irish papers.

The links between the government and the press were more ambiguous in the case of the colonies. Government printing was a major support to pioneering printers in the colonies. Boston's printers did not start the first papers, but they would be as concerned about government attitudes as were the postmasters who did start the papers. William Bradford's experience in both Philadelphia and New York revealed the value of a favorable government to a man who learned his lesson, migrated on the invitation to become an official printer, and did nothing to jeopardize that position when he eventually published a newspaper. The governments of Jamaica, Maryland, Virginia, and South Carolina brought in the men who launched their papers while serving as government printers. The *Weekly Jamaica Courant* was a particularly clear and early demonstration that newspapers with some government support could survive without any local evidence of egalitarianism or mass literacy. The connection with the governments was only reinforced by the special colonial links between the post offices and the newspapers.

Benjamin Franklin's success against the established and satisfactory paper of Andrew Bradford was based on displacing him both as postmaster of Philadelphia and printer to the government of Pennsylvania. These links to the colonial governments did not, however, bring the pioneering newspapers into local politics quickly or obviously.[165] Official proclamations and speeches were printed in newspapers that emphasized the events of the Atlantic world and thereby encouraged a larger view of some issues, a view usually shared by the governor and the imperial authorities who had sent him. Yet local politics was not the purpose or the subject of the newspapers. The harassment of Benjamin Harris, William Bradford, James Franklin, and John Peter Zenger were all related to their venturing into local politics. The central place of the colonial assemblies in these controls, except in the unsuccessful attempt of Governor Cosby to silence Zenger, emphasized the ambivalence of colonial governments. They subsidized colonial printers but would not tolerate criticism in the press.

As has been seen, there were several forces prompting colonial and English provincial newspapers to emphasize cosmopolitan news and themes in their essays. In the English provincial towns, there were pressures from local authorities, but the news market also demanded that stale local gossip was not provided by papers struggling for broader geographic distribution and sustained readership. The prominent place of war in the timing of new papers suggests the same tendency in the market for news. Certainly, the same preoccupation is as evident in Dublin and Edinburgh papers as it is in the colonial papers. Indeed, London papers were the only ones that indulged in much local news, and the most bizarre of this became a regular, if minor, theme in English-language newspapers everywhere else at this time. Censorship may have ensured that colonial newspapers, like those of Dublin and Edinburgh, avoided sensitive political issues, but governments were not the markets for the papers. The overwhelming impression given by the papers printed down to 1740 is one of local markets for such news of the outside world as was available and at all of interest. As a result, the newspapers were a growing force in the integration of isolated communities. The exchange of news stories between papers, the preoccupation with London as a source and broker of news for the colonies, and the attending improvement in colonial post and shipping exchanges—all these contributed to this tendency. Later newspapers throughout the English-speaking Atlantic may well have fostered and supported local identity. In the period down to 1740, newspapers were making the English Atlantic community better informed about political, economic, and social events of consequence to the whole.

9 · The Packet Boats, 1702–1715

Mail packet boats contributed to Atlantic communications quite differently from the posts and the papers. Although the posts and the papers expanded, however irregularly, down to 1740, the packet boats were an extraordinary initiative that was not sustained. Yet during the War of the Spanish Succession, the English government launched two experiments in transatlantic mail services that went far beyond the occasional hiring of a sloop to deliver despatches. The origin, performance, and fate of these experiments, in particular the West Indies packets of Edmund Dummer, demonstrate something of the purposes and presumptions of those involved and the nautical and financial possibilities, as well as the limitations, of English Atlantic communications.

Edmund Dummer's remarkable West Indies packet service did not begin because of the sufferings of the English West Indian colonists in the previous war. In the summer of 1701 the English government was sure that a war with France over the Spanish empire was coming—sure enough to instruct Admiral Benbow to seize the Spanish treasure fleet in the West Indies on its homeward passage and then notify the English empire that the war had begun.[1] The prospect of provoking war in the Caribbean for export to Europe was the first of a series of circumstances that would give Edmund Dummer his opportunity.

While the future duke of Marlborough and Sidney Godolphin were exchanging notes about the bellicose instructions for Benbow, Edmund Dummer approached Robert Harley, Speaker of the House of Commons, with a proposal for "monthly intelligence" between London and the West Indies.[2] Dummer was an accomplished shipwright, a noted dockyard expert, a surveyor of the Royal Navy, MP for Arundel, and already concerned with packet boats between England and the Netherlands.[3] Robert Harley had been receiving information from Dummer for years, and Dummer chose well in beginning with the Speaker.[4] Harley had influence with the ministry that went well beyond his formal position, and he was particularly susceptible to Dummer and his proposal. Although a moderate Tory without great attachment to war at sea, Harley had an interest in the West Indies and was as preoccupied with intelligence networks as he was with domestic political intrigue.[5] Harley would later hear Dummer's accounts of the political progress of the scheme, would be urged to help, thanked, and claimed as Dummer's particular friend.[6] Yet Harley was most important initially as a means of obtaining the support of Sidney Godolphin. As partner of Marlborough in English political management and custodian of the Treasury through much of Queen Anne's first decade, Godolphin was vital to the beginning and the continuation of the packet service. Godolphin had been pressing for military initiatives in the Caribbean in 1700 and 1701, had a good opinion of Dummer, and would have the Treasury bail him out of financial difficulties several times.[7]

Dummer's connections through Harley would be central to the launching of the packet service and vital in its survival, but his rather fortuitous usefulness to the earl of Nottingham was also initially helpful. Daniel Finch, second earl of Nottingham, might well be regarded as the first secretary of state for the English empire. With his appointment as secretary of state for the Southern Department in May 1702, he immediately invited colonial governors to funnel all correspondence through himself, and he fought for increased control of colonial offices.[8] His commitment to war with Spain was considered too rigid on more than one occasion and very vigorous from the moment war was declared. His position made him pivotal in the development of a West Indies packet service, and his interests did much to help the project.

Problems of imperial communications were revealed to Nottingham promptly on his entering office. His reasonable request, that the Admiralty send out duplicates of his letters announcing the declaration of war, met with a surprising response. A secretary of the Admiralty replied that duplicate orders for Jamaica could be sent by two men-of-war bound there.

> But as to the Lres to Berbadoes, New England, Virginia, Pensilvania, Leeward Islands Carolina & Bermuda I do not know what way to contrive to send them forward, for the Vessell that carryed the originalls to the Continent (which were all forwarded from Virginia) Sayled Some time before his Lordps Intentions to Send Duplicates, And so did the Vessell to Berbadoes, and at present I cannot find any others within Reach to take charge of them;[9]

Surely sending duplicates by the same ships as the originals was not sending duplicates at all. Sudden wartime demand for naval vessels was evident here as elsewhere. Admiralty Secretary Burchett went on to suggest the equally useless idea that the duplicates for the eastern Caribbean be sent to Benbow at Jamaica for forwarding. Whether or not Nottingham remembered it, a Jamaican Council had told him nearly a decade before that it was quicker to send mail from Jamaica to England than from Jamaica to Barbados.[10] A series of negotiations with shipmasters produced a way to send the duplicates and revealed what war did to communications.

Sending news to the West Indies was uncertain, and hearing from Jamaica on a regular basis became more difficult just when it became more necessary. Before the end of May, a secret committee, including Nottingham, Godolphin, William Blathwayt, and Sir David Mitchell, began strategic planning of a major West Indian expedition.[11] As the summer progressed, this expedition, to be headed by the earl of Peterborough, was replaced by a preoccupation with capturing the Spanish treasure fleet under the escort of a French fleet commanded by Châteaurenault. The excited English missives to a squadron in the Soundings and to their fleet besieging Cadiz demonstrate the crumbs of Caribbean information available concerning the sailing of a Franco-Spanish fleet of more than 30 major ships.[12] The time between the known sailing and the effective posting of the squadrons spoke volumes on the need for better communication with the West Indies to accomplish a prime object in the strategic considerations of the English. A secretary of the navy lamented that storm damage to the Soundings fleet would hurt the hunt.

> However there is hopes that Wee shall not alone suffer, but that Monsr. Chateau Renault, with his Floating Magazines of Silver, will be soe divided and Shatter'd, as that some of his Ships at least may fall into our hands, or bribe God Neptune with part of the Treasure which Lewis is gapeing after, to enable him the longer to disturb Europe.[13]

The silver was landed at Vigo Bay before the English attacked the Franco-Spanish fleet so successfully. Better information from the West Indies could have made the difference.

Nottingham did not need most of this evidence to set the bureaucracy to thinking about a packet service. Less than a week after Burchett had told him there were no ships for the duplicate declarations of war and the day after the first known meeting of the Secret Committee planning the Peterborough expedition, Nottingham sent the Board of Trade a copy of Edmund Dummer's proposal to provide a monthly packet service to the West Indies.[14]

In Dummer's plan, four vessels of 130 tons would leave London at monthly intervals on a voyage of less than four months during which they would stop at each of the five major English islands in the Caribbean.[15] Dummer displayed his characteristic confidence when he pointed out:

> This constant course of going out & coming home after ye first four or five Months, will answer for all Incid. Occasions of state & Trade & effectually conduce to the Security of the publick Interest depending between this Kingdome and thos Islands in Peace and Warr.[16]

Presenting the proposal as "A Scheam for Forreign Advice" was a clear indication of Dummer's grasp of the strategic needs that would have a wider appeal than Nottingham's administrative interests. As the plan ran the gauntlet of administrative review, it was known to have support from three powerful politicians. As will be seen, the service would survive until two of those were out of office and the third had converted to a peaceful Spanish policy.

When Dummer's proposal went to the Board of Trade, they showed an understandable interest in turning it into a system of more general colonial communication. They were impressed with what the proposal could do for government correspondents and for merchants in the West Indies trades but were unhappy with much of the proposal. Dummer would never let them forget that they regarded his proposed round-trip time of 111 days as "more than can be perform'd in the time limited or in a much longer time." The board suggested an alternative involving three separate packet routes: one to Antigua and Barbados; one via Nevis for Jamaica, which "for the importance of the Place, deserve a distinct Settlement of the same kind"; and one for the North American colonies, using Cape Henlopen as a centrally located western terminus. If maintaining 12 packets might be unrealistic, the board preferred fewer packets per year on those three routes rather than Dummer's West Indian packet-a-month. Only one of their suggestions affected the service, and that was the sensible idea of Falmouth rather than London as the English terminus of the service, and this suggestion was probably politically motivated.[17] The West Indies packets were not undertaken with any serious concern for routine colonial administration.

Experts at the Navy Board and the Post Office provided careful scrutiny of the proposal from other angles. Dummer had originally suggested that he would rent his sloops to the queen at 10s. per ton a month, with her providing men, victuals, and guns. He was talked into another version that had him cover these other costs and be paid at just over £1 a ton a lunar month for each ship. Both the Navy Board and the postmasters general were satisfied that the service was cheaper than could be provided otherwise, and royal approval was given promptly.[18] The government had approved an annual expenditure of more than £6000 after less than a month of departmental review.

As was frequently the case, royal approval was not enough. When the Navy Board was instructed to complete the arrangements with Dummer, the Admiralty rejected any notion that the funds would come from the Royal Navy.[19] When reporting this impasse to Harley, Dummer showed shrewdness by suggesting that the Admiralty should oversee the other conditions but that the Treasury should provide the money. He added that the unexpected delay could affect his chance of reelection as MP for Arundel.[20] But the political managers were even shrewder. Only after Edmund Dummer was again MP for Arundel did they undertake the rather easy task of securing him in the government interest. Henry Guy, political manager for Godolphin,[21] made it all sound simple in a letter to Harley.

Mr. Dummer came to me about his proposal for sending vessels still to the West Indies, which hath hung so long. I brought him to the Lord Treasurer, who upon a full discourse of the matter, went so heartily into it, that he despatched and settled the thing that very day at the Council, and I think Mr. Dummer's first boat sails on Monday next. I find that without this method the proposal had never took effect, or at least not in a long while.[22]

As will be seen, the financial arrangements were quite unlike the negotiated position of Dummer and the experts,[23] but the last hurdles had been overcome in August 1702, and the packet service was to begin.

Dummer's West Indies packet service was born of war and politics. At one level, it was born of the "blue water" strategy of Nottingham, Rochester, and lesser Tories like Blathwayt. Such support could be expected to weaken with the abandonment of the Peterborough expedition, as well as giving a precarious political cast to the enterprise. At another level, the packet service bound its author to Lord Godolphin and the moderate Marlborough-Godolphin ministry. Yet the sustained and expensive packet service survived longer than Dummer's good timing and good connections. The packets were not designed to solve the communications problems of the Board of Trade although they would later claim a major role in launching the service and remark that the service to the West Indies brought regular opportunities to correspond with all the mainland colonies.[24] With all the purposes that found use for Dummer's packet service, the origins are understandable. What is more intriguing is that the service outlasted several of these purposes, yet continued to draw financial support from a hard-pressed wartime government.

During its nearly nine years of life, the West Indies packet service went through three distinct phases, each revealing particular aspects of the adventure. During the initial two years, the experimental service ran close to its founding purpose. Thereafter the packets became more significant as scheduled carriers of small valuable cargoes from Plymouth, and in its final years the packet service was slower, more erratic, and less profitable as was English participation in the Spanish colonial trade. Because the major dificulties of the service proved to be financial rather than navigational, it is not surprising that these three phases were related to the terms of the agreement between Dummer and the crown.

Whatever he might have thought about the difficulties that arose when the Admiralty refused to fund the packets, the outcome was a blessing for the supposedly naive Dummer. In the final arrangement, the packets were to be run under agency at the queen's expense. Dummer was to be advanced money to fit out the vessels, pay wages, and provide victuals; and the queen would repay Dummer the appraised value of sloops captured or lost. In return, the queen was to have the postage, freight, and passage money earned by the packets. With the Post Office and the Navy Board in a position to oversee all aspects of the experiment, both Dummer and the crown were undertaking a well-monitored experiment. Under these terms, Dummer could win a good reputation for his packets, and his venture seemed relatively free from risks.

Dummer had proposed a monthly sailing to the West Indies, disregarding seasons, and claimed to be able to perform the round-trip in about 100 days. It was this proposal that Dummer undertook in the face of the incredulity of the Board of Trade and "many of the Best Seamen in England."[25] Although he never managed a monthly sailing, the nine sailings in the first year defied the seasons and averaged 104 days. On the second voyage of the service, the 134-ton *Mansbridge* would achieve the best time for the whole service, 93 days from leaving Falmouth to return. (See Table 9.1.) To Dummer's continuing and understandable pleasure, the sloops he transferred from his other packet services (to Brielle and Lisbon) proved entirely able to travel the North Atlantic circuit in the time he had promised.

The 13 voyages completed under the agency arrangement and the 3 vessels lost to French privateers should have provided more than enough evidence to allow a full understanding of the possibilities and the problems of the packet service. With both Dummer and the Post Office possessed of the full details of costs and proceeds, both parties should have been able to decide sensibly whether the service would be better integrated into the Post Office, contracted to Dummer, or dropped. In view of Dummer's eventual bankruptcy and his charming capacity to appear as a simple shipwright trying to serve his country, historians have been too ready to make the government the villain of the piece.[26]

The sloops had demonstrated that the passages were possible, yet they also revealed that Dummer's plan for three round-trips per year for each packet was unrealistic. The best time for three trips in a row for the same vessel was about 13 months.[27] Although Dummer never admitted that the mere 3 weeks he allowed between voyages was unrealistic, his recognition of the problem came with his later proposals for 5 sloops instead of 4.

The revenue possibilities of the service could also be estimated from the initial operations. Under the agency, the Post Office handled the postage, but Dummer was in a position to learn what was collected. The very first packet brought home about 1500 private letters, yielding something over £56.[28] Two years later the return mail on a single packet boat yielded postage of £316.19.0. This was excellent growth of the service, which was now bringing home the equivalent of about 8500 private letters per packet. Yet the Post Office remained correct in claiming that the service was still very far from being able to pay its own way.[29] Dummer's reaction was to propose a massive increase in rates, assuming this would not affect volume. Passenger revenue on the first packets was slight, as the cramped quarters of the single-decked sloops that launched the service could not attract many travelers simply by promising quick passage. Dummer would reflect on this with his usual optimism, estimating a major increase in passenger traffic with the introduction of larger ships.[30]

Freight earnings were deliberately low under the agency. The initial agreement stipulated that only gold, silver, and cochineal could be brought home in the packet boats. Dummer's instructions to his commanders stipulated that there was to be no freighting of goods, and he made it clear that hauling goods would delay the service.[31] As the freight and passenger earnings for the first six voyages totaled less than £400,[32] it would not appear to be a very promising part of the packet service.

There were some things about the freighting that Dummer was not sharing with the postmasters general. Of the 13 completed voyages under the agency, fully 11 brought some return cargo into English customs. The beginnings were miniature cargos of a few hundredweight of indigo, sugar, and lime juice.[33] Indigo became a substantial part of this small traffic. If the first entries were without Dummer's knowledge, he probably knew of the shipments imported by his son, William.[34] The trend seemed complete when the *Prince* returned in February 1705 after her slowest passage (116 days) to unload five tons of cargo. With wartime freight rates from Jamaica at about £16 per ton, this was a tidy bonus.[35]

Commodity imports from Jamaica could not be a major aspect of the economics of the packets, however, and could not have been much of an incentive for Dummer to seek the right to carry small cargoes, as he would do as part of renegotiating his arrangement with the crown. It was the regular, convoy-free export of valuable cargoes to Jamaica—and through Jamaica for the Spanish Main—that would be a growing incentive late in the agency period. There had been small cargoes earlier, but from the summer of 1704 the packet boats were carrying valuable cargoes of cloth and manufactures outward bound.[36] The abrupt shift in home port from Falmouth to Plymouth early in 1705 is clearly related to this new opportunity that Dummer saw and the Post Office did not. Freighting out manufactured goods and freighting home bullion may have been important calculations that Dummer could do and his Post Office counterparts could not. Certainly, some of his arguments make more sense if these possibilities are kept in mind.

Whereas the agency period had allowed Dummer to see some of the possibilities, it also revealed the problems. The most dramatic and obvious problem was the loss of packet boats to French privateers. Even during this period of minimum cargoes and maximum speeds, 3 of 16 voyages ended with capture in the Channel. The crown covered these losses completely, but the rate of loss should have warned Dummer. A 19 percent loss rate was exactly what the service would suffer throughout its nine-year history (see Table 9.2), yet Dummer was repeatedly dismayed and distraught and in need of special assistance because the loss rate remained the same after he took the risks of the service on himself.

The packet service also had difficulty attracting and keeping mariners despite some inducements. Crewmen were paid premium wages for duties that were comparatively light, for the sloops were overmanned for their size even if they carried extra sail, and the men were immune from the navy press gangs.[37] These advantages were more than offset by several shortcomings. Crewmen were not allowed the small freighting ventures that were common on merchantmen, and privateering was strictly forbidden even though the sloops had letters of marque.[38] It was also true that crewmen were given no "smart money" if injured, nor did they have access to Greenwich hospital, which was reserved for wounded naval seamen. Therefore men aboard the packets were exposed to considerable risk as targets for privateers without any compensation arrangements.[39] Finally, though Dummer did not mention it until he wanted to use larger sloops, crewmen did not like sailing the Atlantic in all seasons in a single-decked sloop. Although the death rate was low, Dummer mentioned that crewmen often suffered from "languishing distempers" on their return.[40] It was also true that there would be little shore leave in this service unless one could skip the occasional voyage. Long before nonpayment of wages made one crew refuse to sail,[41] the problems of manning the packets were considerable. As early as April 1703, Dummer was seeking press warrants for his commanders in order to man the packets.[42]

The most serious problems of the agency arrangement were becoming clear by the summer of 1703; Dummer's accounting was inadequate enough that he was losing money even on the agency system. By the time the first anniversary approached in August 1703, Dummer had received accountable advances from the Post Office totaling £5500 and had not yet submitted any receipts.[43] It is hard to sustain the notion that the simple and ingenious shipwright was about to be crushed by the accountants of the Royal Navy. When he applied for an additional emergency allocation of £2500 to meet imminent expenses and promised that this would be his last such call before settling his accounts, he received the money promptly. When his inadequate receipts were received, the legitimate concern about their deficiencies did not prevent another advance of £1500 in December.[44] The Post Office referred the accounts to the navy, thinking that accounting methods might be different there, but the truth was no different when seen from that angle. Despite 30 years with the navy, including several years as a surveyor, Dummer had failed to gather or keep what appear to have been receipts proving expenditures approaching £1500.[45] Once this was known in January of 1703/4, the auditing of Dummer's accounts stalled and no additional grants were made from the Treasurer.[46]

Dummer's three reactions to these new difficulties were revealing. He petitioned Godolphin to have his accounts processed after the manner of merchants rather than the stricter methods of the Royal Navy Comptroller's Office, and he urged both Godolphin and the postmasters general to sympathize with his distress and remember his selfless service.[47] These petitions had little visible effect. Although the packet service all but stopped in the first five months of 1704, Dummer managed to raise enough money to send out the *Diligence* in April.[48] Here was more proof of his dedication to the government's packet service if more proof were needed. The third reaction to his impending troubles confirms his reputation as a "projector." When Dummer submitted his accounts to the Post Office, he also sent along a proposal for a new and improved service.[49] His proposal would be better received than his accounts, but nothing would be determined as long as he was under a cloud at the Treasury.

Dummer's situation improved almost as soon as Robert Harley became secretary of state in May 1704. Before the end of the month, the postmasters general authorized their Falmouth agent to pay the wages of the crew of the

Prince, and funds were made available for the next sloop, too, if necessary. The agent was also to learn comparable costs for the kind of service provided, as the government was considering a contract with Dummer.[50] The packets were sailing again, and there were other less obvious signs of the improvement in Dummer's fortunes. Harley was asked to remind Godolphin to audit the outstanding accounts. Through his favorite secretary of state, Dummer also petitioned the queen for "such reward as shall be thought fit."[51] He promptly received the salary of a surveyor of the Royal Navy retroactive to the beginning of the packet service to the West Indies and payable by the Admiralty. Finally, nearly a year after he proposed a new basis for the packet service, he won a contract that would launch a new phase of the packet service.

The agency period ended as a qualified success. The sloops had sailed to the West Indies and back at something very close to the scheduled speeds. The number of sailings was more disappointing, but this seemed related primarily to Dummer's financial management. Although all parties concerned were anxious to see the financial arrangements reformed, all assumed that something quite like the service should be continued.

The packet service that emerged after Dummer gained his 1704 contract was quite different from the one that had run for nearly two years previously. In the long negotiations, it became evident that the Post Office was anxious to preserve as much as possible of the original intent whereas the Treasury and Dummer wanted significant changes. New priorities were accepted that made the continuation of the packets possible, but these concerns would eventually ruin the packet service. Treasury insistence that a cheaper and more regular method be found for the packets to the West Indies ensured that the Post Office priorities were sacrificed. Dummer's desire for larger sloops than those currently in service was a problem in itself and a clue to a greater difficulty that would result.[52]

Dummer gained two new conditions that the postmasters general rightly saw as threats to the service. Dummer argued that five two-decked vessels of 150 tons would give more certainty to the service, reduce risks, and better protect the crew. The postmasters general, who were given the task of negotiating the contract for the government, agreed with the second deck but argued that the current size and number of vessels had proved appropriate.[53] Dummer's second new condition, that he be permitted to carry 5 tons of cargo outward and 10 tons homeward from Jamaica, brought equally sensible replies from the Post Office. Cargoes would make the packets more attractive to enemy privateers and would cause delays in the service, and the quantity limits would be hard to enforce.[54] Although they were cautious, the Post Office officials rightly feared that the packet service would become a handsomely subsidized freighting operation offering a monthly service to the West Indies at a time when competitors would be held up by convoy restrictions and the depredations of the press gangs.[55]

With remarkably good timing, Dummer was quietly moving into the freighting of valuable small cargoes through Jamaica to Spanish America. In the summer of 1704, the English government sought to encourage trade with the Spanish American colonies despite their being enemy territory. Trade to these starved markets flourished for nearly three years, focusing on Jamaica and making the packet boats especially important.[56] The prospect of this trade in the summer of 1704 solved Dummer's financial problems and allowed him to offer terms that satisfied the Treasury even if the Post Office was less convinced. A secret partnership between Dummer, his brother, his son, and the Mears brothers, Jacob and Sampson, at once saved the packet service and changed it. Jacob Mears had just returned from 16 years of trading in Jamaica, and he and his brother would provide the capital for the new ships and the knowledge of the trade. As members of the Jewish community in London and Jamaica, the Mears brothers apparently had contacts with coreligionists in the Spanish empire.[57] Dummer was now able to end the negotiations with a decisive and attractive offer to the government. Not only did he undertake the costs and risks of the ships himself, but he also guaranteed post and passenger revenues so that the cost to the crown would not exceed £4500 a year. The lure of the Spanish American trade was funding a new packet service from the beginning of 1705.[58]

New priorities produced a number of changes in the packet service that did not initially justify the skepticism of the postmasters general. As soon as the new contract went into effect, the packets began sailing from Plymouth rather than Falmouth. Plymouth afforded more stores and men, and a community of merchants and agents, including Dummer's son William, who traded with Jamaica for London merchants or on their own account.[59] Plymouth also was better located for land carriage from London of the expensive luxury goods that became important in the new trade to Spanish America. Returning packet boats continued to drop the mail at Falmouth before proceeding to Plymouth to unload, but Post Office objections to the change of port had no effect.[60]

The five new sloops that Dummer had built especially for the Atlantic packet service in 1705–1706 showed his improved funding. The vessels were each 200 tons rather than the 140 tons agreed to in the contract and were armed with 20 guns and equipped with 24 oars. The size and armaments both meant increased initial cost and running costs, with the armaments indicating that the object was not to defend the mails, which were to be thrown overboard when any packet was in danger of capture. These sloops actually made excellent buccaneering vessels, and governors would worry that the *Queen Anne* packet would make a particularly threatening French privateer after she was captured in November 1705.[61]

The service record of the five new ships and the *Kingston*, which may well have been designed on similar lines,[62] was sad indeed. The most successful made five voyages before being captured, two were taken on their fourth voyage, and both the *Barbados* and the *Kingston* were wrecked on their maiden voyages. (See Table 9.1.) These, the only wrecks of the service, did not shake the Post Office's confidence in Dummer's ship design abilities; but at least one of his commanders, two of his partners, and one colonial governor claimed the vessels were "crank" or overloaded.[63] The sailing speeds of the new sloops tended to be a little slower than those accomplished by the sloops used earlier, but the differences were inconsiderable. The loss of the new sloops was not proof that they were poor ships, but the shifting priorities made the packets among the most attractive and predictable of prizes traveling without convoy.

Preoccupation with the Spanish American trade ensured that the packets sailed more regularly than before, and attempts to free the packet commanders from postal duties led to the appointment of deputy postmasters in the islands, appointed by the postmasters general and paid by Dummer. Detailed instructions to the deputy postmasters emphasized security, speed, and efficiency in mail handling. Lists, labels, and sorted mailbags from different locations were attempts to keep close control of revenues, allow checks on the hour of packet-boat arrival and departure, and encourage mail from other parts of America.[64] The islands gained an internal postal service as a corollary of the new packet contract.

Although Dummer had new capital, new ships, and good prospects under his contract, his packet service was losing money badly from the beginning. Before the contract had been in effect nine months, there were renewed gaps in the sailings, and Dummer was pleading with Godolphin for a six-month postponement to the operation of the postal deficiences clause. The government's continuing interest in this service would be demonstrated throughout the contract, as it had been under the agency, by giving Dummer concessions to which he could hardly claim entitlement. The six-month postponement in the due date for nearly £4000 was granted with Post Office support.[65] When that six months had expired, Dummer successfully petitioned for an additional six months before having any deductions made from the quarterly payments of the government that were providing the operating costs of the packets.[66] Dummer had been allowed two full years without any deficiency payments whatsoever.

When the last extension had expired, Dummer again petitioned Godolphin, revealing some of his difficulties and seeking a basic change in the contract. Negotiation would again go on for nearly a full year, ending with the government's absolving Dummer of some of his obligations and granting him a new contract. In two petitions submitted in February 1706/7, Dummer laid out the terms of the first contract and the trouble he had suffered since. Initially, he sought complete remission of all the deficiencies owing and the crown's assumption of the risks of the sloops. Here was the kernel of the trouble; lost sloops had cost postage, delays, and the faltering of merchant confidence and use of the packets. The new terms Dummer suggested at this point included making the packet service an integral part of the Post Office, a crown subsidy of £12,000 p.a. with the crown receiving the postage and Dummer the other revenues, and Dummer's appointment as manager rather than contractor—which he felt would improve his capacity to borrow money.[67]

The postmasters general, to whom Dummer's petitions to Godolphin were always referred, responded with their customary respect and concern for Dummer. They accepted his argument that the losses had discouraged merchant freighting. The Post Office presented detailed figures on the service in the first two years under contract, specifying the total deficiencies as £5063.10.1. They objected to the idea that the queen accept the loss of those vessels taken, remarking that their size was an extravagance determined by "other Views and designs than what relates to this Office." They opposed taking over the service directly because it would continue to lose money in the foreseeable future.[68] Godolphin's response to this first exchange was a further delay in the deficiencies, thereby granting Dummer six months payment and allowing the packets to sail after another halt of three months.[69] The first of Dummer's petitions of February 1707 had given him a reprieve once more; the second one, specifying his new terms, was not studied seriously until May and would receive review through the summer. The postmasters general admitted that Dummer could not be expected to go on at present terms but reiterated that the service would be a drain if taken over directly by the Post Office. The Postmaster general wanted a new contract for Dummer running for five years, with him to receive revenues, excepting postage, plus annual crown payments to Dummer of £12,000 in war and £8,000 in peace. The owed deficiencies might be forgiven except for moneys that Dummer had received for freighting passengers, and the new contract would not include deficiency clauses.[70] Dummer would be offered a much better contract.

Dummer had seemed better than his arguments once again. His proposals ever since 1704 had always included the calculation of insurance, and he would certainly have complained if he could not get insurance at all or if the rates had become impractical. So the losses of ships were primarily the losses of postage, and he had been receiving allowances for that. He also claimed in 1707 that merchants were no longer shipping cargoes with him because of the loss rate, and the postmasters general agreed. Certainly, the *Barbados* and the *Queen Anne* were heavily loaded when they set out on what proved to be their last packet voyages. Yet even bigger loads were to come within a few months of these losses.[71] There is no sign that the Royal African Company was worrying unduly about the packets; they sent 2000 pieces of eight on almost every homeward-bound packet through 1706, and some later when higher colonial prices made silver less advantageous as a form of return.[72]

The most serious weakness was the waning of the Spanish-American trade on which the packet service had come to depend. Dummer had had two losses in a row during the winter of 1705–1706, yet 1706 would see the packet service at its best with 10 monthly sailings. Although Dummer was already postponing the deficiency payments, he was not so short of cash that the lost packets were not promptly replaced and fitted out in time for the scheduled trips. (See Table 9.1.) While Dummer's postponements were expiring, so was the boom in the Spanish-American trade. The summer of 1707 proved poor in this trade. Merchant recriminations against a naval commodore, a parliamentary inquiry, and the American Trade Act of 1708 were all part of an attempt to lay blame and cure weaknesses, but the position could not be restored.[73] The packet service dropped visibly as 1707 wore on. If the Mearses were his source of capital, it is not surprising that the three losses in 1707 hurt Dummer's service much more than had the loss of two ships in a row a year earlier.

The three years under the first contract were the best of the packet service although Dummer had plenty of reason to be anxious about financing until his deficiency payments were finally forgiven. More regular service had been accomplished, though the individual packet speeds had not bettered those of the smaller sloops that had sailed under the agency. The good years of the Spanish-American trade had been good years for the crown to attempt the marriage of some trading and some postal services into a single carrier service at lower cost.

Yet cost to the government had been the clearest weakness of the contract period when finally assessed. By any calculation, the crown had paid a great deal more for the West Indian packet service under contract than it had under the agency.[74] The first contract had proved the earlier wisdom of the Post Office position on the size and cost of the vessels. The link with trading was going to be as bad for the regularity of the sailings as it had been good for the service in the boom years. Yet the crown would renew its contract with Dummer on terms that were deliberately less favorable to the Treasury.

The decline and final collapse of the West Indian packet system under the second contract were in themselves the clearest demonstration of why and how the service had been maintained. The terms of Dummer's second contract were better than anything offered him in his previous year; the five-year contract offered Dummer £12,000 a year plus the same freighting privileges afforded earlier. Most important, Dummer no longer guaranteed the postal revenues, and he was even allowed the passenger revenues. The articles of agreement were rather full on a number of requirements, in some places reflecting on the service to date. The appointment and dismissal of commanders were specified, giving Dummer the nominations but the Post Office and the Admiralty the right to veto new appointments or demand resignations. Perhaps Dummer's attempt to shift some of the blame for the interruptions in service to the commanders had come back to haunt him. The contract twice insisted that all damage and loss were Dummer's, and no help could be expected from the crown or the government. Dummer was also accountable for any breaches of trading laws, and overloading of packets would result in a fine of three times the value of the overloaded goods. Yet the contract called for the same size and number of ships as before, and Dummer's fleet seemed well able to continue the task.[75]

Politics had played a major part in the creation of the packet service and were about to pull the packets into the partisan whirlpool with other government business as the Marlborough-Godolphin-Harley combination came apart. A month before Dummer won his new contract, his friend Harley was driven from office. In the general election of May 1708, Dummer was defeated and suddenly became vulnerable. If Dummer should need major capital backing for new sloops, the evaporation of the Spanish-American trade and his own political weight would make his task more difficult.

Dummer's finances were already in trouble before exclusion from the House of Commons made him an easier target. In 1707 he had already mortgaged four of his packets in raising £5000.[76] Before Dummer had been out of the House of Commons a month, the Mears brothers petitioned Godolphin that Dummer's new contract violated the secret partnership they had with Dummer, and Dummer's haughty reply did not remove or answer the charges.[77] Whether he needed Harley in office or himself in the House of Commons, Dummer was certainly in need without either.

Having committed some of his quarterly payments in advance to his creditors, Dummer had funds for only seven voyages in 1708 although he drew the full £12,000 from the government. The packets were also noticeably slower under the second contract, averaging a full two weeks longer in their round-trips. At that speed, the monthly packet service was not likely if there were any captures at all. Cargoes were still substantial, but the luxury trade and the bullion traffic were down.

As has been seen, Dummer had thus far received remarkably gentle treatment from the postmasters general, Frankland and Cotton. On 13 March 1708/9, Frankland and his new associate, John Evelyn, Jr., sent Dummer a stinging denunciation of the first year's packet service under the new contract. Assailing the "great disorder and irregularity" that made the packets of little use to the government or the merchants, the postmasters general told Dummer that there must be "a great defect and mismanagement some where" and went on to list some of the places to look. They wanted to know if the ships or commanders were inadequate for the task or whether moneys that should have paid tradesmen and crew had been misapplied. Dummer was told that no further payments would be made until the lord high treasurer had a full explanation. This threat was not carried out, and a more restrained call for an explanation was made again nine months later.[78] This time the postmasters general ordered Dummer's quarterly payment cut to bring his support closer to the half a service he was actually providing.

If the financial rigging of the packet service was already in tatters by the autumn of 1709, many of its remnants were torn away by the news of two packets lost in a single month. The loss of two packets in a row was not only possible; it had happened twice before.[79] This time, however, Dummer was in no position to build or buy replacements. The service limped through the winter with three ships, and the postmasters general's order to cut the quarterly payments was inevitable.

Dummer again tried the approach that had worked before. He petitioned Lord Godolphin for formal permission to move the terminus of the packets to the safer port of Bideford, pointed out his continuing losses, and asked that the full quarterly payments be paid. At that point, Godolphin was dismissed, robbing Dummer of a staunch and powerful friend whose enthusiasm for Dummer was still real.[80] But Godolphin's eclipse was the occasion of Robert Harley's return to power, initially as Chancellor of the Exchequer and

10 months later as lord treasurer. Dummer continued to receive his full payments despite the drop in the service. The shift to Bideford was accepted as safer[81] and represented the final admission that the Plymouth-based Spanish-American connection was moribund.

The collapse of the packet service and of Edmund Dummer cannot legitimately be blamed on the dangers of the task or government parsimony to a servant of the crown. It was a series of related bankruptcies that brought the end. Jacob Mears, the surviving brother of the pair whom Dummer had outmaneuvered in 1707, went bankrupt in March 1711.[82] Less than a month later, Nicholas Goodwin, who held the mortgages of four of Dummer's packets against an outstanding debt, went bankrupt.[83] Although Dummer had just survived yet another stop to his quarterly payments, the truth was not long concealed. Dummer had been making over the Post Office payments to Goodwin in advance rather than using them for the operating costs of the service. The payments were ordered stopped, the mortgaged boats were seized by one of Goodwin's creditors,[84] and the last of the packets straggled home in December 1711.

By the time his last contract came to an end in March of 1712, Dummer was being sued by one creditor and imprisoned at the instigation of a second, and bankruptcy proceedings were initiated by a third.[85] The kind of resilient "projecting" that he had shown before was evident once again. During 1712 he capped his career as a packet-boat projector with a scheme to revive his West Indian service plus packets to the American mainland; another line to Lisbon and the Groyne; and a new version of his third earlier packet service, that to the Netherlands.[86] He could not rouse any government interest in these proposals and died amid his difficulties in April 1713. When his widow applied for a government pension, it was supported by magnanimous testimonials to Dummer's contribution to the country from those government departments that knew his work.[87]

The second contract between Dummer and the government had proved a disaster for both parties. Dummer's scale and methods of operation had come to presume the trade to New Spain, which did not revive. In these circumstances, all the Post Office fears, that the union of trading and postal delivery were unwise, proved entirely justified. Although fewer vessels were taken and none foundered under the second contract, the service was averaging a sailing every two months, which was half of the expected service, and the voyages were averaging two weeks longer than previously.

The West Indies packet service did much more than indicate communication possibilities although 66 sailings in more than 9 years was below the expectations of Dummer and the postmasters general. Dummer made a revealing comment about the service, early in 1704, when he offered:

> It seems the Gen[ll] Humour of Men to Judge of such Intricate undertakings off hand, and to despise what they do not easily Comprehend, but if a Just reflection be made upon the article [Time], in

all Humane [*sic*] affaires this Service well perform'd will be as acceptable in peace as now in Warr for 'tis but commanding time & every
mans Inclination and Intrest is commanded with it.[88]

The packets seemed to have done something toward "commanding time"
along its route, and their impact reached well beyond the sugar routes of the
English Atlantic. The service reinforced the clockwise circle of English Atlantic communications and defied the seasons as the sugar routes could be
expected to do. The packets served for military intelligence at a time when
governors were reluctant to send any sensitive information by any vessel
other than a man-of-war.[89] The packet-boat scheduled stop at Jamaica even
allowed a Leeward Islands governor to send a sloop to catch a packet boat
with news of a French squadron's arrival at Martinique.[90] The packet boats
occasionally transported as many as 50 reinforcements for the Jamaica regi-
ment in a single voyage. The packets were particularly useful in coordinating
ship movements and arranging convoys although the Admiralty did have
numerous opportunities of its own to keep up the links between the squadron
in Jamaica and the administrators in London.[91]

Although the packet boats were primarily continuing in wartime the correspondence level that was possible in peace, the packets had a clear impact on
colonial administrators. As the packets were at government expense and were
on fixed schedules and routes, the Board of Trade was prompted to write
West Indian governors regularly and came to expect letters from governors
by each packet boat. The Board of Trade wrote more often than was customary before or after the packet service,[92] and they were accusatory when noting
that letters from some governors were missing from returning mails. Expectations were being transformed while the packets ran with some regularity. A
Jamaican governor was accused of not writing for two months, and so was
the Board of Trade,[93] and Royal African Company agents were chastised for
failing to write by one packet boat.[94] Normally, such charges would have
been absurd. These reactions occurred during wartime, when the same Board
of Trade would address governors in North America with letters that opened
simply by noting that since their last letter of seven months earlier, they had
received governors' letters of four months earlier or none at all. Thomas
Handasyd, governor of Jamaica throughout the whole packet service, would
come to resent the frequent official requests for a variety of detailed information. His attempt to claim that answering such queries was not his job
provoked a sharp rebuke, but there is evidence here of the pressure that
regular communications brought to those to whom power was delegated.[95]

Dummer's packet service had cost the Post Office some £86,000 in accountable advances and contract payment over a nine-year period.[96] Even with an
optimistic reading of the postal revenues, the Post Office lost at least £45,000
in the operation.[97] Why had the British government invested so much in this
packet service? Military considerations were initially dominant, as with other
communications innovations, and would remain important. When the early
initiatives had been diverted, the fear of enemy initiatives remained. Politics

had played a prominent part in founding and sustaining the packet service; Dummer had been shrewd or fortunate in his choice of patrons, for they provided him with almost uninterrupted support from the heart of the government, the Treasury. Dummer was fortunate to have his last contract in hand before he lost his seat in Parliament in 1708. Perhaps Edmund Dummer, MP, was being financed as well as his packet service, and the eventual lapse of the contract could be presumed. The Spanish-American trade had been essential to continuing the service in 1704, had languished from 1707 on, and was enmeshed in the complexities of peace negotiations by the time Dummer's service was fading.

As the packet boats became less frequent and reliable, correspondents reverted to alternatives that proved adequate in the closing years of the war. The decline of the packet service was more troublesome than its final collapse for many of those who had benefited from the mails. When asked to consider how important the correspondence was to merchants, the postmasters general reported that the collapse of the service had brought no petitions from merchants and that conversation with prominent traders to the West Indies made it clear that by 1711 the packets were not of any great use to them.[98] Postage increases in 1704 and in 1711 had discouraged some users of the packet service, but the postmasters general admitted that they had a thousand letters for the islands on hand when the service ended.

Of all the things that were conspiring to end the West Indian packet service by 1711, one that has been overlooked is the emergence of North America in the overseas military preoccupations of the British government. Dummer had never suffered from a narrow view of the packet boats to the New World, for he was anxious to have the West Indies packets carry mails from other parts of America, and he was periodically interested in a packet service to North America. Although he was more successful at the first of these ambitions than the second, the service that was launched between Bristol and New York in 1710 owed much to the example of Dummer's service.

From the beginning of serious discussion about establishing the West Indian packet service, there had been some thought about a parallel service to the English North American colonies. Dummer's West Indian packets had brought a proposal from Sir Jeffrey Jeffreys for a packet service to New York. Suspicion that a regular merchantman would be getting a subsidy for doing what all merchantment did would quash the proposal—illustrating the value to Dummer of the lean agency years in earning his later contracts.[99]

In the autumn in 1704, when he had new capital, new political influence, and was on his way to turning the agency into the first contract, Dummer had returned to the idea of a packet service to North America. He estimated that 100,000 letters a year went each way, and the service of three vessels would make an annual profit of £3,000.[100] There was no administrative enthusiasm for this at all, perhaps because North American affairs had little impact on government strategy at this point in the way, and Dummer's financial mess made his optimism less than convincing. In any case, within six months Dummer was advertising that his West Indian packets were particularly valuable for North American correspondence with England. The new deputy postmasters in the West Indies were seen as valuable here. Letters from England to North America were bagged and forwarded from the West Indies at the first opportunity. Replies from North America "may be almost daily sent" by ships leaving North American ports for any of the English West Indian islands, from whence they would be forwarded to England at no more charge than that of the General Post Office in London. Dummer added that the deputies in the islands were under orders to keep in touch with each other and with the postmasters in North America.[101]

Dummer's concern for North American mails in 1705 did receive the support of the Board of Trade to the point of their issuing a circular letter to the colony governors. These were urged to give "Your incouragement and assistance as there may be occasion."[102] This rather vague support passed with the limited response that it deserved from most governors. Governor Dudley of Massachusetts replied that he had passed the matter on to the House of Representatives, adding too hopefully, "I suppose they will offer something thereupon."[103] The *Boston News-letter*, itself a major beneficiary of the West Indian packets, carried a massive advertisement for the service in October 1705 but included a devastating error. It claimed that the service was a 150-day schedule; it was seven months later before the notice was repeated with a correction.[104] North American use of the West Indian packets increased in the next couple of winters.[105]

Governor John Seymour of Maryland went far beyond the faint call of duty in support of Dummer, producing a telling incident in the story of intercolonial communication. His own passage to Maryland in the winter of 1703–1704 had been horrendous, and his wartime difficulties in corresponding with England were serious indeed. In March 1707 he received a Board of Trade letter of 11 months earlier, which had been lying in a punchhouse in Kiquotan, Virginia, for six weeks when it was picked up by a chance traveler.[106] Before that month was out, Seymour addressed the Maryland Assembly on the need to support Mr. Dummer's packet boats. He went beyond the materials at hand to suggest that the service and the rates were dependent on the support of the colonial governors. The assembly was not impressed even with the favorable postal rates that Seymour presumed and defeated a proposal of formal support.[107] The chagrined governor wrote the Board of Trade:

> Nowithstanding we heare not from England in 7, 8, or 9 months, during this warr, the Assembly with the like reason, that they might still continue irregular and gainsaying, rejected Mr. Dummer's proposalls for better and more speedy advice and intelligence by way of his pacquett-boats.[108]

The board's sympathy became less vocal once they learned that Dummer had not made any proposals beyond sending his advertisements along with the Board of Trade's circular letters.[109] Seymour's communications troubles would continue,[110] and his judgment of the assemblymen may have been unfair. Those who needed no more harassment from English creditors or had better control over their governor if he were isolated from the sources of his power could not be expected to be enthusiastic about a packet service. Resistance to packets and posts came easily in the Chesapeake colonies—for whatever reasons. Throughout the colonial period there would be no packet-boat service to the Chesapeake despite the vital tobacco trade.

Proposals to operate a packet service to North America were offered spasmodically from the outbreak of the War of the Spanish Succession. If most were rejected on the grounds that they were not offering more than the service already available from ordinary merchantmen, it was also true that the government had no special cause for interest.[111]

One promising exception to the general lack of enthusiasm occurred during discussions with Dummer in the late summer of 1707. The lord high treasurer wanted serious consideration given to extending the West Indian packets to continental North America as a means of increasing the postal revenue and making the service pay. He asked the opinion of the most experienced colonial administrator alive, auditor-general of colonial revenues, William Blathwayt.[112]

Blathwayt's usually subdued language was set aside in a remarkable report on the empire and the packet service. Blathwayt began by asserting the primacy of the continental colonies in the strength of the realm and repeated his long-held position that they deserved their own packet service. Merchants would benefit from regular information, opportunities for quicker returns, cheaper insurance, and warnings of enemies. He claimed that many tobacco ships lost to privateers in the previous year would have been saved if their sailing times could have been coordinated by packet boat. As for the royal advantages, Blathwayt asserted, "Her Majesty who is truly the greatest Merchant in her Dominions and more especially with respect to those [tobacco] colonies" would gain considerably. Eight packets of the 12 sent to the islands each year might go on to the continent, providing a six-week service around the calendar. His doubts about winter passages were not entirely gone, but Dummer's service had shown them possible, and Blathwayt felt they should be attempted. He insisted that the regular sailing of the packets was crucial if they were to be of any use. Here he was reflecting on Dummer's experience, and Blathwayt argued that matters of state should cause extra packets, not hold up the regular ones. He also wanted some vessels to carry mails between North America and the islands, assuming that the service would be very inexpensive in view of the traffic levels on those routes. In the shadow of the union with Scotland, Blathwayt's argument for the North American extension of the packets included the suggestion that the service would tend to "a farther Union between Great Brittan & America."[113] The proposal did not find its way into a new contract for Dummer, perhaps because the postal revenues from North America were checked.[114] Yet this aging administrator's musings were a tribute to what Dummer had accomplished, as well as an indication of what might be done.

The notion of a packet boat to New York was not new in 1709, but what was new was the military planning of an expedition against Quebec. In the spring of 1709, Secretary of State Sunderland hired a 150-ton ship captained by Nathaniel Uring, who had been captain of a West Indian packet until captured by the French in 1707. Uring carried despatches to Boston, with information for neighboring governors announcing the intended invasion of Canada.[115] Like the earlier Peterborough expedition, the intended expedition was diverted to Spain but helped in the development of a packet-boat scheme. At the end of the year, Lord Godolphin sent the postmasters general a plan by William Warren, who described himself as a mariner of Bristol but may well have been a Plymouth merchant and shipping agent who had used Dummer's packets. Warren proposed a monthly service from Bristol to New York, using a minimum of four small vessels. He was to receive the equivalent of nine pence per single letter, be allowed to carry passengers, and have the same freedom from impressment and freighting privileges as Dummer had received. The contract was to run for several years with the option of ending it on six-months' notice.[116]

There were at least 7—and perhaps 10—sailings connected with this contract (see Table 9.3), but the service never approached a monthly opportunity to write. Between September 1710 and March 1712 there was a sailing approximately every three months. One winter crossing westward was attempted each winter, with each one taking as long to reach New York as the West Indian packets had averaged for a whole circuit of the North Atlantic. In the year ending March 1712, Warren's compensation from the Post Office was the equivalent of some 6720 single letters delivered by four packet boats.[117] Although the packets were sometimes carrying Irish servants,[118] it would appear as though the service did not meet Warren's expectations, and the contract may well have ended as early as the spring of 1712. Yet the *Harley* packet continued to run between Bristol and New York for another three years. Despite the miserable winter passages westward and the tragic shipwreck of a naval advice boat sent to Boston in 1714,[119] this packet-boat service suffered no losses or captures. With the ending of the war, the limited advantages of a packet boat on this route evaporated.

Warren's packets, like Dummer's, had commenced because the English government needed to coordinate plans for a military operation. Warren had no additional support for his venture, and his experiment did not last long after the failure of the Walker expedition to Quebec in 1711. Dummer had begun with considerable experience in the mail packet business, as well as having both political place and connections. Dummer's experiment lasted longer because of his own ingenuity, the emergence of a lucrative trade to Spanish America between 1704 and 1707, and the influence and immunities that went with being a member of the House of Commons. When all his major props had fallen, Dummer still managed to continue a reduced service for most of the life of his last contract, but that could not be continued indefinitely.

Postage could not sustain a transatlantic packet service at the opening of the eighteenth century. Newspapers could be livelihoods, post offices could be expected to pay their way, but packet boats needed subsidies that a government needed special reasons to grant. Warren's terms, of a grant of most of the postage, was bound to be inadequate. The large subsidies granted to Dummer were exceptional commitments that ultimately proved inadequate and could not be expected to continue.

Dummer's packet service had a considerable impact on English Atlantic communications. Predictably, there was not much comment on the fact that the packets were sustaining levels of political, commercial, and personal contact during war that were comparable to peacetime opportunities. Nor would many comment that communication disruptions between England and the West Indies that were endemic during the War of the League of Augsburg were not repeated during a war with more focus on the West Indies. The packets not only sustained existing levels of communications, but they also represented a new level of efficiency. The impressive speeds of the early packets were beyond expectations, and the seasons of the North Atlantic were disregarded without consequence. The regular and predictable service, while it lasted, was the most significant innovation of the packets. Not only could correspondents prepare mails for expected packets or forward mails to points along the route, correspondents could also be expected or required to write at specific times by particular vessels on predictable routes to known post offices. Although this predictability also made the packets particularly vulnerable to enemy privateers, it represented a level of metropolitan supervision that some correspondents found unsettling, if not excessive. Dummer's packets had demonstrated the possibility of sailing to his schedule, as well as the impossibility of sustaining the service without substantial subsidy. He had also revealed that there was substance as well as vision to his claim that the packet service was "commanding time & ever mans Inclination and Intrest is commanded with it."

10 · Sending Peace and War Beyond the Line, 1667–1739

"No Peace Beyond the Line" is not an ancient proverb but rather an apt anachronism summarizing the diplomatic state of nature that existed in the New World for nearly two centuries after the first discoveries of Columbus.[1] Although remnants of this doctrine survived, it was being adjusted and gradually superseded in the seventeenth century. Inclusion of colonies in formal peace treaties redefined meaningful space, initially in terms of communications possibilities. Peace was an innovation of Europe's New World, transforming colonial warfare from an endemic local condition into a transatlantic event to be declared by monarchs on behalf of all their subjects. Spread of the news of war became a contest, with forts, fleets, and colonies as potential prizes for those who learned of war before their opponents. In a sketch of the diplomatic integration of the English Atlantic, the spread of peace deserves first attention. It was only after the concept of a transatlantic peace was established that sending news of war came to represent the most strenuous effort governments made to communicate with their colonies.

Changing perceptions of the North Atlantic were evident in the changing views of "the line," which made some revealing migrations in the more than two centuries before "the line" eventually settled down to be a harmless synonymn for the equator. Initially, Spain's claims to the Americas were to be protected by two lines, a parallel of latitude and a meridian of longitude. If all meridians of longitude are imaginary lines, those drawn on the ocean before the invention of the chronometer and intended to claim exclusive ownership of vast unexplored lands were particularly imaginary. In the most spacious days of Iberian discovery, Spain and Portugal were able to partition the Atlantic zones of discovery along a demarcation line that approximated the 50° W meridian. Yet this bilateral agreement[2] was never intended to define Spain's pretensions in the face of other challengers.

The only other Spanish diplomatic effort to divide the temperate North Atlantic along a meridian had occurred in negotiating the Franco-Spanish Treaty of Cateau-Cambrésis of 1559. French challenges to the Spanish monopoly in the New World had been serious, particularly during this war, which had included a French capture of Havana. Although conflicting interests were not negotiable, there was an oral agreement that the treaty would not apply beyond the "lines of amity." Although evidence on precisely what these lines were is limited, they apparently were the Tropic of Cancer and the prime meridian.[3] The prime meridian was most likely the longitude of Ferro (modern Hierro in the Canary Islands, longitude 18° W) although as late as 1614 French officials claimed the agreement promised that

> however many hostile acts occur beyond the meridian of the Azores
> to the west, and the Tropic of Cancer to the south, there shall be no
> occasion for complaints and claims for damages, but whoever proves
> the stronger shall be taken for the lord.[4]

As Garrett Mattingly has pointed out, it is entirely possible that the same prime meridian that Spanish cartographers were placing at Ferro Island might then have been thought to pass through the Azores.[5]

Despite numerous acts of piracy and undeclared war in the North Atlantic west of the Azores, there was no further development of the notion that a meridian of longitude divided waters subject to European international law and convention from temperate American waters of anarchy. As late as 1655, Oliver Cromwell was reported to have attempted to justify Sedgwick's capture of the French Acadian forts of St. John, Port Royal, and Penobscot with a flippant "every one could act for his own advantage in those quarters."[6] If Cromwell genuinely believed that Acadia and Jamaica were in the same sphere of anarchy, it is doubtful that many other heads of state did. However much Spain would protest the seventeenth-century North American settlements of her rivals and however ragged were the boundaries between peace and war in the New World, the notion of a meridian of longitude as a boundary between peace and war never gained written diplomatic consummation in a treaty. It was as politically impractical as it was scientifically impossible. The "lines of amity" had been a whisper without an echo. North America came to be included in Europe's war and peace, and Spain continued to assert her pretentions "beyond the line."

The parallel of latitude that divided European waters from those of the outer world proved remarkably easy to determine. The range of options used in diplomacy from the middle of the fifteenth century was comparatively narrow[7] and the Tropic of Cancer was an obvious navigator's reference point that was a particularly valuable boundary for Spain because it helped protect all her vital Caribbean interests while maximizing the value of Havana as a center from which to police them. A sector of the central Atlantic sailing circle was monopolized. Despite all the explorations, raids, and colonization efforts of Phillip II's enemies, Spain had been able to make separate peace settlements with France (Vervins, 1598) and England (London, 1604), as well as a truce with the Dutch (Antwerp, 1609) without any formal weakening of her diplomatic position on the Caribbean. Spain could still believe that the Caribbean was her mare clausum; the intruders did not agree to anything but the tacit acceptance that all that happened there was "behind God's back."[8]

The Tropic of Cancer remained the boundary of Europe's peacemaking efforts as long as this arrangement served the powers involved. If English, French, and Dutch colonies were initially defiant ventures into Spain's preserve, the most impudent could be dealt with by force, and most of these colonies would become hostages of a sort as soon as they became valuable in themselves. For Spain, the beginning of interest in peace beyond the line did not come until she paid mightily for its absence. The capture of almost the entire treasure fleet by Piet Heyn in 1628 was a blow that shook the Spanish empire all the way from its Manilan merchants to its German mercenaries. The first response was a powerful Spanish squadron sent out in 1629, a squadron that captured and dispersed most of the English settlers of Nevis and St. Christopher as a minor part of its assignment. Within two years, however, a slight fracture could be seen in the Spanish position on "the line." In a treaty with the English, signed late in 1630, England and Spain agreed to return prizes taken beyond "the line" later than nine months after the publication of the peace in Europe.[9] Although not a substantial concession, this was a portent. How little could be presumed from it was evidenced by a question posed to the English Privy Council by the Providence Island Company late in 1635.

> how far it stands with the treaty to suffer His Majesty's ships to defend themselves and to offend if they be offended, being beyond the Line.[10]

This was a very good question to be asked by the leaders of a colonizing company whose Caribbean business had turned toward privateering. They seem to have received no reply from the Privy Council, but in May 1641 the Spaniards answered with the conquest of the island. The tropics were still behind God's back.

It was not until 1648 that Spain concluded a peace treaty that specifically included the New World. Entirely appropriately, it was the Dutch who first were granted formal Spanish permission to navigate, trade, and enjoy their possessions in the Caribbean by virtue of the Treaty of Munster. It was 1667 before the Spanish conceded the same rights to the English[11] although the buccaneers of Jamaica did not get the message. Henry Morgan's sacking of Puerto Bello in 1668 brought an understandable protest from the Spanish and, in April 1669, a remarkable order to Spanish West Indian governors to proclaim war against the English *only* beyond the Tropic of Cancer. The Anglo-Spanish Treaty of Madrid (1670) concentrated on colonial differences and elaborated more fully. Governor Thomas Modyford and Morgan would contrive to sack Panama City before the new peace was proclaimed, but the will to taste whatever peace Europe could arrange was growing with the English sugar industry.[12] French filibusters would be the last to be leashed by their home government; the Franco-Spanish war they provoked in 1683 ended within six months with the Truce of Ratisbon. For the English the Peace of Breda in 1667 had been the significant change in diplomatic treatment of the outer world. Thereafter she had treaties with the French and Dutch, as well as the Spanish, all extending to the New World and beyond. Violations of the peace would be frequent enough, and governments were not above ordering squadron commodores to take valuable prizes and then declare war, but a change had definitely come over international treatment of the North Atlantic. New World rivalries would henceforth contribute more to disturbing the peace of Europe, but Europe's needs for peace brought patches of calm to the colonies.

English use of the term "the line" would not end, but it increasingly became identified with that boundary of the English Atlantic, the equator. Richard Ligon, who had been in the Caribbean in the 1640's, later referred to the equator as the line. Dr. Henry Stubbs, reporting to the Royal Philosophical Society in 1667 about a trip to the West Indies six years earlier, called the equator the line. William Dampier, Woodes Rogers, and Daniel Defoe all reveal the same usage.[13] There were some very persistent doubts, like those intimated by a governor of Barbados on receiving a proclamation of truce with France in 1712. The governor correctly stated:

> The line that's mentioned in the Queen's Proclamation, and your Lordshipe's letter, I take to be the equinoctial line, and not the Tropick of Cancer as some conjecture.[14]

The governor was right, and the privateers were conveniently wrong once again.

The spread of peace and war beyond the Tropic of Cancer was a stage in the expansion of European power. The comparative ease with which the notion of a meridian bisecting the North Atlantic was abandoned was both a tribute to Spanish preoccupation with areas of immediate value and an indication that the North Atlantic was early, if loosely, comprehended within European maritime boundaries. The time it took to extend this understanding to include the Caribbean had nothing whatever to do with travel time or frequency but rather to the intense rivalries that could not be curbed effectively until it became of value for all negotiating parties to do so. The whole North Atlantic was becoming subject to this transformation from the 1670's. With it would come both Europe's peace and Europe's war.[15]

Export of Europe's peace presented practical problems that were serious enough to be part of the treaties. The Treaty of Westminster expressed the difficulty in 1674 as follows:

> But since the distances of places are so various that the commands and directions of the respective superiors cannot reach all their

subjects at the same time, it has seemed proper to assign the following limits for the acts of hostility or violence that might be committed against each party . . .[16]

The English government had first become involved in pacing the application of a peace treaty in the 1630 negotiations leading to the Treaty of Madrid. Previously, it had been assumed that ships, goods, or territories that had been captured after the signing of a treaty were to be returned. The Spanish were interested in maintaining that approach, whereas the English proposed that the effective date of the peace be phased in from the publication. Captures made within the "Narrow Seas" would be valid within 15 days of the publication; those between there and "the Islands," within three months; and effective peace would come beyond the line within a year. The Spaniards changed the last item to provide only nine months' grace to privateers operating beyond the line.[17]

Once revised to specify four separate peace zones, this staged spread of peace became a diplomatic convention with a pace that did not change between 1667 and the end of the eighteenth century. The "Narrow Seas" became more fully described as from the Soundings to the Naze in Norway, and peace was to reach this area within 12 days in treaties down to and including the Peace of Paris in 1783. The second zone extended from the Soundings to Cape St. Vincent[18] and was uniformly agreed as a six-week zone in treaties between 1667 and 1762. The third zone, supposedly one of latitude like the second, reached from Cape St. Vincent to the equator. In England's negotiated peace settlements of 1667, 1674, and 1697, this area was always expected to come under the terms of treaties within ten weeks. Ironically, this zone, which included the West Indies, would receive the benefits of peace more slowly in several eighteenth-century treaties than had been the case earlier. The Anglo-French truce of 1712 was to apply there in 12 weeks, as was the Aix-la-Chapelle settlement of 1748. The slowest projection of peace to the West Indies was negotiated in 1762, when three full months were allowed before peace would be effective in the Carribbean.[19] Spread of peace beyond the equator was allowed nine months in the Anglo-Spanish treaty of 1630, but eight months became a convention of the seventeenth century and six months in the eighteenth.[20] Evidently, a convention had developed about the reasonable pace of news sent out to the world beyond Europe. Variations occurred, reflecting immediate strategic considerations, but no significant changes occurrred in these conventions throughout the seventeenth and eighteenth centuries.

The actual spread of news of a particular peace was a test of these diplomatic conventions that had devised latitudinal zones with no apparent appreciation for the length of a westward crossing in the temperate latitudes. The relationship between conventional and actual communication of peace can be seen in the spread of the major settlements of 1697 and 1713. The long-awaited Peace of Ryswick was finally proclaimed in London on 19 October 1697, very late in the shipping season of the western routes.[21] According to

Article 10 of the treaty, the peace would be effective in the West Indies about 27 December. The place of American colonies that were north of the latitude of Cape St. Vincent, those north of the Carolinas, was not specified at all. Certainly, these colonies could not all be reached within the six-weeks' zone that their latitude suggested, and Canada could not be reached at all in that season. Whether it was accepted that the North Americn colonies were part of the West Indies for these purposes or not, that was where they would be in terms of the possibilities.

Two days after peace was proclaimed in London, the Lords Justices ordered that the peace be circulated to the colonial governors. On 30 October the letters and copies of the treaty were sent to the Admiralty, which had hired the *Hope*, Thomas Driffield master, to carry dispatches to Barbados where notification for the Leeward Islands and for Jamica was left for forwarding. The *Hope* reached Barbados on 28 December, so that the peace proclaimed there two days later met the expectations of the treaty. It is noteworthy that the French at Martinique had already heard of the peace and consequently released a prize taken as early as 7 December. The peace had been rumored in the Leeward Islands from the beginning of December. The official packet with the treaty, including the rather unwelcome requirement to return the French portion of St. Christopher, was at least a week later than the treaty deadline in reaching Governor Codrington at Nevis. Jamaica's Governor Beeston, by contrast, received a packet of duplicate letters and orders direct, on 11 December, and peace was proclaimed there the same day.[22] Peace for the English West Indies had been close to the treaty specifications.

If it can be assumed that the North American peace was expected to commence at the same time as the West Indian one, the English government accomplished that assignment with ease. Captain Gillam delivered the Massachusetts packet on 9 December, allowing proclamation there the next day and the forwarding of the packets for New Hampshire, Rhode Island, and Connecticut.[23] Although the formal packet for New York was sent out with Governor Bellomont and stranded with him at Barbados after a North Atlantic storm, copies of the treaty were in New York in December. These were, no doubt, received by way of Boston.[24] As with the packets sent to Barbados and to Boston, the Admiralty put the messages for the Chesapeake governors aboard hired merchantmen.[25] In this case, as in the others, the merchantman delivered the packet within the time required. Governor Nicholson of Maryland received the news on 16 December, but it was nearly a month before the accompanying packet for Governor Edmund Andros reached him across the bay in Virginia.[26] All the English colonies that were directly involved in the war had received the peace in what the treaty had regarded as an appropriate time for peace to reach the "West Indies."

Peace could come no faster than anything else to the farther north; Canada, Newfoundland, and Hudson Bay would be actively fighting at the end of the war and the last to hear of the coming peace. Treaty timetables took no account of what the seasons did to communications with Canada. Even if a special messenger had been sent to New York with orders to proceed by land to Montreal that winter, peace could not have reached Canada within the 10 weeks that were allowed for the nethermost reaches of the North Atlantic.[27] News of the peace went from Albany to Montreal to reopen the trade route. The first mission left Albany at the end of December. Governor Fletcher had received word of the peace and the text of the treaty, but the formal packet was delayed at Barbados with Lord Bellomont. New York emissaries to Montreal carried no letter from Fletcher, who knew he had been succeeded by Bellomont, and no prisoners were returned. Consequently, the emissaries were received in Canada early in February with less enthusaism than might have compensated their pains.[28] After Governor Bellomont arrived at New York in April 1698, a second mission was sent north to Montreal and Quebec. Peter Schuyler led the small party, including released prisoners of war, which reached Montreal only 12 days after leaving Albany on 8 May. By 25 May they were in Quebec City. Peace had come although the French royal orders would not come until late summer.[29] With all Canada's enemies informed of the peace, it is not surprising that the French court made no extraordinary effort to send peace and end Canadian strikes against Newfoundland and Hudson Bay.

The English involved in the fishing and fur gathering from Newfoundland and Hudson Bay were divided into those in England who heard of the peace promptly and those in the New World who could not hope to hear anything before the next year. An effort by the Board of Trade to have a packet sent to the commander in chief at Newfoundland was returned from the Admiralty with the comment that the Admiralty "does not think it proper to send any ship thither at this time of the year."[30] For the Hudson's Bay Company, which would have liked to forestall their enemies with peace, remoteness was more impressive. Not only was the battle of York Fort fought and lost while the peace was being concluded, but this peace never became operative in the bay at all.[31]

It seems clear that, as the news of peace was sent out, the latitudinal zones established by the treaty were not possible. The 6-week zone could bring peace to the Bay of Biscay, the Azores, and the Atlantic coast of the Iberian kingdoms. The temperate coasts of North America were occasionally referred to as an integral part of the West Indies; the spread of the Peace of Ryswick certainly put this area in the same 10-week zone. For a peace declared in the fall, Canada, Newfoundland, and Hudson Bay were effectively "beyond the line." Acceptance of these zones did not presume any panicked scampering for peace, and the spread of the news by merchantmen to the English colonies adequately fulfilled expectations.

The most complex and enduring European peace in the early eighteenth century, the Peace of Utrecht, began as a four-month truce agreed to in August 1712. English, French, and Spanish forces were to refrain from war between 12 August and 12 December 1712. Carrying this brief respite to the transatlantic empires presented particular problems that were addressed in clause 3 of the truce. Seizures at sea would be valid prizes if taken within 12 days in the Channel or the North Sea; within 6 weeks between the Channel and Cape St. Vincent; within 12 weeks between Cape St. Vincent and the line; and within 6 months beyond the line. On the face of it, this truce would not apply beyond the equator at all, and a separate declaration was signed to establish that there would be a truce in the outer world between 22 February and 22 June of the following year.[32] The general truce was extended for an additional four months, and peace would come without renewed hostilities. The truce itself provides a revealing case study in the spread of urgent news of a suspension of hostilities.

News of the truce with France was sent out to the English Atlantic empire with the speed and efficiency that suggests a genuine anxiety to end hostilities. At the same time, the perfidiousness that is rightly associated with the English government in these peace negotiations was also evident. The original agreement clearly stated that Britain extended the truce to Spain (though Spain did not sign), but the first letter of orders from Lord Dartmouth to the colonial governors did not mention Spain. One week later, after receiving the supplementary agreement on the peace beyond the line from Paris, Dartmouth again wrote the governors to convey this news and to point out that the Spanish were included in the truce.[33] The difference in conveyance of these two letters, dated only one week apart, may have had many causes. The results were to prevent any damaging French actions without reining the English privateers active against Spain for most of the subsequent winter.

The communications structure of the Atlantic and the British Empire always meant that the most efficient communications were usually those that were undertaken by England's government when it was willing to pay for ships to take news to the colonies. The spread of the late summer news of the truce with France was an excellent demonstration of this capacity. Three Royal Navy vessels were lavished on the transmission of news of the truce to the colonies, and these were ready to sail when Dartmouth's initial letters of 21 August were put aboard.[34] Newfoundland's naval commodore that year, Sir Nicholas Trevanion, received one of the packets by HMS *Solebay*, which apparently reached its destination early in October. Trevanion sent copies to the French governor of Placentia and to Governor Dudley of Massachusetts. As a result of this private conveyance, Boston proclaimed the truce on 27 October, and the Boston newspaper of that day would scatter the news in New England just as the official messenger was arriving.[35]

The intended messenger for Massachusetts was Captain Graves of HMS *Dunwich*, who had sailed from Harwick on 26 August. His first destination was Bermuda, which he reached on 1 October. Two weeks later he presented the packet to Governor Spotswood of Virginia, leaving the Maryland packet there for forwarding. The *Dunwich* continued on her peace-giving mission, arriving at New York with Governor Hunter's orders on 26 October. The *Dunwich* then proceeded easterly to bring the message to Newport, Rhode Island, where Captain Graves learned that he did not need to go on to Boston; Boston and New York had both proclaimed the truce on the same day. Rhode Island's proclamation of the truce on 3 November was the last, and the *Dunwich* sailed for England about the time the truce had been promised for the colonies.[36]

HMS *Blandford*, which had set out about the same time as the *Solebay* and the *Dunwich*, was the last to make a landfall, reaching Barbados after a seven-week crossing. Barbados began the truce on 11 October; in four more days the *Blandford* delivered the news to the governor of the Leeward Islands. When the *Blandford* reached Jamaica on the twenty-fourth, Governor Lord Hamilton had already received word from newly arrived Bristol merchantmen, and had called in his privateers.[37]

The efficiency and apparent ease with which the news of the truce was delivered within the deadline, even by a man-of-war that was visiting four colonies as far apart as Bermuda, Virginia, New York, and Rhode Island, argued for the reasonableness of the agreement and English interest in carrying it out.

In sending out the notice that Spain was included in the peace and that a time had been settled for truce beyond the line, the English court was less speedy, whether by accident or design. It was the eighth of December before the *Success* arrived in Boston bringing Dartmouth's letter of 28 August. The North Atlantic truce with Spain was nearing expiry when Dudley or Hunter would hear of it.[38] For the West Indian governors, who were in a position to inflict considerable damage on the Spaniards through privateers, the delay was scandalous. HMS *Nightingale* did not bring this message to the Leeward Islands until 17 February 1712/13. This was just in time to catch the commencement of the four-month truce operating further south beyond the line but was a very tardy inclusion of Spain in the truce. The *Nightingale* then went on to deliver the same message to Jamaica.[39] The governors of Barbados and Jamaica made local agreements with their French neighbors to extend the truce beyond its deadline until word arrived from the courts.[40] Here was evidence that governors had not lost all local initiative on peace by this time even if they had on war. The formal extension of the truce fitted with these local initiatives and prevented action until peace was declared next spring.

In ending the two greatest wars of an era, England applied the diplomatic conventions about the pace of peace on the Atlantic. What this made clear was that the line was the equator and that the zones established for the spread of peace within the North Atlantic could not be latitudinal bands. European coastal waters were all that could be included in the 12-day and 6-week zones. Most of the North Atlantic was in actuality included in the broad zone from Cape St. Vincent to the equator, a 10-week zone in 1697 and a 12-week zone in 1713. Peace was to go out to the New World like some barely seaworthy English sugar ship that would clear the Channel in 12 days but not reach Madeira until it had been at sea for 6 weeks. The pace from there to Jamaica or Virginia matched usual expectations. English North America, with the exception of Hudson Bay, was not 12 weeks away from England by advice boat. Improving postal and newspaper connections between the continental colonies in the eighteenth century meant that the spread of peace within

Europe's actual expectations could become effortless, but the diplomatic conventions adjusted neither to the impossibilities of some of the zones nor to the easy continuation of hostilities beyond first news in the West Indies.

Establishment of the notion that there would be peace between European powers in American waters and the development of a conventional pace at which peace would spread were both signs of the growing importance of the colonies and their increasing integration into the life of major western European states. This civil and civilizing development brought with it the prospect of a transatlantic race to arms whenever peace evaporated. The spread of the news of war would, in an age without major developments in ship speed, represent a frantic effort to warn colonial officials of dangers or opportunities. Barbadians fearing the outbreak of war, for instance, could rest comparatively easy until a small, lone sloop flying Royal Navy colors arrived from the east, invariably with a bellicose packet for the governor.[41] Not only was the usual speed of dispersing war faster than the spread of peace, as the cynic might expect, but the spread of war was an attempt at the minimum practical passage time from metropolis to colony.

Inclusion of the English colonies within the orbit of the royal declaration of war and peace is a stage that is clearly demonstrated by the evolution of the royal instructions to governors. Beginning with the instructions to Sir Charles Wheler, dated 31 January 1670/71, the governors of the Leeward Islands were ordered not to declare war on any colonists "without our knowledge and particular commands therein."[42] This order would become a regular part of the instructions to Barbados governors from 1672 and for Jamaican governors from 1674.[43] It was as though the establishment of peace in the West Indies had more priority than the same problem farther north, for Virginia's governors did not get the comparable order until 1679.[44] Although all of this corresponds sensibly with the diplomatic developments already discussed, the same cannot be said for the very significant power to grant letters of marque and reprisal to privateers. It was only in 1687 that the governor of Jamaica finally received a prohibition against issuing letters of marque "without our special commands." By 1689 all West Indian governors were restrained from granting letters of marque and reprisal "against any prince or state or their subjects in amity with us," and by the following year this had become standard for all English royal governors.[45]

Framers of royal instructions to governors were placing considerable faith in Atlantic communications by preventing governors from committing warlike acts without "particular command." Delivery of a specific message was thereby being promised; governors could not act on confirmed news of the outbreak of hostilities. Outbreak of war was a troubled time for maritime communications. Shipping embargoes were regularly imposed until the naval vessels were fully manned. It was also a time when naval vessels, including the small frigates and advice boats that might be assigned to carry news to the colonies, were needed for scouting and communication work in European waters. The race to bring news of war to the colonies was a contest between priorities as well as a contest with the enemy.

Changing perspectives on the approach of war can be illustrated by comparing the coming of each of the Anglo-Dutch wars during the third quarter of the seventeenth century. Although the first of these was caused in part by colonial commercial rivalries, and the consequences were important for colonial development, the war of 1652–1654 was not carried to the English colonies. Most of these colonies had recently been forced to accept the Cromwellian revolution at gunpoint and valued their trade with the Dutch, which the New English regime was attempting to stifle. Tacit or negotiated neutralities preserved relative calm in colonial waters while the battle raged in the Channel.[46] No colonial government was ordered to declare war, and none did so on their own initiative.

When the second war between the English and the Dutch was approaching in 1664, commercial and colonial rivalries were both a cause and stage in the development of the European war. English attacks on Dutch West African trading posts in 1663 marked an unofficial opening to aggression of a kind both parties had disavowed in treaties twice within the previous five years.[47] Charles II's brazen grant of the New Netherlands to his brother in March 1664 was a declaration that the colonies were all beyond the bounds of European diplomatic behavior, and his intention was reinforced by successful invasion in September. The Dutch response was to send Admiral De Ruyter's Mediterranean squadron secretly to West Africa.[48] Early in January, 1664/5 the English government was preparing legal documents to allow colonial governors to grant letters of marque against the Dutch. By the end of January, all the English colonies were ordered to look to their own defense against De Ruyter, whom the English government rightly expected to raid the English New World colonies on his way home from Africa. The same circular letter that advocated defense authorized the governors to issue letters of marque.[49] The warning arrived in time to save Barbados from attack by De Ruyter in March 1664/5, and the mainland colonies were put on their guard as well. The raids and counterraids in West Africa, the Caribbean, and Newfoundland all demonstrated once more that the outer world could host battling Europeans without the principals being at war in Europe or at least that the deterioration of a peace was an opportunity best exploited out there. In any case, the various English colonial governments took measures for their defense that did not include declaring war. It is understandable that there was no perceived need to convey the news of war to the colonies when the formal war was finally declared by the English government in March 1665.[50]

The third Anglo-Dutch war was not inspired or commenced by colonial rivalries. Although this war was planned and provoked by the courts of England and France, the English officials made no effort to exploit news of the war in the New World. Virginia's governor was ordered to send off tobacco vessels in convoy three times a year, but no special urgency or specific enemy was mentioned in an order dated only 18 days before the declaration of war on the Dutch and only 3 days before an English attack on a Dutch merchant fleet in the Channel marked the beginning of hostilities.[51] War in the colonies generally came in its own time. William, Lord Willoughby, governor designate for Barbados, was still in London in the summer of 1672, actively seeking military supplies for his colony. Defenses were put in readiness in his absence, but he was still able to launch the first expedition of the Caribbean campaign when he arrived there later in the year.[52] Jamaica's governor would learn of the war by way of a Bristol merchantman[53] and there would be plenty of the same sort of news available in Virginia and New York long before a Dutch fleet brought trade destruction to the Chesapeake and recapture to New York.

This war saw both fighting and peace come slowly to the colonies, with two notable exceptions. The commander of HMS *Mary Rose* received orders, nearly a month after the declaration of war, to join HMS *Richmond* in defending the English fishery at Newfoundland, in convoying the fishing fleet to the Strait of Gibraltar, and in taking as much Dutch commerce as possible without hazarding the other assignments. Here was a modest investment to protect a vulnerable significant trade.

The other exception is more intriguing. Within a week of the declaration of war, Charles II wrote the governor of Massachusetts, giving notice of the event and ordering that war against the Netherlands be declared in Massachusetts.[54] Only 42 days later, the General Court of Massachusetts ordered that the royal declaration of war "be published by the marshall general in the three usual places in Boston, by sound of trumpett." Boston had heard such trumpets proclaiming Charles II and declaring war on France in 1666, but this last Dutch war was the first one to be trumpeted in Boston.[55] It would be over a year before the General Court came to the conclusion that "God doth call them to doe something in a hostile way for their oune defence,"[56] suggesting the lame effects of the king's call to arms. Perhaps it was the Massachusetts Bay colony's demonstrated reluctance to go to war with the Dutch that had prompted this royal order. England had gone to war with the Dutch three times in a generation. The first war did not reach the English colonies, the second came after an official warning, and the last provoked a formal declaration of war in one colony on royal order. This formal event to mark the spread of European hostilities to the New World and the speed displayed in getting the news to that colony would become features of the opening of war subsequently.[57]

The English declaration of war on France in 1689 was a premeditated consequence of the "Glorious Revolution" that had been accepted before the end of the preceding winter. A full month before William III declared war on France, the English Privy Council decided that the Admiralty should prepare two of its best-sailing smaller vessels to be ready to sail for the plantations "on receiving notice."[58] A complete shipping embargo was put into effect on 15 April, the same day Secretary of State Shrewsbury wrote circular letters to all the governors and the proprietary colonies, announcing that the king intended to declare war on France and urging that measures be taken for defense.[59] On 24 April, two weeks before war was declared,[60] hired advice boats instead of the naval vessels sailed with dispatches. The *Crane*, Samuel Gillam master, was to go directly to Bermuda, then on to Virginia and Maryland before being discharged. The *John*, Francis Dykes master, was to follow the "sugar route" to Barbados, Nevis, St. Christopher, Jamaica, and Carolina.[61] As was the case with the news of the accession of William and Mary, no news was to be sent to the Dominion of New England. Partisan politics seemed to have provoked remarkable irresponsibility in this case if administrators were convinced that there was no point in sending word of a French war to a governor at Boston or to his lieutenant governor at New York simply because both men were likely to be replaced.[62] Delay would not soften the ferocity of war when it came to the northern colonies, but war would come slowly.

Despite the obvious advantages the English government had when Captain Dykes sailed off for the West Indies bearing warnings of the war that the English government would declare two weeks later, the English lost the race to send official news to the Caribbean. Dykes lost six weeks fighting bad weather in the Channel and putting into Plymouth, and his six-week passage from that port to Barbados was not outstanding either. Although news of the English declaration of war only reached Paris after Dykes was three weeks into his grueling struggle to get out of the Channel, the prompt French response gave Governor-General Count de Blénac at Martinique news first by a swift packet boat that was only 20 days at sea, as the English lieutenant-governor of Barbados, Edward Stede, reported later with some envy.[63] Blénac, who was already at war with the Dutch, gathered a miscellaneous fleet of 43 sail, which reinforced the French resources of the Anglo-French island of St. Christopher on 17–27 July 1689. Although confirmed reports of the declaration of war had reached Barbados and Antigua as early as mid-June, a month later Stede could only fume, "If I knew at this moment that I might make war on the French I would undertake to reduce the whole of the French Islands to the King's obedience."[64] Such were the bounds that the new imperial instructions had tied firmly. Captain Dykes did not arrive until 24 July, a full week after the successful French siege of St. Christopher had begun.

Dykes dutifully went on to Nevis to present the new lieutenant governor, Christopher Codrington, with news of a war with France for which he already had much painful local evidence. According to his instructions, Dykes was then to go to St. Christopher. The besieged remnant of the English settlement in St. Christopher, running out of powder and provisions in their fort while the French controlled the whole island and its waters, might conceivably have had a visit from an embarrassed Captain Dykes to tell them to prepare for war with the French. To the benefit of all, it was judged impossible to get through to the defenders because of French maritime strength.[65]

Captain Dykes's arrival in Jamaica received little immediate official notice, for the island was not in obvious danger from significant French forces as

England joined the War of the League of Augsburg.[66] The president of the Jamaican Council, Sir Francis Watson, was particularly cautious in view of the political difficulties attending the spread of the Glorious Revolution to his island, and he rightly regarded the message as a warning and not an actual declaration of war. The defense of Jamaica against French-commissioned privateers was primarily in the hands of HMS *Drake*, which Watson detained though it had been ordered home. The *Drake* was cruising "with special commissions, as we had then no orders as to war with France." Watson eventually declared war on the king's behalf, on his own authority, in mid-January of 1689–1690.[67] Except for the Jamaican president of the council, warning of impending war was all that was necessary. Despite the tightening of the governor's instructions, the process of going to war in the West Indies was not entirely formalized by 1689. No formal declaration of war was sent out to be proclaimed in the empire.

The voyage of the *Crane* to Bermuda and the Chesapeake colonies was an indication of the trouble and expense that were accepted as necessary for colonies that were not in obvious danger. Captain Samuel Gillam probably had some difficulties with the same Channel weather that had disrupted the transmission of the news to the Caribbean. Gillam delivered the warning of the war to Governor Sir Robert Robinson at Bermuda, who was the only English governor in America actually in place to receive the warning. In keeping with Shrewsbury's instructions, the *Crane* sailed for Virginia the day after her arrival in Bermuda,[68] and Gillam delivered his packets to the president of the Council of Virginia on 9 September. A vessel that took 24 weeks to arrive at Virginia was still able to bring news to the colony that was farthest along the Atlantic shipping routes and most likely to suffer complete interruptions in traffic owing to both embargoes and convoys. It was good fortune that there were no enemies of consequence poised to bring war to Virginia.

By the time Captain Gillam arrived in Maryland, that colony's revolution had occurred, and the royal messenger was reporting to, and thereby supporting, Captain John Coode.[69] From Maryland, the *Crane* went on to Philadelphia, where Gillam delivered a packet to a disappointed Governor Blackwell. The governor had hoped that orders to proclaim the king would be enclosed. Because these were not received, unwilling councillors could delay any serious response to the earl of Shrewsbury's warning of war "until he knows who is King."[70] It is not clear whether the *Crane* visited any other colonies with packets, but by mid-November she was back in Maryland and ready to sail for England. She sailed for London a month later with letters and, no doubt, with many impressions of the animated colonial scene.[71]

The deliberate exclusion of the Dominion of New England from the itinerary of the *Crane* or even the inclusion of a packet to be forwarded by land to Lieutenant Governor Nicholson or to Governor Andros reinforces the impression of a compelling influence to the contrary. Unlike the Chesapeake colonies, these more northerly ones could be expected to be most in need of warning of the impending war with France. If vessels were hired expressly to see that colonies were not to be ignorant victims of the event the English government was engineering, why were these colonies excluded? By the end of July 1689, it was learned in Boston that a French fleet had arrived at Quebec and that war had been declared between England and France.[72] Within a week the news had reached New York as "serious reports," but, as late as mid-October, Leisler was passing on to Maryland what he thought was news of the war. His source had been French prisoners, taken in raids on New England, who reported that the war had been proclaimed in Canada.[73] News of a war declared in May traveled the North Atlantic very differently from a truce declared in August. On the northern frontier, as on the West Indian, the French messengers arrived more quickly than the English. Whatever the Channel weather did to frustrate the cleverness of the English, it is also clear that the voyage of the *Crane* was planned to warn those North American colonies that were least in need of the warning.

The spread of the news of war to the English empire in 1689 could not have met the expectations of many of the people involved. Although the English government's quiet preparations gave them a month's advantage over the French, the French succeeded in informing their colonial governors first. Admittedly, the English revolution had reduced the efficacy of the colonial executives in any case. Bermuda was the only colony that had a governor in place to receive the news of war, and the revolution and its consequences in the northern colonies had ensured that no formal notice would even be sent there. It took three months for news to reach the West Indian English governors and about the same time for New England and New York to hear of the war by way of Canada. The Chesapeake colonies did not learn of the coming war for nearly five months after the packet boats were sent. It was fortunate that most of the empire did not face aggressive French colonial governors poised to exploit their advantage. The English at St. Christopher paid for the spread of peace to the New World once again. A number of administrators who were involved would be in power the next time war approached between England and France, and something appears to have been learned.

The Peace of Ryswick was particularly short and uneasy in the Caribbean. In the course of the War of the League of Augsburg, there was a perceptable shift in focus within the West Indies. The war had opened in the eastern Caribbean, but the emphasis had shifted westward with the French invasion of Jamaica in 1694 and De Pointis's raid on Cartagena. The English would have a squadron based at Jamaica from 1695 on, a significant stage in the development of local imperial power that would culminate in the establishment of a naval base at English Harbour, Antigua, some 40 years later. The Peace of Ryswick would come late to the Caribbean and would not be accepted by all the privateers cum pirates who lived off the shipping of that sea. In addition, the English and French governments both maintained comparatively large squadrons of men-of-war that patrolled the Caribbean like circling vultures waiting for the anemic peace to die.[74]

The climax of English naval adventures on the edge of war came in 1701, when Vice Admiral John Benbow was returned to the West Indies with a strong squadron and what amounted to permission to start a war. Initially, Benbow commanded a combined Anglo-Dutch fleet of 35 men-of-war cruising west of the Azores with orders to seize the homeward-bound Spanish flota. Once the flota had been encountered and attacked, successfully or otherwise, Benbow was to send a ship to Newfoundland with the warning "that there are great apprehensions of a speedy break with France and Spain" and the men-of-war and merchantmen at Newfoundland were to be ordered home.[75] The order was not only an evaluation of the fishery; it was a comment on the routes of the Atlantic. Failing to meet the flota, which had been delayed, Benbow set off to the West Indies with a 10-vessel squadron. The possibility that Benbow could begin the war was certainly incentive enough for regular communications with Benbow. The concern would only heighten when it was learned that the French government had sent out a massive fleet of 35 men-of-war, the largest armament ever sent to the Caribbean.

Benbow's correspondence with the Admiralty and the secretary of state during his last year was very regular indeed. He used returning men-of-war, merchantmen, and even a navy longboat when he was particularly anxious for orders. Benbow sent 11 letters in as many months, averaging a delivery time of 85 days.[76] Although Benbow's communications with the English government were conducted effectively, the same cannot be said for the other half of the correspondence. Benbow was more dependent on his instructions and his own judgment than he thought his very delicate situation warranted. A set of additional instructions dated 23 October 1701 were sent out with a reinforcing squadron under Captain Whetstone. Although the latter was ordered to send the packet ahead to Benbow in the event of any significant delay, Benbow did not receive the change in his orders until the ill-fated reinforcing squadron finally reached Jamaica in May 1702.[77] Seven months was too long to wait for delivery of important instructions to a commander in a position to commit his country to war. Although no comparable delays occurred in other efforts to contact Benbow, this difficulty would be one factor encouraging the founding of the West India packet service later in 1702. For all the concern for the West Indies and all the parrying there, the new war began in Europe on 4–15 May 1702, when England, the Netherlands, and the Hapsburg Empire declared war on France.

Imperial aspects of the English declaration of war in 1702 were in sharp and efficient contrast with the same process 13 years earlier. The orders sent were orders to proclaim war against France, which conformed properly with the governor's existing instructions and completed the process of diplomatic extension of war and peace to the colonies. The formal orders to proclaim war and the arrangement of their conveyance also showed speed and coordination of officers of several departments. Within 5 days of the declaration of war, HMS *Swift* and HMS *Express* had put to sea, compared to 12 days of preparation on the last occasion of war with France. Improved political conditions in the colonies and the intercolonial post between the northern colonies meant that the two naval sloops bound to the closest major ports of Bridgetown and Boston had prospects of prompt dispersal of news to colonies likely to face immediate danger. Although the season matched that in which war had been declared in 1689, the weather also cooperated in conveying the packets to their destinations.[78]

The most practical and immediate consequence of the efficient and fortunate transmission of war to the colonies was English success in the Leeward Islands. HMS *Express* reached Barbados on 23 June, where war was declared that day, and delivered the same news five days later to Governor Christopher Codrington at Antigua. News that had taken three months to reach the eastern Caribbean in 1689 was there in seven weeks in 1702. Within a week, Codrington had fulfilled an ambition in conquering the French portion of St. Christopher. A timely packet boat to a zealous governor achieved more than the squadrons that were sent to the islands in the next decade.[79]

Jamaica received the news in good time from Vice Admiral Benbow, whose packet was sent directly by the Admiralty rather than by way of Barbados. Benbow passed the news to Jamaica's Lieutenant Governor Beckford, who was grateful that "our inhabitants might not be surprised or our vessels unhappily taken as they were the last war, before we had any notice of it here."[80]

HMS *Swift* reached Boston on 29 June, and the colony was at war the next morning. From Boston the news and the official packets for governors traveled quickly along the post road. Portsmouth, New Hampshire witnessed the formal declaration on 7 July. The regular weekly post that ran west from Boston to Philadelphia carried the packets for the governments of Rhode Island, Connecticut, New York, and Pennsylvania.[81]

Bermuda and the Chesapeake colonies, which had been favored with expresses by packet in 1689, were understandably treated with less concern in 1702. Governor Nicholson of Virginia heard confirmed reports of the hostilities before the end of July but could only wait with embarrassment until the autumn.[82] His unsuccessful efforts to open a postal service to Philadelphia could only make his waiting a little worse, yet neither Virginia nor Maryland were in any immediate danger. Bermuda again revealed its isolation from the rest of the empire. The Bermuda packet, sent by way of Barbados, was forwarded to Jamaica, where it waited for a vessel bound directly for Bermuda, and war was not declared there until 28 September. Colonies were seldom prepared to hire sloops, especially to send packets along to other colonies. It is not necessary to postulate intercolonial rivalries in privateering for this; simple economy may have been enough reason.

If news of war were to give vulnerable colonies a chance to prepare their defenses or to give the prepared a chance to strike an unsuspecting enemy, the spread of news to the English Atlantic empire in 1702 was satisfactory. The passage times of the sloops bearing the official packets was no better than average for those routes, but the speed of preparation in Whitehall, the choice of destinations, and the growing intercolonial communication facilities all combined to demonstrate improving possibilities.

For the English authorities, the process of going to war with Spain seemed essentially different from going to war with France. A predatory privateering emphasis in all English conflicts with Spain had retarded the development of peaceful conventions in America before 1670. The outbreak of the War of the Spanish Succession had been anticipated by bellicose instructions to England's Admiral Benbow. English tardiness in conveying news of the truce with Spain in 1712 was further evidence of the aggressive confidence of the English government in combating Spain. Nor was there fear that Spain might attack English colonies when England declared war on Spain again in December 1718. HMS *Deal Castle*, a man-of-war bound for Jamaica, carried news of the war in a most unusual pattern that suggests the English government was anxious to encourage the Jamaica squadron to take prizes. After delivering the formal news to Jamaica in mid-March, the *Deal Castle* visited the new government of the Bahamas, then Virginia, and finally New York. This odd distribution of news, given sailing patterns in the English Atlantic and the formal instructions not to declare war without specific orders, meant that Boston went to war nearly three months after it had been proclaimed in Kingston, Jamaica.[83] When England went to war with Spain once again in 1727, there was no formal notification of that fact at all for the colonial governors.[84] In the eighteenth century, English colonial governors were not only unable to declare war without express orders, but they were also, after 1702, unable to issue letters of marque without "our special commands."[85] This arrangement allowed the English government to allot the news and privateering advantages. It also allowed the crown to give permission to issue letters of marque without declaring war. This had been initiated—and then aborted—in December 1718. It would be the method used when England again attacked Spain in 1739.

Anglo-Spanish relations were chronically tense throughout the 1730s, particularly in the Caribbean. Spanish colonial *guarda costas* bullied British merchant shipping whether the latter were engaged in legal or illegal trade. Abuses by Spanish privateers often amounted to something very close to the old mare clausum in practice and brought understandable howls of protest from its victims. On the other hand, British and colonial shipmasters blatantly disregarded Spanish law. In these circumstances, the will to peace survived remarkably long, especially as the two powers had been at war three times in the previous 40 years. As late as January 1738/9, the second Convention of Pardo promised a peaceful settlement of British merchant grievances.[86] The Jamaican squadron commodore, Charles Brown, followed instructions with a caution that reduced the diplomatic temperature in that area.[87]

During the four months that the Convention of Pardo allowed the Spanish government to repay some £95,000 compensation to British merchants and shipowners, the British government's will to keep the peace all but evaporated. A parliamentary debate early in March was weathered by the government, but public opposition to the Convention of Pardo probably contributed to a reversal of orders for a homeward-bound Mediterranean squadron. Their continuing presence, in turn, contributed to Spanish resistance to the terms, the Spanish failure to pay within the prescribed time led to a prompt and belligerent British response.[88]

On the very first day on which the Spanish government could legally be regarded as in default of the agreement of Pardo, the British Privy Council issued orders that made war probable. Commadores of the Mediterranean and the West Indian squadrons were to seize the Spanish treasure fleet as acts of reprisal rather than of war. The distinction was not being relied on to mean much, for the home fleet was to be strengthened, the land forces increased, and the appropriate method devised to issue letters of marque. By midmonth, the Privy Council ordered letters of reprisal against property of the king of Spain and all his subjects. A general shipping embargo was imposed to help man a fleet under Edward Vernon and to control the news by naval advice boats for the commadores, by a ship preparing to go to New England with the news, and by two ships being sent to support the fishery at Newfoundland.[89] Commadores Haddock and Brown were given the opportunity to strike long before general reprisals were authorized. By the time Vernon sailed from Spithead for Finisterre and the West Indies and the general embargo was lifted, Commadore Brown had received his orders at Jamaica urging him to take the galleons. Governors of the eastern Caribbean, by contrast, would not hear any of these developments until early September.[90]

Distribution of specific permission to commence raiding Spanish property was swift and effective enough to serve as a demonstration of the communication improvements that had been building for a generation. HMS *Tartar*, Captain George Townshend, left Spithead for Boston at the beginning of July, carrying permissions to grant letters of marque addressed to the North American colonial governors. After a quick passage of 38 days, the packets were landed for dispersal along postal routes that now reached from Boston to Charles Town, South Carolina. Bostonians, quite naturally, heard and read their governor's proclamation first, dated 10 August.[91] A week later, similar proclamations were issued by the governors of Rhode Island, New York, and New Jersey.[92] On 20 August, Pennsylvania's governor issued his proclamation to the same effect, and 10 days later Lieutenant Governor Gooch issued his proclamation in Williamsburg.[93] By 8 September the editor of the *South Carolina Gazette* printed a copy of Boston's proclamation that had come by post in one month, and his next issue carried the local proclamation, for the *Tartar* had arrived in Charles Town four days earlier to take up station duties there as well as bring the news for South Carolina and Georgia.[94] These proclamations inviting English colonists to raid Spanish commerce were not exactly the same as declarations of war, yet they were subject to the same rules of procedure, required specific documents rather than confirmed news, and had similar practical consequences.

The contrast between the effort made to send out permission to raid Spanish commerce and the leisurely spread of the formal declaration of war confirms the suspicion that the latter was anticlimactic. False rumors that heralded the truth were reported in colonial newspapers throughout the summer of 1739, and war was finally decided on in London on 19 October and declared on the twenty-third. There was no special dispatch of the declaration to the colonies at all. Predictably, the news spread along the sugar routes first during the winter season, and the West Indian colonies went to war in January.[95] News of the declaration reached Charles Town and New York before the end of the year, and the London declaration was printed in a Boston paper on 10 January.[96] Most of the North American colonial governments declared war in April 1740, on receipt of the formal orders that had been carried out to Virginia with the regular tobacco convoy.[97] Formal declaration of war was of little urgency in this instance and was used primarily to promote colonial recruiting for the Cartagena expedition. In coming to war or peace with Spain, the English government often displayed little concern for formalities and a confidence that more would be gained than lost by confusion or delay. The contrasts between English diplomacy toward France and Spain indicate that it was not the Caribbean that was "beyond the line"; it was the vulnerable Spanish empire. Communication to the Caribbean could be an excuse but was not a legitimate problem.

By the third quarter of the seventeenth century, war in the New World was no longer a constant potential threat. Oceanic peace and war were another part of the shrinking of the oceans that is more usually called the expansion of Europe. War was increasingly a global event initiated by Europe's governments. Diplomatic conventions about the pace at which peace would spread developed rather quickly and remained unaltered by the changing possibilities of distributing news.

Having accepted the notion that peace and war would be carried to the New World and having included the Caribbean in the conventions, the English government entered a new type of race with her rivals. The complete inadequacy of English arrangements in 1689 demonstrated the consequences when hired ships and bad luck combined to give French colonial governors a usable advantage. When war came again in 1702, two English naval ketches won the race to war in America. Although the English usually gave peace less priority, the truce with France in 1712 occasioned the sending of three British naval advice boats to the colonies. The effort lavished on this occasion demonstrated the possibilities of communication with the colonies when there was sufficient official commitment.

Although diplomatic developments made news of war essential, it also made that news unlike all others; nothing except the official packet could allow a governor to go to war or issue letters or marque. Delivery of the official packet to Massachusetts would take nearly as long in 1739 as in 1672, a reminder of continuities. Yet even this kind of news spread in ways that revealed the development of the intervening period. In Pennsylvania, for instance, the change had been dramatic. The passivist colony would hear the unwelcome news of war in 170 days in 1689, 81 days in 1702, and only 49 days after letters of marque were authorized in London in 1739. That same news reached Charles Town from Boston even faster than the *Tartar* sailed on the same route.

Distribution of this kind of news was changing in another basic way. Once the colonial posts and newspapers were operating, the unofficial news of war and peace circulated much more regularly, uniformly, and farther than before. Those who invested in privateers or ventured merchantmen could make or change their plans with the arrival of news of the progress of diplomatic negotiations, news of campaigns won or abandoned, or treaties signed. Although the Anglo-Spanish war of 1727–1729 was not formally proclaimed in the colonies, its progress and the long negotiations of peace were followed in the colonial newspapers down to the Treaty of Seville of November 1729, with its peculiar clause promising the restitution of all prizes taken less than 15 months *before* the final agreement. Colonial newspaper reports of the tortuous peace negotiations would cool colonial investment in privateering during the time that was eventually declared most unprofitable. Atlantic communications had changed the military context from the "two spheres" to a race to war and then to a level of communication in which the advent of war or peace could be anticipated rather than being announced by the surprizing arrival of a lone sloop bearing Admiralty colors.

Of the efforts made to command time in the English Atlantic, government-sponsored voyages exclusively to deliver news to colonial governors were the most dramatic and expensive but not the most important. Edmund Dummer's packet boats to the West Indies were a more substantial and sustained effort by the government to maintain a satisfactory level of correspondence with the West Indian governors throughout much of the War of the Spanish Succession. The packets had transformed the pace at which some business was done and strengthened metropolitan claims on colonial representatives, but the service was an extended emergency measure to be replaced briefly by a packet to New York and forgotten in peacetime. The development of the postal services and the newspapers throughout the English Atlantic owed something to government support and license, but they were ventures that were encouraged and limited by the support of the literate public. The expansion of postal services in England, North America, and the West Indies improved the flow of public and private news. The rigid connection, which merchant shipping had maintained between the movement of goods and of information, was broken, altering the comparative advantage of those in various centers who were competing in politics, business, or society. The post office, particularly in North America, was linked directly to the emerging newspapers, and both of these innovations transformed the spread of news in the generation after the Peace of Utrecht. The English Atlantic was being drawn together in sectors, and it was also being drawn together as a whole by the increasing number of merchantmen and by the written and printed news that they, the postriders, and the newspapers carried.

PART III

The English Atlantic
Aspects and Implications

THIS is to inform (as well as to Recommend) All Persons bound from this and the Neighbouring Colonys, who may happen to Land at or near Dover in England, That they may be Accomodated with suitable Entertainment: Also with Coaches and Horses to go from then[ce to] any part of England, by Mr. Thomas Jennings, at the Ship Inn and Post House in Dover aforesaid.

An advertisement in the *Boston Gazette* of 28 August 1738

11 · Commerce and Communications

The English Atlantic was being shrunk, not by dramatic technological innovation, but by the growth of oceanic merchant shipping and by the development of the news businesses of the post and the newspapers. In one sense,
these changes occurred because of the needs of people whose horizons
included this Atlantic community. Yet consequences were also causes. The
communications developments encouraged more people to enjoy, exploit,
and suffer from gaining such horizons. If commerce were crucial to these
improvements in communications, the improvements would, in turn, change
the methods and expectations of those doing business.

In moving surpluses to scarcities, which was the epitomy of profitable
trade, the early modern merchant sought prompt and private information.
The novice English factor abroad in the Elizabethan period was instructed to
write and deliver letters secretly to any ship that he learned was bound for
England, telling no one of the opportunity and thereby advancing himself in
the opinion of his English employer by offering first news of a ship's safe
arrival, price changes, or political developments.[1] The Boston merchant
Thomas Fitch's efforts to gather profitable returns for his London correspondents during the War of the Spanish Succession were frustrated regularly
by competitors who received information on London prices earlier than he
did. Letters sent directly to Boston by the convoyed fleets did not help "for
when any thing is in demand[,] wch y^e and every body knows[,] it is advanced
in price and catcht up immediately."[2] Two years later he had London letters
come on a ship that put into Piscataqua for 10 days before coming on to
Boston. The captain refused to send the mails on by post, but a passenger or
two carrying private letters took the post road down to Boston and gave a
couple of merchants there an advantage over Fitch and the others.[3] His desire
for letters by Lisbon, by Barbados packet boat, or by way of New York
became even more insistent in 1709, when rumors of peace made his custom-

ers reluctant to buy from his stock of goods bought at higher wartime prices. Fitch summed up the place of correspondence pointedly:

> My advices come too often too late, occasion'd partly by You[r] Contenting Yo[r]selves with haveing wrote per a ship, when as perhaps that ship tarries a long while after, and those of my Neighbours that have later letters and advices of all materiall occurrencies get the start of me here, which is very irksome as also disadvantageous. Be so kind therfore hence foreward as to favour me with the latest advices possible how things governe by opportunities, for my right managem[t] here has an absolute dependance upon it.[4]

Merchants would be understandably anxious to promote improvements in communications, would use them more regularly than other correspondents, and would have their methods of business affected by the developments. Changes in the costs of acquiring information changed profits,[5] usually, though not always, to the benefit of the merchant. The development of posts, papers, and packets all separated communications from freight. This, in turn, increased the possibility of planning and reduced risk. A late eighteenth-century merchant, firmly within the new methods, could offer a reminder of the alternatives.

> I can only say this that if we do not pay strict attention in writing & answering our Letters per every post, we had better leave writing at all and trust all to Chance.[6]

For an illustration of how modest improvements in communications affected commerce, there is merit in considering the general features of the circle of a simple transaction and then examining the impact of improvements on the shipping industry, which affected all English Atlantic trades.

Commercial ventures began with some effort to predict markets even if the merchant was without fresh advice from the destination. The rate of profit and the speed of returns depended on how well a shipment met market needs. In the early days of colonization, chartered companies not ony spread risks widely and drew on the legal and mercantile traditions of merchant "factories," but they also had commercial immortality allowing the completion of trading exchanges, debt collection, and profit sharing on a time scale that could outlast the earthly span of individual venturers in strange places. The joint stock companies could also endeavor to control their market by monopoly and thereby reduce their risks a little. The Hudson's Bay Company held a comparatively effective monopoly of market information and sales through much of this period, minimizing the disadvantages of correspondence only by annual fleets. The East India Company struggled to maintain a monopoly on the English markets for oriental goods, thereby reducing its vulnerability to market changes. The Royal African Company at its strongest had no monopoly on the African coast and no monopoly of its returns of sugar to England but attempted to monopolize the import of African slaves to the English colonies. Trading monopolies were a limited protection against price changes, were allowed only on trade with the peripheries, and were not available to most of those who traded within the English Atlantic.

In predicting a market without fresh information, a merchant gained something from watching export activity from his own port. Embargoes, convoys, spells of calm, contrary winds, as well as local prices for export cargoes, were all market indicators. Merchants were understandably curious about customhouse export records as signs of what was going where. Some false or vague customs entries might well have been inspired by efforts to keep an opportunity to oneself, and the general picture of the despised customs officer would seem to overlook this significant function. As late as 1729, Jamaican correspondents of Bristol merchant Isaac Hobhouse reported a poor market in the island for what might be called a West Country provisions shipment including beer, ale, cider, herring, butter, and claret. The correspondents left the selection of a cargo to Hobhouse but advised that it be sent only if two or three months went by without a vessel leaving Bristol for Jamaica. This small and specialized Jamaican market for Bristol goods might be overseen from Bristol better than from Jamaica, but such advantages only applied to outward-bound cargoes from ports with something approaching a supply monopoly.[7] No English Atlantic port was even close to such a position in any significant commodity.

Another basic method of trading without immediate knowledge of the market in advance of the voyage was to go, or have someone else go, as a supercargo to oversee the marketing of goods directly. For a merchant of any substance with various simultaneous ventures, it would be customary to send a kinsman, apprentice, or junior partner in this capacity, urging him to use the opportunity to become acquainted with customers of worth and local conditions in the markets. A supercargo would have some freedom to choose markets, but the supercargo or the shipmaster who often acted in that capacity for his freight customers was subject to those same economic restraints that made so many trades simple, bilateral exchanges. Tramping from colony to colony in search of the best market cost wages and victuals and was not good ship utilization unless very favorable trading circumstances could be found.[8]

Masters of merchant ships often acted as supercargoes. This was most effective if the vessel were owned or chartered by a single merchant and the captain could be given instructions and an interest in conducting a shrewd and successful voyage. Some of the clearest expressions of market expectations, alternatives, and business methods that survive are captains' letters of instructions, and the changes in these over time are equally instructive.[9] The place of correspondence in the direction of the masters is a particularly interesting development. Like governors bound out with their instructions, masters might be asked to correspond by every opportunity. Letters, orders, or advice from agents were to be picked up at specified ports of call. For example, in 1724, Jonathan Belcher of Boston, merchant and later governor of Massachusetts, sent the *Dove* to Honduras for a load of logwood. The master was then to make for Lisbon. Meanwhile, Belcher asked a London contact to insure the ship and cargo; to keep abreast of the prices of logwood in the Straits, at Lisbon, and in Holland; and to send advice to Lisbon for the master of the vessel. Four years later, Samuel Appleton, another Boston merchant, ordered the master of his small schooner to make for Falmouth, England, when loaded with fish, and there he would receive orders.[10] Appleton included the option of delivering the cargo to agents in Bilbao if there were no orders waiting for the master at Falmouth, providing an early example of the "Falmouth for orders" voyage that would become commonplace for American transatlantic carriers in the nineteenth century.[11] In 1735 the master of a London-owned vessel bound from New York to the Mediterranean with wheat and flour was to stop at Gibraltar to collect the owners' orders.[12] The trade by supercargo and particularly by master as supercargo would continue and improve as postal facilities improved, but it was not the dominant method of trade after 1675.

Supercargoes, whether they were merchants, aspiring merchants, or shipmasters, all faced major problems at their market. Whether or not their cargoes were perishable, it was axiomatic that merchant vessels had to hurry at ports of call if they were not to be ruined by operating costs. In the sugar and tobacco colonies, especially in the seventeenth century, it had been customary for vessels to load over several months, but even here there was pressure to sell remaining goods at lower prices as the last days of the stay approached. Supercargoes often were landed with the cargo in order to allow the ship to proceed while the sale of goods continued. In addition, the sale of goods on credit was often unavoidable, and this was hazardous for a visiting merchant whose knowledge of local people was limited. These were among the reasons that led to the development of agencies in the colonies and in England. Kin and coreligionists were prominent in these arrangements throughout the seventeenth century, and both of these reinforcers of trust were renewed by the Quaker and Huguenot diaspora near the end of the century. Yet business connections were increasingly ruled simply by established merchant practice and defended by laws that were comparable and related in the whole English Atlantic community. In most of the captains' orders that have survived, alternatives usually included turning the cargo over to an agent at one or more destinations.

An agent had much to recommend him as a marketing aid. Inspired by a commission of approximately 5 percent,[13] if not bound by additional ties of kinship or religion, the agent would advise his principal about goods judged appropriate for the local market and would keep up a regular correspondence that included current prices of both the goods being traded and the local commodities that would constitute returns. An agent could store goods that arrived in quantity and sell them at more favorable prices without delaying vessels. Goods that were expected could be promised to buyers in advance, and cargo and freight for a vessel could be assembled before its arrival, thereby lessening port times and operating costs for ships. Under an agency arrangement, the bulk of the profits remained with the principal whose capital was at risk, but agents earned income, gained experience, and often traded on their own account as well. The relationship between an agent and his principal became complex, for the same people would operate different types of accounts with each other, including reciprocal agency arrangements. Correspondence was essential to the functioning of these relationships and to confirm the honesty of the agent.[14] In the transition from annual to seasonal and even to monthly correspondence, shipments could fit markets better; agents' inventories could be smaller, more timely, and less likely to remain unsold for years. Although there was continuing possibilities for trade by "adventure" without the latest market information, those with orders or advice were in a position to gain more, sell for less, and generally harry their less diligent competitors who were not willing or able to correspond as frequently. The competent agent gave his principal a decided advantage in marketing cargoes.

A trading system involving English merchants and their agents in the colonies or colonial merchants and their English agents would meet a new competitor in the last third of the seventeenth century—the commission system. This method emerged first in the sugar trade and reflected the increasing capital position of the larger planters. Under this method, the planter retained ownership of his produce and shipped it to his English commission agent who, for a 3 percent commission, oversaw the landing, storing, and marketing of the planter's crop and arranged return cargoes, holding balances that could be used in England or the West Indies through the planter's drawing a bill of exchange.[15] This increasing complexity and interconnectedness had eliminated the colonial merchant or supercargo from the transaction but presumed that more knowledge of men and markets was available to all parties in the arrangement. The commission system was sustained by the increased communication facilities although it clearly required the colonial capital that came first to prominent Barbados planters, became common to the leading planters of the islands, and became a feature of that part of the tobacco trade that was centered on London. For those who could not afford to wait for their produce to find a good market and did not have the credit or capital to build the necessay contacts, it was the local merchants, merchant planters, and storekeepers who were essential to marketing. The commission system was, nonetheless, an economic arrangement that reflected the opportunities to reinforce trust with information, opportunities that had become much better in the staple trades in general and in the newer colonies in particular. Reciprocal commission selling, a form of factoring that was not necessarily exclusive, represented the apex of this interdependent system.

A further development in the transatlantic marketing system was the emergence of the "storekeeper" in the tobacco trade. "Factors," or exclusive agents of a single mercantile house, were a standard feature of the major monopoly companies that dominated English trade with India, West Africa near the end of the seventeenth century, and Hudson Bay. As paid employees subject to company discipline, the factors represented tighter control in theory. The development of the Scottish tobacco trade and Piedmont tobacco cultivation combined to facilitate a factory marketing system. Although this development was stronger as the eighteenth century progressed, some signs of it were evident before 1740. This business structure could work well enough in the monopoly trades without regular price news, but the Scottish tobacco houses were running a related system without monopoly. In these circumstances, the communications advantages of the routes between Glasgow and the Chesapeake were an element in the success of this whole marketing system.[16]

Marketing methods in the English Atlantic were changing in response to changing circumstances, but none of them could be predicated on a seller on one side of the North Atlantic knowing the price current of his product on the other side at the time of shipping. Those who needed an exact and instant selling price paid for it and sold for cash to someone else who risked the freight and the market. Yet there were constant and strenuous efforts to exploit news even if those were seldom as obvious as the postrider laden with coin who rode out of New York for Boston in 1705 carrying someone's reward for anticipating a price differential imposed by the crown's new proclamation on the price of the coin.[17] The changing marketing arrangements were designed to shorten a ship's stay and increase the amount of negotiating and arranging that could be done subsequently and reported by mail.

The struggle to plan economic advantage and exploit the latest intelligence was undertaken even if the results were not always commensurate with the effort. An illustration can be drawn from Philadelphia's *American Weekly Mercury* of 8 January, 1725–1726, which carried the inviting story that provisions were very scarce at Barbados, with flour selling at two pistoles a barrel and no pork or beef available. This enticing item ended with an implied time limit on the opportunity by noting "but the Irish Vessels were Daily Expected." The report was probably quite fresh when printed and was offered to the public by someone who saw no more private advantage in it.[18] Although Philadelphia heard the news first, ice in the Delaware prevented any sailing for nearly two months because of an uncommonly long cold spell. A week after the news item appeared in Philadelphia, the *Norris* sloop left New York for Barbados, no doubt intending the voyage before the news had arrived there. The *Norris* would arrive too late for the happy market she had not been prepared for; by the time the sloop left New York, ships were leaving Barbados to bring Philadelphia the news that the price of flour had fallen by more than 50 percent, presumably because the Irish provisions had arrived. Yet the tale of opportunity still had a life of its own. The *Boston Gazette* retold the story of the high prices at Barbados a month after that news had appeared in Philadelphia.[19] The scarcity of grain in Boston would have precluded responding to the news item even if it had not been dated a month earlier at a rival port. When the chance had long gone, Isaac Norris wrote from Philadelphia to his Barbados correspondent to apologize for failing to use the news that had come. He recounted that another ship intended for the voyage arrived late for preparation the previous autumn and that the dry weather prevented the mills from grinding flour and kept prices high. When a cargo was offered, Norris accepted it, but the ship was held in the ice. Despite the fact that Norris had sent to London by way of New York to have the vessel insured for the voyage to Barbados, the trip had to be abandoned. Here was a demonstration of an imperfect information system but one struggling to perform. Without any news, Norris would have felt no need to apologize. Without a postal service that allowed him to send to London for insurance while his own port was iced up, he would have saved the entire cost and trouble of insuring a voyage that aborted.[20]

Although marginal advantages in market information could yield great profits, Norris's experience is but a very gentle reminder that improving communications could also hurt merchants. In 1754 a Jamaican correspondent was accused of "a piece of folly" when others at his port learned that he had a ship bound for Philadelphia just after a hurricane had hit the island. His Philadelphia contact, who lost enormous windfall profits when many of his competitors heard of the opportunity by the same ship and sent out 39 vessels with cargoes that glutted the island market, insisted that letting others write by your ship was not "Bristol policy".[21] At another level, improved communications over broader areas tended to build more price uniformities, bring price differentials down toward the shipping costs, and reduce the scale and duration of surplus-to-scarcity profits.

Although predicting markets rather than knowing them remained unavoidable even in simple retail mail orders, interest in prices current was very strong. Not only was it customary to append lists of current prices to business letters, but in 1707 Thomas Fitch noted: "There are short printed Lists of American goods, which some persons here have the prices added to by their friends in writing. Such Lists per Every possible opporun[ity] would be a great advantage."[22] A year later he was sending copies of the printed list to London to be filled in and returned. The intercolonial posts began to build united markets. When asked about the Boston market for cocoa in 1710, Fitch replied to his New York contact that quantities recently imported into New York and Carolina were already affecting the Boston market.[23] For English colonial staple producers, the prices of sugar, tobacco, and furs were set in London at the opening of the eighteenth century. The fish, timber, rice, and provisions trades were less clearly dominated by the setting of a price anywhere, making ventures more risky and current market information even more valuable. In the case of the colonial provisions trades, Irish provisions were the major component in determining West Indian provisions prices. Until about 1720 the resulting West Indian prices would usually determine prices in Philadelphia, New York, and Boston. Thereafter, the transformation of Boston into a provisions importer and the emergence of the southern European markets for colonial grain and flour would tend to change this simpler picture while increasing colonial dependence on English correspondents to report Mediterranean prices and arrange returns.

It may be simple coincidence that the launch of the *Boston Gazette* and the Philadelphia *American Weekly Mercury* late in 1719 also brought the first efforts at providing prices current for colonial produce. Both papers intended to offer current prices in Boston, New York, and Philadelphia. Some merchant opposition was predictable, and neither paper fulfilled the hopes of those looking for regular and full prices current for major commodities at these three centers. Yet markets were enlarging and unifying although this tendency was not very strong in the surviving data for the next 20 years.[24] The oceanic range of prices current thought to be of interest to readers was also instructive although none of these were given regularly. Philadelphia readers were occasionally given Barbados or Jamaica prices current in addition to general comments on the markets there. Provision prices at Trinity Bay, Newfoundland, were once offered to Philadelphia newspaper readers, and the *New York Gazette* of 30 May 1737 was the first colonial newspaper—and the only one before 1740—to give London prices current. This issue offered the prices at Bear Key, London, as of just over two months previously, for grains, malt, hops, tallow, and several teas.[25] The *Boston Gazette* of the 1730's gave the prices at Boston, New York, and Philadelphia with more frequency than had become common once a newspaperman's initial enthusiasm wore off, and South Carolina prices were occasionally included. All this lacked enough regularity and persistence to be of much service to someone attempting to predict prices systematically (or for someone trying to reconstruct price movements carefully), but the whole venture represents an imitation of English prices current and a move toward market sensitivities and equalizers that attended the later improvements of communication.[26]

Although the marketing methods that developed during the middle years of the first British Empire reflected the keen mercantile interest in the exploitation of available information, the improvements from chance to planning were gradual and limited, and earlier methods persisted because the newer ones were not so superior as to force themselves on everyone trading in the English Atlantic. The evolution of the agency, factoring, and commission systems, as well as "storekeeping," were all facilitated by the developing communications. More frequent prices current and letters on market conditions tended to improve selection of goods to fit markets and speed returns.

Returns were the central purpose of all trading, and communications affected returns in a number of essential ways. Consideration of the subject as separate from marketing is itself a useful, but artificial, dissection of a united process. One of the major drawbacks of transatlantic trade was that someone involved in every transaction had to tie up their money for a considerable time. This cost, together with the risks of both shipping and bad debts, would, quite naturally, be borne by the trading partner who stood to gain most of the profits of the predicted but uncertain market. The colonial producer of a marketable staple or the colonial merchant reselling the same in England usually did not bear the costs of credit even if they sold on their own account. The English merchant or the colonial retailer of staples in the colony tended to carry these costs. For both of these groups the speed of returns, as well as their quality and security, was a central ingredient in their rate of profit and ultimately in their prices. As London merchants never tired of reminding their colonial correspondents and as Adam Smith would later formalize in his assessment of the trade of the first empire, the American trades compared unfavorably with the European markets because of the slowness of returns.[27]

In the marketing done within the English Atlantic, the colonial seller was usually able to have his money rather quickly if he did not have it in advance. In local markets the quickest returns, though not the best ones, were provided by selling to local merchants, to merchant planters who resold the produce of their neighbors, or to agents or factors of metropolitan merchants either for goods or to cover goods already received. These methods had their price but were the only methods available to those without the capital or credit that could be tied up in their own commodities. Indeed, even those who did have such capital would weigh ready prices against other uses of funds on the capital-short frontiers of the English Atlantic.

The colonial who could accept the costs and risks of the commission system was also in a position to have a good part of his money quickly if it had not been spent in advance. As he shipped a cargo of sugar, tobacco, fur, or fish to his London commissioned agent, the colonial seller could also send a bill of exchange drawn on that agent and made payable to a third party in his own colony, in England, or elsewhere. Provided he had not overdrawn his account by overestimating the yield on his cargo, or by having a copy of the bill arrive safely after the cargo itself was lost or captured by enemy privateers, the colonial seller could have the use of his money immediately.

In drawing up his bill of exchange, the colonial planter or shipper of furs, deerskins, fish, or flaxseed would indicate the time at which the bill was to be honored. The time allowed the agent between the sight of the bill and its payment came to be called the "usance" on the bill. The time was to allow for arrival of goods forwarded to cover the bill; for the sale of goods already arrived; or at least for an explanation to arrive that would induce the commission agent, trading partner, or relative to make good the payment agreed to by the drawer of the bill. Usance could also be used as a credit instrument and was, therefore, subject to influences other than communications times as evidenced by the tendency for West Indian bills of exchange to carry longer usance in the eighteenth century than the seventeenth, but distance was a factor. Charles Molloy instructed merchants that usance was normally one month from London to nearby European cities like Amsterdam, Antwerp, Bruges, Rotterdam, Lisle, Rouen, and Paris; two months from some southern European cities; and sometimes three months between London and Florence, Venice, Leghorn, Zante, Aleppo, and Lucca. In assembling the business perception of the English Atlantic, it is noteworthy that English, Irish, and colonial bills of exchange were usually drawn at one month after sight.[28] The Atlantic was not seen to be significantly wider than the Irish Sea for usance and, as has been noted previously, the West Indies were closer than Aleppo.

Bills of exchange were themselves a particularly worthy commodity in English Atlantic trading because they were more transferable than currency and were safer than any other method of payment. Some New England merchant letterbooks could be read as though business were primarily a contest for good bills on London, a quest that sent ships to Amsterdam, Jamaica, Newfoundland, or Zante. Traders at Boston, New York, and Philadelphia who imported English goods for resale always valued good West Indian and Chesapeake bills of exchange on London and especially prized these when war or slump made commodity returns risky. In the staple colonies, the local market for bills of exchange fluctuated, with supply likely to outpace demand at peaks of staple shipment. Yet bills of exchange were a postman's commodity, and the development of the intercolonial posts expanded the markets for the bills and thereby improved their selling prices. Even before the colonial posts reached southward to the Chesapeake, tobacco producers' bills on London were a commodity in Boston.[29]

For the merchant in England or the colonies, the speed of returns was a crucial consideration in the pricing of goods in exchange for staples. Communications facilities would play an important part in the initial terms of transactions, as well as in the process of debt collection. Almost inevitably, any discussion of returns must end with a consideration of the broader allocations of credit, which would have great consequence for those able to get and keep metropolitan credit as well as for those who were denied this plasma, which was essential to economic and social success in some colonial economies and an asset in all of them.

Prices of tools, laborers, provisions, furniture, and luxuries sold to colonists naturally included all the cost connected with their delivery and the costs of waiting for returns. Given the annual cycles of much natural resource production anywhere, it is not surprising that the English Atlantic traders usually expected returns within nine months to one year.[30] The charging of interest did not always begin with the passage of that time, but dunning letters about the lack of returns might be expected thereafter.

Collection of overdue accounts was a major concern of merchants operating across the Atlantic. Charging interest on overdue accounts became more regular as time went on but was not in itself an assurance of payment. With the differentials between legal interest rates and the prices capital could command in the colonies, there was a disincentive to repay commercial debts. When a merchant gave up on sending dunning letters, the options open to him were limited. Those who operated through a locally based agent or factor would have some important advantages. The agent or factor would have little difficulty establishing his right to collect the debt as a rule and could better determine whether the debtor was able to pay, a central consideration in deciding whether to start legal proceedings. An agent or factor could participate in the legal process, blunting the tendency for colonial law and practice to favor local debtors and creditors before overseas claimants. In bankruptcies, seizures of effects to cover debts, or the settlement of estates, there was a real possibility that local creditors would strip the property long before more distant creditors heard of the event.[31] Colonial laws unfavorable to overseas creditors had provoked the introduction of suspending clauses into governors' instructions in 1706, and the whole matter had been a part of the imperial review of colonial legislation and judicial proceedings since the 1670's. The British Parliament passed an act in 1732, an Act for the more easy Recovery of Debts in his Majesty's Plantations and Colonies in America,[32] which revealed some of the major remaining difficulties in the process of offering remedies. By this law, proof of debt was to be sworn before an English magistrate and carry the seal of a city, borough, or township. Such affidavits were to have the same force in a colonial court as if they had been sworn there. The act also specified that lands, tenements, and Negroes were liable for debts, as in England, and slaves could be separated from the lands to satisfy debts. These problems had harried merchants who tried to collect debts as did matters of personal identification of debtors and runaway debtors. All these problems would translate themselves into higher prices, of course, but the evolution of the commercial system and especially the reciprocal commission trading involved increased confidence that debts could not be evaded easily.

Legal changes helped the developing commercial methods, and so did communications improvements. Failure to make returns by opportunities that occurred more frequently was an earlier signal that a bad debt might be developing. Increased opportunities to send out letters of attorney and proof of debts meant more chance of participating in the distribution of the effects of a bankrupt or deceased debtor. The advent of colonial newspapers, which regularly carried estate notices, details of counterfeiting, frauds, and other mercantile scams, shrank the world for debtors and debt collectors, to the decided advantage of the latter. The debtors could, however, skim the same pages for those exciting advertisements seeking colonial kin who had inherited English estates. Few creditors would be quite as fortunate as those of Thomas Bourdeaux, director of the Royal Prussian and Brandenburg Company, who died in the West Indian island of St. Thomas in 1735. Two months later an advertisement appeared in the *New York Gazette* inviting creditors

> either in New York, or any adjacent Islands, or elsewhere in America,
> to bring in their Claims, by their Attorneys, within one Year and six
> Weeks, after the Date of the Decease of Mr. Bourdeaux, in Order to
> be intitled and secured for their just Dues in the Bill of Partage. And
> if any one is excluded the Benefits he might have, or suffer Damage
> for want of Regulation, he can blame no Body but himself for his
> Neglect.[33]

Such full notice and ample time to submit debts were not common, but the estate notices of the newspapers circulated this type of essential business information more rapidly and equitably than it had traveled before.

Credit, on the scale of extended commercial loans or more formal investment in colonial development, was not only crucial to the English Atlantic economy, but it was also a resource that determined the social advantages of the colonial elites. Access to credit was an essential prerequisite for the large-scale colonial merchant, planter, shipowner, or land speculator. Capital was initially only available from outside the new colonies, and the London source was natural and necessary. This relationship would be altered in connection with some colonies by 1700 or 1740, but metropolitan credit was still a central source of power. The communications that were essential to that system would increasingly be able to moderate losses, distinguish responsible from irresponsible debtors, and allow creditors legal and mercantile recourse with some hope of success if debtors proved reluctant to repay. In one sense, the improving communications helped the metropolis to police its economic hinterland more effectively. In another sense, this improved control of the debt system was a prerequisite for credit on the scale that was accomplished in the eighteenth century.

The shipping industry itself, which affected all seaborne trade through freight rates, was a considerable beneficiary of evolving communications facilities. Recent scholars have established that the shipping industy of the American colonies improved its productivity noticeably over time. The improvements have been attributed largely to security against pirates and to economic organization.[34] These studies have mentioned reductions in "information costs" as an aspect of the improvements they discuss, but it seems appropriate here to highlight some of the benefits improved communications brought to shipping. These improvements were not sudden and did not apply uniformly to all trades and to all participants, but they can be seen as establishing features that would become trends. Improved communications were also central in the development of those two features scholars have isolated as paramount in cutting shipping costs, the reduction of piracy and changing economic organization.

Operating costs while a vessel was away from its home port constituted the major cost in freighting, and the victuals and pay of crewmen was a major ingredient in those costs. As has been seen, the development of primarily bilateral shipping patterns was one way to reduce these costs, and the changes in the tobacco shipping seasons and organization were another. Market information about the expected size of a staple crop helped merchant-shipowners to deploy their fleets more effectively. Here, too, the number of ships intent on a voyage from one's own port was less useful than a reliable correspondent's estimate of the crop expected. The emergence of agents and factors in the colonies, the commission system, and joint ownership of vessels by merchants and planters reduced loading times for ships. Outbound cargoes could be described to agents and customers in advance of their delivery. Agents could begin collecting return cargoes or at least negotiate freight and returns before the ship arrived. The agency was predicated on trust but grew more effective with the increasing opportunities to exchange information. Improving information flows would also tend to fill freight shortages faster at well-connected ports, as well as prevent gluts. Yet there were limits to what could be accomplished. A Charles Town agent explained to a Boston ship-owner in 1739 that freight for London was only 25s. per ton, and the port crowded with ships "come here now to Seek Freight from France, Spain,

Portugal, the Straits, & West Indies from all which Countries we have Shipping Seekers for Freight here."[35] This most multilateral American port could be expected to have more surprises than most because its rice fleets gathered from such disparate places. Yet here, as well as elsewhere in the English Atlantic, the improvements in the scale of shipping, the communications links to other ports, and the methods of business would all tend to make shipping somewhat more efficient, and efficiencies in that highly competitive industry would ultimately translate into lower costs for freight.

Another major cost advantage after 1720 was the reduction of armament on merchantmen. Savings in the costs of guns were much less significant than the cuts in crew size that became possible once the handling of the guns was eliminated as the expensive determinant of the size of a merchantman's crew. The spread of Europe's peace to the New World was not complete; maritime demobilization had been accompanied by surges in piracy after the treaties of Ryswick and Utrecht. As a crime that disrupted commerce and maritime social order, piracy was the target of vigorous government initiatives in which the Admiralty justified some of its peacetime establishment through its politically helpful role as protector of commerce. The development of overseas naval bases at Gibraltar and Port Mahon were part of the effective pressure against the Barbary pirates, and the development of the naval bases at Jamaica and Antigua provided similar help for the West Indies trades. In the development of the naval base at Antigua, for instance, it was the local assembly that bought the land and built the fortifications in the 1720's as protection for their trade.[36] More permanent naval operations in the West Indies meant that the navy was confident that communications with these overseas naval resources were adequate so that effective English control was not sacrificed. The stifling of piracy after 1720 was also assisted by the emergence of colonial and English newspapers, where incidents of piracy were reported with as much relish as the hangings, and men pressed into service with the pirates were exonerated in ads placed by their more fortunate mates. The detailed descriptions of runaway ships and crews amounted to a fingerprinting of pirated vessels and, given the growth of ocean commerce and communications, there were fewer safe havens for pirates.

Shipowning became less risky in another important respect—and one that was particularly dependent on the quickening exchange of accurate shipping news. Underwriters of marine insurance needed current knowledge of ships, routes, and diplomacy in order to estimate risks effectively and competitively. The most spectacular policies were "lost or not lost" insurances on vessels that were overdue. Premiums here could run to 40 percent in wartime, with payment due even if the ship was later known to have been cast away before the policy was subscribed. Naturally, fraud would be claimed if the person who sought the insurance knew that the ship had been wrecked while gathering insurance. Underwriters would need good sources of information to be able to catch a fraud who asked his colonial correspondent to send notice of a lost or captured vessel in the form of a brief coded message wishing the satisfactory and safe return of the ship.[37] Most insurance policies were purchased in advance of a specified voyage and subscribed by a number of insurers, each taking a small "line" or part of the total insured amount.

Writing insurance and purchasing it required effective correspondence, and so did insurance claims. There was not much English case law concerning marine insurance in this period, and it tended to favor the insurer. No compensation was paid if ships were unseaworthy, crews negligent, or destinations changed.[38] Proving that a ship was completely lost with all hands was an uncommon claim, but one with special problems. Whereas insurers tried to insist that proof of loss was needed, by the 1730's it was accepted that a vessel missing for a year and a day was presumed lost.[39] In 1736 the Bristol owner of a lost ship could hear from a Barbados correspondent that a sea captain had reported that there were men on what he called "Bananoes Islands on the Coast of Guinea" who had found "the Cabin doore, Table, and Other things wch they could Sweare was Poor Capt Franc^s Quirke^s, wch in my Oppinion is Sufficient to Recover the Insurance, as there was noe body Sav'd belonging to her."[40] Although there would not likely be any proof presented to insurers before this vessel had been lost for a year and a day, marine insurance was probing the lesser-known fringes of the English Atlantic.

The English marine insurance business had not developed much of a reputation in the later Stuart period. During the wars of William III and Queen Anne, when much of French naval power was devoted to attacking commerce, the insurers suffered great losses. Indeed, the English marine insurance trade lost most of its reputation and many of its writers in the wake of the French capture of the large Anglo-Dutch Smyrna fleet in 1693. The business operated with major discounts from the nominal insured amounts, capricious settlement of claims in a system that favored the underwriters, and a general belief, which appears to have been well founded, that the majority of premiums were retained as profit.[41] A minor London merchant summarized his feelings about the underwriters in 1712 by noting that their rates were too high and "the Ensurers want insureing."[42]

Ironically, it was the revival of a failed Tudor attempt to monopolize marine insurance that led directly to its improvement. Although the private writing of insurance by merchants was widespread in the seventeenth century, there were pressures toward centralizing the business. Underwriters themselves needed to spread risks and share information, particularly to prevent overinsurance and fraud. Acquiring insurance from a number of writers would also be easier if they were gathered on a walk of the exchange or at a tavern or coffeehouse. A grandiose *Proposal for Incorporation of Insurance* (London, 1672) had been very premature. In the stockjobbing fever of 1717 to 1720, two rival groups sought incorporation as monopolies of marine insurance in England. Merchant resistance was vocal and well organized, and the claim that monopolies would raise prices and create powerful companies, against which the insured could not hope to contend at law, gained some sympathy but did not prove entirely successful. The "Bubble Act" of 1720 would grant both companies a charter to be the only corporations or partnerships in the marine insurance business. Quite contrary to the intent, however, the act promoted the development of individual underwriters who had been gathering at Lloyd's coffeehouse for some time. The London marine insurance business, which was now beginning to attract foreign business because of its favorable rates, would be built on a sound footing in the subsequent generation of peace.[43]

Most of the insurance purchased on English Atlantic voyages between 1675 and 1740 was written in London, but some colonial underwriting became organized after 1720. Soon after Philadelphia gained its first newspaper, its publisher's partner opened a marine insurance office. In advertising his service of bringing underwriters and owners together, John Copson commented that the need to go to London for insurance "has not only been tedious and troublesome, but even very precarious."[44] Perhaps Copson's venture was even more precarious, for nothing more was heard of it. Boston seems to have had a similar office from late in 1724. Joseph Marion, who had established himself as a Boston notary in 1720, started an "Office of Insurance and Bottomrey," which he was still operating in 1739, when a rival office was opened by another notary.[45] These colonial insurance ventures did not command much attention from colonial merchants but suggested a confidence in the marine intelligence becoming available at the leading colonial ports.

London's marine insurance rates late in the seventeenth century were designed to be profitable, with about two thirds of the premiums being retained as profit and the other third used to cover all partial and full loss claims. As the business stabilized in the early eighteenth century, the rates improved dramatically. The portion of the insured amount that was actually payable on a claim rose from as little as 75 percent up to 98 or 99 percent, and transatlantic one-way rates fell near to 2 percent in peacetime.[46] The risks of shipowning had been noticeably reduced and were readily shared with underwriters without diluting control of the vessel in the way that the multiple ownership of vessels had required. Larger merchant firms could gain further advantages with economics of scale as shipping risks were lessened.

The shipping industry had benefited from a number of developments that reduced risks and cost. Improved insurance; suppression of piracy; and better marketing organization through agents, factors, and storekeepers all contributed to savings that would be passed on to freighters and customers because of the decentralized structure of the shipping industry. Improving communications had contributed to all these efficiencies.[47]

Commercial methods current within the English Atlantic changed markedly between 1675 and 1740. Developing communications did not cause these changes but were presumed by them. Emergence of the commission system in the major staple trades presupposed that both parties would correspond at least as frequently as their competitors and that both parties could independently confirm market conditions at the other end of their transactions. The contest for price information was most ferocious within and between the major colonial ports of the western routes, where the struggle for returns to England was continuous and an entrepôt trade in a variety of colonial products enhanced the possibilities and the problems of trading. New World fish was an exception to mercantilist preferences as this perishable product was shipped directly to a wide variety of markets with the growing assistance of letters of advice at Lisbon or Gibraltar. Improving communications helped the shipping industry become more efficient and secure by estimating needed tonnage, shortening port times, advertising measures against pirates, and supporting the marine insurance industry. The growing traffic in news helped to stabilize peacetime freight rates and some commodity prices and generally improved the predictability and control that merchants exercised over their business.

All the benefits of improving communications could not be held as profits by merchant, shipowners, or those who were both. These livelihoods remained comparatively decentralized and competitive, ensuring that their customers could claim a share of the reduced costs. Customers also gained more directly from the improvement in public news. Although the postal services were relatively private and expensive, the developing newspapers were a public challenge to these same private advantages. A newspaper was an economic document and not simply because it revealed prices current, ship movements, goods for sale, and estate settlements. International diplomatic and military news, which was so prominent in the papers, had consequences for business confidence, credit, prices, and profits.[48] Admittedly, the news printed in colonial newspapers was often much older than news that could be received privately through the post, and the postmaster-publishers could be expected to appreciate this gap as long as their own newspaper held a local monopoly. Yet the trend toward "fresher advices" helped newspaper readers whether they were buyers or sellers. Increased merchant shipping, postal services, and newspaper circulation all contributed to more efficient commerce.

Integration of the English Atlantic economy proceeded impressively after 1675. Growing specialization and interdependence, especially in the staple trades and their subsidiaries, meant that more lives and livelihoods became dependent on oceanic trade and communications. In some respects, communications developments were a product of this economic transformation, which attracted increased shipping and made posts and papers feasible. Nonetheless, economic specialization could be undertaken only when large enough markets could be anticipated and the risks were deemed bearable. Improving communications reduced some risks and allowed the sharing of others.[49] Communications improvements were both cause and consequence of increased participation in the complex English Atlantic economic community.

12 · Governors, Agents, and the Communication of Politics

As a polity, the English Atlantic was transformed between 1675 and 1740. Metropolitan concerns that initially fueled the changes included the desire to control colonial staple trades that were of fiscal importance to the restored Stuarts. English provinces everywhere were being drawn into an increasingly complicated and interdependent political system by administrative and judicial initiatives, by equally centralized opposition to those initiatives, then by the overwhelming demands of the generation of war that followed 1689, and by the rewards and punishments of patronage politics in the subsequent generation. Provincial leaders in counties and colonies were provided with opportunities as well as conflicting pressures. Especially in the new colonial settlements (although also in most chartered cities of England), local order, legitimacy, and power could not be sustained by traditions of social deference. Comparatively new elites sought to gain, consolidate, and bequeath power by many means, including the invocation of the crown to bless their judicial and political dominance. Locally prominent men were lured to seek offices and honors from the crown, and at the same time they could parade their substance as a guarantee that they would protect the locality from undue impositions from the metropolis. Although full of inherent tensions and contradictions, the objectives of the English government and of colonial elites promoted the emergence of an integrated English Atlantic polity.

The emerging political culture of the English Atlantic had special effects on two groups of interpreters, the royal governors and the colonial agents. The emergence and regularizing of both of these positions illustrate the political integration of the empire. New governors and agents both represented fresh political connections with their employers and were political communicators even if they also represented the limits of communication. In certain aspects, improving oceanic communications benefited these representatives in their task, but the general tendency was for the delegating groups in the relationships to strengthen their position by using the increasing opportunities to supplement, correct, admonish, and interfere. Increased communications also undercut both governors and agents by allowing opposing interests and alternative versions of events to be heard. Neither group had ever had a monopoly of news despite some efforts by royal governors, but the posts, the papers, and the increased oceanic traffic made it increasingly difficult for governors or agents to interpret positions with any freedom or to negotiate compromises without detection.[1] As insulators, or shock absorbers between the English administration and the local colonial elites who dominated the emerging colonial assemblies, the governors and the agents could be expected to become progressively less effective. At the same time, the English government and the colonial assemblies were represented with increasing accuracy.

English politics and political ideas would also affect the role of governors and agents. Whiggery may owe debts to the English Civil War, but it was born as opposition to the restored Stuarts, it grew through the political fireworks of Queen Anne's reign, and it became the orthodoxy of those who held power in the generation after 1715. The Whig focus on Parliament as the legitimate counterweight to the monarch prompted echoes in the colonies. By the end of the seventeenth century, colonial assemblies were customary and were drawing on Whig rhetoric and English precedence to challenge royal governors. After 1714 all royal governors had to be Whigs to get their positions, but none of them were regarded as Whig by their colonial challengers. The colonial agents in London would find the Whig political milieu increasingly receptive to the politics of interest that they represented. Although there was a noticeable growth of imperial politics in London, the exercise of the political power being assembled at the center was not always at the expense of the periphery.

English colonial administration was transformed as the seventeenth century closed. The volume of correspondence, legislation, and formal documentation grew as did the number of colonies under royal control, the number of crown officials in those colonies, and the number of English government offices with interest in colonial affairs. The Privy Council was a formal coordinator of executive business concerning the empire, though the conduct of business there was slow, capricious, and labyrinthine. Although Parliament's role in imperial legislation would grow, the center of colonial administrative business became the Lords of Trade in 1675 and, its successor after 1696, the Board of Trade. Improving communications can be seen gradually transforming the imperial business of other offices of government, perhaps nowhere more dramatically than the development of Admiralty involvement in the West Indies from visiting to permanent squadrons and then to naval bases.[2] Yet it was in the "Plantations Office" itself that administrative consequences of improving communications were most obvious.

In the development of both the imperial machinery of supervision and the role of royal governor, an ambitious new beginning was made in 1670. A new council of plantations was then established to "inform themselves" on a wide variety of matters relating to America, the West Indies, the Guiana coast "or within any of that Circuit of the Globe, that is generally knowne or called by the name of the West Indies." In several specifics, the instructions for this council sought to establish a new level of control, presumed a new level of effort, and would have enduring significance because the instructions were inherited by the council's successors for more than a century. Three specific assignments deserve attention here: helping prepare governors' instructions, scrutinizing colonial laws so that they could be disallowed if contrary to English law or unjust to colonists, and maintaining a steady correspondence with governors.[3] In all three of these responsibilities, new levels of communications with the governors and the colonial political elites would be invited if not required.

Royal instructions to the governors of the four royal colonies of 1670 (Barbados, the Leeward Islands, Jamaica, and Virginia) would not suggest the scope and consequence of what would become the most systematic and regular effort at royal control. Instructions to governors, like those to ship captains, were intended to place some limits on the use of the power that was being delegated. The assumption was that no communication could be presumed while decisions were being made. The private, if not secret, nature of the instructions would eventually make them harder to follow in the face of local opposition even if the instructions themselves had not become stylized and urged unpopular and impossible executive policies on new governors of a much larger collection of royal colonies. Yet "government by instruction" was a means of describing and controlling the role of royal governor that was actively developed to the end of the Stuart period. The general process has been described well elsewhere.[4] Here it is necessary only to note the changes in governors' instructions that particularly presumed or imposed new levels of communications on the council of trade, the governors, or those interested in the administration at either end.

The 1670 council has been short-lived but made two innovations of particular interest in preparing the instructions for the first governor of the Leeward Islands the following year. Governor Sir Charles Wheeler was the first governor who was expressly ordered not to declare war on any of his neighbors without explicit order. As has already been discussed, this order would soon spread from the Leeward Islands to all the colonies, provoking an urgent concern with communicating news of war.[5]

Another new instruction, again in keeping with an instruction the council itself had received, required Wheeler to send all existing and new laws to the Council of Plantations "by the first opportunity."[6] This would be the first of a series of measures designed to curb the power already gathering in the colonial assemblies in royal colonies. Instructions represented a rein on the governor's capacity to make his own compromises and the call for complete collections of existing laws and prompt conveyance of new ones meant that imperial authorities were intent on discovering how well the governors kept their instructions. This provision would become standard for the West Indian royal governors in the 1670's and for all royal governors in the next decade.[7] Although much less obvious and dramatic than the instruction about declaring war, the review of colonial legislation brought a great deal of communication in its wake. The origin of the colonial agents owed much to the particular threat of higher sugar duties in 1670,[8] but a major regular part of their responsibilities would concern explaining, defending, and smoothing the Whitehall review of the work of the colonial legislatures who paid the agents. Those London merchants who were not agents made invited and unsolicited contributions to this legislative review, both in their own interest and on behalf of colonial dissidents or victims anxious to destroy harmful legislation. Governors found it expedient, even before it became a matter of regular instruction, to explain and justify laws being transmitted; nor was it uncommon for a governor to ask London to veto a law he found bad but too politically expensive to veto in the colony himself. The emergence of this method of intended control reflected the growing sophistication of the political economy of the English Atlantic.[9] The information required for an effective review of colonial legislation was not always available, but the limits of this method of controlling the colonial legislatures did not result from weaknesses in communications.

Before the 1670's had ended, the new Lords of Trade and Plantations made a more ambitious attempt to control colonial legislation, again through royal instruction. The new Jamaica assembly had proved particularly aggressive in extending its liberties, and a clash had been shaping between it and the assertive Lords of Trade and Plantations.[10] The instructions sent with the earl of Carlisle in 1678 as governor of Jamaica included a clause that would carry to the colonies the Poynings method, used in Ireland from 1494 to 1800. No assembly was to be called without special royal order. The governor, when applying to the king for such an assembly, was to send along drafts of acts that he and his council thought fit to pass. The drafts would be amended in Whitehall and then presented to the assembly to accept or reject without amendment. Here was aggressive centralization at the expense of assembly and governor. Some 40 proposed acts were also forwarded to provide Jamaica with a new basis for royal government. As the Jamaicans mustered arguments to defeat this initiative and as the governor was soon allied with them, it is not surprising that the distance from London was part of their argument. Jamaica was farther from London than Dublin had been in 1494, but it is ironic that the colony chosen to pioneer this experiment was one of the farthest from England. The unsuccessful scheme to apply a similar "Poynings Law" to Virginia the following year represented another attempt to reach out to the farthest colonies from London with an ambitious and oppressive method of direct control.[11] The Lords of Trade's reach definitely exceeded their grasp, but neither they nor their opponents doubted that their arbitrariness could be imposed on a colony that was 12 weeks away by sea.

Control of colonial legislation emerged again two years later in the preparation of a charter for the only new proprietary colony launched after 1670. The most unusual requirement of the charter, when compared with others that were used as its model, was that laws passed in Pennsylvania were to be sent to England within five years of their passage and the crown's officers were to have six months thereafter for royal disallowance of any laws found objectionable. If not declared void within six months, a law was confirmed. This provision fitted well with the preoccupations of the Lords of Trade although the time limits proved to be much more restrictive for Whitehall than for Pennsylvania.[12] When the opportunity arose to design a new charter for Massachusetts Bay, it, too, became subject to a similar provision. This time, however, the timetable was made more realistic for the long journey through the offices of Whitehall. The acts were to be forwarded from the colony by the first opportunity after their passing, and the crown officers were to have three years after receipt during which the laws could be disallowed.[13] Even this provision proved too ambitious for the resources that Whitehall gave to reviewing colonial legislation. Several Massachusetts acts were confirmed only to prove a later embarrassment to imperial interests.[14] It was also evident that by the end of the century there were too many laws being received to be handled properly by the Board of Trade. Because of the charter requirements, Pennsylvania and Massachusetts laws continued to receive more attention than those of the other colonies. A new approach was needed, and it would emerge after 1702.

The solution was simple enough but probably could not have been accepted without the 35 years of trying to do more or without the improvements in communications in the meantime. Provoked by a Barbados law prejudicial to creditors, the Board of Trade issued a circular letter to all royal governors in November 1706 ordering them to give special attention to all laws that affected the royal prerogative or the private property of subjects. Such laws must either by sent to London in draft for royal approval (that is, to follow the Poynings system, which would be most unpopular), or all acts of this kind must include a suspending clause that would postpone their operation until they had been approved in London.[15] Here was a solution to several problems. Governors could avoid unpopularity by moving sensitive decisions to London. The Board of Trade could pinpoint acts that were most likely to offend simply by finding suspending clauses, and the suspending clause would also make colonial agents in London draw attention to such acts by seeking their confirmation. Should the administrators fail to notice such an act and the agents miss it as well, no harm would be done because the act was inoperative without express attention and approval. This method was a prerequisite for the development of the more general "lye by" system for handling all colonial legislation. Without fearing that offensive laws were in force without being noticed, the Board of Trade and its legal advisors did not need to review all colonial legislation regularly.[16] Colonial laws were allowed to sit unconfirmed but with the potential of being disallowed should objections to them be raised later. The only laws that would need immediate attention were those containing suspending clauses or those laws subject to special provisions, the laws of Pennsylvania and Massachusetts. In one form or another, this instruction became standard for all royal colonies, and a number of other specific categories of legislation came to be treated similarly.[17] Not only were the kinds of legislation subject to the suspending clauses increased, but the provision that all laws repealing others must have suspending clauses (1728) also greatly expanded the amount of colonial legislation subject to this provision by the middle of the eighteenth century.

The suspending clause presumed that no essential legislation would be unduly held up in the process of imperial review, but in one case the speed of the process was made explicit. In instructions of 1714, the governor of Maryland was not to assent to any law that concerned the property of a subject resident in Great Britain unless it included the proviso that the law

> shall not be in force there till after the expiration of eighteen months
> in time of war and twelve months in time of piece . . .[18]

This peculiar variation undermined the whole function of the suspending clause, but it revealed what was thought an acceptable time for imperial review by 1714. The weakness of the suspending clause was, like much else in the ambitions of imperial administration, the needs and weaknesses of the royal governors. Their compromises severely undermined the method, but the suspending clause was still an active form of restraint on colonial assemblies in 1770, when the Georgia Commons objected to the process as tending "to annihilate the Rights of any Assembly."[19]

Imperial review of colonial legislation developed without any apparent concern for the mechanics of Atlantic communications. From the first orders of 1671 to send acts by the first vessels through the aggressive attempts to impose Poynings' law on Jamaica and Virginia to the suspending clauses after 1706, there were no serious hesitations caused by worries about the speed, frequency, or risks of Atlantic shipping. In 1682, Pennsylvania's review process was allowed 5½ years. A decade later a Massachusetts charter gave the process a little more than 3 years. By 1714 it was feasible to talk of a 12- to 18-month limit for disallowing Maryland laws. The review of colonial legislation was part of the centralization of authority for which an acceptable level of communications was one prerequisite.

Paralleling the legislative review was the emergence of judicial appeals to the Privy Council from the colonies in the generation after 1664. In this process, parties were allowed a year and a day to prosecute their appeal, with the months of December, June, and July favored for hearings, and little likelihood of any action in the three months following 1 August.[20] Like legislative review, legal appeals increased dependence on transatlantic delivery of advocates, witnesses, laws, letters, briefs, and affidavits, to colonial and personal agents and to Whitehall offices on the one hand and on letters of query or warning to governors, a growing host of minor officials, and colonists on the other.

Government by instruction had emerged quickly in the 1670's and 1680's into a formal executive system of rather standardized powers and responsibilities. Delegation of royal authority became more cautious in this process, for the Plantations Office itself and the legislative and judicial reviews all contributed to more direct Whitehall involvement in the regular governance of the colonies. The general pattern of governors' instructions had stabilized by 1700 and ossified thereafter. Although a governor's instructions remained important, he could no longer be described as governed by instructions. Instructions were supplemented by additional instructions as well as royal proclamations, Acts of Parliament, orders and judgments of the Privy Council, and orders and inquiries from the Lords of Trade and then the Board of Trade. Emergence of the order that governors write to the Board of Trade by every opportunity accompanied and supported the other developments that tended to centralize colonial affairs.

Correspondence between colonial governors and the Lords of Trade and their successor, the Board of Trade, constitutes one of the largest, most accessible, and most influential sources of the history of the English Atlantic before 1740. The sheer size of the collection allows some meaningful attention to general patterns and significant variations. It is also possible to compare the frequency of letters from most governors with the individaul performance of some and with a proprietary governor's correspondence with his master and also to compare the correspondence of some governors with that of agents of a major trading company.

Governors were expected to be guided by their instructions, not by correspondence. Governors were not chosen with any eye to their capacity as clerks although a number of them proved to be prolific and literate correspondents. It was 1702 before the governors of most colonies received explicit instructions to correspond regularly with the appropriate secretary of state and with the Board of Trade, and that order was probably inspired by the particular ambitions of the new secretary of state as well as the institution of the West Indies packet boat service that year.[21] It can also be argued that the letters exchanged between governors and the Board of Trade were not really correspondence at all. Governors received few replies, wrote subsequent letters before the previous ones were answered (or perhaps even received), and seldom asked for advice, which indicated that they did not wait for a reply before taking action. The governors were reporting, explaining, defending, justifying; they were also petitioning, but they were not usually asking questions, and they were not usually being sustained by a regular correspondence from Whitehall.

For all that, correspondence was very important to the governors. The Lords of Trade and Board of Trade were corporate entities that survived political storms whatever happened to their membership. A governor could write his case to this group without fearing that the recipient would be out of office. As a central agency likely to have most colonial business either directly or by referral, the Lords of Trade could provide a nascent lobby for a governor, one that could effectively delay or disrupt the designs of opponents from the colony or aspirants for the governor's job.

There was another significant function of correspondence for the governor that should not be overlooked. Although his letters to London represented a force in local politics, a letter from the London government could have special powers beyond its contents. Two governors of Massachusetts who were most avid correspondents reveal something of this power of the post. Richard Coote, earl of Bellomont, complained to Secretary of State Vernon:

> There came hither two ships from London, the last week in May, which brought me not a letter from any of the ministers, and another ship four days ago, but not a letter by that neither. What must people here and in New York think, but that either the King and his ministers have no sort of care or value for these plantations, not minding whether they fall into French hands or no; or else that I am in disgrace with the King, and that all this neglect proceeds from a personal slight to me. I never in all my life was so vexed and ashamed as now; I put the best face I can on it, but I find other people take the liberty to judge of the present conduct of affairs in England.[22]

Thirty-four years later Governor Jonathan Belcher urged his London correspondent, Richard Partridge,

> and when our fall ships are all come away I hope you will write me in the winter season by S° Carolina, Virginia, Maryland, Philad[a], York, & Lix[a] [Lisbon], or by any other ways you may think probable for letters to get to me before the arrival of our spring ships. A letter from London in the winter may be of great service.[23]

The change from Bellomont's concern for a letter on the first spring ships to Belcher's desire for a letter in the winter indicates the growth that occurred in expectations. The reasons behind the desire for a letter remained similar; a letter represented live political connections as well as marketable information.

In times of major political change in England, governors had political urgencies of their own that went beyond the formal problems of their office. Although of less dramatic proportions than the revolution of 1688, the accession of a new monarch could send waves of personal and political uncertainty across the Atlantic. Public awareness and enjoyment of this uneasiness can be seen by a London newspaper item, reprinted in the *American Weekly Mercury*, on the political anxieties attending the accession of George II.

> A certain Governour desires leave to come to England on his private Affairs. Another Governour wants an Exchange. Some Commanders abroad, that have got enough, want to be call'd home; others, to be continued; or removed to better Stations. But the worst is these Gentlemen being afar off, and not understanding how Matters stand since his Majesty's Death, are at a Loss to know where to make a

proper Application; and therefore are angry with us for not telling them when they received the News of the said Turn, what great Changes would ensue upon it.[24]

It was no wonder that governors cultivated friends to whom they sent letters to be distributed to government offices when and if appropriate in the current circumstances.[25] To keep his position amid political change, a governor needed to be more accomplished with his pen than with his sword.

In a consideration of the actual frequency of correspondence of the governors and the London bureaucrats, it is useful to notice evidence of expectations. It was not usual for the Lords of Trade or their successor to require, as they did of Governor Atkins of Barbados in December 1676, that the governor write "by every single ship."[26] Three years later, discovering that the earl of Carlisle was remiss as a correspondent as well as unreliable as an agent of sterner control of the Jamaica elite, the Lords of Trade ordered governors to submit quarterly reports. Although no order this specific became a part of the governors' instructions, the term "upon all occasion" did become standard.[27] Lord Cornbury was not governor of New York for long before he was told by the Board of Trade in April 1703 that "we do expect from your Lordship a constant account by every conveyance of all matters and transactions within your Government."[28] Reprimands to governors who did not write often enough were uncommon but not unheard of. Although the Board of Trade gathered much of its information from the governors' letters—and specific questions were often put to the governors—there were relatively few occasions on which the board paced its work in order to hear specific replies from governors. "General Heads of Inquiry," naval officers' lists, and other major sources of information were not usually seen as urgent. During the operation of Dummer's West Indies packets, there was noticeable pressure on both the governors and the Board of Trade to increase the frequency of letters, but governors were not usually expected, as were eighteenth-century British diplomats abroad, to correspond by every post.[29]

Those acting as royal governors exchanged some 3124 letters with the Lords of Trade, the Board of Trade, or the secretaries of these bodies in the 63 years between 1675 and 1737.[30] Colonial governors wrote an average of three letters for every one sent them by the colonial authority in London, and the total correspondence was comparable to a letter a week being written in 1 of 14 Atlantic colonies or in Whitehall.[31] (See Table 12.1.) Seen another way, this very general picture suggests that governors wrote Whitehall on the average about once every three and one-half months and received an average of a letter a year in return. Although no one calculated these levels of performance or expectation and although the mere counting of letters can hide more than it reveals, some aspects of political communications can be sensed by a general overview of this correspondence.

There were three distinct groups of colonies in terms of the frequency of correspondence with the Lords of Trade at the Plantations Office. Governors of the five royal colonies of Jamaica, the Leeward Islands, Barbados, New

York, and Massachusetts wrote the Plantations Office approximately a letter every two months and received a letter in return twice a year. (See Table 12.1.) The five colonies in this category were all major ones although the absence of Virginia confirms that the communications seasons of the tobacco trade and limited postal services were affecting communications there through much of this period.

The second group of royal colonies, comprising South Carolina, Virginia, Bermuda, Bahamas, and Maryland, seems to have had chief executives who operated on a rather different basis from the other five. (See Table 12.1.) With the notable exception of the Chesapeake colonies, all these might be regarded as lesser colonies in terms of trade, population, and political and administrative business in London. The place of the Carolinas in these findings is exaggerated by the fact that Francis Nicholson, by then an aging but very experienced governor, defended himself with a flurry of 15 letters to the Plantations Office in 1724.[32] Nova Scotia, the most marginal royal colony, had correspondence to match. Governors of these other royal colonies wrote the Lords of Trade approximately once every four months and received an average of a letter a year in return.

Proprietary and charter governments had no reason to correspond regularly with the Lords of Trade or the Board of Trade and did not do so. Governors of Pennsylvania, Connecticut, and Rhode Island wrote to the Plantations Office about once in two years on average and received a direct letter from that source about every third year. Naturally, both the Plantations Office and the proprietary governors did more of their limited exchanging of information by the correspondence each had with the proprietors. However, the proprietary and charter colonies were very marginal in terms of direct correspondence.

When the frequency of governors' letters is surveyed for change over time, very little is found. (See Table 12.2.) Although individuals differed greatly, the very general rhythms of the correspondence of later Stuart West Indian governors were quite like those of their successors half a century later. Although the French wars disrupted the regularity of correspondence, governors maintained nearly the same levels of correspondence, and the West Indies packet-boat service enhanced the number of letters sent to the Whitehall authorities from Jamaica. Certainly, the earlier period must have been marked by greater effort on the part of governors in order to establish expectations that would become easier to meet later. The only notable improvement in frequency of letters was in those of the governors of Virginia and New York. The improving North American posts would be particularly helpful for governors of Virginia. Whether or not governors, secretaries, or Whitehall bureaucrats consciously noticed the number of letters sent by governors of colonies with varying levels of consequence in London, it would appear that some sense of what was expected did develop. Although the number of letters written remained similar as time went on, governors were actually using fewer of the available opportunities to write.

The suspicion that governors did not write to the Plantations Office "by every opportunity" can be tested from a number of sources. Despite the growth of mail services in the colonies and in England, despite the impressive general increases in the levels of transatlantic shipping, there is no sustained growth in the number of letters written by governors of the colonies between 1675 and 1737. Gubernatorial correspondence seemed to have an accepted pace of its own. Three separate tests will provide a more direct method by which this suspicion can be judged. The correspondence of Richard Coote, earl of Bellomont, provides a graphic example of how often a governor could write from either New York or Boston at the end of the seventeenth century. Secondly, a run of correspondence between James Logan and William Penn will be examined as another example of maximized opportunities. And finally, the correspondence of West Indian governors will be compared with those of Royal African Company agents at the same places and times.

Richard Coote, earl of Bellomont, was a compulsive letter writer who showered the Board of Trade with long, detailed letters throughout his period as governor of both New York and Massachusetts.[33] From his arrival in New York early in Arpil 1698 until his death there 35 months later, Bellomont wrote a phenomenal 43 letters to the board and its secretary. Despite the light and seasonal traffic between New York and England, Bellomont succeeded in writing the "Plantation Office" in 12 of the 20 calendar months he spent in New York. Although the months he missed were generally predictable, he did manage letters in midwinter of both 1700 and 1701.[34] Bellomont managed his vast territory from Boston for 15 months beginning in May 1699, and his performance confirmed the evidence about seasons of shipping out of Boston. December 1699 was the only month in which he did not date a letter to the Board of Trade or its secretary.

Bellomont sought the same diligence in his correspondents that he revealed himself. Although he never gained this from the Board of Trade, he tried hard—and with some success. Winter was to be no excuse, for he urged Secretary Popple to send letters by way of Virginia or Barbados at either end of the winter season and

> excepting in the dead of winter, there comes sloops hither from Barbados every month in the year, and two or three months earlier in the beginning of the year than any ships come from England to Boston or this place.[35]

When his political fortunes soured with the Kidd affair and the Tory victory in England, Bellomont became more insistent. "I never longed to hear from England so much as now. 'Tis a long time since I have heard from your Board," he wrote Popple.[36] His wait had just begun. He was more upset when the first letter to arrive from the Board of Trade the next spring was eight months old, and his London agent had misdirected his packet. Bellomont began to hint at deliberate delays in his mail, as other governors would do at times of personal political tension.[37] Most governors did not seek so close a correspondence with the Board of Trade, and no doubt it was as well. The limited response to Bellomont's letters derived from English administrative practices and priorites, not from lack of shipping opportunities. Although they could not satisfy Governor Bellomont, the Board of Trade did write him 16 letters in his two complete years in office, which was unmatched by their correspondence with any other governor although hardly a full response to his 29 letters. In this instance, writing more letters yielded more replies.

Bellomont's correspondence from New York also shows the impact of the postal service rather starkly. Thirty years earlier, Governor Lovelace complained to an English correspondent that sending letters from New York was like producing elephants, "once allmost in 2 yeares."[38] Although this may have been a literary flourish, it seems obvious that New York's links to London had improved mightily during the subsequent 30 years or even in the decade after Francis Nicholson was there as lieutenant governor of the Dominion of New England.[39] Admittedly, Bellomont governed in peacetime and from ports on the intercolonial post routes of North America. Yet his successful efforts to correspond with the Board of Trade at a time when New York's economy was weak and there were no transatlantic packet boats demonstrate possibilities that were seldom realized.

The correspondence between William Penn and his colonial factotum, James Logan, provides another measure of the possibilities of transatlantic communications. Logan's reputation as a careful and skillful defender of the proprietor's interest is reinforced by his regular correspondence with Penn between the latter's second return to England and Logan's visit to him early in 1710. In these eight years Logan wrote an average of eight letters a year and received five a year from Penn. It is no surprise that both men wrote often, even though it was wartime, but it is surprising that Logan wrote Penn as often as the Jamaican governors wrote the Board of Trade in this period. The governor of Jamaica had a monthly packet leaving for England as well as a naval squadron that provided extra opportunities to correspond with London.[40] Many of Logan's letters were sent by the West Indies, and several mention specifically that they went by the packet boats. Although the Delaware River was usually clogged with ice for three or four weeks during the winter,[41] Logan managed to write one fourth of his letters to Penn in the coldest third of the year. If Logan managed this pace of correspondence, with so few concessions to the seasons, royal governors of New York, Massachusetts, or New Hampshire could have exploited the overland mail route south to Philadelphia more than any of them, except Bellomont, did. Certainly Lord Cornbury's defenses against Board of Trade claims that he did not write often enough,[42] lose something from a comparison with the efforts of Logan in the same period at a port connected by postrider with New York.

If Logan's pace of correspondence reflects on royal governors, William Penn's rate of reply is a sharp reminder that the royal colonial officials in London were making very little effort to correspond by available shipping or in all available seasons. Aging, ailing William Penn managed five letters a year to Logan. No royal governor could expect that kind of attention from the "Plantation Office" on a regular basis.[43] Penn's letters were also distributed rather evenly throughout the year.[44] The Penn-Logan correspondence, like the letters of Lord Bellomont, suggest that the surviving correspondence between royal colonial governors and the Plantations Office are not a fair indicator of the communications facilities available and used by those in more immediate need of transatlantic correspondence.

Comparisons between the letter writing of British West Indian governors and the agents of the Royal African Company at the same places and times constitute a third test of the proposition that governors were not corresponding by every opportunity. Table 12.3 confirms that the governors and the Plantation Office were not making every effort to correspond. The Royal African Company records provide comparisons seldom available for business over a number of decades, and they substantiate that this company of slave traders made much fuller use of the communications facilities than did the government. At both ends of the London-Barbados correspondence, for example, the slave traders wrote more than twice as often as did the colonial administrators. The well-known and well-used collection of official colonial correspondence clearly underrepresents the opportunities of communication in the English Atlantic.

A variety of reasons might explain why the pace of gubernatorial correspondence with the Board of Trade failed to respond to improved opportunities except for the use of Dummer's packet boats during the War of the Spanish Succession. As has been suggested earlier, governors were seldom chosen for clerical skills. Although few expressed their objections to the harrying impositions of large and troublesome questions from Whitehall quite as directly as Governor Handasyd,[45] a governor had reason to resist having his time taken up providing London bureaucrats with information that would then be used directly against him or would allow policy decisions in Whitehall that previously were within the governor's power. Governors found correspondence necessary, but it was part of the struggle to build and hold power, to fend off both local and London contenders and critics. Governors lost the battle in the long run to both forces, partly because increased information flows destroyed the governor's place as interpreter of empire to the local elites. Governors were not only being challenged by informed bureaucrats in London and by informed leaders of emerging colonial assemblies. The victory of English Whiggery would enlarge the place of Parliament in colonial affairs, and that legislative authority would not display much concern for governors, who could be represented as the executive remnants of dread Stuart tyranny.

Parliamentary concern for the empire was limited in the lifetime after 1675, and the focus remained on trade. Of 95 acts of Parliament between 1660 and 1753 that were cited in governors' trade instructions, only 19 had been passed in the 47 years down to 1707, and exactly 4 times as many were passed during the next 47 years.[46] Parliament had established colonial trade policy in the second half of the seventeenth century and developed a structure for its enforcement. Parliament became the forum where the early eighteenth-century administrators sought tighter control of what could still be seen as a royal empire. Parliament's role was ambiguous; it set the English duties on colonial staples with considerably more alacrity than it would support administrative centralization by a bureaucracy that was not within its own direct power. Lobbying Parliament was one of the purposes for the creation of colonial agents, and this became an increasingly significant part of their work after 1689.

Parliament's pace of business was usually one within which the English Atlantic political community could function by the end of the seventeenth century. Parliament, like the law, had developed over centuries in which England itself was more loosely tied by communications. Improved communication within England did not bring major changes in pace or procedures although the total volume of work handled by existing methods increased. The legislative year could involve a brief, if optional, pre-Christmas session of three to six weeks, a sustained session from mid-January to Easter, and a resumption for a few weeks after the Easter recess to dispose of unfinished business.

Short parliamentary sessions were never preoccupied with colonial matters, so that intended colonial legislation often died on the order papers as the session wound down in May or June, followed by a long recess in which the parties could prepare for a possible return in November. Lobbyists, agents, government officials, as well as friends and associates, all had time to gather evidence, supporters, or moneys in anticipation of renewed discussion in the House of Commons. Spring and summer communications on the Atlantic did not serve all colonies equally well, but there were opportunities for interested parties in most colonies to hear of proposed legislation and attempt to influence the outcome through the London merchant community or more directly through contracts with Parliamentarians. This would be true from the 1690's on and commonplace after the turn of the century. The effective use of news during a parliamentary session would be limited and would favor nearer colonies like Massachusetts and Barbados. The stately pace of Parliament, a pace that did much to determine the general "seasons of business," could cause hardship and irritating delays for those who had traveled to England to have something accomplished or prevented, as was particularly evident later, in the 1760's and 1770's, when Parliament became more central to colonial management.[47] Yet the leisurely pace of Parliament, compared even to the pace of Whitehall, allowed colonials plenty of opportunity for lobbying. Parliament's pace had not changed much in the course of the seventeenth century, but the development of the colonial trades and communications allowed better presentation of colonial concerns. Legislation central to colonial economic life, like the Navigation Acts of 1651 and 1660, reached the colonies as unanticipated fiat. By the time of the last of the Navigation Acts of 1696, a close network of transatlantic political and administrative exchanges had anticipated the law. The prolonged struggle to defeat a bill to resume control of proprietary and charter governments at the end of the seventeenth century and the fierce intercolonial lobbying that preceded the Molasses Act were just two of the fuller demonstrations of the merging transatlantic politics of Parliament.[48]

Parliaments had little direct and formal concern with the speed and reliability of Atlantic communications, but their activities did show some assumptions on this matter. Firstly, Parliament established the effective dates of its legislation for the colonies. In the case of the principal Navigation Acts, there is no evidence of a recognized convention. The 1660 act had no less than four different effective dates for different provisions of the act, ranging from less than three months for the English monopoly of colonial shipping to more than six months for the beginning of the enumeration of major colonial staples.[49] Most of the subsequent additions and modifications to the act were to take effect within five to eight months of royal assent, with the notable exception of the ship registry provisions of the 1696 Navigation Act.[50]

Effective dates of parliamentary legislation were little challenge to the pace of Atlantic communications. A second, more indirect indicator of parliamentary perceptions of Atlantic communications can be read in the same legislation. The system of bonds by shipmasters and reports by colonial naval officers on ship movements in their colonies was designed to create a network of information on ships and cargoes that would prevent and detect violations of the Navigation Acts. A shipmaster's bond, promising to trade in conformity with the laws, was forfeit unless proof of compliance were received at the port of bonding within 18 months.[51] Here was confidence in transatlantic communications, a confidence that was not usually misplaced.

Colonial interest in Parliament's activities naturally exceeded Parliament's interest in the colonies. The correspondence of regular and special colonial agents in London included self-justification in their detailed information about lobbying, but the reports presumed understanding of the people and patterns of metropolitan politics among the colonial elites. As colonial newspapers emerged, they reported parliamentary activities and devoted space to court appointments and reprinted, in the paper or as separate pamphlets, laws affecting the colonies. They even indulged in the apparent extravagance of long lists of the MPs elected, all indicating a presumed interest in such matters among their readers.[52]

In the half century after 1688, Parliament came to play a more important role in legislating for the empire. As the royal prerogative lost its potency in England, the king's servants needed parliamentary authority to bolster royal proclamations. The results were ambiguous. Parliaments proved less than enthusiastic for stronger control over the colonies on occasion. The lobbying network that had begun to defend colonial interests against the taxation of colonial staples developed into something quite different. Indeed, Parliament became a defense against centralization early in the eighteenth century. Parliament's pace of business helped make colonial lobbying effective as well as expensive. As the lobbying developed at Westminster and at Whitehall, the network of transatlantic political patronage also became more explicit and more political. Taken together, these developments would ameliorate the centralizing consequences of improving Atlantic communications. Governors, customs officers, and revenue collectors were increasing in numbers as were the opportunities to tie them more closely to their London superiors. At the same time, the ships that carried these reports carried agents, funds, and letters designed to coordinate the lobbying of planters and merchants in the interest of London patronage for colonial elites and against London exercise of close supervision at the same time. The integration of politics and patronage was definitely centralized in London, but so were those efforts to resist centralization. The colonial agents had a vital role to play in this process.

Colonial agents in London were performing functions analogous to some roles of the royal governors. Governors were to interpret imperial attitudes, priorities, and initiatives to the colonial leaders; colonial agents worked to make administrators, legislators, and judges in England appreciate colonial views and needs. As interpreters, both governors and agents were at once essential connections in the imperial polity, and they were also insulation in that system as long as they dominated the flow of political information to their employers, again both as servants and interpreters. There are no surviving collections of the correspondence of agents at all comparable to the surviving governors' letters, so the changes over time are more a matter of conjecture in the case of the agents. The increases in private, political, and economic correspondence that seems evident from this study and the increasing numbers of crown officers in the colonies are both trends that would damage the attempt of anyone to claim anything resembling a monopoly of reliable information. Yet it was within the time period explored in this study that the colonial agents became necessary for all colonies because they were effective.

Sending well-connected people from the colonies to London to accomplish some specific tasks was a form of agency that was as old as the colonies themselves, but a noticeable change occurred in the 1670's. London merchants trading with the colonies and London coreligionists of colonials had functioned as private agents on political as well as economic assignments and had been known to band together to inform and influence Parliament as early as 1643. Both sugar and tobacco traders were active more often after the Restoration and were particularly prominent in efforts to avert new duties on their commodities in 1670.[53] Merchant and gentleman lobbies would have specific colonial interests to represent, or did so as part of their own interest. Yet, like the special agents of the colonies, the lobbies could not sustain the task of providing the government with information or providing the colonial governments with constant friends at court or Westminster. The need for a regular agent, whose responsibilities might well include rousing the merchant lobby as individuals or as a group, was being created by the administrative reforms of the Plantation Office in the 1670's.

It is telling that there were several initiatives from Whitehall itself, urging colonial governors to have their assemblies provide for a regular agent in London. Just after the Restoration, a new Council of Plantations urged the governor of Virginia to join his council in appointing agents from time to time to travel to London and facilitate the colony's business there. At this point, the assumption was that colonial travelers would serve the purpose but that Whitehall wanted them more often than had been common. Twenty years later, the Lords of Trade wanted an agent from Jamaica badly enough to make procuring one an item in the governor's instructions.[54] After 1696 the Board of Trade found colonial agents so important as sources of information and also as facilitators of business within the government that they actively and successfully urged that authorized agents be appointed from all the colonies to be available for consultation regularly.[55]

Despite Whitehall's interest in colonial agents, there was never any doubt about whom they were to serve. Colonial governments would be divided on who should hire and instruct the agent or who should be the agent, but he was a paid officer of the colonial government.[56] The actual work of the agent was outlined by Lord Bellomont when he was trying to recruit John Champante to accept the task on behalf of New York.

> Tis not unreputable; and tho the salary be but £100 per annum yet there is this to be said for the Imployment, that there is not much to do: and it will give you frequent opportunities of accesse to the Ministers, and offices of businesse at Court.[57]

A more strenuous description of the task was provided the following year by Sir Henry Ashurst, who had been agent for Massachusetts for more than a decade.

> I am here looked upon as your agent and am sent for often to all the Officers of the Council, Committee of Trade, Treasury and Admiralty etc. to answer to questions and solicite prator relating to your Affaires, and tis from me that the Officers Expect all fees and gratifications for doing your Business which are not inconsiderable for Every common reference is 52 Shillings, the Sollicitour has had fourteen pounds att a time and the attorney severall fees in passing your laws . . . I can't imagine that you ever needed an Agent more than now . . . in so uncertain a time where interests are often pushing att one another there may happen thinges to be offer'd which att so great a distance you can't avoid being ignorant of and without an Agent to watch every turn it may be impossible for you to prevent.[58]

Ashurst was not backward in arguing the importance of his position, but his emphasis on the processing of colonial laws, providing information, and protecting colonial interests against initiatives of government is a fair representation of the tasks. Particularly between 1696 and 1706, the processing of colonial laws was a regular assignment. It also became clear that the reliance on the colonial agent gave him the effective power to slow or stall the processing of laws and judicial appeals simply by refusing to pay fees.[59] Providing government offices with information and explanations was occasionally onerous but often very helpful. It was also useful for colonial government officers to forward their letters through the colony's agent, giving him the option of delivering them at the most appropriate times and ensuring that agent and correspondent were arguing the same perspective. Such work, together with writing to their colonial employers frequently, made the colonial agency no sinecure.

The work of the colonial agent in influencing Parliament was much more difficult and not usually fully recorded, but one revealing exception shows something of the methods and the transatlantic communications. William Penn had served effectively as his own political agent for some 20 years when, while in Pennsylvania, he heard of threatened legislation to deprive him and all proprietary and charter governments of their powers. The warning shot had been fired in the House of Commons near the end of March 1700, but Parliament was prorogued within two weeks and then dissolved. Nine months later, Penn outlined a detailed strategy of defense for Charleswood Lawton, his London agent. Patrons of the antagonists were to be sweetened; named men of influence were to be approached; the arguments Penn outlined were to be printed if Parliament took any notice of the issue. In urging Lawton to take specific actions, Penn made clear that the object was to "give us time, at least a session or two to be heard before condemned."[60] This hope, which proved realistic, suggests a pace of Parliamentary business that allowed a lobbyist to operate a transatlantic interest. When the bill was introduced later the next spring, Lawton seems to have done his work, the Society of Friends had lobbied on Penn's behalf, and the other intended victims of the legislation organized their efforts. The House of Lords was the more manageable object for the lobbyists. The bill slipped off the busy order paper of the House of Lords despite a vote that revealed the intention to proceed further with the matter. By July 1701, Penn had three letters from Lawton but did not yet know of the final disposition of the issue for that session. In mid-August the suspense on this crucial matter was finally broken when Penn received a letter by way of Boston that made him want to know more. Penn told Lawton that "next to those comeing Directly to Our own River there is no conveyance safer than by Vessells to New York and Boston & from thence by post hither." Although Penn had succeeded and he would be back in England to face what was left of the challenge the following year, his correspondence of August 1701 included mention of "our New Shipp the Messenger Designed as a Packet boat between this and England," aboard which he sent "a small Cargoe of Letters" for Lawton to distribute.[61]

The fiercest and most telling colonial lobbying war of the period was actually between the West Indian and North American interests. For two and one-half years the two groups, each gradually coalescing for the purpose, fought over what became the Molasses Act. The Barbadians, who initiated the whole matter with petitions against the trade between the North American colonies and the French West Indies, could be expected to have the best transatlantic communications for the contest. Whether they were exploiting this or simply initiating matters at the opening of the "season of business," the

Barbadians petitioned the crown for relief in the autumn of 1730. Agents for the northern colonies responded with counterpetitions on their own initiative and, when the delayed Privy Council hearing finally occurred at the beginning of February 1731, the northern colonies representatives succeeded in winning a further three-month postponement to allow North Americans to respond to the charges. Privy Council consideration for this sort of problem was predictable, and the Barbadians then moved the struggle to another front by approaching Parliament. Here it was the House of Lords, as it had been for Penn at the opening of the century, that proved susceptible to so full an investigation so late in the season that nothing was done with the Sugar Bill that had passed the Commons readily. The same story repeated itself the next year, when the House again adjourned for the summer without ending its consideration of the reviewed Sugar Bill. When a modified act, which became popularly known as the Molasses Act, finally passed through both Houses of Parliament by May 1733, this major victory of the West Indian interest over their fellow colonials was accomplished only after 30 months of lobbying. Whatever defeated the American interest here, it was not the seasons of the Atlantic. The pace of the House of Lords was no imposition on the pace of the Atlantic communications of the empire the lords occasionally considered.[62]

In one sense, the colonial agency represented the limitations on Atlantic communications, yet in another sense the agents were only necessary once the colonial government had ceased to be simple "government by instruction." Agents needed to keep abreast of changes in the colony they represented, but their expertise was in English politics as far as their employers were concerned. In contest with English interests, the colonial agent could be expected to suffer from the limited contact he could have with the government he represented. As has been seen, the seasons of business in London tended to equalize some aspects of this situation. In an instance in which the colonial interests were pitted against each other, as in the Molasses Act debates, the bias of Atlantic communication could be just one more advantage Barbadian interests had over those of some of their rivals. Yet for more than half the year, Massachusetts correspondents could hear from London and reply faster than could those writing from Barbados. The colonial agents represented a stage in the development of both government and communications. When later British governments decided that they did not need the agents to help them understand what was happening in the colonies, the change was one of attitude. Improved transatlantic communication had encouraged the development of colonial agents, but more political integration and even better Atlantic communications could eventually erode the agent's position as spokesman as surely as the reprinted items from the London press competed with the governor's interpretation of the English government's proceedings.

Imperial politics of this period can be subdivided into three phases, the first of which lasted from 1675 to 1688. The English crown was an unusually active agent of political integration. From the fiscal, diplomatic, and political rubble of the last Dutch war, a sobered Charles II and his more sober and industrious brother, James, began rebuilding the monarchy's position. Opposition to royal resurgence crystallized into Whiggery, developed new weapons in electoral management, but lost the long and bitter fight to exclude James from the throne. Customs revenues on imported colonial staples were a significant part of growing royal revenues and were particularly important as free from parliamentary scrutiny. Bacon's Rebellion in Virginia had interrupted that revenue and invited closer royal management of the colonies. From 1675 on, the new Lords of Trade and Plantations began an administrative centralization, and launched the careers of William Blathwayt and Edward Randolph who became synonymous with this centralization for the next generation. James II became king in 1685, gaining life revenues that proved more generous than intended and allowed him more freedom from Parliament. The Glorious Revolution was an admission of failure by James's opponents: They had failed to stop the king by parliamentary action, they had to resort to unconstitutional means to change that constitution, yet they insisted that they were preserving tradition by their coup.

Some aspects of English Atlantic government and politics were affected by the changes in communication in this period. The developing imperial government of the later Stuarts still made gubernatorial instructions central to its method, a pattern that did not presume much regular correspondence at all. Nonetheless, after 1675 there were developments that presumed a level of communications that had not been available for any colony a generation earlier and that was still not available for all colonies. Executive review of colonial laws and judicial appeals to England both required more transatlantic communication. Closer English supervision of governors and assemblies was feared and occasionally accomplished in this period. The pace of English courts and Parliament, the pace of executive government in England and governors' correspondence with Whitehall all seem to have contributed to a conventional rhythm of imperial political business that would remain through the decades that followed. It is also noteworthy that though Parliament built and reinforced the Navigation Acts between the Restoration and 1673, it did nothing to improve enforcement of those provisions between the emergence of Whig opposition in the 1670's and the fiscal revolution of the 1690 Act of Settlement, after which Parliament rather than the monarch was a direct beneficiary of more effective collection of increased duties on colonial staple products imported into England. Yet even before that time, the executive bureaucracy had strengthened political communications with the colonies and began a process of political integration that would have rather different results.

War is an international test of the ability of a government to marshal resources; the war of 1689 brought unexpected political changes. William III brought England a war against the powerful centralizing French monarchy, and that war effort required some extensions of state power that both the revolution and the war were ostensibly against, for the better-organized enemy had to be imitated. Although there were political concessions to "country" interests in the now annual Parliaments, they were also voting unprecedented taxes for an expanding government. The fiscal drain within England was from the north and west to the southeast, from the landed to the manufacturing and service groups in the nation, and from the provinces to the metropolis. For the colonies, the war and its successor would bring more military responsibilities than resources for the governors, but would increase the roles of the governors as well as the naval commanders of station ships. Colonial assemblies bargained for privileges, paper money issues, and other concessions in return for defense funds, but an echo of the processes at work in England could be heard in the colonies when, rather intermittently, they were roused to war. Colonials fought the French and did so as provincial Englishmen. As with the English governments of these war years, governors had varied success in harnessing factions for the war effort. Assemblies would emerge stronger, and the prerogative weaker, as was true in England, but the wars made colonial dependency on metropolitan war-making and peacemaking painfully obvious. The new Board of Trade and Plantations lost most of its efforts to tighten colonial administration, but it served as a magnet for developing interest groups concerned with the English Atlantic empire.

In the generation of warfare after 1689, royal power was extended to many more colonies and developed new features that utilized the new post and packet-boat services that reduced the disruption of communications attending the war. Parliament now proved willing to complete the legislative efforts to police the colonial trading system with a combination of bonds, naval records, and vice-admiralty courts that presumed the regular and safe exchange of information. This same assumption stood behind the insistence that whole categories of colonial legislation were to include suspending clauses. It also becomes clear in this period that the governors were not corresponding as often as they might. They learned that their correspondence and that of other new crown officials, local political leaders, London agents, and merchants were all tending to cost them power. At its least troubling, this was the visible indignity of not being better informed than others in the colony. At its worst, it became a desperate scramble to keep one's place after information was used against an incumbent by the ambitious and unscrupulous. In what appeared to be yet another aspect of closer scrutiny of colonial affairs in London, each colony was to have a regular agent who would be ready to answer for the colony before Whitehall's various boards and offices. Although English political convulsions in the second half of Queen Anne's reign would rather quickly change the purposes of some of these developments, the changes themselves were further integrating the politics of the English Atlantic.

Peace after 1713 brought a respite from the government drive to assemble resources, eased the tax burden, and promised fewer initiatives at the expense of provincial and colonial life or at least meant that local leaders could manage these initiatives. The Whig political triumph was reinforced by helping the Tories commit political suicide and by reducing the size of the electorate and the frequency of elections. Although a few radical Whigs pursued their wars of ideas, the managers of government focused on patronage as the purpose of power. Frank acceptance of the enjoyment of office brought consequences that were particularly evident in colonial administration. The quality of the duke of Newcastle's governors was uneven, but that was less surprising or uncommon than was the tendency for appointees to avoid unpopular initiatives and make compromises for personal peace and profit that permanently shrank the power of governorships. Power that was not being sacrificed to placate local interests that could coalesce to oust a governor was increasingly being subjected to blatant political pressure from England. Patrons of a governor offered him candidates for those few offices still in his gift, offices he should have used to buy or keep political supporters from within the local elite. The management of colonial politics had always reached to Whitehall; under Walpole and Newcastle, the management of the House of Commons extended all the way to Jamaica and Virginia.

In the generation after 1714, English Atlantic communications continued to improve with increased shipping, extended postal services, and the flourishing of newspapers in English provinces on both sides of the ocean. The victory of English Whiggery in this period was the victory of the legislature over the executive and of local elites over metropolitan elites. "Political stability" and "salutary neglect" are both pleasant euphemisms for this pattern of political dominance. The same communications developments that earlier contributed to the centralization of executive power over the colonies were now centralizing the resistance to that central authority. Colonial agents, sometimes supported by merchant lobbies, became accomplished users of Whig rhetoric and "interest politics" in defense of colonial assemblies, which could institutionalize Whiggery in ways that English counties and cities could not. While colonial assemblies were gathering precedents, trimming executive authority, and integrating local colonial power, English politicians were encouraging decentralization by the intensified patronage politics of the period. Opposition to imperial power was now centralized as well, but its efficacy depended on the reigning English assumptions about the uses of politics. Effective agents and lobbies gained accommodations in this period, but their work was itself an admission that the political hub of the English Atlantic was increasing its access to information and hence to power. The pace of imperial affairs, which once strained communications facilities, now permitted organized transatlantic opposition when threats arose. This cursory sketch of these phases in the political culture of the English Atlantic suggest that political communications were increasingly important as the machinery became more centralized, complex, and sensitive.[63]

13 · Communication and Community

Social aspects and implications of improving communications within what was the English-speaking social world seem obvious, if alloyed. Life rightly refused to be trapped in the conceptual cages that would make things simple for historians. Economic and political considerations not only melted into each other, but they also melted into cultural meanings without any consistent dominance of economic, political, or cultural factors in determining how everyone behaved at any time or how anyone behaved on a regular basis.

Direct links between communications and community have long been asserted by those believing that

> there is more than a verbal tie between the words common, community, and communication. Men live in a community, in virtue of things which they have in common; and communication is the way in which they come to possess things in common.[1]

Venturing into the complexities of modern sociology of communications and theories of social change is beyond the purpose of this study, but Thomas Bender has offered an important reminder in claiming, "Community, then, can be defined better as an experience than as a place. As simply as possible, community is where community happens."[2] What follows is a sketch of some obvious social consequences resulting from improving English Atlantic communications between 1675 and 1740.

Changes in English Atlantic communications affected all who lived within the empire or on its fringes, but four very general groups of people can be distinguished by their different opportunities to react to some of those changes. Those who understood little or no English shared some of the changes that were common to everyone, but they were increasingly insulated and excluded from other experiences. Those English-speaking people who were not functionally literate would also sense a number of changes in the lifetime between 1675 and 1740, some broadening and others narrowing their horizons and their opportunities. Those who could read and write in English and especially those with the time and resources to participate fully in the increased opportunities might be expected to be those who were best served by the communications improvements. All four of these groups would be affected differently, and their size and relationships with each other would also change.

Migration, itself a significant part of communication within a large-scale community, was changing the relative size of these cultural groupings. The greatest migration into the English Atlantic between 1675 and 1740 was not English-speaking nor European nor voluntary. By 1660, Barbados had a Negro slave majority. The same was true of Jamaica by 1670, the Leeward Islands by 1680, and South Carolina before 1710.[3] By 1740 five out of six people living in the British West Indies were slaves, as were two out of three people in South Carolina. The plantation economy of these "sugar routes" had revolutionized their society. If Quaker migration illustrated how close a sense of community could be maintained with kin and coreligionists, slavery illustrated how much of ones' social context could be taken away. Africans and their children could preserve more African culture in those colonies where they constituted a majority of the people, yet even there the specific inheritances of family, clan, and tribe were effectively lost, and their customs were homogenized into a new "Creole" culture with its own language and a new context for family and work.[4] Cut off entirely from their Old World, Africans were forced to make a more complete cultural commitment to the New World than any other migrants. Their slavery, not the Atlantic Ocean, made theirs the newest of the New Worlds.[5]

Improving English Atlantic communications helped intensify some cultural aspects of slavery. These "plantation societies" supported English minorities leading lives that were radically different from those of the English at home, yet these colonial minorities were increasingly determined to preserve and assert their "Englishness." With a color-coded exclusiveness that ignored their own acculturation and what they were forcing on Africans and those born in slavery, the white minority was attracted to the claim that they were the civilized remnant in an increasingly barbarous land. Whether they aspired to retire to England or simply to live well in the tropics, these English put a premium on their English Atlantic connections. Intensifying English cultural identity limited compromises, so that interracial cultural exchanges became increasingly "ascriptive."[6]

Admittedly, some economic efficiencies improved food supplies for slaves, and improving navigation would reduce the death rate in the "middle passage." But these marginal changes would not be known to the Africans landed in Caribbean slavery, nor would they hear those first faint whispers of doubt about slavery voiced by Quakers whose own communication network was among the best in the English Atlantic.[7] Slaves could suffer from the strengthening martial machines in the islands, from the wars between alien masters who were English and French, but they would most likely suffer from an invisible aspect of increased English Atlantic shipping, the spread of disease.

Disease was the great tragic "leveler" of the English Atlantic, for one need not speak English, see anyone who spoke English, or even acquire an English-made gun or blanket in order to be visited by the seaborne diseases of the English Atlantic. Migration was a very unhealthy activity; most natural immunities are only to those diseases already encountered in childhood. When people were gathered from a variety of locations into ships or colonies, they could destroy each other with the variety of germs among them. In some of the more northern colonies, immigration had slowed by 1675, and the development of a locally born population with immunities to some of the most common diseases meant a healthier community. The "seasoning" of newcomers, particularly to malaria, which was endemic in most of the English colonies and in West Africa but was unknown in England except for Kent and Essex, would continue.[8] Malaria thinned the ranks of immigrants to the northern colonies and destroyed visiting English seamen, but it did not spread further than the habitat of the carrier mosquitoes and never became an extensive epidemic on the North-American continent.[9] In the English West Indies and in the southern mainland, where forced African immigration continued throughout the period, malaria continued to take a major toll of immigrants as well as the native-born. Visiting mariners and sailors aboard the naval squadrons that were becoming more frequent were all vulnerable to malaria's agues and fevers. However, in this deadly traffic in disease, seamen could infect as well as be infected. They were vulnerable to malaria and yellow fever but could be carriers of smallpox. Smallpox and yellow fever warrant special attention, as they did then because they were readily identifiable, fatal, and often imported into vulnerable communities from infected ships.

Smallpox was a special scourge of the English Atlantic in the seventeenth and eighteenth centuries. Although the disease already had a long history, it emerged in its modern and most virulent form in the England of the early Stuarts and became endemic in London after the last outbreak of bubonic plague. London's first major epidemic of smallpox was in 1628, and during the next three decades there were major epidemics at least once every seven years. After the Restoration these epidemics gradually became more frequent until, by the 1680's, smallpox was a permanent hazard of London life. This meant that the city's new immigrants, numbering about 10,000 per year, were at special risk as were all visitors and all children.[10] Whether England's other major ports also had endemic smallpox or whether they suffered the more deadly but less frequent attacks of epidemics, most English seamen and soldiers had been exposed to this disease and had developed some immunity. The major ocean voyages of the English Atlantic were all long enough to make most outbreaks aboard ship very obvious before port was reached.[11] The disease was carried to North America long before it came in the Winthrop fleet of 1630, but it did not become endemic or even regularly epidemic as yet in New England. Instead, the occasional epidemic would rage through this colonial population, which possessed little immunity, costing many lives and ravaging their even more susceptible Indian neighbors, trading partners, and enemies. To all of English America, its non-English-speaking communities, and its Indian and French neighbors, smallpox was a threatening epidemical disease that generally did not come often enough to leave substantial groups with immunity.

Smallpox was also common in West Africa in the seventeenth century and may even have orginated in central Africa in early historical times. Existing sources do not make it easy to determine whether the disease was endemic there, but it must have been at least epidemic, both because experience and immunity were advertised attributes of some Africans newly arrived in the American colonies and because one source of information about inoculation was its practice among the Coromantin, as related to Cotton Mather by Onesimus, a slave of his own. It is also evident, however, that Africans died in New York epidemics in approximate proportion to their share of the total population, supporting the notion that fewer Africans were regularly exposed to smallpox than to yellow fever in their native land.[12]

Smallpox would hardly rank with malaria or yellow fever among the diseases that were deadly to the English in the West Indies, but the presence of the disease was attested to by reported epidemics,[13] by carriage of the disease to North America from the West Indies, and by the confluence of English and African "travel routes" in the eastern Caribbean. Smallpox was present in the islands and may well have been endemic, but it would not provoke much comment there. It was not the disease that would spread to visiting English seamen or soldiers. Although smallpox was less important there than were other diseases, this particularly contagious killer could spread easily to North America from these islands.

Smallpox was not common among colonists in English North America before the Restoration, but the disease was passed on to the more vulnerable Indian communities. A smallpox epidemic occurred in several Massachusetts towns in 1648–1649, but a connection between these and an epidemic occurring in London at the same time cannot be proved. The next major Massachusetts epidemics hit Boston in 1666 and again in 1677, when between 200 and 300 of the townspeople died. Both of these outbreaks were linked to arriving shipping from England and centered on the port. Increasing trade with London, where the disease was now endemic, as well as West Indian trading on a larger scale, increased the risks of smallpox for New Englanders.[14]

The first extensive epidemic of smallpox among English colonists in North America occurred in 1689 and 1690. The outbreak of 1689 seems to have begun when a ship came into Boston from Barbados carrying Negro slaves who had smallpox. Although the ship was quarantined on arrival in October, the disease escaped into Boston and adjoining towns that winter and increased in intensity the following summer. New York City had been relatively free from epidemical diseases in the seventeenth century although an outbreak of smallpox had occurred in 1679 and 1680.[15] Whether there were separate new infections in New York and in Canada in 1690 or whether the troop movements associated with the Wood Creek expedition disseminated the smallpox, a general epidemic developed that included New England, New York, the Iroquois tribes, Canada, and Acadia. Apparently, the Iroquois were infected by emissaries who came to solicit their pariticipation in the expedition northward by land.[16] This very extensive epidemic reveals the connections between New France and New York through their Indian allies, links that would make this a regular corridor for smallpox in the eighteenth century.

Colonial mariners were more exposed to smallpox than were their farming relatives and more vulnerable than most English sailors. The story of Captain John Gore, who died a lamented Boston hero in 1720, illustrates the danger. John was from a respected family and had received a B.A. and M.A. from Harvard as well as becoming college librarian, and in 1706 he went to sea as a chaplain. By 1711 he was a sea captain, and nine years later, as he was bringing his ship home from London, all seven members of his crew fell ill with "contagious distemper." John stayed aboard to care for the sick but soon contracted the illness, which finally revealed itself on a crewman three days after the ship had anchored in Boston's Nantasket Roads. Within eight more days the good captain was dead and buried on Spectacle Island. None of the eight men aboard the ship had previously suffered from smallpox.[17]

Smallpox reached Boston again by sea the following spring, this time to launch the most famous colonial epidemic. HMS *Seahorse* returned in April from convoying a fleet of New England merchantmen to Barbados. The ship had passed a health inspection before proceeding to the town dock, but it was learned that two Negroes from the ship had smallpox. Later it was evident that many of the crew had the disease, and by the end of May there were so many cases that the selectmen abandoned the posting of guards at each infected house. The disease spread to neighboring towns and on to Connecticut and Rhode Island. Half of Boston fell victim to the disease, a gruesome reminder that Boston had been free of it for nearly 20 years. This was the epidemic that caused inoculation to become a major local political and religious issue. Inoculation, like smallpox, came to Boston by sea. It was the Royal Society *Transactions* of 1714 and 1716, printing Turkish reports of inoculation, that reinforced what Cotton Mather had learned from Onesimus and led the cleric to champion an experiment that frightened the professionals. In this well-known story, the English Atlantic intellectual community spread Turkish and Coromantin preventative inoculation, then successfully encouraged inoculation in London.[18]

The most extensive smallpox epidemic in English America occurred between 1729 and 1732. Although separate infections from elsewhere were possible, like the ship that brought smallpox to Maryland from Lisbon in July 1731,[19] there was a fairly continuous presence of the disease between the autumn of 1729 and the spring of 1732. The first outbreak was in Boston once again, apparently brought in from Ireland, where the disease was endemic in the major ports. From Boston the infection spread to the towns of Massachusetts and Connecticut and then on to the Indian settlements of Connecticut. Almost a year later there was a major epidemic in Albany, New York, as well as in parts of New Jersey and Pennsylvania. By summer the epidemic was raging in New York City, where 549 died of the disease before winter.[20] The disease returned to Boston during the autumn as well as spreading to Long Island and New Jersey, where considerable numbers were inoculated. By February 1731/2 reports had reached New York City that smallpox was active again in Albany and western New Hampshire and was reportedly among the Iroquois and had spread to Canada.[21] Smallpox epidemics would thereafter be less frequent in Boston and more frequent in the "middle colonies." A major smallpox corridor developed from Pennsylvania northward through the New Jerseys, New York, Iroquois country, and on to Canada. From the 1730's, this whole area seldom escaped a smallpox epidemic for longer than five years. This was in spite of the increased resistance posed by survivors of the disease and from those successfully inoculated. By the 1770's, smallpox was endemic in New York City, as it was in major English cities, and had conferred lifetime immunity on enough survivors to transform the disease into a deadly childhood risk there.[22]

Comparative isolation of the Chesapeake colonies from those further north was often lamented but not when smallpox was considered. English and African sources of smallpox had ready access to the portless riverine trading world of the Chesapeake, and localized outbreaks were not uncommon.[23] Indians of Virginia's eastern shore suffered a smallpox epidemic in 1667, contracted from an English sailor. The only major Virginian epidemic started in Jamestown in 1696 and spread south and west among the Indian community hundreds of miles in the interior. The Pemlico Indians were virtually destroyed by this epidemic, which also spread through the Carolinas to Charles Town. Yet Virginians had no quarantine legislation before the 1740's and would continue to be among the most vulnerable visitors to London although they were also more numerous than visitors from other North America colonies.[24]

Charles Town would not receive any other epidemic by land from the north, but it would be one of the most unhealthy ports of the English Atlantic early in the eighteenth century. The burgeoning rice economy rested on imported slave labor, swampy cultivation, and increased shipping from a variety of places, all of which helped to make Charles Town a major victim of smallpox, malaria, and yellow fever. Charles Town would have four major smallpox epidemics between that of 1711–1712 (which coincided with a yellow fever outbreak) and that of 1738, which resulted in 2100 cases in a town of less than 7000 people and went on to kill half of the Cherokee nation.[25] Charles Town's smallpox came by sea and could be controlled by quarantine and eventually by inoculation. As was true elsewhere on the sugar routes, however, smallpox was not the major enemy.

Yellow fever, known to many colonials as the "plague of Barbados" or the "Barbados distemper" was another deadly disease that rode the ships of the

English Atlantic. The disease was African in origin and was prevalent enough there in the seventeenth and eighteenth centuries to provide noticeable immunities to many of the Africans taken to the New World as slaves. It is a mosquito-borne disease with a very short incubation period of about three days and promptly kills most of its victims. The demonstrable transmission of the disease after long maritime voyages seems explicable only by the survival of the mosquito carriers breeding in the water barrels or fire buckets aboard ships. However the disease was kept active, the result could be most devastating as an occasional plague in North American ports, as a regular visitor to Charles Town early in the eighteenth century, and as a principal killer in the West Indies much of the time after the first major epidemic swept through Barbados, Cuba, and the Yucatan in 1648–1649, less than a decade after the sugar revolution began the forced African migration to Barbados.

Yellow fever never reached England, so English migrants, mariners, and soldiers were prime targets for yellow fever at West Indian anchorages whether the arrivals were intent on settling there, taking a break in the southerly passage to North America, or participating in a naval expedition. The naval expedition led by Sir Francis Wheler in 1693, intending the conquest of Martinique, was a dramatic illustration of the might of yellow fever. Wheler's fleet was prepared for some trouble and was accompanied by two physicians and a hospital ship, and the 4500 sailors and soldiers reportedly arrived at Barbados in good health in March 1693. Yellow fever had rampaged through the islands in the preceding year. A month before Wheler arrived, Barbados Governor Kendal lamented that he had not heard from Europe in four months and that the last ships that did visit had

> frightened all mankind away from us. It is sad but real truth that I have now lived almost three years in the region of death, and that two-thirds of those that arrived, together with one half of the inhabitants, have since my being here paid their tribute to the Sovereign Prince of Terrors.

He went on to add that the disease had been particularly bad among the troops he had raised to join the intended expedition.[26] Wheler's fleet took on the colonial levies and yellow fever during a month at anchorage. More than a third of a 2300-man landing party on Martinique died there from disease in the failed attack of April. Whether they brought more yellow fever than they found in Martinique, it was reported later that summer that disease was raging in that island with the usual result—ships avoided the island, and provisions were very expensive. If the yellow fever did more damage to Martinique and St. Pierre than the English did directly, the disease was far from finished with the English. HMS *Falcon* had gone on to Jamaica and appeared to have revived the yellow fever infection that had just subsided there. The man-of-war's losses were made up by pressing from merchantmen, revealing yet another reason why word of epidemic caused merchantmen to keep their distance from infected islands.[27] Having abandoned the West

Indies campaign unknowingly to the microbes, Wheler took his fleet north for Boston, where he expected to refresh and recover his men and launch the second phase of his assignment, an attack on Canada. Before they reached Boston, Wheler's fleet had lost two thirds of its men. More would die in Boston, and the fleet brought the first known epidemic of yellow fever to North America and the only known epidemic of that disease to Boston.[28]

In North America, yellow fever proved to be a visitation on major ports. Boston had no other known epidemic of yellow fever, but the cities of New York, Philadelphia, and especially Charles Town, would become very familiar with the disease after the first epidemic of 1699. The mosquito-borne disease was repeatedly introduced from the West Indies but failed to take hold on the continent despite seven epidemics in Charles Town and four each in New York and Philadelphia.[29] The West Indies trade of Philadelphia and New York brought the disease to them although it is interesting that the Boston-Barbados trade did not carry yellow fever. Perhaps the somewhat longer voyage home from Barbados to Boston, which was an economic disadvantage, shielded Boston from yellow fever as did the town's comparatively strict quarantine regulations. The slave trade, which gave South Carolina a black majority by 1708, together with the proximity and links between South Carolina and the Caribbean, puts it much closer to yellow fever; but it is also interesting that Virginia did not suffer from yellow fever to a degree that made its distinctive characteristics noteworthy among commentators there. Isolated cases were reported, like that of Robert "King" Carter, who died in 1732 of "the Flux" three days after boarding a vessel to buy slaves.[30] Yellow fever, like smallpox, made victims of all cultures within its range although yellow fever's more limited range made it less an English Atlantic disease than was smallpox.

Quarantine did not hold mosquitoes and, therefore, was less effective against malaria and yellow fever than against smallpox. Some natural immunities to both malaria and yellow fever could be built up where these diseases were endemic, but the English Atlantic was sharply divided into tropical areas, where these were endemic; colonial North America, where malaria was endemic; and England and New England, where neither was endemic. The killing of merchant and naval seamen in the tropics was inevitable, and the seasoning of African and European immigrants remained brutal. The epidemics of yellow fever in English North American ports were a threat that was not adequately controlled by quarantine although the disease would reveal itself very quickly on even the shortest intercolonial voyage.

The growing maritime trade through English Atlantic ports, the increasing size of the populations of those ports, and the traffic in black and white laborers all contributed to the intensifying exchanges of deadly diseases within the English Atlantic community. Most of these problems proved more intractable than the sharing and eventual stemming of smallpox. Smallpox was endemic in London between 1675 and 1740 and may have been endemic in parts of the West Indies and West Africa. Colonial quarantine acts certainly helped in controlling smallpox. Boston was protected by such acts as early as 1647, but most of the other major English North American ports did not begin systematic quarantine before the end of the century.[31] Seamen and adult inhabitants of New York, Philadelphia, and Charles Town became safer from smallpox because of increased exposure in childhood and increased inoculation. For most Indian communities and for English colonists from the more scattered populations of the New England hinterland or Virginia, the risks remained higher. Those Virginia gentry and Connecticut Anglicans bound to England for enjoyment, education, or ordination were justified in their continuing fear of London's smallpox, and so were Iroquois and Cherokee chieftains. "The destroying angel" whom Cotton Mather sensed was hovering over his own town in the dreadful summer of 1721 was not only mighty and invisible but also one of the fastest travelers of the English Atlantic.[32]

For the Indian neighbors of English North America, there were powerful social consequences of the continuing epidemics, of the growing relative strength of the English communities, and of the increasing economic connections between themselves and the European traders. As the English Atlantic empire became more fully integrated, even Indian diplomacy was transformed. Indian communities that had been able to negotiate local compromises with colonial governors found that initiatives in war and peace were increasingly from across the Atlantic. Those famous delegations to England by the Iroquois (1710) and the Cherokee (1730) were significant cultural events in themselves but also evidence of the integration of the English Atlantic.[33] Indian dependence on European trade goods can be exaggerated, for frontiersmen's axes, fishermen's hooks, and planters' hoes bound people to the Atlantic economy as surely as an Ibo's manacles or the musket of a Cherokee or an Iroquois. Yet there were graphic illustrations of Indian dependence on this traffic. For example, the Woodland Cree and Assiniboin people living on what are now the Canadian prairies nearly a thousand miles inland from York Factory, had become accomplished hunters with muskets by the end of the seventeenth century. French conquest of York Factory (1697–1714) severely disrupted the supply of guns, powder, and shot for these hunters. These Indian musketeers, who had terrified enemies who were farther away from the source of guns and still dependent on the bow and arrow, were suddenly defenseless. They were almost entirely obliterated by the arrows of their enemies, who took prompt revenge on the technologically adventuresome.[34]

The misadventures of Isaac Pummatick and his friend, Peter, discussed earlier, not only indicate the effectiveness of English communications in capturing runaways; these two men were also among those of Indian and African origin or ancestry who had become Anglicized to some degree. Both spoke English fluently, as did many slaves born in the colonies. Both were dressed in English-style clothing. The increasing opportunities of travel would invite English-speaking slaves and servants to consider running away as surely as it invited their masters to send newspapers after them. An East Indian ship rigger named Thomas Tamerlane had come even further from home to be an indentured servant in Philadelphia at the age of 23. When he ran away from his master in June 1730, he was reported as speaking and writing good English and dressed rather flamboyantly for an indentured servant, or a fugitive, in "speckled Shirt, strip'd blue and white flannel Jacket, Tarry Trowsers, good Shoes, and a Felt Hat."[35] Like Peter and Isaac, Thomas Tamerlane ran away but did not run home. Such fugitives had to be familiar with the English colonial language and life to run away effectively at all, and their realistic hopes had to be to find a better status somewhere else in that empire. Even those southern slaves who ran away to Spanish Florida or escaped Caribbean slavery to join a Maroon settlement were going to create a new life, not restore an old one. Those who ran away protested the life the English colonists allowed them, but even they were bound to much of it.

Europeans who did not speak English survived in North American communities throughout this period and added to their numbers without becoming a significant sector of any colonies save New York and Pennsylvania. The Dutch, German, Swiss, or French Huguenot communities could be divided into the oral and the literate as could the English. Those who were fully literate in their mother tongue were able to use the improving postal facilities and shipping frequencies to correspond with families and business contacts in their mother country. *The Pennsylvania Gazette* was the only colonial newspaper to run advertisements in German before 1740, and Franklin published a short-lived German-language newspaper in Pennsylvania. Although the connections that reinforce identity would be weaker for these people than for the English colonists, they could benefit from improving English Atlantic communications in sending messages through England, by shipping from New York to Dutch ports, and by European visitors to America. Those who could not read or write would here, as everywhere else, need the occasional services of those who could. Yet even those who stayed outside the English culture entirely were affected by what increasing English Atlantic contacts were doing to them and to the English-speaking community.

In its many dialects and accents, English was the language of the first British Empire. For all the people most of the time and for many of the people all the time, this was an oral culture. Social historians have rightly emphasized the overwhelmingly local nature of most people's lives. For those who could not read or write or did either with difficulty, the effective boundaries of experience were their own travels, the accounts of other travelers as related and improved by many mouths, and whatever was shared by the literate in conversation, sermons, or the oral proceedings of courts and local government. For most people in Stuart and Georgian England, their county was their country. "England" was usually functional reality only for those landowners, merchants, and professionals who had economic, political, or social ties beyond the local level. Migration, however, scattered, mixed, and linked people rather differently.

The English Atlantic had been created by two sorts of English migration before 1660. Long-distance migration within England, within Britain, and to the new colonies had included many poor people seeking subsistence amid food shortages, economic dislocations, and political chaos.[36] Much of the early settlement of the English Caribbean and Chesapeake Bay rested on the labor of male migrants, most of whom had little chance of establishing families because of sex ratios, the devastation of disease, and the terms of their migration. Few survivors could gain more than a sufficiency in this period. The other type of migration, that of religious and political dissidents, had mingled with subsistence migration and had brought the migration of families, especially to New England settlements. The demographic advantages of family migration produced an indigenous "Creole" society much earlier than was possible elsewhere in the new settlements.

Patterns of English migration changed between 1660 and 1730, and so did the English Atlantic. The size of England's population stabilized without significant emigration, there were no major famines, and there were fewer religious or political exiles than had been the case earlier in the seventeenth century. Fewer of the English poor ranged farther than 25 miles from their birthplace than had been the case in the preceding half century. Those who had moved a considerable distance in their lives were more likely to be gentlemen, merchants, and professionals. For the landed and moneyed people, the demographic stability meant consolidation of estates, reduced political competition, an export trade in foodstuffs, and comparative social peace, all of which facilitated the political and social victory of whiggery.[37] There was less long-range migration, and more of that was drawn to the city of London. The metropolis that needed an average of 7000 to 8000 immigrants a year to maintain its population was growing as was its economic role in the country.[38] Some migration to the colonies continued, but the scale and type of migration were different.[39]

Although the demography of the colonies varied greatly and differed from that of the communities from which the original migrants had come, there was a strong trend in most of English North America toward communities with sex ratios, age distributions, marriage ages, and wealth distributions that were more like those in England than had been true earlier in these colonies. In colonies that had attracted family migration early, provincial populations of locally born people were emerging. Although their family links with England were less immediate than those of their parents, their communities were developing patterns of life that were less peculiar. The Chesapeake colonies had been so unhealthy that the establishment of a locally born elite took until the end of the seventeenth century, and the English West Indies failed to establish a locally born elite even in the eighteenth century. English indentured servants were recruited for these colonies in considerable numbers late in the seventeenth century, and Irish migrants became significant in the population of colonies like the Leeward Islands and Maryland. Intercolonial migrations, like those from Barbados to Jamaica and South Carolina, also built new networks of kin, business, and politics that would be much easier to sustain than had been the connections of the initial migrants of an earlier period. Developments in the colonies limited the opportunities for social mobility for new migrants of limited means, as well as establishing dynasties of local community leadership against newcomers, be they immigrants or locals. Improving Atlantic communications encouraged and supported this trend.[40] However, advertisements in colonial newspapers included those seeking poorer migrants who had inherited English estates. People who had not written to relatives frequently enough to be located privately were not presumed dead because they had gone by sea to English America.[41]

Not only had the population of English North America quintupled from 1675 to 1740, numbering well over a million souls by 1740, but the growing settlements were actively engaged in building what they took to be civilized existences. An English visitor to North America in 1740 would be much more at home and needing to learn less to make a living, than would have been the case 65 years earlier. The new "Creole elites" would show some signs of cultural anxiety and some fear of barbarism. Although this fear legitimately included the fear of Indians in 1675, by 1740 it was a fear that the English-speaking colonials were not sufficiently cultivated or educated.

Mariners who sailed the merchantmen, fishing vessels, men-of-war and privateers of the English Atlantic were one numerous and growing group for whom oral culture was not local culture. Between 10,000 and 15,000 English-speaking seamen were employed on transatlantic merchantmen and fishing vessels in the 1680's, and this group numbered between 25,000 and 30,000 by the late 1730's.[42] A ship's company was itself an oral community that often represented the accents and memories of a variety of English Atlantic localities. A striking example was the crew of the *Ranger*, a pirate ship captured off Rhode Island in 1723. Public curiosity about these doomed men was high enough to prompt the *Boston Gazette* to print the birthplace of the 29 crewmen. The birthplaces read like a tour of the English Atlantic. Five were born in London or Westminster, three came from Devon, and the crew also included men born in Durham, Gloucester, Lancashire, Rutland, and Suffolk. In addition, there were three Welshmen, two Irishmen, a Scot, and one sailor born on the Isle of Man. The colonies were also represented, with men born on Barbados, on the eastern shore of Virginia, in New York, in Connecticut, and in Boston, as well as an Indian who had been born on Martha's Vineyard.[43] Although such a varied crew may have had peculiar cause or purpose on this ship, providing the pirate with more accents than flags and a wealth of local knowledge, merchant ships in the overwhelmingly bilateral English Atlantic trades were bound to include someone who would be coming home or bringing news from home at most English Atlantic anchorages. In major ports of England and the colonies, the sailors constituted a sizable enclave themselves, as well as relating to many local people whose livelihoods were meshed with theirs. Whether literate or not, these travelers were a way for the unlettered to share news of kin, acquaintances, and localities that were remembered.

Christian churches of the English Atlantic were very influential as part of oral as well as literate culture. Improving Atlantic communications accompanied a number of religious developments that benefited from closer contacts and contributed to them. Anglicanism was the British Empire's official faith, and its place in the colonies grew with the age of the settlements, with the conscious sponsorship of the government, and with the notable efforts of the Society for the Propagation of the Gospel (S.P.G.). English clergy were sponsored for colonial parishes by the S.P.G. and provided with salary and a small library. Although most of these men and the other Anglican clergy in America were part of the English professional migration to America, a few colonial candidates for ordination came to England for orders before 1740.[44] The founding of Georgia was a major transatlantic charity and one that would attract John and Charles Wesley and then, in 1738, George Whitefield, making the first of his seven visits to America. This powerful evangelist of the English-speaking world helped launch a major Christian revival that was transatlantic, though it disrupted the harmony of many Anglican, Congregational, and Presbyterian communities. In the preceding half century of latitudinarianism, Anglican progress in the colonies had seemed to parallel the growth of ministerial authority in several denominations.[45] It was this growing colonial strength of the Church of England in the colonies that would make the proposal of an Anglican bishop for America into a major controversy later.

The largest group migration within the English Atlantic between 1675 and 1740 was that of the Quakers. The Quakers had first come to English America as zealous touring missionaries. In the eight years after 1655, some 60 men and women carried the ideas of the infant Society of Friends to all corners of the English colonies, from Newfoundland to the tiny settlements in Surinam. In this phase, local residents were being converted to Quakerism and organized into meetings. After a hiatus of eight years, during which the Quakers were severely persecuted in England, a second phase of American missionary work began with the celebrated voyage of the group's founder, George Fox. Quaker colonization, as distinct from conversion, began soon thereafter with the settlement of West Jersey after 1675 and of Pennsylvania after 1682. As with the earlier migration of New England Puritans, most of these Quakers moved in families into temperate climates, founding settlements that would soon increase with migrants' children and would successfully transfer the fruits of their lives' work to their children. The Quakers of English America escaped careful numbering because Pennsylvania never had a colonial census and religion was not usually distinguished in other censuses. One informed estimate suggests that there were at least 40,000 Quakers in the colonies by 1700, and at that time they were already close to outnumbering those who were in the British Isles.[46]

The Quakers displayed a remarkable preoccupation with English Atlantic communications. As members of a faith that emphasized personal inspiration and objected to trained "hireling" clergy, the Quakers were held together by local and regional meetings that were, in turn, linked to the London Yearly Meeting. There was a very strong oral bias to meetings where members were encouraged to share thoughtful "openings," and this was reinforced by the visits of "travelling Friends" who undertook extensive voyages to share their faith, their friendship, and their news with coreligionists who were fellow countrymen, acquaintances, or kin. Between 1655 and 1700 an average of three English Friends a year visited Quaker meetings in the English West Indies, Bermuda, the continental North American colonies, and Newfoundland. Colonial Quaker missionaries were also visiting other colonies and the British Isles by the opening of the eighteenth century.[47]

Although the Quakers were very strenuous in linking their face-to-face community around the Atlantic[48] and were also somewhat suspicious of higher education, they did make impressive use of the written word. Like their founder, George Fox, many of the most effective traveling Friends published their lives and travels as exemplars. These and printed discourses were prominent in packets of books sent out to colonial meetings.[49] The London Yearly Meeting established separate committees of correspondence for each colonial Quaker yearly meeting, and a general annual epistle was supplemented by a particular letter for each colony, usually answering a letter that had been directed to the London Yearly Meeting. Although an annual report seemed adequate for general spiritual accounting, the committees of correspondence and especially the London weekly "Meetings for Sufferings" represented standing facilities to lobby at government offices against persecutions or unfavorable colonial legislation. Although their complex network of communications could falter, especially in wartime or in settlements with very few Quakers, it seems likely that its success helped to prompt those Anglican missionary efforts that began at the end of the seventeenth century. The Quaker Atlantic community was a religious, political, and economic fraternity that demonstrated a level of communication between migrants and their English brethren that had been quite impossible for migrating dissenters half a century earlier.[50]

Oral Protestantism in the English Atlantic empire found its most talented practitioner in George Whitefield. Once an Anglican priest and missionary in Georgia, once a follower of John Wesley, Whitefield was the leading revivalist among English-speaking Calvinists by 1740. His large outdoor meetings in England, Scotland, Ireland, and North America were communications revolutions in themselves. Nathan Cole recounted his frenzied 12-mile run and ride to bring his wife and himself to hear Whitefield preach in Middletown, Connecticut, in 1740. Along the way the fields were all deserted, and what at first seemed to be clouds and thunder proved to be dust and the sound of horses' hooves. Thousands of people, wearing unwanted uniforms of leveling dust, converged for this entirely unprecedented event. Whitefield was the best known of numerous itinerant preachers who were a new challenge to religious stability and a breath of religious egalitarianism that countered the dominant trends of the previous half century. The apparent absence of this revival in the English West Indies seems to hint at the extent to which English society was diverging there. Whitefield's travels and his ability to attract as well as captivate huge audiences demonstrated effective use of improving communications. His success was predicated on religious curiosity, enthusiasm, and vocabulary that were thoroughly shared by unlettered Christians on both sides of the English Atlantic.[51] Calvinism was not enough to unite Congregationalists, Presbyterians, and Baptists in church government, but they all helped make the psalms and hymns of the English nonconformist preacher Isaac Watts immensely popular. Connections between Scottish and colonial Calvinists would grow after 1740 to include a transatlantic "Concert for United Prayer" as well as an offer of a Presbyterian congregation in Scotland for Jonathan Edwards, an offer that he considered seriously.[52]

The Protestantism of the English empire was gradually drawn into a more tolerant brotherhood by conscious latitudinarianism, by the Union with Scotland, and by popular perceptions of being beleaguered. Although the "popish" plots revealed around the English Atlantic in the seventeenth century proved more ethereal than Jacobite plots thereafter, the wars with Catholic France and Spain were very real. After 1689 a long series of wars fought against Catholic enemies promoted a sense of an embattled English Protestant community. The religions they shared were living and changing experiences, not just common inheritances, and defenses of these beliefs against Catholicism helped rouse the literate and illiterate to defend their culture while they defended their families and themselves.

As migrants came to be outnumbered by the locally born in most English colonies, most of those who did not learn to read were villagers again. Reduced migration after 1675 reduced the links that had been kept alive by transfusions of kin and neighbors and countrymen. Illiteracy became a barrier to social mobility in the restoration empire, foreclosing the kind of opportunity that had been evident in a less complicated earlier time of foundings. Yet English oral culture in the colonies meant sharing much more than trade goods, diseases, and wars. As family, church, and county court urged and demanded submission and deference, they fostered respect for models and individuals who were literate, with economic and political resources, and with broader horizons. Illiteracy was a badge of dependence for most slaves and for many women, servants, and children. These people belonged to the English Atlantic empire after 1675, but the English Atlantic did not belong to them.

Ultimately the English Atlantic was a literate empire, a paper empire. Laws and instructions to governors, sea captains, agents, and attorneys, as well as letters and newspapers or even mundane bills of lading—all indicate that the English Atlantic was a society that rewarded literacy, indeed required literacy for full membership. Literate culture encouraged patterns of thought, styles of argument, and views of life that were quite different from the oral traditions that had been inherited and that continued to condition the minds of the illiterate members of the same society.[53] (This division was not sharp, however, for oral traditions affected everyone, and there may have been a sizable group of readers who never mastered writing or lost that skill from lack of use).[54] For some, literacy was a badge of reformed Christianity; for others, literacy was a prerequisite for participation in the economic, social, and political leadership of the English Atlantic empire. A telling distinction has been made between the "great tradition" and the "little tradition" as coexisting and competing perspectives within societies.[55] In the English Atlantic, the little tradition was oral and local; the great tradition was literate and cosmopolitan. Not only did the two compete within society, but they also competed *within* many people.

A bare majority of white adult male householders and about one third of white adult female householders were literate in colonial North America in 1660 if the signing of wills is adequate evidence of literacy. This general picture was true of English-speaking householders in England, the West Indies, or North American colonies at this time. Adult male literacy in New England rose dramatically to 70 percent by 1710 and to 85 percent in 1760, the eventual fruit of Congregational concern with "the Book." Elsewhere in English America there seems to have been no comparable transformation. It seems safe to suggest that only a minority of the English-speaking adults in England or America could read and write well enough to do so regularly. Whenever information was power, the written word was quicker, more accurate, more complete; was exclusive; and also allowed careful rereading. In religion, in politics, in family life, and in business, the English Atlantic functioned primarily through and for the literate. Improvements in communications only served to strengthen the comparative advantages of the literate.[56]

Literate colonials became more numerous while maintaining their proportion of the growing population in most colonies. The newspapers, cautiously avoiding most local news, lured their subscribers and casual readers to the broader perspective of the English Atlantic world or to aspects of the world beyond that as filtered through the London papers. The traffic in imported pamphlets, tracts, and books was overwhelmingly English as was the small but growing production of the colonial presses.[57] Clergymen's libraries, parish libraries, and those donated by missionary groups or patrons gave some access to books for those who could not afford them. Towns like Boston, Dorchester, Concord, and New Haven had public libraries in the seventeenth century. The Artillery Company of Boston had a library of nearly 3000 books in 1724. Some 29 Church of England parishes in Maryland had libraries in 1702, with a sizable provincial library in Annapolis.[58] Some six years after Allan Ramsay started a circulating library in Edinburgh in 1726,[59] the Library Company of Philadelphia provided access to a library for what was initially a modest fee. Books could also live much longer than people, making heirloom Bibles, secondhand prayerbooks, and other popular titles accessible to the literate (or illiterate) of modest means. All this could bring real and imagined social mobility; it also allowed the literate increasing opportunities to find, in books, new English-speaking companions among the dead and distant with whom their neighbors were compared.

The greatest social beneficiaries of increasing English Atlantic communications were the growing group of those with the time and money to educate themselves and their children, to write and post letters, and to read and buy books. The increasing traffic in written business information made literacy mandatory for competition in the world of merchants, customs officers, and sea captains. Education was needed to gain imperial, colonial, or even local offices that provided profit in apparent return for creating records. Courting aristocratic English patrons was done with clever literary allusions, curios, and comments that were relatively au courant. Planters and merchants bought, read, and kept their copies of the *Spectator* and the *Gentleman's Magazine*. These improved and displayed a person's link with the metropolis while including clever jibes at metropolitan extravagance, triviality, and decadence that put heart into English provincials everywhere. Colonial gentlemen also joined together to sponsor editions of works to be published either in London or the colonies. Colonial bibliophiles like Cotton Mather, James Logan, and William Byrd II built impressive personal libraries, revealing a good grasp of current publications as they ordered books. Through English periodicals like the monthly *History of the Works of the Learned*, established in London from 1699, and especially through its successors, colonial bibliophiles and scholars could keep abreast of scholarship and contribute to it. As a very general reflection of developments, it is interesting that only 3 English colonial fellows were elected to the Royal Society of London between 1661 and 1700, but 23 were elected in the next 40 years.[60]

There was a small but significant migration from England and Scotland, which can be seen as part of the trend in migration within England itself around the end of the seventeenth century. Merchants, professionals, and landowners were then the people in England likely to have traveled farthest from their place of birth.[61] Virginia's developing elites late in the seventeenth century owed more to newly arrived men of substance than to families that had survived the earlier "starving time." Massachusetts became home for a number of English merchants in the same period, men who would help bring the colony into closer political and economic contact with London. A prominent London family like the Heathcotes established its own transatlantic trading world, with brothers in New York, Jamaica, Lisbon, and London.[62] Only 2 of 276 clergyman working in colonial South Carolina were native-born—and only 8 of some 37 qualified physicians. Officeholders, physicians, and lawyers arrived in established colonies with the education, resources, and connections to be automatically admitted to their professions and to the homes and families of the leading colonials.[63] Atlantic communications allowed these arrivals to maintain and use their English connections and to arrange contacts for colonials. All migrations create wider horizons and interest in communication, but these migratory elites were especially well placed to profit from the improving communications within the English Atlantic.

The leaders of Massachusetts might be regarded as the English colonial elite least in need of English gentry values early in the eighteenth century. More than any other colony, this community of second- and third-generation colonials had English foundations that were firmly laid in opposition to the English court. Yet some strange things were happening in Boston. In the midst of a major fire that destroyed much of central Boston in 1711, witnesses observed: "Some gentlemen took care to preserve Her Majesties Picture that was in the Town-House."[64] This gallantry occurred in the same town that had harbored regicides, resisted Charles II, and rebelled against James II. In 1730, Massachusetts-born Governor Jonathan Belcher returned from London to take up his post, bringing full-length portraits of George II and Queen Caroline as royal gifts to the province. These were hung, presumably with Queen Anne's portrait, in the council chamber. The new governor had asked their majesties for the portraits, perhaps to stand as a visual aid to patriotism and a labeled notice of Belcher's political connections. In 1740, portraits of the long-since departed King William III and Queen Mary "at full length, which were done in London by the best Hands, at the Charge of the Province" were added to the council chamber.[65] William and Mary had a special appeal as defenders of liberties, but it remains interesting that the Massachusetts Bay colony now paid to add to the royalty who watched over (or did they look down on?) the proceedings of the only elected legislative council in the empire. The social changes could also be sensed from the duels fought by sword-wielding young "gentlemen-merchants," the horse races, and the growth of trades like that of Mrs. Elizabeth Hatton, who arrived from London in 1733 promising to make "all sorts of Women's Apparel after the newest Mode. . . . She also has new Patterns of Sleves by the last Ships, from the Queen's Manteau and Scarf Maker, from whom she'l constantly be supply'd as the Fashion alters."[66] A visitor to Boston seven years later could report that "the ladies here visit, drink tea and indulge every little piece of gentility to the height of the mode and neglect the affairs of their families with as good grace as the finest ladies in London."[67]

In pursuit of civility and gentility, as in fulfilling their related political and economic ambitions, the emerging colonial oligarchies of merchants and planters needed their English connections. Cultural legitimacy had special urgency for those seeking to consolidate and justify their social leadership in communities where deference was not a presumption based on centuries of local existence, and for those fearing that their positions could be destroyed by African, Indian, papist, or their own community's "barbarisms." English models of civility were inevitable, and London fashions in clothes, houses, furnishings, and carriages were among the most visible signs of connections with London. Lineages and cousinages would be explored during trips to England, and marriages could support or create usable family connections.[68]

Provincial social links to London were not idle flourishes grounded in lack of imagination, nor were they uncritical. Provincials who cultivated people and habits that demonstrated London connections were often ambivalent about them. Cotton Mather revealed resentment amid his cultural cringing when he referred to his son as "a tame Indian, for so the Europeans are pleased to denominate the children that are born in these regions."[69] English county or colonial gentry held and enhanced their positions by serving as conveyers of metropolitan influences, exploiting imperial legitimacies but also defending their localities. Denunciations of London fashion and foppery could also be imported in either secular or religious form. Diseases, which were among the fastest travelers of the English Atlantic, could readily be connected to the presumed sinfulness of life in major ports. Even the most urbane colonials could not resist references to Arcadian colonial simplicity for the benefit of English correspondents although these same people would speak of English correspondents and colonial barbarism to their local peers.[70]

The general social dynamics of the English Atlantic empire between 1675 and 1740 included countervailing forces and trends. Falling English migration and continuing African immigration represented real and potential divergence between colonies and metropolis. On the other hand, trends in demography and wealth distributions in other parts of the empire reinforced the integration that was evident in political, economic, and social spheres.

The clearest social divergence occurred in the English West Indies, which had become African colonies ruled by English elites. The attachment of these English to their homeland served to reassure themselves and their English connections. A Barbados planter could insist that his island was as English as fenland reclaimed from the sea, minimized the ocean when he opposed English duties on sugar by fuming:

> So that we must lose our Country upon the account of Space, a thing little more than imaginary: a thing next neighbour to nothing.
> The Citizens of *Rome*, though they lived in the remotest Parts of the World then known, were still *Roman* Citizens to all Intents. But we poor Citizens of *England*, as soon as our backs are turn'd, and we are gone a spit and a stride; are presently reputed Aliens, . . .[71]

The commitment to English culture had a narrower social purpose here than it would in colonies of major English settlement, for English perceptions of the gentry could not provoke much deference from Africans or even colonial-born slaves. Yet the sustained power of these elites to determine life in those islands, despite demographic disaster and a coerced alien majority, is stark evidence of the social possibilities of power. In the face of overwhelming social divergence, an English minority sustained an effective, if sometimes frantic, commitment to an integrated English Atlantic community.

By way of contrast, changing demography and wealth distributions in most of English North America tended toward English patterns over time. The sons and daughters of adventurers or dissident migrants were born the native inhabitants of English colonial provinces, counties, towns, and villages. As those of substance sought to consolidate and bequeath their positions, the attractiveness of the values of English gentry was practical as well as aesthetic. In these colonies the elites could hope to do more than impress themselves and their English counterparts. Here the symbols of the monarchy had more than legal currency, and civility could appeal to those who hoped for accomplishment in these terms for themselves or their children. With some misgivings and some dissent, the leading families in the colonies were drawn toward a set of values and attitudes that were shared by English-speaking leaders everywhere. Colonial communities were becoming more hierarchical, and the values and attitudes that gave support to those realities promised deference for leaders and aspirations and explanations for others. Colonial leaders whose position was built and maintained on transatlantic political and economic connections did not need to do any elaborate social calculus to recognize that their social regard for English gentry culture was a small and profitable investment to encourage civility and deference, as well as loyalty, at the local level.

The English Atlantic was a social innovation, and improving communications accompanied more social change. It has become customary to examine social change by invoking pairs of ideas that are thought to contrast "traditional" and "modern" societies and then to calibrate discernible changes in terms of these dichotomies. Hence there is concern about transitions from homogeneous to heterogeneous, from communal to individualist, from oral to literate, from ascribed to achieved status, or from communal to associational relationships. Such abstractions are more useful if they are not seen as sequential stages in some cosmic historical social development but rather as competing tendencies within people and societies. Improving English Atlantic communications were not unalloyed support for any of these tendencies.

The contrasts between oral and literate culture were considerable and significant within the English empire; but it is essential to appreciate that parts of the English Atlantic were becoming less literate, parts were maintaining the same proportion of literates in stable populations, some areas were maintaining the proportion of literates in a growing population, and increased literacy was evident in very few places. The economics of gaining, keeping, and particularly of effectively using literacy needs emphasis. It is also clear that some benefits of literacy were increasing whereas others were diminishing in the course of a single lifetime. The division between "genteel" and "vulgar" literacy was just becoming noticeable by 1740.[72]

If a move from ascribed to achieved roles for people in society is modernization, improving English Atlantic communications were not modernizing. Increasing opportunities to communicate served to homogenize English-speaking culture and to consolidate membership in it. The social barriers between planter and slave, settler and Indian, master and servant, and between "the gentle sort" and "the common sort" were being intensified by the developing communications available to local social leaders. Even those whose participation in English culture was entirely oral and local would sense the increasing solidarilty of a shared culture and the advantages as well as the need to enhance perceived differences between themselves and those of different religions, languages, and races.

Increasing English Atlantic communication was serving to assist the development of many associational relationships in spite of its simultaneous service to ethnic solidarity. New settlements were, in the vast majority of cases, gatherings of strangers who were building new neighborhoods and new kinships at a local level. Yet they and their children were also building associational connections based on the transatlantic divisions of labor, specialization, and association of common interest that could be political, economic, and social. Associational communities, unlike communal ones, "can be just as strong when they are supra-local" and will not disintegrate because of distances but rather from conflict of interests.[73] English Atlantic communications improvements strengthened both an ethnic and an associational community.

The English Atlantic was coming closer together as a community. Epidemics were a tragic and little understood price of this process—and one paid by many who suffered much else from the growing solidarity of the English-speaking. These English-speaking people shared a language and a culture as well as a political economy. In the English Atlantic, as elsewhere, much of everyday life was oral and local, yet the influences that drew people to the broader society were not just political and economic. The religion of Quakers and Anglicans was consciously transatlantic, and Presbyterians and Congregationalists maintained spiritual and secular friendships that tied people across oceans. In sectarian rivalries and in subsequent interdenomination "awakenings," the ocean proved to be no social barrier. For the literate, the newspapers no less than the books were invitations to the wider community of the English-speaking. Colonial leaders in politics, commerce, religion, and science gained and defended their personal success with English connections. Although they claimed that their substance and English connections made them effective defenders of local rights, privileges, and values, they were local exemplars of success who propagated the value of a civility and a culture that was common throughout the English Atlantic empire.

14 · Conclusion

This exploration of the integration of the English Atlantic ends in 1740 to avoid preoccupation with the countervailing trend that later dominated. Much changed in the next 20 years between the attack on Cartegena and the conquest of New France. The British Army in America between 1755 and 1760, accompanied by a monthly packet boat that continued to run until the American Revolution, displayed massive resources and illustrated further the shrinking of the Atlantic. The process of expanding shipping, extending postal services and mail packets, and founding of newspapers continued in the last years of the colonial period. In a village or an empire, people can share more or less than they want to share. Those who have, with the aid of instantaneous twentieth-century communications, witnessed the evaporation of empires built in the age of sail will have no difficulty sensing the interplay of integration and disintegration in the destruction of the first British Empire. The North Atlantic united that empire more than it divided; American separatism was not an unfolding of the inevitable but a revolutionary achievement. Because the English Atlantic was a functional economic, political, and social universe, no simple unilateral declaration of independence could suffice. The empire did not evaporate like a quaint and formal connection that had become irrelevant. The struggle within people, within colonies, and within the empire was bloody, and it left many loyalist émigrés and royal colonies as indicators that the ocean was not the divide. Poor communication had not dissolved the empire; consciously dismissing that notion is a helpful beginning in studying the emergence of American social and political identity and in understanding the lives of those who had lived within the English Atlantic empire.

Any informed adult living within the English Atlantic empire in 1739 knew that the Atlantic Ocean was traversed regularly, whether or not that person had crossed it. This same person also knew that the North American continent had never been crossed by anyone. If he or she were as old as William Byrd II (1674–1744), Jeremiah Dummer (1679–1739), James Logan (1674–1751), Lewis Morris (1676–1746), John Oldmixon (1673–1742), Alexander

Spotswood (1676–1740), Isaac Watts (1674–1748), or Robert Walpole (1676–1745), that person also knew that Atlantic communication had improved in his or her lifetime and was faster than it had ever been. What was obvious at that time has, for a variety of reasons, become obscured; this study has sought to recover the realities and perceptions of English Atlantic communications in the lifetime before 1740.

Early modern communications within the English Atlantic are now too easily assumed to have been dangerous, slow, infrequent, and unchanging before the invention of the steamship and telegraph. These four assumptions seem to find support in much of the surviving evidence of tragedies, complaints, and excuses; and they are invisible foundations on which most theories of the colonial origins of the United States are based.[1]

In the lifetime before 1740, the dangers of North Atlantic travel were considerably reduced, though marine disasters still occurred. Maritime risks were always higher along coasts, particularly those that were unknown, than on the open seas. Better charts and maps, the construction of lighthouses, and breakwaters and port facilities (as well as the increased number of local pilots at growing ports) did more for marine safety than the improvements in navigational instruments or the invention of headsails and the helm wheel. Improved safety in sailing into Hudson Bay was one dramatic illustration of the victory of accumulated knowledge over a most treacherous new English Atlantic route. Mariners and fishermen who sailed for a livelihood were not suicidal. Members of the colonial elites behaved rationally in sailing to seek offices, collect debts, settle estates, sell cargoes, or even to recover their health. Declining rates for marine insurance, which have been rightly celebrated for improving productivity in shipping and trade, showed both the increased safety and the effective communications on which those industries depended.

The speed of English Atlantic communications could be good, bad, or indifferent. Legitimate expectations developed over time and were related to the very different passage times likely on each route and to the different types of communication. Routes of the English Atlantic had their own various rhythms, and serious concern for a ship would begin only when it had not arrived at its destination in approximately twice the time of a good passage on the same route.[2] War disrupted normalcy, bringing the capture of merchantmen, delayed sailings (which were often unreported because of shipping embargoes), and convoys that tended to slow fleets to the pace of the slowest vessels. Correspondents (and historians, who are their captives) have shown an understandable tendency to comment on communications only when they were disappointing.

The English Atlantic was a very different ocean on its different routes or at either end of the same route. Average peacetime passages from England to the colonies ranged from 5 weeks (Newfoundland) to 12 weeks (Albany Fort in Hudson Bay), and passages from England Atlantic colonies to England averaged from 3 (Newfoundland) to 14 weeks (Jamaica). Not only were voyages from North America to England approximately half as long as the return, but sailings eastward could be made in seasons when westward voyages could not be risked for fear of the possible icing of North American ports between the Chesapeake and Maine. During the lifetime before 1740, there had been a noticeable shift in sailing routes toward challenging the westerlies, prompted by war with France and minor navigational improvements, possibly assisted by minor changes in climate. The winterless eastern Caribbean colonies were 8 weeks from England when viewed from either end of the routes. Jamaica was the only colony that could hear from England more quickly than a ship could take an answer back. The speed of a voyage was not predictable within a week, but expectations could be met often enough to remain legitimate and could be exceeded as well as disappointed.

Expectations also varied because different kinds of communications functioned at different paces. For some government, business, and personal correspondents, as well as institutions like the Quaker Yearly Meeting, an annual letter remained customary. Commercial correspondents were more likely to use the increasing opportunities available to send market information, shipping news, and other "freshest advices" affecting business along to employers, partners, agents, and preferred customers. Government displayed a range of tempos depending on function. As the imperial administrative machinery developed at the end of the seventeenth century, officials established rates of correspondence that reflected possibilities, but the pace of correspondence did not exploit subsequent improvements. Colonials who once were unheard victims of administrative fiat were increasingly able to operate transatlantic lobbies, finding political advantage as well as irritating delay in the leisurely pace of English administrative, legislative and judicial proceedings. In international treaties the English government agreed to increasingly anachronistic conventions for the spread of peace, but government military considerations could lead the same government to sponsor expensive monthly mail service to the colonies in all seasons.

More numerous sailings helped shrink the English Atlantic between 1675 and 1740. Increased shipping meant that more ships would better the average passage time and bring news earlier, and the number of ships that extended or defied the "optimum" shipping seasons also increased on several major routes. The growing maritime commerce, particularly of the Leeward Islands, Jamaica, South Carolina, and Pennsylvania, increased the flow of transatlantic news and narrowed the space and time between colonies. The tripling of intercolonial shipping multiplied the flow of news impressively, if unevenly. The doubling of the number of transatlantic voyages in this same period represented a major improvement.

More deliberate initiatives to improve communications changed the possibilities for correspondence within the English Atlantic even more than did the increased shipping. The development of postal services in Britain, the English West Indies, and English North America immediately multiplied the opportunities to correspond with numerous ports. The birth and growth of newspapers throughout the English Atlantic did even more to hasten the exchanges of public news. Edmund Dummer's West Indies packets illustrated the possibilities and the price of a wartime mail service that allowed correspondents from Boston, Barbados, or Bristol to defy the seasons and the convoys. The posts and the papers, linked as they were in a variety of ways, magnified the increased communications afforded by more numerous shipping to create a striking improvement in the pace of news. The fourth modern assumption about English Atlantic communications between 1675 and 1740, that they did not change, is as misleading as the assumptions of danger, tardiness, and infrequency. Communications changed, and their bias was away from local concerns, favoring perspectives and preoccupations that connected the broader English Atlantic community.

Were developing communications an agent of broader change or an innovation in the service of stability and continuity? Although the provincial period of American colonial history is often characterized as fairly static (for nothing very "revolutionary" happened there), the creation of a consolidated English Atlantic was an innovation. Communications, which can too easily be represented as formative because they touch all aspects of life, were part of that integration process. Simplistic causal connections *cannot* be drawn, for the improvements in communications were at once causing more imperial integration, accompanying it, and resulting from it. Developing communications helped create a united Atlantic empire, helped stabilize and defend it, and may eventually have helped to undermine it.

The growing English Atlantic economy changed communications and was changed by them. Although trading remained a venture, more opportunities to gain market information allowed better planning of cargoes and better utilization of ships. The development of the commission system of trading and the use of factors and storekeepers where there were no monopolies presumed adequate communications. Emergence of the marine insurance business depended on information to prevent fraud and prove claims. As these efficiencies reduced costs in the highly competitive shipping industry, the benefits were passed on to traders and customers as lower freight rates. While the postal services conveyed private information that could give private advantage, the newspapers and the postal services both tended to reduce windfall profits, to equalize prices over broader areas, and to allow more people to calculate advantages and fewer people to have them. Economic integration was discernible in a number of features of the English Atlantic in 1675, but these became dominant realities by 1740.

The English Atlantic polity that developed by 1740 was the creation of the previous lifetime. There is unity to the whole period in the patterning of administrative machinery and in the emergence of Whig political philosophy, but these had been new notions in 1675 that became translated into power systems by 1740. Innovation by the restored Stuarts provoked resistance most clearly in Virginia in 1676 and in both England and the Dominion of New England in 1688–1689. The wars with France that came with William III brought some accomodation of local liberties and some acceptance of central authority. Whig political triumph and peace relaxed some of the centralizing pressures after 1715, giving special opportunities to local elites in a polity whose leaders saw patronage as the purpose of power. English Atlantic communications had been fully exploited in the elaboration of administrative and legal structures late in the seventeenth century, and government military concerns provoked the challenging experiment with Edmund Dummer's packet boats to the West Indies and its faint echo in a New York packet service. Although political communications continued to improve in the first third of the eighteenth century, the legal and administrative pace of business did not usually exploit the quickening pace of English Atlantic communications.

Social transformation of the English Atlantic colonies was impressive. The population increased fivefold between 1675 and 1740, with the forced migration of Africans constituting the greatest addition and English-speaking migrants being succeeded by their colonial-born offspring. Social implications of improving communications, like the economic and political implications, varied according to people's access to information. African immigrants demonstrated the full social cost of lost connections with culture, kin, and language; they were the instant Americans who were forced into a new Creole culture.[3] All those who did not speak English were affected by the increasingly frequent epidemics, by the more intense participation of the colonies in Europe's wars, and by the growing tribalism of the English. Illiterate English colonists were increasingly locally oriented and socially dependent whereas their demographic trends were away from pioneer exceptionalism and toward English patterns. Their embattled Protestantism, their language, their possessions, and the very social facilities and institutions that they developed in keeping with their notion of civilization were all comforting evidence that they belonged to the dominant English culture. Literacy in English gradually became a prerequisite for most social mobility, and improving communications strengthened the advantages of the literate. Newspapers generally sold their readers a world view filtered through the London papers, encouraging a cosmopolitan perspective as did the traffic in English periodicals and books.

Colonial elites stood to gain the most social advantage from the integration of the English Atlantic. In communities without ancient patterns of deference, with very little history and its attending amnesias to bless inequalities of ancient origin, with labor expensive and citizens armed, new men of "substance" sought enough social order to allow them quiet possession of visible inequalities. These men sought to provide services a brokers of political, economic, and social power between their locality and the colony and empire of which it was a part. Cosmopolitan political connections, London credit, and status demonstrated by taste in possessions were used to convince their neighbors that the elite had the substance to offer protection against what they would willingly call provincial or imperial "tyrannies." Yet these same people also sought to convince provincial and imperial managers that, as people with an interest in order, these local magnates should hold the offices that could be trusted only to those with broader loyalties. When colonial gentlemen and merchants adopted gentry patterns of consumption, they were not risking political and economic status with self-indulgent social pretense.[4]

These were not alien and alienating gestures by people who no longer needed customers, voters, or friends. There was characteristic provincial ambivalence to the import of the cosmopolitan, but the cultural support for values that accepted inequality was even more attractive to leaders of increasingly stratified colonies of English-speaking people than it was to the Barbados plantocracy. It is entirely appropriate that colonial leaders initiated changes in the meaning of the word "empire" to include themselves and their localities in an organic union with the British Isles in what, by 1740, was coming to be called the "British Empire."[5] Improving Atlantic communications brought some challenges to the local elites, but the trend in the early eighteenth century brought many advantages and few sacrifices for the colonial elites. At their best, these leaders could serve themselves while claiming to serve both their neighbors and their monarch. Improving communications helped agile local leaders; even better communications would force their heirs to make some hard choices.

Between 1675 and 1740 the development of communications encouraged, accompanied, and resulted from the creation of an English Atlantic economic, political, and social community. In a family or an empire, being identical is neither required nor desired of members although attempts to become similar might be signs of solidarity. In the progress of economic, political, and social inequality that attended colonial development; in the replication of mental and material culture that constituted progress from pioneer deprivation; in the import of credit that could also be seen as debt, of patronage that could also be called corruption, and of fashion that could also be dubbed foppery, English Atlantic communications provided the context. The English Atlantic was not just a shared inheritance; it was also a shared experience.

ABBREVIATIONS

AAS   American Antiquarian Society, Worcester, Massachusetts
AHR   American Historical Review
APCC   Acts of the Privy Council of England, Colonial Series
BIHR   Bulletin of the Institute of Historical Research
BL   British Library (formerly British Museum), London, England
BNA, British North America
BNL   Boston News-Letter
BWI   British West Indies
CSPC   Calendar of State Papers, Colonial Series, America and the West Indies
CSP Dom   Calendar of State Papers, Domestic Series
DAB   Dictionary of American Biography
DNB   Dictionary of National Biography
EHR   English Historical Review
EconHR   Economic History Review
FWI   Foreign West Indies
GPO   General Post-Office Archives, London, England
HBC   Hudson's Bay Archives, Winnipeg, Canada
Historical Statistics   Historical Statistics of the United States, U.S. Bureau of the
        Census, 2d ed., 2 vols. (Washington, D.C., 1975)
HMC   Publication of the Historical Manuscripts Commission
HSP   Historical Society of Pennsylvania, Philadelphia
JEconH   Journal of Economic History
MHS   Massachusetts Historical Society, Boston
NMM   National Maritime Museum, London, England
NYCD   Documents Relative to the Colonial Historical of the State of New York
OED   Oxford English Dictionary
PAC   Public Archives of Canada, Ottawa
PMG   Postmasters general
PMHB   Pennsylvania Magazine of History and Biography
PRO   Public Record Office, London, England
TRHS   Transactions of the Royal Historical Society
VMHB   Virginia Magazine of History and Biography
W&MQ   William and Mary Quarterly

APPENDIX: TABLES

TABLE 1.1 Calendar of the Transatlantic Trade of English Ports, 1696-1700[a]

	j	f	m	a	m	j	j	a	s	o	n	d	TOTAL
Clearances to colonies	54	41	51	26	46	26	41	46	40	50	73	114	608
Entries from colonies	67	21	25	30	54	100	138	106	78	101	89	78	887

SOURCE: PRO, E 190 series, port books.

a.   Outport records for entire period, London for 1696 and 1697 only.

TABLE 2.1 Some Average England-Barbados (Barbados-England) Passages

Ship type	from (to)[a]	Avg. days	Avg. knots	No. of cases
Merchantmen[b] 1698-1700	Channel ports	62.9 (56.8)	2.5 (2.8)	20 (5)
Merchantmen[b] 1698-1700	West of England	80.2 (64.2)	2.0 (2.5)	26 (9)
Mail Packets 1702-1711	Channel ports	33.7	4.7	36
Mail Packets 1702-1711	West of England	38.6	4.1	7

SOURCES: PRO, CO 33/13 and E 190 series for merchantmen. For mail packets
          see Table 9.1

a. Barbados to England evidence in parentheses.

b. These are customs-to-customs times.

TABLE 2.2 Shipping at Barbados – 1681–1738

Annual Entries (Clearances)

From (to)	1681–1682	1684–1685	1685–1686	1699	1700	1715–1716	1720–1721	1736–1737	1737–1738
Britain and Ireland	76	116	135	113(61)	126(109)	(103)	(91)	67(32)	69(12)
BNA	141	134	178	152(87)	188(136)	(208)	(250)	160(123)	170(126)
BWI	38	57	37	38(47)	76(91)	(212)	(96)	23(44)	20(30)
FWI	22	7	16	35(26)	41(67)	(122)	(80)	31(17)	35(17)
Africa	18	13	13	17(10)	28(15)	(6)	(3)	19(-)	15(-)
Other	31	25	41	15(1)	22(6)	(3)	(14)	36(1)	28(-)
TOTAL	326	352	420	370(232)	481(424)	(654)	(534)	336(217)	337(187)

SOURCE: PRO, CO 33/13–16. Each column is exactly one year, but terminal days are varied to gain as many complete years as possible from records that are generally incomplete.

284

TABLE 2.3 British North American Shipping at Barbados, 1681-1738

Annual Entries (Clearances)

	1681-1682	1684-1685	1685-1686	1696	1697	1698	1699	1700	1715-1716	1720-1721	1736-1737	1737-1738
New England	16	74	53	15	3	2	6(4)	1(1)	(1)	(-)	3(-)	2
New Hampshire	6	2	7	-	11	11	16(4)	18(6)	(7)	(12)	8(3)	4(-)
Massachusetts	63	8	41	37	30	46	52(17)	87(35)	(40)	(46)	44(22)	35(18)
Rhode Island	3	2	8	5	7	9	11(9)	13(14)	(22)	(28)	6(3)	9(3)
Connecticut	6	-	5	2	2	4	6(1)	3(1)	(13)	(18)	14(10)	16(12)
Total New England	94	86	114	59	53	72	91(35)	112(57)	(83)	(104)	75(38)	66(33)
Newfoundland	5	3	7	4	1	8	6(5)	5(10)	(11)	(12)	4(7)	6(7)
New York	14	15	11	5	9	9	12(3)	19(12)	(21)	(14)	10(5)	6(4)
New Jersey	-	-	-	-	-	-	-	-	-	-	1	-
Pennsylvania	-	2	9	10	14	17	18(6)	23(11)	(19)	(20)	22(8)	32(21)
Maryland	1	6	2	3	2	1	3(6)	7(13)	(9)	(26)	14(20)	15(15)
Virginia	18	13	17	1	4	7	14(24)	8(25)	(55)	(49)	23(28)	34(32)
Carolinas	9	9	12	4	5	5	8(8)	4(8)	(10)	(25)	11(17)	11(14)
TOTAL	141	134	178	86	88	119	152 (87)	188 136	(208)	(250)	160 (123)	170 (126)

SOURCE: PRO, CO 33/13-16. Each column is exactly one year, but terminal days were varied to gain as many complete years of shipping as possible from records that are generally incomplete.

285

TABLE 2.4   English Imports of Colonial Sugar by Source, 1683-1740

Annual Average	Barbados tons (%)[a]	Leewards tons (%)	Jamaica tons (%)	Avg. Annual Total tons (%)	Estimated Ships[b]
1683	c.10000 (54.9)	c.3300 (18.1)	4902 (26.9)	18202 (99.9)	143
1701-1710[c]	7638 (40.3)	6485 (34.2)	4798 (25.3)	18920 (99.8)	149
1711-1720	9501 (33.7)	10674 (37.9)	7946 (28.2)	28122 (99.8)	221
1721-1730[d]	9189 (23.8)	17036 (44.2)	12287 (31.9)	38512 (99.9)	303
1731-1740	6197 (15.0)	18799 (45.7)	16074 (39.1)	41069 (99.8)	323

SOURCE: R. S. Dunn, Sugar and Slaves (Chapel Hill, 1972), p. 203 for 1683.
Others from Noel Deerr, The History of Sugar, 2 vols. (London,
1949), I, 193-98.

a. % of the total sugar imported annually from that source during designated
period.
b. At an average of 127 tons. This is the average of 615 ships entering
Barbados between 1696 and 1700 from Britain. The assumption that ship
size remained fairly constant through this period is supported by Ralph
Davis, The Rise of the English Shipping Industry (London, 1962), pp.
280-81. Estimate is conservative, as full lading is presumed.
c. No figures for 1705. St. Kitts figures averaged without 1701-1703 as
well.
d. No figures for 1727.

TABLE 2.5 Calendar of British Shipping at Jamaica 1685-1687[a]

	j	f	m	a	m	j	j	a	s	o	n	d	total
Entered	11	7	9	15	13	9	4	5	4	8	10	6	101
Cleared	1	4	14	17	14	14	14	14	1	2	8	3	106

SOURCE: PRO, CO 142/13, fols. 1-30, 111, 117.

a. For two years beginning 29 September 1685.

TABLE 2.6 British North American Shipping at Jamaica 1685-1729

Annual Average Entries (Clearances)

from (to)	1685-1688[a]	(1685-1687)[b]	(1689-1700)[c]	(1703-1704)[d]	1718-1719[e]	1728-1729[f]
New England	23.3	(17-5)	(11)	(8)	20(13)	41
New York	10.6	(7)	(13.5)	(11)	22(14)	21
Pennsylvania	-	(-)	(1.5)	(2)	10(9)	16
Chesapeake	1	(3)	(1.5)	(2)	1(6)	8
South Carolina	1	(-)	(1.5)	(8)	7(10)	9
TOTAL	35.9	(27.5)	(2.9)	(31)	60(52)	95

SOURCE: PRO, CO 142/13, 14.

a. Average of three years commencing 29 Sept. 1685.

b. Average of two years commencing 29 Sept. 1685.

c. Average of two years commencing 25 Dec. 1698.

d. One year commencing 25 Dec. 1703.

e. One year commencing 25 Dec. 1718.

f. One year commencing 25 Dec. 1728.

TABLE 2.7 Shipping at Charles Town 1717-1739: Entries (Clearances)

From (to)	1717-1718[a]	1724-1725	1731-1732	1732-1733	1734-1735	1735-1736	1736-1737	1737-1738	1738-1739
Britain and Ireland	33(57)	49(79)	43(94)	49(76)	36(81)	42(86)	47(87)	22(87)	17(76)
BNA	33(41)	40(27)	44(25)	39(35)	73(57)	62(65)	77(57)	81(55)	74(57)
BWI	54(39)	46(38)	64(55)	69(57)	76(55)	59(50)	76(53)	46(51)	69(62)
FWI	6(2)	2(1)	3(-)	4(-)	1(-)	4(1)	3(1)	1(1)	4(-)
Southern Europe[b]	6(2)	6(1)	6(19)	9(18)	13(27)	25(25)	17(17)	16(5)	16(9)
Africa	6(-)	5(-)	7(-)	3(-)	7(-)	10(-)	13(-)	4(-)	10(-)
Other	6(5)	-(-)	6(2)	7(1)	16(3)	23(7)	19(3)	5(2)	7(5)
	144(146)	148(146)	173(195)	180(187)	222(225)	225(234)	252(228)	175(192)	197(207)

SOURCE: PRO, CO 5/508-10.

a. All years commence 25 March except 1717-1718, which commences Christmas 1717.

b. South of Cape Finisterre, including the Wine Islands.

288

TABLE 2.8 Calendar of Charles Town Shipping with Great Britain and Ireland

Entries	j	f	m	a	m	j	j	a	s	o	n	d	Total
1724-1725[a]	1	1	10	9	1	2	2	2	-	8	7	6	49
1731-1732	8	6	-	3	2	2	3	1	-	5	2	11	43
1732-1733	12	5	3	4	5	3	-	1	3	2	2	9	49
1734-1735	2	1	7	1	3	2	-	1	4	3	7	5	36
1735-1736	4	5	-	6	4	-	3	1	2	5	10	2	42
1736-1737	3	6	4	5	3	-	1	7	6	4	2	6	47
Clearances													
1724-1725	12	10	11	4	13	6	4	-	1	4	5	9	79
1731-1731	6	14	15	22	10	6	3	3	2	1	2	10	94
1732-1732	8	15	17	5	5	7	4	-	1	3	4	7	76
1734-1735	11	11	8	14	7	3	1	4	1	3	10	8	81

SOURCE: PRO, CO 5/508-10.

a. All years are from Christmas to 24 December.

TABLE 2.9   Calendar of English and Irish Shipping with Barbados, 1697

Entries	j	f	m	a	m	j	j	a	s	o	n	d	Total
From England	*	1	*	*	1	3	*	*	6	2	1	6	20
From Ireland	*	2	3	*	1	3	2	1	1	*	*	4	17
Into England from Barbados	3	*	1	*	*	1	7	5	2	3	2	*	24

SOURCE: PRO, CO 33/13, and E 190/Series.

TABLE 2.10   War and Shipping at Barbados 1696-1700

Annual Entries[a]					
	1696	1697	1698	1699	1700
Britain and Ireland	54	37	110	113	126
BNA	86	88	119	152	188
BWI	10[b]	10[b]	37	38	76
FWI	6	2	38	35	41
Africa	9	10	18	17	28
Other	16	7	27	15	22
Total	181	154	349	370	481

SOURCE: PRO, CO 33/13-14.

a. All years commence 25 December of previous year.

b. Entries from Bermuda totaled 9 of these entries in 1696 and 8 in 1697.

TABLE 3.1   American Tobacco Shipments to Great Britain,[a]
             Annual Averages 1686-1740

	1686-1688	1697-1700	1701-1710	1711-1720	1721-1730	1731-1740
Pounds (millions)	28.0	32.0	27.5	28.7	33.6	40.0
Ships (estimated)[b]	221	252	217	226	265	316

SOURCE: <u>Historical Statistics</u>, Series Z, 449, 458.

a. Scottish imports included where available (1708-1711, 1715-1717,
    1721-1731, 1738-1740).

b. For average ladings see J. M. Price, <u>France and the Chesapeake</u>, 2 vols.
    (Ann Arbor, 1972), II, 901-2.

TABLE 3.2 Calendar of Tobacco Convoys 1693-1715

	j	f	m	a	m	j	j	a	s	o	n	d
Passed Lizard Outward	1	1	6	2	2	1	1	-	1	4	1	1
Left Capes Home	1	-	2	-	-	5	3	1	4	5	-	-

SOURCE: PRO, Adm 51/series.

TABLE 3.3 Calendar of Virginia's Trade with Great Britian
and Ireland 1699-1700 vs. 1737-1738

	j	f	m	a	m	j	j	a	s	o	n	d	No. of Cases
Virginia Entries													
1699-1700[a]	13	10	11	5	3	1	-	1	5	8	17	13	87
1737-1738[b]	3	9	10	13	18	13	6	2	-	1	4	4	83
Virginia Clearances													
1699-1700[a]	4	8	22	36	34	27	4	6	2	-	-	-	143
1737-1738[b]	-	-	4	5	10	20	13	21	22	4	2	-	101

SOURCES: PRO, CO 5/144; Virginia Gazette.

a. Christmas 1698 to Christmas 1700. Includes Ireland.
b. 1, January 1737 to 31, December 1738. Includes Ireland and Scotland.

TABLE 3.4 Calendar of British Shipping at Maryland, 1695-1700[a]

	j	f	m	a	m	j	j	a	s	o	n	d	Total
Entered	12	20	30	15	7	7	8	18	8	17	15	6	163
Cleared	2	8	36	46	55	76	43	9	6	7	5	7	300

SOURCE: PRO, CO 5/749.

a. Christmas 1694 to Christmas 1700.

TABLE 3.5   Bermuda Shipping 1729-1737[a]

	1729-1730	1730-1731	1731-1732	1732-1733	1733-1734	1734-1735	1735-1736	1736-1737	Annual Average
Britain									
from	3	2	5	3	2	3	1	3	2.8
to	1	0	0	0	1	2	1	1	.8
BNA									
from	48	39	49	51	49	52	46	57	48.9
to	60	63	54	70	62	52	48	57	58.3
BWI									
from	38	38	41	36	59	47	44	44	43.4
to	62	62	78	61	88	85	76	86	74.8
Other									
from	10	7	20	20	19	8	13	14	13.9
to	1	2	4	1	0	1	4	3	2.0
TOTAL									
Entered	99	85	115	110	129	110	104	118	108.8
Cleared	124	127	136	132	151	140	129	147	135.8

SOURCE: PRO, CO 41/6.

a.   Each year commencing 25 March.

TABLE 4.1   Population of Major English Colonial Ports, 1660-1760

	Boston	New York	Philadelphia	Newport	Charles Town
1660	3000	2400	----	700	----
1680	4500	3200	----	2500	700
1700	6700	5000	2500	2600	2000
1720	12000	7000	4885	3800	3500
1741	16660	10000	9515	6200	6800
1760	15631	13045	17060	7500	8000

SOURCES: Gary B. Nash, Urban Crucible (Cambridge, Mass., 1979), pp. 407-9; Carl Bridenbaugh, Cities in the Wilderness (New York, 1938), pp. 5, 143, 303; Cities in Revolt (New York, 1955), p. 5.

TABLE 4.2   Shipping at Boston by Region 1687-1738
Annual Entries (Clearances)

from (to)	1687-1688[a]	1718-1719[b]	1729-1730[c]	1732-1733[d]	1737-1738[e]
Britain & Ireland	30	66(68)	75(39)	63	46(55)
BNA	46	126(151)	372(440)	379	347(387)
BWI	94	86(123)	95(131)	74	81(98)
FWT	29	28(26)	67(69)	62	24(77)
Southern Europe	13	26(24)	27(30)	28	25(25)
Other	6	9(2)	6(6)	3	32(40)
TOTAL	218	341(394)	642(715)	609	555(682)

SOURCES: a. For year commencing Michaelmas 1687; from PRO, CO5/848.
b. For period 29, July 1718 - 14, July 1719; from same source.
c. For period 1 December 1729 - 5 December 1730; Pennsylvania Gazette, no. 112.
d. For year commencing 5 April 1732; from PRO, CO5/848.
e. For year commencing 1 April 1737; from Boston Weekly News-letter, nos. 1726-1775.

TABLE 4.3 Calendar of Boston's Shipping with Great Britain and Ireland
1687-1738

	j	f	m	a	m	j	j	a	s	o	n	d	Total
Entries													
1687-1688[a]	2	-	-	1	5	6	6	3	2	4	1	-	30
1718-1719[b]	1	-	3	9	3	4	9	10	7	14	2	4	66
1737-1738[c]	-	-	2	6	4	7	3	2	3	3	15	1	46
Clearances													
1718-1719[b]	7	5	2	5	3	9	3	6	3	9	4	12	68
1737-1738[c]	4	-	4	2	4	7	7	6	3	3	7	8	55

SOURCES:

a. PRO, CO 5/ 848, year commencing 29 September 1687.

b. Ibid., year commencing 17 July 1718.

c. Boston Weekly News-letter, nos. 1726-75, year commencing 1 April 1737.

TABLE 4.4 Passages to Boston from London by News-bearing Ships

1711-1739, by month of arrival

	j	f	m	a	m	j	j	a	s	o	n	d	Average (total)
Average Passage (weeks)	8.3	8	7.6	6.7	6.9	7.7	7.6	8	6.5	7.8	6.5	8.8	7.5
Range of Passages (weeks)	7-10	6-10	5-12	5-10	4-9	5-13	5-9	6-11	6-8	6-9	4-8	6-11	(4-13)
Number of cases	3	2	3	29	12	17	8	15	10	10	15	8	(132)

SOURCE: Boston News-letter.

TABLE 4.5   Boston Shipping and the West Indies 1687–1738

Number of Entries (Clearances)

From (to)	1687–1688	1718–1719	1729–1730	1732–1733	1737–1738
Barbados	33	35(57)	19(34)	9	7(2)
Leeward Islands	30	32(49)	34(48)	28	13(29)
Jamaica	14	13(14)	23(47)	30	37(52)
Honduras	-	-(-)	17(-)	5	18(-)
Other BWI	17	6(3)	2(2)	2	6(5)
Salt Tortuga	21	12(1)	-(-)	7	5
Other FWI	8	16(25)	67(69)	55	19(77)
TOTAL	123	114(149)	162(200)	136	105(175

SOURCE: As in Table 4.2.

TABLE 4.6 Boston Shipping and North America

Number of Entries (Clearances)

From (to)	1687-1688	1718-1719	1729-1730	1732-1733	1737-1738
Newfoundland	3	8(7)	24(42)	21	19
Nova Scotia[a]	-	18(21)	43(54)	26	24
New Hampshire	-	-	-	-	4
Rhode Island	1	1(-)	26	32	37
Connecticut	-	-	89 (79)	91	68
New York[b]	7	15(19)	31(36)	39	46
New Jerseys	-	-(1)	9(5)	8	3
Pennsylvania[c]	12	12(9)	17(16)	18	20
Maryland	5	8(11)	30(26)	23	33
Virginia	13	9(25)	16(23)	20	25
North Carolina	5	41(40)	66(75)	88	59
South Carolina		14(18)	12(16)	13	9
TOTAL	46	126(151)	363(372)	379	347

SOURCE: As in Table 4.2.
      a. Annapolis, Canso, Cape Breton, Chignecto, and Louisbourg.
      b. Including Long Island.
      c. Including Delaware.

TABLE 4.7 Shipping at New York by Region 1701–1738

Number of Entries (Clearances)

From (to)	1701[a]	1718[b]	1728[c]	1738[d]
Britain and Ireland	10	22(14)	25(10)	21(22)
BNA	24	59(57)	72(82)	94(92)
BWI	37	76(94)	55(62)	77(81)
FWI	1	35(20)	38(27)	27(27)
Southern Europe	5	4(8)	12(13)	13(15)
Other	1	2(-)	-(3)	11(2)
TOTAL	78	198(193)	202(197)	243(239)

SOURCES:

a. Julius Block et al., eds., An Account of her Majesty's Revenue in the Province of New York (Ridgewood, N.J., 1966). Year 1 January – 31 December.

b. PRO, CO 5/1222. Year following Christmas 1717.

c. PRO, CO 5/1224. Year following Christmas 1727.

d. PRO, CO 5/1225-26. Year following Christmas 1737.

TABLE 4.8 Calendar of New York Shipping with Great Britain and Ireland

	j	f	m	a	m	j	j	a	s	o	n	d	Total
Entries													
1701	2	1	2	-	-	1	1	-	-	-	1	2	10
1718	-	-	-	-	5	1	3	1	1	6	4	1	22
1728	-	-	-	-	4	6	1	4	2	3	2	3	25
1738	-	-	3	3	2	1	-	1	2	4	4	1	21
Clearances													
1718	1	-	-	-	3	1	1	2	1	1	1	3	14
1728	-	-	-	-	2	-	3	2	-	1	-	2	10
1738	-	-	1	-	1	3	2	-	-	2	10	3	22

SOURCES: as in Table 4.7.

TABLE 4.9 Passages to New York from London by
News-bearing Ships 1711-1739

	j	f	m	a	m	j	j	a	s	o	n	d	Average (total)
Average Passage (weeks)	15	10.5	10.7	6.8	9	9.6	9.6	9	7.4	8.6	7.5	15.4	9.2
Range of Passages (weeks)	15	10.5	10.7	5-9	8-11	7-11	8-12	8-10	7-8	7-10	4-10	13-19	(4-19)
Number of cases	1	1	1	6	8	9	4	3	2	4	5	3	(47)

SOURCES: Boston News-letter, American Weekly Mercury.

TABLE 4.10 New York Shipping and the West Indies, 1701-1738
Number of Entries (Clearances)

From (to)	1701	1718	1728	1738
Barbados	13	33(42)	14(24)	8(9)
Leeward Islands	9	15(18)	13(14)	16(25)
Jamaica	13	15(23)	15(17)	25(38)
Bermuda	2	6(5)	9(6)	18(5)
Other BWI	-	7(6)	4(1)	10(4)
Surinam	1	3(4)	5(2)	-(1)
Curacao	-	9(11)	17(19)	11(21)
Other FWI	-	23(5)	16(6)	16(5)
TOTAL	38	111(114)	93(89)	104(108)

SOURCES: As in Table 4.7.

TABLE 4.11 Calendar of New York Entries from the British Caribbean

	j	f	m	a	m	j	j	a	s	o	n	d	total
1701	-	-	3	6	6	2	3	8	3	4	-	-	35
1718	-	3	5	8	12	8	6	13	3	7	5	-	70
1728	2	3	3	5	8	4	5	2	5	2	5	2	46
1738	1	-	2	5	7	11	6	4	10	6	3	4	59

SOURCES: As in Table 4.7.

TABLE 4.12   Shipping at Philadelphia by Region, 1720-1739

Annual Average Entries (Clearances)

	1720-1724	1725-1729	1730-1734	1735-1739
Britain and Ireland	16(7)	30(15)	27(27)	40(30)
British North America	29(31)	30(33)	55(52)	66(69)
Caribbean	58(63)	62(73)	80(87)	74(80)
Southern Europe	4(9)	4(14)	11(19)	24(38)
TOTAL	107(110)	126(135)	173(185)	204(217)

SOURCE: Calculated from James G. Lydon, "Philadelphia's Commercial Expansion 1720-1739," PMHB, 91 (1967), 401-18. These figures are derived from Pennsylvania newspapers and have been compared with more fragmented data from Historical Statistics, Series Z, nos. 266-85; NYCD, V, 615; Bodleian Library, Oxford, Rawlinson MSS C 379, p. 45; Pennsylvania Gazette, no. 112; American Weekly Mercury nos. 795, 900; A. L. Jensen, The Maritime Commerce of Colonial Philadelphia (Madison, 1963), pp. 43, 70, 88; and Pennsylvania Archives, 8th ser., III (1931), pp. 1794-1795.

TABLE 4.13   Passages to Philadelphia from London by News-bearing Ships 1705-1739

	j	f	m	a	m	j	j	a	s	o	n	d	Average (total)
Average passage (weeks)	–	–	–	6.4	9.4	9.5	–	13	11	9.6	11.6	6.6	9.8
Range of passages (weeks)	–	–	–	5.7-7	9.4	6.9-11	–	13	8-15	7.3-12	10.6-13.1	6.6	(5.7-15)
Number of cases	–	–	–	2	1	4	–	1	3	2	3	1	(17)

SOURCES: American Weekly Mercury, Boston News-letter.

TABLE 5.1   Newfoundland Fishing, the English sector 1675-1741

	Fishing Ships	Sack Ships	Total Ships	Fishing Boats	Catch (quintals)	Source
1675			175	965	241,250	a
1682	32			482		b
1684	43			598		b
1694	40	30	70	1000	100,000	c
1698			252	929	215,922	c
1699	166	68	234	1241	372,300	d
1700	171	49	220	1564	312,000	d
1701	75	46	121	993	216,320	d
1702	16	25	41	415	82,140	e
1703	23			258	75,000	f
1705	20				78,000	g
1706			46	260	106,270	g
1713	46			725		b
1714	106			936	115,000	b
1715	108			981	88,622	b
1716	86			911	88,469	b
1738-1741				1310	450,000	h

SOURCES: a. H. A. Innis, The Cod Fisheries, 2d ed. (Toronto, 1958), p. 101.
          b. House of Commons Sessional Papers for the Eighteenth Century,
              ed. Sheila Lambert, vol. 90 (Wilmington, 1975), pp. 14, 237.
          c. PRO, CO 390/6 fol. 5.
          d. PRO, CO 389/17, pp. 261-66.
          e. L. E. Stock, Proceedings and Debates . . ., II, 5.
          f. CSPC 1702-1703, no. 1379.
          g. PRO, CO 195/4, pp. 341-57.
          h. Annual average estimates from R. G. Lounsbury, The British
              Fishery at Newfoundland, 1634-1763 (New Haven, 1934), p. 312.

TABLE 5.2   Calendar of Some English Ships
in the Newfoundland Trade, 1695-1700

	j	f	m	a	m	j	j	a	s	o	n	d	No. of Cases
Cleared England 1695-1700 [a]	27	36	68	52	43	44	19	4	1	1	1	8	304
Entered England 1696-1700 [b]	6	3	2	2	1	1	3	0	2	60	27	19	126

SOURCE: PRO, E 190/ series of port books.

       a.   London clearances for 1695 and 1696 only. Most vessels bound for Newfoundland did <u>not</u> clear customs, as they had nothing to declare.

       b.   London entries for 1696 only. Most vessels did <u>not</u> enter customs from Newfoundland because of their cargoes.

TABLE 7.1   Gross Revenues of the General Post Office
1686-1744

Year Ending 25 March	Gross Postal Revenues
1687	£ 94,644.19.6
1694	108,000
1704	156,000
1714	unknown
1724	178,071
1734	176,334
1744	194,461

SOURCES: <u>First Report of the Post Master General on the Post Office</u> (1855) for 1687; Howard Robinson, <u>The British Post Office: A History</u> (Princeton, 1948), p. 81 for 1694 and 1704; J. C. Hemmeon, <u>The History of the British Post Office</u> (Cambridge, Mass., 1912), Appendix I.

TABLE 7.2 New England Postal Revenues, 1693-1697[a]

Year Ending 1 May	Salaries	Postal Receipts	Total Revenue
1694	£ 20	£ 87[b]	
1695	42	147.1.7[b]	£ 296.1.7
1696	nil	227.11.8½	227.11.8½
1697	25	273.4.1	298.4.1

SOURCES: GPO Post 1/2, fol. 265. The salaries, granted by the Massachusetts and New Hampsire governments, are mentioned in: MHS Collections, 3d ser., 7 (1838), pp. 57-60; CSPC 1693-1696, nos. 1580, 2368; CSPC 1696-1697, no. 23; N. Bouton, ed., Documents & Records relating to the Province of New Hampsire, 1686-1772, pt. 1, vol. 2, pp. 157-58, vol. 3, p. 61.

a. All sums in colonial currency. Those of New York and Massachusetts were both about £130 for £100 sterling at this time. John J. McCusker, Money and Exchange in Europe and America, 1600-1775 (Chapel Hill, 1978), pp. 139-62.

b. Numbers are estimates. The revenue for 1694 and 1695 was not distinguished.

TABLE 7.3 Estimated Annual Business of the North American Post Office, 1693-1704
(Estimated in Parentheses)

Year	Net[1]	Mail Revenues Costs[2]	Gross	Estimated No. of Letters[3]	Estimated Annual Letters per 100 persons
May 1693– May 1697	-263.7.6	590.2.0	326.14.7	(12,069)	(9.0)
1699	-227.3.10¼	(626.6.0)	(399.2.1¾)	(15,964)	(11.1)
1700	-224.1.2¼	(644.8.0)	(420.6.9¾)	(16,813)	(11.5)
1701	-217.17.1½	(662.10.0)	(444.13.10½)	(17,787)	(11.8)
1702	-187.3.5½	(680.12.0)	(493.8.6½)	(19,737)	(12.8)
1703	-156.7.0	(698.14.0)	(542.7.0)	(21,694)	(13.7)
1704	-116.9.6	(716.16.0)	(600.6.6)	(24,013)	(14.9)

SOURCES: GPO, Post 1/2 fols. 264-65 for 1693-1697 revenues; GPO. Treasury 4, pp. 34-35 for net revenues 1699-1704.

1. Net revenues 1699-1704 reduced by £260 N.Y. to account for unpaid deputy postmaster's salary.
2. Costs estimates for 1699-1704 interpolated from 1693 figures and those of 1706, given as £711.12.3 in GPO, Post 1/4, p. 197. This becomes £771.12.3 when all items are converted to £N.Y.
3. Estimated at an average of 6d. per letter. The rate at New York was 4½d. within 80 miles and 9d from the West Indies, Europe, or Maryland. See J. T. Dixon, "The Problem of Imperial Communication During the Eighteenth Century, with Special Reference to the Post Office," M.A., thesis, University of Leeds, 1964, p. 83.
4. Populations of colonies having postal services, Delaware to Maine, are interpolated from decennial figures in Historical Statistics, Series Z, 2-12.

TABLE 8.1   Copies per week of London Papers

	Copies per week	London Population	Copies per 1000
1620's	500	300,000	1.7
1644	6,000	400,000	15.0
1704	43,800	575,000	76.2
1712	66,979	600,000	111.6
1750	c.100,000	675,000	148.1

SOURCES: Population from E. A. Wrigley, "A Simple Model of London's Importance in Changing English Society and Economy, 1650-1750," Past & Present, 37 (1966), p. 44 with derived estimates.   Copies per week: 1620's and 1644, Joseph Frank, The Beginnings of the English Newspaper, 1620-1660 (Cambridge, Mass., 1961), pp. 13, 57-58; 1704, J. R. Sutherland, "The Circulation of Newspapers and Literary Periodicals, 1700-1730," The Library, 4th ser., 15(1934), p. 111; 1712 figures are averages for the six weeks before the Stamp Act came into effect, from J. M. Price, "A Note on the Circulation of the London Press, 1704-14," Bulletin of the Institute of Historical Research, 31(1958), p. 220, with the Spectator calculated as a daily; 1750, G. A. Cranfield, The Development of the Provincial Newspaper, 1700-1760 (Oxford, 1962), pp. 175-79.

TABLE 8.2   Age of London Datelines in Boston Papers
                         for Year Ending 22 April 1721

	Range	Average	No. of Cases
Boston News-letter	54-374 days	114.3 days	161
Boston Gazette	54-249	101.0	103

SOURCES: Boston News-letter; Boston Gazette.

TABLE 9.1 Sailings of Edmund Dummer's West Indies Packets, 1702–1711

Voyage Number	Sloop	Left England	Passage Out	Isles	Back	Total	Arrived England	Notes
1	Bridgman	Needles 21 Oct 02	28	27	49	104	Falmouth 2 Feb 02/3	
2	Mansbridge	Plymouth 8 Dec 02	35	24	34	93	Plymouth 10 Mar 02/3	
3	King William	Falmouth 30 Jan 02/3	39	23	44	106	Falmouth 16 May 03	
4	Bridgwater	(TAKEN by French privateers off Dungeness 25 Feb 02/3)						
5	Bridgman	Falmouth 4 Apr 03	(TAKEN off Scilly Is. on way back 27 July 03. 114 days out)					
6	Mansbridge	Falmouth 9 May 03	36	22	42	100	Falmouth 17 Aug 03	
7	King William	Falmouth 30 June 03	32	26	42	100	Mount's Bay 8 Oct 03	
8	Prince	Falmouth 3 Aug 03	30	29	43	102	Mount's Bay 13 Nov 03	
9	Mansbridge	Falmouth 25 Sept 03				116	Falmouth 19 Jan 02/3	into Kinsale 12 Jan by storm
10	King William	Falmouth 12 Dec 03				104	Falmouth 26 Mar 04	

Voyage Number	Sloop	Left England	Passage — Out	Isles	Back	Total	Arrived England	Notes
11	Prince	Falmouth 6 Jan 03/4				103	Falmouth 19 Apr 04	
12	Diligence	St. Ives 19 Apr 04	32			104	Penzance 1 Aug 04	formerly the Mansbridge
13	Prince	Falmouth 1 June 04	28	30	39	97	Plymouth 6 Sept 04	
14	King William	Falmouth 22 July 04				108	Falmouth 7 Nov 04	
15	Diligence	Falmouth 14 Sept 04	(TAKEN off the Lizard the next day)					
16	Prince	Falmouth 13 Oct 04	33	34	49	116	Falmouth 6 Feb 04/05	
17	King William	Plymouth 3 Jan 04/5	25	32	44	101	Falmouth 14 Apr 05	
18	Cotton	Plymouth 4 Mar 04/5	32	(TAKEN 12 April between Nevis and Montserrat)					
19	Six Islands	Plymouth 8 Apr 05	30	47	37	114	St. Ives 31 July 05	formerly the Prince
20	Frankland	Plymouth 19 May 05	32	30	40	102	Falmouth 29 Aug 05	
21	Queen Anne	Plymouth 14 May 05	28	31	46	105	Plymouth 27 Sept 05	
22	Jamaica	Plymouth 19 Sept 05	29	35	44	108	Falmouth 6 Jan 05/6	

Voyage Number	Sloop	Left England	Passage Out	Isles	Back	Total	Arrived England	Notes
23	Barbados	Plymouth 13 Oct 05					(LOST 28 Dec. in the Windward Passage)	
24	Queen Anne	Plymouth 14 Nov 05					(TAKEN in the Soundings on return 25 Feb 05/6)	
25	King William	Falmouth 21 Dec 05	29	29	49	107	Studwell Roads, Wales 8 Apr 06	
26	Prince George	Plymouth 21 Jan 05/06	40	31	46	117	Penzance 17 May 06	
27	Antigua	Plymouth 26 Feb 05/06			36	113	Mount's Bay 20 June 06	stopped by governors
28	Jamaica	Plymouth 12 Apr 06	37	31	39	107	Plymouth 29 July 06	
29	King William	Liverpool 19 May 06	40	34	41	115	Liverpool 11 Sept 06	north about Ireland homeward
30	Frankland	Plymouth 5 Jun 06	31	31	36	98	Plymouth 11 Sept 06	
31	Prince George	Plymouth 10 Jul 06	33	35	41	109	Plymouth 27 Oct 06	
32	Antigua	Plymouth 9 Aug 06	37	42	44	123	Falmouth 11 Dec 06	
33	Jamaica	Plymouth 17 Sept 06	28	36	42	106	Falmouth 2 Jan 06/7	
34	Frankland	Plymouth 20 Oct 06	36	32	35	103	Milford Haven 1 Feb 06/7	

Voyage Number	Sloop	Left England	Out	Isles	Back	Total	Arrived England	Notes
35	King William	Liverpool 17 Nov 06	42	31	39	112	Plymouth 11 Mar 06/7	out via Lough Swiley, Ireland
36	Prince George	Falmouth 14 Jan 06/7	24	32	41	97	Plymouth 21 Apr 07	overloaded
37	Antigua	Plymouth 13 Feb 06/7	36	33	35	104	Falmouth 28 May 07	
38	Jamaica	Plymouth 26 Mar 06/7	(TAKEN second day out)					
39	Frankland	Plymouth 20 Jun 07	36	35	52	123	Plymouth 22 Oct 07	
40	Prince George	Plymouth 22 Aug 07	(TAKEN off Scilly 23 Dec coming back)					
41	Antigua	Plymouth 23 Sept 07	39	35	44	118	Plymouth 20 Jan 07/8	
42	King William	Plymouth 6 Nov 07				121	Plymouth 5 Mar 07/8	return via Kinsale
43	Kingston	Plymouth 6 Nov 07	(LOST off Scilly 5 Apr 08)					
44	Frankland	Plymouth 31 Jan 07/8	28	32	50	110	Milford Haven 21 May 08	return via Kinsale
45	Antigua	Plymouth 31 Mar 08	46	38	39	123	Bristol 31 July 08	
46	King William	Plymouth 24 May 08	31	31	50	112	Plymouth 13 Sept 08	

Voyage Number	Sloop	Left England	Passage Out	Isles	Back	Total	Arrived England	Notes
47	Resolution	Falmouth 9 July 08				135	Falmouth 21 Nov 08	See PRO, E 190/ 1067/21, fols. 34-36
48	Cotton	Plymouth 7 Aug 08	45	36	82	163	Plymouth 16 Jan 08/9	Windward Passage failed
49	Frankland	Bideford 20 Sept 08	39	36	37	112	Milford Haven 11 Jan 08/09	
50	Antigua	Bristol 13 Nov 08	(TAKEN 22 Nov, into St. Malo)						
51	Resolution	Plymouth 22 Mar 08/9	46	38	50	134	Penzance 2 Aug 09	
52	Sophia	Plymouth 10 Apr 09	31	40	45	116	Falmouth 4 Aug 09	
53	Frankland	Plymouth 16 May 09	31	34	48	113	Mount's Bay 7 Sept 09	
54	King William	Plymouth 4 July 09	(TAKEN in Soundings on return 23 Oct 09)						
55	Pearle	Plymouth 19 Aug 09	(TAKEN off Martinique 3 Oct 09)						
56	Sophia	Plymouth 10 Oct 09	36	33	41	110	Clovelly 28 Jan 09/10	
57	Resolution	Plymouth 13 Jan 09/10	48	42	77	167	St. Ives 28 June 10	through Gulf of Florida

Voyage Number	Sloop	Left England	Passage Out	Passage Isles	Passage Back	Passage Total	Arrived England	Notes
58	Frankland	Plymouth 31 Mar 10	34	32	37	103	Bideford 11 July 10	
59	Sophia	Bideford 8 May 10	45	31	44	120	Bideford 5 Sept 10	into Kinsale by storm outward
60	Evelyn	Plymouth 23 July 10				123	Bideford 23 Nov 10	
61	Union	Plymouth 23 Sept 10				133	Falmouth 6 Feb 10/11	
62(a)	Frankland	Bideford 21 Nov 10						Lost mast, returned to port after 16 days
63	Sophia	Bideford 29 Dec 10	47	35	44	126	St. Ives 3 May 11	
62(b)	Frankland	Bideford 2 Feb 10/11						(Lost mast, returned to port after 7 days
64	Evelyn	Bideford 13 Mar 10/11				100	Bideford 22 July 11	
62(c)	Frankland	Bideford 16 Apr 11	(TAKEN in Soundings third day out)					
65	Resolution	Bristol 15 June 11	27	35	40	102	Bideford 25 Sept 11	
66	Martlet	Portsmouth 20 July 11				152	Tenby, Wales 19 Dec 11	

SOURCES: Dummer's letters to the Board of Trade, PRO, CO 323/5-7, passim; same to Harley 28 September 1711, Dummer Papers, NMM. These were, in the few cases of discrepancies, taken as more reliable than Dummer's "an abstract" of 15

TABLE 9.2   Average Passages of Dummer's West Indian Packets 1702-1711

| | ---- Average Days Passages (no. of cases) ---- | | | | | | |
	to Barbados	in the islands	from Jamaica	voyage total	captured	lost	total sailings	sailings per annum
Under Agency (Oct. 1702- Oct. 1704)	32.6(9)	26.9(8)	42.8(8)	104(13)	3	0	16	7.7
First Contract (Nov. 1704- Feb. 1708)	33.0(21)	33.7(20)	42.0(21)	109.7(22)	4	2	28	8.5
Second Contract (Mar. 1708- Mar. 1712)	38.9(13)	35.5(13)	48.8(13)	124.7(18)	4	0	22	5.4
TOTAL	34.7(43)	32.9(41)	44.3(42)	113.5(53)	11	2	66	7.0

SOURCE: Table 9.1

313

TABLE 9.3: Sailings of William Warren's New York Packets, 1710-1715

Voyage Number	Ship (Captain)	Left Bristol	Days to New York	Days at New York	Days from New York	Arrived Bristol	Total Days	Notes
1	Royal Anne (Shorter)	c. 5 Sept. 1710	72	28	28	c. 10 Jan. 1710/11	128	
2	Bristol (Ball)	c. 5 Jan. 1710/11	103	19	34	c. 9 June 1711	156	via Charles Town, S.C., westward
3	Royal Anne (Shorter)	9 Mar. 1710/11	59					
4	Harley (Palmer)	16 July 1711	34	30	30	c. 17 Oct. 1711	94	
5	Harley (Palmer)	11 Dec. 1711	110	87	33	28 July 1712	230	
6	Edgley Galley	5 Mar. 1711/12	60					to Philadelphia
7	Harley (Palmer)	c. 25 Oct. 1712	109					via Rhode Island
8?	Harley (Totterdell)							at N.Y. May 1714
9?	Harley (Totterdell)				35	23 April 1715		
10?	Harley (Totterdell)	19 June 1715	100					

1. CSPC 1710-1711, nos. 503, 512, 517, 555; BNL, no. 369. Five days are allowed here for delivery between London and Bristol, a two-day trip.

2. CSPC 1710-11, nos. 832, 834; CSPC 1711-12, no. 14 (i); BNL, nos. 359-62, 365-368.

3. CSPC 1710-11, nos. 859, 872; BNL, nos. 369, 374.

4. BNL, nos. 383-5, 387-9; CSPC 1711-12, no. 95.

5. BNL, nos. 410, 411, 416-9, 429, 445.

6. BNL, nos. 417, 421, 426.

7. BNL, nos. 452, 455, 458, 462.

8. BNL, nos. 526, 528.

9. BNL, no. 589.

10. BNL, nos. 592, 598; PRO. CO 5/1222, n.p. This customs clearance from New York lists the Harley Pacquet as a ship of 80 tons, 2 guns and 10 men, Edward Totterdell mr. She was built in Bristol in 1711, presumably expressly for the packet service and registered there 9 June 1711. The owners were given as Richard Champion, Jonathan Teague, and others. Her cargo certainly exceeded 10 tons, and included rice, logwood, pitch, turpentine, cocoanuts and indigo, plus furs, skins, and cranberries.

TABLE 12.1   Average Number of Letters per Annum Exchanged Between Governors
and the Plantations Office 1675-1737

Colony	A Governor to Plantations Office (no. of cases)		B Plantations Office to Governor (no. of cases)		A/B
Jamaica	6.8	(428)	2.0	(123)	3.4
Leeward Islands	5.8	(368)	2.1	(134)	2.8
New York[a]	5.8	(242)	2.0	(86)	2.9
Barbados	5.5	(343)	2.2	(135)	2.5
Massachusetts[b]	4.9	(229)	2.0	(92)	2.5
South Carolina[c]	3.8	(68)	.8	(14)	4.8
Virginia	3.2	(200)	1.4	(89)	2.3
Bermuda[d]	3.0	(160)	1.0	(55)	3.0
Bahamas[e]	2.8	(55)	.6	(11)	4.7
Maryland[f]	2.7	(62)	1.7	(39)	1.6
Nova Scotia[g]	1.8	(50)	.5	(15)	3.6
Pennsylvania[h]	.6	(36)	.2	(14)	3.0
Connecticut	.4	(23)	.3	(18)	1.3
Rhode Island	.3	(17)	.3	(18)	1.0
Average (Total)	3.4	(2281)	1.2	(843)	2.8

SOURCE: CSPC.   For criteria for inclusion, see earlier, chap. 12, notes 30,

a.   1693-1697, 1701-1737   b.   1691-1737   c.   1720-1737
d.   1685-1737   e.   1718-1737   f.   1692-1714
g.   1710-1737   h.   1682-1737

TABLE 12.2   Changing Frequency of Governors' Letters to the
              Plantations Office 1675-1737

Colony	Annual Average No. of Letters		
	1675-1688	1689-1713	1714-1737
Jamaica	6.5	7.2	6.2
Leeward Islands	5.6	5.8	5.8
New York[a]		4.3	6.1
Barbados	6.0	5.8	4.6
Massachusetts[b]		5.0	4.4
South Carolina[c]			3.8
Virginia	.6	3.4	5.0
Bermuda[d]	2.5	3.1	2.8
Bahamas[e]			2.8
Maryland[f]		2.5	
Nova Scotia[g]		.0	2.0
Pennsylvania[h]	.0	.6	.8
Connecticut	.1	.6	.3
Rhode Island	.2	.4	.1

SOURCE: CSPC. For criteria for inclusion, see earlier, chap. 12, notes 30, 31.

a. 1693-1697, 1701-1737   b. 1691-1737   c. 1720-1737
d. 1685-1737   e. 1718-1737   f. 1692-1714
g. 1710-1737   h. 1682-1737

TABLE 12.3.   Average number of letters exchanged:
                    Royal government vs Royal African Company 1675-1737

                             Letters per annum sent by

to/from	governors	vs	company agents	Plantation Office	vs	Royal African Company
Barbados	5.5		11.4[a]	2.2		6.7[b]
Jamaica	6.8		10.3[c]	2.0		4.7[b]

Sources: CSPC; PRO, T 70/8, 12-14, 57, 58.

a. 1684-1719   b. 1687-1715   c. 1689-1715

NOTES

PREFACE

1. Quoted in O. H. K. Spate, *The Pacific Since Magellan*, vol. I, *The Spanish Lake* (Minneapolis, 1979), p. ix.
2. Thomas Paine, *The Writings of Thomas Paine*, ed. M. D. Conway, 4 vols. (New York, 1967), I, 89.

Chapter 1. INTRODUCTION

1. The fullest description of the *Palm Tree* was made by the naval officer of the Lower James District of Virginia when entering the vessel on 25 January 1699/1700. (Public Record Office [hereafter PRO], CO 5/1441). The dimensions are estimated by using the customs service calculation for tonnage found in Henry Crouch, *A Complete Guide to the Officers of His Majesty's Customs in the Outports . . .* (London, 1732), p. 289.
2. See Plymouth customs records: PRO, E 190/1057/1, p. 44; E 190/1058/2, pp. 17, 28; E 190/1059/4, pp. 11, 31; and E 190/1060/6, p. 11.
3. See Figure 2.
4. PRO, CO 33/13, n.p.
5. Although a Bristol ship came in the very same day, there had not been a West Country entry into Barbados since the *Hope* of Bideford on 28 August (ibid.).
6. PRO, CO 5/1441; The log of Captain Aldred of the *Essex Prize* is in PRO, Adm 51/291.
7. She cleared customs 15 May 1700—see PRO, CO 5/1441, and A. P. Middleton, *The Tobacco Coast* (Newport News, Va., 1953), Appendix E.
8. She entered customs at Plymouth 18 July 1700 (PRO, E 190/1060/6, p. 11). For average traveling times, see Chapter 3.
9. United States Navy Department, Hydrographic Office, *Table of Distances Between Ports* (Washington, D.C., 1948), has been used to estimate that the voyage approached 8960 nautical miles, or 10,304 statute miles, or 17,173 km.
10. *Calendar of State Papers, Colonial Series, America and the West Indies*, ed. W. N. Sainsbury et al. 43 vols. (London, 1860-1963). Hereafter *CSPC*.
11. *CSPC 1702-3*, no. 323, and E. Dummer to Thomas Pitt, 10 March 1702/3 in British Library (hereafter BL), Add. MSS. 22852, fols. 111-12, are examples.
12. *CSPC 1704-1705*, no. 1343; *CSPC 1706-1708*, no. 973; *CSPC 1708-1709*, no. 396.

*All references to "Cambridge" are to be understood as England unless otherwise noted.

13. J. Piaget, *Le Développement de la notion du temps chez l'enfant* (Paris, 1946).
14. A. H. Cole, "The Tempo of Mercantile Life in Colonial America," *Business History Review*, 33 (1959), esp. pp. 280, 282, 284. Clarence S. Brigham shows the same impatience with "delay" and "little improvement" in his haste to get to the next century with its magnetic telegraph and Atlantic cable (*Journals and Journeymen: A Contribution to the History of Early Newspapers* [Philadelphia, 1950], pp. 55–59).
15. *The Torrington Diaries*, ed. C. B. Andrews, 4 vols. (London, 1934), III, 39–40.
16. Piers Mackesy, *The War for America, 1775–1783* (Cambridge, 1964), p. 473. According to the *Guinness Book of Records, 1976* (London, 1976), p. 285, George Osbaldeston covered 200 miles in 8 hours 42 minutes at Newmarket in 1831. He used 50 mounts to average 22.9 mph (37 kph).
17. See J. Crofts, *Packhorse, Waggon and Post* (London, 1967), and Joan Parkes, *Travel in England in the Seventeenth Century* (Oxford, 1925), chap. 4.
18. Dummer's packets averaged 35 days from the west of England to Barbados—or just over 120 miles a day. See Table 9.2. The nineteenth-century clipper ship *Lightning* made 436 miles in one 24-hour period on her maiden voyage east to England from the United States. See G. R. Taylor, *The Transportation Revolution, 1815–1860* (New York, 1951), p. 111. For other sailing records, see Carl C. Cutler, *Five Hundred Sailing Records* (Mystic, Conn., 1952).
19. Board of Trade to Nottingham, 22 June 1702, PRO, CO 318/3, fols. 164–65; PRO, T 1/89, fol. 319.
20. Ralph Davis, *Aleppo and Devonshire Square* (London, 1967), p. 3.
21. Fernand Braudel's *La Méditerranée et le monde méditerranéen à l'époque de Philippe II*, rev. ed., 2 vols. (Paris, 1966), I, 370, suggests some comparisons. The longer westward English Atlantic passages to the Chesapeake averaged close to 70 days, and the voyage from the Downs to York Fort or Churchill in Hudson Bay averaged 75 days.
22. H. H. Lamb's *Climate: Present, Past and Future*, vol. 1, *Fundamentals and Climate Now* (London, 1972), and vol. 2, *Climatic History and the Future* (London, 1977), are a good introduction. The articles of E. LeRoy Laduire, "Aspect historique de la nouvelle climatologie," *Revue Historique*, 225 (1961), 1–20, and "Climat et récoltes aux xviie et xviiie siècles," *Annales*, 15 (1960), pp. 434–65, are excellent general discussions. See also the "Climate and History" special number of the *Journal of Interdisciplinary History* (Spring 1980).
23. Carl O. Sauer, *Northern Mists* (Berkeley, 1968), esp. pp. 155–57.
24. H. H. Lamb, *The Changing Climate* (London, 1966), pp. 210–12. These differences would affect the Arctic routes most.
25. See T. F. Gaskell, *The Gulf Stream* (New York, 1973); Henry Stommel, *The Gulf Stream: A Physical and Dynamic Description*, 2d ed. (London, 1966); and Henry Chapin and F. G. W. Smith, *The Ocean River* (New York, 1952).
26. See Middleton, *Tobacco Coast*, pp. 35–37, regarding teredo worms; and Darrett B. Rutman and Anita H. Rutman, "Of Agues and Fevers: Malaria in the Early Chesapeake," *William and Mary Quarterly* (hereafter *W&MQ*), 3d ser., 33 (1976), pp. 31–60, on fevers. For discussion of the shipping seasons, see Middleton, *Tobacco Coast*, chap. 4; Ralph Davis, *The Rise of the English Shipping Industry* (London, 1962), pp. 190–91, 279; H. Heaton, "The American Trade" in C. N. Parkinson, ed., *The Trade Winds* (London, 1948), chap. 9; C. S. S. Higham, *The Development of the Leeward Islands Under the Restoration, 1660–1688* (Cambridge, 1920), p. xi.
27. Gillian Cell, *English Enterprise in Newfoundland 1577–1660* (Toronto, 1969), p. 4.
28. Of 76 vessels known to have entered English ports from the colonies in the months of February to April from 1696 to 1700, 35 were from the West Indies; 22, from the Chesapeake; 7, from Newfoundland; 3, from New England; 1, from New York; 5

came in by way of the Netherlands or Spain; and 3 cases give inadequate information (PRO, E 190 series).

29. P. 31.

30. *A True & Exact History of the Island of Barbadoes*, 2d ed. (London, 1673), p. 111. The first edition was in 1657. Nicholas Foster, a Barbadian planter, argued in 1650 that the island had "a very fair correspondency" with England, New England, Hamburg, Holland, and other parts, estimating that more than a hundred ships a year arrived at the colony (*A Briefe Relation of the Late Horrid Rebellion in the Island Barbadas* [London, 1650], p. 3).

31. *Publick Occurrences, both Foreign and Domestick* (Boston, 1690).

32. *American Weekly Mercury*, no. 743, 28 March 1734.

33. Archibald Laidlie, quoted in Michael Kraus, *Atlantic Civilization: Eighteenth Century Origins* (Ithaca, N.Y., 1949), p. 25.

34. An entire five-vessel fleet under John Cabot was lost in 1498. J. A. Williamson notes that through the whole sixteenth century "there is no instance of a multi-ship expedition having been entirely wiped out by an unknown disaster; and we are entitled to say that the odds were heavily against it in 1498" (*The Cabot Voyages and Bristol Discovery Under Henry VII* [Cambridge, 1962], p. 105).

35. The natural development is evident from Edward G. Cox, *A Reference Guide to the Literature of Travel*, 3 vols. (Seattle, 1935–1946), esp. I, 6–15; II, 34–105. William Dampier and Woodes Rogers, the most popular nonfiction seafarers of the early eighteenth century, took their readers beyond the North Atlantic.

36. *Of Plymouth Plantation*, ed. Harvey Wish (New York, 1962), pp. 57–59. See E. S. Morgan, ed., *The Founding of Massachusetts* (New York, 1964), pp. 204–25.

37. See Sacvan Bercovitch, "Colonial Puritan Rhetoric and the Discovery of American Identity," *The Canadian Review of American Studies*, 6 (1975), pp. 131–50, and his *The Puritan Origin of the American Self* (New Haven, 1975), esp. pp. 117–19. Increase Mather assembled *An Essay for the Recording of Illustrious Providences* (Boston, 1684), the first chapter of which records remarkable sea deliverances of New England men.

38. See Frederick B. Tolles, *Quakers and the Atlantic Culture* (New York, 1960), esp. pp. 12–16, 25–29, and his *The Atlantic Community of the Early Friends*, supplement no. 24 to the *Journal of the Friends' Historical Society* (London, 1952). See also Daniel B. Sea, Jr., *Spiritual Autobiography in Early America* (Princeton, 1968), chaps. 1 and 2.

39. *The Journal of George Fox*, ed. John L. Nickalls (London, 1975), pp. 592–93, 612, 615, 659–61; *Narrative Papers of George Fox*, ed. Henry J. Cadbury (Richmond, Ind., 1972), p. 109. Fox also recorded a miraculous passage from the Netherlands to Harwich in 1677 (ibid., p. 146). Also see *Journal of the Life of Thomas Story* (Newcastle, 1747), pp. 152–53; *Collection of the Works of . . . Thomas Chalkley* (London, 1791), p. 13; and *An Account of the Life of . . . John Richardson* (London, 1843), p. 61, for other contemporary examples of providential assistance at sea.

40. *The Journal of the Reverend John Wesley*, ed. Nehemiah Curnock, 8 vols. (London, 1909–1916), I, 138–39. Wesley noted that his fear of the sea was both uncommon and unbecoming of a Christian (ibid., p. 435). I am grateful to Professor Frederick Dreyer, who kindly provided this reference.

41. Cotton Mather's *The Sailour's Companion and Counsellour* (Boston, 1709) is a good example of this perspective.

42. William L. Sachse, *The Colonial American in Britain* (Madison, Wis., 1956) discusses colonial travel to Britain.

43. Michael G. Hall, *Edward Randolph and the American Colonies 1676–1703* (Chapel Hill, N.C., 1960), passim.

44. C. K. Shipton, *Sibley's Harvard Graduates*, VII (Boston, 1945), pp. 121–24. An established merchant who undertook sea voyages could expect legitimate complaints from correspondents who expected regular business services from him. See Harry D. Berg, "The Organization of Business in Colonial Philadelphia." *Pennsylvania History*, 10 (1943), p. 160.

45. Sachse, *Colonial American*, p. 8. Between 1765 and 1775 the Sea Captains Club of Philadelphia accumulated 274 members. Sixty-eight members died during that decade, only 9 of whom were lost at sea. See William Bell Clark, "The Sea Captains Club," *Pennsylvania Magazine of History and Biography* (hereafter *PMHB*), 81 (1957), pp. 47–49.

46. *Barlow's Journal*, ed. Basil Lubbock, 2 vols. (London, 1934) is replete with these understandable feelings. *Adventures by Sea of Edward Coxere* (London, 1946), pp. 81, 119–21 is another example from a sea journal first published in the twentieth century.

47. This preliminary, conservative, estimate is based on an English fleet in the American trades of about 70,000 tons and a colonial fleet of some 25,000 tons. The first figure is taken from Davis, *Shipping Industry*, p. 17, and the second is calculated from the surviving English port books and colonial naval officers' lists for the years 1695 to 1700. In order that 10,000 men handle those 95,000 tons, they would accomplish an optimistic tons-per-man ratio of 9.5. Davis, *Shipping Industry*, pp. 59, 71, and James F. Shepherd and Gary M. Walton, *Shipping, Maritime Trade and the Economic Development of Colonial North America* (Cambridge, 1972), Appendix III, Tables 12–16, 23–25, indicate tons-per-man ratios that would result in some 10,000 to 12,000 active mariners in the English Atlantic.

48. Daniel Defoe, *Robinson Crusoe*, ed. M. Shinagel (New York, 1975), p. 8.

49. Davis, *Shipping Industry*, p. 136. Smart money was compensation paid Royal Navy sailors for injuries received in action. Crewmen of the *Royal Hudson's Bay* refused to sail without the company's assurance that smart money would be paid in case of an engagement (*Hudson's Bay Copy Booke of Letters Commissions Instructions Outward 1688–1696*, ed. E. E. Rich [London, 1957], p. 79 and 252). Crewmen of the Falmouth-Lisbon mail packet acted similarly in February of 1705/6. (General Post-Office Archives [hereafter GPO], Falmouth Packet Book, fol. 35, 88). See also *The Voyages and Travels of Captain Nathaniel Uring* (London, 1928), pp. 66–67.

50. James Henretta found 188 propertyless adult males in Boston according to the tax lists of 1687 ("Economic Development and Social Structure in Colonial Boston," *W&MQ*, 3d ser., 22 [1965], p. 76). After a decade of war the town had 6443 tons of locally owned shipping (B. Bailyn and L. Bailyn, *Massachusetts Shipping, 1697–1714* [Cambridge, Mass., 1959], Table V). What the intervening decade had done to tonnage is not clear. What is evident is that the fleet of 1698 would employ some 678 men, presuming the optimistic tons-man ratio mentioned in note 47 and also presuming full utilization of the fleet at some point in time. On seamen's wages, see Gary B. Nash, *The Urban Crucible* (Cambridge, Mass., 1979), pp. 64–65, 392–94.

51. Eric G. Forbes et al., *Greenwich Observatory*, 3 vols. (London, 1975), I, esp. chap. 1; Derek Howse, *Greenwich Time and the Discovery of Longitude* (Oxford, 1980), pp. 1–67; "Directions for observations and experiments to be made by masters of ships, pilots, and other fit persons in their sea voyages," *Philosophical Transactions*, 2 (1667) pp. 433–48. For a broader context for the Royal Society's interest in empire, see J. R. Jacob, *Robert Boyle and the English Revolution* (New York, 1977), pp. 143–59.

52. Margaret Espinasse, "The Decline and Fall of Restoration Science," *Past & Present*, 14 (1958), pp. 71–89; Margaret Deacon, *Scientists and the Sea, 1650–1900* (New York, 1971), chap. 8; and E. G. R. Taylor, *The Haven-Finding Art* (London, 1956),

chaps. 10–11. Halley launched his long career with observations at St. Helena between 1676 and 1678 while recording the transit of Mercury and plotting a star map of the southern sky. See Angus Armitage, *Edmond Halley* (London, 1966).

53. "An historical account of the trade winds, and monsoons, observable in the seas between and near the Tropicks, with an attempt to assign the physical cause of the said winds," *Philosophical Transactions*, 16 (1686–1687), pp. 153–68.

54. E. G. R. Taylor, *The Mathematical Practitioners of Tudor and Stuart England* (Cambridge, 1954), p. 402. H. L. Burstyn, "Early Explanations of the Role of the Earth's Rotation in the Circulation of the Atmosphere and the Oceans," *Isis*, 57 (1966), 167–87. See also John Atkins, *A Voyage to Guinea, Brazil & the West Indies* (London, 1735), pp. 141–45.

55. *The Three Voyages of Edmond Halley in the Paramore, 1698–1701* (London, 1981), passim. Halley's "New and Correct Chart Shewing the Variations of the Compass in the Western and Southern Oceans . . . 1700" appeared continuously in the fourth book of *The English Pilot* in every edition from 1721 to 1749. On changes in compass variations in the early modern period, see A. H. W. Robinson, *Marine Cartography in Britain* (Leicester, 1962), p. 45.

56. Forbes et al., *Greenwich Observatory*, I, 86–88.

57. See C. Verner, *A Carto-Bibliographical Study of the English Pilot. The Fourth Book* (Charlottesville, Va., 1960), and his "John Seller and the Chart Trade in Seventeenth Century England" in Norman J. W. Thrower, ed., *The Compleat Plattmaker: Essays on Chart, Map, and Globe Making in England in the Seventeenth and Eighteenth Centuries* (Berkeley, 1978), pp. 127–57. This volume also includes Thomas R. Smith's "Manuscript and Printed Sea Charts in Seventeenth-Century London: The Case of the Thames School," pp. 45–100. See also Sarah Tyacke, "Map-sellers and the London map trade c. 1650–1710," in Helen Wallis and Sarah Tyacke, eds., *My Head Is a Map: A Festschrift for R. V. Tooley* (London, 1973), pp. 62–80.

58. John Seller's *Atlas Maritimus* begins ' ith a plate that divides the Atlantic at the equator into "Mar del Nort" and "Oceanus Aethiopicus." Edward Wright (1683) does not label the North Atlantic at all but calls the portion south of the equator the "Aethiopian Sea," as does John Thornton's "A New Map of the World" (1703). Maps of the North Atlantic usually labeled the ocean "The Western or Atlantic Ocean." For examples, see those of Edward Wells (1700), John Senex (1720), Henry Popple (1733), and John Senex again (1739).

59. William Dampier, *Voyages and Discoveries*, ed. N. M. Penzer (London, 1931), p. 4; Joseph C. Shipman, *William Dampier, Seaman-Scientist* (Lawrence, Kans., 1962), p. 24.

60. Dampier, *Voyages*, p. 233.

61. Beyond the North Atlantic basin, the later Stuarts seemed willing to leave matters in the hands of the Hudson's Bay Company, the Royal African Company, and the English East India Company, while royal pressure was put on charters in England and America. When planters on St. Helena rebelled against the East India Company in the name of the king in 1684, the royal response was that they should be dutiful subjects to the company (Philip Gosse, *St. Helena 1502–1938* [London, 1938], pp. 84–91).

62. If the travels of George Roberts are also Defoe's creation, their setting in the Cape Verde Islands is comparable.

63. D. Alan Stevenson, *The World's Lighthouses before 1820* (London, 1959), chaps. 7–11; Douglas B. Haque and Rosemary Christie, *Lighthouses: Their Architecture, History and Archeology* (Llandyssul, Wales, 1975), esp. Figure 6.

64. Letter of 17 February, 1694/5, quoted in J. B. Hewson, *A History of the Practice of Navigation*, 2d ed. (Glasgow, 1963), p. 101.

65. *A Character of the Province of Maryland* (*1666*), ed. N. D. Mereness (Cleveland, 1902), pp. 63–64.
66. *A Two Years Journal in New York* . . . (London, 1701), reprinted in Cornell Jaray, ed., *Historical Chronicles of Newe-Amsterdam, Colonial New York and Early Long Island* (New York, 1968), pp. 60–61.
67. *Life and Errors*, 2 vols. (London, 1818), 1, 86–89, 137.
68. Sachse, *Colonial American*, pp. 8, 44. For example, see Elizabeth Usher to John Usher, 12 October 1685, Massachusetts Historical Society (hereafter MHS), Jeffries III; *Boston Gazette*, nos. 757, 767; *Boston Weekly News-Letter*, no. 1830; Davis, *Shipping Industry*, p. 112; and Public Archives of Canada (hereafter PAC), HBC C 2/1–3.
69. Wolley, *A Two Years Journal*, p. 63.
70. H. Chaunu and P. Chaunu, *Séville et l'Atlantique*, vol. VIII, *Les Structures; Structures Géographiques 1504–1650* (Paris, 1959), p. 6.
71. Davis, *Shipping Industry*, pp. 47–54.

Chapter 2. SUGAR ROUTES

1. H. Chaunu and P. Chaunu, *Séville et l'Atlantique, 1504–1650*, 8 vols. (Paris, 1955–1959), VIII, Part I, pp. 95–97; see also VII, pp. 22–27 of this work.
2. See Mathew Edel, "The Brazilian Sugar Cycle of the Seventeenth Century and the Rise of West Indian Competition," *Caribbean Studies*, 9 (1969), pp. 42–44.
3. James A. Williamson, *The English Channel, a History* (New York, 1959), chap. 11; Nathaniel Bowditch, *American Practical Navigator*, rev. ed. (Washington, D.C., 1962), p. 798.
4. A report from the Customs Commission to the Treasury of 5 October 1692 divided English shipping into three zones: Thames to Berwick, Carlisle to Land's End, and Land's End to the Thames. The Land's End to Thames section was held longer than the others (*CSPC 1699*, no. 1272). This indicator is tentative but is supported by the passage time for ships that cleared customs for Barbados in 1696. Six outport ships entered Barbados customs an average of 76 days after clearing English customs (range 48 to 120). Eight London vessels average 153 days (range 48 to 181). Even this does not adequately reflect the differences, for six vessels that came out with the 1696 convoy had cleared customs before the end of 1695. These ships, which were not slavers, averaged a pathetic 214 days from London to Barbados customs (range 195 to 239). See PRO, E 190 series and CO 33/13.
5. See Sir Francis Russell to the Lords of Trade, 30 August 1694, *CSPC 1693–1696*, no. 1266. Russell, an admiral's brother, was in the convoy on his way to become governor of Barbados.
6. PRO, E 190 series, port books. Outport records are complete, but London records are only for 1696 and 1697.
7. The *Shrewsbury Galley* made an 8-day passage completed 27 November 1697 (*The Bolton Letters* [London, 1928], p. 89).
8. Of 227 entries and clearances at Funchal for the years 1682, 1687, and 1699, 142 were from the English Atlantic; 51 were French; 21, Portuguese; and 13, Dutch (T. Bentley Duncan, *Atlantic Islands* [Chicago, 1972], p. 74). Four years later, for instance, the governors of Barbados and Bermuda, as well as the lieutenant governor of St. Christopher, all happened to be at Madeira at the same time and spent 8 days together there (*The Bolton Letters*, p. 106).
9. For a Barbados prejudice against Canary wines and preference for those of Madeira, see [Daniel Defoe?] *The Four Years Voyages of Captain George Roberts* (London, 1726), p. 11.

10. Five merchantmen leaving Madeira between September 1697 and February 1699/ 1700 can be timed from *The Bolton Letters* and the Barbados naval officer's lists in PRO, CO 33/13. Passages ranged from 14 to 27 days, averaging 20.2 days or 5.4 knots. The fastest of them, the 165-ton *Mary* of Bristol, averaged 7.8 knots. For the 1694 convoy, see *CSPC 1693–1696*, no. 1266, and Edward Barlow, *Barlow's Journal*, ed. Basil Lubbock, 2 vols. (London, 1934), II, 446.

11. John Atkins, *A Voyage to Guinea, Brazil & the West Indies* (London, 1735), p. 145.

12. James Logan, "An Account of Mr. Thomas Godfrey's Improvement of Davis's Quadrant, transferred to the Mariner's Bow," *Philosophical Transactions* of the Royal Society, 38 (1734), p. 443.

13. W. Penn to C. Codrington, 31 March 1701, Historical Society of Pennsylvania (hereafter HSP), Penn Letterbook 1699–1703, p. 97. See also Richard S. Dunn, *Sugar and Slaves: The Rise of the Planter Class in the English West Indies, 1624–1713* (Chapel Hill, N.C., 1972), p. 5.

14. Duncan, *Atlantic Islands*, p. 189, Atkins, *Voyage*, pp. 31–32; *Captain Roberts*, p. 401. Apparently the slavers did not load salt here, though Accra salt was significant in the Gold Coast trade. See K. Y. Daaku, *Trade and Politics on the Gold Coast 1600 to 1720* (Oxford, 1970), pp. 25–26.

15. William Dampier, *Voyages and Discoveries*, ed. N. M. Penzer (London, 1931), pp. 231–33, and K. G. Davies, *The Royal African Company* (London, 1957), chap. 5.

16. *CSPC 1693–1696*, no. 1266, and Barlow, *Journal*, II, 446.

17. See Russell's letter to the Lords of Trade, 24 October 1694, *CSPC 1693–1696*, nos. 1446, 1446i; Robert H. Schomburgk, *The History of Barbados* (London, 1848), pp. 45–46; and Barlow, *Journal*, II, 447–50. For destruction of the mole, see *CSPC 1693–1696*, no. 1592. For the usual tracks of Caribbean hurricanes, see John Macpherson, *Caribbean Lands: A Geography of the West Indies*, 3d ed. (London, 1973), p. 15.

18. Merchant petitions concerning Barbados convoys are discussed in I. K. Steele, *The Politics of Colonial Policy: The Board of Trade in Colonial Administration 1696–1720* (Oxford, 1968), pp. 32–34; and seasons of shipping in *CSPC 1693–1696*, nos. 986, 1758; and *CSPC 1696–1697*, nos. 267, 287. See also Publication of the Historical Manuscripts Commission (hereafter *HMC*), *House of Lords Manuscripts*, new series, 11 vols. (London, 1900–1963), III, 77. For historians, see, for instance, Ralph Davis, *The Rise of the English Shipping Industry* (London, 1962), pp. 190–91, 279; Richard Pares, *Yankees and Creoles* (London, 1956), pp. 17, 18; C. N. Parkinson, ed., *The Trade Winds* (London, 1948), p. 183; David Syrett, *Shipping and the American War* (London, 1970), p. 223.

19. In 1696, 22 of 52 entries into Barbados from Britain were with the convoy in July. The rest were scattered in every month of the year except August and October. Irish ships and also English ships coming via Ireland arrived every month from January to July of that year, with the September, November, and December arrivals coming directly from London or Bristol (PRO, CO 33/13).

20. In the years of peace, 1698–1700, a total of 349 ships entered Barbados directly from British ports, for an average of 116.3 p.a. (PRO, CO 33/13). Between Christmas 1714 and Christmas 1717, 347 ships left English ports for Barbados, or 119 p.a., excluding Irish clearances (CO 390/8). For evidence of the absolute decline in Barbados shipping, see Tables 2.2 and 2.4.

21. See, for instance, *Lloyd's News*, nos. 25 and 26, for 27 and 29 October 1696. The delivery time of 343 letters from Barbados governors to the Lords of Trade between 1675 and 1737 averaged 11 weeks (78 days), and the quickest time was 3 weeks.

22. Halley's chart is in the British Library and is reproduced in Angus Armitage, *Edmond*

Halley (London, 1966), facing p. 148. Of 345 New England entries to Barbados from 1696 to 1700, none were specifically via the Azores, and only 9 were by way of Madeira.

23. The route is described in Byron Fairchild, *Mssrs. William Pepperrell: Merchants of Piscataqua* (Ithaca, N.Y., 1954), pp. 50–51. The average passage time for 123 voyages from 1686 to 1688 and from 1715 to 1719, was 43.3 days (derived from James F. Shepherd and Gary M. Walton, *Shipping, Maritime Trade, and the Economic Development of Colonial North America* [Cambridge, 1972], p. 197). Shepherd and Walton's figures for speed, averaging only 1.8 knots, ignore the length of the arc into the Atlantic. Thaddeus Maccarty performed a superb 25-day passage in June of 1719, allowing no arc to the east of Barbados at all. See his sea journal for 1718–1719 in American Antiquarian Society (hereafter AAS).

24. PRO, CO 33/13; Pares, *Yankees and Creoles*, p. 49.

25. PRO, CO 33/13.

26. Pares, *Yankees and Creoles*, pp. 20, 75, 103–4, 158.

27. See above, p. 163.

28. The distribution was uneven, but the 105 clearances from Barbados for the Leeward Islands in 1699–1700 were as follows: January (13), February (15), March (7), April (9), May (7), June (5), July (10), August (8), September (5), October (6), November (11), and December (9) (PRO, CO 33/13). See Ruth Bourne, *Queen Anne's Navy in the West Indies* (New Haven, 1939), p. 32.

29. See Davis, *Shipping Industry*, p. 277; C. S. S. Higham, *The Development of the Leeward Islands Under the Restoration* (Cambridge, 1921), pp. ix–xiii; Dunn, *Sugar and Slaves*, pp. 128–29, 204, 206–10. C. Jeaffreson reported in May of 1677 that he believed "no less than forty or fifty saile of ships" came to Nevis and St. Christopher in a year, but the latter's trade was almost all in shallops working to and from the ships at Nevis (*A Young Squire of the Seventeenth Century: From the Papers of Christopher Jeaffreson of Dullingham House, Cambridgeshire*, ed. John Cordy Jeaffreson, 2 vols. [London, 1878], I, 216).

30. PRO, CO 318/1, fol. 6. See also *CSPC 1699*, nos. 1217, 1335.

31. Thirty-seven of 130 entries were from Britain as were 44 of 115 clearances for Britain (PRO, CO 157/1). In the three years after Christmas 1714, an average of 66 vessels a year cleared English customs for the Leewards, of which an average of 37 were bound for Antigua (PRO, CO 390/8).

32. A list of customs clearances from major North American ports for the year ending early December 1730 indicates a total of 111 clearances for the Leeward Islands, of which 50 were for Antigua and 25 were not specific as to which of the Leewards was intended (*Pennsylvania Gazette*, no. 112, 5 January 1730/31. Cf. Pares, *Yankees and Creoles*, p. 49, who uses the same list, as reprinted in the *Boston Weekly Newsletter*).

33. For royal instructions to the governor of the Leeward Islands dated 21 November 1729, see *Royal Instructions to British Colonial Governors*, ed. L. W. Labaree, 2 vols. (New York, 1935), I, 408–9. See Daniel A. Baugh, ed., *Naval Administration, 1715–1750* (London, 1977), chap. 8, and esp. pp. 329, 368–77. I also thank Professor Baugh for his conversation on this matter.

34. Barlow, *Journal*, II, 304–50; PRO, CO 142/13 and E 190 series. Packet passages ranged from 44 to 75 days, including both departure and arrival days. The packets ran the 870 nautical miles from the Leeward Islands to Jamaica at an average speed of 5 knots. See Tables 9.1 and 9.2.

35. Barlow, *Journal*, II, 346.

36. When the homeward-bound South Sea Company ship *Luxborough* caught fire and sank in June of 1727, she was about 100 leagues off the Newfoundland coast (Archibald Duncan, *The Mariner's Chronicle*, 4 vols. [London, 1804], II, 349–53.

37. Barlow, *Journal*, 317–18.
38. The powerful northerly current in the Straits of Florida was well known. See *The Journal of Jasper Danckaerts, 1679–1680*, ed. J. F. Jameson and Bartlett B. James (New York, 1913), pp. 37–38; *The English Pilot, the Fourth Book* (London, 1689), p. 46; and Dampier, *Voyages*, p. 294. John Atkins discusses the "Florida current" in 1735 but does not suggest awareness of the Gulf Stream further north (pp. 230–33). Walter Hoxton's "This Mapp of the Bay of Chesepeack" (London, 1735) included a description and chart of the Gulf Stream. Francis Goelet, a New York merchant and experienced sea traveler, noted in his journal of a trip to London under the date 25 August 1750: "Saw a great many Porposses & some gulf wheed, from thence conclued we where near in with the Gulf Stream" [and two days later] "Haveing a good observation, found we had driffted at N.E. From thence conjectured had got in the Gulf Stream" (*The Voyages and Travels of . . . Francis Goelet . . . 1746–1758*, ed. Kenneth Scott [New York, 1970]). This was 19 years before Benjamin Franklin's well-known supervision of the first chart of the Gulf Stream. It is not possible to reconstruct what variabilities there might have been in the Gulf Stream to account for an apparent delay in confirming its location. For a discussion of the variability of Europe's climate in the late seventeenth century and beyond, see Christian Pfister, "The Little Ice Age: Thermal and Wetness Indices for Central Europe," *Journal of Interdisciplinary History*, 10 (1979–1980), pp. 665–96.
39. The average of 16 merchant passages in 1699 and 1700, linked by using the Jamaican naval officers' lists and the port books of West Country ports, was 95 days (PRO, CO 142/13 and E 190 series). The packets averaged 43 days in 42 trips. One packet was lost in the Windward Passage. See Table 9.1.
40. *The Weekly Jamaica Courant*, began in May 1718.
41. Barlow, *Journal*, II, 347.
42. The figures of R. S. Dunn, *Sugar and Slaves*, p. 203, for Jamaican sugar exports to England from 1680 to 1683 and from 1686 to 1688 average 5026 tons a year. PRO, CO 390/6, 31–32 shows 101 ships clearing Jamaica for England in the two years from 5 April 1682 to 25 March 1684. See also W. A. Claypole and D. J. Buisseret, "Trade Patterns in Early English Jamaica," *Journal of Caribbean History*, 5 (1972), pp. 1–19. In the years 1698–1699, 121 English ships arrived (PRO, CO 390/6, 18–19), and a tabulation of 114 can be made from the naval officers' lists for 1699 and 1700. (PRO, CO 142/13). English exports to Jamaica in the three years after Christmas 1714 were made in 50, 66, and 46 ships respectively (PRO CO 390/8).
43. *CSPC 1689–1692*, no. 2715.
44. For passages between New England and Jamaica and between New York and Jamaica, see Shepherd and Walton, *Shipping*, Table 17, p. 197. For a Boston-to-Kingston winter passage of less than a month, see Thaddeus Maccarty Sea Journal 1718–1719 in AAS. The nautical distances to Kingston, by way of the Windward Passage, are instructive: Boston, 1657 nautical miles; New York, 1474; Philadelphia, 1446; Norfolk, 1279; Charles Town, 1064 (U.S. Navy, Hydrographic Office, *Table of Distances Between Ports, 1943* [Washington, D.C., 1948], pp. 214–15).
45. PRO, CO 142/13. Robert Pringle urged his English correspondents to trade by way of Barbados and Antigua (*The Letterbook of Robert Pringle*, ed. Walter B. Edgar, 2 vols. [Columbia, S.C., 1972], pp. xvii, 31).
46. Converse D. Clowse, *Economic Beginnings of Colonial South Carolina, 1670–1730* (Columbia, S.C., 1971), passim; PRO, E 190 series for years 1695–1700; *Historical Statistics*, Series Z, 15–16. More than 17 ships cleared the Carolinas in 1707 according to John Archdale, *A New Description of . . . the Province of Carolina* (London, 1707), reprinted in B. R. Carroll, *Historical Collections of South Carolina*, 2 vols. (New York, 1836), II, 97.

47. PRO, CO 33/13.
48. Bernard Bailyn, *The New England Merchants in the Seventeenth Century* (Cambridge, Mass., 1955), pp. 147–48, 151; Ralph Earle Moody, "Massachusetts Trade with Carolina, 1686–1709," *North Carolina Historical Review*, 20 (1943), pp. 43–53.
49. See especially *Pringle Letterbook*, I, xv–165. Pringle wrote to eight London correspondents by a ship bound *via* Cowes to Holland or Hamburg (ibid., 75–80, 84–85. See also George C. Rogers, *Charleston in the Age of the Pickneys*, rev. ed. [Columbia, S.C., 1980], p. 12). On the legalizing of rice exports to southern Europe and its consequences, see Lawrence A. Harper, *The English Navigation Laws* (New York, 1939), pp. 262, 398–99; "Representation of the Lisbon merchants concerning Rice from Carolina" in the William Blathwayt Papers, Colonial Williamsburg, vol. XVIII; Gary M. Walton, "New Evidence on Colonial Commerce," *Journal of Economic History* (hereafter *J. Econ H.*), 28 (1968), p. 371 note. For the rules derived from 3 Geo. II, cap. 28, see Henry Crouch, *A Complete Guide to the Officers of His Majesty's Customs in the Outports . . .* (London, 1732), pp. 93–96.
50. *Pringle Letterbook*, I, pp. 83, 116, 117. Vessels could retreat up the Cooper or Ashley rivers to fresh water.
51. *Historical Statistics of the United States*, U.S. Bureau of the Census, 2d ed., 2 vols. (Washington, D.C., 1975) (hereafter *Historical Statistics*), Series Z, 15–16.
52. See J. S. Bromley, "The French Privateering War, 1702–13," in H. E. Bell and R. L. Ollard, eds., *Historical Essays 1600–1750* (London, 1963), pp. 205–9; G. S. Graham, *Empire of the North Atlantic*, 2d ed. (Toronto, 1958), pp. 62–64.
53. See *HMC, House of Lords Manuscripts*, New Series, 11 vols. (London, 1900–1963), II, 76–77, 79, 88–89; John Cary, *An Essay of the State of England in Relation to Its Trade* (Bristol, 1965), p. 28; and Steele, *Colonial Policy*, 32–34.
54. There were only 32 merchantmen in from England and 20 from Ireland in 1696. The island's agents laments of November 1696, including the loss of 40 provision ships in 12 months, are in *CSPC 1696–1697*, no. 400. For the loss of the packet boat, see *CSPC 1696–1697*, no. 104.
55. William Bolton noticed the dearth of English shipping at Madeira that summer and the lack of colonial vessels (*The Bolton Letters*, pp. 82, 84).
56. Richard Pares, *War and Trade in the West Indies, 1739–1763* (Oxford, 1936), p. 242.
57. *CSPC 1696–1697*, no. 978.
58. *CSPC 1696–1697*, no. 192. There were two convoys out of Barbados that summer. See *CSPC 1696–1697*, nos. 138, 166, and 178, and *Lloyd's News*, nos. 12, 15, 16, 18, 21, 25, 26, 35, and 40.
59. *Lloyd's News*, nos. 25 and 26; *CSPC 1696–1697*, no. 349.
60. Barbadian entries from Massachusetts were these: (1696) 37 ships; (1697) 30 ships; (1698) 46 ships; (1699) 52 ships; and (1700) 87 ships (PRO, CO 33/13).
61. An embargo was imposed on 9 July 1696, extended on 27 July, and lifted on 4 September (*CSPC 1696–1697*, nos. 84, 114, 185). News of a French squadron's arrival in the West Indies reached Boston 15 August (*The Diary of Samuel Sewall*, 3 vols. [Boston, 1878–1882], I, 431). The embargo cut entries from Massachusetts to Barbados to two in August, two in September, and none during the next two months (PRO, CO 33/13). In 1697 there was a Massachusetts embargo on 1 May, and another was imposed on 12 August (see *CSPC 1696–1697*, nos. 991, 1217, 1219, 1238). No Barbados entries from Massachusetts were recorded for April, May, or August that year (PRO, CO 33/13).
62. Barbados entries from the West Indies including Bermuda were these: (1696) 16; (1697) 12; (1698) 75; (1699) 73; and (1700) 116 (PRO, CO 33/13). Of the 28 entries in the two war years, 17 were from Bermuda; and 7, from Surinam.

63. University of Bristol, Pinney Papers, Letters of Azariah Pinney from Nevis, 1688–1720, fol. 14.
64. See Richard B. Sheridan, *Sugar and Slavery* (Epping, Essex, 1975), p. 407, and K. G. Davies, *The Royal African Company* (London, 1957), p. 366.
65. William Burt to Edmund Dummer, 25 June 1702, *CSPC 1702–1703*, no. 849.
66. PRO, CO 157/1.
67. *CSPC 1689–1692*, nos. 2254, 2261, 2302. It was 59 days before the news of the quake arrived in Boston via Salem and 4 days later (8 August) before the first ripples of the disaster hit London. See *Diary of Samuel Sewall*, I, 362, and *Diary of Cotton Mather*, ed. Worthington C. Ford, 2 vols. (Boston, 1911–1912), I, 142–143; *CSPC 1689–1692*, no. 2278, endorsed as received 8 August 1692.
68. Governor Beeston sent three expresses. The first reached London in 56 days, the second was captured, and the third was over 3 months in transit. See Trenchard's letter to Blathwayt of 17 August and 12 October 1694 in National Maritime Museum (hereafter NMM), Southwell/3, pp. 295 ff.
69. *CSPC 1696–1697*, nos. 48, 101, 130, 639.
70. Naval officers' returns for Christmas 1703 to 1704 show that 72 vessels entered Jamaica from England in the year, but none came in March, and only one came in each of January, August, November, and December. Thirty-one North American vessels entered that year. Although there were none in January, at least one came every other month despite the low traffic. (PRO, CO 142/24, fols. 174–75).

Chapter 3. Tobacco Routes

1. *Historical Statistics*, Series Z, 458, 459. The annual average London importation for 1676–1682 was 12,758,140 lbs. This would employ about 100 ships at J. M. Price's estimated average of 126,750 lbs. per ship (*France and the Chesapeake*, 2. vols. [Ann Arbor, Mich., 1972], II, 901–2). The outports imported about two thirds of the quantity of tobacco that went to London, and outport vessels were generally smaller than those from London.
2. J. M. Price, "The Economic Growth of the Chesapeake and the European Market, 1697–1775," *JEcon H*, 24 (1964), pp. 494–511; Russell R. Menard, "The Tobacco Industry in the Chesapeake Colonies, 1617–1730: An Interpretation," *Research in Economic History*, 5 (1980), pp. 136–42; John M. Hemphill, Jr., "Virginia and the English Commercial System, 1689–1733. Studies in the Development and Fluctuations of a Colonial Economy Under Imperial Control," Ph.D. dissertation, Princeton University, 1964; *Historical Statistics*, Series Z, 449.
3. See William Tatham, *An Historical and Practical Essay on the Culture and Commerce of Tobacco* (London, 1800), pp. 14, 111–12. Tatham argued that tobacco would last for three years if properly cured. A century earlier, William Fitzhugh grew some sweet-scented tobacco because it weighed heavier for the same freight charges and would be less susceptible to damage if high freight or poor prices made storage preferable (R. B. Davis, ed., *William Fitzhugh and his Chesapeake World* [Chapel Hill, N.C., 1963], p. 257). The year was 1689, an appropriate time for such reflections.
4. The evidence is not unanimous on this matter. When Governor Nicholson complained about frosts and deep snow in the winter of 1697–1698, it was clear that he was concerned with processing the tobacco, not shipping it (*CSPC 1697–1698*, no. 517). In February 1700, however, his successor claimed that the bay itself was almost frozen over (*CSPC 1700*, no. 85). The log of the royal guard ship *Essex Prize* demonstrated that it and dozens of other ships sailed within the bay throughout that

winter and the previous one (PRO, Adm. 51/291. See also Edmund S. Morgan, *American Slavery, American Freedom* [New York, 1975], p. 184). On ice damage later, when vessels wintered in the fresh water upriver, see note 17. See also D. W. Pritchard, "Salinity Distribution and Circulation in the Chesapeake Bay Estuaries System," *Journal of Marine Resources*, 11 (1952), pp. 106–23.

5. William Bullock, *Virginia Impartially Examined* (London, 1649), p. 11; *CSPC 1661–1668*, no. 1084; log of the *Bristol*, convoy escort 1676–1677, PRO, Adm. 51/134; Dalby Thomas, *An Historical Account . . .* (London, 1690), p. 26. See also P. A. Bruce, *Economic History of Virginia in the Seventeenth Century*, 2 vols. (New York, 1896), I, 622–23.

6. On freight rates, see John M. Hemphill, "Freight Rates in the Maryland Tobacco Trade, 1705–1762," *Maryland Historical Magazine*, 54 (1959), pp. 36–58, 154–87; and A. P. Middleton, "The Chesapeake Convoy System 1662–1736," *W&WQ*, 3d ser., 3 (1946), pp. 188–91. For prices, see Menard, "Tobacco Industry," Appendix. In July of 1690, William Byrd I was urging his London agents to shift to earlier sailings from West Country ports. He argued that their winter passage home would not need convoys although he did specify that the ships be small (Marion Tinling, ed., *The Correspondence of the Three William Byrds of Westover Virginia, 1684–1776*, 2 vols. [Charlottesville, Va., 1977], I, 118–19).

7. Henry Hartwell, et al., *The Present State of Virginia and the College*, ed. H. D. Farish (Charlottesville, Va., 1964), pp. 10–11. See also *CSPC 1702–1703*, no. 773.

8. Full-scale discussions, involving the Board of Trade, the Privy Council and the Admiralty as well as the tobacco interests, occurred in 1696–1697, 1702–1703, and 1706–1707. See *CSPC 1702–1703*, nos. 55i, 763, 773; *Journal of the Commissioners of Trade and Plantations*, 14 vols. (London, 1920–1938), I, 297; Board of Trade representation of 20 December 1706, PRO CO 5/1362, pp. 88–91; Middleton, "Convoy System," pp. 189–91; and M. S. Morriss, *Colonial Trade of Maryland, 1689–1715* (Baltimore, 1914), pp. 40–41.

9. *CSPC 1706–1708*, no. 295i.

10. *CSPC 1696–1697*, no. 1253; *CSPC 1701*, nos. 423, 434; *CSPC 1702–1703*, no. 103.

11. PRO, CO 5/1362, p. 410.

12. See log of the *Lincoln* for 1698, PRO, Adm. 51/4240, and that of the *Essex Prize* returning to England in 1700 with 57 merchantmen in midsummer, PRO, Adm 51/291. Sailing from England were not affected, and merchantmen were not obliged to sail in convoy.

13. Of 139 voyages, 122 (87 percent) began from English outports between August and January. Fully 29 percent of outport sailings occurred in October and early November (PRO, E 190/series).

14. Calculated from PRO, CO 5/1441.

15. Ralph Davis charts the changes in the arrival months of tobacco ships entering English ports from the Chesapeake in his *The Rise of the English Shipping Industry* (London, 1962), pp. 285–86.

16. *The History and Present State of Virginia*, ed. L. B. Wright (Chapel Hill, N.C., 1947), pp. 121–22. Some wood sheathing was done as early as 1696 (A. P. Middleton, *The Tobacco Coast* [Newport News, Va., 1953], p. 236).

17. *Boston Weekly Newsletter*, nos. 1721, 1727; *American Weekly Mercury*, no. 898. In December of 1728 a ship had to break its way through ice to reach Annapolis, but the difficulty was short-lived (*Maryland Gazette*, nos. 66, 73, 74; *American Weekly Mercury*, no. 471). It was reported from Annapolis in December of 1732 that the rivers were "all froze over and the Bay near stopt up with ice" (*American Weekly Mercury*, no. 681).

18. See J. M. Price, "The Rise of Glasgow in the Chesapeake Tobacco Trade, 1707–1775," *W&MQ*, 3d ser., 2 (1954), p. 183.
19. D. B. Quinn notes that the direct route to Virginia was not developed by 1606 ("James I and the Beginning of Empire in America," *The Journal of Imperial and Commonwealth History*, 2 [1973–1974], p. 137). See also Table 2.3.
20. See PRO, E/190/155/5, p. 5 for clearance of 14 January 1695/6 and PRO, CO 5/1441 for entry of 25 November 1699 and clearance of 2 March 1699/1700. The log of the *John* is in the Bodleian Library, Rawlinson MSS, C 967. See Hugh Jones, *The Present State of Virginia*, ed. Richard L. Morton (Chapel Hill, N.C., 1956), p. 86, for reflections on the contest between wines circa 1724.
21. See the logs of the *Essex Prize* and the *Dreadnought* (PRO, Adm. 51/291 and 4171 respectively). W. B. Blanton, *Medicine in Virginia in the Seventeenth Century* (Richmond, Va., 1930), p. 37, lists the medical hazards of this longer route.
22. The log of the *Dreadnought* makes it clear that this story lost nothing in the telling. Governor Seymour, Governor Granville of Barbados, and Colonel Ingoldsby (who came out in the same fleet) all exaggerated the length of this very long passage (*CSPC 1704–1705*, nos. 343, 73, and 389, respectively).
23. Bruce, *Virginia*, pp. 623–24; and Sir Samuel Argal in *Dictionary of American Biography* (hereafter *DAB*).
24. PRO, Adm. 51/4341.
25. Bullock, *Virginia*, p. 51; PRO, Adm. 51/915, 4282, 4341, and Adm. 52/412.
26. See J. S. Bromley, "The French Privateering War, 1702–13," in H. E. Bell and R. L. Ollard, eds., *Historical Essays, 1600–1750, Presented to David Ogg* (London, 1963), pp. 203–31. Logbooks of the *Garland* (1708) and *Maidstone* (1708–1709) show the westerly route whereas the *Oxford* and *Guernsey* (1708), *South Sea Castle* (1709) and *Oxford* (1712) went via Madeira (PRO, Adm. 51/384, 571; 4781 and 423, 915, and 4282 respectively).
27. The 1787 map is reproduced as an endpaper of Lillian Penson, *The Colonial Agents of the British West Indies* (London, 1924).
28. Bullock, *Virginia*, p. 51.
29. P. 10.
30. One case is cited in *The Voyages and Travels of Captain Nathaniel Uring*, ed. Alfred Dewar (London, 1928), p. 5. The *Boston Gazette*, no. 523, for 1 December 1729, gives an account of a Virginia fleet hit by a hard gale on the banks of Newfoundland.
31. Nineteen convoy logbooks indicate an average of just over 81 days westward passage, and the 6 via the Azores averaged 77 days. However, the larger group of cases includes the two horrendous voyages mentioned earlier in note 21.
32. Two convoys touched at Bermuda: the *Lincoln* in 1701 and the *Woolwich* in 1705. Although the two convoys never dropped below the 36° parallel, the *South Sea Castle* had observations of 23.25° in its very good passage of 66 days. See PRO, Adm. 51/4240, 4399, and 915 respectively. For Byrd, see *Virginia Magazine of History and Biography* (hereafter *VMHB*), 25 (1917), pp. 258–59; *The Journal of John Fontaine*, ed. Edward Porter Alexander (Williamsburg, Va., 1972), pp. 67–81; Jones, *Virginia*, p. 72.
33. PRO, Adm. 1/3863, n.p. For another tobacco ship, taken by French privateers off the Orkney Islands in this period, see *Essex Institute Historical Collections*, 41 (1905), pp. 184–85. Isaac Norris was very upset early in 1700 because "Those Prodigall Scotts James & Heraclus Coutts have spoilt our Tobacco Trade this year" by overpaying for tobacco (HSP, Isaac Norris Letterbook 1699–1702, p. 137).
34. See J. E. Williams, "Whitehaven in the Eighteenth Century," *EconHR*, 2d ser., 8 (1956), pp. 393–404; Paul G. E. Clemens, "The Rise of Liverpool, 1665–1750,"

EconHR, 2d ser., 29 (1976), pp. 211–25, and especially Price, "The Rise of Glasgow," as well as his *France and the Chesapeake*, I, chap. 23.

35. Price, "The Rise of Glasgow," p. 187; W. Iain Stevenson, "Some Aspects of the Geography of the Clyde Tobacco Trade in the Eighteenth Century," *Scottish Geographical Magazine*, 89 (1973), pp. 19–20. See the eloquent statement of Daniel Defoe on this matter in *A Tour Through the Whole Island of Great Britain*, intro. by G. D. H. Cole and D. C. Browning (London, 1974), p. 339.

36. On three modern routes from Norfolk, Va., to Bishop Rock in the English Channel, the distances are 3202, 3168, and 3107 nautical miles. For three routes from Norfolk to Inishtrahull Island, off northernmost Ireland, the distances are 3235, 3191, and 3100 (U.S. Navy, Hydrographic Office, *Table of Distances Between Ports via the Shortest Navigable Routes* [Washington, D.C., 1948], pp. 285–86).

37. J. B. Hewson, *A History of the Practice of Navigation*, rev. ed. (Glasgow, 1963), p. 198; Davis, *Shipping*, p. 75.

38. Middleton found Chesapeake references to a schooner in 1717 and 1718. (*Tobacco Coast*, p. 408 note 8). The first references in the *Boston News-letter* are 18 August, 26 September, and 14 November 1718. See also Joseph A. Goldenberg, *Shipbuilding in Colonial America* (Charlottesville, Va., 1976), pp. 78–82, and A. P. Middleton, "New Light on the Evolution of the Chesapeake Clipper-Schooner," *American Neptune*, 9 (1949), 142–47.

39. John H. Harland, "The Early History of the Steering Wheel," *Mariner's Mirror* 58 (1972), pp. 41–68; G. F. Howard, "The Early Steering Wheel," *Mariner's Mirror*, 64 (1978), pp. 188–89. The earliest ship model with a helm wheel is in NMM, and I am grateful to Dr. Alan McGowan for information concerning it. Jack Cremer's memoirs mention having an old 300-ton merchantman refitted with a wheel in Boston sometime after 1714 (*Ramblin' Jack*, ed. R. R. Bellamy [London, 1936], p. 87). The earliest printed reference cited in the *Oxford English Dictionary* (hereafter *OED*) under "wheel" is 1743. The 12-gun *Antelope* was equipped with a wheel as she set out from New York for London late in 1746. See entry for 18 January 1746/7 in Francis Goelet, *The Voyages and Travels of . . . 1746–1758*, ed. Kenneth Scott (New York, 1970), and *Falconer's, Marine Dictionary*, pp. 150–54.

40. Byrd was 33 days from Deal to Virginia. See *Byrd Correspondence*, I, 79, 81. C. M. Andrews suggested "five weeks to the Capes was considered a fine passage" (*Colonial Folkways* [New Haven, 1919], p. 207). The *Boston News-letter* mentioned two such springtime passages in its early years, one from Bristol and the other from London. See nos. 50, 421. The same paper carried a report from Philadelphia in January of 1713/14 of a truly incredible passage of 19 days from England to Maryland (ibid., no. 512).

41. Cited in Carl Bridenbaugh, *The Spirit of '76* (New York, 1976), p. 35.

42. Yet William Byrd II, in this letter of 10 October 1735 to Mrs. Jane Pratt Taylor, notes that this is his fourth letter to her within a year (*Byrd Correspondence*, II, 461).

43. *Calendar of State Papers, Domestic Series* (hereafter *CSP Dom*) *Charles II*, ed. Everett Green et al., 28 vols. (London, 1860–1947), XXIII, p. 182.

44. Ship logs from PRO, Adm. 51 series. Comparing Maryland naval officers' lists (PRO, CO 5/749) with English outport port books (PRO, E 190 series) for the years 1698–1700 yielded 17 eastward passage times: to Barnstable and Bideford, 10 passages averaging 49 days; to Liverpool, 4 passages averaging 63 days; and to Plymouth, 3 passages averaging 58 days. As these are customs-to-customs passages, they may lengthen the voyages somewhat; the 17 passages averaged 54 days. The *John* made a 37-day crossing from the capes to Ushant in July 1701 (Bodleian Library, Rawlinson MSS, C 967).

45. See chap. 7.

46. *Historical Statistics*, Series Z, 1–19, 121; PRO, CO 5/1441; and the *Virginia Gazette* for 1737 and 1738. See David C. Klingaman, *Colonial Virginia's Coastwise and Grain Trade* (New York, 1975), pp. 32–36, 73; Middleton, *Tobacco Coast*, pp. 178 ff.; Paul G. E. Clemens, *The Atlantic Economy and Colonial Maryland's Eastern Shore* (Ithaca, N.Y., 1980), chap. 6; and Tables 2.3 and 2.5.

47. Twenty-one vessels indicating a Virginia home port are mentioned in surviving naval officers' lists and port books of the English Atlantic empire for the period 1696–1700. Of these, 10 were less than 30 tons, and 9 others were under 100 tons. At a depreciation rate of 5 percent, Governor Andros's estimate of 15 craft in 1697 and 27 the following year (including 17 sloops) remains plausible. (*CSPC 1696–1697*, no. 1131, and *CSPC 1697–1698*, no 550).

48. William Byrd wrote Nathaniel Seldon, newly arrived attorney general of Barbados, in May 1691 that in Virginia "wee scarce expect any ships here till Christmas, so that wee shall have a long vacation, and possibly may have certain news round your way sooner than directly from England" (*Byrd Correspondence*, I, 146). In 1699 and 1700, 13 of 15 clearances from Virginia for the British West Indies occurred between April and August (PRO, CO 5/1441. CF. Middleton, *Tobacco Coast*, p. 184). In 1737 and 1738 the pattern seems to have been different, with only 7 of 16 clearances in those summer months and as many in the first 3 months of the year (*Virginia Gazette* for 1737 and 1738). The general pattern and the difference in 1738 are supported by the seasons of Virginia entries into Barbados summarized in Table 2.3 (PRO, CO 33/13–16).

49. *Historical Statistics*, Series Z, 13. M. S. Morriss, *Colonial Trade of Maryland, 1689–1715* (Baltimore, 1914); the works of Hemphill and Clemens; and Gloria Main, "Maryland and the Chesapeake Economy, 1670–1720," in A. Land et al., eds., *Law, Society, and Politics in Early Maryland* (Baltimore, 1977), pp. 134–52 have been particularly useful.

50. Morriss, *Colonial Trade*, pp. 31–35, 85–87, and V. J. Wycoff, "Ships and Shipping in Seventeenth Century Maryland," *Maryland Historical Magazine*, 34 (1939), p. 273. The English customs records for the seven years commencing October 1694 indicate a lower figure—of just over 50 ships for England and 9 for other plantations (PRO, CO 390/6, fols. 73–74).

51. Of 108 arrivals from North American colonies in the six years commencing Christmas 1694, two thirds came in in the last six months of the year although there were entries in every month (PRO, CO 5/749). See C. P. Nettels, *The Money Supply of the American Colonies before 1720* (Madison, Wis., 1934), p. 111.

52. Morriss, *Colonial Trade*, pp. 114–15.

53. "Maryland in 1699: A Letter from the Reverend Hugh Jones," ed. M. Kammen, *Journal of Southern History*, 29 (1963), pp. 367–68. See Fontaine, *Journal*, pp. 114–22, concerning a trip from New York to Williamsburg by way of Maryland's eastern shore.

54. Wycoff, "Ships and Shipping," pp. 276–77.

55. See Henry C. Wilkinson, *The Adventurers of Bermuda* (Oxford, 1933), and L. H. Gipson, *The British Empire before the American Revolution*, 15 vols. (1936–1970), II, 230–38. Sir Thomas Day, commenting on shipping to Bermuda in 1698, said, "It is very rare to find a ship bound thither." (*CSPC 1697–1698*, no. 625). For the minuscule annual trade between England and Bermuda between 1697 and 1750, see Charles Whitworth, *State of the Trade of Great Britain in Its Imports and Exports Progressively from the Year* 1697 . . . (London, 1776), Part 2, pp. 51–52. See also Table 3.5.

56. See Robert V. Wells, *The Population of the British Colonies in America before 1776* (Princeton, 1975), pp. 172–81.

57. To William Blathwayt, 7 October 1690, Colonial Williamsburg, Blathwayt Papers, vol. 36, n.p.

58. Ian K. Steele, "Time, Communications and Society: The English Atlantic, 1702," *Journal of American Studies*, 8 (1974), pp. 13–15.

59. Henry C. Wilkinson, *Bermuda in the Old Empire* (Toronto, 1950), p. 20.

60. *CSPC 1693–1696*, no. 192. See also *CSPC 1689–1692*, no. 1484 xv; *CSCP 1693–1696*, no. 51; *CSPC 1700*, no. 936.

61. *CSPC 1700*, no. 936; survey of British and colonial shipping records for Christmas 1695 to Christmas 1700. Robert Dinwiddie estimated that there were 75 vessels belonging to Bermuda in 1740. See Jack P. Greene, ed., *Settlements to Society, 1584–1763* (New York, 1966), p. 277.

62. In the eight years after 25 March 1729 there was an average of 23 entries a year from Virginia, of 13.9 from the Bahamas, and of 12.3 from the Leewards. Clearances for the Leewards averaged 42.2 a year whereas those to the Bahamas and to Virginia averaged 17.4 and 17.3 respectively (PRO, CO 41/6). Governor Bennett outlined the patterns of Bermuda intercolonial trade in a long letter to the Board of Trade, dated 10 February 1707/8. (*CSPC 1706–1708*, no. 1330).

63. *CSPC 1693–1696*, nos. 1354, 1372. See Nellis M. Crouse, *The French Struggle for the West Indies 1665–1713* (New York, 1943), pp. 190–96, for a clear account of the raid.

64. *CSPC 1708–1709*, no. 411; Verner W. Crane, *The Southern Frontier, 1670–1732* (Ann Arbor, Mich., 1929), pp. 87–88; *Boston Weekly News-letter* of 19 November 1730, no. 1399.

65. Richard Pares, *War and Trade in the West Indies, 1739–1763* (Oxford, 1936), pp. 432, 449–50; Gipson, *British Empire*, II, p. 238.

Chapter 4. WESTERN ROUTES

1. MHS, John Erving Sea Journal, 1727–1730. *A Logg-Book for the Use of Mariners. To which Is Added, Proper Columns for the Better Working a Traverse at Sea* was published by Samuel Butler of London in 1710. For an example of the use of this by a Massachusetts shipmaster, see Thaddeus Maccarty Sea Journal, 1718–1719, AAS.

2. The term "galley" had outgrown associations with power by oars and had come to mean a flush-decked ship, often comparatively slender in line.

3. See entries for 1 April, 20–21 April, and 6 May 1730 in Erving's Sea Journal.

4. R. G. Albion, "Sea Routes," in Critchell Rimington, ed., *Merchants Fleets* (New York, 1944), p. 22. Erving averaged 34 days from Boston to the Channel and 61 days return on three round-trips in the *Sarah Galley* between 1727 and 1730 (Erving Sea Journal).

5. *American Weekly Mercury*, 22 May 1729.

6. *Boston Gazette*, 11 August 1729, and 11 January, 12 February, and 5 March 1732/3.

7. See earlier, pp. 49–50.

8. See Jacob M. Price, "Economic Function and the Growth of American Port Towns in the Eighteenth Century," *Perspectives in American History*, 8 (1974), pp. 123–86; and C. P. Nettels, *The Money Supply of the American Colonies Before 1720* (Madison, Wis., 1934), chap. 4.

9. Allan R. Pred, *Urban Growth and the Circulation of Information: The United States System of Cities, 1790–1840* (Cambridge, Mass., 1973).

10. U.S. Navy, Hydrographic Office, *Ice Atlas of the Northern Hemisphere*, rev. ed., (Washington, D.C., 1955).

11. *Pennsylvania Gazette*, nos. 208, 210, 213, 220, 222, 223; *American Weekly Mercury*, nos. 673, 675, 684, 686.

12. *American Weekly Mercury*, 18 January 1732/3.

13. *Boston Gazette*, 22 January 1732/3; *Boston Weekly News-letter*, nos. 1510, 1512.
14. Isaac Norris to William Righton, 11 seventh month 1699, and similar sentiments expressed to Jeffrey Pinnell of Bristol, England, later the same year (HSP, Isaac Norris Letterbook 1699–1702, pp. 72, 123).
15. *American Weekly Mercury*, passim. For reference to freedom from ice in January, see issues for 8 January 1722/3 and 14 January 1723/4. See also *Pennsylvania Gazette*, 16 January 1733/4. New York harbor's difficulties can be calendared from *American Weekly Mercury* of 23 February 1719/20, 23 January 1721/2, 8 March 1725/6, and 29 January 1727/8; *Boston Gazette* for 14 March 1725/6, 26 February 1727/8 and 24 December 1732; and the *New York Gazette*, 29 January 1727/8. Concerning the freezing of Boston harbor, see *Boston News-letter* of 15 February 1719/20; *Pennsylvania Gazette* of 7 January 1728/9; *American Weekly Mercury* of 8 February 1731/2; *Boston Weekly News-letter* of 4 January 1732/3. Gary Warden, *Boston 1689–1776* (Boston, 1970), pp. 17, 121, notes a freeze-up in 1737, and he suggests that the harbor often froze. S. E. Morison, *The Maritime History of Massachusetts* (Boston, 1921), p. 6, suggests that Boston harbor "freezes but once a generation," which may indicate increased water processing rather than significant changes in weather in the intervening period.
16. Ironically, this is despite average annual river ice days at Philadelphia limited to 40 whereas New York had 60 and Boston area 80 (*Ice Atlas of the Northern Hemisphere*).
17. For Boston's dominance of Massachusetts ship owning, see B. Bailyn and L. Bailyn, *Massachusetts Shipping 1697–1714* (Cambridge, Mass., 1959), esp. pp. 88–89.
18. The war with Spain after 1739 disrupted the fish market just as a series of bad harvests in southern Europe opened markets for American grain. Philadelphia and New York merchants thereby gained the credit balances in England to allow the expansion of their direct imports. See Price, "Economic Function," pp. 140–44.
19. On modern navigational charts, three main "tracks" to Bishop Rock, Cornwall, allow comparisons between the three cities.

Nautical Miles to Bishop Rock from

	Boston	New York	Philadelphia
Track A (extra southern)	2860	3019	3159
Track B (southern)	2816	2986	3124
Track C (northern)	2744	2922	3066

Source: U.S. Navy, Hydrographic Office, *Table of Distances Between Ports via the Shortest Navigable Routes* (Washington, D.C., 1948), pp. 51, 53.

Boston's advantages over New York seem to be over a week for westbound vessels if passages reported in the local press are compared. In 32 reported passages of news bearing ships to New York from London between 1724 and 1739, the average passage was 62 days. See *American Weekly Mercury*, nos. 18 to 1007. Compare Table 4.4, indicating that an average passage to Boston from London by 132 news-bearing ships between 1711 and 1739 averaged 52.5 days. Philadelphia-bound news-bearing ships from London averaged four days longer than those bound for New York. See Table 4.13. Cf. westward crossings from Liverpool, London, and Le Havre between 1818 and 1857. In 4160 passages of these nineteenth-century clipper ships, the average length of time to New York was 36.2 days (R. G. Albion, *Square Riggers on Schedule* [Princeton, 1938], Appendix XI).

20. Nettels, *Money Supply*, p. 107.
21. From Christmas 1716 to Christmas 1719, London sailings: for New England, 101; for New York, 19; for Pennsylvania, 25; for South Carolina, 26. Voyages in the opposite

direction to London: from South Carolina, 91; from Pennsylvania, 8; from New York, 44; from New England 123 (Nettels, *Money Supply*, p. 101 note).

22. *Pennsylvania Gazette,* 5 January 1730/31.

23. *Historical Statistics,* Series Z, 277; John J. McCusker, "The Current Value of English Exports 1697 to 1800," *W&MQ,* 3d ser., 28 (1971), pp. 623–24.

24. See Richard B. Morris, *Fair Trial* (London, 1953), pp. 33–68, and G. F. Dow and J. H. Edmonds, *The Pirates of the New England Coast, 1630–1730* (Salem, Mass., 1923), pp. 73–83; R. Yard to W. Blathwayt of 1 and 5 September and reply of 8/18 September 1699, Boston Public Library, MS. K. 5.3.

25. *CSPC 1700,* nos. 14, 22; PRO, CO 391/12, pp. 269–70; *The Diary of Samuel Sewall,* 3 vols. (Boston, 1878–1882), II, 3; PRO, Adm. 3/15. The HMS *Advice* made a second voyage westward in 1700, arriving in New York on 17 September (*CSPC 1700,* no. 845). By way of contrast, however, the *Hazard Galley,* Captain Richard Green, left Deal 14 August 1714 bound for Boston with news of the accession of George I. A summer passage ended as a winter wreck on 12 November on the Massachusetts coast about 10 leagues from Boston. She was lost with all hands and no surviving detail of her three-month passage (*CSPC 1714–1715,* no. 88; *Boston News-letter,* no. 553).

26. Price, "Economic Function," pp. 140–50. For Salem, see James D. Phillips, *Salem in the Seventeenth Century* (Boston, 1933), and his *Salem and the Indies* (Boston, 1947), as well as William I. Davisson and Dennis J. Dugan, "Commerce in Seventeenth-Century Essex County, Massachusetts," *Essex Institute Historical Collections,* 107 (1971), especially pp. 124–42. On New Hampshire shipping, see David E. Van Deventer, *The Emergence of Provincial New Hampshire, 1623–1741* (Baltimore, 1976), pp. 98–99, 104–5, 175; William G. Saltonstall, *Ports of Piscataqua* (Cambridge, Mass., 1941). Boston apparently had a considerable place in the whaling industry in the 1730's. Between 1 April 1737 and 31 March 1738 some 38 vessels cleared Boston for the Arctic (*Boston Weekly News-letter,* nos. 1726–1775; see also E. A. Stackpole, *The Sea Hunters: The New England Whalemen During Two Centuries, 1635–1835* [Philadelphia, 1953], pp. 18, 32).

27. For the salt gathering on the island off the Venezuela coast, see Richard Pares, *Yankees and Creoles* (London, 1956), pp. 103–4; Byron Fairchild, *Messrs. William Pepperell: Merchants at Piscataqua* (Ithaca, N.Y., 1954), pp. 35, 42, 107. Government concern, in Barbados as well as in Massachusetts, for the protection of salt gatherers from pirates and privateers is evident from *CSPC 1693–1696,* no. 1740; *CSPC 1697–1698,* no. 41; *CSPC 1699,* nos. 72, 343, 890; *CSPC 1700,* no. 66.

28. *Pennsylvania Gazette,* no. 112; *Boston Weekly News-letter,* 31 March 1712.

29. Thomas C. Barrow, *Trade and Empire: The British Customs Service in Colonial America, 1660–1775* (Cambridge, Mass., 1967), pp. 142–44.

30. The Massachusetts figures in Table 2.3 include Salem and Marblehead shipping.

31. See James F. Shepherd and Gary M. Walton, *Shipping, Maritime Trade, and the Economic Development of Colonial North America* (Cambridge, 1972), p. 197. Notice their warning that customs-to-customs times are not passage times, but realize that this distortion *overstates* the length of voyages and *understates* ships' speed rather than the reverse.

32. Ibid.

33. See Table 4.1 for Boston's population. For Massachusetts' population, see *Historical Statistics,* series Z, 6. For current values of New England-destined English exports, see John J. McCusker, "The Current Value," pp. 623–24.

34. Shepherd and Walton, *Shipping,* pp. 49–53; William I. Davisson and Lawrence J. Bradley, "New York Maritime Trade: Ship Voyage Patterns, 1715–1765," *New York Historical Society Quarterly,* 55 (1971), pp. 309–17.

35. The enumeration of rice in 1705 and the licensing system instituted in 1730 were

designed to control this major new staple. Boston's entrepôt services would be of little use to an area with so major a transatlantic traffic. Boston's need was for wheat, not rice, and this would expand traffic between Boston and ports in the Chesapeake and further north. See Gary M. Walton, "New Evidence on Colonial Commerce," *JEconH*, 28 (1968), p. 371 note. Apparently, the links did not grow in the generation after 1740. See J. J. Malone, *Pine Trees and Politics* (Seattle, 1964), p. 172 note 42.

36. Malone, *Pine Trees*, pp. 33–38. Also see Ralph Earle Moody, "Massachusetts Trade with Carolina, 1686–1709," *North Carolina Historical Review*, 20 (1943), pp. 43–53. North Carolina's population rose from 5430 in 1680 to 10,720 by 1700, to 21,270 by 1720, and to 51,760 by 1740 (*Historical Statistics*, series Z, 15).

37. In the year 29 July 1718–14 July 1719, ships entered Boston from North Carolina in all months save January and February (with 27 of 41 entries between March and June), and the 40 clearances for North Carolina included none in January or March (PRO, CO 5/848). The *Boston Weekly News-letter*'s accounts of ships entering and "cleared out" in the year after 1 April 1737 suggest entries from North Carolina in all months save February (with 37 of 49 entries in months March to June) and clearances for North Carolina in all months (with 36 of 69 leaving between September and December).

38. See A. P. Middleton, *The Tobacco Coast* (Newport News, Va., 1953), p. 201.

39. Paul G. E. Clemens, *The Atlantic Economy and Colonial Maryland's Eastern Shore: From Tobacco to Grain* (Ithaca, N.Y., 1980), passim; David C. Klingaman, "The Coastwise Trade of Colonial Massachusetts," *Essex Institute Historical Collections*, 108 (1972), pp. 217–34.

40. *Boston Weekly News-letter* for the year beginning 1 April 1737 recorded 58 Boston entries from the Chesapeake, with a minimum of 1 a month and a focus on late spring and early summer. Clearances for the Chesapeake in the same period totaled 55, in every month save March 1737/8 with emphasis on midsummer and early winter. See nos. 1726–1775.

41. I. K. Steele, "Time, Communications and Society: The English Atlantic, 1702," *Journal of American Studies*, 8 (1974), pp. 9–11. On Massachusetts relations with Nova Scotia throughout this period, see George A. Rawlyk, *Nova Scotia's Massachusetts: A Study of Massachusetts–Nova Scotia Relations 1630–1784* (Montreal, 1973), chaps. 3–8.

42. By a *Boston Gazette* account there had been 671 entries into the port of Lisbon between 1 January and 31 December 1725. These included 391 English, 103 Portuguese, 66 Dutch, and 57 French entries. See no. 337 for 16 May 1726.

43. See PRO, CO 5/848, for the year commencing 5 April 1732 and that commencing 1 April 1737.

44. In 1680 New York City's population (3200) approached one third of that of the colony of New York (9830), and this was after a decade of much more rapid growth in the colony than in the city (1670 populations were c. 2800 and 5754 for city and colony respectively). See earlier note 6 and *Historical Statistics*, series Z 9.

45. Thomas J. Archdeacon, *New York City, 1664–1710: Conquest and Change* (Ithaca, N.Y., 1976), esp. chap. 5. The figures for 1695 (£49,657) and 1701 (£44,230) support the contemporary laments that associated the decline with the War of the League of Augsburg. Figures are from Gloria Main's discussion in *Reviews in American History*, 4 (1976), p. 383.

46. See Fletcher to the Admiralty, 19 November 1694, *CSPC 1693–1696*, no. 1519; Chidley Brook's report of 24 January 1698/9 in *CSPC 1699*, no. 51; and Bellomont to Board of Trade, 5 January 1699/1700, *CSPC 1700*, no. 14. Lord Bellomont described the New York fleet in 1700 as composed of 14 ships, 2 ketches, 27 brigs, and 81 sloops (*CSPC 1700*, no. 953). Using the average size of each class of vessel in the

Massachusetts fleet of 1698, as detailed in Bernard Bailyn and Lotte Bailyn, *Massa-chusetts Shipping, 1697–1714* (Cambridge, Mass., 1959), pp. 82–83, Bellomont's list would come to some 5232 tons of New York shipping. The Bailyns are rightly convinced that Bellomont's estimates were exaggerated (ibid., p. 21). My own efforts to gather references from English port books, surviving colonial officers' lists, and a list of vessels at Newfoundland in 1698 certainly are incomplete on the total number of active vessels operating in the English Atlantic between 1696 and 1700. This method produced a total list of Massachusetts shipping that exceeded the size of the Massachusetts fleet of 1698, as described carefully by the Bailyns, by some 18 percent (12,117 tons vs. 10,202 tons). Assuming that the New York fleet's appearance in these same places bore anything like the same relationship to the size of New York's fleet of 1698, the New York fleet of 1698 was approximately 1734 tons, or about one-third the size that would be derived from the Bellomont list. For the end of the century decline in New York traffic at Barbados, see Table 2.3.

47. Bellomont's shipping totals for the Michaelmas quarters for the years 1695–1698 show no increase with the coming of peace (*CSPC 1697–1698*, no. 978iv).

48. *Historical Statistics*, Series Z, 9. New York's imports from Britain tripled between 1720 and 1739, but growth of return cargoes in value was very weak (McCusker, "The Current Value," pp. 623–24, and *Historical Statistics*, Series Z, nos. 217–18).

49. Seven of the entries of 1718 were from Cowes and seven of the 1728 entries were from Dover. Patricia Bonomi discusses this in *A Factious People* (New York, 1971), pp. 60–63. For an illustrative and large Dutch cargo aboard a New York brigantine being processed through Southampton in October 1697 on its way to New York, see PRO, E 190/839/10.

50. Eight of the 22 clearances were for Ireland in 1738 although there had been none earlier. All but one were in the last three months of the year (PRO, CO 5/1225–1226). There had been no clearances from New York for Irish ports in the year ending 5 December 1730, and only 5 in the 15 months ending 25 March 1735. See *Pennsyl-vania Gazette*, no. 112, and *New York Gazette*, no. 494, respectively.

51. See Herbert Heaton, "The American Trade," in C. N. Parkinson, ed., *The Trade Winds* (London, 1948), p. 210, and Pred, *Urban Growth*, pp. 28–31.

52. James Birket, *Some Cursory Remarks . . . in his Voyage to North America, 1750–1751* (Freeport, N.Y., 1971), p. 43. *The Journal of Jasper Danckaerts, 1679–1680*, ed. J. F. Jameson and Bartlett B. James (New York, 1913), p. 166, is an earlier descrip-tion. Newport, R.I., was similarly blessed.

53. *Boston News-letter*, no. 824.

54. Letter of 12 December 1702, *Documents Relative to the Colonial History of the State of New York*, ed. E. B. O'Callaghan and Berthold Fernow, 15 vols. (Albany, 1856–1887), hereafter *NYCD*, IV, 1017. William Penn reported that the meeting of colonial governors held at New York in 1700 agreed to petition the king for two or three packet boats in the off-season for shipping (PRO, CO 5/1289, pp. 21–25).

55. See chap. 9.

56. The fastest westward passages from Liverpool by sailing packets were 15 days and 14 hours by the *Emerald*, arriving in Boston early in 1824, and 15 days by the *John Stuart*, arriving in New York in October 1852 (Carl C. Cutler, *Five Hundred Sailing Records* [Mystic, Conn., 1952], pp. 23–24).

57. The crossings of three men-of-war, all in the summer, were noticed as being by way of Madeira. See *Boston Gazette* of 26 September 1720 and 5 August 1734 and *Ameri-can Weekly Mercury* of 6 July 1721. Systematic study of PRO, Adm. 51 series, would yield a clearer picture of convoy routes and those of guard-vessels.

58. To William Popple, 14 November 1698, *NYCD*, IV, 432.

59. The surveyor general of New York's report on the trade on New York, which includes no statistics, is in *NYCD*, V, 685–90.

60. The proportion, expressed as a fraction and a percentage of total entries, can be offered for the following years: 1701: 38/78 or 49 percent; 1718: 111/198 or 56 percent; 1726: 85/202 or 42 percent; 1727: 95/215 or 44 percent; 1728: 93/202 or 46 percent; 1729–1730: 112/211 or 53 percent; 1733: 97/217 or 44 percent; 1734: 78/213 or 36 percent; 1735: 83/196 or 42 percent; 1738: 104/243 or 43 percent; 1739: 105/261 or 40 percent (*sources:* Table 4.7; *Historical Statistics*, Series Z, 276, 283; and *Pennsylvania Gazette*, no. 112). Given the somewhat more multilateral trading patterns of New York ships compared to those of other English colonies, entries from the Caribbean represent a conservative measure of the place of that trade in the life of the port.

61. Cf. John Watts, quoted in R. Pares, *Yankees and Creoles*, p. 47.

62. *The Bolton Letters* (London, 1928), pp. 86–87; *Boston News-letter*, no. 362. Rumors of peace in Europe arrived in Boston via Jamaica and New York in March 1734/5 (ibid., no. 1620. See also Table 2.3).

63. Average passage times were comparable although the seasons affected New York much more than Jamaica.

64. See Table 4.6 for New York to Boston traffic. New York entries from Massachusetts, expressed as a fraction of all traffic in from North American colonies were these: 1701, 16/24; 1718, 14/59; 1728, 24/72; 1738, 14/94. See sources for Table 4.7.

65. Rhode Island entries into New York as a fraction of that city's total entries from North America: 1701, 1/24; 1718, 20/59; 1728, 26/72; 1738, 31/94. For Rhode Island traffic into Boston, see above Table 4.6. For the eighteenth-century growth of Rhode Island commerce coastwise and to the West Indies, see Carl Bridenbaugh, *Fat Mutton and Liberty of Conscience* (Providence, 1974), esp. chap. 5, and Price, "Economic Functions," pp. 149–51; Lynn Withey, *Urban Growth in Colonial Rhode Island: Newport and Providence in the Eighteenth Century* (New York, 1984), esp. pp. 7, 21, and Appendix B. A rather vague, but suggestive official description of Rhode Island seaborne trade is printed in *Records of the Colony of Rhode Island and Providence Plantations, in New England*, ed. John Russell Bartlett, 10 vols. (Providence, 1856–1865), IV, 60. With so few statistics of Rhode Island shipping available, it is unfortunate that the lists for 1729–1720 published in the *Pennsylvania Gazette*, no. 112, show so little traffic to New York or Massachusetts. Perhaps the recording of coastwise trade there had fallen off at the customhouse. James Coden sailed his *Hester* back and forth between New York and Rhode Island with such regularity that it was called a packet service. He made nine round-trips in the year after 29 September 1723, for instance, and New York shipping returns in the newspapers would read "Only Coden" for weeks when no other traffic entered New York harbor. See *American Weekly Mercury*, passim.

66. See Gary B. Nash, "The Quest for the Susquehannah Valley: New York, Pennsylvania and the Seventeenth-Century Fur Trade," *New York History*, 148 (1967), pp. 3–28.

67. See *Historical Statistics*, series Z, 11, concerning the population of the colony; Table 4.1 for population of Philadelphia. For shipping in the early 1730's, see A. L. Jensen, *The Maritime Commerce of Colonial Philadelphia* (Madison, Wis., 1963), p. 290, and *Historical Statistics*, series Z, 266–85; J. T. Lemon, *The Best Poor Man's Country* (Baltimore, 1972), pp. 219 ff.

68. PRO, CO 33/13.

69. Of 73 entries from the Caribbean in the year ending 3 December 1730, there were 17 from Barbados, 17 from Jamaica, 28 from the Leewards, 4 from Tortuga, 4 from Turks Island, and 3 from Surinam (*Pennsylvania Gazette*, no. 112). Seven years later there were 65 entries for the year ending 24 March 1736/7. Of these, 32 were from the Leewards, 20 from Barbados, 7 from Jamaica, and 6 from other West Indian islands (*American Weekly Mercury*, no. 900). See also Barbados clearances in Table 2.3.

70. *Virginia Gazette*, 28 April 1738.

71. The direct distance to Barbados in nautical miles is 1829 from New York, 1839 from Philadelphia, and 1899 from Boston (U.S. Navy, Hydrographic Office, *Table of Distances*, pp. 65–66). The comparable figures for Kingston, Jamaica, are 1446 nautical miles from Philadelphia, 1474 from New York, and 1657 from Boston (ibid., pp. 214–15). For comparisons between Boston and New York passages to the Caribbean, see Shepherd and Walton, *Shipping*, p. 197. Philadelphia to Barbados passages cannot be accurately gathered in any quantity. In nine "news-bearing" passages from Barbados, the average time was 29 days, and the range was from 16 to 34 days. A comparable group of 34 arrivals at New York from Barbados averaged 24 days and ranged from 15 to 34 days (from *American Weekly Mercury, Pennsylvania Gazette, New York Gazette, Boston News-letter*, and *Boston Gazette*). It was this last paper that carried a story from Philadelphia in December 1736 noting that Captain Bordman of the *Hampshire* had

> compleated three Voyages since the River clear'd it self of Ice last Spring; one of which was from hence to Ireland and the West-Indies, and the other two from this Place to Antigua, which two last Voyages he has made since the middle of July last [*Boston Gazette*, no. 885].

Bordman sailed again for Antigua early in December. Such a pace was clearly beyond expectations, but three West Indian voyages a year were not.

72. See Jensen, *Maritime Commerce*, chap. 4.

73. Jensen, *Maritime Commerce*, chap. 6; James H. Levitt, *For Want of Trade: Shipping and the New Jersey Ports, 1680–1783* (Newark, 1981); *Pennsylvania Gazette*, no. 112; *American Weekly Mercury*, no. 900.

74. Gary B. Nash, "Maryland's Economic War with Pennsylvania," *Maryland Historical Magazine*, 60 (1965), p. 239. See also HSP, Isaac Norris Letterbook 1699–1702, pp. 122, 163. The provisioning of the tobacco and sugar fleets bound for Britain must have constituted a considerable avenue of commerce although it escapes documentation by escaping customs concern.

75. *Pennsylvania Gazette*, no. 112; *American Weekly Mercury*, no. 795; Jensen, *Maritime Commerce*, pp. 79–83.

76. Jensen, *Maritime Commerce*, chap. 5; James G. Lydon, "Philadelphia's Commercial Expansion, 1720–1739," *PMHB*, 91 (1967), pp. 412–14. Of 30 clearances from Philadelphia for Lisbon, Madeira, and Gibraltar in 1729 and 1730, there were 6 in June and again in December. January and October were the only months without a sailing (*Pennsylvania Gazette*).

77. New York exports to the Wine Islands and southern Europe involved 8 clearances in 1718, 13 in 1728, and 15 in 1738 (PRO, CO 5/1222, 1224–1226; see also *Pennsylvania Gazette*, no. 112, and *American Weekly Mercury*, no. 795).

78. See the entry of the *Isaac* of London, Francis Walton master into Newcastle customs (PRO, E 190/207/13). All outport records for 1696–1700 have been checked in this connection, and London records for 1696–1697 revealed no entries from Pennsylvania either.

79. *CSPC 1704–1705*, no. 1446; Jensen, *Maritime Commerce*, pp. 85–106.

80. For the extent of this imbalance in direct trade see *Historical Statistics*, Series Z, nos. 219–20; Lydon, "Philadelphia's Expansion," p. 409.

81. *American Weekly Mercury*, nos. 499, 1039. For subsequent ads for the *Constantine* bound for London, see *American Weekly Mercury*, nos. 500, 502, 504, 550–53, 556, 559, 609, 713, 761, 921, 962, 972, 1030. She was also advertised in the *Pennsylvania Gazette*, nos. 146–47, 155–56, 197–99, 248–53, 295, 297, 299.

82. The *Stork Galley*, William White commander, was one that claimed intention to sail

"precisely the 25th of November next" in 1726 (*American Weekly Mercury*, no. 355). The preparation of the *Charming Nancy*, John Stedman master, can be followed in *American Weekly Mercury*, nos. 936, 947–49, 953.

83. In the years 1729 and 1730 some 38 ships entered Philadelphia from England and Scotland, 20 of them from London. There was only one entry in two years during the first three months of the year. As an English correspondent of Isaac Norris was reminded in 1699, Philadelphia's fairs were on the sixteenth of May and November and "Goods goe off best against those Times . . ." (HSP, Isaac Norris Letterbook 1699–1702, p. 124).

84. Four of these 17 crossings were said to be by way of the Azores; and one, by way of Madeira. As naval convoys did not sail to Philadelphia, little is known about which routes were the most frequented.

85. See further on, pp. 240–41.

86. *American Magazine*, 1 (February 1741), p. vii.

Chapter 5. Northern Routes and the English Atlantic

1. For the population, see Robert V. Wells, *The Population of the British Colonies in America before 1776* (Princeton, 1975), p. 47, and C. Grant Head, *Eighteenth Century Newfoundland, a Geographer's Perspective* (Toronto, 1976), chaps. 2 and 5. For government policy on Newfoundland's inhabitants, see, for instance, I. K. Steele, *Politics of Colonial Policy* (Oxford, 1968), pp. 43, 161, 168.

2. See James R. Coull, *The Fisheries of Europe* (London, 1972), especially Figure 3 on p. 32.

3. Gillian T. Cell, *English Enterprise at Newfoundland* (Toronto, 1969), pp. 4–5. In planning the Newfoundland convoys for 1706 and 1707, the Board of Trade sought one vessel with salt ships by way of Lisbon; two vessels by way of the "south channel" early in March; one by the "north channel," leaving from Milford Haven about March 10; and two with the sack ships, leaving 20 May. It is not clear whether wartime risks revived the northern route or whether this was still regularly used. (PRO, CO 195/4, pp. 119–205, 363–65; CO 389/19, pp. 490–91, 498). On the polar easterlies, see U.S. Navy, *Marine Climatic Atlas of the World*, vol. 1 *North Atlantic Ocean* (Washington, D.C., 1974) pp. 2, 30, 58, 86, 114, 142, 170, 198, 226, 254, 282, 310. It is probable that both these winds and currents were stronger and active in slightly lower latitude in 1675–1740 than they are today. See H. H. Lamb, *The Changing Climate* (London, 1966), pp. 15, 18, 201.

4. Samuel E. Morison, *The European Discovery of America: The Northern Voyages* (New York, 1971), pp. 136, 157–209, describes Cabot's course as westerly, but the controversy about his course and landfall continues. See D. B. Quinn, *England and the Discovery of America, 1481–1620* (London, 1974), pp. 93–111 for another reading of the evidence.

5. *The English Pilot*, p. 10. The logbook of HMS *Bristol*, convoying the sack fleet in June 1676 suggests that the fleet set out WSW, but, as the winds backed to NW, they were able to hold closer to W and kept north of the 45th parallel on their whole passage (PRO, Adm. 51/134). HMS *Guernsey*, on the same assignment in 1709, reached an observed latitude of 40° 20″ before heading northwesterly (PRO, Adm. 51/423). Only 8 of 247 English ships at Newfoundland in 1698 were listed as in from the Azores (Colonial Williamsburg, Blathwayt Papers, vol. xix. See also in PRO, CO 360/6, f. 5). Very few ships cleared São Miguel, Azores, for Newfoundland in surviving evidence for the seventeenth century (T. B. Duncan, *Atlantic Islands* [Chicago, 1972], Table 18, p. 110).

6. PRO, E 190/927/9, p. 10; Blathwayt Papers, vol. xix. Only two vessels were reported

into Newfoundland directly from Salt Tortuga. Most of this salt came to Newfoundland via Massachusetts ports.

7. Ibid. Norris recorded 40 ships entering from Irish ports: Cork (14), Dublin (13), Waterford (4), Belfast (2), Kinsale (2), Sligo (1), and Ireland (4).

8. Head, *Newfoundland*, chaps. 1, 3. This level represented a drop from early Stuart participation by the English. See Josiah Child, *A New Discourse of Trade*, 2d ed. (London, 1694), p. 205; H. A. Innis, *The Cod Fisheries*, 2d ed. (Toronto, 1958), pp. 95–111; R. G. Lounsbury, *The British Fishery at Newfoundland, 1634–1763* (New Haven, 1934), pp. 126–272.

9. Quoted in James A. Williamson, *The Cabot Voyages and Bristol Discovery under Henry VII* (Cambridge, 1962), p. 225.

10. Passage times to Newfoundland are not available in large numbers for the early period. Spring passages of 22 days or less were "commonly performed" in the sixteenth century (ibid., pp. 63, 226). Cabot's trip of 1497 included a westward passage of 35 days from Bantry Bay to landfall. John Rut (1527) had a 41-day passage. In June 1676 HMS *Bristol* convoyed sack ships to Newfoundland from Plymouth in 20 days (PRO, Adm. 51/134). By contrast, HMS *Guernsey* and its charges took twice as long in 1709 (PRO, Adm. 51/423). The distance from Bishop Rock, southwest of the Lizard, to St. John's, Newfoundland, is 1804 nautical miles. A direct passage of three weeks would be at 3.6 knots average. Traversing against the westerlies could easily bring the average running speed up to 4 knots (PRO, E 190/974/4, p. 30).

11. Charles Davis letter, Lambeth Palace, London, England, Fulham Papers, vol. I, fol. 7.

12. Head, *Newfoundland*, pp. 16, 23–25, 54–137; Morison, *European Discovery*, p. 272.

13. *CSPC 1704–1705*, no. 1031. The Board of Trade regularly advocated that convoys sail before the end of March and May for the fishing and sack fleets respectively. See, for instance, PRO, CO 391/10, pp. 406–7; and CO 195/3, pp. 161–66, 400–2.

14. *The Journal of James Yonge, Plymouth Surgeon*, ed. F. N. L. Poynter (Hamden, Conn., 1963), p. 54.

15. See D. W. Prowse, *A History of Newfoundland* (London, 1895), pp. 211 ff., and G. S. Graham, *Empire of the North Atlantic*, 2d ed. (Toronto, 1958), pp. 76–77.

16. See *Lloyd's News*, 20–24 October 1696, 10–16 January 1696/7.

17. It is not surprising that the outward-bound fishing vessels clearing customs, as indicators of the mood of the whole industry, were cautious. The surviving port books for 1695 to 1700 suggest the trends although not the figures: 1695 (46 clearances for Newfoundland), 1696 (52), 1697 (20), 1698 (59), 1699 (69), and 1700 (59).

18. Colonial Williamsburg, Blathwayt Papers, vol. xix. The other 32 vessels were bound to: North American colonies (14); the West Indies (11); the "Wine Islands"; and Ireland (1).

19. Ian K. Steele, "Time, Communications and Society: The English Atlantic, 1702," *Journal of American Studies*, 8 (1974), pp. 9–11.

20. *Boston News-letter*, nos. 422 and 423. London reports of 6 March were reprinted in Boston 19 May.

21. Colonial Williamsburg, Blathwayt Papers, vol. xix. See also the evidence gathered in Table 28, p. 128, of W. B. Stephens, *Seventeenth-Century Exeter* (Exeter, 1958).

22. This was one case in which customs officials actually did survey colonial naval officers' lists to answer a query from the Board of Trade about the extent of the colonial trade at Newfoundland. Of the eight "other" colonies represented in the traffic, there were three voyages from Philadelphia, two from New York, and one each from New Hampshire, Rhode Island, and Antigua (PRO, CO 194/6, fol. 192).

23. *CSPC 1704–1705*, no. 1409.
24. See E. E. Rich, ed., *Hudson's Bay Copy Booke of Letters, Commissions Instructions Outward 1688–1696* (London, 1957), p. xxxi note 6 concerning six wrecks 1678–1686 (hereafter cited as *Letters Outward, 1688–1696*). For a detailed account of the early years of the company, see E. E. Rich, *Hudson's Bay Company*, 3 vols. (Toronto, 1960), I, 61–237.
25. E. E. Rich, ed., *Copy-book of Letters Outward Etc. 1679–1694* (Toronto, 1948), p. 43.
26. E. E. Rich, ed., *Minutes of the Hudson's Bay Company 1679–84; first series 1679–82* (Toronto, 1945), Appendix A, p. 295.
27. The sailing orders that survive for 1696 and before are printed in *Letters Outward, 1679–1694*. Those for 1697–1740 are in Hudson's Bay Archives, Winnipeg, A 6/3–6, microfilms of which are in PAC, with the prefix MG20.
28. In 1706, Captain Joseph Davis was ordered to sail out with the Newfoundland convoy by way of Plymouth (Hudson's Bay Archives [hereafter HBC] A 6/3, pp. 150–51). For 1715–1719, see HBC A 6/3, pp. 269, 273; HBC A 6/4, pp. 7, 10, 29, 30–33, 47–48, 66–70.
29. *Letters Outward, 1688–1696*, pp. 106, 131. The ships sent out in 1689 via the Channel had failed to get through. For 1708–1712, see HBC A 6/3, pp. 178–80, 199–200, 210, 229–31. For 1727–1728, see HBC A 6/5, pp. 19–22, 23–26, 39–41, 42–44, 45–47. The orders for 1732–1740 are in HBC A 6/5, pp. 129–32, 163–68, 182–84, 201–5, 227–33, 252–57; HBC A 6/6, pp. 47–54, 101–18, 161–72. Captain William Coats, *The Geography of Hudson's Bay: Remarks of Capt. William Coats*, ed. J. Barrow (London, 1852), pp. 5–13.
30. Orders to Michael Grimington, 6 June 1698, HBC A 6/3, pp. 77, 84–85, 96–97. See Figure 1. Cape Farewell is at 59°45′ N.
31. HBC A 6/3, pp. 150–51, 178–80, 199–200, 210–19, 229–31, 239–41, 251, and HBC A 6/4, p. 126.
32. The Ship Movement Book 1719–1929, HBC C 4/1, abstracts from the logbooks of 39 westward passages from the Downs to Resolution Island between 1719 and 1740. The average time was 45 days; the range, 32 to 64; the median, 44.
33. Ibid., fol. 5; Coats, *Geography*, p. 19.
34. Coats, *Geography*, p. 19. Three outward-bound vessels in 1740 made Cape Diggs on or before 5 July, having gathered at Resolution Island by 30 June. HBC C 4/1, fol 5.
35. Canadian Hydrographic Service (Ottawa, 1955), p. 13. See also Charles Swithinbank, *Ice Atlas of Arctic Canada* (Ottawa, 1960), and F. Kenneth Hare and Margaret R. Montgomery, "Ice, Open Water, and Winter Climate in the Eastern Arctic of North America," *Arctic*, 2 (1949), esp. pp. 153–55.
36. Coats, *Geography*, pp. 18–22, 24.
37. Thirty-eight passages are recorded in HBC C 4/1 for the years 1740 and earlier (A. B. Becher, *Navigation of the Atlantic Ocean*, 5th ed. [London, 1892], p. 73).
38. K. G. Davies and A. M. Johnson, eds., *Letters from Hudson Bay* (London, 1966), pp. 34–35, 56.
39. Coats, *Geography*, pp. 90–91. The captain's sailing orders for Michael Grimington dated 31 May 1697 were uncommon in specifying that he stay at Hayes River no longer than 15 September. Grimington was also told that if he could not make Hayes river by 15 August because of contrary winds, he was to go for Albany River at the bottom of the bay (HBC A 6/3, pp. 60–62). The ships sent out in 1694 were ordered to leave by 16 September. See *Letters Outward 1688–1696*, p. 233.
40. In the 50 years before 1740, only once, in 1692, did ships sent to York Fort winter in the bay. That year three ships were sent from York Fort to winter at Gilpin's Island in

James Bay. With the French in control of the bottom of the bay, as they were from 1689 to 1695, this wintering was to trade on the Eastmain, not because the season prevented the ships' return to England. See *Letters Outward, 1688–1696*, p. 332.

41. The logs of 22 return voyages from York Fort and Churchill between 1720 and 1740 suggest an average of 42.8 days to the Downs, with a range of 29 to 57 and a median of 44.5 (derived from the Ship Movement Book 1719–1929, HBC C 4/1, fols. 4–5).

42. A modern description of this is in *Labrador and Hudson Bay Pilot* (Ottawa, 1955), pp. 13–14.

43. Betwen 1719 and 1740 the averages were 81.6 vs. 75.0, the ranges 60 to 102 vs. 57 to 92, and the medians 83 vs. 78. On the problems of navigation at the Albany River, see Rich, *Hudson's Bay*, I, 112, 387, 502, 506.

44. To Richard Staunton, 28 June 1715 (HBC A 6/4, p. 14).

45. To Thomas Maclish, 15 May 1716 (HBC A 6/4, pp. 3–4). The same point was made that year in the letter to Knight at Churchill River or York Fort (HBC A 6/4, pp. 18–22).

46. The contributions of Baffin Bay (Arctic ice), Foxe Channel, and winter ice to this process are outlined in *Labrador and Hudson Bay Pilot*, pp. 13 ff.

47. The years were 1706, 1708, 1710–1712, 1727, 1734, 1738, and 1740.

48. HBC C 4/1, fols. 4–5. The captains were paid 12 months a year. All other officers and crew were hired on in May and discharged in stages in October. See HBC C 2/1–3, Seamen's Wage books.

49. No ships were sent out in 1695, 1700, 1703, 1704, 1707, and 1709.

50. In 1719 the *Hudson's Bay III* was wrecked off Cape Tatnam. In 1724 the *Mary I* was wrecked as she left Albany. In 1727 the *Mary II* was lost off Cape Farewell. In 1736 the *Hudson Bay IV* went down in the strait.

Chapter 6. COMMUNICATING REVOLUTION, 1688–1689

1. *The Diary of Samuel Sewall*, 3 vols. (Boston, 1878–1882), I, 240. On 12 November 1688 Governor Andros granted a license for this 140-ton ship, William Clarke master, to sail for London (Massachusetts Archives, Boston, vol. 7, Commercial 1685–1714, p. 61).

2. *Sewall Diary*, I, 242, 245, 246.

3. The crisis is here considered as beginning with the royal proclamation of 28 September, printed in the *London Gazette* of 1 October. The new monarchs accepted the throne on 13 February 1688–1689.

4. For Maryland, see *The Declaration . . . of their Majesties Protestant Subjects in the Province of Maryland* (St. Mary's, Md., and London, 1689), reprinted in C. M. Andrews, *Narratives of the Insurrections, 1675–1690* (New York, 1915), p. 311, and "Mariland's Grevances Wiy The Have Taken Op Arms," ed. B. McAnear, *Journal of Southern History*, 8 (1942), pp. 392–409. For Boston, see *The Declaration of the Gentlemen, Merchants and Inhabitants of Boston and the Country Adjacent*, also reprinted in Andrews, *Narratives*, p. 181. Concerning New York, see *NYCD*, III, 660.

5. C. D., *New England's Faction Discovered* (London, 1690), reprinted in Andrews, *Narratives*, p. 257. For the collapse of the case against Andros, see Theodore B. Lewis, ed., "Sir Edmund Andros's Hearing before the Lords of Trade and Plantations, April 17, 1690: Two Unpublished Accounts," AAS *Proceedings*, LXXXIII, Part 2 (1974), pp. 241–50.

6. Among recent works on the subject, the following deserve special note: L. G. Carr and D. W. Jordan, *Maryland's Revolution of Government, 1689–1692* (Ithaca, 1974); Robert C. Ritchie, *The Duke's Province: A Study of New York Politics and*

Society 1664–1691 (Chapel Hill, N.C., 1977); T. J. Archdeacon, *New York City, 1664–1710: Conquest and Change* (Ithaca, N.Y., 1976); D. S. Lovejoy, *The Glorious Revolution in America* (New York, 1972). Lovejoy has succinctly restated this argument in "Two American Revolutions, 1689 and 1776," in J. G. A. Pocock, ed., *Three British Revolutions, 1641, 1688, 1776* (Princeton, 1980), pp. 244–62. Richard R. Johnson's *Adjustment to Empire: The New England Colonies 1675–1715* (New Brunswick, N.J., 1981), chaps. 2–4, is sensitive to developments on both sides of the Atlantic.

7. See B. C. Steiner, "The Protestant Revolution in Maryland," American Historical Association *Annual Report for 1897* (Washington, D.C., 1898), p. 290; Bernard Mason, "Aspects of the New York Revolt of 1689," *New York History*, 30 (1949), p. 166.

8. *CSPC 1685–1688*, no. 1910.

9. *London Gazette*, nos. 2409–2415.

10. Sir Nathaniel Johnson, governor of the Leeward Islands.

11. Blackwell to Penn, 8 April and 1 May 1689. HSP, Penn Papers, reel 6, acc. nos. 503, 1617.

12. *CSPC 1689–1692*, nos. 8, 20, 22, 25; PRO, CO 324/5, p. 38; *Acts of the Privy Council of England, Colonial Series*, ed. W. L. Grant and J. Munro, 6 vols. (London, 1908–12), II, 122 (hereafter *APCC*).

13. *CSPC 1685–1688*, no. 1929. In sharp contrast, two advice boats were sent 24 April 1689 to warn West Indian and North American governors that England would declare war on France (PRO, CO 324/5, pp. 41–43).

14. Colonial Williamsburg, Blathwayt Papers, XXXII, Stede to Blathwayt, 16 August 1688 and to Lords of Trade, in *CSPC 1685–1688*, nos. 1876–1876 (iii).

15. There was an embargo that affected colonial trades between 19 and 29 October (*APCC*, II, 116). Existence and survival of the naval officers' list were signs of stability in themselves (PRO, CO 33/13, fol. 20).

16. Edward Hill was master of the *Blake*. She had a crew of 20 and a cargo of hardware and metal goods (PRO, CO 33/13, fol. 20; *CSPC 1689–1692*, nos. 3, 14, 15, 34, 35).

17. PRO, CO 33/13, fol. 20; Blathwayt Papers, XXXII, Stede to Blathwayt, 16 March 1688/9; *CSPC 1689–1692*, no. 43.

18. Clearances from Barbados directly for North America in the quarter commencing 25 December 1688 were two each for Maryland, Virginia, New York, and Newfoundland and one for Pennsylvania. Unfortunately departure dates were not recorded (PRO, CO 33/13, fol. 20).

19. *CSPC 1689–1692*, nos. 88, 256; R. S. Dunn, *Sugar and Slaves* (Chapel Hill, N.C., 1972), pp. 133–34.

20. John Winslow's oath is printed in *Andros Tracts*, ed. W. H. Whitmore, 3 vols. (Boston, 1868–1874), I, 78.

21. *CSPC 1689–1692*, nos. 88, 255, 256.

22. Agnes M. Whitson, *The Constitutional Development of Jamaica 1660–1729* (Manchester, 1929), pp. 131–32; Dunn, *Sugar and Slaves*, pp. 160–62; *CSPC 1685–1688*, nos. 1940, 1941, 1943; *CSPC 1689–1692*, nos. 6, 7.

23. *CSPC 1689–1692*, nos. 50–52; Smyth Kelly to Blathwayt, 27 May and 5 June 1689, Blathwayt Papers, XXII.

24. On 15 March Watson wrote the Lords of Trade of being affronted and abused "so that in view of the danger from French and Spaniards and to secure the peace and quiet of the Island, I proclaimed martial law" (*CSPC 1689–1692*, no. 52). On 6 June he wrote Blathwayt that martial law was proclaimed in keeping with King James's order of 16 October 1688 (Blathwayt Papers, XXVII).

25. *CSPC 1689–1692*, no. 397.

26. The proclamation was covered by a letter dated 1 March 1688/1689, *CSPC 1689–1692*, no. 42. On 18 October 1690 the Lords Proprietors acknowledged a letter of 11 August, bringing word that the proclamation had occurred (Alexander S. Salley, ed., *Records in the British Public Record Office relating to South Carolina, 1685–1690* [Atlanta, 1929], p. 292. See M. Eugene Sirmans, *Colonial South Carolina, a Political History, 1663–1763* [Chapel Hill, N.C., 1966], esp. chap. 3).

27. N. Spencer to Blathwayt, 1 March 1688/9, Blathwayt Papers, XVI; *Executive Journals of the Council of Colonial Virginia*, ed. H. R. McIlwaine and W. L. Hall, 5 vols. (Richmond, 1925–1945), I, 101.

28. *CSPC 1685–1688*, no. 1929. Cf. the Virginia colonial entry book, PRO, CO 5/1357, which suggests that the message was sent 25 October.

29. This tentative connection presumes that Andries Greveraet's report to Nicholson derived from this packet (*NYCD*, III, 660). Nicholas Spencer's letter to Blathwayt of 1 March, which mentions "this most unhappy Conjunction of Affairs," presumes more news than appeared in the council minutes of 27 February (Blathwayt Papers, XVI).

30. *Virginia Executive Journals*, I, 104–6.

31. Ibid. Spencer to Blathwayt of 10 June 1689 mentions "a Rescue lately made in Stafford County by a Rabble of abt. two hundred . . ." (Blathwayt Papers, XVIII).

32. *Archives of Maryland*, ed. W. H. Browne et al., 72 vols. (Baltimore, 1883—), VIII, 56–57, 62–65; *CSPC 1685–1688*, no. 1910. Cf. Lovejoy, *Glorious Revolution*, p. 260. Two vessels are recorded as clearing Barbados for Maryland before Christmas of 1688 (PRO, CO 33/13, fol. 19). Three other vessels, which cleared customs from Maryland in the first quarter of 1689 (for which only fragmentary lists survive), had previously come in from Barbados (PRO, CO 5/749, fol. 4).

33. *Archives of Maryland*, VIII, 65.

34. Ibid., p. 88.

35. F. E. Sparks, *Causes of the Maryland Revolution of 1689* (Baltimore, 1896), p. 572.

36. Carr and Jordan, *Maryland's Revolution*, chap. 1; M. G. Kammen, "The Causes of the Maryland Revolution of 1689," *Maryland History Magazine*, 55 (1960), pp. 293–333.

37. Gary N. Nash, *Quakers in Politics* (Princeton, 1968), pp. 114–26.

38. *Minutes of the Provincial Council of Pennsylvania*, 10 vols. (Harrisburg, Pa., 1852), I, 246–47.

39. "Minutes of the Councill att New York, Mr. 1, 1689," New York Historical Society *Collections*, I (1868), 241–42. Blackwell and Andros had discussed improving communications before the Puritan soldier left Boston to take up the governorship of Pennsylvania (Blackwell to Penn, 20 November 1688, Penn Papers, reel 6, acc. no. 2615; *Pennsylvania Council Minutes*, I, 287–88.

40. *Pennsylvania Council Minutes*, I, 299–300. It is surprising that Queen Mary's position was still not clear in Philadelphia four months after the Virginia proclamation.

41. Ibid., A public reading of the duke of Shrewsbury's circular letter of 15 April was needed to quell popular concern that orders to proclaim William and Mary may have arrived.

42. Ibid., I, 302–11.

43. Richard Wharton letter of 18 October 1688, quoted in T. B. Lewis, "Massachusetts and the Glorious Revolution, 1660–1692," Ph.D. dissertation, University of Wisconsin, 1967, p. 290. Andros's proclamation of 10 January is reprinted in *Andros Tracts*, I, 75–76 note.

44. Andries Greveraet apparently brought the initial news by sea (*NYCD*, III, 660).

45. MHS *Collections*, 6th ser., 3 (1889), pp. 495–96.

46. John West to Fitz-John Winthrop, 23 February 1688/9. MHS *Collections*, 6th ser., 3 (1889), 496–97. The only ship that could have brought the news to Barbados in

accordance with West's details was the *Friendship* of Bristol, Jeremiah Pearce master, arriving in Barbados on 2 January (PRO, CO 33/13, fol. 20).

47. MHS *Collections*, 6th ser., 3 (1889), pp. 496–97. In all the subsequent oath taking designed to discredit Andros and his officers, there was nothing relating to this incident. What "seditious & rebellious libells" could have been gathered at Barbados and St. Christopher at the end of January? The preceding discussion suggests that the confirmed information available there would be the same news Nicholson was sending Winthrop.

48. West would certainly have informed Andros as fully as he did Winthrop. It was a three-day trip from Boston to the governor. Although Andros destroyed his papers, it seems reasonable to estimate that he heard of the news into Boston as early as 19 February and certainly before the end of the month.

49. New York Historical Society *Collections*, I, 241–42.

50. "Autobiography of Increase Mather," ed. M. G. Hall, AAS, *Proceedings*, 51 (1961), pp. 331–32; PRO, CO 5/905, p. 42; Andrews, *Narratives*, p. 277; *CSPC 1689–1692*, no. 21. Lewis, "Massachusetts," p. 290. Wait Winthrop's correspondence with his brother in New London has a comparable gap (MHS, Winthrop Papers).

51. Mather regarded stopping the letters to Andros as justifying his agency in itself ("Autobiography," p. 332). Besides this news and the accession of the king and queen, Mather also knew by 22 February that both Andros and Nicholson were to be recalled (*CSPC 1689–1692*, nos. 28, 37; *APCC*, II, 124–25). The embargo, to man the fleet in anticipation of war with France, was not imposed until 15 April (*APCC*, II, 117–19). Randolph later claimed that "the revolt here was pushed on by the Agent in England, Mr. Mather, who sent a letter to Mr. Bradstreet encouraging him to go cheerfully to so acceptable a piece of service to all good people" (*CSPC 1689–1692*, no. 407). This claim was made later; it was unconfirmed and partisan. Mather is not likely to have urged Bostonians to take for themselves what he wanted to bring them from London, although this does not preclude the possibility that his news, if received, would have helped provoke the local initiative. The only vessel known to be bound from London to Boston late that winter, a ship captained by Benjamin Guillam, was still registering cargo on 11 March (PRO, E 190/148/4, p. 3). Even if he sailed immediately and enjoyed one of the best spring crossings recorded for news-bearing ships (see Table 4.4), he would have arrived in Boston only in time to witness the rising there.

52. John Nelson to _____ (Boston Public Library, Prince Collection, Mather Papers, VII, 81). The letter, to an Acadian correspondent who may well have been Jean-Vincent d'Abbadie de Saint-Castin, was mutilated so that any later news of the English scene was removed. On Saint-Castin's trade with New England, see *Dictionary of Canadian Biography*, ed. George W. Brown et al., 8 vols. (Toronto, 1966—), II, 4–7. See also George A. Rawlyk, *Nova Scotia's Massachusetts* (Montreal, 1973), pp. 35 ff.

53. The tract, *A Narrative of the Miseries of New England* (London, 1688) by Increase Mather, was reprinted in Boston and dated "1688" in the reprint (Charles Evans, ed., *American Bibliography: A Chronological Dictionary of all Books, Pamphlets and Periodical Publications Printed in the United States . . .*, 14 vols. (Chicago and Worcester, Mass., 1903–1959), no. 450. The Boston reprint also included an application to Prince William by the bishop of London dated 21 September 1688. The Boston reprinting of these items together with *An Address* would occur between the end of February (giving six weeks passage and one week at each end for conveyance and printing) and 25 March (the official end of "1688").

54. Winslow's oath, taken 10 months after the event, was printed in *The Revolution in New England Justified* (Boston, 1691), pp. 16–17, reprinted in *Andros Tracts*, I, 78–79.

55. *Further Quaeries upon the Present State of the New-English Affairs* (London, 1690), p. 4, reprinted in *Andros Tracts*, I, 196.

56. *CSPC 1689–1692*, no. 256. For a very different view of what news Winslow brought, see Viola F. Barnes, *The Dominion of New England* (New Haven, 1923), p. 239, and Guy H. Miller, "Rebellion in Zion: The Overthrow of the Dominion of New England," *Historian*, 30 (1968), p. 450.

57. Samuel Wyllys to Mary Wyllys, Connecticut Historical Society *Collections*, 21 (1924), p. 307. In Newport, R.I., on 1 April it was known that "Prince William was in command in England" (Lovejoy, *Glorious Revolution*, p. 238).

58. *The Revolution in New England Justified* (Boston, 1691), p. 56, reprinted in *Andros Tracts*, I, 118.

59. *Andros Tracts*, I, 9.

60. J. P. Kenyon, "The Revolution of 1688: Resistance and Contract," in *Historical Perspectives: Studies in English Thought and Society in Honour of J. H. Plumb*, ed. Neil McKendrick (London, 1974), pp. 46–47.

61. *London Gazette*, no. 2409, and Evans, *Bibliography*, no. 465 and microedition of same.

62. *Andros Tracts*, I, 18.

63. Harris was supposedly protected from abuse by a guard of Whigs. Harris's paper soon became *True domestick intelligence* and by March 1681 was replaced by the *Loyal Protestant and true domestic intelligence* (R. S. Crane and F. B. Kaye, *A Census of British Newspapers and Periodicals, 1620–1800* [Chapel Hill, N.C., 1927], p. 33. See also Winthrop S. Hudson, "William Penn's *English Liberties*: Tract for Several Times," *W&MQ*, 3d ser., 26 [1969], pp. 578–85, and the unsympathetic J. G. Muddiman, *The King's Journalist, 1659–1689* [London, 1923], pp. 214–19).

64. See Evans, *Bibliography*, no. 474.

65. Evans, *Bibliography*, no. 453.

66. For Plymouth colony, see *Records of the Colony of New Plymouth in New England*, ed. N. B. Shurtleff and D. Pulsifer, 12 vols. (Boston, 1855–1861), VI, 208–9, and *CSPC 1689–1692*, no. 183. For Rhode Island, see *CSPC 1689–1692*, no. 99, and *Records of the Colony of Rhode Island and Providence Plantations in New England, 1632–1792*, ed. J. R. Bartlett, 10 vols. (Providence, R.I., 1856–1865), III, 257. For Connecticut, see Gershom Bulkeley, *The People's Right to Election* (Philadelphia, 1689), and his *Will and Doom* (London, 1692) and R. S. Dunn, *Puritans and Yankees: The Winthrop Dynasty of New England 1630–1717* (Princeton, 1962), chap. 13. See also Lovejoy, *Glorious Revolution*, pp. 196–208.

67. Robert Livingston to Randolph on 22 March 1688/9. *Edward Randolph . . . , Including his Letters and Official Papers, 1676–1703 . . .* 7 vols. (Boston, 1898–1909), IV, 262.

68. *CSPC 1689–1692*, no. 104; *NYCD*, III, 574–76, 591. See Ritchie, *The Duke's Province*, especially chap. 9, and J. R. Reich, *Leisler's Rebellion* (Chicago, 1953), chap. 3.

69. *NYCD*, III, 585–86.

70. Ibid., III, 583–84.

71. *Hudson's Bay Copy Booke of Letters Commissions Instructions Outward, 1688–1696*, ed. E. E. Rich (London, 1957), p. 50.

72. Ibid, pp. 50–53, 59, 75–76, 93–104.

Chapter 7. THE POSTS

1. Alexander Spotswood in the *Virginia Gazette* of 28 April 1738. The casual reference to "one or other" island should not, of course, be understood as including Jamaica.

2. Louis B. Wright attempted a balance in his exploratory *The Cultural Life of the American Colonies* (New York, 1957), chap. 11.

3. The postal monopoly did not suffer any serious legal challenge after 1656. See William Smith, *History of the Post Office in British North America 1639–1870* (Cambridge, 1920), p. 3.

4. Peter Fraser, *The Intelligence of the Secretaries of State and Their Monopoly of Licensed News, 1660–1688* (Cambridge, 1956), esp. pp. 20–27; Kenneth Ellis, *The Post Office in the Eighteenth Century: A Study in Administrative History* (London, 1958), chap. 5. See also Lawrence Hanson, *Government and the Press, 1695–1763* (Oxford, 1936), especially pp. 42, 109–10.

5. Howard Robinson, *The British Post Office: A History* (Princeton, 1948), pp. 27–47; J. C. Hemmeon, *The History of the British Post Office* (Cambridge, Mass., 1912), chap. 2; J. W. Hyde, *The Early History of the Post Office in Grant and Farm* (London, 1894), chaps. 2–8. See also the Post Office Acts: (1657) *Acts and Ordinances of the Interregnum*, 3 vols. (London, 1911), II, 1007–13; and (1660) *Statutes at Large*, 12 Car. II c. 35.

6. Hemmeon, *British Post Office*, p. 22; Robinson, *The British Post Office*, pp. 49–50.

7. The bulk of the king's portion of £5382.10s. went to the duchess of Cleveland. Of the balance, some £3700 p.a. was spent on secret service in the 1660's (Robinson, *The British Post Office*, p. 53). Under James II, though nearly £20,000 p.a. was granted to his consort, the Exchequer receipts from postal revenues were approximately £60,000 p.a. See D. C. Chandaman, *The English Public Revenue, 1660–1688* (London, 1975), pp. 117, 120–21, 360–61.

8. The rates increased from 2d to 3d for the first 80 miles and from 3d to 4d for inland letters over 80 miles (Robinson, *The British Post Office*, p. 96). If these and other increases are averaged at approximately one third overall, the gross revenue for 1703–1704 of £156,000 was produced by mails that would have yielded £208,000 at the rates in effect after 1711. That revenue was equaled for the first time, in 1747. See Hemmeon, *British Post Office*, Appendix 1.

9. Thomas De Laune, *The Present State of London* (London, 1681), reprinted in Frank Staff, *The Penny Post, 1680–1940* (London, 1964), p. 164.

10. Ibid., chap. 2; Robinson, *The British Post Office*, chap. 6.

11. Robinson, *The British Post Office*, p. 17.

12. Charles Wilson, *Anglo-Dutch Commerce & Finance in the Eighteenth Century* (Cambridge, 1941), p. 28. See also Robinson, *The British Post Office*, pp. 160–61; Emanuel Bowen, *Britannia Depicta* (London, 1720), pp. 44–46; Daniel Defoe, *A Tour through the Whole Island of Great Britain* (London, 1974), I, 34–35.

13. J. A. J. Housden, "Early Posts in England," *English Historical Review* (hereafter *EHR*), 18 (1903), p. 714.

14. This was rivaled only briefly during war in the late 1670's, when a similar level of service was provided on the Harwich Road. See Brian Austen, *English Provincial Posts, 1633–1840: A Study Based on Kent Examples* (London, 1978), p. 20.

15. The post service to Sheerness ended in 1705 (ibid., p. 22).

16. Garrett Mattingly, *The Defeat of the Spanish Armada* (London, 1959), pp. 92–93. Certainly, the courier to Plymouth and those responsible for sending the pinnace after Drake were very quick, for a London order of 9 April resulted in a pinnace's sailing from Plymouth on the eleventh. For a comparable ride, conducted two centuries later, and after improvements to the London-Exeter Road halved the coach time, see A. S. Turberville, ed., *Johnson's England* 2 vols. (London, 1933), I, 136. Pigot had been named to replace Rodney and had set out when news of Rodney's sea victory arrived. The courier bound for Plymouth with the counter-manding orders made the trip in 28 hours but failed to catch Pigot (Piers Mackesy, *The War for America, 1775–1783* [Cambridge, Mass., 1964], p. 473).

17. During the wars with France, the division of news coming in from the Falmouth and from the Harwich packets would correspond roughly with the division of responsi-

bility associated with the secretaries of state for the Southern and the Northern departments, respectively.

18. See especially J. Crofts, *Packhorse Waggon and Post: Land Carriage and Communications Under the Tudors and Stuarts* (London, 1967), pp. 98–101.

19. Robinson, *The British Post Office*, p. 59. The speeds achieved on this road averaged less than the 4 to 4½ mph. accomplished on the Dover Road in the same period.

20. See further on, pp. 176–77.

21. See earlier, p. 84.

22. See, for example, "Instructing the Master of a Newfoundland Sack Ship, 1715," *Mariner's Mirror*, 63 (1977), pp. 191–93.

23. Exeter was another rival of Plymouth in the colonial trades. Yet Exeter's trade was oriented even more toward European markets, and her strategic location was less advantageous when there was sea war in the Channel. At the end of the seventeenth century, some of Exeter's investment in Atlantic trades would pass through Barnstable and Bideford on the Bristol Channel.

24. Robinson, *The British Post Office*, p. 60. A series of letters between Bristol and its MPs in December 1695 is an impressive illustration of the speed and reliability of the postal service. See BL, Add. MSS. 5540, fols. 78–93.

25. See GPO, Treasury Letter Book, II, 156–58, 160–61. The Treasury warrant of 2 November 1696 said that the service was being instituted for "the convenience and benefitt of trade." With a scheduled 24 hours from Exeter to Bristol and about 30 hours from Bristol to London, the new service would not reduce the travel time of news from Falmouth, Plymouth, or Exeter to London. Bristol was the intended beneficiary.

26. See GPO Treasury Letter Book, II, 268–69, and Hemmeon, *British Post Office*, p. 103.

27. Housden, "Early Posts," pp. 713–18; Robinson, *The British Post Office*, p. 20.

28. See Defoe, II, 68–69.

29. A. R. B. Haldane, *Three Centuries of Scottish Posts* (Edinburgh, 1971), pp. 39–40.

30. Robinson, *The British Post Office*, p. 139.

31. See, for example, Ian K. Steele, ed., *Atlantic Merchant-Apothecary: Letters of Joseph Cruttenden* (Toronto, 1977), pp. 66, 107–8.

32, The Barbados Council appointed John Dallison as postmaster in 1681 and ordered that all incoming letters be delivered to him. Carl Bridenbaugh and Roberta Bridenbaugh, *No Peace Beyond the Line* (New York, 1972), p. 334.

33. Ibid.

34. *CSPC 1685–1688*, no. 1848. The deputy postmastership of Jamaica was thought to be a lucrative enough appointment by 1781 that Francis Dashwood then offered to pay £200 sterling a year for it. Ellis, *Post Office* p. 93.

35. The instructions are in GPO, Falmouth Packet Book, I, fols. 53, 77. These include no mention of keeping financial accounts or forwarding funds to the GPO.

36. The appointees were Alexander Skene at Barbados, Richard Buckeridge at Antigua, Colonel Anthony Hodges at Montserrat, William Burt at Nevis, John Helding at St. Christopher, and Thomas Wood at Jamaica (ibid., fol. 53).

37. George Saint Lo, a commissioner of the Chatham dockyard, had the powers assigned to him, and he successfully presented John Hinton to replace Alexander Skene (ibid., fols. 99–100). The Neale patent itself does not obviously include the Caribbean islands. See Mary E. Woolley, *The Early History of the Colonial Post-Office* (Providence, R.I., 1894), pp. 27–33.

38. Fairbanks had been the town's cattle herder from 1635 to 1638. See Darrett Rutman, *Winthrop's Boston* (Chapel Hill, N.C., 1965), pp. 175, 190, 194 note, 206. See also Woolley, *Early History*, p. 4.

39. The General Court did fix the price at which oats and hay could be sold to public messengers in January 1673/4 (MHS, *Collections*, 3d ser., 7[1838], p. 49).

40. M. G. Hall, *Edward Randolph and the American colonies, 1676–1703* (Chapel Hill, N.C., 1960), pp. 95, 177. Randolph's incidental expenses, dated 22 December 1687, included these (from MHS, Jeffries MSS, I, fol. 101).

for postage of letters to Rhode Island, etc.	10s.
paid Simon Messanger for carrying Andros's letter to Gov. of Connecticut	£4.15s.
paid Mr. Massey for carrying letter to Piscataqua	£1.15s.

These rates were so high that they must have been expresses, except perhaps for the first item.

41. See J. T. Dixon, "The Problem of Imperial Communications During the Eighteenth Century, with Special Reference to the Post Office," M.A. thesis, University of Leeds, 1964. John Perry's activities as a messenger from 1686 to 1689 may have been regularized. Woolley, *Early History*, pp. 7–8.

42. Lovelace to Secretary of State Joseph Williamson, 3 October 1670, *NYCD*, III, 189.

43. Lovelace to John Winthrop, 27 December 1672, in J. R. Brodhead, *History of the State of New York*, 2 vols. (New York, 1853–1871), II, 196–98. Cf. Smith, *History of the Post Office*, p. 6.

44. Stewart H. Holbrook, *The Old Post Road* (New York, 1962), pp. 1–2, puts the distance at 250 miles. Seymour Dunbar, *History of Travel in America* (New York, 1947), p. 177 note, offers no source for the suggestion that the trip took three weeks each way.

45. Woolley, *Early History*, pp. 6–7.

46. *NYCD*, III, 355; Woolley, *Early History*, pp. 7–8; *CSPC 1681–1685*, no. 1848.

47. See *Dictionary of National Biography* (hereafter *DNB*); Henry Horwitz, *Parliament, Policy and Politics in the Reign of William III* (Manchester, 1977), pp. 111, 129, 130, 137, 190, 207, 212, 220; P. G. M. Dickson, *The Financial Revolution in England* (London, 1967), pp. 45, 52; Ming-Hsun Li, *The Great Recoinage of 1696–9* (London, 1963), pp. 42–43, 74. Neale's petitions to the crown are incredible in their variety, their frequency, and their continuity through three reigns. The colonies interested him only briefly and never exclusively, but he sought the patent for mining gold and silver in Maryland and Virginia (4 August 1691, *CSP Dom 1690–1691*, p. 470); the right to salvage a Spanish ship lost between Florida and Cape Henry (1 October 1691, ibid., p. 535); the right to unclaimed escheated estates in the plantations, rather prematurely noting "the petitioner having now settled a postage in those countries, and having thereby a better opportunity than others" (11 January 1691/2, *CSP Dom 1691–1692*, p. 92); and the right to all mines in the American plantations outside of New England, Virginia, and North Carolina (14 January 1691/2, ibid., p. 98).

48. See John E. Pomfret, *Colonial New Jersey, A History* (New York, 1973), pp. 60, 66–67. Hamilton was reelected governor of East Jersey on 27 March and governor of West Jersey on 11 April and dated his employment under Neale from 24 June 1692. See GPO, Treasury Letter Books, 1/2, p. 264. Cf. Woolley, *Early History*, p. 8, and William Smith, "The Colonial Post Office," *American Historical Review* (hereafter *AHR*), 21 (1915–1916), p. 262.

49. Wooley, *Early History*, Appendix 1, p. 28.

50. Ibid., pp. 10–11; *Colonial Laws of New York from the Year 1664 to the Revolution*, 5 vols. (Albany, 1894–1896), I, 293–96.

51. Hamilton estimated that his trip eastward from New York in March 1693 had cost him £50 New York (GPO, Treasury Letter Books, 1/2, p. 264). For his negotiations with New Hampshire, see N. Boulton, ed., *Documents and Records Relating to the Province of New Hampshire*, 7 vols. (Concord, Mass., 1867–1873) II, 100, 101. On the various colonial acts, see Smith, "The Colonial Post Office," pp. 262–63.

52. The route is described by Daniel Leeds, *An Almanack for the Year . . . 1698* (New York, 1698). It is noteworthy that neither the earl of Bellomont nor Dr. Benjamin Bullivant used the post road when traveling between Boston and New York in that decade. The justly celebrated *The Journal of Madam Knight* describes the trip in 1704 and suggests reasons why it was not popular. See also *The Vade Mecum for America* (Boston, 1732), pp. 195 ff. The GPO list of deputy postmasters in America after 1706 included men at Saybrook, New London, and Stonington (GPO, Post 1/4, 1706–1712, p. 197).

53. Quoted in D. H. Flaherty, *Privacy in Colonial New England* (Charlottesville, Va., 1972), p. 120. On the experiment, see *Boston News-letter*, nos. 555–57, 661 (misnumbered as 658). The fortnightly posts between December and the end of February were first noted in *Boston News-letter*, no. 33.

54. Deputy postmasters, each paid £2 New York money p.a., were on the GPO list after 1706 (GPO Post 1/4, p. 197).

55. John Campbell repeatedly claimed that the post office saved the Massachusetts government about £150 p.a. in express charges (MHS, *Collections*, 3d ser., 7[1838], pp. 61–63, 66–67, 69–70, 81–82).

56. The population of New England in 1700 is estimated as 92,763 in *Historical Statistics*, Series Z, 1–19. Approximately 66 percent of adult males and about 40 percent of adult females could sign their name. See K. A. Lockridge, *Literacy in Colonial New England* (New York, 1974), passim, and compare William J. Gilmore, "Elementary Literacy on the Eve of the Industrial Revolution: Trends in Rural New England, 1760–1830," AAS *Proceedings*, 92 (1983), 87 ff.

57. Seamen in the service of the Massachusetts government had their pay fixed at 24s. per month in 1694. (C. P. Nettels, *The Money Supply in the American Colonies before 1720* [Madison, Wis., 1934], p. 71 note).

58. The Massachusetts Post Office Act of 1693 was disallowed in 1696, the year it expired, but it provided the postal rates in the meantime. Key rates (to or from Boston) were as follows: Rhode Island, 6d.; Connecticut, 9d.; New York, 12d; Pennsylvania, 15d. It would take 10,928 letters paying 6d. to generate the postal revenues of the New England post roads and offices in the year ending 1 May 1697. See *CSPC 1693–1696*, no. 228. A memo, probably by John Campbell, placed the postal revenues for the month of June 1703 at £21.17.4 for the New England posts. If such a revenue were generated each month, it would amount to £262.8s., approximate to the revenues of the 1696–1697 year (MHS, *Collections*, 3d ser., 7[1838], pp. 65–66).

59. One intriguing comparison with yet another unsubstantiated estimate for the United States in 1790 "puts the total number of letters carried at 265,545. This figure, if correct, would mean that scarcely one letter per fifteen persons was delivered over the full twelve-month period" (Allan R. Pred, *Urban Growth and the Circulation of Information* [Cambridge, Mass., 1973], p. 79). By 1840 there were two letters per person delivered in the United States per year (ibid., p. 81).

60. See Governor Cornbury to Board of Trade, 19 February 1704/5. *CSPC 1704–1705*, no. 876. The proclamation was entirely ineffective because the trading links between colonies forced governments that attempted to enforce the proclamation to face the mass export of coin to places that were more flexible. For examples, see PRO,

CO 5/1263, fol. 153–54 (Pennsylvania); CO 5/1362, pp. 269–70 (Virginia); CO 28/10, fol. 95 (Leewards). The failure prompted legislation that was not effective either (PRO, CO 324/9, pp. 143–45); *Statutes of the Realm*, VIII, 792–93; C. M. Andrews, *The Colonial Period of American History*, 4 vols. (New Haven, 1934–1938), IV, 166.

61. Cornbury rightly claimed on 10 August 1706 that Boston merchants controlled the bulk of New York's trade to England (PRO, CO 5/1049, fol. 94).

62. The pay of the postrider and of the man who kept the post office in Philadelphia was dated from 22 August 1693 (GPO, Post 1/2, fol. 265).

63. Smith, "The Colonial Post Office," p. 262, and W. E. Rich, *The History of the United States Post Office to the Year 1829* (Cambridge, Mass., 1924), p. 16.

64. The receipts of the Philadelphia post totaled only £115.13.1 for the 54 months down to February 1698. At an average of only £25.11.0 per annum, this would amount to only about 1/5d. per person for the inhabitants of Pennsylvania, New Jersey, and Delaware without considering any mail paid for at Philadelphia that would be bound further south (GPO, Post 1/2, fol. 265; *Historical Statistics*, series Z, 1–19).

65. After the patent was bought out in 1706, the GPO calculated the annual costs on this route as follows (GPO, Post 1/4, p. 197).

	£ s. d.
A boat from New York to Elizabethtown point	40
Deputy at Perth Amboy	5
Deputy at Burlington	5
Deputy at Philadelphia	30
Rider from New York to Philadelphia	45
TOTAL (New York currency)	£125

66. For a description of the road, see Daniel Leeds, *An Almanack for . . . 1694* (New York, 1694).

67. HSP, William Penn's Letterbook, 1699–1703, p. 106.

68. Sharpas, who described himself as a gentleman and was rather wealthy, was also New York City clerk (GPO, Post 1/2, fol. 264; Thomas J. Archdeacon, *New York City 1664–1710: Conquest and Change* [Ithaca, N.Y., 1976], p. 62).

69. The proceeds were (for year ending 1 May) these: (1694) £61.4.0, (1695) £82.11.3, (1696) £93.12.2½, and (1697) £122.17.0 (GPO, Post 1/2, fol. 265).

70. These calculations are based on the New York population as 19,107 as per *Historical Statistics*, series Z, 1–19.

71. Andrew Hamilton's account of the post office finances from 1693 to 1697 is as instructive here as elsewhere. Hamilton, who certainly would regret Heyman's appointment by 1697 regardless of what he thought of it initially, noted:

> To an allowance of £100 sterling per annum given by Mr. Neale himself to Peter Hayman Deputy Postmaster of Virginia & Maryland 2 years and 11 months and settling Ferrys & incident Charges £436.3.4 sterling is in New York money with an allowance of £30 Per Cent Exchange —— £530.17.0 [GPO, Post 1/3, fol. 264].

72. *CSPC 1693–1696*, nos. 175, 188, 201, 220, 235; W. W. Hening, ed., *The Statutes at Large Being a Collection of All the Laws of Virginia*, 13 vols. (Richmond, Va., 1809–1923), III, 112–15.

73. The council referred a petition for a subvention to the House of Burgesses in

November 1693 and 17 months later would claim that they had done all they could with the assembly in the matter and could suggest nothing further (*CSPC 1693–1696*, nos. 671, 1430, 1454, 1804).

74. *CSPC 1693–1696*, no. 1975.
75. Council minute of 24 September 1694, *Archives of Maryland*, XIX, 35, 46, 54, 176. The matter came up again in 1697 (ibid., p. 563; XXIII, 69).
76. *CSPC 1693–1696*, nos. 1816, 1832, 1833, 1849; *Archives of Maryland*, XX, 246–47. See also note 41 earlier concerning Perry.
77. *CSPC 1693–1696*, no. 2091; *Archives of Maryland*, XX, 370–71, 376, 402; XXII, 64, 124, 171, 176, 188, 191–92, 235, 255, 258, 259; XXIII, 9, 221–22, 295–98, 345–46, 432, 507.
78. GPO, Post 1/2, fols. 252–55, 264–65. Neale's price was £5000 or £1000 a year for life.
79. See further on, pp. 150–51.
80. Hugh Jones, *The Present State of Virginia*, ed. R. L. Morton (Chapel Hill, N.C., 1956), p. 73.
81. Andrew Hamilton sought British government support for a post from Newcastle (Delaware) to James City in 1699. He estimated the cost at £300 a year for two years, which was as optimistic as his hope that this service would be self-supporting within two or three years (GPO, Treasury 2, p. 258).
82. See PRO, CO 5/1289, pp. 21–25, Penn to the Board of Trade 13 December 1700.
83. See *CSPC 1702–1703*, nos. 761, 944.
84. *CSPC 1704–1705* no. 427. The cost of sending an express from Virginia to New York in the mid-1690's was, according to William Byrd, £15 (Marion Tinling, ed., *The Correspondence of the Three William Byrds of Westover Virginia 1684–1776*, 2 vols. [Charlottesville, Va., 1977], I, 177).
85. The governors were on their way north for yet another governors' conference in New York. See *Boston News-letter*, nos., 702, 704, 705; cf. Smith, "The Colonial Post Office," pp. 268–69. For Alexander Spotswood's interest in such a service as early as 1710, see further on, note 101.
86. See *Boston News-letter* no. 708. The first news item from Williamsburg that appeared in the paper was datelined 56 days earlier than printing (ibid., no. 723).
87. Quoted in Rich, *History of U.S. Post*, p. 28.
88. Dixon, "Imperial Communications," pp. 195–96.
89. 9 Anne ch. 10.
90. The main grievance was the charge for delivery of ship letters that were not directly trade related and the monopoly of delivery of the same that belonged to the post office by the act. In several important respects, the act accomplished changes that Andrew Hamilton had pleaded unsuccessfully for in reporting to the postmasters general in 1699. See GPO, Post 1/2, fols. 252–55, 264–65.
91. For Spotswood's account of this, see *CSPC 1717–1718*, no. 568.
92. *American Weekly Mercury* for August 1720, no. 33. This ad was repeated in no. 35, and an earlier version had appeared 21 July 1720 in this same paper. In this version, Hill gave "Notice to all Gentlemen, Merchants or others that have Occasion to send a Messenger to any part of the British Continent."
93. James Craggs, Jr., was a friend of George I before his accession to the English throne, and the family was in considerable favor until the bursting of the South Sea Bubble. See *DNB*; John Carswell, *The South Sea Bubble* (London, 1961), passim.
94. A John Lloyd served as one of Barbados's agents for the whole period 1715–1720, but it is not clear whether this was the same man. In 1720 the South Carolina government allowed him £1000 for a trip to England. See L. Penson, *The Colonial*

Agents of the British West Indies (London, 1924), p. 250; Ella Lonn, *The Colonial Agents of the Southern Colonies* (Chapel Hill, N.C., 1945), pp. 71, 277, 308–9.

95. *Boston News-letter*, no. 974.

96. Lloyd was active in South Carolina politics within four months of arriving in Boston (Lonn, *Colonial Agents*, p. 255; M. Eugene Sirmans, *Colonial South Carolina: A Political History 1663-1763* [Chapel Hill, N.C., 1966], pp. 139, 141, 146, 151, 181-82.

97. *American Weekly Mercury* for 26 February 1722/3 and the *Boston Gazette* of 11 March following. The advertisements were placed by a William Atkinson.

98. *American Weekly Mercury* of 4 April 1728, repeated in ibid., no. 433, and *New York Gazette* of 8 April 1728.

99. In addition to the papers cited in footnote no. 98, see *American Weekly Mercury*, nos. 436, and especially 441, where the details of the service are given, including stages and rates.

100. Parks's *Maryland Gazette* for 31 December 1728 notes that the post would set out for Philadelphia a week later.

101. In addition to the earlier discussion, see his letter to the Board of Trade of 24 October 1710, printed in *Collections of the Virginia Historical Society*, new series, I, 21.

102. *New York Gazette* for 31 July 1732 is the fullest account. See also the *American Weekly Mercury*, nos. 653, 655.

103. The project was probably an instant disappointment to its initiator; the silence in the newspapers after July 1732 contrasts ominously with the enthusiasm of the previous month, and nothing direct or incidental appears to suggest the service continued. In March 1735/6 Andrew Bradford advertised for a postrider for the Philadelphia-to-Annapolis route (*American Weekly Mercury*, no. 846). This ad appeared only once but could not have resulted in a service of any regularity without such being advertised in the same paper. All these various brief initiatives do not challenge J. T. Dixon's claim ("Imperial Communications," p. 145) that there was no postal service south to Williamsburg before 1738.

104. See Fairfax Harrison, "The Colonial Post Office in Virginia," *W&MQ*, 2d ser., 4 (1924), p. 21.

105. *Virginia Gazette* of 28 April 1738, Harrison, "Colonial Post Office," p. 83.

106. Spotswood's salary was to be £300 sterling per year plus 10 percent of clear profits. The proceeds of the post office had doubtlessly grown very considerably to provide for salaries of postmasters and riders on additional routes and provide for the deputy postmaster general's salary as was not the case early in the century. See Table 7.3. Franklin's sending a surplus revenue to England earned him plaudits at the expense of his predecessors but exaggerates his contribution and underestimates what had been achieved earlier.

Chapter 8. THE PAPERS

1. See Bernard Bailyn and Lotte Bailyn, *Massachusetts Shipping* (Cambridge, Mass., 1959), especially pp. 82–87, 94–97, 102–5, 122–23.

2. *Boston News-letter* (hereafter *BNL*), no. 105. The ads had appeared in nos. 86, 87, and 89.

3. I. K. Steele, "Time, Communications and Society: The English Atlantic, 1702," *Journal of American Studies*, 8 (1974), pp. 9–10.

4. R. S. Crane and F. B. Kaye, *A Census of British Newspapers and Periodicals, 1620-1800* (Chapel Hill, N.C., 1927), and K. K. Weed and R. P. Bond, *Studies of British Newspapers and Periodicals from Their Beginning to 1800: A Bibliography* (Chapel

Hill, N.C., 1946), are particularly useful concerning British newspapers as are the following general works: H. R. Fox Bourne, *English Newspapers*, 2 vols. (London, 1893); Laurence Hanson, *Government and the Press* (London, 1936); Stanley Morison, *The English Newspaper: Some Account of the Physical Development of Journals Printed in London Between 1622 and the Present Day* (Cambridge, 1932). The provincial English press has been particularly well served by G. A. Cranfield, *The Development of the Provincial Newspaper, 1700–1760* (Oxford, 1962), and by R. M. Wiles, *Freshest Advices: Early Provincial Newspapers in England* (Columbus, Ohio, 1965). Robert Munter's *The History of the Irish Newspaper, 1685–1760* (Cambridge, 1967)—hereafter *Irish Newspapers*—is sound, and one could wish for a comparable work on the Scottish press. For the American colonial press, the basic finding aid is still Clarence S. Brigham, *History and Bibliography of American Newspapers, 1690–1820*, 2 vols. (Worcester, Mass., 1947); and the following general works are particularly helpful: Sidney Kobre, *The Development of the Colonial Newspaper* (Pittsburgh, 1944); James M. Lee, *History of American Journalism* (Boston, 1923); Leonard Levy, *Legacy of Suppression: Freedom of Speech and Press in Early American History* (Cambridge, Mass., 1960); Frank L. Mott, *American Journalism* (New York, 1941); and Isaiah Thomas, *The History of Printing in America*, 2 vols. (Albany, 1874).

5. This definition is derived from Joseph Frank, *The Beginnings of the English Newspaper, 1620–1660* (Cambridge, Mass., 1961), pp. 1–2. In the context of time-perception, two items are worthy of note here. When Roger L'Estrange launched his *The Intelligencer* in August 1663, he suggested that "once a week may do the business, for I intend to utter my news by weight and not by measure." See Fox Bourne, *English Newspapers*, I, 35–36. Benjamin Harris, that transplanted London publisher, launched his one and only issue of the Boston, Massachusetts, paper *Publick Occurrances Both Forreign and Domestick*, dated 25 September 1690, with the more leisurely claim that the paper would be "furnished once a moneth (or if any Glut of Occurrences happen, oftener)" (Mott, *American Journalism*, p. 9).

6. Frank, *Beginnings*, pp. 2–3.

7. By the 1586 Star Chamber ordinance there were to be no more than 20 master printers in the realm. One could be in Oxford, one in Cambridge, and one in York, but all others except the queen's printer were to be in London, supervised by the London Stationers Company.

8. Frank, *Beginnings*, p. 13.

9. Ibid., pp. 57–58, 146. The London population estimate of 400,000 in 1650 is from E. A. Wrigley, "A Simple Model of London's Importance in Changing English Society and Economy, 1650–1750," *Past and Present*, 37 (1967), p. 44. This is not to suggest that copies of London papers were not sent out by mail, carriers, and travelers to the countryside. Yet Frank's study presents ample evidence to support his conclusion that "the vast majority of weeklies were addressed to Londoners, permanent and transient, for it was only in the city that enough people, interest, and news existed to justify printing a newspaper" (*Beginnings*, p. 271).

10. There was a brief suspension of effective control late in 1679 and early the following year until the legal gap was filled by royal proclamation. Upon James II's flight from England in December 1688 there was a brief flurry of new, unlicensed newspapers, but they quickly disappeared. See Fox Bourne, *English Newspapers*, I, 50.

11. See Frank, *Beginnings*, chaps. 11–14; Fox Bourne, *English Newspapers*, I, 20–26; and P. M. Handover, *A History of the London Gazette 1665–1965* (London, 1965), pp. 3–4.

12. Fox Bourne, *English Newspapers*, I, 28–29; 13 and 14 Car. II, c. 33.

13. For the case of one Twyn, see Fox Bourne, *English Newspapers*, I, 37–39.

14. The impeachment of Chief Justice Scroggs showed the Commons' reaction to this method of licensing, but the approach worked in England and in the colonies, where instructions to governors became the initial vehicle for control.

15. It has been claimed that Muddiman had "hundreds of correspondents, and . . . he invariably refused a less fee than £5 a year for his news-letters," and a list of some 134 letters of his sent in one week suggests a very wide service running the length of each of the major post roads, and including Irish and Scottish recipients. See J. G. Muddiman, *The King's Journalist, 1659–1689* (London, 1923), pp. 166, 258–64. Hanson, *Government*, p. 84, mentions that the newsletters accepted the *London Gazette*'s coverage of foreign news (and presumably its wide circulation) by making a point of not covering foreign news at all.

16. In the first year, the *London Gazette* had six stories datelined from the English West Indies and numerous mentions of ships into the outports from North American and West Indian colonies. In the year beginning 18 November 1675, which was particularly eventful in North American English colonies, there were only five stories dated from English colonies, and these did not include anything specifically on Bacon's Rebellion. The outport shipping notices were gone from the paper by this time, being replaced by advertisements.

17. "Except in its emptiness and worthlessness there was nothing notable about 'The London Gazette' in these or later years," wrote Fox Bourne, *English Newspapers*, I, 41.

18. *The Lives of the Norths*, ed. A. Jessop, 3 vols. (London, 1890), II, 292. Kirk kept a coffeehouse in Cambridge.

19. Hordesnell to William Blathwayt, Bermuda, 29 September 1688 (Blathwayt Papers, Colonial Williamsburg, vol. xxxvi). For an earlier example, see Thomas Lynch to Joseph Williamson, Jamaica, 7 March 1671/2, *CSPC 1669–1674*, no. 776.

20. Matthias A. Shaaber, "Forerunners of the Newspaper in America," *Journalism Quarterly*, 11 (1934), pp. 339–47, cites several items of interest. The *London Gazette* was directly reprinted in Boston on the death of King Charles II (no. 2006, 9 February 1684–5); in New York in 1696 concerning a naval engagement with the French; and in Boston twice in 1714 concerning the accession of George I; and an account of the marriage of the Prince of Wales was reprinted in New York from the same source in 1736. See Charles Evans, *The American Bibliography of Charles Evans*, 14 vols. (Worcester, Mass., 1959), nos. 388, 746, 4031, and Roger P. Bristol, *Supplement to Charles Evans' American Bibliography* (Charlottesville, Va., 1970), nos. B448, B451. B. Green of Boston reprinted an account of the Hapsburg victory over the Turks, which was a broadside reprinted from Ichabod Dawk's *Dawk's Newsletter* (Evans, *American Bibliography*, no. 787). York was the only English county town with a printer during this period, and no such broadsides are known to have been printed there. For Ireland, see further on, note 69.

21. See Hanson, *Government*, pp. 7–10.

22. Robert Munter has emphasized that the Irish press grew at approximately the same time but not because of the changes of 1695. See his *Irish Newspapers*, pp. 15 and 100. The Scottish and colonial presses seem also to emerge in the wake of this legislative change, but again the connection does not seem direct and may be no more than coincidence.

23. On Harris, see *DAB*; Winthrop S. Hudson, "William Penn's *English Liberties*: Tract for Several Times," *W&MQ*, 3d ser. 26 (1969), pp. 578–85, and see earlier, p. 106.

24. J. R. Sutherland, "The Circulation of Newspapers and Literary Periodicals, 1700–1730," *The Library*, 4th ser., 15 (1934), p. 116. The total circulation amounted to 43,800 per week.

25. Fox Bourne, *English Newspapers*, I, 69; G. Holmes, *British Politics in the Age of Anne* (London, 1967), p. 30.
26. Hanson, *Government*, pp. 93, 97–98.
27. Frank, *Beginnings*, pp. 156–57; Wiles, *Advices*, pp. 4–9.
28. By 1704 these two papers accounted for 20,600 of the 43,800 total weekly production of newspapers in London. See Sutherland, "Circulation," p. 111.
29. Later issues of *Warwick and Staffordshire Journal* were no longer printed in London. Wiles, *Advices*, p. 7.
30. See Hanson, *Government*, pp. 135–38, and J. A. Downie, *Robert Harley and the Press* (Cambridge, 1979), passim.
31. Hanson, *Government*, p. 42.
32. Ibid., p. 109; Cranfield, *Development*, pp. 147–48.
33. Fox Bourne, *English Newspapers*, I, 124.
34. Cranfield, *Development*, pp. 176–80.
35. Lawrence C. Wroth, *The Colonial Printer* (New York, 1931), pp. 12–13. Wroth was under the impression that the Licensing Act expired in 1693, but there was a two-year extension beyond that year. This adds only William Bradford's New York press to his list.
36. Wiles, *Advices*, pp. 14–16; Cranfield, *Development*, p. 8.
37. Wiles, *Advices*, Appendixes B and C.
38. Ibid., pp. 14, 23.
39. The *Oxford Journal* seems to have appeared briefly in 1736, and the *Oxford Flying Weekly Journal* did not appear until a decade later. Cambridge had no paper until the *Cambridge Journal* appeared in 1744 (Wiles, *Advices*, pp. 396, 477). The York printer John White, succeeded by his wife, Grace, may have helped with the local circulation of *The Newcastle Courant*, published by John White, Jr., from August 1711. When Grace White published York's first paper, the *York Mercury* in February 1718/9, it was not for sale in Newcastle. See R. Davies, *A Memoir of the York Press* (London, 1868), pp. 132–33; Wiles, *Advices*, p. 452.
40. Penelope Corfield, "A Provincial Capital in the Late Seventeenth Century: The Case of Norwich," in Peter Clark and Paul Slack, eds., *Crisis and Order in English Towns 1500–1700* (London, 1972), pp. 263–310.
41. See Howard Robinson, *The British Post Office: A History* (Princeton, 1948), pp. 30, 32, 66, 82.
42. His name was George Rose. Wiles, *Advices*, pp. 5–6.
43. Cranfield, *Development*, p. 12.
44. Corfield, "Norwich," p. 288; Wiles, *Advices*, pp. 463–68.
45. W. E. Minchinton, "Bristol—metropolis of the west in the eighteenth century," *Transactions of the Royal Historical Society* (hereafter *TRHS*), 5th ser., 4 (1954), pp. 69–89.
46. Dr. Wild, quoted in John Dunton, *The Life and Errors of . . .* , 2 vols., 2d ed. (London, 1818), I, xxxii.
47. Cranfield, *Development*, pp. 8, 247–48.
48. Ibid., p. 169, and J. M. Price, "A Note on the Circulation of the London Press, 1704–1714," *Bulletin of the Institute of Historical Research* (hereafter *BIHR*), 31 (1958), p. 220. New information suggests that the paper lived two years longer than the last surviving copy indicates. Wiles, *Advices*, p. 383. *Sam. Farley's Bristol Post Man* began in February 1712/3.
49. Bristol had two papers during the lifetime of the *Bristol Weekly Mercury* (October 1715–May 1727).
50. Wiles, *Advices*, pp. 412–19.

51. See W. G. Hoskins, *Industry, Trade and People in Exeter 1688–1800*, 2d ed. (Exeter, 1968), chap. 1.
52. In 1671 the population was approximately 11,234. In 1800, when the town was in decline, it numbered 16,827 souls (ibid., pp. 114, 127).
53. See earlier, pp. 117–18; Hoskins, *Exeter*, p. 27.
54. Wiles, *Advices*, pp. 14–16, 23.
55. Ibid., Appendixes B and C.
56. Ibid., pp. 198, 226, 252–53; Cranfield, *Development*, chap. 4.
57. Cranfield, *Development*, chap. 8.
58. Ibid., chap. 9. Andrew Hooke's *Bristol Oracle* is an exception to this general practice.
59. Ibid., pp. 205–6.
60. Ibid., pp. 66, 82.
61. The stories concerned ship arrivals, loss of a ship to pirates, and a report of rain falling on one particular tree. They appeared in no. 28, 28 January 1715/6. The six surviving issues, nos. 24–29, are in the Bristol Reference Library.
62. The stories are datelined 3, 10, and 14 October 1715, as they were in *BNL*, nos. 559–61, 10–24 October 1715. When reprinted in Bristol, these accounts were between three and four months old. Such a time lapse was acceptable enough at the time to make R. M. Wiles's derision (*Advices*, p. 62) anachronistic.
63. Cranfield, *Development*, p. 263.
64. Quoted in ibid.
65. *Boston Gazette*, no. 72.
66. *BNL*, no. 51, 9 April 1705.
67. L. C. Wroth, *William Parks, Printer and Journalist of England and Colonial America* (Richmond, Va., 1926), pp. 9–11.
68. L. M. Cullen, *An Economic History of Ireland Since 1660* (London, 1972), p. 19; Munter, *Irish Newspapers*, pp. 12, 16; Robert Munter, *A Handlist of Irish Newspapers 1685–1750* (London, 1960), p. 1 (hereafter *A Handlist*).
69. Ten issues of the *London Gazette* were reprinted between December 1700 and March 1702/3, and many more papers including *The London Post-man, The Medley, The Tatler, The Examiner, The Observator, Englishman, The Daily Courant, The Country Gentleman*, were reprinted in Dublin. See Munter, *A Handlist*, pp. 1–29.
70. Munter, *Irish Newspapers*, p. 17.
71. Munter, *A Handlist*, passim.
72. Ibid., pp. 30–31.
73. Ibid., pp. 29–30.
74. W. J. Couper, *The Edinburgh Periodical Press*, 2 vols. (Stirling, Scotland, 1908), I, 40–53, 163–78; Munter, *Irish Newspapers*, pp. 5–6.
75. Couper, *Edinburgh*, I, 52–53, 170–74, 184–87.
76. Ibid., pp. 188–89.
77. J. D. Mackie, *A History of Scotland* (Harmondsworth, 1964), p. 247.
78. Couper, *Edinburgh*, I, 120.
79. If three hours of press time is estimated and if a single press was used, a run of 375 could have been ready for sale. A second press, printing the reverse side of this single sheet, would nearly double the output. See D. Nichol Smith, "The Newspaper" in A. S. Turberville's, *Johnson's England*, 2 vols. (Oxford, 1933), II, 333–34. Even a run of 375 would have been very substantial for an English-language newspaper outside London in that generation.
80. Couper, *Edinburgh*, I, 40.

81. Ibid., I, 236.
82. Glasgow had a population of 30,000 before 1700. Mackie, *Scotland*, p. 247. Aside from the rather short-lived *Glasgow Courant* of 1715, the city had no newspaper before the *Glasgow Journal* began in 1741. Couper, *Edinburgh*, pp. 44, 119.
83. See Thomas, *Printing in America*, I, 42–84.
84. C. Bridenbaugh, *Cities in the Wilderness* (New York, 1938), p. 6.
85. C. A. Duniway, *The Development of Freedom of the Press in Massachusetts* (New York, 1906), pp. 42–61.
86. See Evans, *American Bibliography*, I, no. 388. This was the only issue of the *London Gazette* that was printed in colonial Boston. For reactions to the news, see *Letterbook of Samuel Sewall*, 2 vols. (Boston, 1886–1888), I, 2; *The Diary of Samuel Sewall*, 3 vols. (Boston, 1878–1882), I, 69, 70; *Diary of Cotton Mather*, 2 vols. (New York, 1957), I, 93, 94.
87. See earlier, pp. 104–6.
88. Duniway, *Development*, pp. 67–68; Evans, *American Bibliography*, no. 492.
89. This source cannot be traced, but it was not likely a printed paper. Nothing like it is listed in Crane and Kaye, *Census*.
90. Cf. Lee, *American Journalism*, p. 17.
91. Examples of Harris's publishing for the Mathers include Evans, *American Bibliography*, nos. 535, 540, 563, 566, 568, 623. As printer to the government, Harris printed *The Acts and Laws of Massachusetts* in 1692 and 1693, as well as small tasks. See Evans, *American Bibliography*, nos. 616–620.
92. The manual, by Harris's hero James Fitzroy, duke of Monmouth, was entitled *An Abridgement of the English Military Discipline Printed by Special Command for the use of Their Majesties Forces* (Boston, 1690). See Evans, *American Bibliography*, no. 508.
93. Ibid., no. 513.
94. Quoted in Thomas, *Printing in America*, p. 94.
95. The paper is conveniently reprinted in Lee, *American Journalism*, pp. 10–15.
96. See Evans, *American Bibliography*, no. 545.
97. Cotton Mather to John Cotton, 17 October 1690, printed in V. H. Paltsits, "New Light on 'Publick Occurrences' America's First Newspaper," AAS *Proceedings*, 59 (1949), pp. 87–88.
98. Duniway, *Development*, p. 69.
99. Duncan had been a confidant of Governor Bellomont when the latter was in Boston, had been chosen as the town's postmaster by his fellow Scot Andrew Hamilton, and would serve as the earl's negotiator in the entrapment of another Scot, Captain William Kidd. Duncan died early in 1702. John cannot have been his son and most likely was his brother. See *Acts and Resolves Public and Private of the Province of Massachusetts Bay, 1869–1922*, ed. A. C. Goodell, 21 vols. (Boston, 1869–1922), VIII, 283 note, and John Dunton, *Letters Written from New England a.d. 1686* (Boston, 1867), p. 80 note.
100. Letters of 12, 27 April; 3, 17 May; 1, 7 June; 12 July; 20 September; and mid-October 1703 are printed in MHS *Proceedings*, 9 (1867), pp. 485–501. Kobre, *Colonial Newspaper*, p. 17, goes well beyond the evidence on the extent of the service.
101. *Newsletter* was an uncommon name for a newspaper, perhaps because of the competition between newsletters and newspapers. *Dawk's Newsletter* and the *Limerick Newsletter* are two examples, the one before (1696) and the other after (1716) Campbell's venture began. Benjamin Green had reprinted Dawk's account of the imperial victory over the Turks in 1697: *Yesterday Morning Arrived Three Holland*

Mails . . . (Boston, 1697). Bostonians had some earlier acquaintance with something called the "London newsletter," which was probably handwritten.

102. MHS *Proceedings*, 9 (1867), pp. 488, 489, 499.
103. Campbell listed obtaining official approval among his onerous tasks as publisher (*BNL*, no. 51). He still managed to be reprimanded by the governor for offending the Quaker community on one occasion (*CSPC 1706–1708*, nos. 510, 511).
104. See Lee, *American Journalism*, p. 19.
105. *BNL*, no. 51, 9 April 1705. The Exeter paper was probably cheaper, at 2d. sterling, but Campbell said that it cost 20s. a year delivered whereas his paper cost only 12s. He undoubtedly meant sterling, which would translate at about 16s. in Massachusetts currency, according to John J. McCusker, *Money and Exchange in Europe and America, 1600–1775, A Handbook* (Chapel Hill, N.C., 1978), p. 140. Campbell had, of course, the advantages of being postmaster whereas Farley had not.
106. MHS *Collections*, 3d series, 7 (1838), pp. 67–68.
107. Ibid., p. 80.
108. *BNL*, no. 799, 10 August 1719.
109. In the summer of 1706, his list of prints for sale included individual copies of Bills of Entry and Prices Current as well as these (*BNL*, no. 112).
110. *BNL*, no. 51, 9 April 1705.
111. Ibid., no. 672, 4 March 1716/17.
112. Ibid., no. 1412, 18 February 1730/31.
113. "Domestick Intelligences" was the title used in no. 616 to introduce items from Virginia, Pennsylvania, New York, and Rhode Island. Then, after a small space but no new heading, was news from Edinburgh and London, which probably arrived late (*BNL*, no. 952, 30 April 1722). In no. 938, news from Boston and from Albany, New York, were both considered "Home news."
114. One striking example of this occurred in the *Boston Gazette*, no. 342, on 20 June 1726. One item reports that the HMS *Greyhound*, Captain Solgard, had touched at Madeira according to a recently arrived vessel. Another item in the same issue reported that this popular naval commander and his ship had arrived at Jamaica. This report, by a sloop into New York in 19 days from Jamaica, was 2 months younger than the other, yet they were contemporaneous in Boston.
115. *BNL*, no. 137, 2 December 1706. This method was followed perfectly in the year ending in April 1712. See *BNL*, nos. 366–418.
116. Ibid., no. 216, 7 June 1708.
117. Ibid., nos. 948–52. This kind of concern is not evident in English provincial newspapers. The *Northampton Mercury* of 4 April 1721 was interested in having news come in order, was confident that this was happening, and urged readers to keep their copies in their libraries as a newsman's diary (Cranfield, *Development*, p. 258).
118. The problem was particularly acute in wartime. For an elegant statement of the problem later and a determination to tell a coherent story, see the *Pennsylvania Gazette* for 22 January 1744/5, no. 841.
119. *BNL*, nos. 799, 806, 10 August and 28 September 1719.
120. R. M. Wiles, *Advices*, pp. 68–71.
121. *BNL*, no. 849.
122. *BNL*, no. 852, 11 July 1720.
123. *BNL*, no. 882, 6 February 1720/21. The other story was an item about Jamaica in no. 880, 23 January 1720/21. In this case, the item was seven months old and received via the London *Daily Courant* of September date, an indication of the severe loss of intercolonial news that came after Campbell lost his postmastership.
124. Nine issues of the *Courant*, ranging from 30 July 1718 to 24 June 1730, are known

to have survived. On the ingenious restoration of the first two issues, see *British Museum Quarterly*, 9 (1936), pp. 20–21. The other issues, from 11 February 1719 to 24 June 1730, are in the PRO, CO 127 series. Citations in North American newspapers before 1740 are *BNL*, no. 889; *Boston Gazette*, nos. 159, 369; *American Weekly Mercury*, nos. 157, 659, and 967. Isaiah Thomas, *Printing in America*, II, 185, suggested that the paper survived at least until 1755. See also Frank Cundall, *A History of Printing in Jamaica from 1717 to 1834* (Kingston, 1935), corrected by Douglas C. McMurtrie, *The First Printing in Jamaica* (Evanston, Ill., 1942).

125. Daniel J. Boorstin, *The Americans: The Colonial Experience* (New York, 1958), p. 327. On the population of Kingston, see Colin G. Clarke, *Kingston, Jamaica: Urban Development and Social Change, 1692–1962* (Berkeley, 1975), p. 141, Table I.

126. Although Green shifted his publication day from Monday to Thursday because the intercolonial post was less crucial to him now, the two papers were serving a larger audience than the *News-letter* had in 1719. See Thomas, *Printing in America*, II, 22. If a minimum number of 200 copies is accepted for viability, Boston was buying something approaching 400 copies a week in 1720.

127. *BNL*, nos. 783, 790, 791.

128. See Wiles, *Advices*, Appendix B. For Nottingham's population, see J. D. Chambers, "Population Change in a Provincial Town: Nottingham 1700–1800," in L. S. Pressnell, ed., *Studies in the Industrial Revolution* (London, 1960), p. 122.

129. *Boston Gazette*, nos. 1, 3, dated 21 December 1719 and 4 January 1719/20.

130. Ibid., nos. 310, 396, 448, 515, 754, 777.

131. Andrew Bradford advertised in the *Boston Gazette* for a servant of his, Nicholas Classon, in June 1728 (*Boston Gazette*, nos. 448–50). William Parks advertised for a runaway in October 1729, inviting those who took him up to deliver him to Andrew Bradford in Philadelphia, William Bradford in New York, or to "Mr. Marshall, Post-Master in Boston" (ibid., nos. 515–16). Henry Marshall published the paper and served as postmaster, between 1727 and his death in May 1732.

132. Issue of 28 August 1738. The *Boston Gazette*, no. 59, of 30 January 1720/21 carried what was probably an unpaid public service announcement that the government of Ireland had erected a lighthouse at Loop Head at the mouth of the Shannon River.

> It is thought proper to Advertise the Publick thereof, that the Merchants of these and other Parts may give Notice of it to the Commanders of the Ships which may come on that Coast by Night, in order to prevent the ill Consequences of their being Surprised, or thinking themselves on any other Coast.

133. The *Pennsylvania Gazette* put the matter even more directly when recording in May 1733 that a ship had arrived in six weeks "but as he has brought no Prints, we have no Intelligence that can be depended on" (No. 235).

134. The paper had been published for William Brooker in its first few weeks, for Philip Musgrave from 1720 to 1726, for Thomas Lewis before his early death in May 1732, and then for John Boydell, who, like Campbell, continued his paper after he lost the postmastership in 1734. He continued to publish it until his death in 1739, and his heirs carried on for two more years.

135. Franklin printed the first 35 numbers of the *Gazette* before being replaced by Samuel Kneeland (Thomas, *Printing in America*, II, 28–29).

136. Duniway, *Development*, pp. 93–103; Perry Miller, *The New England Mind: From Colony to Province* (Cambridge, Mass., 1953), pp. 333–42.

137. The *Boston Gazette* stayed with the post-related Monday; the *Boston News-letter* moved to the second most popular day for newspapers, Thursday; and the *Courant* appeared on Saturday. Boston had no fixed market days despite attempts. See G. B. Warden, *Boston, 1689–1776* (Boston, 1970), pp. 53–55, 74, 76–77.

138. J. R. Pole, *The Gift of Government: Political Responsibility from the English Restoration to American Independence* (Athens, Ga., 1983), p. 121.

139. Thomas, *Printing in America*, II, 43; Kobre, *Colonial Newspaper*, pp. 48–49.

140. James Franklin and Samuel Kneeland.

141. See Wiles, *Advices*, Appendix B.

142. Nos. 341–43.

143. Ibid., nos. 611, 614.

144. *American Weekly Mercury*, no. 136, 19 July 1722.

145. *American Weekly Mercury*, No. 1, 22 December 1719. Postmasters would receive the papers post-free.

146. See nos. 117, 197, 245, 323, 363, 532, 583.

147. See Thomas, *Printing in America*, II, 132–33. The names appeared again on the paper between December 1739 and November 1740.

148. See Lee, *American Journalism*, p. 36. For Bradford's own explanation for beginning the paper and his account of his losses in running it, see no. 137 for 17 June 1728.

149. James Franklin's *Courant* may have served those unhappy with the existing order in Boston, but the paper was launched by yet another displaced printer of the *Gazette* there, not by the political opposition group.

150. Kobre, *Colonial Newspaper*, pp. 63–69; Thomas, *Printing in America*, II, 99–104; Stanley N. Katz, *Newcastle's New York: Anglo American Politics, 1732–1753* (Cambridge, Mass., 1968), chap. 4.

151. The first surviving issue is number 64 of December 1728.

152. War had been declared in February. George I died 15 June 1727, and his son was proclaimed: in Boston, 16 August; New York and Portsmouth, New Hampshire, 21 August; Perth Amboy, 25 August; Philadelphia, 31 August. See *BNL*, no. 33; *American Weekly Mercury*, nos. 399, 400; *Boston Gazette*, no. 405. All these appear to have had their official packets by way of the HMS *Drake*, sent out to Boston. See *Boston Gazette* of 15 April 1728, no. 438. The news arrived in Virginia on 6 September, with the arrival of Governor Gooch in the *Randolph*, Captain Bowling, in from London (*Boston Gazette*, no. 431). The flow of news south from Philadelphia remained at a different rate from movement of news to the north.

153. *DAB* and Wroth, *William Parks*, passim.

154. *American Weekly Mercury* of 4 April 1728; *New York Gazette* of 8 April 1728.

155. Cf. Kobre, *Colonial Newspaper*, p. 77.

156. See Thomas, *Printing in America*, I, 229–33; II, 134, 188–90; L. W. Labaree et al., *The Autobiography of Benjamin Franklin* (New Haven, 1964), pp. 77–79, 108–12, 287; *American Weekly Mercury*, nos. 209, 213, 252, 320, 348, 473. See also Stephen Bloore, "Samuel Keimer," in *PMHB*, 54 (1930), 255–87, and C. Lennart Carlson, "Samuel Keimer: A Study in the Transit of English Culture to Colonial Pennsylvania," ibid., 61 (1937), 357–86.

157. Keimer, in explaining his own difficulties, including imprisonment for debt, claimed, "I had at least at the rate of 120 l. per Annum clear of all Charges secur'd to me by my News-Paper, and Leed's Almanack" (*Pennsylvania Gazette*, no. 27, 3 July 1729).

158. Edward McGrady, *The History of South Carolina Under Royal Government, 1719–1776* (New York, 1899), p. 144. An advance of £175 sterling was offered to be paid off by printing for the government at rates of 125 percent of current English printing rates. The search went on at least until early 1724. See Hennig Cohen, *The South Carolina Gazette* (Columbia, S.C., 1953), p. 3.

159. Bridenbaugh, *Cities*, p. 303, estimates the population in 1730 as 4500. The advance of 1722 had now become an outright grant of £1000 in Carolina currency, amount-

ing to approximately £142.17.0 sterling. See McCusker, *Money and Exchange*, p. 223.

160. Cohen, *Gazette*, p. 4 and note; Thomas, *Printing in America*, II, 169; Carl Van Doren, *Benjamin Franklin* (New York, 1938), p. 116.

161. The pioneering *Philadelphische Zeitung* of May and June 1732 (Edward Connery Lathem, *Chronological Tables of American Newspapers 1690–1820* [Barre, Mass., 1972], p. 3).

162. *South Carolina Gazette*, no. 1, 8 January 1731/2.

163. See A. M. Schlesinger, *Prelude to Independence* (New York, 1958), and Richard L. Merritt, *Symbols of American Community, 1735–1775* (New Haven, 1966), as well as Philip Davidson, *Propaganda and the American Revolution, 1763–1783* (Chapel Hill, N.C., 1941), pp. 170–72, 225–45, 332–37, 394–408.

164. Private conveyance of London newspapers to the colonies was commonplace, as Chapter 6 illustrates. Evidence of intercolonial shipment of London papers is scarce. In August 1701, Isaac Norris of Philadelphia wrote the following to a business associate in Maryland, Abraham Johns.

W^t publick News I hear being Included wth more in y^e Newspaper I send y^e a Coppy—Let thy fath^r & Sam^{il} Chew see it. I have not time or would send Saml a Coppy. If thou'l send him one for me I$^{·l}$ take it kind [HSP, Isaac Norris Letterbook, 1699–1702, p. 329].

Thomas Fitch of Boston sent an issue of the *Boston News-letter* on to Edward Shippen in Philadelphia in March 1710 (AAS, Thomas Fitch Letterbook, 1702/3–1711).

165. Stephen Botein's convincing argument is in "'Meer Mechanicks' and an Open Press: The Business and Political Strategies of Colonial American Printers," *Perspectives in American History*, 9 (1975), 127–225.

Chapter 9. THE PACKET BOATS, 1702–1715

1. See *The Marlborough-Godolphin Correspondence*, ed. H. L. Snyder, 3 vols., (London, 1973), I, 15, 19, for the formulation of the policy in August 1701. For the instructions, dated 23 October 1701, see NMM, Southwell/5, pp. 315–17. Benbow's seizures of French merchantmen were causing embarrassment to the Barbados government by the following January. See PRO, CO 28/6, fols. 132–33.

2. *HMC Portland*, VIII, p. 90.

3. See John Ehrman, *The Navy in the War of William III 1689–1697,* (Cambridge, 1953), pp. 183 note, 207–8; John H. Kemble, "England's First Atlantic Mail Line, Part I," *Mariner's Mirror*, 26 (1940), pp. 35–36; James H. St. John, "Edmund Dummer and his West India Packets," *University of Iowa Studies in the Social Sciences*, 11 (1941), 125–26; E. G. R. Taylor, *The Mathematical Practitioners of Tudor & Stuart England* (Cambridge, 1954), pp. 272–73; Robert Walcott, *English Politics in the Early Eighteenth Century* (Oxford, 1956), pp. 196, 217; Dummer to Nottingham, 12 May 1702, *CSP Dom 1702–1703*, p. 61.

4. Dummer to Harley, 11 August 1701, *HMC Portland*, VIII, p. 90.

5. H. L. Snyder, "Godolphin and Harley: A Study of Their Partnership in Politics," *Huntington Library Quarterly*, 30 (1967), p. 258.

6. Dummer to Harley, 31 May; 6, 21 July; 20, 21 August; 24 September 1702 (*HMC Portland*, VIII, pp. 101, 102, 104, 108, 109, 110); Dummer to Thomas Pitt, 10 March 1702/3, BL, Add MSS 22852, fols. 111–12.

7. W. G. Bassett, "English Naval Policy in the Caribbean, 1698–1703," *BIHR*, 11 (1933), 123–24; Godolphin to Harley, "Monday night 15" in BL, Loan 29/64.

8. I. K. Steele, *Politics of Colonial Policy* (Oxford, 1968), pp. 86–92; cf. H. Horwitz, *Revolution Politicks* (Cambridge, 1968), p. 181.

9. Burchett to Aglionby (Nottingham's secretary), PRO, Adm. 2/403, pp. 282–83.

10. President and Council of Jamaica to Nottingham, 23 December 1692. *CSPC 1689–1692*, no. 2715.

11. H. Richmond, *The Navy as an Instrument of Policy, 1558–1727* (Cambridge, 1953), 294–95; minutes of the Secret Committee meetings are in BL, Add MSS 29591, fol. 11 ff. Colonials still anticipated sailing as late as May 1703 (MHS *Proceedings*, IX [1867], 488, 491, 493).

12. BL, Add MSS 29591, passim. See also H. Kamen, "The Destruction of the Spanish Fleet at Vigo in 1702," *BIHR*, 39 (1966), pp. 165–73.

13. BL, Add MSS 29591, fol. 113.

14. Nottingham to Board of Trade, 27 May 1702, PRO, CO 324/8, pp. 160–61.

15. St. Christopher was not mentioned in any of the recorded discussions although it would be served by the packets from the beginning.

16. "A Scheam for Forreign Advice," PRO, CO 324/8, p. 161.

17. Board of Trade to Nottingham, 22 June 1702 (PRO, CO 318/3, fol. 164–65). Sir Philip Meadows of the Board of Trade and Sir Robert Cotton, joint postmaster general, were the MP's for Truro in Cornwall. See Walcott, *English Politics*, p. 209; *The Parliamentary Register Containing Lists of the Twenty Four Parliaments from 1660 to 1741* (London, 1741), pp. 242, 243.

18. Dummer's terms as of 18 June 1702 are in PRO, CO 324/8, pp. 168–69. The Navy Board report on the new terms, which mentions that RN vessels would need more officers for the crew size proposed, is in PRO, Adm. 1/4087, fols. 287–88. The postmaster generals' report to Nottingham of 13 August 1702 estimated costs of a one-way voyage at £150 (*CSP Dom 1702–1703*, p. 211; Nottingham to Admiralty, 20 August 1702, PRO, Adm. 1/4088, fol. 56).

19. J. Burchett to Nottingham, 3 July 1702, PRO, Adm. 2/404, p. 39.

20. Dummer to Harley, 6 July 1702, *HMC Portland*, VIII, p. 102.

21. See Walcott, *English Politics*, p. 219.

22. Guy to Harley, 22 August 1702, *HMC Portland*, IV, p. 45.

23. Nottingham to Admiralty, 20 August 1702, PRO, Adm. 1/4088, fol. 56.

24. Report of 20 November 1702, *HMC House of Lords*, V (1702–1704), pp. 67–68.

25. The Proposition, 1 October 1705, CO 137/9, no. 66(i). The packet service that would be operating in 1813 between Falmouth and Jamaica had a 17-week, or c. 119-day, schedule (Arthur C. Wardle, "The Post Office Packets," in C. N. Parkinson, ed., *The Trade Winds* [London, 1948], p. 287).

26. See St. John, "Dummer," pp. 133–34 and Kemble, "Mail Line," passim.

27. See Table 9.1: the *Mansbridge* (voyage numbers 2, 6, and 9) and the *Prince* (voyage numbers 11, 13, 16).

28. The rates were 9d. for a single letter and 1s. 3d. for a double. See postmasters general (hereafter PMG) to Godolphin, 20 January 1704/5, GPO, Post 1, vol. 3, p. 242. Postage outward consistently produced about one-sixth the yield of the homeward-bound mail (GPO, Post 1, vol. 4, p. 14). West Indian correspondents were not charged to send or receive mail under the agency (GPO, Post 1/3, 1699–1705, p. 233).

29. GPO, Post 1/4, p. 14. The postage earned on the *Prince* returning in February 1704/5 was still at the old rates. For costs per voyage, see further on, note. 74.

30. See PMG to Godolphin 20 January 1704/5, GPO, Post 1/3, 1699–1705, p. 241–42. On passengers, see Nathaniel Uring, *Voyages and Travels* (London, 1928), pp. 60–69; and *A Journal of the Life of Thomas Story* (Newcastle, 1747), p. 443. On shipment of troops via packet, see below note 91. An indication that postage costs

were high in 1703 can be drawn from the Royal African Company orders to their West Indian agents not to send weighty journals, accounts, or routine material by the packet boats because of cost although letters were expected by each packet (PRO, T 70/58, pp. 70, 90, 92, 93).

31. Instructions to Commanders, 2 September 1703, PRO, CO 318/3, fol. 213, and Dummer to Nottingham, of same date, ibid., fols. 210–11.
32. Account enclosed with PMG to Godolphin, 9 July 1704, GPO, Post 1/3, 1699–1705, p. 226.
33. Captain Ralph Corbett importing into Falmouth customs from the *Bridgman* (PRO, E 190/1062/14, n.p., and E 190/1062/25, n.p.).
34. See entries in PRO, E 190/1062/25, n.p., for 31 August 1703.
35. See PRO, E 190/1064/2, n.p., entries for 7–9, 12, 15, 17, 19, and 23 January, as well as 2 March 1704/5.
36. See the Penryn customs clearance for 2 April 1703 in PRO, E 190/1064/14 n.p. The more substantial Falmouth clearances of 22 and 23 June 1704, and 4 and 6 of September are in E 190/1063/36, n.p.
37. GPO, Falmouth Letter Book, I, 33. The use of 28 men aboard ships of about 120 tons approximates 4.3 tons per man compared to 11.7 tons per man for non-slaving ships of London ownership and 101–150 tons burthen entering Barbados between 1696 and 1700. See author's unpublished paper "Harmony and Competition." Officers aboard a Dummer packet in 1709 were captain, first mate, and second mate. There was also a doctor, a gunner, and a steward according to Story, *Journal*, p. 443.
38. Instructions to commanders included with Dummer to Nottingham, 2 September 1703 (PRO, CO 318/3, fol. 213). Despite Dummer's insistence that his vessels be issued letters of marque, he dismissed Richard Simpson for taking a prize. See GPO, Post 1/3, 184, and PRO, CO 318/3, fol. 208.
39. Although J. H. Kemble's discussion, "Mail Line," part II, pp. 186–87, frequently confuses the West Indian and Lisbon services, his account of "smart money" is applicable to both. See Uring, *Voyages*, pp. 66–67.
40. Dummer to PMG, 1 December 1703, PRO T 1/89, fol. 144. Writing the Board of Trade on 10 January 1705/6, Dummer claimed that the 6 men lost on the latest voyage of the *Jamaica* was a higher toll than in all the previous voyages together. The only surviving muster sheet notes 3 of 30 men were "discharged or run" on one voyage (NMM, Dummer Papers, dated 1 March 1703/4 to 31 August 1704).
41. In May 1704 the *Prince* could not sail for this reason. See PMG to Rogers, their agent at Falmouth, 25 May 1704, GPO, Falmouth Letter Book, 1703–1709, Part 1, pp. 13a, 14.
42. PMG to Burchett, 12 April 1703, PRO, Adm. 1/4071, n.p.
43. The state of Dummer's account can be gained from PMG to Godolphin of 6 July 1704, GPO, Post 1/3, p. 226.
44. Dummer to PMG 19 August 1703, GPO, Post 1/3, p. 186; PMG to Lowndes, 19 August 1703, GPO, Post 1/3, p. 186; and entry for 26 August 1703 in account statement of 6 July 1704, GPO, Post 1/3, p. 226.
45. PMG to Lowndes, 26 November 1703, GPO, Post 1/3, pp. 198–99. Dummer claimed he had spent £920:9:0 beyond the impressed amounts whereas the final tally of proved expenses left Dummer owing the Post Office £490:12:9. See GPO, Post 1/3, p. 227.
46. See Dummer to Godolphin, 10 January 1703/4, PRO, T 1/89, fols. 21, 23.
47. See Dummer to Godolphin, 8 February 1703/4 in PRO, T 1/89, fol. 42, and Dummer to PMG, 31 January 1703/4 in PRO, T 1/89, fol. 145.

48. See Table 9.1, voyage no. 12, and Dummer to Harley, 7 June 1704, in *HMC Portland*, VIII, p. 122.
49. The introduction of the spar-decked *Prince* in August 1703 represented the first sign that Dummer was interested in better-protected vessels, but this one was no bigger than the others. On 17 November 1703 Dummer mentions the need for better vessels (PRO, CO 318/3, fol. 216), but it was on 1 December 1703, a few days after he submitted his accounts, that he gave the PMG a detailed plan for the use of bigger sloops with two decks (PRO, T 1/89, fol. 144).
50. PMG to Jones, 25 May 1704, GPO, Falmouth Packet Book, Part 1, fol. 14.
51. Dummer to Harley, 7 June 1704, *HMC Portland*, VIII, pp. 122, 319; Kemble, "Mail Line," pp. 41–42.
52. Dummer to Nottingham, 17 November 1703, PRO, CO 318/3, fol. 216; Dummer to PMG, 1 December 1703, PRO, T 1/89, fol. 144.
53. Dummer to PMG, 1 December 1703, PRO, T 1/89, fol. 144; PMG to Godolphin, 15 February 1703/4, 15 July 1704, and 11 October 1704, PRO, T 1/89, fols. 252–53, and GPO, Post 1/3 1699–1705, pp. 232–34.
54. PRO, T 1/89, fols. 317–20, and GPO, Post 1/3, 1699–1705, p. 235. For the three PMG replies see note 53 earlier.
55. In 1704 the Royal African Company paid an average of 16s. per ton from Jamaica to London, and the rate stayed higher than that for the next five years. See R. Davis, *The Rise of the English Shipping Industry* (London, 1962), p. 283. If he did not overload, Dummer would be able to sell 120 tons a year homeward for £96. The small freights out would gain even more by arriving at markets free of competition although outward freight was usually cheap. The usual rate for shipping bullion was 50s. per £100, and there is considerable evidence that bullion returns by the packets were very substantial. The Royal African Company shipped bullion regularly during the war years; London merchants preferred bullion to staples that had no markets or to a long wait until the end of the war for their money. When the *Barbados* was lost in the Windward Passage, the crew reportedly salvaged £30,000 of bullion from her only to lose it to a privateer. Nathaniel Uring, *Voyages* (p. 67), recalled breaking open a cask of merchant money to encourage his crewmen to fight off privateers.
56. See Jean O. McLachlan, *Trade and Peace with Old Spain, 1667–1750* (Cambridge, 1940) pp. 36–45; C. P. Nettels, "England and the Spanish American Trade, 1680–1715," *Journal of Modern History*, 3 (1931), pp. 1–32; and Steele, *Politics*, pp. 88–92.
57. The government became aware of the partnership only when a dispute arose between the Mearses and the Dummers in the summer of 1708. The charges, countercharges, and PMG report of 18 January 1708/9 are in GPO, Post 1/4, pp. 120–35.
58. The contract iself has not survived. The draft contract, dated 6 November 1704, is in GPO, Post 1/3, pp. 236–38, and its basic requirements are repeated by Dummer to Godolphin, 15 February 1706/7, GPO, Post 1/4, p. 40.
59. While the West Indies packets ran, there were 15 agents who acted for others on three or more occasions: Daniel Gwyn of Falmouth; John Bourn, George Buck, and William Kelly of Bideford; and 11 Plymouth agents—John Addis (Royal African Company agent), Richard Burlace, James Cooke, Josiah Ceane, Amos Doidge, William Dummer, Robert Hewer, Phillip Pentyre, John Stevens, William Warren & Co., and Nathaniel White (derived from the records of cargoes in the port books of the period 1702–1711).
60. See GPO, Post 1/4, pp. 19–23. For PMG protests, see GPO, Falmouth Packet Book, Part I, fols. 124, 141. Acceptance is clear in GPO, Falmouth Packet Book,

Part II, fols. 21, 56. Falmouth was also struggling to keep the Lisbon packets based there (ibid., Part II, fols. 37–42, 44, 45, 59).

61. Lord Cornbury to Board of Trade, 20 July 1707, PRO, CO 5/1121, p. 114; Handasyd to Board of Trade, 31 March 1708, *CSPC 1706–1708*, no. 1423. The packet-turned-privateer reputedly captured seven vessels off the capes of Virginia in 1707 and was feared to be "designing for our coast" the following year after refitting at Martinique (*BNL*, nos. 168, 212). On the rumor that she was retaken, Post Office agents were told to buy up the prize (GPO, Falmouth Packet Book, Part 1, fol. 152). On the size of the packets, see GPO, Post 1/4, pp. 44, 120.

62. Dummer freighted the *Kingston* on his own account and carried over 22 military recruits for Jamaica. Governor Handasyd was asked to let her clear customs promptly because she was intended to join the packet service on her return. Handasyd calls her a galley, but little else is known except that she was wrecked on the Scilly Isles on her return. See *CSPC 1706–1708*, nos. 837, 1250, 1339.

63. GPO, Post 1/4, pp. 125–29; Uring, *Voyages*, pp. 66–70, 74–75; Handasyd to Board of Trade, 14 January 1705/6 and 16 February 1705/6, CO 137/7, nos. 20, 21. The *Barbados* was reported to have carried 150 casks of indigo when she was wrecked on "Heneago" (*BNL*, no. 110). For Dummer's defense before the Board of Trade, see *Journal of the Lords Commissioners of Trade and Plantations*, 14 vols. (London, 1920–1938), I, 250 (hereafter cited as Board of Trade *Journal*).

64. Heads of a Contract, 6 November 1704, GPO, Post 1/3, p. 237; Instructions of July 1705, GPO, Falmouth Packet Book, Part I, fol. 53.

65. Dummer to Godolphin, 16 October 1705, and PMG to Godolphin, 3 December 1705, GPO, Post 1/3, p. 263–65; PMG to Godolphin, 18 June 1706, GPO, Post 1/4, pp. 6–8.

66. Dummer to Godolphin, 18 June 1706, GPO, Post 1/4, pp. 6–8, and PMG report dated 10 July 1706, GPO, Post 1/4, pp. 11–13. Godolphin's decision, dated 3 August 1706, gave Dummer a credit of £400.17.0 for delays in postal rate increases, allowance for mails lost with ships, and postponement of deficiency payments until after 25 January 1706/7. In March 1706, Dummer was granted a sinecure clerkship of the Wardrobe, worth £300 p.a. (Kemble, "Mail Line," pp. 41–42).

67. Dummer to Godolphin, 15 February 1706/7 and 20 February 1706/7, GPO, Post 1/4, pp. 37–42, 56–58.

68. Ibid., p. 44.

69. Godolphin's orders of 7 April 1707, GPO, Post 1/4, p. 45, and Table 9.1.

70. PMG to Godolphin, 13 June 1707, GPO, Post 1/4, pp. 60–62.

71. For the Plymouth port-book materials on the *Barbados*, loading 6 to 11 October 1705 and including parcels belonging to Bartholomew Gracedieu, the Mears brothers, and seven others, see PRO, E 190/1064/8. The *Queen Anne*'s lading of reexported cloth, silks, English bone lace, 50 barrels of foreign corn powder (granulated gunpowder), and so on, is recorded in PRO, E 190/1064/8, 2–7 November 1707. The very large export loading of the *Antego*, voyage 37, is recorded in the Plymouth port book, 29 January–12 February 1706/7 (PRO, E 190/1066/37, fols. 22–23).

72. For record of deliveries for the Royal African Company, 17 December 1703 to October 1708, see PRO, T 70/8, pp. 1–79, and T 70/971–72, n.p. The company had at least 42,150 pieces of eight delivered by Dummer's packets in this period, or roughly £9483.10.0.

73. Handasyd to Board of Trade, 19 June 1707 (*CSPC 1706–1708*, no. 998). For the charges against Commodore Kerr, see PRO, CO 138/12, pp. 150–53; PRO, CO 137/7, nos. 64, 65, 70. Board of Trade responses to Parliament on the matter are 21 November 1707 in PRO, CO 138/12, pp. 171–79; and 4 December 1707, PRO, CO 389/20, p. 17. The American Trade Act of 1708 was no solution, as both

Dummer and Handasyd made clear between the summer of 1708 and the autumn of 1710. See Board of Trade *Journal*, I, 534; PRO, CO 138/12, pp. 318–24, 365; CO 138/13, pp. 40–41, 291, 301–2. See also Dummer to Popple, 1 April 1709, *CSPC 1708–1709*, no. 445; and J. M. Treadwell, "William Wood of Jamaica, a Colonial Mercantilist of the Eighteenth Century." *The Journal of Caribbean History*, 8 (1976), pp. 42–64.

74. The costs to the government were about £633.33 per sailing under the agency and £1500 under the first contract although that was not what was agreed to. With a conservative estimate of postal revenues for 1702–1704 of £6000, the net cost to the government under the agency was £233 per sailing compared with £900 under the first contract.

75. Articles of Agreement between PMG and Dummer, 19 March 1707/8, Dummer Papers, NMM.

76. Kemble, "Mail Line," p. 46.

77. The Mears petition, Dummer's reply, the Mears retort, dated June 17 to July 27 1708 are copied in GPO, Post 1/4, pp. 119–29, followed, pp. 130–35, by the PMG report on the same, dated 18 January 1708/9.

78. PMG to Dummer, 13 March 1708/9 and again 26 January 1709/10, GPO, Falmouth Packet Book, Part II, fols. 126–27, 169–70; GPO, Post 3/4, figures for year ending 25 March 1710 include the full £12,000 for Dummer.

79. See Table 9.1, voyages no. 4, 5; 23, 24; and 54, 55.

80. For Godolphin's praise of Dummer's new Gravesend-to-Ostend packet, see his letters to Marlborough of 12 July and 20 August 1710 (Snyder, *The Marlborough-Godolphin Correspondence*, III, 1566, 1611).

81. Dummer's petition, of 22 July 1710, and the PMG report of 21 August 1710, are in GPO, Post 1/4, pp. 155–59. Dummer's £12,000 for the year ending 25 March 1711 is entered in GPO, Post 3/5, p. 36.

82. A commission of bankruptcy was established 13 March 1710/11. Dummer missed the proceedings but won the right to be heard by the commissioners of bankruptcy four months later (PRO, B 4/1, p. 43). The successful petition for Dummer, his brother Thomas, and his son William to be heard in the case, dated 21 July 1711, is in PRO, B 1/1, pp. 77–78.

83. The commission for Goodwin's bankruptcy hearing was established 9 August 1711 (PRO, B 4/1, p. 74) though Dummer's printed *The Case of Edmund Dummer Esq.* claims it was earlier (copy in Dummer's Papers, NMM). By 10 September 1711, Goodwin had been declared a bankrupt (GPO, Post 1/4, p. 203).

84. Petition of 2 August 1711 and PMG report of 6 August 1711, GPO, Post 1/4, pp. 200–1; PMG report of 10 September 1711, GPO, Post 1/4, p. 203.

85. *The Case of Edmund Dummer Esq.* tells of the suit and the imprisonment. The commission of bankruptcy was established 16 February 1711/12 at the initiative of John Grove, a London merchant (PRO, B 4/1, p. 127).

86. In February 1711/12 Dummer tried to interest Thomas Harley in a new Netherlands packet (BL, Add MSS 22617, fols. 138–40). In July he sought Board of Trade support for a revived West Indies packet involving a separate route to Jamaica (PRO, CO 138/13, pp. 392–393). By the end of 1712, Dummer was suggesting to Thomas Harley a "Universal Correspondence" of 16 vessels on routes serving northern Spain, Portugal, southern Spain, the West Indies, and North America. Incidentally, the sloops were to be of 120 tons, worth £1400 apiece, and mounting only four guns. Perhaps he had learned something from his bigger sloops. Dummer's letters of 8 November 1712 and 14 January following tie together well with the undated proposal for "Universal Correspondence." All are in Dummer Papers, NMM.

87. The petition of his wife, Sarah, and daughter Jane received sympathy and support from Mr. Sergison, secretary of the Admiralty; from the PMG; and from the Navy Office. The petition and three responses are in Dummer Papers, NMM.

88. "The Explication to the Proposall of Carrying on a Correspondence with the West Indies. . . ," 24 February 1703/4. (PRO, T 1/89, fol. 319).

89. *CSPC 1704–1705*, nos. 390, 426. Governor Handasyd, for instance, withheld details from a letter of 1 February 1708/9 for transmission by man-of-war or packet boat (*CSPC 1708–1709*, no. 339).

90. *CSPC 1706–1708*, no. 1201. Parke's letter, sent six days after the *Antigua* packet left Antigua, was successfully put aboard the packet boat at Jamaica and came into the Board of Trade with that mail.

91. *CSPC 1706–1708*, no. 1250; *CSPC 1708–1709*, no. 912; and *CSPC 1710–1711*, no. 313, discuss shipment of recruits. For the smooth coordination of men-of-war for a tobacco convoy in 1703, see log of HMS *Falmouth*, PRO, Adm. 51/341.

92. See Table 12.2.

93. *CSPC 1702–1703*, no. 496; *CSPC 1706–1708*, no. 493.

94. PRO, T 70/58, p. 59, 118. Like the Board of Trade, the Royal African Company initially wrote its agents more often because of the packets, soon had the secretary write, and within two years was often sending nothing but copies by half the packets (PRO 5 T 70/57–58, *passim*).

95. See *CSPC 1702–1703*, no. 496; "The Queries etc. for Jamaica," PRO, CO 323/6, fol. 25; *CSPC 1706–1708*, nos. 1180, 1317. Governor Crowe of Barbados, under attack from members of his council in 1708, was accused by the Board of Trade of failing to answer questions by two opportunities, one 17 days and another 35 days after Crowe promised his answers by the next conveyance (*CSPC 1708–1709*, no. 248).

96. The funds afforded Dummer were these.

under agency	£ 9,500
first contract	37,500
second contract	39,000
TOTAL:	£86,000

This calculation does not assume that the predating of the second contract included payment for 1706. If it did, the total would be £98,000.

97. The postal revenues are not available for each year. See note 74 earlier for agency period. If revenues remained thereafter at the 1704–1705 levels of £5000 p.a.

1702–1704	£ 6,000
1704–1711	35,000
TOTAL:	£41,000

This is very optimistic. The PMG reported in October 1711 that the service was not earning a quarter of the cost, that is, not £3000 p.a. See PMG to Harley, 2 October 1711, GPO, Post 1/4, p. 210.

98. PMG to Harley, 31 October 1711, GPO, Post 1/4, pp. 218–19.

99. See PRO, CO 323/5, fols. 1, 3, 8, 14, 16, and CO 324/8, pp. 215–18, 220, 222–24; GPO, Post 1/3, pp. 126, 127.

100. *HMC Portland*, VIII, p. 147.

101. Advertisement of 10 February 1704/5, CO 323/5, fol. 213; *HMC Portland*, VIII, p. 170.

102. Circular letter of 29 October 1705, PRO, CO 324/9, p. 112.

103. Dudley to Board of Trade, 23 April 1706, *CSPC 1706–1708*, no. 288; Handasyd to Board of Trade, 16 February 1705/6, *CSPC 1706–1708*, no. 116.

104. *BNL*, nos. 79, 111, 123.

105. *Ibid.*, nos. 45, 51, 114–19, 136, 153, 207, 370; *CSPC 1706–1708*, nos. 443, 1186; *Letterbook of Samuel Sewall*, 2 vols. (Boston, 1886–1888), I, 390.

106. *CSPC 1704–1705*, nos. 73, 343; *CSPC 1706–1708*, no. 792.

107. PRO, CO 5/746, fols. 30, 35, 40.

108. 10 June 1707, *CSPC 1706–1708*, no. 975.

109. Ibid., no. 1113; Board of Trade *Journal*, I, 410.

110. See *CSPC 1706–1708*, no. 1570, for his letter of 23 June 1708, and PRO CO, 5/727, p. 99, for his letter of September 7 following.

111. Besides Jeffreys, Dummer, and William Warren, there was also an attempt by the holders of the Neale patent to have approval for a North American packet service in 1706. See GPO, Post 1/4, pp. 32–33.

112. See G. A. Jacobsen, *William Blathwayt: A Late Seventeenth Century English Administrator* (New Haven, 1932); Stephen S. Webb, "William Blathwayt, Imperial Fixer," *W&MQ*, 3d ser., 25 (1968), pp. 3–21 and 26 (1969), pp. 373–415; and Barbara C. Murison, "William Blathwayt's Empire: Politics and Administration in England and the Atlantic Colonies, 1668–1710," Ph.D. dissertation, University of Western Ontario, 1981.

113. Blathwayt to Godolphin, 6 September 1707, PRO, T 64/89, pp. 378–82.

114. See GPO, Post 1/4, pp. 34–35.

115. Uring, *Voyages*, p. 76; *CSPC 1708–1709*, nos. 475, 476, 478, 503.

116. GPO, Post 1/4, pp. 136–38. See earlier note 59 about William Warren & Co.

117. GPO, Post 3/5, n.p., entry for 25 March 1712.

118. The *Edgley Galley*, voyage no. 6, reportedly stopped in Ireland and went to Philadelphia with more than 100 passengers, chiefly servants (*BNL*, no. 421). The *Harley*, voyage no. 7, was reported as carrying several servants (*BNL*, no. 455). On voyage no. 10, the *Harley* went west via Ireland and loaded much more than 10 tons of cargo at New York (*BNL*, no. 598, and PRO, CO 5/1222).

119. The *Hazard*, Captain Richard Green, left Deal 14 August 1714 for Boston with packets proclaiming George I for all the governments north of Virginia. The vessel was wrecked, with all hands lost, on the coast of Massachusetts on 12 November following. The mail washed ashore and was recovered (*CSPC 1714–1715*, no. 88; *BNL*, no. 553).

Chapter 10: SENDING PEACE AND WAR BEYOND THE LINE, 1667–1739

1. Garrett Mattingly, "No Peace Beyond What Line?" *TRHS*, 5th ser., 13 (1963), 145–62.

2. The Treaty of Tordesillas of June 1494. See Frances G. Davenport, *European Treaties Bearing on the History of the United States and Its Dependencies*, 4 vols. (Washington, D.C., 1917–1937), I, 84–100.

3. Mattingly, "No Peace," p. 148. See also A. Pearce Higgins, "International Law and the Outer World, 1450–1648," in J. Holland Rose et al., eds., *The Cambridge History of the British Empire*, I (1929), chap. 6.

4. Mattingly, "No Peace," p. 149.

5. Ibid., pp. 150–51.

6. Davenport, *European Treaties*, II, 42.

7. Ferro Island, Cape Bojador, and the Tropic of Cancer are within 4° 30″ of each other.

8. The phrase is A. P. Thornton's (*West-India Policy Under the Restoration* [Oxford, 1956], p. 73).

9. See Higgins, "International Law," p. 191, Davenport, *European Treaties*, I, 313.

10. *CSP Dom, 1635*, p. 600. Sir Richard Fanshawe, when negotiating with the Spanish court in 1664, argued that the treaty of 1630 had not extended beyond "the line."
11. Davenport, *European Treaties*, I, 360; II, 94.
12. Violet Barbour, "Privateers and Pirates of the West Indies," *AHR*, 16 (1910–1911), 529–66. For royal instructions to the Jamaican governor in 1670, see L. W. Labaree, ed., *Royal Instructions to British Colonial Governors 1670–1776*, 2 vols. (New York, 1935), I, no. 643. In the spring of 1655, however, Philip IV argued that the English attack on Hispaniola and conquest of Jamaica constituted a declaration of war in Europe (Max Savelle, *The Origins of American Diplomacy: The International History of Angloamerica, 1492–1763* [New York, 1967], p. 90). Spanish reaction to Morgan's sacking of Puerto Bello in 1668 suggests a return to the "two spheres."
13. *A True and Exact History of the Island of Barbados* (London, 1673), pp. 15, 18, 19, 85, 106; *Philosophical Transactions*, 2:27 (1667), p. 496. See also William Dampier, *Voyages and Discoveries*, ed. N. M. Penzer (London, 1931), p. 231; Woodes Rogers, *A Cruising Voyage Round the World* (London, 1712), p. 35; Daniel Defoe, *Robinson Crusoe*, ed. Michael Shinagel (New York, 1975), p. 52. John Senex's 1739 map of "The Western or Atlantic Ocean" labels the "Equator or Line."
14. *CSPC 1712–1714*, no. 106.
15. There were a number of treaties or agreements between colonial governors in the seventeenth century that represent an unfulfilled alternative to the integration of peacemaking. These agreements included the Massachusetts and Acadia agreement of 8 October 1644; New England and New Netherlands, 19 September 1650; Virginia and New Netherlands, April 1660; and the treaty of neutrality between governors of English and French sectors of St. Christopher, 9/19 May 1678. The most significant aberration in European diplomacy in this connection was the Anglo-French Treaty of Neutrality of 1686, which sought to separate the colonies from European dangers (Davenport, *European Treaties*, I, 347–52; II, 1–6, 53–56, 256–60, 309–23).
16. Ibid., II, 238–39.
17. Ibid., I, 306, 313. Davenport claims that the "line" was the equator in this case, which would mean that the islands included the West Indies and not just the Azores and the Canary Islands.
18. In the Anglo-Dutch Treaty of 1674, this zone reached to Tangier but did not include the Mediterranean (ibid., II, 238–39).
19. Davenport, *European Treaties*, passim. In 1783 peace was to reach the area between the Canary Islands and the equator within two months (ibid., IV, 148–49).
20. Exceptions were the Anglo-French treaty at Breda in 1667, which allowed six months for peace between powers that then had few interests east of the Strait of Malacca; and the 1783 peace settlement, which was to reach the ends of the earth in five months.
21. See *CSP Dom, 1697*, pp. 387, 409–10, 413, 423, 425, 432.
22. *APCC*, II, p. 317, and *CSPC 1696–1697*, no. 1399; *CSPC 1697–1698*, nos. 10, 12, 14, 30, 91, 143, 168, 220.
23. For Massachusetts, see *Letterbook of Samuel Sewall*, 2 vols. (Boston, 1876–1878), I, 194; *The Diary of Cotton Mather*, 2 vols. (New York, 1957), I, 243; *CSPC 1697–1698*, no. 95; *CSPC 1696–1697*, no. 1421. Connecticut proclaimed the peace on 24 December; *The Public Records of the Colony of Connecticut*, 15 vols. (Hartford, 1850–1890), IV, 234. The packet arrived in New Hampshire by 13 December; *CSPC 1697–1698*, no. 108 ii.
24. On the special efforts of the Board of Trade and Bellomont to speed the news to New York, see *CSPC 1696–1697*, no. 1413; *CSPC 1697–1698*, nos. 13, 159. On 29 December, messengers were sent north from Albany for Montreal, bearing a copy of the treaty forwarded by Governor Fletcher (*NYCD*, IV, 338).

25. Nicholas Lydston, though called a captain in the receipt for the packets, was the master of the *Speaker* of London and was recorded as being at Sandwich on 12 October bound for Virginia. See *CSPC 1697–1698*, no. 15, and PRO, E 190/674/4, n.p.

26. *Maryland Archives*, XXIII, 341; *CSPC 1697–1698*, no. 291.

27. Davenport's comment, that "the French government was very dilatory in notifying Canada of the peace" (*European Treaties*, II, 358), seems a bit harsh.

28. *NYCD*, IV, 338. Although the mission returned with Callières' understandable response that he hoped for a confirmation of the peace and a return of prisoners, Frontenac later claimed that, on receiving this first news of peace, he send out orders for the Abenaki raids to cease (ibid., IV, 343).

29. *NYCD*, IV, 347–51. The party was eight days in getting to Crown Point and four days from there to Montreal.

30. *CSPC 1697–1698*, no. 14.

31. See G. S. Graham, *Empire of the North Atlantic*, 2d ed. (Toronto, 1958), p. 80; W. J. Eccles, *Canada under Louis XIV* (Toronto, 1964), pp. 196–99; E. E. Rich, *Hudson's Bay Company*, 3 vols. (Toronto, 1960), I, 333–67.

32. Davenport, *European Treaties*, III, 165, 166. This clause was dated 14/24 August 1712.

33. *CSPC 1712–1714*, nos. 50, 51, 66.

34. The letters were carried to the Admiralty on 22 August. The HMS *Dunwich* sailed from Harwick on the twenty-sixth. (*CSPC 1712–1714*, no. 50, and *BNL*, 3 November, no. 446.)

35. Captain Owen was her master (*CSPC 1712–1714*, nos. 114, 114i., 117; *BNL*, nos. 445–46).

36. *CSPC 1712–1714*, nos. 89, 144; PRO, CO 5/1363, pp. 475–77; *BNL*, no. 446, of 3 November 1712, which notes that Connecticut proclaimed the truce on 30 October; and New Hampshire, the next day. See also *BNL*, nos. 447–49.

37. See *CSPC 1712–1714*, nos. 94, 106, 148, 282.

38. Ibid., no 164.

39. Ibid., nos. 282, 307.

40. Ibid., nos. 180, 176.

41. See *American Weekly Mercury*, no. 743, 28 March 1733/4, for an example.

42. Labaree, *Royal Instructions*, I, no. 132.

43. Ibid. In the case of Jamaica, this was a very sharp reduction in the discretionary powers that the governor had held in the previous five years (ibid., no. 131).

44. There is, for instance, nothing comparable in the royal instructions to Governor Yeardley (1626) or Governor Berkeley (1641 and 1662). See *VMHB*, 2 (1894–1895), pp. 395, 281–88; 3 (1895–1896), pp. 15–20 respectively.

45. Labaree, *Royal Instructions*, I, no. 642. The power to grant or withdraw commissions to privateers was formally authorized for Governor Thomas Modyford in the summer of 1665. (*CSPC 1661–1668*, no. 1264).

46. A. P. Newton, *The European Nations in the West Indies, 1493–1688* (London, 1933), pp. 208–9; Savelle, *Origins*, p. 163. The Massachusetts General Court did prohibit trade with the Dutch between 18 May 1653 and 22 August 1654 but firmly resisted the urgings of the Connecticut settlements to wage war on the Dutch. The commissioners of the united colonies of New England were, momentarily, denied the power "to determine the justice of an offensive or vindictive warr, & to ingage the colonyes therein" (N. B. Shurtleff, ed., *Records of Massachusetts*, 5 vols. [Boston, 1853–1854], III, 297–98, 311, 354). An English force was sent out, but nothing was accomplished before the peace (A. B. Hart, *Commonwealth History of Massachusetts*, 5 vols. [Boston, 1927], I, 242–45).

47. Charles Wilson's *Profit and Power: A Study of England and the Dutch Wars* (London, 1957), chap. 8, is particularly helpful. Also see Savelle, *Origins*, pp. 54–55; Davenport, *European Treaties*, II, 73–85.

48. The secret orders to proceed to the West African forts reached De Ruyter 1 September 1664 (New Style). See P. Blok, *The Life of Admiral De Ruyter*, trans. by G. J. Renier (London, 1933), p. 179.

49. *CSPC 1661–1668*, nos. 910, 920, 926, 953.

50. Ibid., nos. 927, 983, 992; Shurtleff, *Records*, IV, pt 2, 153. For Virginia, see *VMHB*, 19 (1911), p. 27; 20 (1912), pp. 357–59; 18 (1910), 426–27. When France became an enemy a year later, however, a warning was accompanied by a declaration of war (*CSPC 1661–1668*, nos. 1132–34). The Massachusetts Council discussed the royal suggestion that Canada be attacked, but their conclusion was "that it is not feasible, as well in repect of the difficulty (if not impossibility) of a land march ouer the rocky mounteines & houling desarts about fower hundred miles, as the strength of the French there accoring to report" (Shurtleff, *Records*, IV, pt 2, p. 316).

51. *VMHB*, 20 (1912), pp. 127–28.

52. *CSPC 1669–1674*, no. 823; V. T. Harlow, *A History of Barbados, 1625–1685* (Oxford, 1926), pp. 208–12.

53. *CSPC 1669–1674*, no. 885.

54. Ibid., no. 793.

55. Shurtleff, *Records*, IV, part 2, pp. 30–31, 517.

56. Ibid., 572–73.

57. Massachusetts Bay would be deliberately excluded from similar proceedings in 1689.

58. *APCC*, II, 128. Shrewsbury relayed the order to the Admiralty on 12 April, by which time it was to be two hired ketches ready "for immediate despatch to the West Indies" (*CSPC 1689–1692*, no. 66).

59. *APCC*, II, 117–119 regarding the shipping embargo, most of which was lifted 8 July and the remaining controls ended 2 September 1689. The circular letters are calendared in *CSPC 1689–1692*, nos. 69–70.

60. See PRO, CO 324/5, pp. 41–43, and *CSPC 1689–1692*, nos. 81, 105.

61. The letter to Lord Baltimore, however, claimed that the *Crane* was to go on to Carolina from Maryland (*CSPC, 1689–1692*, no. 78).

62. Ibid., nos. 28, 37.

63. Apparently, Dykes sailed in the *Bonetto* sloop from Plymouth, suggesting that the *John* had been damaged (*CSPC 1689–1692*, no. 397).

64. Ibid., nos. 262, 200, 230.

65. Ibid., no. 333.

66. Sir Francis Watson acknowledged receipt of the letters of 15 and 19 April 1689 in his letter to Shrewsbury of 27 October (ibid., no. 514).

67. Ibid., nos. 714, 873.

68. See ibid., nos. 76, 472.

69. Apparently the *Crane* had arrived by 22 September 1689 (*Maryland Archives*, VIII, pp. 123–24).

70. *Minutes of Provincial Council of Pennsylvania*, I, 301–11.

71. *Maryland Archives*, VIII, pp. 127, 151–52.

72. Robert N. Toppan and Alfred T. S. Goodrick, eds., *Edward Randolph: Including His Letters and Official Papers . . .* , 7 vols. (Boston, 1898–1909), VI, 295; *CSPC 1689–1692*, no. 336. The contrast with the declaration of war with France in 1666 is striking. Although all governors had then been warned of the likelihood of war and urged to be bellicose, formal orders to proclaim war on France were sent to none but the governors of Massachusetts, Connecticut, and Nova Scotia (*CSPC 1661–1668*, nos. 1130, 1132, 1134, 1136, 1166, 1181, 1209, 1212, 1263, 1299, 1302.)

73. *CSPC 1689–1692*, nos. 320, 322; *Documentary History of the State of New York*, ed. E. B. O'Callaghan, 4 vols (Albany, 1849–1851), II, 36.

74. See G. H. Guttridge, *The Colonial Policy of William III* (Cambridge, 1922), pp. 68–74; Nellis M. Crouse, *The French Struggle for the West Indies* (New York, 1943), chaps. 6–8.

75. *CSP Dom, 1700–1702*, pp. 407–8; NMM Sergison/44, n.p. Also see W. G. Bassett, "English Naval Policy in the Caribbean, 1698–1703," *BIHR*, 11 (1933), pp. 122–26, and Sir H. Richmond, *The Navy as an Instrument of Policy 1558–1727* (Cambridge, 1953), pp. 280–81.

76. On 6 November, 9 December, 24 December 1701, calendared in *CSP Dom 1700–1702*, pp. 439–40, 464, 473; 13, 30 April; 13 May, 1, 30 June 1702 in *CSPC 1702*, nos. 333, 473, 560; 11, 24 September 1702, in *CSPC 1702–1703*, nos. 123, 124; 20 October 1702, *CSPC 1702*, no. 1066.

77. *CSP Dom, 1700–1702*, pp. 431–32; NMM, Sou/5, pp. 315–17; PRO, Adm. 2/401, pp. 165–66, 227–28; *CSPC 1702*, no. 473. Ruth Bourne's *Queen Anne's Navy in the West Indies* (New Haven, 1939), pp. 64–66.

78. *CSPC 1702*, nos. 431–49; I. K. Steele, "Time, Communications and Society: The English Atlantic, 1702," *Journal of American Studies*, 8 (1974), pp. 15–16.

79. Ibid, p. 16. On Codrington's intention and French fears, see Père Labat, *The Memoirs of . . .* trans. and ed. by John Eaden (London, 1931), pp. 213–15. When, in April 1666, the English governor on St. Christopher had honorably warned the French that war had been declared, in accordance with a previous agreement, the results were disastrous for him and his colony. See *CSPC 1661–1668*, no. 1179.

80. Beckford to Board of Trade, 20 July 1702, *CSPC 1702*, no. 743.

81. Steele, "Time, Communications," pp. 17–21.

82. War was formally declared in September (Executive Journals of the Council of Colonial Virginia, II, 266, 296–97).

83. An initial intention to issue letters of marque was reversed (*APCC*, II, 854. See *CSPC 1717–1718*, nos. 803, 804, 814; *CSPC 1719–1720*, nos. 132, 205, 227; *BNL*, nos. 783, 790, 791).

84. *CSPC 1726–1727*, pp. viii–ix.

85. Labaree, *Royal instructions*, I, 446.

86. The Convention of Pardo was reprinted in full in the *New York Gazette* of 30 April, no. 703, and the *American Weekly Mercury* of Philadelphia on 3 May, no. 1009.

87. The same cannot, however, be said of Brown's relations with Governor Trelawney of Jamaica, who wanted more aggressive action. See G. Metcalf, *Royal Government and Political Conflict in Jamaica 1729–1783* (London, 1965), p. 63; Sir Herbert Richmond, *The Navy in the War of 1739–48*, 3 vols. (Cambridge, 1920), I, 6–8, 11.

88. Richmond, *The Navy in the War of 1739–48*, I, 12–13.

89. *APCC*, III, 630, 636.

90. Vernon's orders to Capt. Richard Herbert of the *Norwich*, 2 September 1739, *The Vernon Papers*, ed. B. McL. Ranft (London, 1958), p. 23.

91. Although the formal authorization was dated 10 July and was approved by the Privy Council meeting of that date, the *Tartar's* reportedly superior passage time of five weeks and three days meant that she had sailed by 3 July to arrive on 8 August (*APCC*, III, 636; *BNL*, nos. 1826–27).

92. The "universal joy" of Newport, Rhode Island, was reported in Boston and New York papers of 20, 23, 27 August. See *New York Gazette*, nos. 718–19, 20 and 27 August, about the New York and New Jersey proclamations.

93. See *Pennsylvania Gazette* of 23 August and *Virginia Gazette* of 31 August. Gooch received his formal packet via Boston on 28 August, and the next day a sloop from Barbados brought rumors that war had been proclaimed.

94. See *The Letterbook of Robert Pringle*, ed. Walter B. Edgar, 2 vols. (Columbia, S.C., 1972), I, 134–135, and *Stephens' Journal 1737–1740*, ed. Allen D. Candler, vol. IV of *The Colonial Records of the State of Georgia*, 26 vols. (Atlanta, Ga., 1904–1916), IV, 406–7.
95. Barbados by 7 January and Jamaica on 21 January. See Board of Trade *Journal*, VII, 323; *New York Gazette* of 31 March 1740.
96. *The Letterbook of Robert Pringle*, I, 163; *American Weekly Mercury*, no. 1046, 15 January 1739/40; *BNL*, no 1868.
97. The HMS *Colchester* also brought orders for raising colonial troops for the Cartagena expedition. Most of the colonies in British North America went to war between 14 and 21 April though South Carolina did not do so until 13 May (*South Carolina Gazette*, 17 May 1740).

Chapter 11. COMMERCE AND COMMUNICATIONS

1. John Browne, *The Merchant Avizo*, ed. P. McGrath (Cambridge, Mass., 1957), p. 9.
2. To Robert Plumsted & Co., 11 October 1706, AAS, Thomas Fitch Letterbook 1702/3–1711, n.p.
3. To John Crouch and Samuel Arnold, 22 September 1708 (ibid.).
4. Thomas Fitch to John Crouch & Samuel Arnold, 15 November 1709. See also letters of 20 May 1703 and 14 December 1708 (ibid.). Fear of war could also make the "Country people" in frontier areas reluctant to buy, as Philip Livingston assured his London correspondents Storke & Gainsborough on 21 July 1735, AAS, Livingston Family Papers 1734–1738, n.p. Apprehension that war would come made Philadelphia shopkeepers increase their stock and their customers buy more in July 1701, however (HSP, Isaac Norris Letterbook 1699–1702, p. 324).
5. D. North and R. P. Thomas, "An Economic Theory of the Growth of the Western World," *EconHR*, 2d ser., 23 (1970), p. 6.
6. Quoted in Stuart Bruchey, *The Roots of American Economic Growth, 1607–1861* (New York, 1965), p. 56.
7. Tyndall and Asheton to Hobhouse, Kingston, Jamaica, 16 November 1729, Hobhouse Papers 1722–1755, Bristol Central Library.
8. Slavers, with valuable cargoes and a variety of markets, were sometimes given considerable latitude to test markets. Captain William Barry of the brigantine *Despatch* was to sell his slaves at Trinidad, Antigua, Nevis, or South Carolina. Significantly, contacts were named only for the English colonies (Orders of 7 October 1725, Hobhouse Papers 1722–1755, Bristol Central Library).
9. For an example in the Newfoundland trade, see "Instructing the Master of a Newfoundland Sack Ship, 1715," in *Mariner's Mirror*, 63 (1977), pp. 191–93, and compare one of 1634 in Ralph Davis, *The Rise of the English Shipping Industry in the Seventeenth and Eighteenth Centuries* (London, 1962), pp. 236–38. For the New England-West Indies trades, there are examples among the Joshua Hull, William Pepperrell, and Moses Brown papers. See John Hull Letterbook 1670–1685, AAS; Byron Fairchild, *Mssrs. William Pepperrell: Merchants of Piscataqua* (Ithaca, N. Y., 1954), pp. 52–53; and Moses Brown Papers, I, p. 4, Rhode Island Historical Society. For slavers, see Hobhouse Papers in Bristol Central Library.
10. MHS, Belcher Letterbook, I, 225–26; MHS, MSS Bound, 1728–1733, Appleton to Joseph Brandon, 24 June 1728.
11. R. G. Albion, "Sea Routes," in Critchett Rimington, ed., *Merchant Fleets* (New York, 1944); p. 24. This technique might be seen as supporting the notion that English market information was of value to American colonials who might, for other

good reasons, resent the imposition of English entrepot functions on some of their trade with Europe.

12. Entry for 10 April 1735 in Livingston Family Business Papers 1734–1738, AAS.

13. A "Boston Merchant" charged London merchant accounts 5 percent commission, 1 percent for storage in addition to cash paid for customs and port lodge (MHS, Account Book of a Boston Merchant, 1688–1694). The Royal African Company West Indian agents seem to have had from 7 to 10 percent in Barbados in 1697 (PRO, T 70/57, fols. 133–34).

14. This point was noted in Max Weber, *General Economic History* (New York, 1961), p. 218.

15. K. G. Davies, "The Origins of the Commission System in the West India Trade," *TRHS*, 5th ser., 2 (1952), 89–107.

16. For an exposition of this complex world of tobacco marketing, see Jacob M. Price, *France and the Chesapeake*, 2 vols. (Ann Arbor, Mich., 1973). See also T. M. Devine, *The Tobacco Lords* (Edinburgh, 1975), chap. 4.

17. See earlier, pp. 123–24.

18. The Barbados trade had been rather languid (HSP, Isaac Norris Letterbook 1716–1730, pp. 445, 446, 449).

19. See *American Weekly Mercury*, 18 January 1725/6, and 15 February 1725/6; *Boston Gazette*, 14 February 1725/6 and 14 March 1725/6.

20. HSP, Isaac Norris Letterbook 1716–1730, pp. 449. He would not pay the full premium. William Bolton, part owner of the *William*, bound from Madeira to Barbados in 1696, wrote to London for insurance on a voyage projected from Barbados to London. He claimed that if the voyage did not occur, the premium actually charged would be only one half of 1 percent (*The Bolton Letters*, I, p. 35). For a more excruciating failure, involving an attempt to fill a Boston provision shortage from Ireland in 1763, see W. T. Baxter, *The House of Hancock* (Cambridge, Mass., 1945), pp. 203–4.

21. Arthur L. Jensen, *The Maritime Commerce of Colonial Philadelphia* (Madison, Wis., 1963), pp. 52–53.

22. Thomas Fitch to William and John Crouch, 15 March 1706/7, Thomas Fitch Letterbook 1702/3–1711, AAS.

23. Thomas Fitch to John Crouch and Samuel Arnold, 4 March 1707/8, 29 April 1708; Thomas Fitch to Adrian Hooglant, 6 November 1710 (ibid.).

24. Arthur H. Cole, *Wholesale Commodity Prices in the United States 1700–1861* (Cambridge, Mass., 1938), pp. 94–101. Isaac Norris was frequently called on to explain to West Indian customers why his flour was more expensive than that from New York (HSP, Isaac Norris Letterbook 1699–1702, passim).

25. *American Weekly Mercury* of 7 September 1721, 20 February 1727/8, and 6 November 1729; *New York Gazette*, no. 603.

26. Of related interest was the colonial printing of London stock prices. The *American Weekly Mercury* carried these with some regularity during the summer and fall of 1720, usually running nearly three months behind. The *Boston News-letter* carried some account of the South Sea Bubble in November of that year, nos. 881–82, but showed little interest in this type of information. Cf. no. 980 for 12 November 1722. The *Boston Gazette* carried occasional lists of London stock prices in the early 1730's. See nos. 532, 574, 594, 611, 616, 648, 690, 871. There is not much evidence of colonial losses of consequence related to the South Sea Bubble although colonial victims of later economic crises of the century were plentiful enough. In this respect, the colonial integration into the London money market was as yet incomplete.

27. See Adam Smith, *Essay on Colonies* (London, 1901), pp. 53–55, and Andrew

Skinner, "Adam Smith and the American Economic Community: An Essay in Applied Economics," *Journal of the History of Ideas*, 37 (1976), p. 72.

28. Davies, "Commission System" pp. 98 and 98 note; Richard B. Sheridan, *Sugar and Slavery* (Epping, Essex, 1975), pp. 285, 290; Charles Molloy, *De Jure Maritimo et Navali: or A Treatise of Affairs Maritime and of Commerce*, 7th ed. (London, 1722), pp. 293–94. The general tendency for usance to be related to the distance of a trade is also supported by the fact that later in the eighteenth century supercargoes at Canton drew bills on the East India Company Court of Directors at 365 days' sight (Vincent T. Harlow, *The Founding of the Second British Empire*, 2 vols. [London, 1952–1964], II, 543). For Irish usance, see L. M. Cullen, *Anglo-Irish Trade 1660–1800* (New York, 1968), pp. 98–99. Cullen notices the tendency toward some longer bills later in the eighteenth century in the Irish trade as in the West Indian.

29. James H. Soltow, "The Role of Williamsburg in the Virginia Economy," *WM&Q*, 3d series, 15 (1958), pp. 478–79, discusses the intercolonial market in bills later in the eighteenth century. Thomas Fitch, who seemed to exploit the commercial advantages of the intercolonial posts quite effectively by 1703, bought Maryland bills on London by mail (Thomas Fitch Letterbook 1702/3–1711, AAS).

30. Conditions varied, of course. At a sale of slaves at Barbados in 1719, nearly two-year's credit was allowed the purchasers. See Elizabeth Donnan, *Documents Illustrative of the History of the Slave Trade to America*, 4 vols. (Washington, D.C., 1930–1935), II, 242.

31. The point is made regarding estate settlements by Sheridan, *Sugar and Slavery*, pp. 274–75.

32. 5 Geo. II, c.7, L. E. Stock, ed., *Proceedings and Debates of the British Parliaments Respecting North America*, 5 vols. (Washington, D. C., 1924–1941), IV, 128, 130, 145, 150, 153–54, 156. See Sheridan, *Sugar and Slavery*, pp. 288–89.

33. *New York Gazette*, 8 September 1735.

34. James F. Shepherd and Gary M. Walton, *Shipping, Maritime Trade and the Economic Development of Colonial North America* (Cambridge, 1972), and Douglass C. North, "Sources of Productivity Change in Ocean Shipping, 1600–1850," *Journal of Political Economy*, 76 (1968), pp. 953–70. Gary M. Walton, "Sources of Productivity Change in American Colonial Shipping, 1675–1775," *EconHR*, 2d ser., 20 (1967), pp. 67–78.

35. *The Letterbook of Robert Pringle*, ed. Walter B. Edgar, 2 vols. (Columbia, S. C., 1972), I, 112–13.

36. See Daniel Baugh, *Naval Administration 1715–1750* (London, 1977), pp. 325–32.

37. Molloy, *De Jure Maritimo*, pp. 283–84. This seems to be the intent of G. Prankard of Bristol writing to Thomas Wyer of Philadelphia, 28 February 1717/18. Prankard Letterbook 1712–1718, Somerset Record Office, Taunton, England.

38. Morton J. Horwitz, *The Transformation of American Law, 1780–1860* (Cambridge, Mass., 1977), pp. 226–33.

39. See case described in *New York Gazette*, no. 358, 4 September 1732; case of *Charming Peggy* (1739), described in James Allan Park, *A System of the Laws of Marine Insurance*, 2d ed. (Boston, 1799), p. 63. In the disappearance of the *Milk-maid* (1729) and her subsequent reappearance and seizure for the insurers in London and Amsterdam, the insurance money appears to have been paid in less than a year (*American Weekly Mercury*, no. 574, 29 December 1730).

40. Samuel Salmon to Isaac Hobhouse, 6 June 1736 (Hobhouse Papers, 1722–1755, Bristol Central Library).

41. Discounts of 16 percent were regular; and those of up to 30 percent, possible. See Violet Barbour, "Marine Risks and Insurance in the Seventeenth Century," *Journal of Economic and Business History*, 1 (1928–1929), pp. 561–96; R. Grassby, "The

Rate of Profit in Seventeenth Century England," *EHR*, 84 (1969), p. 742; A. H. John, "The London Assurance Company and the Marine Insurance Market of the Eighteenth Century," *Economica*, 25 (1958), pp. 126–41.

42. Joseph Cruttenden, *Atlantic Merchant Apothecary: Letters of Joseph Cruttenden, 1710–1717*, ed. I. K. Steele (Toronto, 1977), p. 37. For the Royal African Company experience, see K. G. Davies, *The Royal African Company* (London, 1957), pp. 208–9. Some insuring of insurers apparently occurred betwen 1689 and 1713. See Board of Trade *Journal*, IV, 340.

43. Board of Trade *Journal*, IV, 339–40; *Journals of the House of Commons*, XIX, esp. 355, 367; Charles Wright and C. Ernest Fayle, *A History of Lloyd's* (London, 1928), pp. 44–78; John "Marine Insurance," passim.

44. *American Weekly Mercury*, 25 May 1721.

45. See *BNL*, 31 October 1720, and *Boston Gazette*, 25 June and 10 December 1739. Benjamin Pollard was his new rival.

46. Grassby, "Rate of Profit," p. 742; Shepherd and Walton, *Shipping*, pp. 88–89; John, "Marine Insurance," p. 138; and J. R. Ward, "The Profitability of Sugar Planting in the British West Indies, 1650–1834," *EconHR*, 2d series, 31 (1978), p. 200.

47. For several series of freight rates relevant to these comments, see Shepherd and Walton, *Shipping*, Appendix III.

48. A related argument concerning English provincial newspapers is made by John Brewer in *The Birth of a Consumer Society* by N. McKendrick, John Brewer, and J. H. Plumb (Bloomington, Ind., 1982), pp. 215–16.

49. James E. Vance, Jr., in *The Merchant's World: The Geography of Wholesaling* (Englewood Cliffs, N.J., 1970), p. 49; William N. Parker, *Europe, America, and the Wider World: Essays on the Economic History of Western Capitalism*, vol. I, *Europe and the World Economy* (Cambridge, 1984), pp. 152–53.

Chapter 12: GOVERNORS, AGENTS, AND THE COMMUNICATION OF POLITICS

1. Edward Barlow, commander of a ship entering Port Royal, Jamaica, in 1679, explains a common practice.

> And coming to an anchor, I was ordered to go to the Governor to relate what news and from whence we came and what was our business, which is a thing usual when any ship arrives, for the commander to present himself before the Governor the first thing he doth; and my next thing was to enter the ship in the Custom House [*Barlow's Journal*, ed. B. Lubbock, 2 vols. (London, 1934), II, 321].

On the matter of governors' interfering with the mails, see K. Ellis, *The Post Office in the Eighteenth Century* (Durham, 1958), pp. 64–65; David H. Flaherty, *Privacy in Colonial New England* (Charlottesville, Va., 1972), pp. 120, 123, 124–27.

2. I am grateful to Professor Daniel Baugh of Cornell University for this insight.

3. See the commission, instructions, and additional instructions of the council in PRO 30/24, Bdle, XLIX, no. 10, pp. 1–19, and R. P. Bieber, "The British Plantation Councils of 1670–4," *EHR*, 40 (1925), pp. 93–106, as well as C. M. Andrews, *British Committees, Commissions and Councils of Trade and Plantations, 1622–1675* (Baltimore, 1908), pp. 96–105.

4. L. W. Labaree, *Royal Government in America* (New Haven, 1930).

5. The instruction was more prohibitive than seems to have been intended by the instruction to the Council of Plantations, which was to exhort governors to live in peace with their neighbors (PRO 30/24, Bdle. XLIX, p. 11, and see earlier, chap. 10).

6. L. W. Labaree, *Royal Instructions to British Colonial Governors 1670–1776*, 2 vols.

(New York, 1935), I, 133. The Jamaica assembly had been a subject of special concern since 1662, when Lord Windsor's instructions insisted that no law could remain in force for more than two years unless it was confirmed by the king (*CSPC 1661–1668*, no. 259). The same was repeated in Thomas Modyford's instructions of 1664 (ibid., no. 664) and in Thomas Lynch's instructions when he was sent out as lieutenant governor of Jamaica. (*CSPC 1669–1674*, no. 367). Nothing comparable was ordered in the instructions for Governor Berkeley of Virginia in 1662 or Lord Willoughby of the "Caribee Islands" in 1663 (*CSPC 1661–1668*, nos. 368, 489).

7. Labaree, *Royal Instructions* I, 133–36. Governor Sir Jonathan Atkins of Barbados learned just how seriously this was meant in 1677. See A. P. Thornton, *West-India Policy Under the Restoration* (Oxford, 1956), p. 178.

8. L. M. Penson, *The Colonial Agents of the British West Indies* (London, 1924), pp. 46–52.

9. The Board of Trade asked Governor Granville of Barbados for the reasons for passing an *Act to supply the want of cash*, the size of the majority in favor of it, and public sentiment of the matter. This inquiry of 26 September 1706 led to a circular letter (*CSPC 1706–1708*, nos. 50–52, 529, 578, 582, 583). Standing instructions on this matter were first issued to the governor of New Jersey in 1708 and spread gradually to become standard by 1715 (Labaree, *Royal Instructions*, I, 136–37, Elmer B. Russell, *The Review of American Colonial Legislation by the King in Council* [New York, 1915], esp. chap. 1).

10. See Thornton, *West-India Policy*, pp. 167–78. A. M. Whitson, *The Constitutional Development of Jamaica, 1660–1729* (Manchester, 1929), pp. 70–109.

11. For the instructions, see Labaree, *Royal Instructions*, I, 125. See S. S. Webb, *The Governors-General* (Chapel Hill, N.C., 1979), pp. 280–89, 295–98, 301–4, 321–24 regarding Jamaica and pp. 378–80, 382–83 regarding Virginia.

12. On subsequent difficulties, see I. K. Steele, *Politics of Colonial Policy* (Oxford, 1968), p. 144. For the text of the charter, see Merrill Jensen, ed., *English Historical Documents*, IX, *American Colonial Documents to 1776* (London, 1964), pp. 93–101.

13. *Acts and Resolves Public and Private of the Province of the Massachusetts Bay*, 2 vols, (Boston, 1868–1922), I, 17.

14. On the Massachusetts piracy act of 1696, see Bellomont to the Board of Trade, 28 August 1699, PRO, CO 5/860, fols. 203–4. On the consequences of comfirming the Massachusetts Act for Ascertaining the Value of Coyns Currant within this Province, of October 1697, see PRO, CO 323/5, fol. 34.

15. *CSPC 1706–1708*, nos. 502, 529, 582–583, 632; Labaree, *Royal Instructions*, I, 142–43. When the Carolina proprietors had been stung by a law from their colony suspending the prosecution of debts owed to individuals outside the colony, they responded by ordering that no law in their colony would be in force more than two years unless it had been confirmed by the proprietors (J. M. Sosin, *English America and the Restoration Monarchy of Charles II* [Lincoln, Neb., 1980], p. 212). This was the type of restriction the crown used in Jamaica's case at the Restoration.

16. E. B. Russell's discussion of the timing of royal disallowance (*Colonial Legislation*, pp. 222–23), suggesting an average life of three years and five months for colonial laws that were disallowed, must be understood in the context of this "lye bye" method.

17. Eighteen such instructions are indexed in Labaree, *Royal Instructions*. The categories are summarized in his *Royal Government*, pp. 227–28 note.

18. Labaree, *Royal Instructions*, I, 151. Early in 1734, the House of Lords considered a proposal to require all colonial governments to submit all legislation for royal approbation within 12 months of passage and none but emergency laws to be in force

until such approbation was received. See L. E. Stock, ed., *Proceedings and Debates of the British Parliaments Respecting North America*, 5 vols. (Washington, D.C., 1924–1941), IV, 224–26, 230, 232–33, 236–37.

19. *Georgia Colonial Records*, XV, 152; see also Russell, *Colonial Legislation*, pp. 214–15.

20. See J. H. Smith, *Appeals to the Privy Council from the American Plantations* (New York, 1950), p. 289. He also discusses the times allowed (ibid., esp. pp. 272–74, 662). Colonial criminals might also be granted a stay of execution a year and a day in order to discover the bounds of royal mercy. See, for instance, *Boston Gazette*, 18 May 1724.

21. S. S. Webb, *The Governors-General*, has rightly emphasized the importance of military connections in gubernatorial appointments. On the aggressive administration of the earl of Nottingham, see Steele, *Colonial Policy*, pp. 86–92.

22. Quoted in J. G. Palfrey, *History of New England* 5 vols. (Boston, 1858–1890), IV, 196–97. A related problem was revealed by Governor Atkins of Barbados in April 1677, when he complained that most orders from the Lords of Trade came "from the Exchange here sometimes two or three months before your orders come to me" (PRO, CO 29/2, p. 173).

23. MHS *Collections*, 6th ser. vol. VII, *The Belcher Papers*, Part 2 (Boston, 1894), p. 107.

24. London story, datelined 28 October, 1727, reprinted in *American Weekly Mercury* of 6 February 1727/8. On similar concerns at the accession of Queen Anne, see the author's "Time, Communications and Society: The English Atlantic, 1702," *Journal of American Studies*, 8 (1974), pp. 1–21.

25. William Blathwayt was a private correspondent as well as a self-interested public servant. His handling of governors' letters addressed to the Board of Trade, of which Blathwayt was a member, was particularly evident in the case of Governor Fletcher of New York. See James S. Leamon "Governor Fletcher's Recall," *WM&Q*, 3d ser., 20 (1963), pp. 527–42. In April 1719 the secretary of the Board of Trade complained about governors who sent their letters through agents in London who would petition the king on some matter, using the letters to the Board of Trade in the case, letters that still had not been delivered to the board. (PRO, CO 153/13, pp. 405–6).

26. PRO, CO 29/2, fol. 76.

27. Thornton, *West-India Policy*, pp. 194–95; Labaree, *Royal Instructions*, II, 747–50.

28. He was also advised to have his letters delivered by persons prepared to sink mail packets with weights if in danger of the enemy (*CSPC 1702–1703*, no. 554).

29. See K. L. Ellis, "British Communications and Diplomacy in the Eighteenth Century," *BIHR*, 31 (1958), p. 162.

30. Correspondence of lieutenant governors or presidents of councils was considered while they were acting governors. Only one executive officer was counted for the Dominion of New England or the Leeward Islands. Correspondence to the secretaries was considered only if the letter was presented to the senior body. Circular letters, which never occurred more than twice a year, were considered as letters although covering notes and letters written within a week of each other were not counted separately.

31. New Hampshire and New Jersey are excluded from this study because they were formally under the governor of Massachusetts and of New York respectively.

32. This level of letter writing was matched only once by another governor, Jonathan Belcher of Massachusetts in 1731.

33. Bellomont made his dependence on correspondence with the Board of Trade clear in his of 5 January 1699/1700 (*CSPC 1700*, no. 14). See S. S. Webb, "Willaim Blathwayt, Imperial Fixer: Muddling Through to Empire, 1689–1717," *WM&Q*, 3d ser., 26

(1969), p. 395; S. H. Friedelbaum, "Bellomont: Imperial Administrator—Studies in Imperial Administration During the Seventeenth Century;" unpublished Ph.D. dissertation, Columbia University 1955, pp. iii, 63.

34. There were no letters dated in April or August 1698; January–March 1699; or August, September, and December 1700. See his letter of 5 January and 28 February 1699/1700 and those of 16 January and 21 February 1700/01 (*CSPC 1700*, nos. 14, 167; *CSPC 1701*, nos. 38, 188).

35. 14 November 1698, *NYCD*, IV, 432; *CSPC 1697–1698*, no. 992.

36. 30 November 1699, *CSPC 1699*, no. 1015, and John D. Runcie, "The Problem of Anglo-American Politics in Bellomont's New York," *WM&Q*, 3d ser., 26 (1969), pp. 191–217.

37. Bellomont's letters of 7, 25 May and 22 June 1700, printed in *CSPC 1700*, nos. 402, 466, 581.

38. *NYCD*, III, 189.

39. See earlier, chap. 6.

40. Logan wrote Penn 66 letters in 8 years, or 8.25 per year. Between 1702 and 1713, the Jamaican governors wrote the Board of Trade and its secretary an average of 8.6 times a year (*Correspondence Between William Penn and James Logan*, ed. Edward Armstrong, 2 vols. [Philadelphia, 1870–1872]).

41. A. L. Jensen, *The Maritime Commerce of Colonial Philadelphia* (Madison, Wis., 1963), p. 6. See also earlier, p. 59.

42. For Cornbury's continuing exchanges with the Board of Trade concerning correspondence, see *CSPC 1702*, no. 995; *NYCD*, IV, 1017; *CSPC 1702–1703*, no. 554; *CSPC 1704–1705*; nos. 427, 523, 878, 1230; *CSPC 1706–1708*, nos. 823, 1213; *CSPC 1708–1709*, no. 10.

43. Bellomont received seven letters in 1699 and nine in 1700. Cornbury had six in 1703. Most of the exceptionally high rates of letters to governors were those to West Indian governors in this same period via Dummer's packet boats.

44. September was his favorite month, when he wrote twice as many as in any other month. He only wrote one letter in eight years in each of the subsequent months of October and November, however.

45. *CSPC 1702–1703*, no. 496; *CSPC 1706–1708*, no. 493.

46. Seventy-six acts are cited from the years 1708 to 1753. See Labaree, *Royal Instructions*, II, 752–60.

47. For a sensitive study of this problem, see Michael Kammen. "The American Colonies and the 'Seasons of Business' in Eighteenth-Century Britain," in *Anciens Pays et Assemblées d'États. Etudes Publiées par la Section Belge de la Commission Internationale pour l'Histoire des Assemblées d'États*, 53 (Louvain, 1970), pp. 243–59.

48. See M. G. Hall, "The House of Lords, Edward Randolph, and the Navigation Act of 1696," *WM&Q*, 3d ser., 14 (1957), pp. 494–515. On the resumption of proprietary charters, see Alison G. Olson, "William Penn, Parliament and Proprietary Government," *WM&Q*, 3d ser., 18 (1961), pp. 176–95; Philip S. Haffenden, "The Crown and the Colonial Charters, 1675–1688," ibid., 15 (1958), pp. 297–311, 452–66, and the author's "The Board of Trade, The Quakers, and Resumption of Colonial Charters, 1699–1702," ibid., 23 (1966), pp. 596–616. On the Molasses Act, see Richard B. Sheridan, "The Molasses Act and the Market Strategy of the British Sugar Planters," *Journal of Economic History*, 17 (1957), pp. 62–83.

49. The act, passed 13 September 1660, also ordered foreign merchants out of the colonial trades as of the next 1 February and a system of bond for ships trading in colonial enumerated commodities (Danby Pickering, *The Statutes at Large*, VII, 452–54, 459–60).

50. The law rightly anticipated some difficulties, and nearly two years were allowed. This

proved inadequate, and nine additional months were later allowed. See Pickering, *Statutes*, IX, 428–37; Labaree, *Royal Instructions*, II, 782–83.

51. See Henry Crouch, *A Complete Guide to the Officers of His Majesty's Customs in the Outports* . . . (London, 1732); Lawrence A. Harper, *The English Navigation Laws* (New York, 1939), pp. 119–23, 165, 216–17; Thomas C. Barrow, *Trade and Empire: The British Customs Service in Colonial America, 1660–1775*, (Cambridge, Mass., 1967), pp. 85–87.

52. For lists of MPs, see, for instance, *BNL* nos. 368, 505; *Boston Gazette*, nos. 757, 759; *American Weekly Mercury*, no. 762.

53. Lillian M. Penson, *The Colonial Agents of the British West Indies* (London, 1924), pp. 46–48. For a parallel case study, see Francis G. James, "The Irish Lobby in the Early Eighteenth Century," *EHR*, 81 (1966), pp. 543–57.

54. B. L., Egerton, MSS. 2395, fol. 335; Labaree, *Royal Instructions*, I, 386–87.

55. PRO, CO 391/10, p. 311. On the emergence of the colonial agents, see Penson, *Colonial Agents*; Ella Lonn, *The Colonial Agents of the Southern Colonies* (Chapel Hill, N.C., 1945); J. J. Burns, *The Colonial Agents of New England* (Washington, D.C., 1935); Michael G. Kammen, *A Rope of Sand* (Ithaca, N.Y., 1968), chap. 1; Alison G. Olson, "The Board of Trade and London-American Interest Groups in the Eighteenth Century," *Journal of Imperial and Commonwealth History*, 8 (1980), pp. 33–50.

56. Jack P. Greene, *The Quest for Power: The Lower Houses of Assembly in the Southern Royal Colonies, 1689–1776* (Chapel Hill, N.C., 1963), pp. 266–86, discusses the struggles over control of the agent in the southern mainland colonies.

57. Boston, 6 September 1699, Bodleian Library, Rawlinson MSS. A 272, fol. 60.

58. MHS, Miscellaneous MSS, quoted by John D. Runcie in *W&MQ*, 3d ser. 26 (1969), p. 192.

59. For a Massachusetts appeal in 1699, see PRO, CO 391/12, pp. 61, 88, and CO 391/93, fol. 227. Four years later, Attorney General Edward Northey complained about a general unwillingness of the colonial agents to attend his office to discuss colonial laws (CO 323/5, fol. 66).

60. Penn to Lawton, 21 December 1700, HSP, William Penn's Letterbook, 1699–1703, p. 79.

61. Ibid., pp. 106, 114–15. For a fuller discussion, see the author's "The Board of Trade, the Quakers, and Resumption." A Captain Joshua Guy was master of the *Messenger* according to the Isaac Norris Letterbook, 1699–1702, HSP, pp. 349, 350.

62. *APCC*, II, 297–99. The best discussion of this struggle is still Frank Wesley Pitman, *The Development of the British West Indies, 1700–1763* (New Haven, Conn., 1917), pp. 242–70 although aspects have been developed further by Sheridan, "The Molasses Act" pp. 62–83. The letters of Richard Partridge tell something of the costs and pace of matters, in G. S. Kimball, ed., *The Correspondence of the Colonial Governors of Rhode Island, 1723–1775*, 2 vols. (Boston, 1902), I, 19–34.

63. The preceding sketch of the politics of empire is derived from the sources cited and those discussed in the author's "The Empire and the Provincial Elites: An Interpretation of some Recent Writings on the English Atlantic, 1675–1740," in *The British Atlantic Empire Before the American Revolution*, ed. Peter Marshall and Glyn Williams (London, 1980), esp. pp. 13–18.

Chapter 13. COMMUNICATION AND COMMUNITY

1. John Dewey, *Democracy and Education* (New York, 1966), p. 4. Robert E. Park, "Reflections on Communications and Culture," *American Journal of Sociology*, 44 (1938), pp. 187–205; Karl W. Deutsch, *Nationalism and Social Communication; An*

Inquiry into the Foundations of Nationality (Cambridge, Mass., 1958); and Edward Shils, *Center and Periphery: Essays in Macrosociology* (Chicago, 1975), are prominent exponents of the sociology of communications. Harold A. Innis, *Empire and Communications* (Oxford, 1950), and *The Bias of Communications* (Toronto, 1964), emphasize technological and historical aspects.

The social history of the English Atlantic during the lifetime after 1675 has received comparatively little direct attention. Noteworthy general examples include M. Kraus, *The Atlantic Civilization—Eighteenth-Century Origins* (Ithaca, N.Y., 1949); F. B. Tolles, *Quakers and the Atlantic Culture* (New York, 1960); and C. Bridenbaugh, *Mitre and Sceptre: Transatlantic Faiths, Ideas, Personalities, and Politics 1689–1775* (London, 1962). Particularly helpful articles include John Clive and Bernard Bailyn, "England's Cultural Provinces: Scotland and America," *WM&Q*, 3d ser., 11 (1954), pp. 200–13; Jack P. Greene, "Search for Identity: An Interpretation of the Meaning of Selected Patterns of Social Response in Eighteenth Century America," *Journal of Social History*, 3 (1970), pp. 199–220; and J. M. Price, "One Family's Empire: The Russell-Lee-Clerk Connection in Maryland, Britain, and India, 1707–1857," *Maryland Historical Magazine*, 72 (1977) pp. 165–225.

2. *Community and Social Change in America* (New Brunswick, N.J., 1978), p. 6.
3. R. S. Dunn, *Sugar and Slaves* (Chapel Hill, N.C., 1972), esp. pp. 237, 311–14; Peter H. Wood, *Black Majority* (New York, 1974), chap. 5.
4. Dunn, *Sugar and Slaves*, chap. 7; Wood, *Black Majority*, chaps. 4–6. John W. Blassingame, *The Slave Community*, 2d ed. (New York, 1979), provides a provocative argument and a useful bibliography on the general subject.
5. Sidney W. Mintz and Richard Price, *An Anthropological Approach to the Afro-American Past: A Caribbean Perspective* (Philadelphia, 1976), passim; Gary B. Nash, "Social Development," in Jack P. Greene and J. R. Pole, eds., *Colonial British America: Essays in the New History of the Early Modern Era* (Baltimore, 1984), p. 255.
6. Dunn, *Sugar and Slaves*, chap. 8. For population estimates in 1740, see Robert V. Wells, *The Population of the British Colonies in America before 1776* (Princeton, 1975), chap. 6, and *Historical Statistics*, Z, 16; T. H. Breen, "Creative Adaptions: Peoples and Cultures," in Greene and Pole, eds., *Colonial British America*, p. 221.
7. See Epistles Received, vol. 2, pp. 132–34, 172–73, 236, and Epistles Sent, vol. 2, pp. 195–97, in Friends House Library, London, for exchanges of views on slavery and the slave trade 1712–1718.
8. Philip D. Curtin, "Epidemiology and the Slave Trade," *Political Science Quarterly*, 83 (1968), pp. 190–216; Darrett B. Rutman and Anita H. Rutman, "Of Agues and Fevers: Malaria in the Early Chesapeake," *WM&Q*, 3d ser., 33 (1976), pp. 31–60; Mary Dobston, "'Marsh Fever'—the geography of malaria in England," *Journal of Historical Geography*, 6 (1980), pp. 357–89; Carville V. Earle, "Environment, Disease, and Mortality in Early Virginia," in Thad W. Tate and David L. Ammerman, eds., *The Chesapeake in the Seventeenth Century: Essays on Anglo-American Society* (Chapel Hill, N.C., 1979), pp. 96–125; Wood, *Black Majority*, pp. 88–90; Dunn, *Sugar and Slaves*, chap. 9; John Duffy, *Epidemics in Colonial America* (Baton Rouge, 1953), pp. 204–14.
9. Malaria increased in New York City toward the end of the seventeenth century and became a major problem for the colony and neighboring New Jersey in the eighteenth century, by which time it was less evident in New York City itself (J. Duffy, *A History of Public Health in New York City, 1625–1866* [New York, 1968], pp. 35–36). Apparently, the malaria mosquitoes were arriving in increasing numbers aboard ships in the developing West Indies trade and became established in swamps over a wide area whereas New York land drainage was reducing the threat in the city itself.

10. There were major outbreaks in both London and Norwich in 1681 and again in 1710. There were epidemics in Yorkshire in 1721 and in Plymouth in 1724–1725. See Charles Creighton, *History of Epidemics in Britain*, 2 vols. (Cambridge, 1891–1894), II, 434–557.

11. Smallpox virus, transmittable by inhalation directly or from clothing or utensils, has a 12-day incubation period and 3 further days before the pustules appear.

12. For this well-known story, see, for instance, Ola Elizabeth Winslow, *A Destroying Angel: The Conquest of Smallpox in Colonial Boston* (Boston, 1974), pp. 32–33. See also Wood, *Black Majority*, p. 77. On New York mortalities, see *New York Gazette*, nos. 305–16, for example.

13. There were epidemics in St. Christopher in 1723, and in Barbados in 1738 and 1759. The disease was also common in Jamaica. See Pitman, *Development*, pp. 373, 384, 387; Marion Tinling, ed., *The Correspondence of the Three William Byrds of Westover, Virginia, 1684–1776*, 2 vols. (Charlottesville, Va., 1977), II, 529. Cf. Dunn, *Sugar and Slaves*, p. 302.

14. Bruce Trigger, *The Children of Aataentsic: A History of the Huron People to 1660*, 2 vols. (Montreal, 1976), II, 588–98. Creighton, *Epidemics*, II, 437. John Duffy, *Epidemics in Colonial America* (Baton Rouge, 1953), chap. 2 and his *History of Public Health in New York City, 1625–1866* (New York, 1968); John B. Blake, *Public Health in the Town of Boston, 1630–1822* (New Haven, 1959).

15. There had been a general problem with typhoid or malaria in 1668, but the city deserved its healthful reputation. See Duffy, *Public Health*, chap. 1.

16. See Duffy, *Public Health*, pp. 48, 72–73; Winslow, *Destroying Angel*, pp. 26–27; Allen W. Trelease, *Indian Affairs in Colonial New York: The Seventeenth Century* (Ithaca, N.Y., 1960), pp. 304–5; John J. Heagerty, *Four Centuries of Medical History in Canada*, 2 vols. (Toronto, 1928), I, 31.

17. John was not the first of the 14 members of his Harvard class to die, and his former classmate William Hutchinson would die of smallpox the following year without ever traveling. Hutchinson would contract smallpox from a member of the Massachusetts General Court, holding its session at Cambridge in order to avoid the epidemic raging in Boston. Boston's quarantine procedures had worked when Gore and his men came in a year earlier; the outbreak was confined to the unfortunate ship (*BNL*, no. 876; Clifford K. Shipton, ed., *Sibley's Harvard Graduates*, V, (Boston, 1937), pp. 135–79; William Cooper, *A Sermon Concerning the Laying the Deaths of Others to Heart* (Boston 1720), especially the Appendix by Mr. Colman on Gore.)

18. The last previous outbreak had been in 1702–1703, Duffy, *Epidemics*, pp. 49–50; Blake, *Public Health*, chaps. 2–4; John B. Blake, "The Inoculation Controversy in Boston, 1721–1722," *New England Quarterly*, 25 (1952), pp. 489–506; Winslow, *Destroying Angel*; Dr. Zabdiel Boylestone, *Some Account of What Is Said of Inoculating or Transplanting the Small Pox by the Learned Dr. Samuel Timonius and Jacobus Pylarinus* (Boston, 1721); and Cotton Mather, *An Account of the Method and Further Success of Inoculation for the Small Pox in London* (Boston, 1721), and especially Mather's letter to Dr. John Woodward of 12 July 1716, printed in *Selected Letters of Cotton Mather*, ed. Kenneth Silverman (Baton Rouge, La., 1971), pp. 213–14.

19. The arrival prompted an immediate quarantine act. See *American Weekly Mercury*, no. 606.

20. Duffy, *Epidemics*, pp. 52–55, 78–82. Fairs in Salem, Pa., and in Burlington, N.J., were canceled and prohibited because of the fear of smallpox (*American Weekly Mercury*, nos. 588, 590). On the Albany outbreak among the "High Dutch People," see *Boston Gazette*, no. 589; *New York Gazette*, nos. 305–16; *Boston Gazette*, nos. 614–16, 618–21.

21. On Boston, see *Boston Gazette*, nos. 619–23, 632. See also *American Weekly Mercury*, no. 630, 632; *BNL*, nos. 1464. The disease was widespread among French settlers in Canada between 1731 and 1733 (Heagerty, *Medical History*, I, 72). New outbreaks in Connecticut in the spring of 1732 proved to be the last in this rather continuous series of deadly infections and reinfections (*BNL*, no. 1476).

22. Duffy, *Epidemics*, p. 69, and *Public Health*, pp. 57–58.

23. William Byrd I had smallpox within his "family" in 1686, brought by slaves imported from Gambia. He reported that there were at least 23 cases and 4 deaths, but the outbreak did not spread. His daughter-in-law, Lucy Byrd, died of smallpox while visiting London in 1716, in conformity with the legitimate fear of Virginians about the metropolis, but her sister, Mrs. John Custis, died of smallpox contracted in Virginia the year before (Tinling, *Byrd Correspondence*, I, 65–68, 196 note, 291 note; II, 580).

24. B. W. Sheehan, *Savagism and Civility: Indians and Englishmen in Colonial Virginia* (Cambridge, 1980), pp. 179–80; Verner Crane, *The Southern Frontier 1670–1732* (Ann Arbor, Mich., 1929), p. 142; Joseph I. Waring, *A History of Medicine in South Carolina, 1670–1825* (Charleston, S.C., 1964), p. 18. On maritime quarantine, see Arthur Pierce Middleton, *Tobacco Coast* (Newport News, Va., 1953), pp. 11–12, 154.

25. Duffy, *Epidemics*, chap. 2; Carl Bridenbaugh, *Cities in the Wilderness* (New York, 1938), pp. 303, 399.

26. *CSPC 1693–1696*, no. 70. The yellow fever was raging in Jamaica that winter and had killed nearly 800 people in Bermuda the previous summer (ibid., nos. 51, 207, 209i).

27. *CSPC 1693–1696*, nos. 477, 479, 568.

28. Cotton Mather, *Magnalia Christi Americana, or The Ecclesiastical History of New England*, 2 vols. (Hartford, Conn., 1853), I, 226. See John Duffy, *Epidemics*, pp. 141–42; J. J. Keevil, *Medicine and the Navy, 1200–1900*, 2 vols. (Edinburgh, 1958), II, 182–83; and Nellis M. Crouse, *The French Struggle for the West Indies* (New York, 1943), pp. 182–83. Keevil gives a good account of the similar fate of John Neville's squadron in the West Indies in 1696–1697 (*Medicine*, pp. 186–88).

29. Duffy, *Epidemics*, chap. 4.

30. *Boston Gazette*, no. 660. See Wyndham B. Blanton, *Medicine in Virginia in the Seventeenth Century* (Richmond, Va., 1930), pp. 72–74, and his *Medicine in Virginia in the Eighteenth Century* (Richmond, Va., 1931), pp. 52–54.

31. See Duffy, *Epidemics*, pp. 61, 101–4; Waring, *Medicine in South Carolina*, p. 18; *The Laws of the Province of Pennsylvania: Now in Force, Collected into One Volume* (Philadelphia, 1727), p. 18; *American Weekly Mercury*, no. 606, for a hasty Maryland Act in 1731.

32. *Diary of Cotton Mather*, 2 vols. (Boston, 1911–1912), II, 623; Tinling, ed., *Byrd Correspondence*, passim; Joseph Ellis, *The New England Mind in Transition: Samuel Johnson of Connecticut, 1696–1772* (New Haven, 1973), pp. 88, 107; William Sachse, *The Colonial American in Britain* (Madison, Wisc., 1956), pp. 49, 71.

33. The colonial press also reported the visit to England of six commissioners from the Great Mogul in 1720, a delegation of 12 natives of Bengal in 1730, and a delegate from the West African "Emperor of Pau Pau" in London in 1731 (*American Weekly Mercury*, no. 69; *Boston Gazette*, nos. 586, 629).

34. Arthur J. Ray, *Indians in the Fur Trade* (Toronto, 1974), pp. 19–21, as well as his "Indians as Consumers in the Eighteenth Century," in Carol M. Judd and Arthur J. Ray, eds., *Old Trails and New Directions: Papers of the Third North American Fur Trade Conference* (Toronto, 1980), pp. 255–71.

35. See earlier, pp. 132–33 concerning Isaac and Peter. For Tamerlane, see *Pennsylvania Gazette*, no. 83.

36. See Peter Clark, "Migration in England, 1660–1730," *Past & Present*, 83 (1979),

pp. 57–90, and his "The Migrant in Kentish Towns, 1580–1640," in P. Clark and P. Slack, eds., *Crisis and Order in English Towns 1500–1700* (London, 1972), pp. 117–63; P. Slack "Vagrants and Vagrancy in England 1598–1664," *EconHR*, 2d ser., 27 (1974), pp. 360–79; David Souden, "'Rogues, Whores and Vagabonds'? Indentured Servant Emigrants to North America, and the Case of Mid-Seventeenth-Century Bristol," *Social History*, 3 (1978), pp. 23–41.

37. Clark, "Migration in England," p. 81. Substantial landowners did no better than maintain their numbers as T. H. Hollingsworth has shown in *The Demography of the British Peerage* (London, 1965). Some direct social consequences are studied in L. Stone, "Social Mobility in England, 1500–1700," *Past & Present*, 33 (1966), esp. pp. 47–48, and in C. Clay, "Marriage, Inheritance, and the Rise of Large Estates in England," *EconHR*, 2d ser., 21 (1968), pp. 503–18.

38. E. A. Wrigley, "A Simple Model of London's Importance in Changing English Society and Economy, 1650–1750," *Past & Present*, 37 (1967), pp. 44–70. In the estimates of Phyllis Deane and W. A. Cole, *British Economic Growth 1688–1959*, 2d ed. (Cambridge, 1964), p. 118, London needed more than 12,000 immigrants a year to account for its population between 1701 and 1750.

39. See Henry A. Gemery, "Emigration from the British Isles to the New World, 1630–1700; Inferences from Colonial Populations," *Research in Economic History*, 5 (1980), pp. 179–231; and E. A. Wrigley and R. S. Schofield, *The Population History of England 1541–1871* (Cambridge, Mass., 1981), p. 187.

40. This discussion is based on scholarship that has been surveyed in the author's "The Empire and Provincial Elites: An interpretation of some recent writings on the English Atlantic, 1675–1740," *Journal of Imperial and Commonwealth History*, 8 (1980), esp. pp. 9–10.

41. Forty-seven inheritance ads appeared in colonial newspapers before 1740. Forty-three of these were searching for inheritors of English estates, one each for a Scottish, a Swedish, and a Massachusetts estate (seeking an heir in Pennsylvania). Illustrations of the kind of depositions that would result or that hopeful colonials gathered in anticipation of trips to England are printed in *Essex Institute Historical Collections*, 41 (1905), p. 252; 42 (1906), p. 157; 43 (1907), p. 59; 44 (1908), p. 328; 45 (1909), pp. 93, 95.

42. Gregory King estimated that there were about 50,000 common English seamen in 1688. Ralph Davis has calculated that the Atlantic trades of England employed 70,000 tons of shipping in 1686 and that this was about one fifth of the overseas trading tonnage of England. Something approaching 10,000 English seamen could work those ships at a plausible ton/man ratio of 7:1. For Gregory King's estimate, see Peter Laslett, *The World We Have Lost* (London, 1965), p. 36, and see Ralph Davis, *The Rise of the English Shipping Industry in the Seventeenth and Eighteenth Centuries* (London, 1962), p. 17. These fleets approximately doubled in size by 1740. Colonial seamen are much harder to number. A rough estimate of Boston's manning needs, derived from Table 4.2, would suggest that nearly 1000 men would have been occupied most of the year in operating shipping there and nearly 1900 men by 1737–1738. Boston probably represented about one third of all West Indian and North American intercolonial shipping. None of these estimates include Royal Navy vessels, which were worked by 41,940 men in 1688 (Christopher Lloyd, *The British Seaman* [London, 1968], p. 72).

43. *Boston Gazette*, no. 187.

44. See Patricia U. Bonomi and Peter R. Eisenstadt, "Church Adherence in the Eighteenth-Century British American Colonies," *WM&Q*, 3d ser., 39 (1982), pp. 245–86; C. Bridenbaugh, *Mitre and Sceptre: Transatlantic Faiths, Ideas, Personalities, and Politics 1689–1775* (New York, 1962), chaps. 1–3; J. Calam, *Parsons and Pedagogues:*

The S.P.G. Adventure in American Education (New York, 1971), passim; Sachse, *The Colonial American*, p. 72.

45. Norman Fiering, "The First American Enlightenment: Tillotson, Leverett and Philosophical Anglicanism," *New England Quarterly*, 54 (1981), pp. 307–44, and Edwin S. Gaustad, *George Berkeley in America* (New Haven, 1979), passim. Jon Butler, *Power, Authority, and the Origins of American Denominational Order: The English Churches in the Delaware Valley, 1680–1730*, in American Philosophical Society, *Transactions*, 68 (1978) part 2, is very suggestive.

46. Quaker Pennsylvania would also become the home of the largest German-speaking community in English America in the eighteenth century. By 1790 they constituted one third of the colony's population (*Historical Statistics*, Z, 20; Frederick B. Tolles, *Quakers and the Atlantic Culture* [New York, 1960], esp. p. 24).

47. The Quaker community was almost entirely living within the empire of William III. In 1692, for instance the London Yearly Meeting sent epistles out to Amsterdam, Bermuda, Burlington in West Jersey, Dublin, Gloucester, Jamaica, Maryland, Sally (where Friends were prisoners of Algerian pirates), Scotland, Sussex, and Wales (Library of the Society of Friends, London, Epistles Sent, I, 105–31). For a London request for intercolonial "public Friends," issued in 1703, see Library of the Society of Friends, Epistles Sent, I, 443–44; Tolles, *Quakers*, p. 28.

48. The London Yearly Meeting would hear oral reports from "travelling Friends" on their return. This method could prove tiresome as it did in 1700, when Aaron Atkinson was accused of

> taking up time unseasonably by giving a narrative of his travailes with so much indiscretion, as it gave advantage to some, who looke not with the best eye towards America. So it greatly grieved his ffrds, and being that discourse took up an hour and a half of the last two hours we had to spend, the hurt both to himself and the meeting could not be recovered.

This excerpt is quoted in G. L. Willauer, "Public Friends Reports to London Yearly Meeting on their Mission to America, 1693–1763," *Journal of the Friends Historical Society*, 52 (1969), p. 130.

49. In 1700 the London Yearly Meeting showed particular concern about getting books to America, including the urging of reprints in Philadelphia (Epistles Sent, I, 361–63). For a list of 34 titles sent to Rhode Island that year and the number of copies of each (totaling 275 copies), see Epistles Sent, I, 370–71.

50. Puritan connections that survived long after the Civil War are examined in Francis J. Bremer, "Increase Mather's Friends: The Trans-Atlantic Congregational Network of the Seventeenth Century," AAS *Proceedings*, 94 (1984), 59–96.

51. Harry S. Stout, "Religion, Communications, and the Ideological Origins of the American Revolution," *WM&Q*, 3d ser., 34 (1977), pp. 519–41, and Michael J. Crawford, "The Spiritual Travels of Nathan Cole," *WM&Q*, 3d ser., 33 (1976), pp. 92–93.

52. See David D. Hall, "Religion and Society: Problems and Reconsiderations," in Greene and Pole, *Colonial British America*, pp. 322–27; *The Works of Jonathan Edwards*, ed. Edward Hickman, 2 vols. (Edinburgh, 1974), I, cxxi; II, 278–311. I am grateful to Professor Frederick A. Dreyer for this reference.

53. This relates particularly to the work of H. A. Innis and Marshall McLuhan. See Innis, *Empire and Communication*; Marshall McLuhan, *The Gutenberg Galaxy* (Toronto, 1962), and his introduction to Innis's other book on the subject, *The Bias of Communication*. W. J. Ong, *The Presence of the Word: Some Prolegomena for Cultural and Religious History* (New Haven, 1967), is also seminal in this regard. R. Isaac shows the value of this approach in "Dramatizing the Ideology of Revolution: Popular Mobilization in Virginia, 1774 to 1776," *WM&Q*, 3d ser., 33 (1976),

pp. 357–85, and his "Preachers and Patriots: Popular Culture and the Revolution in Virginia," in A. F. Young, ed., *The American Revolution: Explorations in the History of American Radicalism* (DeKalb, Ill., 1976), pp. 127–56.

54. William J. Gilmore, "Elementary Literacy on the Eve of the Industrial Revolution: Trends in Rural New England, 1760–1830." AAS *Proceedings*, 92 (1983), pp. 87 ff., is suggestive.

55. Robert Redfield, *The Primitive World and Its Transformation* (Ithaca, N.Y., 1953).

56. K. Lockridge, *Literacy in Colonial New England* (New York, 1974), pp. 87–97; Lawrence Stone, "Literacy and Education in England, 1640–1900," *Past and Present*, 42 (1969), pp. 69–139; R. T. Vann, "Literacy in Seventeenth-Century England: Some Hearth Tax Evidence," *Journal of Interdisciplinary History*, 5 (1974–1975), pp. 287–93; David Cressy, "Levels of Illiteracy in England, 1530–1730," *Historical Journal*, 20 (1977), pp. 1–23. For cautions about the necessity of literacy in England and a careful discussion of its distribution, see Cressy's *Literacy and the Social Order: Reading and Writing in Tudor and Stuart England* (Cambridge, 1980).

57. Giles Barber, "Books from the Old World and for the New: The British International Trade in Books in the Eighteenth Century," *Studies on Voltaire and the Eighteenth Century*, 151 (1976), pp. 185–224; Stephen Botein, "The Anglo-American Book Trade Before 1776: Personnel and Strategies," in William L. Joyce et al., eds., *Printing and Society in Early America* (Charlottesville, Va., 1983), pp. 48–82. Bookselling in Boston, the leading book town of the colonies, is studied carefully in Worthington Chauncey Ford, *The Boston Book Market, 1679–1700* (Boston, 1917).

58. C. Seymour Thompson, *Evolution of the American Public Library, 1653–1876* (Washington, D.C., 1952), pp. 13–14. See also *BNL*, no. 477; *The Diary of Samuel Sewall*, 3 vols. (Boston, 1878–1882), III, 334–35; Louis B. Wright, *The Cultural Life of the American Colonies* (New York, 1957), pp. 146–47.

59. W. J. Couper, *The Edinburgh Periodical Press*, 2 vols. (Stirling, 1908), I, 28, 129.

60. Norman Fiering, "The Transatlantic Republic of Letters: A Note on the Circulation of Learned Periodicals to Early Eighteenth-Century America," *WM&Q*, 3d ser., 33 (1976), pp. 642–60, and his *Jonathan Edwards's Moral Thought and Its British Context* (Chapel Hill, N.C., 1981). See also Edwin Wolfe II, *The Library of James Logan of Philadelphia, 1674–1751* (Philadelphia, 1974); Alfred C. Potter, "The Harvard College Library, 1723–1735," *Transactions of the Colonial Society of Massachusetts*, 25 (1922), pp. 1–13; and especially Raymond Phineas Stearns, *Science in the British Colonies of America* (Urbana, Ill., 1970); Raymond P. Stearns, "Colonial Fellows of the Royal Society of London, 1661–1788," *WM&Q*, 3d ser., 3 (1946), pp. 208–68.

61. Clark, "Migration in England."

62. Three studies by Bernard Bailyn illuminate this development: "Politics and Social Structure in Virginia," in James Morton Smith, ed., *Seventeenth-Century America* (Chapel Hill, N.C., 1959), pp. 90–115; *The New England Merchants in the Seventeenth Century* (Cambridge, Mass., 1955), chaps. 5–7; and "Communications and Trade: The Atlantic in the Seventeenth Century," *JEconH*, 13 (1953), 378–87.

63. See Richard Waterhouse, "The Development of Elite Culture in the Colonial American South: A Study of Charles Town, 1670–1770," *Australian Journal of Politics and History*, 28 (1982), p. 393. On the automatic qualification of barristers trained in England before Virginia's highest court, see Alan McKinley Smith, "Virginia Lawyers, 1680–1776: The Birth of an American Profession," Ph.D. dissertation, Johns Hopkins University, 1967, pp. 175–80, 301–18.

64. *BNL*, 8 October 1711, and Sewall *Diary*, II, 323–24.

65. *Boston Gazette*, nos. 567, 1093.

66. Ibid., nos. 698, 450, and *BNL*, nos. 594–96. Richard S. Dunn's, *Puritans and Yan-*

kees: The Winthrop Dynasty of New England, 1630–1717 (Princeton, 1962), is a particularly revealing microcosm of this general process.

67. Quoted in Richard L. Bushman, "American High-Style and Vernacular Cultures," in Greene and Pole, *Colonial British America*, p. 358.

68. Ibid., passim. The marriages of the rival Morris and DeLancey families of New York, including three marriages of daughters to Royal Navy captains in the early 1730's, illustrate the possibilities better than the well-known difficulties of colonials seeking English heiresses. See *New York Gazette*, no. 457; Julian Gwyn, *The Enterprising Admiral* (Montreal, 1974), esp. pp. 10–11; Stanley N. Katz, *Newcastle's New York* (Cambridge, Mass., 1968), pp. 111–13; and Eugene R. Sheridan, *Lewis Morris, 1671–1746* (Syracuse, N.Y., 1981), pp. 144–45.

69. To Sir William Ashurst, 29 March 1715 (*Selected Letters of Cotton Mather*, Kenneth Silverman, ed., [Baton Rouge, La., 1971], p. 178).

70. William Byrd II's letters to Charles Boyle, earl of Orrery, are classic examples of the Arcadian myth (Tinling, *Byrd Correspondence*, I, 354–58).

71. Edward Littleton, *The Groans of the Plantations* (London, 1689), p. 24.

72. A. G. Roeber, "'The Scrutiny of the Ill Natured Ignorant Vulgar': Lawyers and Print Culture in Virginia, 1716 to 1774," *VMHB*, 91 (1983), pp. 387–417, is particularly suggestive here. See also David D. Hall, "Introduction: The Uses of Literacy in New England, 1600–1850" in Joyce et al., eds., *Printing and Society*, pp. 1–47.

73. Samuel Clark, *Social Origins of the Irish Land War* (Princeton, 1979), pp. 8–9. I thank Professor Clark for his help with various aspects of this topic.

Chapter 14. CONCLUSION

1. I. K. Steele, "Moat Theories and the English Atlantic, 1675 to 1740," Canadian Historical Association, *Historical Papers, 1978* (Ottawa, 1979), pp. 18–33.

2. I. K. Steele, "Time, Communications and Society: The English Atlantic, 1702," *Journal of American Studies*, 8 (1974), pp. 1–21.

3. Sidney W. Mintz and Richard Price, *An Anthropoligical Approach to the Afro-American Past: A Caribbean Perspective* (Philadelphia, 1977), passim; Gary B. Nash, "Social Development," in Jack P. Greene and J. R. Pole, eds., *Colonial British America: Essays in the New History of the Early Modern Era* (Baltimore, 1984), p. 255.

4. Richard L. Bushman, "American High-Style and Vernacular Cultures," in Greene and Pole, *Colonial British America*, pp. 345–83.

5. Richard Koebner's *Empire* (Cambridge, 1961), chap. 3, remains useful, but more is needed on this and on the cult of Britannia in the mid-eighteenth century. It is entirely possible that large-scale communities are subject to increasing tension as communications "improve." David M. Potter's "Historians and the Problem of Large-Scale Community Formation," in his *History and American Society*, ed. Don Fehrenbacker (New York, 1973), pp. 48–59, is particularly suggestive in this connection. The growing links and tensions between the American South and North in the early nineteenth century suggest parallels with the previous century.

Index